THE CAMBRIDGE COMPANION TO

# CONSTANTINOPLE

From its foundation in the fourth century to its fall to the Ottoman Turks in the fifteenth, "Constantinople" not only identified a geographical location but also summoned an idea. On the one hand there was the fact of Constantinople, the city of brick and mortar that rose to preeminence as the capital of the Roman Empire on a hilly peninsula jutting into the waters at the confluence of the Sea of Marmora, the Golden Horn, and the Bosporos. On the other hand there was the city of the imagination, the Constantinople that conjured a vision of wealth and splendor unrivaled by any of the great medieval cities, east or west. This Companion explores Constantinople from Late Antiquity until the early modern period. Examining its urban infrastructure and the administrative, social, religious, and cultural institutions that gave the city life, it also considers visitors' encounters with both its urban reality and its place in the imagination.

Sarah Bassett is Associate Professor in the Art History Department at Indiana University and author of *The Urban Image of Late Antique Constantinople* (Cambridge University Press, 2004). Her research interests include late antique urbanism, collecting and display in the late antique world, and the historiography of late antique and Byzantine art.

THE CAMBRIDGE COMPANION TO

# CONSTANTINOPLE

*Edited by*

SARAH BASSETT

*Indiana University*

CAMBRIDGE
UNIVERSITY PRESS

# CAMBRIDGE
## UNIVERSITY PRESS

University Printing House, Cambridge CB2 8BS, United Kingdom

One Liberty Plaza, 20th Floor, New York, NY 10006, USA

477 Williamstown Road, Port Melbourne, VIC 3207, Australia

314–321, 3rd Floor, Plot 3, Splendor Forum, Jasola District Centre,
New Delhi – 110025, India

103 Penang Road, #05–06/07, Visioncrest Commercial, Singapore 238467

Cambridge University Press is part of the University of Cambridge.

It furthers the University's mission by disseminating knowledge in the pursuit of
education, learning, and research at the highest international levels of excellence.

www.cambridge.org
Information on this title: www.cambridge.org/9781108498180
DOI: 10.1017/9781108632614

© Cambridge University Press 2022

First published 2022

Printed in the United Kingdom by TJ Books Limited, Padstow Cornwall

*A catalogue record for this publication is available from the British Library.*

*Library of Congress Cataloging-in-Publication Data*
NAMES: Bassett, Sarah, 1954- editor.
TITLE: The Cambridge companion to Constantinople / edited by Sarah Bassett.
DESCRIPTION: Cambridge, United Kingdom ; New York, NY: Cambridge University Press,
2021. | Series: Cambridge companions to the ancient world | Includes bibliographical
references and index.
IDENTIFIERS: LCCN 2021026078 (print) | LCCN 2021026079 (ebook) | ISBN 9781108498180
(hardback) | ISBN 9781108705578 (paperback) | ISBN 9781108632614 (epub)
SUBJECTS: LCSH: Istanbul (Turkey)–History–To 1453. | Istanbul (Turkey)–Civilization. |
BISAC: HISTORY / Europe / General | HISTORY / Europe / General
CLASSIFICATION: LCC DR729 .C346 2021 (print) | LCC DR729 (ebook) | DDC 949.61/
8012–dc23
LC record available at https://lccn.loc.gov/2021026078
LC ebook record available at https://lccn.loc.gov/2021026079

ISBN 978-1-108-49818-0 Hardback
ISBN 978-1-108-70557-8 Paperback

*In memory of Ruth Macrides*

# Contents

# Figures

# Notes on Contributors

**Sarah Bassett** is Associate Professor of Art History at Indiana University. She has published on installations of public sculpture in Constantinople, the materiality of late antique sculpture, and aesthetic issues in early Byzantine art.

**Albrecht Berger** is Professor of Byzantine Studies in the Department for Cultural Studies and Studies of Antiquity at the Ludwig Maximilian University in Munich. He is the author of numerous publications on the monuments and topography of Constantinople, and editor of the *Byzantinisches Zeitschrift*.

**Annemarie Weyl Carr** is University Distinguished Professor Emeritus of Art History at Southern Methodist University. She has published widely on Byzantine icons and the art and architecture of medieval Cyprus, and is currently working on a study of the afterlife of Byzantine icons, especially those in Cyprus.

**James Crow** is Professor of Classical Archaeology at the University of Edinburgh, where he teaches Roman and Byzantine Archaeology. He has published widely on the Anastasian Wall and the water supply of Constantinople. He is also interested in the application of archaeology to the study of urban history in the early medieval period and historic landscape studies especially in the Aegean and Anatolia.

**Koray Durak** is Associate Professor in the Department of History at Boğaziçi University. His publications address Byzantine-Islamic relations, the economic history of the middle Byzantine period, and Byzantine pharmacology. He is currently at work on a book about trade in pharmacological commodities between Byzantium and the Near East in the early middle ages.

**Niels Gaul** is A. G. Leventis Professor of Byzantine Studies at the University of Edinburgh. His research focuses on education and the classical tradition, social performances, and scholarly networks in Byzantine society. He is currently working on a monograph on the sociology of classicizing learning in the Byzantine Empire.

**Andreas Gkoutzioukostas** is Associate Professor of Byzantine History and Institutions in the Department of Ancient Greek and Roman, Byzantine and Medieval History of the School of History and Archaeology at the Aristotle

University of Thessaloniki. His research addresses the institutional history of the Byzantine Empire. He is particularly interested in the administrative structures and officials of the Byzantine state, Byzantine seals and inscriptions, the administration of justice, and the Byzantine prosopography.

**Mark J. Johnson** is Professor of Ancient and Medieval Art at Brigham Young University. His work on late Roman and Byzantine art and architecture includes publications on Roman imperial mausolea in late antiquity, the Byzantine churches of Sardinia, and octagonal churches in the late antique world. He has also published articles on the eleventh- and twelfth-century art and architecture of Norman Italy.

**Çiğdem Kafescioğlu** is Professor in the Department of History at Boğaziçi University. She writes on the urban, architectural, and visual culture of the Ottoman world in the period between 1400 and 1700. Her interests include spatiality and urban imagination, urban water, vernacular architecture and residential patterns, and Mediterranean cartography.

**Anthony Kaldellis** is Professor of Classics at Ohio State University. He has published many books and articles on aspects of Byzantine culture and history, along with many translations of Byzantine texts.

**Nike Koutrakou** is an independent scholar and an external collaborator with the Late Byzantine Hagiography Database Program of the Institute of Historical Research at the Hellenic National Research Foundation, Athens. Her scholarly interests include the history of ideas and *mentalités*, diplomatic history, and foreign relations in history (in particular Byzantium and the Arabs), strategic studies and war, women's studies, and hagiography. She has written on political, social, and military history with a focus on propaganda and perception issues. Currently she is working on Byzantine North Africa.

**Dirk Krausmüller** studied Classics and Byzantine History at the universities of Gießen and of Munich where he obtained a master's degree, and at Queen's University of Belfast for his doctoral degree. He has been a temporary lecturer at Queen's University Belfast, Cardiff University, and Mardin Artuklu University, and was a member of the ERC Project 9SALT at Vienna University. Currently he is working for the Moving Byzantium project, also based at Vienna University. His research interests are Byzantine monasticism and Byzantine theology.

**Paul Magdalino** is Emeritus Professor of Byzantine History at the University of St. Andrews and a fellow of the British Academy. His numerous publications address questions related to the society, culture, and economy of the Byzantine world from the sixth to the thirteenth centuries. He has worked especially on the city of Constantinople; the interface between magic, astrology, and religion in the Byzantine world; and Byzantine religious and political ideology.

**Vasileios Marinis** is Associate Professor of Christian Art and Architecture at Yale University. He has published on a variety of topics, ranging from early Christian tunics decorated with New Testament scenes to medieval tombs, graffiti, and visions of the Last Judgment. He has written two books, both published by Cambridge University Press. His current research interests include the textual construction of sacred space and the cult of the martyr Euphemia in Byzantium.

**Eric McGeer** holds a PhD from the University of Montreal. He teaches in the School for Continuing Studies at the University of Toronto and serves as consultant for Byzantine sigillography at Dumbarton Oaks. His publications include books on Byzantine military history and law, his most recent being *Byzantium in the Time of Troubles: The Continuation of the Chronicle of John Skylitzes* (Brill Press, 2020). He has also published on Canadian military history.

**Timothy S. Miller** is Professor of History at Salisbury University. His work focuses on the history of medicine and philanthropic institutions in the Byzantine Empire. His publications include monographs on the Byzantine hospital and child welfare in Byzantium. He is the coauthor, with John Nesbitt, of a study of leprosy in Byzantium and the medieval west.

**Philipp Niewöhner** is Privatdozent in the Department of Christian Archaeology and Byzantine Art History at Georg August University of Göttingen. He has worked and excavated at Istanbul and in Turkey for over twenty years and edited a volume on the archaeology of Byzantine Anatolia. His current research engages with the interior decoration of Byzantine churches, including early Christian aniconism in Constantinople and Asia Minor and a book on architectural sculpture and liturgical furnishings.

**Marcus Rautman** is Professor Emeritus of Art and Archaeology of Late Antiquity and the Early Middle Ages in the Department of Ancient Mediterranean Studies at the University of Missouri. A specialist in the material culture of daily life in late Rome and early Byzantium, he has carried out a survey and excavation at the village site of Kalavasos-*Kopetra* in Cyprus and has worked for many years at Sardis in western Turkey.

**Sean Roberts** is Lecturer in the School of Art at the University of Tennessee, Knoxville and past president of the Italian Art Society. A specialist in the arts of Renaissance Europe, his research explores interactions between Italy and the Islamic lands and the place of prints in the histories of art and technology.

**Thomas Russell** earned his doctorate at St. Hilda's College, Oxford before taking up a position as Lecturer of Classics and Ancient History at Balliol College. He subsequently became a Classics school teacher, and is Head of Classics at the Royal Grammar School Worcester. He is the author of *Byzantium and the Bosporus* (Oxford University Press, 2017).

**Raymond Van Dam** is Professor Emeritus in the Department of History at the University of Michigan. His publications include *Rome and Constantinople: Rewriting Roman History during Late Antiquity* (Baylor University, 2010), as well as books about late antique Gaul, late antique Cappadocia, and the emperor Constantine.

**Enrico Zanini** is Full Professor of Methodology in archaeological research in the Department of History and Cultural Heritage at the University of Siena. He excavates at Vignale in Italy and at Gortyn on Crete. His publications include work on technology in late antiquity and the fate of cities in the early Byzantine period.

# ACKNOWLEDGMENTS

No book comes about without the help of a variety of individuals and institutions, and one of the great pleasures at the completion of any long-term project comes from the opportunity to thank those who contributed to its realization. This volume is no exception. The project began its life at the suggestion of Beatrice Rehl at Cambridge University Press. I thank Beatrice, not only for the opportunity to put this volume together but also for her steady oversight, patience, and good humor as she guided the project from its first stirrings to completion. Those stirrings took place while I was a member of the School of Historical Studies at the Institute for Advanced Study, Princeton, NJ, during the academic year 2015–16, and I thank the institute and the Andrew W. Mellon Foundation for support during that time. Further work was completed at Williams College during the spring of 2017, where I was a Visiting Croghan Bicentennial Professor in Biblical and Early Christian Studies. My hosts in the Art History Department, Guy Hedreen and Elizabeth McGowan, merit special thanks. No less important has been the support of my home institution, Indiana University, and my colleagues in the Art History Department, most especially the chair, Diane Reilly, for her endorsement of a sabbatical leave in the 2019–20 academic year that facilitated completion of the project. Amelia Berry and Amy Welch provided logistical support, and I am grateful, as always, to Brian Madigan. Finally, my thanks to the contributors without whose work this book would be nothing. Together we offer our labors to the memory of Ruth Macrides, whose untimely death in 2019 has been a loss not only for scholarship but also to her friends and colleagues, many of whom are contributors here. Although previous commitments prevented her from contributing directly to the volume, her advice and counsel as the project was taking shape were invaluable. Moreover, as references to her work throughout the volume make clear, her scholarship has played no small part in shaping the understanding of things Byzantine in general and Constantinopolitan in particular. With this in mind, we dedicate the project to her.

# ABBREVIATIONS

| | |
|---|---|
| *AASS* | *Acta Sanctorum*, 71 vols. (Paris 1863–1940) |
| *AB* | *Analecta Bollandiana* |
| *ActaIRNov* | *Acta ad archaeologiam et artium historiam pertinentia*, Institutum Romanum Norvegiae |
| *AH* | *Art History* |
| *AJA* | *American Journal of Archaeology* |
| *AntTard* | *Antiquité Tardive/Late Antiquity* |
| *AOL* | *Archives de l'Orient latin*, 2 vols. (Paris, 1881–4) |
| *ΑρχΔ / ArchD* | *Ἀρχαιολογικὸν δελτίον/Archaeologikon deltion* |
| *BCH* | *Bulletin de correspondance héllenique* |
| *Belleten* | *Belleten Türk tarıh kurumu* |
| *BMFD* | *Byzantine Monastic Foundation Documents*, 5 vols., ed. J. Thomas, A. Constantinides, and G. Constable (Washington, DC, 2002) |
| *BMGS* | *Byzantine and Modern Greek Studies* |
| *BollGrot* | *Bollettino della Badia greca di Grottaferrata* |
| *BSl* | *Byzantinaslavica* |
| *ByzF* | *Byzantinische Forschung* |
| *BZ* | *Byzantinische Zeitschrift* |
| *CAH* | *Cambridge Ancient History* |
| *CahArch* | *Cahiers Archéologique* |
| CFHB | Corpus fontium historiae byzantinae |
| *CIC* | *Corpus iuris civilis*, ed. P. Krüger et al. (Berlin, 1928–9; repr. 1993) |
| *CIC CI* | *Corpus iuris civilis, vol. 2, Codex Iustinianus*, ed. P. Krüger (Berlin, 1929; repr. 1993) |
| *CIC Dig* | *Corpus iuris civilis, vol. 1, pt. 2, Digesta*, ed. T. Mommsen and P. Krüger (Berlin, 1928; repr. 1993) |
| *CIC Inst* | *Corpus iuris civilis, vol. 1, pt. 1, Institutiones*, ed. P. Krüger (Berlin, 1928; repr. 1993) |

| | |
|---|---|
| *CIC Nov* | *Corpus iuris civilis, vol. 3, Novellae,* ed. F. Schoell and G. Kroll (Berlin, 1928; repr. 1993) |
| *ClMed* | *Classica et mediaevalia* |
| *CMH* | *The Cambridge Medieval History (Cambridge and New York, 1911–36) (note: vol. 4, revised 1966–7 in two parts; entire set succeeded by NCMH)* |
| *CRAI* | *Comptes rendues de l'Academie des Inscriptions et Belles-Lettres* |
| *CTh* | *Theodosiani libri XVI cum constitutionibus Sirmondianis et leges novellae ad Theodosianum pertinentes,* ed. T. Mommsen and P. M. Meyer (Berlin, 1905). Translation, C. Pharr, et. al. *The Theodosian Code and Novels and the Sirmondian Constitutions* (Princeton, 1952) |
| *DOP* | *Dumbarton Oaks Papers* |
| *EHB* | *Economic History of Byzantium,* 3 vols., ed. A. E. Laiou and C. Bouras (Washington, DC, 2002) |
| *FM* | *Fontes Minores* |
| *IstMitt* | *Istanbuler Mitteilungen,* Deutsches Archäologisches Institut, Abteilung Istanbul |
| *JbAC* | *Jahrbuch für Antike und Christentum* |
| *JbBM* | *Jahrbuch der Berliner Museen* |
| *JDAI* | *Jahrbuch des Deutschen Archäologischen Instituts* |
| *JESHO* | *Journal of the Economic and Social History of the Orient* |
| *JHS* | *Journal of Hellenic Studies* |
| *JLA* | *Journal of Late Antiquity* |
| *JMedHist* | *Journal of Medieval History* |
| *JÖB* | *Jahrbuch der Österreichischen Byzantinistik* |
| *JRA* | *Journal of Roman Archaeology* |
| *JRS* | *Journal of Roman Studies* |
| *JSAH* | *Journal of the Society of Architectural Historians* |
| *JWarb* | *Journal of the Warburg and Courtauld Institutes* |
| *MDAI* | *Mitteilungen des Deutschen Archäologischen Instituts* |
| *MÉFRA* | *Mélanges de l'École française de Rome, Antiquité* |
| *MünchJb* | *Münchner Jahrbuch der bildenden Kunst* |
| *NachrGött* | *Nachrichten von der Akademie [Gesellschaft] der Wissenschaften zu Göttingen, Philologisch-historische Klasse* |
| *NCMH* | *New Cambridge Medieval History,* 7 vols. (Cambridge and New York, 1995–2005) |
| *ODB* | *The Oxford Dictionary of Byzantium,* ed. A. Kazhdan et al. (New York and Oxford, 1991) |

| | |
|---|---|
| *OHBS* | *The Oxford Handbook of Byzantine Studies*, ed. E. Jeffreys, J. Haldon, and R. Cormack (Oxford, 2008) |
| PG | Patrologiae cursus completus, Series graeca, ed. J.-P. Migne (Paris, 1857–66) |
| *PLP* | *Prosopographisches Lexikon der Palaiologenzeit*, ed. E. Trapp et al. (Vienna, 1976–) |
| *PLRE* | *The Prosopography of the Later Roman Empire, vol. 1*, ed. A. H. M. Jones, J. R. Martindale, and J. Morris (Cambridge, 1971); vols. 2–3, ed. J. R. Martindale (1980–92) |
| *ProcBrAc* | *Proceedings of the British Academy* |
| *RE* | *Paulys Real-Encyclopädie der classischen Altertumswissenschaft*, new rev. ed. by G. Wissowa and W. Kroll (Stuttgart, 1894–1978) |
| *REArm* | *Revue des études arméniennes* |
| *REB* | *Révue des Etudes Byzantines* |
| *RendLinc* | *Atti dell'Accademia nazionale dei Lincei, Rendiconti, Classe di scienze morali, storiche e filologiche* |
| *RendPontAcc* | *Atti della Pontificia accademia romana di archeologia, Rendiconti* |
| *RH* | *Révue Historique* |
| *RHC HOcc* | *Recueils des historiens des Croisades, Historiens occidentaux* (Paris, 1844–95) |
| *SBMünch* | *Sitzungberichte der Bayerische Akademie der Wissenschaften, Philosophisch historische Klasse* |
| *SBN* | *Studi bizantini e neoellenici* |
| SBS | Studies in Byzantine Sigillography |
| *SpBAN* | *Spisanie na Bŭlgarskata akademiia na naukite* |
| *TM* | *Travaux et Mémoires* |
| *VizVrem* | *Vizantiiskii vremennik* |
| *ZPapEpig* | *Zeitschrift für Papyrologie und Epigraphik* |
| *ZRIV* | *Zbornik radova Vizantološkog instituta, Srpska akademija nauka* |

# INTRODUCTION

## Sarah Bassett

From its foundation in the fourth century, to its fall to the Ottoman Turks in the fifteenth century, the name "Constantinople" not only identified a geographical location, but also summoned an idea. On the one hand, there was the fact of Constantinople, the city of brick, mortar, and marble that rose to preeminence as the capital of the Roman Empire on a hilly peninsula jutting into the waters at the confluence of the Sea of Marmora, the Golden Horn, and the Bosporos. On the other hand, there was the city of the imagination. To pronounce the name Constantinople conjured a vision of wealth and splendor unrivalled by any of the great medieval cities, east or west. The commanding geographical location together with the city's status as an imperial capital, the correspondingly monumental scale of its built environment, the richness of its sacred spaces, and the power of the rituals that enlivened them drove this idea, as its urban fortunes waxed and waned in the course of its millennial history. The devastations of earthquakes, fire, plague, and pillage notwithstanding, the idea of Constantinopolitan greatness prevailed. If there was one thing about which the diverse and often quarrelsome populations of the Middle Ages could agree, it was on Constantinople's status as the "Queen of Cities."

Although tempered by time, the conviction that Constantinople holds pride of place among medieval cities persists, as evidenced by the steady pace of scholarly production devoted to its understanding over the course of the last half century. As if taking its cue from medieval ideas about the city, two basic strands characterize this work. On the one hand, scholarship is archaeological in nature, focusing on the study of the physical place, its overall plan and infrastructure, and the shape and place of individual monuments within the whole. On the other hand, grounded in the evidence of texts, it looks to the written word to identify and understand the events and institutions associated with the city.

Traditionally, both of these exercises in reconstruction have coalesced around the desire to uncover and describe the city as the stage on which the events of Byzantine history have played out, with the result that Constantinople has been conceived almost exclusively in terms of the luster of imperium. While this interest persists, recent work has begun to explore other aspects of urban living with an eye to understanding other sides of life in the capital. As well, there is a growing desire to approach Constantinople less as an isolated entity, and more within the larger context of ancient and medieval Mediterranean life. Thus, new approaches drawing on interest in the medieval Mediterranean together with theories of networking and globalization have combined with old methodologies and new archaeological discoveries to give Constantinopolitan studies a new slant. As a result, a much richer understanding is beginning to emerge, one picturing the city not simply as the blank canvas upon which to paint a description of Byzantine history, but also as a place with a dynamic population whose built environment represented a response to varieties of human experience.

This Constantinople, a multifaceted center built on interlocking tiers of human experience, is the focus of this volume. Its chapters address both the time-honored issues of infrastructure and the newly developed understandings of the city's people and their institutions. It examines the rapport between people and place, with the latter understood to encompass both the natural and the manmade environment. With the exception of Chapter 1, which sets the stage with a discussion of Constantinople's pre-fourth-century history, and Chapters 20 and 21, which conclude with the exploration of early modern antiquarian interest in the city and Ottoman approaches to the Constantinopolitan past, the volume focuses squarely on the period between the city's foundation by Constantine the Great (306–37) in 324 and its capture by the Ottoman Turks under the leadership of Mehmed II Fatih (1444–6/1451–81) in 1453.

As these chronological boundaries suggest, Constantinople began life as an ancient city, founded and built along the lines of late Roman urban tradition, and ended its Byzantine run as a fully medieval urban center. Part of this volume's mandate is to consider both the different ways in which this passage is manifest and the implications of this change. To this end, each chapter pursues its topic along chronological lines, noting aspects of continuity and disruption across the millennium of the city's history.

## HISTORIOGRAPHICAL CONSIDERATIONS: ORGANIZING THE NARRATIVE

History is a matter of storytelling, and all good stories need to organize their narratives. In the case of Constantinople, two dates define the city's history: its foundation by the emperor Constantine on the site of the old Greco-Roman town of Byzantion on November 8, 324, and its collapse in the face of the Ottoman siege on May 29, 1453. This history, derived largely from the testament of Greek literary sources and the sporadic input of archaeological investigation, exists within the larger context of Byzantine studies, and constructs the city's story on the armature of Byzantine history's modern periodization. This volume is no exception. Although period designations are nothing if not artificial, modern historiography's division of late Roman and Byzantine time offers a generally understood structure around which to build discussion of the Constantinopolitan past. The late antique or early Byzantine period (32–c.700), the Dark Age of the eighth and early ninth centuries, which also overlaps with the period of Iconoclasm in which religious images were banned, the Middle Byzantine period (843–1204), the Latin Interregnum (1204–61) in which western powers controlled the city, and the Late Byzantine or Palaiologan Period (1261–1453), named for the empire's last ruling dynasty, constitute its chronological units.

Thus, during the first of these phases, Constantinople became the center of Roman imperial court life and increased in population. The city's physical structure both shaped and responded to these developments. This period saw the establishment of the city limits and an effective infrastructure for feeding, watering, and defending the capital together with the creation of a monumental armature of streets and public spaces that would organize the rhythms of public and private life. When, in the sixth century, an outbreak of plague beset the capital, Constantinople experienced a decline, a Dark Age, which saw a decrease in population and economic, social, and cultural activity, and from which it emerged only in the middle period. From the second half of the ninth century, population growth and renewed economic prosperity led to the restoration of extant infrastructure and social institutions as well as to the construction of new facilities in both the public and private sectors. This resurgence came to a halt in 1204 with the capture of the city by the army of the Fourth Crusade and the establishment of western, Latin rule that not only wrested control of the city from the Byzantines, but also divided the empire. An initial sack destroyed large swaths of the urban building stock, and in the aftermath of the invasion a significant portion of the population fled, leaving the city and its institutions bereft of their customary guidance for the next several decades. Restoration of Greek rule in 1261 introduced the final phase of the capital's Byzantine history, a period that saw renewed, if modest, population growth and with it a concern to revive the institutions and traditions left to languish during the Latin interregnum. While the restoration of these institutions and the infrastructure that supported them came from the imperial house, financial constraints also meant that private initiative was crucial in steering the fortunes of the capital in these last centuries.

## DISCOVERING AND WRITING CONSTANTINOPOLITAN HISTORY

Modern interest in reconstructing a Constantinopolitan past began within a hundred years of the Ottoman conquest. The initial concern, driven by the antiquarian traditions of Renaissance humanism, was to recover the city's monumental architectural past. Subsequent inquiry aimed to bind this building legacy to the larger subject of Byzantine history. These two strands of inquiry, the one rooted in the pursuit of the city's physical structure, the other in historicist thought, continue to shape the study of Constantinopolitan history.

The reconstruction of this history began in 1544, when the French humanist, Pierre Gilles (1490–1555), traveled to Ottoman Constantinople at the behest of his patron, Francis I Valois (r. 1515–47) with the mandate to purchase Greek and Latin manuscripts for French royal collections. Gilles remained in Constantinople for three years, until 1547, exploring the Ottoman city and the dwindling evidence for its Byzantine past in light of his reading in Greek and Latin sources. The enduring legacy of this enterprise, *De topographia Constantinopoleos et de illius antiquitatibus libri quattuor* (Lyon, 1561), represents the first attempt at a systematic description of Byzantine Constantinople.[1]

The interest driving Gilles' study was the basic question of identification. Already in the sixteenth century the Byzantine city was fast disappearing. Only a handful of monuments survived as testament to the city's former status. His concern was therefore two-fold: to recover Constantinople's ancient topography and to identify individual monuments. To do so he used Byzantine sources as his guide, prime among them the document known as the *Notitia Urbis Constantinopoleos*.[2] Written in the fifth century, the *Notitia* offered a summary description of each of the capital's fourteen administrative regions. Walking the city, text in hand, Gilles established the lay of the land, marking the boundaries of each region and identifying the monuments within them. Although he inevitably made mistakes, the project was important because, for the first time, it gave Byzantine Constantinople, to this date known only through the written word, a physical shape and structure.

Gilles's antiquarian interests established the terms by which Constantinopolitan history would be explored over the course of the next several hundred years, most notably in the work of Charles Du Fresne Du Cange (1610–88). An indefatigable editor of Byzantine texts, Du Cange is probably best known for his medieval Greek and Latin dictionaries; however, his *Historia byzantina duplici commentario illustrata* (Paris, 1680) represents an important contribution to Constantinopolitan studies. Written in two parts, *Constantinopolis Christiana*, and *De familiis byzantinis*, the book is at once a topographical study of the city and a genealogical account of Byzantine aristocratic families. Unlike Gilles, Du Cange never visited Constantinople, and his own topographical study, produced in the haven of his own library, relies on that of his predecessor for content and organization. It also provided a model of how close textual analysis could expand upon Gilles' initial contribution, thus cementing the role of purely philological approaches to the city's topographical reconstruction.[3]

Throughout the nineteenth and twentieth centuries, the identification and description of the overall topography and individual buildings within remained the primary concern. In large measure these studies were noteworthy for persisting with a philological approach that located and identified buildings and other elements of the urban infrastructure on the basis of textual reference. This methodology was conducive to the nature of the surviving evidence. Throughout the city, survival of material evidence from the Byzantine period – everything from the great city walls of the fifth century to the ruined or repurposed churches of the early, middle, and late periods – invited above-ground survey and identification of the sort undertaken by Alexander van Millingen in two comprehensive studies, *Byzantine Constantinople, the Walls of the City and Adjoining Historical Sites* (1899) and *Byzantine Churches in Constantinople: Their History and Architecture* (1912). The goal in such ventures was, as Van Millingen saw it, to identify "the historical sites of Byzantine or Roman Constantinople with the view of making the events of which that city was the theater more intelligible and vivid."[4]

Eventually, archaeological excavation came to complement these early surveys. Sir Charles Newton undertook the first excavation, a three-day dig around the Serpent Column in the Hippodrome, in 1855,[5] and there was sporadic discovery attendant upon construction projects throughout the later nineteenth century; however, it was only in the twentieth century that any large-scale systematic excavation took place. By and large the areas targeted were those identified with the monumental imperial core, among them the Hippodrome and the Great Palace. As a result a fair picture of the city's central district had emerged by the middle of the century, confirming Constantinople's status as an imperial capital. This, together with sustained interest in the identification and description of individual structures around the city, set the stage for production of a series of mid-century encyclopedic publications designed to offer the latest word on topographical issues: Raymond Janin's *Constantinople byzantine: dévelopment urbain et repertoire* (Paris, 1964); Rodolphe Guilland's *Études de topographie de Constantinople byzantine* (Berlin/Amsterdam, 1969); and Wolfgang Müller-Wiener's *Bildlexikon zur Topographie Istanbuls: Byzantion, Konstantinupolis, Istanbul bis zum Beginn d. 17. Jh.* (Tübingen, 1977).

Given that so much of the Byzantine city remains a cypher, the interest in topographical study first sparked by Gilles over 400 years ago continues, with the result that much of the most interesting and important work of recent years may be said to stand in a direct line of descent from his efforts. Among the most visible projects of the last two decades have been the excavations at the Great Palace[6] and the archaeological rescue operations at the Theodosian harbor.[7] No less interesting and important is recent work documenting the city's water supply and defense systems.[8] Although less glamorous, the hard work of rescue archaeology has also borne fruit.[9] Finally, above ground, major restoration projects associated with the city's churches, most notably Hagia Sophia, the Chora Monastery (Kariye Camii) and the Pantokrator Monastery (Zeyrek Camii), have shed light on the some of the more historically important and familiar Constantinopolitan monuments.[10]

Although the focus on topographical study became synonymous with the idea of Constantinopolitan history, the emphasis on individual places and buildings that characterized it brought with it an unintended consequence: the city's atomization. Because monuments were identified and described in isolation from any urban or historical context, the history of Constantinople seemed to be little more than a series of disconnected dots on the map. The challenge, then, was to integrate these dots and to consider the city in unified, historical terms, a task first undertaken by Hans-Georg Beck and Gilbert Dagron. Beck did so in an edited volume that included a series of individual essays addressing topics such as urban infrastructure, administration, and housing.[11] Dagron, by contrast, offered a systematic institutional history of the city in the first centuries of its formation.[12] His study cast a wide net, examining Constantinople as an imperial residence, the formation of its senate, and the office of the urban prefect together with issues such as the church, population, patterns of residence, and the food supply.

Together Beck and Dagron built a firm foundation for the historical study of the city in the early centuries of its development, one that pointed to the possibility of a more integrated approach to urban history. They did so, however, largely without recourse to archaeological materials, building their studies in time-honored tradition on philological foundations. A correlation of textual and archaeological evidence was thus in order. That project became the work of Cyril Mango.[13] Without denying the continued importance of topographical or philological inquiry, Mango argued that the time was ripe to build a synthetic approach that would pull observations about individual monuments and places together to construct a history of the city's physical development. Drawing on the combined testimony of words and archaeology, he identified and tracked the growth of the built environment over the early centuries of the city's history, noting not only developmental sequences, but also the political, social, and economic forces that shaped them.

Mango's ability to step back and look for the big picture sparked a new fire in Constantinopolitan studies. Paul Magdalino picked up where Mango had left off to pursue a similar line of inquiry for the city in the middle period.[14] Subsequently, two major conferences and their attend-ant publications expanded upon these initiatives: "Constantinople: The Fabric of the City," organized by Henry Maguire and Robert Ousterhout, the annual Spring Symposium at Dumbarton Oaks in 1998,[15] and, in the following year, "Byzantine Constantinople," directed by Nevra Necipoğlu in conjunction with Boğaziçi University and the Institut Français d'Études Anatoliennes in Istanbul.[16] At both venues papers directed at specific questions related to urban life – streets, housing, commerce, and the like – worked to integrate topographical observation with historical discussion in an effort to see the nuts and bolts of physical evidence in terms of historical contexts.

Although initial studies considered Constantinople as the accumu-lation of monuments within its walls, the interest in developing a more integrated and historicized understanding of the capital also fostered a desire to see it in a larger context. This interest derives in no small measure from the urge to understand such practical aspects of urban living as the water supply and defense, two issues that not only bind the intramural city to its extramural hinterland, but also profit from the combined study of archaeological materials in their historical context. Mango and Dagron joined forces to spearhead the exploration of this relationship with the organization in 1993 of the Oxford Spring Symposium of Byzantine Studies, "Constantinople and its Hinterland."[17] Papers examined the relationship between intramural Constantinople and the surrounding territory in terms of food and water supply, administration, defense, communication, inhabitants, manufacture, export, and cultural relations. Some of the most interesting and important work on Constantinople in recent years comes as an outgrowth of this expanded view. Archaeological survey of the entwined structures of the Long Walls of Thrace and the infrastructure of the water supply has established a concrete basis on which to address both the mechanics of provision and defense, as well as the historical and administrative relationship between city and country.[18]

Scholarship on Constantinople has also profited from the interest in the more integrated approach to the medieval Mediterranean world that began to take shape in the 1990s. The result has been to refine the sense of Constantinople's place within the larger orbit of the Mediterranean and territories beyond. For the Byzantine Empire and the Mediterranean world beyond, the investigation of networks of exchange has replaced a model that spoke in the binary terms of one-way interactions between center and periphery. Thus, the city's monumental infrastructure has been studied in comparison to the design strategies of other late antique cities, with the result that it no longer stands as an isolated example of urban development.[19] Individual buildings and institutions have also benefited from this approach. This is especially the case with the Great Palace of the Byzantine Emperors, a complex whose architecture and court culture have been considered in the context of a larger Mediterranean orbit that includes the medieval west and Islam.[20] Other studies have considered the role of the Constantinopolitan church in the promotion of monasticism within the territories of the larger empire.[21]

## TEXTUAL STUDY AND CONSTANTINOPOLITAN HISTORY

As Pierre Gilles well understood, one of the more profitable avenues into the study of Byzantine Constantinople was that of texts, and written sources have remained crucial to the city's study. During

Gilles's own lifetime, the process of identifying, transcribing, and producing editions of Byzantine historical texts had only just begun. The initial centers of this sixteenth-century editorial activity were at Augsburg in Germany and Leiden in the Netherlands, where interest in the Byzantine past was fueled by commercial trading interests with the Ottoman Empire. In the seventeenth century the interest in Byzantium and with it the editorial hat passed to the French, who, under the patronage of Louis XIV (1643–1715), began the production of the series known as the *Corpus Byzantinae Historiae*. Comprising twenty-eight volumes and as many as ten supplements, the Parisian corpus formed the basis of what was later to become the most comprehensive attempt to edit the texts of Byzantine history, the nineteenth-century series known as the *Corpus Scriptorum Historiae Byzantinae* (*CSHB*) or the Bonn Corpus, after its initial publication venue. The brainchild of the historian Barthold Georg Niebuhr (1776–1831), the project was directed after his death by the philologist Immanuel Bekker (1785–1871) under the aegis of the Prussian Academy of Sciences. At fifty volumes, the *CSHB* represented the most substantial publication enterprise to date. That said, the editions produced after Niebuhr's death were flawed, many of them representing little more than a reprinting of the earlier Parisian texts. In an effort to remedy the situation the International Association of Byzantine Studies (Association Internationale des Études Byzantines), has, since 1966, been working to produce improved editions of materials from the Bonn Corpus together with new editions of unedited texts in a subsequent series, the *Corpus Fontium Historiae Byzantinae*.[22] In addition, new translations of important texts into modern languages on a range of subjects has opened many sources to a wider readership.[23]

Because so much of the study of Constantinopolitan history relies on the evidence of written sources, these philological labors have provided a crucial foundation for the reconstruction of the city's history. Traditionally they have done so by offering the means to identify, locate, and describe monuments, people, and events. Thus, the sixth-century writings of Prokopios of Caesarea have allowed reconstruction of the rebellion that nearly brought down Justinian's reign together with documentation of the emperor's Constantinopolitan building activity in the aftermath of its quelling, while two tenth-century texts, the *Book of the Eparch* and the *Book of Ceremonies*, have been used to examine two poles of Constantinopolitan life: its commercial practices and court environment.[24]

Recent scholarship makes it clear that these written materials can also be a source of information about contemporary mindsets and the attitudes they express toward the city, its monuments, and its history. For example, beyond documenting the nuts and bolts of construction activity, a text such as Procopius' *On Building* may also be understood as an encomium of imperial greatness, which in turn describes larger aspects of Byzantine mentalities.[25]

This understanding of the capacity of texts to document intellectual ideas and attitudes occurred in tandem with the interest in developing a more historicized understanding of Constantinople. It was first manifest in the study of the cluster of texts known as the *Patria Konstantinopoleos*, a set of commentaries on the city of Constantinople with dates ranging from the sixth century through the tenth. Renowned for their problematic language and curious commentary, and dismissed as the poor cousins of more orthodox historical texts, the *Patria* saw a reversal in fortune in the 1980s. A new publication of the eighth-century text known as the *Parastaseis syntomoi chronikai*, together with synthetic studies of the larger collection of *Patria*, looked at these written documents as resources for understanding contemporary ideas and attitudes toward Constantinople and its monuments and through them larger ideas about Byzantine society and civilization.[26] Subsequent study of some Constantinople's more familiar literary resources has proceeded along similar lines to expand the understanding of the Byzantine's own view of their monuments and institutions, together with the use of their city.[27]

As this necessarily superficial overview suggests, recent trends in Constantinopolitan scholarship have continued to build on traditional methods of inquiry while branching into new areas for discussion, with the result that there is much new material that can be brought to bear on the understanding of the city's history. Important advances have been made with respect to the study of the urban infrastructure. Perhaps even more compelling has been the groundswell of interest in the city's populations and institutions, a trend that has invigorated the study of Constantinopolitan history.

Given the ups and downs of the city's fortunes and the long and winding nature of its history, there are many subjects a companion volume might have addressed. Ultimately, the impulse guiding the selection of topics has been the desire to explore the ways in which urban structures and institutions entwined with human lives in this most evocative of late ancient and medieval cities. Cities are arguably one of the great expressions of human experience. They exist because of human beings: populations create their physical environments in response not only to the exigencies of survival, but also to the mandates of social structure, communal identity, and aesthetic vision. As such, the shape and structure of every city reflects both the needs and priorities of its population together with its hopes and aspirations. To understand the nature of an urban population is therefore to understand something of the form and structure of the city and the way it both molds and is molded by its residents. With this idea in mind, this volume aims to examine Constantinople as a vital urban center, a place that informed and responded to overlapping layers of human experience in boom times and bust, across the thousand-year span of its history. To accomplish this task the book is organized in four parts. Part I, "The Place and Its People," has three chapters. The first discusses the history of the site in the period before Constantine's foundation, the second, the development of the urban infrastructure in late antiquity and the middle ages, the third, population. These chapters are designed to introduce the protagonists of the discussion: the environments natural and built and the people who interacted with them. Part II, "Practical Matters," considers the nuts and bolts of urban living in individual chapters devoted to the supply and consumption of water and food, the organization and administration of urban building and maintenance, and urban defense. Part III, "Urban Experiences," looks at different aspects of Constantinopolitan life by focusing on four interconnected spheres of activity: the residential, imperial, commercial, and sacred. A chapter examining the various types of urban populations and the housing solutions available to them opens the section. A closer examination of specifically imperial residences and their implications for Constantinopolitan life follows. A third chapter offers an overview of commercial activity, its participants and venues, and the ways in which such activity shaped the urban experience in both physical and social terms. Three final chapters address the spiritual and sacred experiences of Constantinopolitan life by focusing on the relationship between church building and ecclesiastical practice, monastic experience, and death and burial. Part IV, "Institutions and Activities," includes chapters devoted to urban administration, social services, philanthropy, education, and learning, and, lest we forget that the Byzantines as much as anyone else loved a good time, entertainment. Part V, "Encountering Constantinople," examines the views and expectations of outsiders. Two chapters, one devoted generally to travelers, another specifically to pilgrims, consider the topic from the point of view of medieval visitors. The final two chapters track emerging historical appreciation of the Constantinopolitan past in the early modern period, one from the point of view of western antiquarian interest, the other from the Ottoman perspective.

The picture of the city to emerge from this collection is in many respects familiar. Without doubt it confirms Constantinople as an imperial city, a status made clear not simply by the presence of the emperor and court, but also by the way in which this imperial presence infiltrated all aspects of urban living in ways obvious and unexpected. The population itself was large, perhaps 500,000 in its more prosperous moments, with a healthy portion of aristocrats and administrators to staff the imperial administration and contribute to the tax base. Its infrastructure was nonpareil. An extensive water system supplied fountains, baths, and private residences. Ports on the Marmora shore and the Golden Horn facilitated the food supply and commercial trade, while a network of streets and public gathering places allowed the distribution of these goods throughout the city. Its public amenities and entertainments were unrivalled, as was its status as an educational center. All of this was overseen by the Prefect of the City, an office appointed by and responsible to the emperor. In these ways and others, Constantinople stood out among the cities of the empire as the emperor's city. At the same time, beneath the imperial gloss, it was a profoundly human city, a collection of neighborhoods in which residents and visitors haggled at the market and complained about their neighbors; where builders needed permits; where monks pursued a life of prayer; where professors bickered with one another about who had greater claims to status; where orphans, lepers, the infirm, and the elderly were in need of succor; where children and adults entertained themselves not only by visits to the Hippodrome, but also with games in the privacy of their own courtyards.

In navigating these chapters, readers may find that some discussions overlap with one another. For example, although the food supply has a designated chapter, that subject and the allied issues of diet and food consumption also find a place in the discussions of monastic, commercial, and philanthropic activities. Such repeated appearances should be viewed not as redundancies, but complementary discussions offering insight into the ways in which institutions and activities were intertwined within the urban context.

On a practical note, discussions of things Constantinopolitan often force readers to grapple with the alien terminology of medieval Greek: administrative offices, court titles, and ceremonial practices all had their names. In many instances it is possible to translate these titles. There are, however, occasions when it is impossible to do so. Court titles are particularly intractable, as there is nothing like them in our modern lexicon. In such instances, terms should be understood as a generic aristocratic honorific title. Transliteration of the Greek alphabet and orthography for all names and titles follow the conventions of the *Oxford Dictionary of Byzantium*. Unless otherwise indicated, abbreviations of classical and Byzantine sources follow those of the *Oxford Classical Dictionary* and the *Oxford Dictionary of Byzantium* respectively.

Many are the subjects that might have been covered in a companion volume, and many the ways in which individual discussions might have been addressed, with the result that some readers may feel dismay upon noting the absence of a particular subject or an individual author's approach to material. At the same time, as with all good companions – a friend who accompanies us on a journey, a person with whom we share a meal, someone with whom we share an ongoing correspondence – the goal of this volume is not to provide all of the answers, but to extend the conversation by opening the door to further inquiry. In this spirit, the authors, without whom this volume would be nothing, and I wish you happy reading!

## NOTES

1 For translation and commentary see most recently Kimberly M. Byrd, *Pierre Gilles' Constantinople: A Modern English Translation* (New York, 2008). See also the abbreviated eighteenth-century translation by John Ball, *The Four Books of the Antiquities of Constantinople* (London, 1729; reprint with introduction by R. Musto, New York, 1988).

2 J. Matthews, *Notitia Urbis Constantinopolitanae*, in *Two Romes. Rome and Constantinople in Late Antiquity*, ed. L. Grig and G. Kelly (Oxford, 2012), 81–115.

3 *Historia byzantina duplici commentario illustrata* (Paris, 1680; reprint Brussels, 1964). The dictionaries: *Glossarium ad scriptores mediae et infimae graecitatis* (Lyon, 1688); *Glossarium ad scriptores mediae et infimae Latinitatis* (Frankfurt, 1681).

4 A. Van Millingen, *Byzantine Constantinople, the Walls of the City and Adjoining Historical Sites* (London, 1899), vi.

5 C. T. Newton, *Travels and Discoveries in the Levant*, 2 vols. (London, 1865): 2: 25–8.

6 E. Bolognesi Recchi-Franceschini, *Il Gran Palazzo degli Imperatori di Bisanzio* (Istanbul, 2000); E. Bolognesi Recchi-Franceschini, M. König, and E. Riemer, eds., *Palatia: Kaiserpaläste in Konstantinopel, Ravenna und Trier* (Trier, 2003); J. Kostenec, "The Heart of the Empire: The Great Palace of the Byzantine Emperors Reconsidered," in *Secular Buildings and the Archaeology of Everyday Life in the Byzantine Empire*, ed. K. Dark (Oxford, 2004), 4–36; K. Dark, "Roman Architecture in the Great Palace of the Byzantine Emperors at Constantinople during the Sixth to Ninth Centuries," *Byzantion* 77 (2008): 87–105.

7 A. Karamani-Pekin, ed., *8000 Years Brought to Day Light: Marmaray, Metro, Sultanahmet Excavations* (Istanbul, 2007); A. Karamani-Pekin, *Stories from the Hidden Harbor: The Shipwrecks of Yenikapı* (Istanbul, 2013).

8 J. Crow, J. Bardill, and R. Bayliss, *The Water Supply of Byzantine Constantinople* (London, 2008).

9 K. Dark and F. Özgümüş, *Constantinople: Archaeology of a Byzantine Megapolis* (Oxford, 2013).

10 K. Dark and J. Kostenec, "The Hagia Sophia Project in Istanbul," *Bulletin of British Byzantine Studies*, 35 (2009): 56–68; 36 (2010): 40–9; 37 (2011): 48–68; C. Barsanti and A. Guiglia, "The Byzantine Sculpture of the Ayasofya Müzesi, Istanbul: Ten Years of Researches (1999–2009)," *Ayasofya Müzesi Yıllıgı* 13 (2010): 134–54; R. Ousterhout, *Architecture of the Kariye Camii in Istanbul* (Washington, DC, 1987); S. Kotzabassi, ed., *The Pantokrator Monastery in Constantinople* (Boston, 2013).

11  H.-G. Beck, ed., *Studien zur Frühgeschichte Konstantinopels* (Munich, 1973).

12  G. Dagron, *Naissance d'une capitale: Constantinople et ses institutions, 330–451* (Paris 1974).

13  C. Mango, *Le développement urbain de Constantinople (IVe–VIIe siècles)* (Paris, 1985).

14  P. Magdalino, *Constantinople Médiévale: Études sur l'évolution des structures urbaines* (Paris, 1996).

15  "Constantinople: The Fabric of the City, Dumbarton Oaks Symposium, 1998," ed. H. Maguire and R. Ousterhout, *DOP* 54 (2000): 157–264.

16  N. Necipoğlu, ed., *Byzantine Constantinople: Monuments, Topography and Everyday Life* (Leiden, 2001).

17  C. Mango and G. Dagron, eds., *Constantinople and Its Hinterland* (Aldershot, 1995).

18  J. Crow, J. Bardill, and R. Bayliss, *The Water Supply of Byzantine Constantinople* (London, 2008).

19  F.A. Bauer, *Stadt, Platz und Denkmal in der Spätantike : Untersuchungen zur Ausstattung des öffentlichen Raums in den spätantiken Städten Rom, Konstantinopel und Ephesos* (Mainz, 1996); S. Bassett, *The Urban Image of Late Antique Constantinople* (Cambridge and New York, 2004).

20  H. Maguire, ed., *Byzantine Court Culture from 829 to 1204* (Washington, DC, 1997); F. A. Bauer, ed., *Visualisierung von Herrschaft. Frühmittelalterliche Residenzen- Gestalt und Zeremoniell* (Istanbul, 2006); A. Ödekan, E. Akyürek, and N. Necipoğlu, eds., *The Byzantine Court: Source of Power and Culture* (Istanbul, 2013).

21  D. Caner, *Wandering, Begging Monks: Spiritual Authority and the Promotion of Monasticism in Late Antiquity* (Berkeley, 2002).

22  For a more complete discussion of these developments see D. R. Reinsch, "The History of Editing Byzantine Historiographical Texts," in *The Byzantine World*, ed. P. Stephenson (London and New York, 2010), 435–44.

23  For example: *Byzantine Monastic Foundation Documents: A Complete Translation of the Surviving Founders' "Typika" and Testaments*, ed. J. Thomas and A. C. Hero (Washington, 2000); *The Book of Ceremonies of Constantine Porphyrogennetos*, trans. A. Moffatt and M. Tall (Canberra, 2012); *Constantine of Rhodes on Constantinople and the Church of Holy Apostles*, ed. L. James and I. Vassis (Burlington, VT, 2012).

24  G. Downey, *Constantinople in the Age of Justinian* (Norman, 1960); M. Mango, "The Commercial Map of Constantinople," *DOP* 54 (2000): 189–207; F. A. Bauer, ed., *Visualisierung von Herrschaft. Frühmittelalterliche Residenzen- Gestalt und Zeremoniell* (Istanbul, 2006); J. Koder, "The Authority of the Eparchos in the Markets of Constantinople (according to the Book of the Eparch)," in *Authority in Byzantium*, ed. P. Armstrong (Farnham, 2013), 83–108.

25  Av. Cameron, *Procopius and the Sixth Century* (London, 1985); R. Webb, "Ekphrasis, Amplification and Persuasion in Procopius' Buildings," *AntTard* 8 (2000): 67–71.

26  Av. Cameron and J. Herrin, *Constantinople in the Eighth Century: The Parastaseis Syntomai Chronikaia* (Leiden, 1984); G. Dagron, *Constantinople imaginaire: Études sur le recueil des Patria* (Paris, 1984); A. Berger, *Untersuchungen zu den Patria Konstantinupoleos* (Bonn, 1988).

27  R. Macrides and P. Magdalino, "The Architecture of Ekphrasis: Construction and Content of Paul the Silentiary's Poem on Hagia Sophia," *BMGS* 12 (1988): 47–82; L. James and R. Webb, "'To Understand Ultimate Things and Enter Secret Places': Ekphraseis and Art in Byzantium," *AH* 14.2 (1991): 1–17.

# PART I

# THE PLACE AND ITS PEOPLE

# 1: BEFORE CONSTANTINOPLE

## Thomas Russell

## THE SITUATION AND CHARACTER OF GREEK BYZANTION

Constantinople was founded on the site of its Greco-Roman predecessor, Byzantion, whose fortunes were defined by its relationship to the Bosporos, a strait that simultaneously connected and divided. Running north to south, it linked the Pontus (Black Sea) to the Propontis (Sea of Marmora) and the Mediterranean beyond. At the same time, it split Europe from Asia. Standing at the southern end of the strait, Byzantion both commanded and was commanded by these strategic waters. The history of human habitation of the Bosporos stretches back thousands of years before Constantine (306–337), and this 'prehistory' has an important role to play in shaping the understanding of Constantinople. Cities and communities are defined by their relationship with their environment. Byzantion was no exception. Its inhabitants' lives, and the daily rhythms of its local economies, were formed by human interaction with the Bosporos. Thus, it is with Byzantion and its relationship to the Bosporos that the Constantinopolitan story begins.

In AD 53, a deputation from Byzantion was granted an audience with the emperor Claudius (10 BC–AD 54). At this time, Byzantion was one of many unremarkable Greek cities subject to Roman rule, and the Byzantines had come to Rome to plead for a reduction of their financial burdens. To make their case, they drew upon the rich cultural capital of their provincial town. Byzantion was a Greek city which claimed ancient origins. It possessed, they observed, rich mythological traditions linking it to the journey of the Argonauts and the passage of Io across the Bosporos. The Byzantines also recounted their history, stressing the strategic value of the site, and the various times Byzantion had aided Rome by allowing troops or supplies to be ferried between Europe and Asia.[1]

Tacitus, who recorded these remarks, was not alone among ancient commentators in recognizing the strategic significance of Byzantion's location. One ancient tradition mocked Byzantion's neighbour Chalcedon (modern Kadıköy) as the 'City of the Blind'. Located on the eastern shore of the Bosporos opposite Byzantion, its founders allegedly had overlooked the more favourable location of Byzantion when choosing their own site.[2] In a lengthy excursus, Polybius (second century BC) described the situation of Byzantion and the natural geography and hydrography of the Bosporos strait.[3] His discussion provides a glimpse into how the early city was viewed. While its maritime advantages were long recognized, and the city was, as a consequence, internationally valued, it was also widely known that Byzantion's fraught relationship with its barbarian Thracian neighbours made it difficult for it to enjoy its fertile agricultural territory: Polybius says that it was the most well-sited city in the entire world with regard to the sea, but because of regular raids by its Thracian neighbours, the worst sited with regard to the land.[4] The natural advantages of Byzantion's situation had therefore impressed ancient authors, who also mentioned the city's proverbial wealth in fish.[5]

The city occasioning these comments was centred on a promontory at the tip of a peninsula jutting into the Bosporos at the point where the strait flows into the Propontis (Fig. 1.1). This hilly outcropping, now occupied by modern Istanbul's Topkapı Palace, was lapped by the waters of the Propontis to the south and a secluded, sheltered harbour, the Golden Horn, to the north. Protected by water on three sides, Byzantion was an easily defensible location from which to monitor maritime traffic passing through the Bosporos. The city's territory (*chora*) extended west along the Propontis. At its height in the Hellenistic period it reached the ancient village Selymbria (modern Silviri), 60 km from the entrance to the Bosporos. Byzantine territory stretched northward on the western side of the Bosporos to the opening of the Pontus, and the shore of the strait was littered with small communities which belonged to Byzantion. For a period between the third and first centuries BC the city appears to have also controlled an extended *peraea* (overseas possession) on the southern shore of the Propontis, possessing territory in Mysia and around Lake Dascylitis, near Cyzicus.[6]

The envoys from Byzantion, then, did not come from an insignificant place; yet, despite their city's international fame, its expansive territory, its strategic defensive position and its ability to control Bosporos shipping, it took a long time for it to develop beyond a provincial trading hub of marginal importance. It was not inevitable that Byzantion should become a world capital, and for much of its history it was a backwater. The wit Stratonicus referred to it as the

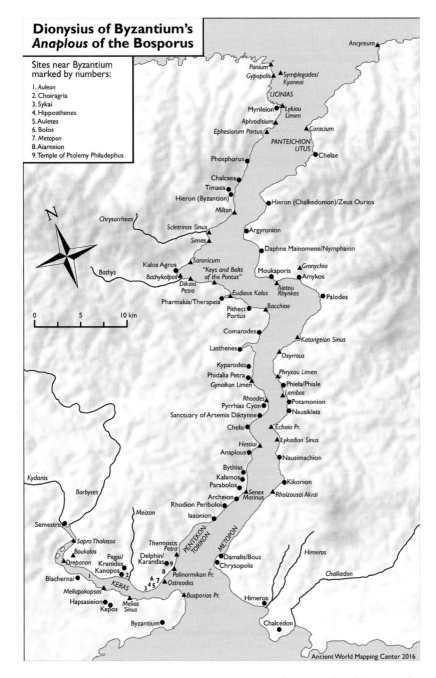

## Dionysius of Byzantium's *Anaplous* of the Bosporus

**Sites near Byzantium marked by numbers:**
1. Auleon
2. Choiragria
3. Sykai
4. Hipposthenes
5. Auletes
6. Bolos
7. Metopon
8. Aianteion
9. Temple of Ptolemy Philadephus

1.1 Dionysios of Byzantion's Bosporos. (Courtesy of T. Russell and G. Moss for the Ancient World Mapping Centre)

'armpit' of Greece.[7] Some of the explanation for this apparent paradox may be found in the natural conditions of the Bosporos. This narrow, winding waterway meanders from the Pontus into the Propontis for 31 km. Whoever controlled the strait could regulate, tax or otherwise extort mercantile traffic passing through it. Consequently, the Bosporos ensured that Byzantion's fortunes were tied to the ebb and flow of trade between Greece and the Pontus.

The natural conditions of the Bosporos could make the strait dangerous. Its dominating currents flow north to south and grow stronger as they rebound at the various indentations and elbows of the Bosporos. They helped to funnel shoaling fish into Byzantion's harbours and its fishermen's nets, but they could also make it difficult for maritime traffic to pass through the strait without an extended stop in one of the city's harbours or its many *emporia* (trading stations) along the Bosporos shores. Hieron, 'the Sanctuary', a religious site located near the strait's northern mouth on the Asiatic coast, functioned as the symbolic entrance to and exit from the Pontus.[8] Jason and the Argonauts were said to have originally established Hieron as a sacred place on their way through the Bosporos towards Colchis. Here, an inscription preserves the words of a thank-offering, which invites sailors to make offerings to Zeus Ourios, the 'fair-winded', in exchange for favourable sailing conditions through the 'dark-blue Cyaneae' (the clashing rocks of Argonautic fame) north into the Pontus, or south to the Aegean.[9] The inscription illustrates one response to the many maritime dangers of the Bosporos. When the currents of the strait conspired with the winds to make the strait treacherous, and when sudden, dense mist obscured both shores of the narrow strait, ship captains had no choice but to seek refuge in a place like Hieron, making numerous stops during their passage for safety, and timing their voyages around the winds. Captains would plan their itineraries around the need to make 'pit stops' along the way, and they would group together with other ships in convoy for safety. These numerous stops must have made maritime traffic easier to tax, and no doubt the local economy depended upon their presence. The passing fleets were also a lucrative source of income in other ways, and attracted the interest of outside powers who could offer them protection.[10] Therefore, the history of pre-Constantinian Byzantion is to a large degree the history of the Bosporos's financial exploitation.

Prior to the institution of Roman rule in 146 BC, Byzantion was considered a frontier city, located at the fringes of Hellenic culture and surrounded by hostile barbarian tribes. As noted, Polybius paid special attention to the Thracian tribes surrounding Byzantion, saying that they launched repeated incursions into the Greek city's territory. Xenophon says that the Ten Thousand, on their return from Persia in 399 BC, viewed Byzantion as the 'first' Greek city at which they arrived, implying that Byzantion served as a final bastion of Hellenic civilisation before the Pontic frontier.[11] Living in a city on the periphery, the Byzantines were fiercely proud of their Hellenic identity. They clung to those mythological traditions which connected them to the wider Greek community, and they consciously preserved those institutions, cults or dialectical peculiarities which underlined this link.

Another feature of the Greek city was its status as a *trading* city. We cannot know what feeling Stratonicus was attempting to evoke when he called the city the 'armpit' of Greece, but it may have had something to do with smell. As a vibrant fish market, Byzantion must have reeked not only of the fish caught in the Bosporos but also of salted fish taken from the Pontus or Propontis and brought to Byzantion for export. In addition, as a rich, international port, Byzantion drew the attention of some moralizing ancient commentators who thought that wealth and luxury incited indolence: the fourth-century BC historian, Theopompus, is reported to have characterized the Byzantines as lazy sots who spent all their time at the market or the pub.[12]

These are the views of outsiders. Unusually, we also know a great deal about what one local thought of his homeland. Sometime during the first or second centuries AD, Dionysios of Byzantion wrote a treatise describing the topography and mythological traditions of the Bosporos, the *Anaplous Bosporou* (*Navigation of the Bosporos*).

The *Anaplous* is a goldmine of topographical and mythological information about Byzantion. Just as interesting as this information is the way in which Dionysios reveals his own feelings towards his home town. In the preface he invites the reader to visit his homeland, claiming that personal autopsy is the only way to gain a true appreciation of the region.[13] Dionysios' tone is one of childlike enthusiasm; he revels in the 'wondrous' qualities of the strait and its currents, and fixates on the dangers created by the 'roiling' and 'spitting' of the waters. He is a proud local welcoming an outsider into a foreign, overwhelming and mysterious world, using native knowledge to explain the inexplicable: the mysterious strength of the unseen Bosporos currents; the reasons for the extreme violence of the water at various bays along the strait. This fixation perhaps reflects the role of Byzantion as an international hub:

Byzantines like Dionysios must have become well versed in explaining these things to visitors, and no doubt a busy tourist industry had emerged in Byzantion by the second century AD.

Throughout the treatise, Dionysios explains the mythological aetiologies which lie behind the names of numerous sites along the Bosporos shores, linking them to famous stories from Greek mythology. He also provides detailed descriptions of the most dangerous locations in the Bosporos, where the currents, winds and fog can make passage difficult for unwary navigators. At these sections, Dionysios betrays a pride in his possession of privileged, local knowledge, which the inexperienced, the naive or the foreign did not share. For example, in his account of Timaea, where a lighthouse aided mariners sailing south through the strait, Dionysios describes how barbarian inhabitants lit rival signals further west from the opening of the Bosporos to lure sailors away from the lighthouse and wreck them on the dangerous shores along the coast at Salmydessos.[14] In Dionysios' day the lights of Timaea had been extinguished and the tower fallen into ruin, meaning that no signals survived to aid navigators. Only those locals, like Dionysios, who knew the lighthouse from oral tradition, would have been aware that signals were ever lit here. Dionysios is thereby sharing this privileged, local information with the rest of world. Again, this focus may reflect Byzantion's role as an international trading hub. While Byzantion may have been a busy cosmopolitan metropolis open to the rest of the Greco-Roman world, locals like Dionysios clung carefully to their specialist knowledge about the dangers of these spots, and the myths and traditions accompanying them. Used to explain the Bosporos to the outside world, these stories distinguished insiders from outsiders and were also a way to claim ownership of the strait. This point of view reflects a city and region which was not only open to the outside world but also possessed a highly developed tourist industry that would accommodate its visitors.

## ORIGINS AND EARLY HISTORY

Many of the myths preserved in sources like Dionysios concern the city's foundation. In myth, Byzantion was founded by the eponymous *ktistes* (founder), Byzas. This founder figure functioned as all things to all people. In one version of his story, Byzas was a demi-god: the son of Poseidon and Ceroessa, the daughter of Zeus and Io.[15] This divine parentage lent cultural prestige to his city. In another, earlier version of the myth, Byzas was a Thracian king who lived at the site during the Argonauts' journey to Colchis.[16] In a third version, he was the son of the local water nymph Semestre, a parentage which emphasized his connection with the area.[17] Such stories were useful; they helped to legitimate the social pretensions of local elites who claimed descent from figures like Byzas, or to solidify territorial claims to spots along the Bosporos in cultural and mythological terms.

Much less is known about the historical settlement of Byzantion than the mythical foundation. The earliest indications of human occupation on the Istanbul peninsula go back to the Palaeolithic period, while coffins and human remains have been discovered dating back some 8,000 years. It is apparent that the site has been occupied through-out human history: excavations in the modern district of Yenikapı and around Lake Küçükçekmece, 20 km west of Istanbul, have reinforced this picture.[18] It is unclear, however, when *Greeks* began to live in the region. The earliest archaeological evidence, proto-Corinthian pottery, dates to the eighth or seventh centuries BC, but the picture is too scanty to determine when a Greek presence originated.[19] Nor are ancient sources clear on who 'founded' Byzantion. The earliest sources are unspecific, while others provide contradictory testimonies. A sixth-century tradition claims that Byzas was the leader of a contingent from Megara in the Peloponnesus, and a number of other ancient sources refer to Megara among other competing claims.[20] Modern commentators tend to uphold the Megarian view. Some explain the contradictory claims as evidence of a 'mixed' foundation involving a majority of Megarians; others suggest a 'staged' foundation, with various settlers arriving from different places in different phases.[21] Modern debates about the nature of Greek 'colonization' have not so much advanced understanding of the phenomenon as they have obfuscated it, and it is now possible to deny the very concept of colonization altogether.[22] Nevertheless, the evidence of prosopography together with that of the local alphabet, cults and the festival calendar of Byzantion indicates that Megarians comprised a significant group among the region's first settlers, and it is clear that Hellenistic and Roman Byzantines were keen to connect themselves with Megara.[23]

Byzantion's early appearances in the historical record reinforce the economic and strategic significance of the strait. For much of its early history Byzantion was the target of opportunistic individuals who hoped to control and profit from the strait. Their involvement in the region limited any potential for the city to develop into a major power in its own right. The first time Byzantion figures in a historical source is as a crossing point between Europe and Asia: Darius is said to have bridged the Bosporos on an expedition against the Scythians in 513.[24] It is likely that the Persians, in common with all subsequent powers who controlled the strait, attempted to profit from merchant traffic in the Bosporos. Dionysios says that Chrysopolis ('City of Gold'), a site on the Asiatic coast opposite Byzantion, took its name from the fact that the Persians used to collect gold here, suggesting that the location was used as a customs house.[25] Byzantion appears to have remained under intermittent Persian control until the onset of the Persian Wars (499–449 BC). At that time, Histiaeus, the tyrant of Miletus who had been expelled from his own city, sailed to the Bosporos and established himself as a privateer. Here he began extorting mercantile traffic passing through the Bosporos by running a protection racket.[26] The episode is one example of the way in which individuals or communities could monopolize protection services and so profit from control of the Bosporos.

This pattern of extortion and protection continued throughout the fifth century BC, with various powerful individuals making intelligent use of the opportunities afforded by the site. Following the Persian Wars, the Spartan regent Pausanias made Byzantion his base. He may have had designs on creating his own power base for a tyranny or was perhaps continuing Histiaeus' example by exploiting the site to extort passing ships. His exact plan is unclear, and the evidence compromised by contemporary hostility for Pausanias. He aroused considerable dislike in Greece, and was ultimately recalled to Sparta, where he was placed on trial for collaborating with Persia. Thucydides' account reflects the negativity with which Pausanias was viewed: he is said to have behaved in Byzantion as a tyrant and a traitor.[27] These accusations all provided a useful excuse for Athens to expel Pausanias from Byzantion and assume leadership of the Hellenic League, the association of Greek city-states that had fought against Persia.

It is clear that a powerful person like Pausanias in sole charge of a region as economically sensitive as the Bosporos made some people outside Byzantion very nervous. Inside Byzantion, however, it is likely that Pausanias was genuinely popular. Herodotus reports that after the Ionian Revolt, an uprising of Greek cities in Asia Minor against Persian control at the start of the Persian Wars, a number of Byzantines fled and founded the city of Mesembria in advance of an attack by the Phoenicians, who were Persian allies. In their absence, the Phoenicians razed Byzantion. Subsequently, Pausanias may have restored the Mesembrian exiles to Byzantion and rebuilt the city.[28] It has been suggested that this act of reconstruction and repatriation resulted in his being hailed as a liberator, accorded cult status and worshipped as a semi-divine 'founder hero' (*heros ktistes*).[29] If true, it is easy to see how Pausanias could have built a strong power base in the strait, threatening those interested in safe passage.

This pattern of opportunistic exploitation continued with limited success during the Peloponnesian War (431–404 BC). In 409 BC, towards the close of the war, Clearchus, the Spartan *harmost* (military governor) of Byzantion, arrived at the city with the aim of controlling the strait and cutting off Athens's Pontic food imports. Like Histiaeus, his purpose was to exploit the city's economically vital position, but once there he installed a brutal military regime and behaved as a tyrant. He returned to Byzantion after the Peloponnesian War at the request of local pro-Spartan oligarchs, and during his second stint he embarked on a reign of terror before fleeing to Persia when the Spartans recalled him.

This pattern of exploitation continued into the fourth century. In 389 BC the Athenian Thrasybulus liberated Byzantion and established a customs house which taxed vessels passing through the strait. His political opponents in Athens viewed this move as an attempt to establish a tyranny, with the result that Thrasybulus' friends advised him to flee to Byzantion, marry a daughter of the Thracian King Seuthes and establish himself as tyrant.[30]

These powerful individuals all controlled the Bosporos for limited periods of time, and earned negative reputations for their actions there. Lacking the maritime resources to enforce a lasting protection racket, their efforts to extort passing trade were sporadic and short lived. In fact, for much of the fifth century BC the Athenian Empire controlled the Bosporos, and its bureaucratic apparatus combined with the naval power of the Delian League, the alliance of Greek states under the leadership of Athens, permitted the Athenians to exploit the strait in a much more thorough way.

Athens's involvement in the strait was transformational, invigorating the local economy and establishing the Bosporos as a key plank among the mechanisms of control in the Athenian Empire. Evidence is fragmentary, but there is enough to suggest that for most of the fifth century Athens exploited Pontic trade on an institutional level by requiring tribute payments. It legitimated this policy by describing it as a tax paid to a benevolent power in exchange for services rendered.[31]

Thus, when Athens assumed leadership of the Greek alliance after Pausanias' expulsion, Byzantion soon became one of the most valuable members of the Delian League. The Athenian Tribute Lists, which record the financial contributions of the league's members, reveal that Byzantion was among the league's highest-spending members, with payments rising steadily from 15 talents in 450/49, to 18 talents 1,800 drachmas in 433/2, and 21 talents 4,740 drachmas in 430/29. Across the empire, only Aegina and Thasos, two 30-talent contributors, regularly outpaid Byzantion.[32]

Such high tribute levels must reflect the wealth and economic capacity of Byzantion, as such payments tend to correlate with the value of local resources.[33] Other evidence suggests that Athenian involvement in the strait went even further. An inscription, concerning Athens's ally Methone, sets out the privileged conditions allowing Methone to import corn from Byzantion. The Methonians were permitted to import a set number of *medimnoi* (grain measures). Officials called *Hellespontophylakes* ('Hellespont Guards') who were charged with preventing outside interference, oversaw the process.[34] The *Hellespontophylakes* appear to have been one cog in the wheel of a wider protective service offered by the Athenian Empire.[35] As the Methone decree makes clear, this service used the strategic position of Byzantion to coordinate and manage transit. In exchange, Athens received a percentage of the value of goods carried by merchants. Evidence from near the end of the Peloponnesian War indicates that the Athenians had established a 10 per cent toll (*dekate*) on Pontic trade, which was administered at Chrysopolis. Although known only from evidence relating to events at the war's end, when the strait passed back and forth between Athens and Sparta, there is no reason to assume that it was a temporary or emergency measure.[36] This *dekate*, then, was the cost of doing business in this region of the Athenian Empire.

It took a centralized imperial bureaucracy backed by the threat of naval intervention to transform the Bosporos into a highly valuable economic resource, and to exploit fully the fleets constantly passing between the Pontus and Greece. During the classical period no single individual was able to achieve this level of success in the region, because each lacked the military dominance and financial institutions of the Athenian Empire. Nor were the Byzantines able to implement fully their own financial strategies in the strait because their happy natural location was too inviting to predators like Pausanias and Histiaeus. In 340 BC, Philip II of Macedon also tried to conquer Byzantion. Though he succeeded in capturing a fleet of corn ships bound for Athens at Hieron, he was not able to capture the city. Byzantion resisted stubbornly, and aid came from a variety of places, including Persia. Byzantion's allies feared that in taking possession of the city Philip might control Bosporos shipping. This role as guarantor of free passage for shipping through the strait would come to define Byzantion in the Hellenistic period.

## THE HELLENISTIC AND ROMAN CITY

During the Hellenistic period, the Byzantines, according to Polybius, functioned as 'common benefactors of all'.[37] Their city, which did not belong to any of Alexander the Great's successor kingdoms, was unusually important in the Hellenistic world, and Byzantion's independent stewardship of the Bosporos was preferable to the dominance of a larger power, because it allowed the strait to remain open and for international trade to continue to pass unmolested. Thus, left in relative freedom, the Byzantines enjoyed a period of sustained economic development. During this time, Byzantion intensified trade links with the cities of the Pontus. Coins from the mint at Byzantion were used heavily in the Propontis and Pontus, becoming a highly valued form of currency.[38] Byzantion's art had a similar impact: funerary banquet motifs on *stelai* (grave markers) from Byzantion's workshops were imitated throughout the Pontic region in the Hellenistic and Roman periods.[39] Finally, it is likely that Hellenistic Byzantion exploited its possession of the Bosporos to establish a closed currency system. By requiring the use of local currency or foreign issues, which had been countermarked and thus validated after payment of a tax, the Byzantines profited from merchants passing through the strait by imposing an indirect tariff on the exchange of currency.[40] This was an ingenious way to profit from the merchant traffic of the Bosporos without interfering with free passage through the strait.

Throughout this period, however, regular invasions by their Thracian neighbours continued to oppress the Byzantines. According to Polybius these raids were yearly occurrences,[41] and together with other sources he characterizes the relationship between the Byzantines and the Thracians as one of continuous conflict. It is, moreover, clear that the Byzantines defined themselves in opposition to their neighbours. Dionysios tells of how the city's original founders were forced to defeat a massed barbarian army before taking possession of the site, while in the sixth century Hesychius recounts mythical battles undertaken by Byzas against his Thracian rivals.[42] Even to late authors, Byzantine self-identity was bound up with opposition to the Thracians.

In line with this oppositional relationship is the limited evidence for Thracian involvement in the political, social or cultic life of Byzantion. For example, there is no hard evidence that the Thracian goddess Bendis was honoured with a festival and a torch race at Byzantion, though some inscriptions preserve theophoric names relating to her worship.[43] Very few of the many funerary *stelai* discovered in

Byzantion's ancient necropolis preserve Thracian iconography.[44] Similarly, Thracian names are barely present in Byzantion's prosopography: one calculation puts the proportion at 4.4 per cent, lower than comparable Greek cities in the Propontis and Pontus.[45]

Finally, citizenship requirements at Byzantion were strict: as at Athens, a dual endogamy requirement left little scope for the children of mixed marriages between Greeks and Thracians to achieve Byzantine citizenship.[46] Consequently, even when Thracian names appear on local inscriptions, it is *exceptionally* rare to find offspring of Thracian parents who also bear Thracian names.[47] That said, our evidence is limited, and may reflect a distorted view. It was advantageous for the Byzantines to accentuate their Hellenic credentials. There are clues that relationships between Thracians and Byzantines may have been closer than the evidence initially admits. For example, the name Byzas (and his city Byzantion) probably derives from a Thracian root, while a series of *stelai* preserve evidence of the worship of a Thracian divinity Stomianos, propitiated as a protector of sailors, along the shores of the Bosporos.[48]

Eventually the pressure of repeated barbarian invasions led to a crisis. In 280 BC a group of Galatians attacked Greece and migrated across to Asia. A splinter group established the kingdom of Tylis in eastern Bulgaria. These Tylians launched invasions of Byzantion's hinterland over an extended period: each time the Byzantines were forced to bribe them to leave, but each time they returned and the 'gift' grew larger. Eventually the Byzantines were paying the equivalent of 80 talents per payment. By 220 BC, unable to bear the pressure, Byzantion was forced to revive the *dekate*, thus earning the ire of the international community. Rhodes, which possessed a vested interest in free trade, demanded an end to the toll. When this request was refused, Rhodes went to war against Byzantion. The Byzantine–Rhodian War did not last long, and consisted mainly of a protracted blockade of the Bosporos, which was enough for the city to surrender and accept terms that restored the status quo in exchange for the toll's removal.[49] The whole episode is instructive because it reveals that Byzantion's neutrality and privileged position in the Hellenistic world were predicated upon the guarantee that it maintain free passage through the strait. The international community would not tolerate Byzantion trying to do what Athens had done; the market could not bear it. Even in the third century, a period of relative freedom, the Byzantines were prevented from fully exploiting the natural circumstances of their situation by outside powers.

Eventually Byzantion fell under the sway of Rome. In 146 BC a formal alliance was concluded, and by the time of the Byzantine embassy to Claudius, Byzantion had been made tributary. At some point the Romans assumed responsibility for extracting tolls on Bosporos shipping: the first clause of the Roman customs law of Asia, inscribed in AD 62, concerns the taxation of imports and exports at the Pontus. During this period Byzantion continued to thrive as a busy trading hub. A notable development during the Roman period was the revival by local Bosporos elites of the region's epichoric myths and traditions, and their connection of their own families with the stories. The phenomenon is linked to the Second Sophistic, and is likewise reflected in the text of Dionysios' *Anaplous*, which itself served to reinvigorate oral traditions. These stories were a useful way to ingratiate oneself with Roman officials, as they created a sense of prestige by linking the city and its inhabitants to hoary antiquity.[50] As a result, references to Byzantion's convoluted foundation myths appear to have been in fashion during the Roman period. A description of Byzantion as the 'land of Inachus' (the father of Io) appears on a funerary inscription of a Byzantine actor discovered in Tomis in the Pontus, while the image of Ceroessa (the mother of Byzas) as a maiden with horns appears on Byzantine coins in the first and second centuries AD.[51] Possibly the invention or elaboration of such stories was a response to the city's circumstances under the Roman Empire. Hadrian probably visited in AD 117/18: epigraphic evidence reveals that he was designated as eponymous magistrate for several consecutive years. The best explanation of this fact is that he was there to agree to the offices in person.[52] If Hadrian did visit, it is not difficult to imagine that the city's mythological traditions enjoyed a renaissance as the local elites tried to ingratiate themselves with the visiting emperor. One sophist from Byzantion, Marcus, who was a contemporary of Hadrian, traced his descent to Byzas.[53] Possibly his kinship claims were a response to the pan-Hellenist emperor's visit, and the genealogy reflects the Byzantines' pride in their prestigious mythological past.

Few traces of this city remained when Constantine founded Constantinople on the site. In AD 193 Byzantion sided with Pescennius Niger, the rival of Septimius Severus (193–211). After the defeat of Niger the Byzantines refused to capitulate, leading to a lengthy siege, which ended with the surrender of the city and its destruction by Severus in 196. As punishment, Byzantion was stripped of its freedom, made into a dependency of nearby Perinthus, and its buildings were razed to the ground. Severus appears to have regretted this decision, and at the urging of Caracalla he refounded the city. Coins from this period bear the legend *ktisis*, 'foundation', and show a unique type which depicts Severus offering before an altar. Severus endowed the city, which was renamed *colonia Antonia* in honour of his own dynastic line, with elaborate building works including a *stoa*, a public bath, an amphi-theatre and a hippodrome.[54] It was this city which Constantine selected for his new capital.

Before it became Constantinople, Byzantion was therefore a city with a long history, rich cultural and mythological traditions, and a thriving tourist industry. It was famous for its fishing industries and for the natural advantages of its location, which offered the potential for profit from ships passing to and from the Pontus. For much of its history opportunistic powers that hoped to exploit the Bosporos for themselves impeded the city's growth. In consequence, Byzantion remained a provincial if wealthy merchant town. This situation would change following the foundation of Constantinople, when Constantine and his successors were able to take control of and exploit the natural advantages that had played so vital a role in the history of old Byzantion to the benefit of the new city's development.

## FURTHER READING

Gabrielsen, V. 'Trade and tribute: Byzantion and the Black Sea straits', in *The Black Sea in Antiquity: Regional and Interregional Economic Exchanges*, ed. V. Gabrielsen and J. Lund (Aarhus, 2007), 287–324.

Mango, C. 'Septime Sévère et Byzance', *CRAI*, 147e année, n. 2, (2003): 593–608.

Robu, A. *Mégare et les établissements mégariens de Sicile, de Propontide, et du Pont-Euxin. Histoire et institutions* (Bern, 2014).

Russell, T. *Byzantium and the Bosporus: A Historical Study, from the Seventh Century BC until the Foundation of Constantinople* (Oxford, 2017).

## NOTES

1 Tac. *Ann.* 12.62.
2 Hdt. 7.144.2; Strab. 7.6.2.
3 Pol. 4.38–53.
4 Pol. 4.38.1.
5 Tac. *Ann.* 12.62–3.
6 T. Russell, *Byzantium and the Bosporus: A Historical Study, from the Seventh Century BC until the Foundation of Constantinople* (Oxford, 2017), 104–12.
7 Athen. 8.351d.
8 A. Moreno, 'Hieron: the ancient sanctuary at the mouth of the Black Sea', *Hesperia* 77 (2008): 655–709.
9 *Die Inschriften von Kalchedon*, ed. R. Merkelbach (Bonn, 1980), no. 14.
10 V. Gabrielsen, 'Trade and tribute: Byzantion and the Black Sea straits', in *The Black Sea in Antiquity: Regional and Interregional Economic Exchanges*, ed. V. Gabrielsen and J. Lund (Aarhus, 2007), 287–324.

11 Xen. *An.* 7.1.29.
12 Athen. 12.526e.
13 Dion. Byz. 1.
14 Dion. Byz. 77.
15 Dion. Byz. 24; Hsch. *FGrHist* 390 F1.6–7.
16 Diod. 4.49.1.
17 Hsch. *FGrHist* 390 F1.5.
18 B. Hughes, *Istanbul: A Tale of Three Cities* (London, 2017), 15–18; S. G. Aydingün 'Some remarkable prehistoric finds at Istanbul-Kucukcekmece', in *SOMA 2008: Proceedings of the XII Symposium in Mediterranean Archaeology*, ed. H. Oniz (Oxford, 2009), 154–7; Z. Kızıltan (ed.), *Istanbul: 8,000 Years Brought to Daylight: Marmaray, Metro Sultanahmet Excavations* (Istanbul, 2007).
19 Moreno, 'Hieron', 666, with n. 36. L. D. Loukopoulou, *Contribution à l'histoire de la Thrace Propontique durant la periode archaique* (Athens, 1989), 52–3.
20 Russell, *Byzantium*, 214–16.
21 A. Robu, *Mégare et les établissements mégariens de Sicile, de Propontide, et du Pont-Euxin: Histoire et institutions* (Bern, 2014), esp. 254–5, 282–5, 409–10; B. Isaac, *The Greek Settlements in Thrace until the Macedonian Conquest* (Leiden, 1986), 218.
22 Russell, *Byzantium*, 205–41.
23 Robu, *Megaré*, esp. 248–92. K. Hanell, *Megarische Studien* (Lund, 1934), 116–204.
24 Hdt. 4.87.
25 Dion. Byz. 109.
26 Hdt. 6.5, 26.
27 Thuc. 1.94–6, 128–35.
28 Hdt. 6.33.
29 Russell, *Byzantium*, 218–19. C. F. Lehmann-Haupt, 'Pausanias, Heros Ktistes von Byzanz', *Klio* 17 (1921): 59–73.
30 Lys. 28.5.
31 Russell, *Byzantium*, 53–90.
32 Russell, *Byzantium*, 69–80; H. Merle, *Die Geschichte des Städte Byzantion und Kalchedon, von ihrer Gründung biz zum Eingriefen der Römer in die Verhältniesse des Ostens* (Kiel, 1916), 17, 21.
33 L. Nixon and S. Price, 'The size and resources of Greek cities', in *The Greek City, from Homer to Alexander*, ed. O. Murray and S. Price (Oxford, 1990), 137–70.
34 *IG* I³ 61.34–41.
35 Gabrielsen, 'Trade and tribute', esp. 300–11.
36 Xen. *Hell.* 1.1.22; Merle, *Byzanz*, 22–3, 28; Gabrielsen, 'Trade and tribute', 293–5.
37 Pol. 4.38.
38 C.A. Marinescu, 'Making and spending money along the Bosporus: the Lysimachi coinages minted by Byzantium and Chalcedon and their socio-cultural context' (PhD diss., Columbia University, 1996), esp. 366–71.
39 M. Dana, '"Le banquet des sophistes": représentation funéraire, représentation sociale sur les stèles de Byzance aux époques hellénistique et impériale', in *Studia Universitatis 'Babeş- Bolyai,' Historia*. 59.1 (2014): 345–71, esp. 357–61.
40 Marinescu, 'Making and spending money'; Russell, *Byzantion*, 91–132; H. Seyrig, 'Monnaies hellénistiques de Byzance et de Calcédoine', in *Essays in Greek Coinage Presented to Stanley Robinson*, ed. C. M. Kraay and G. K. Jenkins (Oxford, 1968), 183–200.
41 Pol. 4.45.5.
42 Dion. Byz. 53; Hsch. *FGrHist* 390 F1.11, 15–18.
43 N. Fıratlı, *Les stèles funeraires de Byzance Gréco-Romaine, avec l'édition et l'index commenté des épitaphes par Louis Robert* (Paris, 1964), 26–7, 37.
44 Louis Robert in Fıratlı, *Les stèles funeraires*, 133–5.
45 Loukopoulou, *Contribution*, 198–207 ; L.D. Loukopoulou, 'Colons et indigénes dans la Thrace Propontique', *Klio* 71 (1989): 78–83.
46 Arist. *Oec.* 1346b 26–1347a 3.
47 Russell, *Byzantium*, 202; Loukopoulou, *Contribution*, 202.
48 Russell, *Byzantium*, 199–200, 235–6.
49 Pol. 4.47–52.

50  Dion. Byz. 24; Hsch. *FGrHist* 390 F1.3–9.

51  A. Avram and C.P. Jones, 'An actor from Byzantium in a new epigram from Tomis', *ZPapEpig* 178 (2011): 126–34.

52  Russell, *Byzantium*, 47; A. Łajtar, *Die Inschriften von Byzantion* (Bonn, 2000), 72.

53  Philostr. *VS* 1.24.

54  C. Mango, 'Septime Sévère et Byzance', in *CRAI*, 147.2 (2003): 593–608.

# 2: Urban Development and Decline, Fourth–Fifteenth Centuries

*Albrecht Berger*

## Ancient Byzantium

Constantinople, ancient Byzantion and today's İstanbul, lies at the southern exit of the Bosporos, the strait separating Europe from Asia Minor and connecting the Black Sea to the Sea of Marmara, on its European side. Surrounded by the waters of the Sea of Marmora and the Golden Horn, it is a peninsular city (Fig. 2.1).

According to tradition, Byzantion was founded by Greeks from Megara around 660 BC.[1] The name of the legendary King Byzas, who led the Greeks to this place and founded the city, was derived from the name Byzantion only much later.[2] The strategic position on the peninsula and the natural harbor in the Golden Horn explain the choice of location: strong surface currents and northerly winds often forced ships traveling from the Aegean to the Black Sea to spend long periods in Byzantion before sailing up the Bosporos. Fishing, especially for tuna, as well as the export of salted fish, was an important source of income. The city's status as a transit harbor brought it high customs revenues and prosperity; it also provoked frequent attacks and led to involvement in wars. Byzantium was temporarily under Persian control after 512 BC, then belonged to first Delian League from 476 BC and, after an interlude under Spartan sovereignty, from 390 to 356 BC to the second Delian League. Philip II of Macedon (359–336 BC) besieged the city in 340–339 BC, and the Galatians threatened repeatedly from 278 BC. Byzantion allied with the Romans in 146 BC and finally became part of the province of Bithynia in 79 BC; however, it retained its autonomy until the age of Vespasian (AD 69–79).

The only source for the topography of Byzantium before Constantine is the *Anaplus Bosporou* or "way up the Bosporos" by Dionysios of Byzantion (second century), a work from the Roman imperial period, which describes the shores of the Golden Horn and Bosporos, the north coast of the city included.[3]

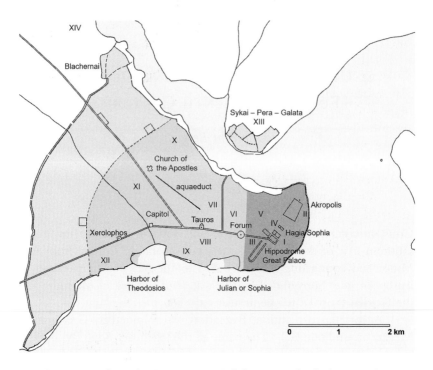

2.1 Constantinople in the Byzantine period showing individual regions (Roman numerals) and the growth of the city from the Akropolis (dark) through the Constantinian (medium) and the Theodosian (light) expansions. (Courtesy of Albrecht Berger)

In a civil war in AD 196, the emperor Septimius Severus (193–211) conquered Byzantion after a long siege. As punishment he destroyed its walls and withdrew its town privileges, transferring them to the neighboring city of Perinthos. Byzantion became a *kome*, a rural community without town rights; however, it soon regained them under the new name Antonina. From the sixth century onward, sources claim that Severus reconstructed the walls and founded the famous baths of Zeuxippos and the Hippodrome: the walls were not yet rebuilt in 240, and this claim is a legend.[4]

The last town walls constructed before Constantine's refoundation were probably built when the Goths threatened the area in 258/259, and are likely to have followed the same course as those destroyed by Severus in 196, enclosing an area of approximately 1.2–1.5 square kilometers. The legendary Wall of Byzas, which reportedly surrounded the area that would later be occupied by Hagia Sophia and the Sultan's

Palace, is the invention the so-called *Patria* of Constantinople, a local history from around 990.[5]

Little is known about ancient Byzantion inside the walls. Most settlement appears to have been at the eastern end of the peninsula, facing the Golden Horn. Sources mention the Acropolis, a square called Thrakion, city walls with the main gate to the west, and a number of temples. Byzantion had three harbors on the Golden Horn. The central harbor was protected with jetties, and west of them there was a massive round tower at the northern end of the city wall.[6] Byzantion's oldest aqueduct dates to the time of Hadrian (117–38).[7]

When Septimius Severus rebuilt the city in the third century it received a roughly grid-shaped street system. Oriented along the main hillsides, this system can still be recognized in the placement of some monuments.[8] Nevertheless, the material remains of pre-Constantinian Byzantion are few: mosaic fragments from private houses, architectural parts reused as *spolia*, and remains of the city wall on the east and south shores which have been incorporated into the Byzantine fortifications.[9]

## THE CITY OF CONSTANTINE, 330–79

Constantine the Great (306–37) founded his new city in November 324. The walls were begun in 328, and the solemn inauguration took place on May 11, 330, when the walls and the main public buildings had been completed: the emperor's new Forum (of Constantine), his palace in the old city center known as the Great Palace, and the adjoining Hippodrome. By moving the wall to the west, Constantine enlarged the city to four or five times its previous size so that it now covered an area of approximately seven square kilometers. Lack of material remains make it difficult to determine the wall's course, beyond the location of its main gate.[10]

Constantinople was initially conceived as a traditional imperial foundation, not as the new capital of the empire, and it is doubtful whether the architectural analogies between the new city center of Constantinople and that of Rome are really as close as it has sometimes been assumed.[11] Constantinople is first called "second Rome" in a poem in praise of Constantine.[12] It is unclear whether Constantine used this expression,[13] but in any case he never called it "new Rome." However, a clear parallel between Rome and Constantinople was drawn on coins and medallions minted between 330 and 347 showing the personifications of both cities.[14] In the later fourth century, rhetors like Libanios and Themistios call Constantinople "new Rome," and the designation appears in the bishop's title even before he received the rank of patriarch in 381.[15] In the fifth century the legend arose that Constantine's move to the "new Rome" had restored the legitimate world rule, that of the Trojans, to the east where it belonged. It was therefore claimed that he had initially considered making Troy his capital, or that a statue of him on the Forum of Constantine had been brought from there. A later addition claims that Constantine also brought the Palladion, the old Trojan cult image, and buried it under his Forum.[16]

In the age of Constantine the status of Constantinople was that of a normal city: its administrative head was a proconsul, not a city prefect as at Rome, and the members of its city council, referred to as a "second-order senate," were "distinguished" (*clari*), in contrast to their "most distinguished" (*clarissimi*) Roman counterparts.[17] Only in the last years of Constantine's successor, Constantius (337–61), was the status of Constantinople changed to that of a second capital, exempt from provincial administration and complete with a city prefect and its own senate.[18]

## PAGAN AND CHRISTIAN MONUMENTS

Constantinople was distinguished from other cities of the Roman Empire bearing their founder's name because of Constantine's overwhelmingly ideological self-presentation. He promoted a syncretic religious concept combining elements of Christian, oriental, and traditional Roman religions, which was so strongly tied to his person that it lost its integrating force soon after his death, and was finally abandoned when his son, Constantius, turned Constantinople not only into a "new Rome" but also into a Christian capital.

The strength of the Christian element in Constantine's later years is disputed; however, it is clear that pagan or semi-pagan monuments associated with his imperial cult dominated the cityscape, not churches. A large porphyry column was set up on a new circular Forum – the Forum of Constantine – outside the gates of old Byzantion. On top stood a statue of Constantine in the shape of the undefeated Sun God: naked, with a crown of rays, a globe in one hand, and a lance in the other.[19] Although the statue disappeared long ago, the column remains.

Later sources call a domed rotunda on the northern side of the Forum a Senate, but it was apparently never used for meetings or receptions, in contrast to the Senate building near the Great Palace. One source says that a statue of Constantine as chariot-driving Sun God, which was carried in procession at the city's May 11 birthday celebrations, was stored there during the year, suggesting that the rotunda was originally built as a temple for Constantine's imperial cult.[20]

When Constantine died in 337 he was buried in a monumental rotunda on a high hill in the west of his city in a sarcophagus surrounded by cenotaphs of the twelve apostles. This self-representation as a Christ-like ruler met with opposition in church circles. Translation of the relics of the apostles Andrew and Luke to the site soon after his death turned these cenotaphs into actual relic shrines, and some decades later the Church of the Apostles was added to the rotunda, which continued to exist as its annex.[21]

The first "Great Church," often claimed as Constantine's foundation, was inaugurated only in 360, more than twenty years after his death. This date suggests that the building was not originally a church, but a palace hall designed for his imperial cult.[22] The "Great Church" is sometimes called Sophia (Wisdom) in the fourth century; the name Hagia Sophia is not attested before the middle Byzantine age.

Another Constantinian monument was the Capitol, which was located at the point where the street to the Church of the Apostles branched off from the city's main road leading out of the city to the west. Capitols served the veneration of Jupiter and the Capitoline Triad, so we may assume that Constantine was worshipped there as a new Jupiter. The Capitol is first mentioned in 425 when it was turned into a law school, without comment on its original use.[23]

Zosimos, the last pagan historian (fl. 490–510), reports more than a century after Constantine that the emperor built two temples in the city center near the market basilica. One housed a Tyche of Rome, the other a Tyche of Constantinople created from a statue of the mother goddess Rhea, the old deity Kybele from Asia Minor by removing lions flanking the figure and changing her hands to a praying position.[24] In fact there was probably only one temple, which should be identified with what is later called the Milion, the "golden milestone" of Constantinople.

The Mesomphalon or "middle navel," another semi-pagan monument which must have been intended as the symbolic center of the city in the tradition of ancient Greek *omphaloi*, must also go back to the age of Constantine, although it is not mentioned before the tenth century. Its position on the northern side of the peninsula suggests that the city's extension to the north rather than to the west was initially considered.[25] Another important element of Constantine's syncretism was the decoration of the Hippodrome and other public buildings and streets with ancient Greek and Roman statues.[26]

It is difficult to determine when the first churches were built. The only known pre-Constantinian church is that of Saint Eirene in the city center where the bishops of Byzantion resided.[27] Later sources portray Constantine as an exclusively Christian emperor and therefore attribute as many churches to him as possible.[28] They also credit him with the conversion of pagan temples or the construction of churches in their place, although all better documented cases happened under Theodosios I (379–95). Around 360 the construction of major churches in Constantinople began outside the old walls of Byzantium, among them the martyr's church of Saint Akakios, the church of Concord (*Homonoia*), the New City (*Neapolis*) church, and the church of Anastasis.

## EXPANDING THE CITY

It took several decades after the foundation of Constantinople to develop the part of the city between the old and new walls. The hilly peninsula required extensive terracing to facilitate construction; in fact, sources report that hills were leveled and earth dumped on the shore. The rhetor Himerios said in 362 that the city "also turns the sea itself into solid land and forces it to become part of the city; in this way it has caused an element to become solid which is actually rocking back and forth and is unstable."[29] Zosimos remarks further that "not a small part of the surrounding sea was turned into solid land by ramming piles in a circle in the ground and placing buildings on it, in a number which was sufficient to form a handsome city."[30] It is unclear, however, how much land was actually reclaimed from the sea.[31]

The first area settled outside the old walls was between the Golden Horn and the main street leading west from the old city.[32] Since the old harbors on the Golden Horn were soon insufficient for the growing population, two large bays on the south coast were turned into artificial harbors with quays and moles. The eastern one, initially called the harbor of Julian after the emperor Julian (361–3), was restored in the late sixth century as the harbor of Sophia, and became the harbor of the imperial navy. The western one, the harbor of Theodosios I (379–95) or of Kaisarios, was mainly built to receive Egyptian grain imports.

Although it disappears from the sources after the seventh century and slowly silted up, shipwrecks from the site demonstrate that it was in use until the twelfth century.[33]

## THE CITY OF THEODOSIOS, 379–450

Urban development speeded up when a new water supply line feeding the upper parts of Constantine's city was completed in 375. Part of this line, the so-called aqueduct of Valens, survives.[34] Under Theodosios I and his successors Constantinople gradually grew to the west. Colonnades were added to the large streets leading out of the city center and public squares were installed at intervals. The first of these squares, the Forum of Theodosios I, was commonly called Tauros (the Bull). Its construction began around 380. In 387 a triumphal column with external spiraling reliefs and an internal staircase was installed, and in 393 the column was crowned with the emperor's statue. This Forum must have been planned long before Theodosios, since a water reservoir on its northern side, the endpoint of the aforementioned water line, was already built in 372/3. The size of the square, which also had a basilican hall on its south side, has often been overestimated because of an erroneous equation with an early Ottoman palace district.[35]

The next Forum was built on the southern branch of the main street which led from the Capitol to the Golden Gate, Constantinople's principle land entrance. Begun in the time of Arkadios (395–408) and later referred to as Xerolophos (the Dry Hill), it was completed around 420 under Theodosios II (401–50). The Xerolophos included an historiated column similar in size and structure to that of the Tauros; its base survives.[36]

Together with the column of Constantine, these columns formed impressive landmarks in the city. At least four more columns were added before the late sixth century, increasing the vertical accents of the Constantinopolitan the cityscape. In this way they fulfilled a function very similar to the minarets of the Ottoman city more than a thousand years later.

Closer to the city center, on the so-called Middle Street (Mese) between the Fora of Constantine and Theodosios, stood another monument, a large tetrapylon covered with bronze reliefs and crowned by a pyramidal roof with a weathervane on top. Sources date it to the time of Theodosios I, referring to it either as the "bronze Tetrapylon" or, after its weathervane, the Anemodulion (servant of the winds).[37]

## THE NEW LAND AND SEA WALLS

When most of the area within the Constantinian wall had been built up, a new city wall was constructed under Theodosios II between 408 and 413. Still largely in place, it marks the final, western limit of the Byzantine city.[38] Placed about 1,500 meters west of the Constantinian wall it runs from the Sea of Marmora on the south toward the Golden Horn on the north, terminating on a hill above the Golden Horn where it connects to an older wall of a fortified village near the sea. A sea wall was added around 438/9 along the shores of the Golden Horn and the Sea of Marmara, but left the big harbors on the south coast outside their circuit. After the Avar siege in 626 another wall was added to the northwest by the Golden Horn to enclose the region known as Blachernai and its famous church of the Mother of God.[39]

Built with alternating courses of ashlar masonry and brick, the Theodosian fortification consists of a main wall about twelve meters high with ninety-four or ninety-five rectangular or polygonal towers, and a front wall about eight meters high preceded by a moat. With this new fortification the city grew to around 12.7 square kilometers, almost doubling its surface area. Building in the newly enclosed area was concentrated along the coast, leaving the inland territory covered with gardens, villas, and monasteries. Because the area was not legally regarded as part of the city for a long time, cemeteries there remained in use, prohibitions against intramural burial notwithstanding. In the sixth century the cemeteries spread beyond the new wall into the hinterland.[40]

The only information about the size of the Constantinopolitan population around 400 is in a sermon by the patriarch John Chrysostom, who mentions 100,000 Christians and 50,000 pagans; but this is only an estimate.[41]

## THE *NOTITIA URBIS CONSTANTINOPOLITANAE*

The most important source for the topography of the city in the early Byzantine age is the *Notitia urbis Constantinopolitanae*, a text written in Latin around 425 and dedicated to Theodosios II.[42] By analogy to Rome, the *Notitia* divides Constantinople into fourteen regions, of which twelve are located in the city of Constantine. Region XIII is Sykai (later known as Galata) across the Golden Horn; region XIV a fortified village nearby. The division of the city into regions is rarely mentioned outside the *Notitia*, and the competences of its top officials, the *curatores*, are not known in detail.

For each region the *Notitia* lists churches, public buildings, and monuments, and gives the number of residential areas (*vici*), houses (*domus*), porticos along with streets, baths, bakeries, and bread distribution points (*gradus*). It also lists officials in each region and the guild members (*collegiati*) who responded to fires. A geographical definition at the beginning of each section allows an approximate identification of individual regions and their boundaries. A summary lists 322 *vici*, 4,388 *domus*, 52 porticos, 153 baths, 20 public and 120 private bakeries, 117 *gradus*, and an overall number of officials and 560 *collegiati*. Occasional discrepancies between the regional list and the summary probably result from errors in textual transmission.

The *Notitia* mentions the new city walls but does not include the added western territory in the regional divisions. The city's length and breadth which are given as 14,075 and 6,150 feet respectively (about 4,080 and 1,780 meters), clearly refer to the Constantinian city.

It is difficult to draw conclusions from the *Notitia* about building development and settlement structure, especially because the meaning of the term "house" (*domus*) is not clear. On the one hand, it was apparently applied to large tenement houses or to their individual storeys, which were rented as apartments; on the other hand, it was also used for free-standing buildings of very different sizes and standards.

Region XIV, which the *Notitia* indicates lay at some distance outside the city walls, has traditionally been identified with the village of Blachernai approximately 1,300 meters from the Constantinian walls; however, the only traceable wall in this northern area at the end of the Theodosian walls did not include Blachernai, which remained outside the city wall until 626. Therefore the *Notitia's* description is best connected to an area near the present suburb of Eyüp, about 2,500 meters from the Constantinian walls.[43] A bridge associated with region XIV is one over the Golden Horn mentioned by Dionysios of Byzantion; in the *Notitia* it is described as wood; it was later replaced by a stone construction.[44]

We might expect the *Notitia* to claim that Constantinople, like Rome, was a city of seven hills; however, it does not. This number could only be reached were the area brought in by the Theodosian expansion included. Constantinople is first called "seven-hilled" in seventh- and eighth-century apocalyptic literature, and a geographical definition of the hills is not given by sources until the tenth century.[45]

After the age of the *Notitia* the city continued to grow within the walls, adding living quarters and public buildings. New triumphal columns were set up, such as that of Marcian (450–7); the column of Leo I (457–74) on the Akropolis, whose statue should probably be identified with a monumental bronze now in Barletta, Italy;[46] and finally the columns of Justinian (527–65) and Justin II (565–78).[47]

## THE HEYDAY OF CONSTANTINOPLE

In 465 a fire severely damaged the central area of Constantinople. An edict of Zeno (474–91) issued before 479 with the intention of promoting reconstruction gives an idea of settlement density at the time.[48] Had the city been built according to these regulations the population can hardly have exceeded 300,000–400,000 people, for the area between the walls of Constantine and Theodosios was still not settled except along the coasts.[49] A similar number can be calculated from an edict of Justinian which mentions that eight million bushels of grain were delivered to Constantinople annually.[50]

During the long reign of Justinian the face of Constantinople changed drastically. In 528 the suburb of Sykai across the Golden Horn, which had been a part of Constantinople, became an independent city. Its sixth-century fortification wall is unknown but may have enclosed roughly the same area as the fourteenth-century Genoese circuit for Galata.[51]

During the so-called Nika revolt of 532 the circus factions and parts of the urban aristocracy tried to overthrow Justinian. When the revolt was suppressed by a loyal military, 35,000 people were killed who had gathered in the Hippodrome, and the newly proclaimed emperor, Hypatios, was murdered. A great fire in the city center destroyed, among other things, Hagia Sophia, Hagia Eirene, the Senate, and the Great Palace entrance, the so-called Chalke.[52] All were rebuilt, most on a greater scale, as were churches in districts unaffected by the fire, among them the Church of the Apostles. On the Augustaion square in front of Hagia Sophia a triumphal column was set up in honor of Justinian; however, the equestrian statue on it was actually a reused piece from the Forum Tauros.

After the Nika revolt Constantinople again became attractive to immigrants, so much so that measures were taken to limit their number. In 535 and 539 new officials were appointed with their own troops both to guarantee order and to reduce foreign presence as far as possible.[53]

In 542 the so-called Justinianic plague reached Constantinople, causing a rapid decline in population.[54] Building activity continued after Justinian's death in 565, but ended almost completely with the great crisis of the seventh century.

## THE DARK AGES

In 619 the Egyptian grain supply ended definitively when the Persians occupied the province. In 626 the Avars and Slavs destroyed the water supply lines of Constantinople during their first great siege of the city. These lines were repaired only 140 years later. This disruption caused further population decline; estimates for the later seventh century hover between 40,000 and 50,000 people.[55]

The building of churches and palaces ended almost completely. New fortifications were constructed instead. The Blachernai region, its famous church of the Mother of God having been damaged during the Avar siege, was enclosed by the city walls. Leo V (813–20) added a heavily fortified bailey to the Blachernai circuit. Under Tiberios II (705–11) the sea walls were heightened; the floating chain across the Golden Horn, which is first mentioned at the Arab siege of 717/18, probably belongs to the same phase.

The recovery of Constantinople began in the age of Constantine V (741–75). New inhabitants were brought from outside and the water supply line was repaired in 766.[56]

## THE SECOND AGE OF PROSPERITY

Despite several early ninth-century political crises the city again began to prosper. A clear sign of this improvement was Theophilos's (829–42) building campaign in the Great Palace which saw the construction of a number of small but luxurious halls and pavilions within the complex,[57] and the addition of an impressive facade of *spolia* on top of the sea walls below.[58] Inscriptions document work on the sea walls in the age of Theophilos and Michael III (842–67).[59] The old, silted-up harbors on the Golden Horn and the eastern half of the harbor of Sophia on the south shore were now abandoned and included within the fortification.

The next major building campaign under Basil I (867–86) expanded beyond the Great Palace to include churches throughout the city.[60]

Many of these, having fallen into ruins or been damaged in an earthquake in 866, were now rebuilt, though mostly on a smaller scale. Although the big cemeteries in the west of the city continued to exist, burials inside the (Constantinian) walls near churches became customary, a habit which Leo VI (886–912) finally sanctioned shortly before 900.[61]

The tenth to twelfth centuries saw steady development. New buildings, especially monasteries, were constructed, among them several imperial foundations intended as family mausoleums: the monastery of the Mother of God Peribleptos by Romanos III (1028–34); Saint George at the Mangana by Constantine IX (1042–55); and Christ Pantokrator under John II Komnenos (1118–43).

In addition to the Great Palace a second imperial palace was established in the Blachernai area. It became the main residence of the emperors in the mid-twelfth century. The old palace remained in use for ceremonial purposes.

## THE LATIN OCCUPATION

In 1204 the army of the Fourth Crusade and the Venetians conquered Constantinople. Parts of the city center were destroyed by fire and many works of art were destroyed or carried off as booty.[62] The city was divided into an imperial zone, including the Great Palace and the Blachernai Palace, and a Venetian zone along the shore of the Golden Horn and its hinterland.[63] Many Greek inhabitants left the city and the population shrank quickly. The Latin empire of Constantinople soon lost most of its territories to the Greek successor states of the Byzantine empire. After 1235 the city was accessible for the Crusaders only by sea, and in 1261 Constantinople was recaptured by the Empire of Nicaea.[64] During the fifty-seven years of Latin occupation almost nothing was built or restored in Constantinople, and the city ended up in a state of complete decay.

## LATE BYZANTINE CONSTANTINOPLE

After the reconquest of the city in 1261 a last phase of rebuilding began. Many churches and monasteries were restored and new ones built. The Great Palace and the Blachernai Palace were repaired, but porticoes along the main streets were not; nor were chariot races in the Hippodrome resumed and the building was left to decay. Sources mention immigration, but the level to which the population rose is unknown.

The Venetians relinquished their large trading concession in the city, and the suburb of Galata was ceded to the Genoese in 1267. Soon thereafter, however, a smaller concession near the shore of the Golden Horn was returned to the Venetians.[65]

This last phase of political recovery ended with the death of Emperor Michael VIII Palaiologos (1262–82). The Chora Monastery, the last major building of this age, was restored between 1315 and 1321 and still preserves its architecture and painted décor.[66]

Foreign visitors to Constantinople in the fourteenth and fifteenth centuries report that the city was half empty, with gardens and fields inside the walls. The Arab traveler Ibn-Battuta says that the city lay "at the foot of a hill" and contained thirteen inhabited villages in its circuit.[67] This observation indicates that the shores of the Golden Horn remained inhabited, while the inner parts of the peninsula were empty. The Monastery of Sure Hope (*Bebaias Elpidos*) had a large walled precinct of about fifteen hectares in the former region X, one of the most densely settled areas of Constantinople in the early Byzantine age.[68]

A treaty of 1304 defined the limits of the Genoese colony in Galata and prohibited its fortification. However, in 1312 a wall was built, and by 1348 the area of Galata extended uphill to a large tower, the so-called Tower of Christ or Galata Tower. Still later two suburbs were added to the walled city, Spiga in the west and Lagirio in the northeast.[69]

As the Genoese's main transit harbor for the Black Sea trade, Galata developed quickly into a densely settled Italian-style city. Although its surface area was less than 3 percent that of Constantinople, Ibn-Battuta described it as one of two parts of the same city separated by a big river, suggesting that both parts were similar in size.

The state of Constantinople in the decades before the Ottoman conquest can best be seen in Cristoforo Buondelmonti's bird's eye view of 1422, which was reproduced in many variants, with and without accompanying text (Fig. 2.2).[70] The city is largely empty, with groups of houses and churches scattered here and there. Five triumphal columns remain standing. Small walled rectangles either with domed or gabled roofs represent the churches. Only Hagia Sophia is shown in some detail with the Hippodrome attached as a forecourt. The Blachernai Palace appears as a multi-storeyed building near the city walls. Galata is far too big, its surface area about a third that of Constantinople. When Constantinople was finally conquered by the Ottomans in 1453 its population was probably on the same level as in the late seventh century and did not exceed 40,000 or 50,000 persons.

2.2 Cristoforo Buondelmonti, view of Constantinople from the *Liber insularum archipelagi* (Marc. XIV.25), 1422, Venice, Biblioteca Marciana (su concessione del Ministero dei Beni e delle Attività Culturali e del Turismo – Biblioteca Nazionale Marciana. Divieto di riproduzione).

## FURTHER READING

Asutay-Effenberger, N., *Die Landmauer von Konstantinopel–İstanbul* (Berlin and Boston, 2007).

Bardill, J., *Constantine, Divine Emperor of the Christian Golden Age* (Cambridge, 2012).

Barsanti, C., "Note archeologiche su Bisanzio romana," in *Costantinopoli e l'arte delle province orientali*, ed. F. De Maffei et al. (Rome, 1990), 11–72.

Bassett, S., *The Urban Image of Late Antique Constantinople* (Cambridge, 2004).

Berger, A., "Regionen und Straßen im frühen Konstantinopel," *IstMitt* 47 (1997): 349–414.

Crow, J. et al., *The Water Supply of Byzantine Constantinople* (London, 2008).

Dagron, G., *Naissance d'une capitale: Constantinople et ses institutions de 330 à 451* (Paris, 1974).

Kocabaş, U., *Yenikapı Shipwrecks* (İstanbul, 2008).

Magdalino, P., "Constantine V and the Middle Age of Constantinople," in P. Magdalino, *Studies on the History and Topography of Byzantine Constantinople* (Aldershot, 2007), no. IV.

Mango, C., *Le développement urbain de Constantinople, IVe–VIIe siècles* (Paris, 1990).

Matthews, J., *Notitia Urbis Constantinopolitanae*, in *Two Romes: Rome and Constantinople in Late Antiquity*, ed. L. Grig and G. Kelly (Oxford, 2015), 81–115.

Nicol, D., *The Last Centuries of Byzantium, 1261–1453* (Cambridge, 2004).

## NOTES

1 The date in Eusebios, *Chronicle*, 185.

2 T. Russell, *Byzantium and the Bosporus* (Oxford, 2017), 19–24.

3 *Dionysii Byzantii Anaplus Bospori*, ed. R. Güngerich (Berlin, 1927).

4 G. Dagron, *Naissance d'une capitale: Constantinople et ses institutions de 330 à 451* (Paris, 1974), 15–19.

5 A. Berger, *Untersuchungen zu den Patria Konstantinupoleos* (Bonn, 1988), 203–6.

6 C. Mango, *Le développement urbain de Constantinople, IVe–VIIe siècles* (Paris, 1990), 13–15.

7 See J. Crow et al., *The Water Supply of Byzantine Constantinople* (London, 2008), 114–17.

8 A. Berger, "Regionen und Straßen im frühen Konstantinopel," *IstMitt* 47 (1997): 349–414, esp. 391–5.

9 C. Barsanti, "Note archeologiche su Bisanzio romana," in *Costantinopoli e l'arte delle province orientali*, ed. F. De Maffei et al. (Rome, 1990), 11–72.

10 A. Effenberger and N. Asutay-Effenberger, "Zum Verlauf der Konstantinsmauer zwischen Marmarameer und Bonoszisterne und zu den Toren und Straßen," *JÖB* 59 (2009): 1–29.

11 For example see D. Chatzilazarou, "Le centre monumental de Constantinople," *TM* 21.1 (2018): 35–54.

12 Optatianus Porphyrius, *Carmen* 4.6.

13 The law quoted by Sokrates, *Church History*, 1.16, where this is the case, is perhaps not authentic.

14 G. Bühl, *Constantinopolis und Roma* (Kilchberg and Zurich, 1995), 10–44.

15 Sozomenos, *Church History*, 7.9.3; Libanios, *Oration* 20.24; Themistios, *Orations* 3.42 and 14.84.

16 C. Ando, "The Palladium and the Pentateuch," *Phoenix* 55 (2001): 369–410; the story first appears in Ioannes Malalas, 13.7.

17 Dagron, *Naissance*, 120–4, 192.

18 A. Skinner, "The Early Development of the Senate of Constantinople," *BMGS* 32 (2008), 128–48.

19 J. Bardill, *Constantine, Divine Emperor of the Christian Golden Age* (Cambridge, 2012), 27–34.

20 A. Berger, "Die Senate von Konstantinopel," *Boreas* 18 (1995): 131–42.
21 *The Holy Apostles: A Lost Monument, a Forgotten Project, and the Presentness of the Past*, ed. M. Mullett and R. G. Ousterhout (Washington, DC, 2020).
22 P. Speck, "Konstantins Mausoleum," in *Varia* 7, ed. P. Speck (Bonn, 2000), 113–56.
23 P. Speck, "Urbs, quam Deo donavimus," *Boreas* 18 (1995): 143–73.
24 Zosimos, 2.31.
25 Berger, "Regionen," 411.
26 S. Bassett, *The Urban Image of Late Antique Constantinople* (Cambridge and New York, 2004).
27 U. Peschlow, *Die Irenenkirche in Istanbul* (Tübingen, 1977).
28 Dagron, *Naissance*, 399–401.
29 Himerios, *Oration* 41.6.
30 Zosimos, 2.35.
31 Mango, *Développement*, 16.
32 Berger, "Regionen," 396–8.
33 U. Kocabaş, *Yenikapı Shipwrecks* (İstanbul, 2008).
34 J. Crow, *The Water Supply of Byzantine Constantinople* (London, 2008).
35 A. Berger, "Tauros e Sigma: Due piazze di Costantinopoli," in *Bisanzio e l'Occidente: Arte, archeologia, storia. Studi in onore di Fernanda de' Maffei*, ed. C. Barsanti (Rome, 1996), 17–31.
36 C. Konrad, "Beobachtungen zur Architektur und Stellung des Säulenmonuments in Istanbul-Cerrahpasa – 'Arkadiussäule'," *IstMitt* 51 (2001): 319–401.
37 A. Berger, "Das Chalkun Tetrapylon und Parastaseis, Kapitel 57," *BZ* 90 (1997): 7–12; B. Anderson, "Leo III and the Anemodoulion," *BZ* 104 (2011): 41–54.
38 N. Asutay-Effenberger, *Die Landmauer von Konstantinopel–İstanbul* (Berlin, 2007), 13–27.
39 Asutay-Effenberger, Die Landmauer von Konstantinopel–İstanbul.
40 *CIC*, 3, 44, 12; Justinian, *CIC Nov* 59; see Mango, *Développement*, 47–8, 57–8.
41 Ioannes Chrysostomos, *Homily on the Acts of the Apostles*, 11.3 (*PG* 60.97).
42 Berger, "Regionen," 350–87; J. Matthews, *Notitia Urbis Constantinopolitanae*, in *Two Romes: Rome and Constantinople in Late Antiquity*, ed. L. Grig and G. Kelly (Oxford, 2012), 81–115.
43 C. Mango, "Le mystère de la XIVe région de Constantinople," in *Mélanges Gilbert Dagron*, ed. V. Déroche (Paris, 2002), 449–55.
44 A. Effenberger, "Brücken über das Goldene Horn," *Millennium* 15 (2018): 157–75.
45 C. Mango, "A Daniel Apocalypse of 716/717," *Rivista di studi bizantini e slavi* 2 (1982): 297–313.
46 U. Peschlow, "Eine wiedergewonnen byzantinische Ehrensäule in Istanbul," in *Studien zur spätantiken und byzantinischen Kunst, Friedrich Wilhelm Deichmann gewidmet*, ed. O. Feld (Bonn, 1986), I, 21–33.
47 C. Mango, "Columns of Justinian," in *Studies on Constantinople* (Aldershot 1997), no. X, esp. 2–13.
48 CIC 8.10.12 ; H. Vetters, "Das Baugesetz Zenons für Konstantinopel," *MDAI* 39 (1989): 575–84.
49 D. Jacoby, "La Population de Constantinople à l'époque byzantine: un problème de démographie urbaine," *Byzantion* 31 (1961): 81–109.
50 A. E. Müller, "Getreide für Konstantinopel," *JÖB* 43 (1993): 1–20.
51 A. M. Schneider and M. I. Nomides, *Galata, topographisch-archäologischer Plan* (İstanbul, 1944), 1–6.
52 G. Greatrex, "The *Nika* Riot: A Reappraisal," *JHS* 117 (1997): 60–86.
53 *CIC Nov* 13 and 80.
54 D. Stathakopoulos, *Famine and Pestilence in the Late Roman and Early Byzantine Empire* (Aldershot, 2004), 10–54.
55 Mango, *Développement*, 53–4.
56 P. Magdalino, "Constantine V and the Middle Age of Constantinople," in *Studies on the History and Topography of Byzantine Constantinople*, ed. P. Magdalino (Aldershot, 2007), no. IV.
57 Theophanes continuatus, 3.42–4.
58 Theophanes continuatus, 3.4; see C. Mango, "The Palace of the Boukoleon," *CahArch* 45 (1997): 41–50.
59 A. M. Schneider, "Mauern und Tore am Goldenen Horn zu Konstantinopel," *NachrGött* (1950): 65–107.
60 Theophanes continuatus, 5.76–94.
61 Leo VI, *CIC Nov*, 53.

62  See, among others, D. E. Queller and T. F. Madden, *The Fourth Crusade: The Conquest of Constantinople* (Philadelphia, 1997); M. Angold, *The Fourth Crusade: Event and Context* (Harlow, 2003).

63  D. Jacoby, "The Venetian Government and Administration in Latin Constantinople, 1204–1261: A State within a State," in *Quarta Crociata: Venezia, Bisanzio, Impero Latino*, 2 vols., ed. G. Ortalli, G. Ravegnani, and P. Schreiner (Venezia, 2006), 1: 19–79.

64  See D. Nicol, *The Last Centuries of Byzantium, 1261–1453* (Cambridge, 2004), 19–38.

65  Nicol, The Last Centuries of Byzantium, 1261–1453, 60–1.

66  R. Ousterhout, *The Architecture of the Kariye Camii in Istanbul* (Washington, DC, 1987).

67  *Ibn Battuta, Travels in Asia and Africa 1325–1354*, tr. and ed. H. A. R. Gibb (London, 1929), 159–60.

68  H. Delehaye, *Deux typica byzantins de l'époque des Paleologues* (Brussels, 1921), 106–36.

69  Nicol, *Last Centuries*, 111–12, 223; Schneider and Nomides, *Galata*, 5–6.

70  G. Gerola, "Le vedute di Costantinopoli di Cristoforo Buondemonti," *SBN* 3 (1931): 247–79; *Cristoforo Buondelmonti, Liber insularum archipelagi*, ed. I. Siebert and M. Plassmann (Wiesbaden, 2005).

## 3: The People of Constantinople

### Anthony Kaldellis

#### Numbers

Who were the people of Constantinople? Let us begin with how many there were. Between 324 and 1204 Constantinople experienced two periods of growth, separated by one of contraction. The first period, which was rapid in pace and massive in scale, occurred in the aftermath of Constantine the Great's (306–37) selection of the site for his new capital. This phase saw the population of ancient Byzantion increase from c.25,000 around 324 to somewhere between 400,000 and 750,000 in 541, just before the arrival of the Justinianic plague. These estimates are produced in three different ways: by guesswork; by correlating the size of the city with guesses about its population density, although it is not known how much of it was residential; and by calculating the number of people who could be fed by the shipments of Egyptian grain stipulated in Justinian's *Edict* 13.8 of c.539. The last produces larger estimates, but assumes that Justinian's expectations were met and used only to feed Constantinople.[1] Conventionally, half a million is understood as the high point in 541.

During the Nika Riots that threatened his rule in 532, Justinian (527–65) slaughtered between 30,000 and 50,000 of his subjects, or up to 10 percent of Constantinople's population. Then plague arrived in 542. An eyewitness, the historian Prokopios, says that thousands died, more than 10,000 per day at the peak. Another eyewitness, Yuhannan (John), Monophysite bishop of Ephesos, says that 16,000 died each day at the peak and that 230,000 bodies were collected, after which counting stopped; he estimates that perhaps 300,000 died in total.[2] Later there were periodic outbreaks. Some modern estimates take sources at face value and postulate a mortality rate of 50 percent. Others argue for a much smaller impact, though it is clear that large cities would have been harder hit than rural districts.[3] Constantinople suffered another demographic blow in the early seventh century when the empire lost Egypt, first to the Persians and then to the Arabs in 642. As a result the Egyptian *annona* (grain supply) was discontinued in 619 in the midst of yet another plague outbreak,[4] causing a significant population drop, probably because of mass exodus to rural districts. Thereafter the city's lowest population estimates, which are probably too low, suggest 40,000 survivors; others argue that the minimum, going forward from the worst days of the seventh century, was 70,000.[5] These numbers are guesses.

After the seventh century Constantinople's population expanded along with the empire itself, albeit more gradually this time. By the end of the twelfth century its population had reached a maximum size of 400,000 according to Geoffrey Villehardouin (d. 1212–18), a contemporary historian of the Fourth Crusade; however, this number seems high.[6] It was downhill again from there, especially during the Latin occupation (1204–61), which led to another exodus. The restoration of Byzantine rule in 1261 is likely to have reversed this trend, at least until the outbreak of the Black Death in 1347–8, which initiated the terminal phase of decline. The empire dwindled in size and resources, and many people must have fled the city during its long blockade and siege by the Turkish Sultan Bayezid (1394–1402). Joseph Bryennios, a monk in the Stoudios monastery in the early fifteenth century, says the capital had upward of 70,000 people; during the final siege of 1453 its population is calculated at *c*.25,000.[7] Perhaps many had fled recently in anticipation.

Constantinople was thus a city of immigrants, and it needed a constant influx of people not only to grow but also to maintain its numbers. Densely populated premodern cities are believed to have lost around 1 per cent of their population annually to disease;[8] therefore, in order to grow from 25,000 to 500,000 in 210 years (330–540) Constantinople would have had to compensate for that loss *and* score a net gain on top of it. For the initial phase of expansion the math works out to an import of 2.43 percent of its total population each year (1 percent to compensate for loss, 1.43 percent to grow). In other terms, if the city's population were 400,000 in the later fifth century, then it would have needed to import almost 10,000 new people *every year* in order to stay on track for its half-million apex in 541. This number was almost as large as the number of recruits required by the imperial army. No wonder Theodoretos of Kyrrhos referred to the "rivers of people that flowed into it from all sides," in the 430s or 440s.[9]

For the second phase of expansion, when the population rose from *c.*70,000 to 400,000 people between 700 and 1200, the growth rate was lower, at 1.43 percent annually. A population of 250,000 in 1000 would have needed around 3,500 new residents every year. All of these calculations, however, assume steady growth, which was certainly not the case. Some events, such as the city's dedication in 330 and the Turkish conquest of Asia Minor in the 1070s, which created a refugee flow, would have brought in disproportionate numbers of new residents.[10] A mandatory relocation of provincials to the capital ordered by Constantine V (741–75) boosted the early stages of recovery in the eighth century.[11] A combination of imperial incentives, relocations, and voluntary internal migration resulted in growth.

## A CITY OF IMMIGRANTS

The constant arrival of people at critical points in the capital's history means that a categorical distinction between Constantinopolitans and provincial Romans was bound to be fuzzy. In the twelfth century the philosopher Stephanos defined "indigenous inhabitants" (*autochthones*) as "people who are not immigrants, or who, if they come from another land, have lived in this land long enough to be like the indigenous inhabitants, for example those who are like the indigenous inhabitants of Constantinople."[12]

Who were these immigrants to Constantinople, whose descendants became its indigenous inhabitants? Famine in the countryside induced some to move to Constantinople temporarily because it was better provisioned, as many Phrygians did under Valens (364–78). Some may have stayed on permanently.[13] Poverty also induced poor provincials to seek a better fortune in the city, as is stated explicitly for two future emperors, Justin I (518–27) who made the move in *c.*470, and Basil I (867–86), in the mid ninth century.[14] Local educated elites also moved in the hope of obtaining a post in the administration, the Church, or the court. Authors of many Byzantine historical sources documented their careers and in so doing their mobility. In the sixth century Prokopios came from Caesarea, John Lydos from Philadelphia, and Agathias from Myrina. Theophylaktos Simokattes came in the early seventh century from Egypt, Arethas in the late ninth century from Patras, Michael Attaleiates in the eleventh century from Attaleia, and Michael and Niketas Choniates in the later twelfth century from Chonai.

Provincial mobility also shaped the capital's monastic and ecclesiastical life, and provided many of the eunuchs who served at the court.[15] To give an example of the capital's provincial nature, Justinian's inner circle – its top generals, jurists, administrators, churchmen, and architects – had only one native Constantinopolitan, the empress Theodora. The generals were mostly from the Balkans, the rest from Asia Minor. Conversely, when the court, between the eighth and the tenth centuries, staged "bride shows" to find future empresses, it sent agents out to the provinces to prospect for suitable candidates.

Although a city of immigrants, there was some order to the chaos: Constantinople's populace had an as yet unrecognized core. Constantine encouraged western senators to move to his new capital – he even built houses for them – and his son Constantius II (337–61) created a senatorial order for New Rome that, by the early fifth century, had c.3,000 members, most of them drawn from the Greek-speaking cities of the eastern provinces.[16] Initially they were required to reside in the new capital, but in the fifth century they were first allowed, and then encouraged, to return to their "native" cities, leaving the functions of the Senate in the hands of the highest senatorial order, the *illustres*.

Let us take 400 as our vantage point. These new senators would not have come alone. They would have had retinues, secretaries, and servants, and many had large or extended families. According to the Cappadocian Fathers, a provincial aristocrat had "stewards, accountants, farmers, craftsmen, cooks, bakers, wine-pourers, hunters, painters, and procurers of every type of pleasure," to say nothing of jesters, mimes, musicians, boys with the hair-style of girls, and let us not forget the "shameless girls."[17] As the richest provincial elites, the senators of New Rome would have had large households. Estimates for individual Roman senatorial households suggest between 200 and 400 slaves plus free attendants and employees.[18] If we give eastern elites smaller followings – perhaps thirty each – then the senatorial order in New Rome accounted for almost 100,000 of Constantinople's population, free and enslaved. If households numbered forty people on average, which is probably still conservative, then we arrive at 120,000. Powerful Romans always had retinues, even in the middle period (843–1204),[19] and the imperial court itself employed a few thousand people above and beyond those of its aristocracy. This group was probably the city's core population throughout its history, adjusting for the size of the court elite in each period.

There were other demographically significant bodies within the general population, most of them discrete. The number of monks living in organized houses in and around Constantinople in the mid-fifth century has been estimated between 10,000 and 15,000, a figure that presumably rose and fell thereafter in proportion to the city's general population.[20] The wealthiest church in the Constantinople, Hagia Sophia, was also one of its most powerful institutions and owned a number of subordinate churches. In 535 Justinian limited its clergy to 425, and allowed for a hundred porters. Herakleios (610–41) raised the number in 612 to 525, plus seventy-five porters. A few thousand, therefore, might be a reasonable estimate for all the clergy of Constantinople.[21] In 1204, at the peak of the city's long recovery, the Crusader Robert de Clari (d. after 1216) estimated that monks and priests together numbered 30,000.[22] In addition to local clergy there was also the Home Synod, which consisted of a few dozen bishops from other, mostly nearby cities, who assembled every year to advise the patriarch and take collective decisions; each of these bishops would have had at least three clerical attendants and other servants.

Soldiers constituted another corporate group, but few were stationed inside Constantinople. The late Roman praesental field armies (I and II) were billeted in Thrace and northwest Asia Minor, whence they could be summoned in an emergency. The palace guard consisted of 3,500 *scholares*, but by the later fifth century they were mostly a ceremonial unit. The real battle-worthy guards were the *excubitores*, 300 strong and founded or reformed by Leo I (457–74) in the 460s. The same was generally true in the middle Byzantine period (843–1204). The military units known as the *tagmata* were not stationed in the city, except possibly for the *Vigla*, an imperial guard with a maximum of 4,000 men, and a contingent of the Varangian Guard after 989.[23] Thus, the city was largely demilitarized. Civilians were also not allowed to bear arms. These circumstances meant that when the field armies revolted or were suborned, as in 602 and 1047, emperors had to scrape a defense militia together from civilians and count on their loyalty and the strength of the city walls.

Each year thousands of litigants, appellants, and petitioners, ranging from farmers and monks to abbots, bishops, and provincial notables, also visited the capital. Their numbers seem to have increased during the first two centuries of the city's existence, as more and more provincials made use of the Roman legal system. "A manifold crowd of people from the whole world comes to the city, on some errand, in hope, or by chance," wrote Prokopios. One historian postulated "tens of thousands" of short-term visitors per year, and Justinian built a huge hostel where they could stay while undertaking their business.[24]

## QUESTIONS OF STATUS: INSIDERS AND OUTSIDERS

If Constantinople was a city of immigrants, was there any difference in civic status between its residents and provincial Romans? In an era when Roman law had universally replaced that of the empire's individual cities, and a common Roman citizenship had been extended throughout imperial territory, did Constantinopolitans enjoy any advantages in the eyes of their own governing institutions?

There appear to have been two, both attested only in the early period. The first was the *annona* of bread loaves, given to citizens of Constantinople. As instituted by Constantine, it allowed for 80,000 daily portions, which could feed between 150,000 and 240,000, depending upon how portions are understood.[25] This allotment exceeded the numbers of 332, but was not enough for the mid-fifth-century population, which means that the right to the bronze token enabling access to the *annona* did not overlap with the distinction between natives and non-natives. Originally given to immigrants who were willing to build or who owned a house in the city, these tokens soon began to circulate beyond that group,[26] until the *annona*'s discontinuation in 619.

A second benefit came in the mid and late 530s, when Justinian overhauled the empire's provincial administration. One of his chief concerns was to delegate more legal business to governors in order to staunch the flow of people to the capital. The emperor appears to have been seriously annoyed by these crowds. In 539 he also instituted the office of the *quaesitor* ('inquirer' or 'inquisitor'), whose task was to interview all new arrivals or non-locals about their city business. If it were a legal matter, the *quaesitor* was to expedite it, by pressuring the relevant judges or local parties to the dispute for a quick resolution so that participants could be sent home. The *quaesitor* also rounded up beggars: if they were able-bodied natives, they were assigned to the public works. Thus, the *quaesitor* somehow distinguished between natives and non-natives. A sixth-century legal scholion suggests that his staff engaged in the ethnic profiling of Syriac and Coptic speakers, presuming that they were non-residents.[27] This observation raises questions of ethnicity and language. From where had people emigrated?

## ETHNICITY

Byzantine Constantinople is commonly described as a multilingual and "cosmopolitan" city in which many ethnic groups rubbed shoulders, and some sources offer statements to this effect.[28] However, the evidence does not support this image, and it is likely that modern scholarship has projected the image of the Ottoman city back onto the Byzantine. In reality Constantinople was overwhelmingly Greek speaking between 400 and 1204. Until about 600 there was a small but powerful minority of Latin speakers, which included many members of the court, but they also spoke Greek.[29] As for other groups, it is likely that there were in Constantinople speakers of every language then known, but their groups were small, transient, or both, and some were viewed with hostility and attacked violently. This was not a cosmopolitan place.

The original Latins of Constantinople stemmed from the Roman senatorial families that Constantine and Constantius enticed to the eastern capital, along with their households and retainers. This group received periodic infusions of western Romans who sought safety in the east as the western empire crumbled during the fifth century. Others left Italy during the war between Justinian and the Goths (536–55) and the subsequent Lombard invasion (568). For example, in the early 460s the *comes* Titus relocated from Gaul to Constantinople with his band of mercenary soldiers.[30] As late as the twelfth century, prominent Byzantine families boasted descent from these western senators. Another early contingent of Latin speakers came from the portion of Illyricum that belonged to the eastern empire. Many served in the armies and mounted the throne of the east, including Justin I and Justinian.[31] Otherwise, the vast majority of new Constantinopolitans probably came from predominantly Greek-speaking provinces, mostly eastern Thrace and Asia Minor. Inscriptions recording their origin convey this impression,[32] and the reception of other groups by the Constantinopolitan people confirms it.

Egyptians are attested in the capital as litigants and as sailors in the grain fleet. In the fourth century Ammianus Marcellinus claimed that they were so litigious that they jammed up the courts. In 361 Julian (361–3) instructed them to go to Chalcedon and, once they were there, he ordered the ferry captains not to bring any back. This reminds us of the ethnic profiling practiced later by Justinian's quaesitor.[33] As sailors in the grain fleet, Egyptians would have been a familiar presence, but not as permanent residents, and their foreignness was readily apparent. In 403, when Theophilos, the bishop of Alexandria, orchestrated the downfall of John Chrysostom, bishop of Constantinople, John's followers fought a street battle with the Egyptians of the fleet, with many casualties on both sides.[34] In the Christological controversy of the fifth century, the Egyptians took the side of Alexandrian One Nature theology, whereas the people of Constantinople were overwhelmingly on the side of the Two Nature theology of the Council of Chalcedon (451). When Timotheos the Cat, bishop of Alexandria, was recalled from exile by the Monophysite emperor Basiliskos (475–6) in 476, he was cheered on by Alexandrian sailors in the city.[35] The Constantinopolitans, by contrast, rose up against his ecclesiastical policy.

Goths were also present in the later fourth and fifth centuries. In 399, a generation after the battle of Adrianople, Synesios of Cyrene said that even moderate households in the capital had a Gothic slave, but he was trying to make the case that Goths were barbarians who should be conquered and denied high positions in the Roman army.[36] The Goths, moreover, were mostly Arians so they were not a good fit for the religious life of the capital. John Chrysostom reached out to them by instituting services in Gothic for those who accepted Nicaean orthodoxy, but this Nicaean Gothic community was small. In 400, when the general Gaïnas, a Roman officer of Gothic origin, brought his army into the city in an effort to dominate the regime of Arkadios (395–408), the people of Constantinople rose up spontaneously and massacred most of the Gothic population, including those who sought sanctuary in the Nicaean Gothic church. This pogrom left 7,000 dead and caused Gaïnas to flee and eventually lose his life.[37]

Prejudice was directed also at the Isaurians, an ethnic group from southern Asia Minor. Although they had long been part of the empire and were Roman citizens, they were regarded as a separate ethnic group and disliked. Tensions rose when a group of Isaurians led by the general Zenon (né Tarasikodissa) was courted by the regime of Leo I. There were at least two mass attacks on Isaurians in the late 460s and early 470s, one of them a large-scale massacre.[38] The people of Constantinople resented the Isaurian nature of Zeno's subsequent reign (474–91). Zeno was unpopular; he survived largely because the many alternatives to his reign were worse, such as Basiliskos, who tried to repeal Chalcedon. When he died, the people demanded a "true" Roman as their next emperor.[39] The latter, Anastasios (491–518), promptly expelled the Isaurians from the capital and waged a long war to pacify finally their homeland.

Syriac speakers in the capital present an interesting case. They made up a large portion of the population of the eastern provinces, and there were surely many in the capital. In 402 John Chrysostom reports that the empress Eudoxia, the wife of Arkadios, led a religious procession of "people speaking different tongues: Latin, Syriac, Greek, and barbaric."[40] But it appears that Chrysostom was here striking one of his favorite notes, the harmonious chord of an apostolic congregation unifying many tongues. He provides no demographic information. Other sources suggest that the city's Syriac speakers were mostly churchmen and monks, such as the group of a hundred monks brought to Constantinople by Alexander the Sleepless in the early fifth century. After an inquiry they were expelled and settled nearby on the Bosporos.[41] Syriac speakers encountered increasing prejudice as the eastern provinces drifted toward the rejection of Chalcedon. Many sources reveal that speaking Syriac was enough to arouse theological suspicion.[42] In a riot of 512, against the perceived Monophysite policies of the emperor Anastasios, the people plundered the house of the former prefect Marinos, a Greek speaker from Syria who was thought to be a Monophysite influence on the emperor. They also killed an eastern monk and paraded his head around on a pole, calling him "the enemy of the Trinity."[43]

The capital's largest concentration of Syriac speakers was probably the Monophysite monastic community that Justinian and Theodora originally sponsored in the Hormisdas palace, and which later appeared in other locations. It had up to 500 members. By the late 530s Justinian was implementing various methods to limit their flow to the capital.[44] It is possible that his quaesitor's "Syrian-catchers" and "Egyptian-catchers" (*Syriopiastai* and *Aigyptopiastai*) were meant to filter out Monophysite monks as well.

There is no evidence for significant ethnic communities in Constantinople during the middle Byzantine period, at least before the twelfth century. Scholars often refer to a "cosmopolitical" or "multiethnic" city, pointing to foreign mercenaries, prisoners of war, diplomats, and transient merchants, whose presence does not justify those terms. There were enough Muslims (probably Arabs) in Constantinople to justify a discrete mosque or two, which often led to intense negotiations with neighboring Muslim powers over its sponsorship. That said, this community probably did not amount to more than a few hundred and was destroyed by the Crusaders who arrived in 1203.[45] There was doubtless a Jewish community throughout the city's history, but it is not firmly attested until the later twelfth century, when the Spanish Jew Benjamin of Tudela reveals that the Jews had their own "quarter" at Pera (later Galata) across the Golden Horn. The community consisted of 2,000 Rabanite Jews and 500 Karaite Jews, who so disliked each other that they had a wall built between them.[46]

Constantinople was not an open city that foreign groups could approach, enter, and live in at will. Approaches by sea, the most common, were monitored by the toll and customs stations in the Hellespont and Bosporos, which made sure that "no one was bringing weapons to the city or attempting to enter without the proper documents."[47] Foreign trade delegations – for example, the Rhos (Rus') – could enter only after their rulers had signed a treaty with the emperor stipulating how many individuals (whose names were recorded) could enter and for how long. People who looked foreign were sometimes arrested by the city watch, and when the Rhos king attacked the empire in 1043 the Roman authorities rounded up all Rhos merchants in the capital; their identities and whereabouts were obviously known.[48] When the Second Crusade arrived, Manuel I Komnenos (1143–80) sent secretaries to record the number of German Crusaders crossing the straits, but they gave up because there were too many.[49]

In the later tenth and eleventh centuries the empire expanded dramatically into the Caucasus, northern Mesopotamia, Syria, Bulgaria, and the western Balkans, and secured its position in Italy, before the arrival of the Normans. This expansion increased the presence of people from those lands in the capital. They came primarily as short-term visitors on diplomatic, commercial, and legal business. Constantinople also began to host many more royal hostages and defeated rebels who were kept close in order to be monitored, including Lombards, Italian "Latins," Croats, Dalmatians, Georgians, and Armenians.[50] The empire also began to employ more foreign mercenaries, especially the Varangian Guard, which included 6,000 men at most, many of them stationed in the provinces. The Guard was recruited initially among Rhos and Scandinavians, but after the Norman conquest of England it included Anglo-Saxons. The whole point of the Guard was that its members would not integrate into mainstream Roman society and so remain dependent on, and loyal to, the emperor. They were a distinctive sight.[51] The emperors also began to employ Norman mercenaries in the later eleventh century, though never more than 2,000 at a time. They were rarely stationed in the capital, though their leaders and personal retinues were often there.

A Latin description of Constantinople, by the "Anonymous Tarragonensis" from the end of the eleventh century, says that Constantinople contained many *gentes*: Greeks, Armenians, Syrians, Lombards, English, Dacians (probably Vlachs), Amalfitans, Franks, Jews, and Turks, but that the Greeks (i.e., Romans) occupied the largest and best part of the capital.[52] If the other groups were as small as we know or suspect that the Jews, English, Franks, Turks, and Amalfitans were, they would not have made up a significant portion of the city's population of 300,000. That said, increasingly more languages could be heard on the streets. In the mid-twelfth century the classical scholar Ioannes Tzetzes wrote a brief poem boasting that he could greet all people in their own tongue; he included some choice insults to use against Jews, and a particularly vulgar phrase in Alanic.[53] The group that grew the most during the twelfth century was that of the "Latins," that is, western European Catholics, primarily Italians. As they began to play an increasingly important role in the empire's trade, foreign policy, and domestic politics, they established a growing presence in most of the advantageous trading locations throughout the empire, including Constantinople. The Amalfitans, Venetians, Pisans, and Genoese were assigned quarters along the Golden Horn wharfs.[54] By the 1180s one probably exaggerated source claims that 60,000 Latins had settled there.[55] The Germans (possibly mercenaries in the emperor's service) and the "French" (identity unknown) were also assigned a small district with wharves along the Golden Horn, but these were folded into the Venetian one in 1189.[56]

Tensions were inevitable, especially as the empire was often at odds with the Italian city-states. In 1171, in an operation of impressive complexity and scope that had been planned in secret, Manuel I Komnenos arrested all Venetians in the empire and threw them in prison; it is said that 10,000 were arrested in and around Constantinople.[57] This operation reveals that in the twelfth century the imperial authorities continued to monitor foreign residents and their locations, no less than when they had been dealing with the Rhos in the early tenth century. In a more indiscriminate operation, in 1182, Andronikos Komnenos (1183–5) incited the people to massacre Latins, mostly those Pisans and Genoese who did not manage to flee in time.[58] By this time religious differences between Latin Catholics and Greek Orthodox Romans made the hatred and suspicion worse, as had the economic ascendancy of the western merchants over their local suppliers and competitors. Along with the massacre of the Goths in 400, this was the largest massacre of foreigners in the city's history. In both cases it is interesting that Constantinopolitans targeted the group posing the greatest danger to the empire at the moment, and by doing so they exacerbated the threat. Their city would survive the Goths but not the Latins.

The Romans of Byzantium were generally reluctant to let foreign groups live among them in large numbers. Isaac II Angelos (1185–95) was telling the truth to the Venetians when he stated, in a chrysobull of 1189, that it was not desirable to let the "nations" spread themselves in

Constantinople, yet he was willing to except the Venetians from this exclusionary policy because they loved Romanía so much that they were virtually like native Romans.[59]

## CONCLUSIONS

This chapter has discussed the people of Constantinople primarily under their demographic and ethnological aspects. Space prevents a full consideration of their civic identity and political roles, which would require a detailed analysis of Roman imperial politics. Suffice it to say that the people of Constantinople were not an inert, passive, or random "population" thrown together by the random movements of history and governed as mere "subjects" by the emperors. They were, from the very beginning, understood and addressed by the emperors as "Roman citizens" and a critically important subset of the *populus Romanus*. Their vocal consent was necessary for any regime to claim legitimacy, and their withdrawal of that consent caused many regimes to topple. Alongside the imperial court, the Church, and the armies, the people of Constantinople were a major and active player in shaping the course of Byzantine history.[60]

## FURTHER READING

Kaldellis, A., *The Byzantine Republic: People and Power at New Rome* (Cambridge, MA 2015).

Kaldellis, A., *Romanland: Ethnicity and Empire in Byzantium* (Cambridge, MA, 2019).

Stathakopoulos, D., "Population, Demography, and Disease," in E. Jeffreys et al., eds., *The Oxford Handbook of Byzantine Studies* (Oxford, 2008), 309–16.

## NOTES

1 Guesswork (low): C. Mango, *Le développement urbain de Constantinople (IVe – VIIe siècles)* (Paris, 1990), 51; urban demography (also low): D. Jacoby, "La population de Constantinople à l'époque byzantine: un problème de démographie urbaine," *Byzantion* 31 (1961) : 81–109; grain-based estimates (high): C. Zuckerman, *Du village à l'empire: autour du régistre fiscale d'Aphroditô, 525–6* (Paris, 2004), 189–212.

2 Prokopios, *Wars* 2.23.2; Yuhannan in W. Witakowski, *Pseudo-Dionysios of Tel-Mahre: Chronicle (Known also as the Chronicle of Zuqnin), Part III* (Liverpool, 1996), 86–7.

3 Higher: K. Harper, *The Fate of Rome: Climate, Disease, and the End of Empire* (Princeton, 2017), chapter 6; lower: L. Mordechai and M. Eisenberg, "Rejecting Catastrophe: The Case of the Justinianic Plague," *Past and Present* 244 (2019): 3–50.

4 *Chronicon Paschale* s.a. 618 (August); Nikephoros, *Short History* 8.

5 40,000: Mango, *Le développement*, 54; at least 70,000: P. Magdalino, "Medieval Constantinople," in *Studies in the History and Topography of Byzantine Constantinople* (Aldershot, 2007), no. I: 1–104, esp. 18–19.

6 Magdalino, "Medieval Constantinople," 61–3 (arguing not only on the basis of Geoffrey, *Conquest of Constantinople*, 12).

7 70,000: Ioseph Bryennios in E. Boulgaris, Ἰωσὴφ μοναχοῦ τοῦ Βρυεννίου τὰ εὑρεθέντα, vol. 2 (Leipzig, 1768), 280; 25,000: K. Moustakas, "Μεθοδολογικά ζητήματα στην προσέγγιση των πληθυσμιακών μεγεθών της υστεροβυζαντινής πόλης," *Οι βυζαντινές πόλεις (8ος-15ος αιώνας): Προοπτικές της έρευνας και ερευνητικές προσεγγίσεις* ed. T. Kiousopoulou (Rethymno, 2012), 225–51.

8 K. Hopkins, "The Political Economy of the Roman Empire," in *The Dynamics of Ancient Empires: State Power from Assyria to Byzantium*, ed. I. Morris and W. Scheidel (Oxford, 2009), 178–204, esp. 192.

9 Theodoretos of Kyrrhos, *Letter* 15, to Proklos of Constantinople.

10 Refugees: A. Kaldellis, *Streams of Gold, Rivers of Blood: The Rise and Fall of Byzantium, 955 A.D. to the First Crusade* (Oxford, 2017), 262–3. For Constantine see below.

11 Theophanes, *Chronographia* a.m. 6247 (p. 429) and 6258 (p. 440) = Nikephoros, *Short History* 68 and 86.

12 Stephanos (possibly Skylitzes), *Commentary on Aristotle's* Rhetoric 1360b31; *Anonymi et Stephani in artem rhetoricam commentaria*, ed. G. Rabe (Berlin: 1896 = *Commentaria in Aristotelem Graeca* v. 21, pt. 2), 263–322, esp. 270.

13 Sokrates, *Ecclesiastical History* 4.16; cf. Ioannes Lydos, *On the Magistracies* 3.70, right before the Nika Riots in 532.

14 Prokopios, *Secret History* 6.2–3; Konstantinos VII, *Life of Basileios I*, 7–9.

15 S. Tougher, *The Eunuch in Byzantine History and Society* (London and New York, 2008), 60–4.

16 P. Heather, "New Men for New Constantines? Creating an Imperial Elite in the Eastern Mediterranean," in *New Constantines: The Rhythm of Imperial Renewal in Byzantium, 4th–13th Centuries*, ed. P. Magdalino (Aldershot and Burlington, 1994), 11–33.

17 Basil the Great, *Homily to the Rich (Homilia in divites)* 2; Gregory of Nyssa, *De beneficentia* (ed. van Heck, v. 9, p. 105).

18 W. Eck, *Roma Caput Mundi* (Wellington, 2001), 9–11.

19 H.-G. Beck, *Byzantinisches Gefolgschaftswesen*, *Sitzungsberichte der bayerischen Akademie der Wissenschaften, Phil.-hist. Kl.*, Heft 5 (Munich, 1965), 1–32.

20 P. Hatlie, *Monks and Monasteries of Constantinople, 350–850* (Cambridge, 2007) 89, 94, 216–9. For skepticism of the figure 300, given for many large monasteries, see D. Caner, *Wandering, Begging Monks: Spiritual Authority and the Promotion of Monasticism in Late Antiquity* (Berkeley, 2002), 147 n. 95, 219 n. 45, 227.

21 Justinian, *CICNov* 3; Herakleios, *Novel* I in I. Konidaris, "Die Novellen des Kaisers Herakleios," *FM* 5 (1982): 33–106, here 62–72, with commentary at 94–100.

22 Robert de Clari, *Conquest of Constantinople*, 92.

23 G. Dagron, *Naissance d'une capitale: Constantinople et ses institutions de 300 à 451* (Paris, 1974), 108–15; B. Croke, "Leo I and the Palace Guard," *Byzantion* 75 (2005): 117–51; J. Haldon, "Strategies of Defence, Problems of Security: The Garrisons of Constantinople in the Middle Byzantine Period," *Constantinople and Its Hinterland*, ed. C. Mango and G. Dagron (Aldershot and Burlington, 1994), 143–55.

24 Prokopios, *Buildings* 1.11.24–7; estimate: Zuckerman, *Du village à l'empire*, 205.

25 80,000: Sokrates, *Ecclesiastical History* 2.13.5; different interpretations discussed by Dagron, *Naissance*, 535–41.

26 *CTh* 14.17.1, 11, 13.

27 *Quaesitor. CICNov* 80; ethnic profiling: A. Laniado, *Ethnos et droit dans le monde protobyzantin, Ve–VIe siècle: Fédérés, paysans et provinciaux à lumière d'une scholie juridique de l'époque de Justinien* (Geneva, 2015), 173–254.

28 E.g., Jordanes, *Getica* 28.143 (sixth century, referring to the late fourth).

29 For the asymmetrical co-existence of Greek and Latin in this context, see F. Millar, *A Greek Roman Empire: Power and Belief under Theodosius II, 408–450* (California, 2006).

30 *Life of Daniel the Stylite*, 60.

31 For Illyrians in Constantinople, see B. Croke, *Count Marcellinus and His Chronicle* (Oxford, 2001), chapter 3.

32  D. Feissel, "Aspects de l'immigration à Constantinople d'áprès les épitaphes protobyzantines," in *Constantinople and Its Hinterland*, 367–77.
33  Ammianus Marcellinus, *Res Gestae* 22.6.
34  Palladios, *Dialogue on the Life of John Chrysostom* 9; John Chrysostom, *Letter* 1 (to Pope Innocent I).
35  Pseudo-Zacharias, *Chronicle* 5.1; Theophanes, *Chronographia* a.m. 5967 (p. 121, from Theodoros Anagnostes).
36  Synesios, *On Kingship* 20.1.
37  Zosimos, *New History* 5.18.10–22.3; Sokrates, *Ecclesiastical History* 6.6; Sozomenos, *Ecclesiastical History* 8.4; Philostorgios, *Ecclesiastical History* 11.8; *Anonymous Funeral Oration for John Chrysostom* 47.
38  Ioannes of Antioch, *History* fr. 229 (Mariev); Marcellinus Comes, *Chronicle* s.a. 473. Among many studies of the Isaurians, see N. Lenski, "Assimilation and Revolt in the Territory of Isauria, from the 1st Century BC to the 6th Century AD," *JESHO* 42.4 (1999): 413–65; for Zenon's reign, R. Kosiński, *The Emperor Zeno: Religion and Politics* (Cracow, 2010).
39  Konstantinos VII, *Book of Ceremonies* 1.92.
40  John Chrysostom, *Homily on the Martyr's Relics* 3 (*PG* 63: 472).
41  Caner, *Wandering, Begging Monks*, 126, 131–2.
42  M. Leontsini, "Views Regarding the Use of the Syrian Language in Byzantium during the 7th Century," *Graeco-Arabica* 9–10 (2004): 235–48, including much material from earlier centuries.
43  Malalas, *Chronicle* 16.19; Marcellinos Comes, *Chronicle* s.a. 512; see J. Dijkstra and G. Greatrex, "Patriarchs and Politics in Constantinople in the Reign of Anastasius (with a Reedition of *O.Mon.Epiph.* 59)," *Millennium* 6 (2009): 223–64, here 260 n. 118.
44  B. Croke, "Justinian, Theodora, and the Church of Saints Sergius and Bacchus," *DOP* 60 (2006): 25–63, esp. 40.
45  For ethnic diversity in the middle Byzantine period, see A. Kaldellis, *Romanland: Ethnicity and Empire in Byzantium* (Cambridge, MA, 2019), esp. 225–7 and 258–60 for Constantinople. Muslims: G. Anderson, "Islamic Spaces and Diplomacy in Constantinople: (Tenth to Thirteenth Centuries C.E.)," *Medieval Encounters* 15 (2009): 86–113, esp. 104–5 for destruction.
46  Benjamin of Tudela, *Itinerary*, 13–14. In general, see *Jews in Byzantium: Dialectics of Minority and Majority Culture*, ed. R. Bonfil et al. (Leiden and Boston, 2012).
47  Prokopios, *Secret History* 25.3; see H. Antoniadis-Bibicou, *Recherches sur les douanes à Byzance: L'"octava", le "kommerkion" et les commerciaires* (Paris, 1963).
48  Treaties: *Russian Primary Chronicle* s.a. 903–7 (English trans. pp. 64–5); arrests: Kaldellis, *Romanland*, 227; Rus' in 1043: Skylitzes, *Synopsis*, 430.
49  Niketas Choniates, *History* 65–6.
50  Details in Kaldellis, *Streams of Gold*.
51  S. Blöndal, *The Varangians of Byzantium*, trans., rev., and rewritten by B. S. Benedikz (Cambridge, 1978).
52  K. N. Ciggaar, "Une description de Constantinople dans le *Tarragonensis* 55," *REB* 53 (1995): 117–40, here 119–20.
53  Ioannes Tzetzes, *Epilogue to the Theogonie*, ed. H. Hunger, *Byzantinistische Grundlagenforschung* (London, 1973), XVIII.
54  P. Magdalino, "The Maritime Neighborhoods of Constantinople: Commercial and Residential Functions, Sixth to Twelfth Centuries," *DOP* 54 (2000): 209–26, esp. 219, 221–6.
55  Eustathios of Thessalonike, *The Capture of Thessalonike* 28.
56  O. Lugovyi, "The Chrysobullos of 1189 and the History of German and French Quarters of Constantinople," in *Proceedings of the Symposium on City Ports from the Aegean to the Black Sea: Medieval-Modern Networks*, ed. F. Karagianni and U. Kocabas (Istanbul, 2015), 71–80.
57  Niketas Choniates, *History* 171–2; Ioannes Kinnamos, *History* 6.10; western sources: D. M. Nicol, *Byzantium and Venice: A Study in Diplomatic and Cultural Relations* (Cambridge, 1988), 97–8.
58  Nicol, *Byzantium and Venice*, 107, citing the main sources.
59  Translated and discussed by P. Magdalino, "Isaac II, Saladin, and Venice," in *The Expansion of Orthodox Europe: Byzantium, the Balkans and Russia*, ed. J. Shepard (Aldershot and Burlington, 2007) 93–106, esp. 102.
60  For a more detailed presentation of this aspect, see A. Kaldellis, "Civic Identity and Civic Participation in Constantinople," in *Civic Identity and Civic Participation in Late Antiquity and the Early Middle Ages*, ed. H. G. E. Rose and C. Brelaz, 2021.

# PART II

# PRACTICAL MATTERS

# 4: Waters for a Capital: Hydraulic Infrastructure and Use in Byzantine Constantinople

## James Crow

### A View from Baghdad

Writing of Al-Mansur's foundation of the city of Baghdad, the eleventh-century chronicler Al-Khaṭīb al-Baghdadi describes how the caliph queried a Byzantine ambassador, asking him to identify the shortcomings of his new city. In reply, the ambassador identified three: the absence of gardens, the proximity of the populous to the palace, and the distance of the palace from water, "which is necessary for the lips of the people."[1] To remedy the last of these deficiencies, the caliph ordered two canals to be dug from the Tigris. The relevance of this tale for the history of Constantinople's water supply is not in the detail, but rather in the date and the perspective it gives on Arab views of the Byzantines, especially as it highlights a competence, water supply and management, normally reserved in modern accounts of the history of water to the Islamic world.[2]

Al-Baghdadi's story is set in the later eighth century, and it is surely no coincidence that it was contemporary with Constantine V's (741–57) restoration of the so-called Bulgarian channel, the long-distance water supply stretching deep into Thrace. Emissaries and prisoners ensured that Baghdad was kept abreast of news from the Byzantine capital, and Arab sources were aware of and impressed by Constantinople's water supply. Indeed, the account of the late ninth-century prisoner, Haroun-ibn-Yahya, was the first to maintain that the city's waters came from Bulgaria. This claim was also found in the tenth-century *Patria*, which also reports on the city's large drains and its forty fountains.[3]

This chapter presents an overview of the exceptional achievement of late antique engineers in what is justifiably claimed to be the longest Roman water supply line.[4] It also shows how maintenance of this system was able to sustain the city into the middle ages. One of the challenges in studying the water history of Constantinople after the late sixth century is that the most informative comments about the hydraulic system derive from foreign visitors or emissaries. Thus, William of Malmesbury's account of the arrival of First Crusade in 1098 observed: "The Danube . . . flows by hidden channels underground into the city; on appointed days it is admitted by opening a sluice, and carries the dirt of the city into the sea."[5] To outsiders the middle-Byzantine (843–1204) water provision was a marvel, certainly in comparison to the primitive plumbing and sanitary infrastructure available in medieval European towns. Other elements, such as the city's great aqueduct, the Bozdoğan Kemer, continued to impress later Islamic commentators.

PREVIOUS RESEARCH

The Byzantine achievement in water engineering is often neglected in wider studies of the history of water. In part, this situation reflects the fact that a clear picture of the complexity and extent of channels outside, and the number of cisterns inside Constantinople has only emerged in the last thirty years. In the sixteenth century, Pierre Gilles could claim to have "rediscovered" the greatest of the covered cisterns, the Yerebatan or Basilica cistern. Others continued to be described by travellers up to the late nineteenth-century study of Forchheimer and Stryzgowski, a pioneering collaboration between an engineer and a classical archaeologist.[6] Although later Ottoman aqueducts and barrages in the Belgrade forest were well known from travellers' accounts, the more distant remains of channels were ignored, apart from a study by a Bulgarian officer during the First Balkan War (1912–13). His study, written in Bulgarian, included a sketch of Kurşunlugerme (Fig. 4.1), the greatest surviving aqueduct bridge from the system.[7] Subsequently a map of Istanbul's water supply produced by the Compagnie des Eaux de Constantinople in 1922 marked the late Roman channels near Çebeçiköy as "Ancienne conduit Romaine."[8] Because Thrace remained a military zone up to the fall of communism in 1989, arch-aeological research outside the city was restricted. Nevertheless, Feridün Dirimtekin, director of the Ayasofya Museum and a former cavalry officer, was able to undertake a number of surveys, including studies of the aqueducts and channels published in 1959.[9] Although he reported his results in an international journal, the Roman archaeological com-munity paid no further attention to the research. One suspects that

4.1 Peter Oreshkov, Kurşunlugerme, c.1912.

those concerned with hydraulic engineering were reluctant to credit such an achievement to the late empire, which was still perceived as an empire in decline.[10]

New research commenced in the 1990s, when Cyril Mango published a characteristically erudite and concise overview of the history of water in Constantinople.[11] Subsequently, the first attempt to map the channels outside the city appeared in Kâzim Çeçen's book *The Longest Roman Water Supply Line*.[12] A professor of hydraulic engineering and an expert on Ottoman water works, Çeçen was the first to document the channels and bridges as far as their sources near Vize. Fieldwork and research over the next two decades increased knowledge both of the extent and chronological development of the system outside the city, and the network of cisterns and channels within it. This work provides the basis for the discussion in this chapter.[13] While Mango's article presented a historical narrative based on the written and topographical sources concerning the water provision in Byzantine Constantinople, the current discussion presents new perspectives on how the complex of water channels and cisterns resourced the great city. Water usage and distribution in large urban centers responded to a suite of social, environmental, and political demands; therefore, water history can serve as a barometer of urban triumph and failure, a test of human resourcefulness in a challenging urban setting.

## WATER AND THE GROWTH OF A GREAT CITY

Byzantion was a medium-sized Roman city in an exceptional physical setting. The decision by Constantine (306–37) to create a new megalopolis required huge human energy and resources. This effort notwithstanding, he left one challenge unresolved for nearly fifty years: the deficiency of water. Byzantion, like many east Roman cities, had benefited from the patronage of Hadrian, who, according to later Byzantine sources, had built it an aqueduct.[14] With the Constantinian development of the site, this supply line proved inadequate. Although Constantinople was surrounded by water, it was saline. On the peninsula itself, there was limited groundwater for wells, and the only water course, the Lycus, was a small perennial stream which flowed into a bay on the Sea of Marmara later occupied by the Harbor of Theodosios. Unlike Rome or Antioch there was no major river to fall back on if the aqueducts were to fail or break.[15] Themistios, the court orator in the 360s, recognized the problem when he wrote, "The city thirsts." This remark had nothing to do with sudden drought or long-term climate change; it was quite simply a response to the fact that the city could not satisfy the demands of the growing numbers of incomers who were extending the urban area. A new aqueduct was needed, and it was built at huge cost.

The response was the "longest water supply system in the Roman world."[16] The channels bringing the waters from distant springs in Thrace can be dated to two main phases: the first initiated *c.*340 by Constantius II (337–61), was completed in 373 under Valens (364–78) (Fig. 4.2). There were two lines, one sourced at springs near Danamandıra, and a second at Pinarca. They joined near the village of Akalan, flowing toward Constantinople, with a total estimated length of 246 km.[17] The channels were cut into the sides of the hills, and were lined with mortared stone and water-proof mortar covered with a stone vault. Most were *c.*1 m wide, and some up to 1.6 m high. The water was gravity-led, and there was a shallow gradient as the channels followed the contours of the Thracian hills. Where the valleys were too deep, bridges were constructed to reduce overall channel length. From this first phase, thirty-six bridges have been identified or interpolated. Two long tunnels were required on this section, one at Akalan to allow the two branches to join. Although no physical traces are known, the topography demands a tunnel 2 km in length. A second tunnel was required further downstream at Tayakadın, where construction of the southwest corner of the new Istanbul airport has obscured part of the

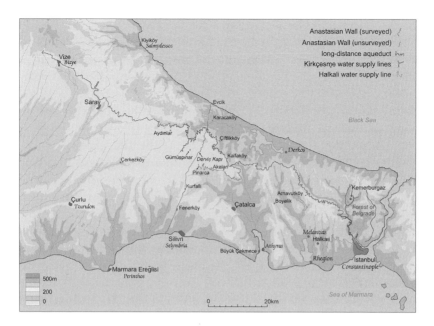

4.2 Thrace and the Byzantine water supply channels. (Courtesy of Richard Bayliss)

line. From there the channels continue along the Alibey valley, a tributary of the Golden Horn, toward the city.[18]

The later, second channel was sourced by springs much further to the west at Pazarlı, west of Vize, at Ergene, and near Bınkılıç (now Fatih). This channel was 180 km in length. East from Bınkılıç it was normally 1.6 m broad, and in places more than 2 m high. In part, it ran parallel to but at a different elevation than the earlier channel. It remains uncertain whether the two channels continued separately as far as the city, since the evidence for the channels and bridges is less complete close to Istanbul's urban sprawl. The combined length of these channels is 426 km; however, calculated separately, the total is 565 km. A total of fifty-seven new bridges are known from the second-phase channel, together with eleven newly built replacements along the first phase, making a working number of around a ninety-three supplied by all the spring sources.

The work of construction was among the most outstanding infra-structure projects executed in the ancient world, an enormous under-taking involving complex planning and resource management.[19] While the cost to the imperial treasury cannot be known, estimates based on length and the construction materials give some idea of the magnitude of the undertaking. Stone required for the channels and the bridges amounted to just over 2.5 million cubic meters, a mass equivalent to the Great Pyramid at Giza. The quantity of mortar required was enough to fill 500 Olympic-sized swimming pools.[20] Such enormous figures demonstrate the new city's ability to command imperial resources in the fourth century, even before Constantinople had become a permanent imperial residence from the Theodosian dynasty (379–450) onwards.

While the construction and arrival of the first channel is well documented by contemporary writers and chroniclers, including Gregory of Nazianzus, who complained of the Constantinopolitans' pride in their civic amenities, "that marvellous work the underground and overhead river" included,[21] construction of the second phase remains obscure. We know of an Aqueduct of Hadrian, an Aqueduct of Valens (later mistakenly referred to as Valentinian), and a reference from 396 in one law code to a Theodosian aqueduct. The text refers to contributions by praetors, who were normally expected to fund the civic games. While the sums mentioned would have been adequate for repairs, they would have contributed little to the construction of the great new bridges and the far-reaching channels of the second phase.[22]

Bridges from both phases vary in size. They range, according to need, from small single-arched structures to majestic multi-tiered aqueducts rising to over 45 m in height and spanning valleys up to 150 m in length. Five bridges of the second phase rank among the monumental aqueducts of imperial Rome. In all cases, they replaced earlier fourth-century structures and in instances such as the new bridges at Kumarlidere and Büyükgerme, they replaced several smaller crossings with longer, higher structures that reduced the earlier, more sinuous route.[23] The largest of these bridges was Kurşunlugerme. Set in a deep, forested valley, this structure remains one of the most dramatic survivals of late antique Constantinople (Fig. 4.1). Faced with metamorphic limestone ashlar blocks, which are almost like marble in appearance and hardness, its three tiers rise to a height of over 40 m (Fig. 4.3). Christian symbols and texts decorate the vaults and keystones. It is a unique monument of a Christian Roman Empire, and of the new city's ambition.[24] The earliest surviving reference to the long-distance channels extending to Vize is in Hesychios' sixth-century text on the birth of Byzantion's mythical founder[25]; however, comparison of distinctive carving from Kurşunlugerme to that on Marcian's column of c.450 points to an earlier date for the completion of the bridge and the extended system.[26] The origin of this monumental phase remains uncertain, although an earthquake in the region of the aqueducts at

4.3 Büyükgerme aqueduct showing the fifth-century construction similar to Kurşunlugerme and the later narrowing of the upper vaults. (Courtesy of J. Crow)

the very end of the fourth century may have accounted for the need to repair and replace the earlier bridges and provided an impetus for the new extended line.[27]

## WATER IN THE CITY

Constantinople itself grew westwards, with the new Theodosian Land walls completed by c.415. This new intermural zone was never as fully urbanized as the city within the Constantinian walls, and much of it was given over to elite houses, monasteries, parks, and horticulture. Shortly after the completion of the new walls, the cistern of Aetios, now occupied by a minor league football stadium, was constructed in 421. It was the first of three great open-air reservoirs to be excavated in the intermural zone. Although there is no direct evidence, it is difficult not to associate this new reservoir and the other two, the Mokios and Asper cisterns of the later fifth century, with the additional provision of water made available by the new long-distance line from Vize. In total these reservoirs could have held over 600,000 m³ of water.[28] While these new resources were intended for the agriculture and gardens of the inter-mural zone, they are best seen as the city's strategic reserve, not only in times of war and crisis, but also with respect to the management of water distribution across the city. Water storage on this scale was unprecedented in the ancient world, but it is significant that in later times when the Ottoman Empire faced few external threats without any obvious need for security, the later water supply system in the Belgrade forest relied on external reservoirs formed behind dams (*bent*). Despite the city's history of sieges, there were only two occasions when the water supply was cut: when Theodoric Strabo revolted against the emperor Zeno (474–91) in 487 and is reported to have cut the aqueduct only to retreat soon thereafter, and the more serious Avar siege of 626, when the city's aqueduct was broken and not reinstated until 767 under Constantine V. This repair represented a turning point in the city's early medieval revival.[29] The water supply does not figure in the city's most serious sieges in 1204 and 1453.

Cisterns are the most numerous surviving structures from Byzantine Constantinople. Cut into the ground and lined with water-proof hydraulic mortar, they survive in a range of locations, reused, among other things, as restaurants, marriage venues, shopping arcades, and hidden storerooms. They vary in size from the massive open reservoirs located in the intermural zone, to small cisterns providing water for individual dwellings.[30] Although the smallest may have bene-fited from rain water collection,[31] the majority were part of the city's water supply and distribution network. Recent research has identified 209 examples, including examples first documented in the nineteenth and early twentieth centuries.[32] The preponderance of cisterns occupies the higher ground in a band north of the Valens aqueduct. There are also clusters around the Column of Marcian, which become more marked toward the Forum Taurii. From there they are more or less uniformly spread across the east end of the peninsula, especially on the First Hill later occupied by the Topkapı Palace (Fig. 4.4).

Historically cisterns were constructed in the city from the fourth century onwards.[33] However, the appearance of large reservoirs and covered cisterns is better documented from the fifth and sixth centur-ies.[34] Anastasios (491–518) may have introduced large, covered cisterns to the heart of the city with the Binbirdirek project, although the chronology of this cistern is uncertain.[35] As the deepest of the large urban cisterns, it reflects the need to create a vast storage space with a limited footprint in what was a crowded urban region. Also credited to

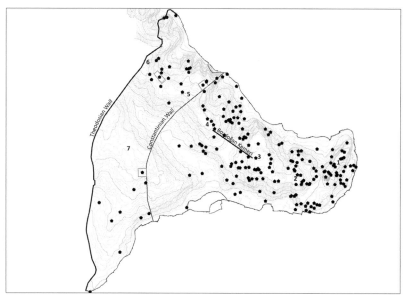

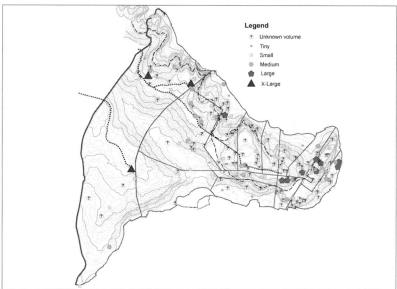

4.4 Distribution of known cisterns in Byzantine Constantinople. (Courtesy of Kate Ward)

Anastasios was the Cold Cistern in the Sphendone of the Hippodrome. The Cold Cistern represents the earliest insertion of a cistern into an existing large building, a practice commonly adopted in later centuries.[36] Soon afterwards, Justinian (527–65) constructed the largest of the covered cisterns, the Yerebatan Saray or Basilica Cistern, below the courtyard of the pre-existing Basilica.[37] It is a massive example of urban infrastructure, with its brick vaults supported on an array of columns often capped by decorated capitals from Prokonessos. The apparently redundant and enigmatic elaboration of its structures far exceeds even the grandest of the imperial Roman cisterns in both scale and design innovation.

In Constantinople the major hydraulic constructions from the mid-fifth century onwards responded to the needs of the city; they were not mere vanity programs like the nymphaea and baths of earlier Roman cities.[38] This new age came to be defined by the pragmatic need to sustain the city's infrastructure. One concern was security, and Anastasios's decision to construct a new barrier wall only 61 km west of the Theodosian walls provided an outer defense for the city through-out the sixth century. [39] The new wall protected the spring sources at Pinarca, part of the water supply network from phase 1, but left exposed those at Danamadırı and the outer line to Vize.

If only a few of the smaller cisterns relied on rain water harvesting, the majority must represent a complex system of water channels which required constant management and maintenance. Water came into the city through the northern end of the land walls at two elevations. Neither point of entry survives today. The elevation of the upper line from more distant Thracian springs can be determined from the 973 m line of the Bozdoğan Kemer, the Aqueduct of Valens, stretching between the city's third and fourth hills. This constant reminder of the water supply remained in use until the early twentieth century. Two channels cross the interior of the bridge; one is seen clearly blocked at the west end. It is not certain if they represent the two channels known in the Thracian hinterland, or if one is a secondary line from the closer but less prolific springs at Halkalı, southwest of the city. It is assumed that water from Thrace ceased to flow across the bridge after the later twelfth century; however, a reference by the early fifteenth-century emissary Clavijo to water flowing across the bridge may represent waters from the smaller springs at Halkalı. Beyond the valley between the third and fourth hills, the channel flowed into the great nymphaeum in the Forum of Theodosios from which it was distributed across the higher parts of the new city including the Binbirdirek Cistern, which from c.500 served as its distribution hub, or *castellum aquae*, at the east end of the line. Stone pipes discovered during road works beneath the modern streets of Ordu Cadessi and Divan Yolu, which follow the line of the Byzantine Mese, were carved out of marble column drums and were intended to lead the water under pressure; elsewhere a range of ceramic pipes are known, some of large diameter.[40] Unlike the western Roman empire, where lead pipes were common, no examples of lead pipes are known to survive from Constantinople, although some are referred to in sources. These were mostly used to monitor the flow of water to large private houses, which were charged according to pipe diameter. The location of these pipes has allowed partial reconstruction of the water distribution system in the city center.[41] In addition to pipes, other buried water channels are reported across the city. Many of these channels, especially those without traces of hydraulic mortar, are likely to have been storm water drains and sewers. Known examples are buried, running beside the Column of Constantine. Another excellent example is visible within the Hippodrome seating now exposed in the Turkish and Islamic Arts Museum in Sultanhamet. This extensive network of drains and sewers continued to impress visitors throughout the Middle Ages.

Recent study of the city's water distribution has also been able to reconsider the route of the Aqueduct of Hadrian. The key historical source is the sixth-century historian John Malalas, who states that the Basilica cistern was supplied by the Hadrianic aqueduct line. This information provides a delivery point and an elevation and is the best evidence for associating earlier channels with the springs closer to the city in the Belgrade Forest and the Kırkçeşme, sources also exploited by the Ottoman channels. Traces of earlier bridges have been recognized in the later Ottoman structures, which incorporated them into their fabric.[42] The Hadrianic channel will have entered the city at around the 35 m contour, and recent study concludes that the channel followed more closely the later Ottoman line than once thought.[43]

## AN AQUEDUCT OF JUSTINIAN?

No aqueduct of Justinian is attested in historical sources, and sixth-century accounts outline a number of water shortages, which created unrest among an urban population reliant on public fountains.[44] In the *Secret History*, the sixth-century historian Prokopios lays the blame not on drought, but on Justinian's frugality and his consequent failure to maintain channels and bridges in Thrace. However, archaeological evidence presents a different picture. The only known building inscription from the entire system still in position was found on a small bridge at Elkaf Dere, west of Çiftlikköy (Fig. 4.2). It reports that construction was overseen by Longinus, ex-city prefect and consul, who as prefect had completed the paving of the courtyard at the Basilica Cistern in 541; the works on the aqueducts must have followed a few years later.[45] With its plainly dressed blocks and the absence of boss work character-istic of the earlier phases, the new construction at Elkaf Dere is struc-turally different from previous work. There is no evidence for reused blocks in the facings, which were newly quarried or redressed. At the springing of the arch there was an unusual downward-sloping chamfer similar to work on other bridges from Lukadere in the west to beyond Büyükgerme. The largest of these was the restored bridge at Talas, where the new works enclosed a two-tier bridge from the fifth cen-tury.[46] A similar but arguably different repair may date to a decade or so later, when the aged Justinian was present in Selymbria (Silivri) to oversee repairs on the Anastasian Wall following an earthquake in 557. The line of the aqueducts crosses the wall, and bridges and channels are likely to have been damaged by the same catastrophic event. Whichever exact period of rebuilding this construction represents, the system clearly underwent a major restoration program during Justinian's reign, one otherwise unattested in the written accounts. As well, the work demonstrates the continuing seismic threat from the nearby North Anatolian Faultline below the Sea of Marmora.

## AFTER THE DRY YEARS

In 626 Constantinople's mighty fortifications resisted the Avar siege, but the long-distance water supply was cut and remained unrestored for nearly one and a half centuries. This situation did not mean that the city was without water. As Theophanes specifically notes, the "City" aque-duct was restored by Constantine V in 767, which means that the aqueduct of Hadrian, the lower-level supply line, had remained avail-able to supply parts of the city. There is, however, little reference to water infrastructures in the years after Herakleios (610–41), although Justinian II (685–95 and 705–11) is reported to have crept into the city through the dry channel to regain power in 705. While cisterns were used for the burial of plague victims in 747, in 713 the emperor Philippikos (711–13) bathed in the city's main public baths, the Zeuxippos, which were known to have been fed by the Hadrianic line.[47] Failure to restore the Valens line must reflect the seventh- and eighth-century downturn in the urban demography; its restoration signals the revival of imperial fortunes under Constantine V.[48] Despite the chronicler Theophanes' hostility to Constantine, he records the extensive workforce drawn from Anatolia and the Aegean, noting the workers' skills in brickmaking, stone cutting and plastering. He also mentions laborers from nearby Thrace.[49] Extensive restoration work is also evident on a number of the major water bridges, and is best documented at Büyükgerme and Ballıgerme[50] (Fig. 4.3). At both bridges the second tiers underwent distinctive repairs, and at the former the arch width was reduced from 7 to 4 m to support the upper arches carrying the channel. Roughly squared and reused blocks laid in courses with surviving springing of brick arches comprised the new work. At Ballıgerme this stonework phase was more extensive, and much of the upper facings were replaced in this fashion. Unlike the sixth-century restorations where new facings were quarried or reworked, the later rebuilding reused existing blocks or bricks from the nearby Anastasian Wall. The association of this work with Constantine V's major building program remains conjectural; however, in the cycle of repairs and renovations recognizable from the main bridges, his is the most extensive intervention after the sixth century and so provides the most compelling context for this major restoration.

Historical accounts up to the twelfth century briefly describe other work on the aqueducts, and a number of later restorations are also apparent. The most significant example is at Ballıgerme. The upper two arches show evidence for further narrowing using brick bonding courses and rubble construction with brick vaults to support the earlier arches. Structurally this is the bridge's latest phase, and it includes the use of vertically set bricks, a form of construction known as cloisonné work that is typical from the eleventh century onwards.[51] The eleventh-century historian John Skylitzes records that Basil II (976–1025) renovated the aqueduct of Valentinian, confusing the later emperor's name with that of Valens. An epigram, from an inscription found in the vicinity but now lost, enigmatically refers to a "wondrous work" restored by Basil II and his brother Constantine VIII (1025–8).[52] The brickwork from Ballıgerme supports the latter suggestion. The epigram spoke that "Time threatened a wondrous work," and both phases of structural intervention on the aqueduct bridges strengthened vaults enfeebled by earthquakes and erosion over five centuries. It is therefore not surprising that the twelfth-century historian John Kinnamos reports that during a drought in the 1170s Manuel I (1143–80) "noted that the old arcades which conveyed water to Byzantium were long since collapsed, and it would be a difficult task to reconstruct them, requiring much time."[53] The maintenance of these antique bridges and water channels from Thrace was too great a challenge, and the city looked to develop water resources closer to hand, in the same region of Kırkçeşme and the Belgrade Forest which was to be the main resource for the Ottoman city.

These springs were the source for the Aqueduct of Hadrian and for the later system repaired by Mehmet Fatih after 1453. There were also major new works built by Sinan in the mid-sixteenth century, including the monumental bridges of the Eğri or Kovuk Kemer and the Uzun Kemer. The latter is 711 m in length with fifty upper arcades.[54] Outwardly these structures appear as Sinan's great monuments, albeit constructed in a manner reminiscent of the great fifth-century Thracian bridges. Many show traces of earlier Roman bridges at their base. If we accept that bridges comparable in height and length to the Ottoman aqueducts were required to bring waters from the Belgrade Forest to Constantinople, then we can imagine that the late Roman works closer to the city were on an equally massive scale, but almost completely refurbished in later Byzantine and, more especially, Ottoman periods.[55]

## WATER IN MEDIEVAL CONSTANTINOPLE

Constantine V's restoration of the Valens line enabled the distribution of water to those high parts of the city left dry since 626. Among the most of significant of these establishments was the church of the Holy Apostles situated on the fourth hill. It is therefore not coincidental that Nicholas Mesarites' late twelfth-century description of the church and its surroundings remarks, "Indeed one can see in it and in the regions surrounding it inexhaustible treasures of water and reservoirs of sweet water made equal to seas, from which as though from four heads of rivers the whole City of Constantinople receives its supply."[56] More than two centuries before, the Arab Haroun-ibn-Yahya had used similar imagery in his description of Constantinople,[57] and water imagery was a mainstay in tenth-century rhetorical descriptions, which included fountains, pools, and especially baths; not the great public baths of imperial Rome, but smaller complexes, among them the ritual baths (*lousma*) associated with monasteries.[58]

None of these features survive, but cisterns continued to be constructed, and later examples can be dated from the reuse of capitals.[59] A continuing feature of new cisterns from the ninth century onwards was their insertion into preexisting elite buildings. The great cistern in the late antique rotunda below the tenth-century palace of

Romanus I Lekapenos (920–44) at the Myrelaion (Bodrum Camii)[60] and the new cisterns inserted into and beside the large hall north of the late antique Palace of Antiochos (later the monastery of St. Euphemia) near the hippodrome demonstrate this trend.[61] One of the most important new middle-Byzantine cisterns which can be dated with some certainty was part of the church complex at Küçükyalı.[62] Now convincingly associated with the monastery of Satyros founded by the Patriarch Ignatios between 867 and 877, it is located outside the city close to the eastern shore of the Sea of Marmara. The monastery survives as a rectangular platform 70 by 51 m set above the level coastal plain. An intricately designed and centrally planned church is located toward the east end of the platform, with an open atrium in front of it to the west. Set into the platform was an extensive cistern, which partly reflects the plan of the church to the east, and the atrium supported by a vaulted roof supported on piers, now lost, to the west. A well-preserved channel enters the pool below the church on the east, a settling tank before the entrance confirming its function as a cistern. This church-cistern complex is now among the best documented middle-Byzantine buildings in Constantinople and its suburbs. With an estimated water volume of 3,000 m$^3$, the cistern makes clear that the monastery's builders were concerned with water storage and distribution from the outset, and that the quantity of water provided will have exceeded the needs of a monastic community. Water was distributed to the surrounding communities for either domestic or agricultural reasons, providing the monastery with a resource it could control. None of the *typika* (foundation charters) from monasteries in Constantinople refers to water usage or rights. However, from Thessalonike there is very clear evidence for the management and control of the city's water resources by the main monasteries, a role that continued into the Ottoman period.[63]

From Constantinople there are a number of cisterns associated with known monastic churches, the Studios and Chora Monasteries included. The Pantokrator Monastery (Zeyrek Camii), one of the city's most important surviving middle-Byzantine buildings, had a significant cluster of cisterns in its vicinity. Below the ecclesiastical complex and close to Attatürk Bulvarı is the cistern of Unkapanı. It was built into the hillside with scalloped buttresses facing the road. While there is no independent dating evidence, such as brick stamps or specific capital types to suggest an early date, comparison of the cistern to late ninth-century construction and design at Küçükyalı suggests that the Unkapanı cistern, with a maximum internal capacity of 3,500 m$^3$, could

4.5 Fountain house near Unkapanı, Istanbul, middle Byzantine period. (Courtesy of Kerim Altuğ)

have been constructed in the same era. The proximity of the monastery to the Unkapanı cistern makes it likely that the Pantokrator foundation was instrumental in the regulation of water distribution from this large cistern supplied either by the Hadrianic channel or the Valens line close by. A well-preserved middle Byzantine fountain (Fig. 4.5), one of the only examples from the city, survives nearby, but there is no direct connection to the line.

The monasteries' involvement in the city's quotidian life was part of a changing pattern of patronage in the middle Byzantine period.[64] It is also seen at the Myrelaion, which on the death of Romanus Lekapenos became a nunnery with a bequest for the regular distribution of bread[65]; the large cistern is not mentioned. This new provision of cisterns associated with monastic foundations may also be reflected in the practice of constructing cisterns below middle Byzantine churches, some of which were for rainwater harvesting, but others, such as those from the Mangana region, were of greater capacity.[66]

Archaeological evidence from Constantinople and elsewhere attests to the maintenance and continued development of Byzantine hydraulic technologies. A feature of the very large reservoirs was the need to control the volume and pressure of outflow. At the Fildanı Reservoir outside of the city and north of the Hebdomen Palace, a tall cylindrical chamber was added to more effectively control outflow and hence reduce friction and erosion to the outflowing water channels. The Fildanı most likely dates to the sixth century or later, while the water tower, which was built using a different construction method, is structurally later in date, and therefore demonstrates continuing developments in Byzantine water technology.[67] Within the city, at another massive late antique reservoir, the Aspar, a circular structure was constructed within the northwest corner, which may have served to manage the outflow, or to aerate the waters. While the reservoir dates from the fifth century, cloisonné brickwork in the tower places its construction in the middle-Byzantine period and indicates the continued use and maintenance of the reservoir into the eleventh century.

## CONCLUSION

For the citizens of Constantinople, public access to water was a right, not a privilege or a commodity. In the late antique city the elite paid for water to be delivered through pipes,[68] but there is no evidence for how supply was managed in later centuries. The shift to the use of cisterns associated with institutions may reflect a more irregular pattern of water supply, a trend that may have begun in the sixth century with the new large cisterns such as those at the Basilica and in the imperial palace. Throughout Constantinople's history, emperors recognized the importance of water to urban life. Indeed, even after the great infrastructure of late antiquity could no longer provide for the city's needs, the memory of the great channels and cisterns survived in the writings of the fourteenth-century diplomat, Manuel Chrysoloras, composed less than fifty years before the city's fall.[69] This legacy went beyond literary memory: the new Ottoman rulers were able to adapt, renovate, and develop the Byzantine system, a system which at its height was unrivalled in the ancient or medieval worlds.[70]

## FURTHER READING

Altuğ, K., "Reconsidering the Use of Spolia in Byzantine Constantinople," in *Di Bisanzio dirai ciò che è passato, ciò che passa e che sarà: Scritti in onore di Alessandra Guiglia*, ed. Silvia Pedone and Andrea Paribeni (Rome, 2018), 3–16.

Çeçen, K., *The Longest Roman Water Supply Line* (Istanbul, 1996).

Crow, J., "The Imagined Water Supply of Constantinople, New Approaches" *TM* 22.1 (2018): 211–36.

Crow, J., J. Bardill and R. Bayliss, *The Water Supply of Byzantine Constantinople* (London, 2008).

Forchheimer, P. and J. Strzygowski, *Die byzantinischen Wasserbehälter von Konstantinopel* (Vienna, 1893).

Magdalino, P., "The Culture of Water in the 'Macedonian Renaissance'," in *Fountains and Water Culture in Byzantium*, ed. B. Shilling and P. Stephenson (Cambridge, 2016), 130–44.

Mango, C., "The Water Supply of Constantinople," in *Constantinople and Its Hinterland*, ed. C. Mango and G. Dagron (Aldershot, 1995), 9–18.

Snyder, R. J., "Manipulating the Environment: The Impact of the Construction of the Water Supply of Constantinople," in *A Most Pleasant Scene and an Inexhaustible Resource? Steps Towards Environmental History of the Byzantine Empire*, ed. H. Baron, and F. Daim (Mainz, 2017), 169–85.

Ward, K., M. Crapper, K. Altuğ, and J. Crow, "The Byzantine Cisterns of Constantinople," *Water Science and Technology: Water Supply* 17.6 (2017): 1499–506.

Ward, K., J. Crow and M. Crapper, "Water-Supply Infrastructure of Byzantine Constantinople," *JRA* 30 (2017): 175–95.

# NOTES

1 Al-Khaṭīb al-Baghdadi, translated in J. Lassner, *The Topography of Baghdad in the Early Middle Ages: Text and Studies* (Detroit, 1970), 58, n. 50. Although Lassner thinks the anecdote may be a later embellishment, he considers it to reflect contemporary events. I thank Antonio Montinaro for this source.

2 See B. Fagan, *Elixir, a Human History of Water* (London, 2011), who devotes a chapter to the Islamic world, but makes no reference to Constantinople or Byzantium.

3 N. M. El Cheikh, *Byzantium Viewed by the Arabs* (Cambridge, MA, 2004), 147; *Patria* I. 69–70. See A. Berger, *Accounts of Medieval Constantinople, the Patria* (Washington, DC, 2013), 43 for translation.

4 K. Çeçen, *The Longest Roman Water Supply Line* (Istanbul, 1996).

5 William of Malmesbury, *Gesta Regum Anglorum*, 4.355.4.

6 K. Byrd, *Pierre Gilles' Constantinople: A Modern English Translation* (New York, 2008), 100–2; P. Forchheimer and J. Strzygowski, *Die Byzantinischen Wasserbehälter von Konstantinopel* (Vienna, 1893).

7 P. N. Oreskov, "Vizantijski starini okolo Carigrad," *SpBAN* 10 (1915): 71–118.

8 A. Köç, ed., *Osmanlı Arşiv Belgelerinde Sultangazi*, Sultangazi Belediyesi Kültür Yayınları 1 (İstanbul, 2012).

9 F. Dirimtekin, "Adduction de l'eau à Byzance dans la région dite 'Bulgarie,'" *CahArch* 10 (1959): 217–43

10 For the persistence of such views, see, I. Moreno Gallo, "Roman Water Supply Systems, a new approach," in *De aquaeductu atque aqua urbium Lyciae, Pamphyliae, Pisidiae, the Legacy of Sextus Julius Frontinus*, ed. G. Wiplinger (Leuven, 2016), 117–27, esp. 123.

11 C. Mango, "The water supply of Constantinople," in *Constantinople and Its Hinterland*, ed. C. Mango and G. Dagron (Aldershot, 1995), 9–18.

12 Çeçen, *Longest Roman Water Supply*.

13 See esp. J. Crow, J. Bardill and R. Bayliss, *The Water Supply of Byzantine Constantinople* (London, 2008); to avoid excessive references the reader is recommended to seek further information and references to texts and structures in this volume.

14 For a discussion of historical sources, see Mango, "Water Supply." For translations of main sources, see Crow et al. *Water Supply*, Appendix 1, 221–47.

15 J. Crow, "Water and late antique Constantinople," in *Two Romes: Rome and Constantinople in Late Antiquity*, ed. L. Grig and G. Kelly (Oxford, 2012), 116–35.

16 Çeçen, *Longest Roman Water Supply*.

17 See the recent estimate in F. Ruggeri, M. Crapper, J. R. Snyder and J. Crow, "GIS based assessment of the Byzantine water supply system of Constantinople," *Water Science and Technology: Water Supply* 17.6 (2017): 1534–1543.

18 Crow et al. *Water Supply*; Ruggeri "GIS-base assessment".

19 J. R. Snyder, "Manipulating the Environment: the impact of the construction of the Water Supply of Constantinople," in *A Most Pleasant Scene and an Inexhaustible Resource? Steps Towards Environmental History of the Byzantine Empire*, eds. H. Baron, and F. Daim (Mainz, 2017), 169–85.

20 Snyder, "Manipulating the Environment," 180–2, tables 3–6 for supporting data.

21 Gregory of Nazianzus, *Orationes* 33, *Against the Arians* 6; see Crow et al. *Water Supply*, 226.

22 Crow et al. *Water Supply*, 16.

23 J. Crow, "The Imagined Water Supply of Constantinople, New Approaches," *TM* 22/1 (2018): 211–36, figs. 3–4.

24 J. Crow, "Blessing or Security? Understanding the Christian Symbols of a Monumental Aqueduct Bridge in The Hinterland of Late Antique Constantinople," in *Graphic Signs of Power and Faith in Late Antiquity and The Early Middle Ages: Essays on Early Graphicacy*, ed. I. Garipzanov, C. Goodson, and H. Maguire (Turnhout, 2017), 147–74.

25 *Patria* I, 7; Berger, *Accounts of Medieval Constantinople*, 7.

26 Crow, et al. *Water Supply*, 161–2.

27 J. Crow, "The Wonderful Works, a history of bridges on the Thracian aqueducts," in *Crossing Bridges in Byzantium and Beyond*, ed. G. Fingarova and A. Külzer (forthcoming).

28 Crow et al. *Water Supply*, 129; Crow, "Imagined Water Supply," 227 for evidence of how water may have been distributed.

29 Crow et al. *Water Supply*, 16–17, 19–20.

30 Crow et al. *Water Supply* 124ff.; K Ward, M. Crapper, K. Altuğ and J. Crow, "The Byzantine cisterns of Constantinople," *Water Science and Technology: Water Supply*: 17.6 (2017): 1499–1506.

31 R. Ousterhout, *Master Builders of Byzantium* (Philadelphia, 2008), 167 for the cistern below the Kariye Museum.

32 Ward et al. "Byzantine Cisterns"; K. Altuğ, "Planlama İlkeleri ve Yapım Teknikleri Açısından, Tarihi Yarımada'daki Bizans Dönemi Sarnıçları (Notes on planning and construction techniques of Byzantine cisterns in the historical peninsula of Istanbul)," *Restorasyon/Konservasyon* 15 (2012): 3–22, with coloured illustrations and plans of many of the city's cisterns.

33 See outline history in Crow et al. *Water Supply*, 15–16; 126–40.

34 Crow et al., *Water Supply*, 128.

35 Also of similar date on the basis of capital forms was the cistern in Divânı Ali Sokağı, J. Bardill, *Brickstamps of Constantinople* (Oxford, 2004), 129–30.

36 Forchheimer and Strzygowski, *Die Byzantinischen Wasserbehälter*, 104–5.

37 Crow et al., *Water Supply*, 17–19.

38 For Constantinopolitan nymphaea, see P. Stephenson and R. Hedlund, "Monumental waterworks in late antique Constantinople," in *Fountains and Water Culture in Byzantium*, ed. B. Shilling and P. Stephenson (Cambridge, 2016), 36–54.

39 J. Crow, "Recent research on the Anastasian Wall in Thrace and late antique linear barriers around the Black Sea," in *Roman Frontier Studies 2009*, ed. N. Hodgson, P. Bidwell, and J. Schachtmann (Oxford, 2017), 131–8.

40 C. Barsanti and A. Guiglia, *The Sculptures of the Ayasofya Müsesi in Istanbul, a short guide* (Istanbul, 2010), 49–55.

41 K. Ward, J. Crow and M. Crapper, "Water-supply infrastructure of Byzantine Constantinople," *JRA* 30 (2017): 175–95, esp.187–90, fig. 6.

42 Crow, "Imagined Water Supply," 222–3, fig. 7.

43 Compare the route shown in Crow et al. 2008, fig 2.2; Maps 12–15; with Ward et al., "Water-supply infrastructure," fig. 4.

44 B. Croke, "Justinian's Constantinople," in *The Cambridge Companion to the Age of Justinian*, ed. M. Maas (Cambridge, 2005), 60–86, esp. 68–9; P. Magdalino, "Medieval Constantinople," in *Studies on the History and Topography of Byzantine Constantinople* (Aldershot/Burlington, 2007) no. I: 1–111, esp. 54, n. 205.

45 Crow et al., *Water Supply*, 18, 62–3.

46 Crow et al., *Water Supply*, 102–3.

47 Ward et al., "Water Supply Infrastructure," fig. 4.

48 P. Magdalino, "The Culture of Water in the 'Macedonian Renaissance'," in *Fountains and Water Culture in Byzantium*, ed. B. Shilling and P. Stephenson (Cambridge, 2016), 130–44, esp. 132.

49 Crow et al., *Water Supply*, 19–20, 236.

50 Crow et al., *Water Supply*, fig. 4.2, 4.12 (elevation drawings).

51 R. Ousterhout, *Eastern Medieval Architecture: The Building Traditions of Byzantium and Neighbouring Lands* (New York, 2019), 413.

52 J. Crow, "The Wonderful Works, a History of Bridges on the Thracian Aqueducts," in *Crossing Bridges in Byzantium and Beyond*, ed. G. Fingarova and A. Külzer (forthcoming) with references to recent discussion of the epigram.

53 Crow et al., *Water Supply*, 239.

54 G. Necipoğlu, *The Age of Sinan: Architectural Culture in the Ottoman Empire* (London, 2005), 140–1, 171.

55 Crow, "Imagined Water Supply," 222–3.

56 Magdalino, "Culture of Water," 130–1; Crow et al., *Water Supply*, 237, 239–40.

57 Quoted in Crow et al., *Water Supply*, 237.

58 Magdalino, "Culture of Water," 134–5.

59 Ward et al., "Byzantine Cisterns"; K. Altuğ, "Reconsidering the Use of *Spolia* in Byzantine Constantinople, *Di Bisanzio dirai ciò che è passato, ciò che passa e che sarà. Scritti in onore di Alessandra Guiglia*, ed. Silvia Pedone and Andrea Paribeni (Rome, 2018), 3–16.

60 W. Müller-Wiener, *Bildlexikon zur Topographie Istanbuls: Byzantion, Konstantinupolis, Istanbul bis zum Beginn d. 17. Jh.* (Tübingen, 1977), figs. 272, 273; P. Niewöhner, "The Rotunda at the Myrelaion in Constantinople: Pilaster Capitals, Mosaics, and Brick Stamps," in *The Byzantine Court: Source of Power and Culture*, ed. A. Ödekan, E. Akyürek, and N. Necipoğlu (Istanbul, 2013), 25–36, esp. fig. 2

61 Müller-Wiener, *Bildlexikon*, fig. 109, C, D; fig. 269.

62 A. Ricci, "Rediscovery of the Patriarchal Monastery of Satyros (Küçükyalı, Istanbul): Architecture, Archaeology and Hagiography," *Bizantinistica: Rivista di Studi Bizantini e Slavi* 2nd ser. 19 (2018): 247–76, esp. 263–5.

63 Ch. Bakirzis, "The Urban Continuity and Size of Late Byzantine Thessaloniki," *DOP* 57 (2003): 35–64.

64 R. Ousterhout, "Constantinople and the Construction of a Medieval Urban Identity," in *The Byzantine World*, ed. P. Stephenson (London, 2010), 334–51 esp. 337.

65 Magdalino, "Medieval Constantinople," 25, 73,

66 Ousterhout, *Master Builders*, 165–9.

67 Crow, "The Imagined Water Supply," fig. 13.

68 Crow, "Water in Late Antique Constantinople."

69 Magdalino, "Culture of Water," 132.

70 Necipoğlu, *The Age of Sinan*, 114; Köç, *Osmanlı Arşiv*, Ottoman legislation retained the Roman requirement for landowners to keep the path of the aqueduct channels clear of trees, *CTh.* 15.2.1; trans. in Crow et al. *Water Supply*, 222.

# 5: THE SUPPLY OF FOOD TO CONSTANTINOPLE

## Raymond Van Dam

Supplying Constantinople would become the largest enterprise in the Byzantine Empire. When Constantine (306–37) refounded Byzantium as Constantinople, he designated 80,000 rations of bread for free distribution, which may have been adequate to feed 200,000 residents or more.[1] Byzantium had been a typical nondescript Greek city, and this allocation would have exceeded its current population by at least twentyfold. Constantine was clearly looking to the future. If his namesake capital were to become an oversized New Rome, if the supply of its provisions were to match that of Old Rome, then it too had to depend upon subventions and a vast infrastructure of acquisition, transportation, storage, and distribution.

Because of these subsidies, Constantinople was imagined to be a city of astonishing abundance. According to a medieval biography of Constantine, the sacred relics moved to the capital had included the leftovers from Jesus' miraculous loaves and fishes, which might again feed more multitudes without limit.[2] The key was access to shipping. Already by the later fourth century, the capital was thought to be "feeding a boundless population." As a result, when harvests failed in landlocked Phrygia, many farmers trekked to the capital, which "greatly flourished because it imported provisions from everywhere by sea."[3] The attractions of Constantinople were difficult to resist. As one visitor in the mid-fourth century noted, Odysseus had had better luck at defying the seductive songs of the Sirens.[4]

This vision of the abundance available at Constantinople cloaked some harsh realities. In antiquity most cities relied primarily on food harvested from their immediate hinterlands, which would support only several thousand residents; in contrast, the population of a very large city could be supplied only from a distance. One option was for the state to play a determinative role through enforced reallocation of resources. In this model, extracting and redistributing surplus food was a consequence of taxation, and outlying provinces were exploited and even oppressed to supply the new capital. Another option was to rely on market forces for buying and selling food and other necessities. In this model the capital was hostage to the caprices of production and distribution, and consumers had to earn enough to purchase the imported supplies.

The provision of food and other necessary commodities was hence more than a fiscal or commercial issue. It also served to define the authority of emperors and the contours of empire. Initially the extraction of food was a strategy for emperors to exert their authority over outlying provinces. Collecting food as taxes and distributing it at the new capital provided leverage for the recognition of Constantinople as the political center. During the medieval centuries, however, emperors devolved authority to great magnates and awarded estates to churches and monasteries. Because these landowners could limit supply and even manipulate the market, they had leverage over the emperors, who might be blamed for food shortages in the capital. As a result, at different moments the supply of food could be a centripetal force enhancing the standing of emperors and making Constantinople the focal point of the empire, or a centrifugal force underscoring the weakness of emperors and the potential fragmentation of the empire.

Because explicit evidence in the Byzantine literary sources is limited, comparisons with the supply of other big cities in antiquity and medieval times can be very helpful.[5] Provisioning Constantinople was inherently fragile, dependent on abundant production in the provinces, susceptible to the disruptions of natural disasters and hostile warfare, and suspended between the demands of a large centralized population and a gossamer network of shippers. As always in premodern societies, the logistics of supplying a large city seemed daunting.

## THE CAPITAL OF AN EASTERN MEDITERRANEAN EMPIRE

In the early fourth century the population of Rome was probably still at its maximum of about one million residents. Supplying this enormous population with food and other necessities required an extended ensemble of officials, sailors, dockworkers, and farmers, and only emperors had the authority, resources, and commitment to maintain such an obligation for centuries.

The most important component of the Mediterranean diet was grain, typically wheat and usually baked into bread. Almost half of the residents of Rome received free doles of grain, and more grain was available at subsidized prices. In addition, by the fourth century the emperors had added olive oil, pork, and perhaps wine to the dole. The pigs walked from central Italy to the slaughterhouses of Rome, but many other foodstuffs came from overseas. Grain was imported from Egypt, North Africa, and Sicily, olive oil from North Africa and southern Spain, and wine from southern Gaul and eastern Spain. On the basis of estimates regarding minimum subsistence requirements and deductions for loss and spoilage, each year during the prime sailing season from April to September about 1,000 shiploads of grain arrived at ports at the mouth of the Tiber River, as well as another 750 shiploads of olive oil and wine. Rome existed as a gigantic city only by commandeering resources from almost all of the regions around the Mediterranean.[6]

Then the population of Rome began to decline precipitously, by perhaps 50 percent in the early fifth century, by perhaps almost 95 percent in the early sixth century. During the same centuries the population of Constantinople increased rapidly, reaching a peak of perhaps half a million or more residents in the sixth century. By then it was probably ten times the size of Rome. Between the reigns of Constantine and Justinian (527–65), Constantinople was a boomtown.

Much of its staple food was imported from overseas. The most important source of grain was Egypt, and by the mid-sixth century more Egyptian grain was being shipped to Constantinople than had previously been shipped to Rome. One observer thought that so many ships were sailing between Alexandria and Constantinople that the sea looked like dry land.[7]

The organization of the grain supply was suitably byzantine. For the collection of taxes from Egypt the praetorian prefect could follow the detailed instructions in an edict from Justinian. Assisted by hundreds of bureaucrats, the regional administrators and provincial governors were to ensure that cities, estates, and small landholdings contributed their assessments, that the grain was barged down the Nile and stockpiled at Alexandria, and that it was shipped to Constantinople before the end of summer. "There is to be absolutely no delay and no shortfall to the providential shipment of grain."[8] Shipping the grain across the eastern Mediterranean and the Aegean would have taken several weeks. Because sailing up the Hellespont against the prevailing current required waiting for favorable winds, emperors constructed a large granary on the island of Tenedos, located at the mouth of the Hellespont. At Constantinople emperors expanded the port facilities along the Sea of Marmara and the inlet of the Golden Horn, which eventually included two and a half miles of jetties with berths for hundreds of ships. Near the docks they constructed more granaries and warehouses; over a hundred public and private bakeries were scattered throughout the city's neighborhoods.[9]

The citizens of Constantinople did not live by bread alone. The demands of supplying an insatiable city compelled farmers in the provinces to become more productive. In Egypt landowners experimented with various techniques of irrigation; in northern Syria the production of olive oil and wine boomed; in southern and southeastern Asia Minor the production of olives expanded and even replaced other crops. At Abydos (on the Hellespont) an inscription recorded the tariffs due from the many ships carrying wine, olive oil, vegetables, lard, and grain to "the imperial city."[10]

While Italy and the western provinces were being overrun by barbarian migrants and invaders, the agrarian economy of the eastern provinces was flourishing. But the premise of this economic expansion was somewhat hollow. The principles encouraging the economic integration of the eastern Roman empire were tribute exaction from provincials and redistribution to the capital. The supply of Constantinople always took priority. During a severe shortage of bread at the capital Tiberios I (578–82) first distributed surplus animal feed and vegetables; then, in desperation, he had more grain imported from Egypt. This confiscation caused a food shortage in Egypt.[11] Just as many secular monuments and sacred relics were pilfered from eastern cities for the enhancement of the new capital, likewise food from the provinces was extracted to feed its still-growing population. The indignant comment of a churchman in Palestine about the monumental despoliation was also applicable to the agrarian economy: "Constantinople was dedicated by stripping bare almost all other cities."[12]

The large size of late antique Constantinople presupposed a fundamental reorientation of the political contours of the eastern Roman Empire. Constantinople was a northern city, closely associated with the frontier along the Danube River. But much of its overseas food was imported from Egypt, Palestine, Syria, and southern Asia Minor. The supply of Constantinople was a redistribution of resources in two dimensions, politically from the provinces to the capital, geographically from the southern Roman Empire to the northern frontier.

As a result, the regions around the eastern Mediterranean, including prominent cities such as Alexandria and Antioch, now seemed peripheral. After the foundation of Constantinople, no emperor ever visited Egypt. Instead, emperors maintained direct contact through the food that appeared on their tables. At the banquet celebrating his accession, Justin II (565–78) enjoyed wines from Syria, Palestine, Egypt, and Cyprus. Because the wines were proxies for "whichever provinces are subject to the Roman empire,"[13] imperial feasts were extravagant examples of the imbalanced relationship between capital and provinces. This was not a trade deficit, because there was no reimbursement. On their return voyages to Egypt and other provinces ships carried not much more than ballast. In late antiquity the hundreds of thousands of entitled residents of Constantinople devoured the surplus of the eastern Roman provinces.

## THE CAPITAL OF AN AEGEAN EMPIRE

Soon the weight of Constantinople lessened considerably. Already during the reign of Justinian the first outbreak of the plague appeared in Egypt; the pandemic arrived in Constantinople in 542. This time the grain ships from Egypt had brought mass death to the capital. Thousands died every day; within a few months up to half of the population had died. The municipal networks of distributing food collapsed. "In a city utterly flourishing with every advantage genuine hunger was on the rise; acquiring enough bread was difficult." "The entire city came to a standstill, so that its food supply stopped; food vanished from the markets."[14] At Constantinople outbreaks of plague reappeared at irregular intervals over the next two centuries, and its population may have dropped by 90 percent or more. According to a patriarch, in the mid-eighth century "the city was almost deserted."[15]

At the same time the emperors had to deal with increased military pressure along both the northern and eastern frontiers. In the Balkans and the Greek peninsula, Avars and Slavs seized numerous cities. Roman armies likewise failed to defend the provinces around the eastern Mediterranean. Those losses severely constrained the supply of the capital. In the early seventh century, when a Persian army occupied Egypt, recipients of the dole at Constantinople had to pay a small fee for their loaves; then the dole was suspended.[16] By the mid-seventh century Syria, Palestine, and Egypt had been lost to the Islamic caliphate, and the grain of Egypt was diverted to Arabia. The Arabs also raided Asia Minor and even menaced Constantinople. In the early eighth century, when the Arabs threatened a siege, Anastasios II (713–15) advised residents to hoard enough food for three years or leave.[17]

Early medieval Constantinople was a much smaller city presiding over a much smaller empire, in which the burden of supplying the capital was focused on the nearby provinces in Europe and Asia Minor. While the north coast of Asia Minor was accessible through shipping on the Black Sea, ports on the Aegean provided access to the fertile western coastlands of Asia Minor and the plains in the Greek peninsula. The Constantinople of Justinian had relied on food and other supplies imported from the entire eastern Mediterranean. In contrast, an Aegean empire would have strained to sustain such a huge megalopolis.

Because of threats to production, other cities might compete over harvests. In the Balkans the Avars, Slavs, and Bulgars made agriculture difficult. Avars attacked residents of Constantinople who tried to harvest crops only ten miles outside the walls.[18] At Thessalonike bands of Avars and Slavs consumed all the grain outside the walls, and their presence frightened merchants. The city's patron saint came to the rescue when an apparition of St. Demetrios convinced a captain to take his cargo of grain to Thessalonike rather than to Constantinople.[19] From the eighth century emperors gradually regained control over territories in the Balkans and Greece, and Basil II (976–1025) was able to incorporate Bulgaria into Byzantine jurisdiction. Already in the ninth century, Constantinople had begun to reclaim its population, to peak at perhaps a few hundred thousand residents by 1200. During the eleventh and twelfth centuries Constantinople was a large city again.

Although emperors once more had to consider the provisioning of a large capital as a top priority, they could not simply extract sufficient resources through taxation in order to distribute free or subsidized food. The equilibrium of authority and economic power in the empire had changed considerably, and emperors had to weigh their need for revenues against their need for the backing of powerful magnates and institutions. On the one hand, imperial officials continued to assess and collect taxes on farmland, pastures, and fisheries. From the perspective of Michael Choniates, bishop of Athens in the later twelfth century, just as God had once inflicted a plague of frogs on Egypt, now "the queen of the cities" was sending out a blight of tax-collectors.[20] On the other hand, emperors tried to acquire support with financial gifts. Provincial magnates, churches, and monasteries had built up extensive landholdings, in part by having absorbed the property of peasants. Emperors compounded the trend by granting large landowners immunities from taxes and revenues from imperial estates. As a result the great landowners, both secular and ecclesiastical, seemed to form a parallel administration that mirrored the imperial government.[21] The devolution of imperial authority and resources left the supply of Constantinople vulnerable.

Food was certainly imported for sale in markets. Since peasants and landowners in the provinces were expected to pay many taxes in money, they had to sell produce to middlemen, who in turn moved it to consumers in the capital. But many people at Constantinople also (or instead) relied on charitable distributions from the emperors, as well as from aristocrats and religious foundations. In his will, Romanos I Lekapenos (920–44) hoped for 30,000 loaves of bread to be distributed every day at his tomb.[22] In the eleventh century the scholar Michael Attaleiates endowed his charitable foundation with various estates as well as a bakery in Constantinople; his poorhouse provided meals and distributed grain to widows and old men.[23] Imperial foundations could be more generous. John II Komnenos (1118–43) endowed the monastery of Christ Pantokrator with estates in Thrace, the Balkans, the Greek peninsula, and Asia Minor. The monastery used its considerable resources to feed monks and the patients in the hospital, and after meals it collected the leftovers for charity "to the brothers in front of the gate."[24]

As a large metropolis dependent on provisions from overseas, Constantinople during the eleventh and twelfth centuries seems to have resembled the sprawling capital of late antiquity. But because the emperors had limited control over supply and distribution, they struggled to manage conflicting pressures. On the one hand, as the capital again became more attractive to immigrants, the population could easily surpass the available resources. When peasants fled central Asia Minor to avoid a famine, Romanos III (1028–34) was so concerned about overcrowding that he paid financial incentives for them to return.[25] On the other hand, the supply of provisions could be interrupted by the powerful officials and churchmen in the outlying regions. As Michael Choniates noted, the "delicate citizens" of the capital relied on the grain harvested in Greece and the grapes pressed into wine on the islands.[26] This comment was both a complaint about the burden of the capital and a veiled threat about its liability.

It was also a warning about the vulnerability of emperors, whose authority might be threatened during food shortages. After a frost that lasted four months, Romanos I Lekapenos could build shelters for the poor but had little food to distribute.[27] During a food shortage Nikephoros II Phokas (963–9) initially took advantage of rising prices to sell grain at a profit, but then was shamed into releasing more grain to end the speculation.[28] The scheme of Michael VII Doukas (1071–8) to impose a state monopoly on the purchase of Thracian grain upset landowners, merchants, and urban consumers.[29]

His successors seem to have learned the lesson. Even though the Komnenian emperors could not regain control over Asia Minor from the Seljuq Turks, they were apparently able to manage the provisioning of the capital. One tactic was granting maritime privileges, including exemptions from custom dues, to encourage powerful landowners and monasteries to import more provisions. Komnenian emperors also granted commercial privileges to traders from Venice, Pisa, and Genoa. Increasingly the supply of the capital was outsourced to foreigners.

## MARKETS, LABOR, STATUS

Medieval Constantinople was a super-sized emporium for food and other materials. Even during the early centuries when the state had expropriated much of the staple foodstuffs for distribution through the dole, other food was imported for sale in markets.

The variety of food available was extensive. The basic Mediterranean diet of bread, olive oil, and wine could be supplemented with meat, fish, eggs, milk, butter, cheese, honey, salt, fresh and dried fruits, and fresh and pickled vegetables. After the termination of the grain dole, meat and fish were a larger part of people's diet.[30] In the twelfth century an anonymous poet suggested that every household should be stocked with grain, vegetables, olive oil, kitchen utensils, firewood, and charcoal.[31]

The duties of the eparch (or prefect), the chief administrative officer in Constantinople, included the supervision of markets, mercantile transactions, and manufacturing activities. The manual known as *The Book of the Eparch*, issued by Leo VI (886–912), established clear boundaries among the commercial guilds engaged in the preparation and distribution of food.[32] Merchants could sell meat in their grocery shops but they did not slaughter the animals; butchers were responsible for buying cattle and sheep but not pigs; pig dealers could not purchase pigs outside the city. Fishmongers sold fresh fish, while merchants could sell salted fish as well as cheese, honey, olive oil, and butter. The eparch also carefully regulated both the prices of grain, meat, and fish for customers and the profits for merchants; his interest was in stabilizing prices for consumers rather than facilitating the acquisition of investment capital by brokers. This sort of enforced specialization and regulated pricing would have prevented the emergence of large supermarkets and department stores. As a result, small retail shops and street stalls were ubiquitous.

The preservation and storage of food were always of concern.[33] Grain could be stored for several years in cool, dry, dark warehouses. Some foods, such as nuts, remained edible for a long while, and others, such as hard vegetables and fruits, for a short while. Fresh fruits and vegetables had to be supplied from gardens along the city's walls or from nearby regions, such as the districts bordering the Bosporos and the Sea of Marmara. Some perishable foods such as milk could be turned into food with a longer shelf life, such as cheese.[34]

Another solution was frequent shopping. Countless boutique stores, workshops, and booths filled the porticoes that lined the streets and surrounded the forums. In the early sixth century the ecclesiastical establishment alone owned over a thousand shops; in 1203 the French crusader Geoffroy de Villehardouin regretted the incineration of "the great streets filled with merchandise."[35] In the late tenth century Leo, a bishop in Phrygia, followed the same route as the pigs, cattle, and sheep from the highlands of Asia Minor to Pylae, a port on the Sea of Marmara.[36] These herds of livestock crowded the streets of the capital on their way to slaughterhouses. The supply of fresh food, especially meat and fish, was something like the just-in-time systems of inventory used to improve efficiency in modern assembly lines.

Much of the raw food was inedible without being grilled, baked, boiled, or roasted. Modern discussions of the nexus of transforming agrarian produce and fresh meat into edible food often overlook the importance of firewood and charcoal.[37] For cooking, baking, and heating the Pantokrator monastery received almost a hundred tons of firewood annually. During its heydays as a megalopolis, Constantinople had to import hundreds of thousands of tons of firewood annually, as well as lumber and timbers. Much of this wood was transported from nearby forests in Thrace and Bithynia on carts and pack animals and from coastal regions by ship.[38]

Emperors and aristocrats could rely on the supply of food from their own estates, and bishops, clerics, and monks on the produce from the estates belonging to their churches and monasteries. But most residents of Constantinople had to buy supplies in shops and markets. How could they afford to purchase food, as well as other necessary goods and services?

Despite its size, the capital was not a center of large-scale manufacture and industry. Most jobs were in trades, crafts, manual labor, and services. In addition to workers in the food industry *The Book of the*

*Eparch* mentioned goldsmiths, silk weavers, candle makers, soap makers, leather workers, tavern keepers, plasterers, painters, and masons. Emperors, ecclesiastics, monks, and aristocrats hired laborers for construction projects and to tend their properties. The Pantokrator monastery employed over a hundred men (and a few women) in its hospital, among them not only medical personnel but also cooks, bakers, a miller, a groomsman for horses, a dishwasher, a cooper, five laundry workers, an ironworker who maintained the surgical instruments, and four gravediggers. Their wages included allowances of grain.

The supply of food hence linked agrarian labor in the provinces with urban labor at Constantinople. The middlemen were the officials and agents of emperors, landowning aristocrats, and the religious institutions. These brokers collected taxes and rents in the provinces, purchased food and other supplies, and transported the commodities to the capital, where the great landowners, including emperors, paid wages to workers who in turn bought the food. Even this simplistic model implies that medieval Constantinople was still largely a consumer city.

The consumption of food created and reinforced social and economic distinctions. Everyday meals for most residents consisted of bread and soup made from cheap vegetables.[39] Better quality food presupposed status and wealth, usually derived from ownership of the agricultural production. Emperors and other powerful notables sometimes flaunted their extravagance and gluttony. Constantine VIII (1025–8) was a gourmet who "painted" his dishes with the textures and fragrances of his rich sauces.[40] A high court official won a wager with Manuel I Komnenos (1143–80) by guzzling a large bowl of wine, "coming up for air only once!"[41]

Now and then emperors shared their opulence with ordinary citizens. Before the wedding of his son to a daughter of the king of France, Manuel I Komnenos distributed loaves of bread throughout the empire "like a welcome rainstorm." At Constantinople, the congratulatory banquet in the hippodrome turned into a carnival. The guests included dignitaries and people collected off the streets; grills were set up in the starting gates; tables covered with platters of meat in "dense mounds, solid heaps, and thick piles" filled the racetrack. The "races" were the diners' sprints to the sumptuous bounty on display.[42] Although the free distribution of grain to the residents of Constantinople had ended long ago and the hippodrome was hardly used for entertainments anymore, for a brief moment this banquet brought back memories of old times: not bread and circuses, but now complimentary meat in the circus.

## A CAPITAL WITHOUT AN EMPIRE

The supply of Constantinople constantly faced competition for the available surplus of food and resources. Other large cities whose requirements had surpassed the production of their hinterlands also had to import food. The most important rival, however, had always been the army. During late antiquity, although the Roman army had been very large, most troops had been stationed in the frontier zones and supplied locally. Back then the Roman Empire had been capacious enough that the frontiers were far away from the Mediterranean and provincial producers rarely had to provision both the army and the large cities.

In the smaller Byzantine Empire troops were also supplied locally. Soldiers were given land to farm in the themes; then the burden was placed directly on peasants, who were expected to billet visiting army units and furnish supplies. After the late eleventh century the emperors also agreed to provide provisions for the armies of the Western crusaders. In this more compact empire the same regions had to supply both the capital and the armies, and provincial producers endured competing pressures. Even regions near the capital or on the Aegean coast were obligated to provide food for the army. In the mid-tenth century, for instance, the theme of Thrakesion in western Asia Minor was expected to deliver enough barley, wheat, and wine for thousands of soldiers, as well as 10,000 livestock.[43] Manuel I Komnenos once requisitioned "an unutterable number" of oxen and carts from villages in Thrace for his military campaign.[44] Because of this competition for food and other resources, the provisioning of Constantinople seemed to be a lower priority.

During much of the thirteenth century the establishment of a Latin empire at Constantinople compounded the problem. Because control over Asia Minor, the Balkans, and the Greek peninsula was fragmented among competing successor states, there were rival capital cities that needed supplying. Nor did the Greek states necessarily share their prosperity with Constantinople. John Vatatzes, emperor at Nicaea (1222–54), preferred to sell grain and livestock to the Seljuq sultans in Asia Minor.[45]

In 1261 Greek emperors returned to Constantinople. Even though the population was now small, supplying the city was difficult. One strategy was the restoration of control over overseas lands and their produce; the most important sources of grain were the neighboring plain of Thrace and the regions around the Black Sea. Another strategy was to appeal to sympathetic states. The Bulgarian tsar Theodore

Svetoslav (1300–21/2) was allowed to marry an imperial princess after having grain shipped to Constantinople.[46] John V Palaiologos (1341–91) even promised to cede to Venice the island of Tenedos, which had once served as a granary at the mouth of the Hellespont.

Increasingly Constantinople was isolated and alone. Rather than attacking the great walls, the Ottoman sultan Bayezid I imposed a military blockade and intended to compel surrender by weaponizing food shortages. In response, Manuel II Palaiologos (1391–1425) appealed for grain from Venice, and merchants smuggled grain through the Genoese port of Galata. The residents of Constantinople also farmed their own food. Some of the large open-air cisterns were filled with dirt and used as gardens.[47] Not surprisingly the prices of fields and vineyards inside the walls soared. When firewood became scarce, bakers stoked their ovens with beams from imperial residences.[48] Late medieval Constantinople had become its own source of food and fuel. To survive the residents had to till the city soil and burn the lumber deposited over previous centuries.

For the final siege in the mid-fifteenth century, the sultan Mehmed II (1451–81) stationed a huge army outside the walls. This army was the equivalent of another large city that was sharing the space and the resources of Constantinople. Because the residents of the capital and the Ottoman soldiers were competing for the same limited food supplies, they fought over nearby fields of grain and vegetables. When the soldiers finally entered the city, they ate off the liturgical plates and roasted meat over fires fueled by sacred icons.[49] The besiegers were as hungry as the besieged.

## CONTINUITIES

The supply of Constantinople was one of the grand achievements of the Byzantine emperors. When huge with a population of hundreds of thousands it was one of the largest cities in the medieval world; when comparatively small with a population of tens of thousands it was still the largest city in the empire. Until its final shrinkage and decline, most of its food and other provisions had to be imported from overseas. The great surviving monuments and buildings, such as Justinian's Hagia Sophia, capture our imagination to evoke the grandeur and the magnitude of Byzantine rule. In fact, the grain alone that had to be imported every year to feed Justinian's megalopolis was almost as expensive as the entire cost of Hagia Sophia.[50] Given the constraints on the production and distribution of food in premodern times, the feeding of Constantinople for so many centuries was an astonishing triumph.

Then the food was chewed, the wine and water were swallowed, and the firewood was burned. Despite its recurrence and its necessity for basic survival, the supply of basic provisions has left few traces. Literally so: the sewers, drains, and garbage of Constantinople remain understudied.

In modern scholarship, although diet, feasting, and nutrition are common topics, the supply of food to Constantinople deserves more consideration. One reason is that it touches on so many other topics in Byzantine studies; another is that it opens the possibility of imagining an alternative Byzantine history. The supply of food shaped the relationship between the political center of the empire and its periphery, whether defined as the links between capital and provinces or as the interactions between emperors and regional magnates. It affected the entire spectrum of the economy, from the agrarian fields and pastures of producers to the urban markets of consumers. It generated wealth and health even as it exacerbated poverty and illness. It influenced the military and diplomatic interactions between the empire and neighboring states. The supply of food is the often-overlooked bedrock foundation for our modern narratives of political, military, diplomatic, and ecclesiastical history.

After 1453 the challenges of supplying a large city intensified again. The sultans encouraged immigration, and the population of Constantinople expanded to hundreds of thousands of residents. The Ottoman administration relied on political redistribution rather than strictly market forces, with price controls over the purchase of grain from producers and its sale to consumers. The primary sources of grain were the coastal plains along the Black Sea and the Aegean Sea, with Egypt as an emergency reserve.[51] Because of these similarities, the supply of food and other provisions can highlight the underlying continuity from Byzantine Constantinople to Ottoman Istanbul.

## FURTHER READING

Brubaker, L. and K. Linardou (eds.), *Eat, Drink, and Be Merry (Luke 12:19): Food and Wine in Byzantium* (Aldershot, 2007).

Laiou, A. E. (ed.), *The Economic History of Byzantium: From the Seventh through the Fifteenth Century* (Washington, DC, 2002).

Magdalino, P. and N. Necipoğlu (ed.), *Trade in Byzantium: Papers from the Third International Sevgi Gönül Byzantine Studies Symposium* (Istanbul, 2016).

Mango, C. and G. Dagron (ed.), *Constantinople and Its Hinterland* (Aldershot, 1995).
Marin, B. and C. Virlouvet (ed.), *Nourrir les cités de Méditerranée: Antiquité – temps modernes* (Paris, 2003).
Mayer, W. and S. Trzcionka (eds.), *Feast, Fast or Famine: Food and Drink in Byzantium* (Brisbane, 2015).
Teall, J. L. "The Grain Supply of the Byzantine Empire, 330–1025," *DOP* 13 (1959): 87–139.
Van Dam, R. *Rome and Constantinople: Rewriting Roman History during Late Antiquity* (Waco, 2010).

# NOTES

1   Socrates, *HE* 2.13; J. Durliat, *De la ville antique à la ville byzantine: Le problème des subsistances* (Paris, 1990), 249–75.
2   M. Guidi, "Un ΒΙΟΣ di Costantino," *RendLinc*, seria quinta, 16 (1907): 337.
3   Socrates, *HE* 4.16.
4   Basil of Caesarea, *Ep.* 1.
5   C. Isendahl and S. Barthel, "Archaeology, History, and Urban Food Security: Integrating Cross-Cultural and Long-Term Perspectives," in *Routledge Handbook of Landscape and Food*, ed. J. Zeunert and T. Waterman (London, 2018), 61–72.
6   R. Van Dam, *Rome and Constantinople: Rewriting Roman History during Late Antiquity* (Waco, 2010).
7   Theophylact Simocatta, *Hist.* 2.14.7.
8   Justinian, *Edicta* 13.
9   J. Matthews, "The 'Notitia urbis Constantinopolitanae'," in *Two Romes: Rome and Constantinople in Late Antiquity*, ed. L. Grig and G. Kelly (Oxford, 2012), 81–115.
10  J. Durliat and A. Guillou, "Le tarif d'Abydos (vers 492)," *BCH* 108 (1984): 581–98.
11  Michael the Syrian, tr. Chabot, 2:351–2.
12  Jerome, *Chronicon* s.a. 330.
13  Corippus, *In laudem Iustini* 3.85–104.
14  Prokopios, *Bella* 2.23.19; John of Ephesus, *HE*, tr. Witakowski, 88.
15  Nicephorus, *Breviarium* 68.
16  *Chronicon Paschale* s.a. 618.
17  Nicephorus, *Breviarium* 49.
18  *Chronicon Paschale* s.a. 626.
19  *Miracula sancti Demetrii* 1.69–72.
20  Michael Choniates, *Ep.* 64.4, ed. Lampros, 2:105.
21  J. L. Teall, "The Grain Supply of the Byzantine Empire, 330–1025," *DOP* 13 (1959): 87–139; P. Magdalino, "The Grain Supply of Constantinople, Ninth-Twelfth Centuries," in *Constantinople and Its Hinterland*, ed. C. Mango and G. Dagron (Aldershot, 1995), 35–47.
22  Theophanes Continuatus, ed. Bekker, 430.
23  P. Gautier, "La Diataxis de Michel Attaliate," *REB* 39 (1981): 5–143.
24  P. Gautier, "Le Typikon du Christ Sauveur Pantocrator," *REB* 32 (1974): 1–145.
25  John Skylitzes, *Synopsis historiarum*, ed. Thurn, 386.
26  Michael Choniates, *Ep.* 50.10, ed. Lampros, 2:83.
27  Theophanes Continuatus, ed. Bekker, 417–18.
28  John Skylitzes, *Synopsis historiarum*, ed. Thurn, 277–8.
29  Michael Attaleiates, *Hist.*, ed. Bekker, 201–4; D. Krallis, *Michael Attaleiates and the Politics of Imperial Decline in Eleventh-Century Byzantium* (Tempe, 2012), 22–7.
30  G. Dagron, "Poissons, pêcheurs et poissonniers de Constantinople," in *Constantinople and Its Hinterland*, 57–73; C. Morrisson and J.-P. Sodini, "The Sixth-Century Economy," in *EHB* 1: 171–220, esp. 201.
31  D.-C. Hesseling and H. Pernot, *Poèmes prodromiques en grec vulgaire* (Amsterdam, 1910), 40–3.
32  J. Koder, ed., *Das Eparchenbuch Leons des Weisen* (Vienna, 1991).

33 M. Grünbart, "Store in a Cool and Dry Place: Perishable Goods and Their Preservation in Byzantium," in *Eat, Drink, and Be Merry (Luke 12:19): Food and Wine in Byzantium*, ed. L. Brubaker and K. Linardou (Aldershot, 2007), 39–49.

34 J. Koder, "Fresh Vegetables for the Capital," in *Constantinople and Its Hinterland*, 49–56; G. C. Maniatis, "The Byzantine Cheesemaking Industry," *Byzantion* 84 (2014): 257–84.

35 Justinian, *Nov.* 43; T. F. Madden, "The Fires of the Fourth Crusade in Constantinople, 1203–1204: A Damage Assessment," *BZ* 84–5 (1992): 72–93; M. M. Mango, "The Commercial Map of Constantinople," *DOP* 54 (2000): 189–207.

36 Leo of Synada, *Ep.* 54.

37 B. Graham and R. Van Dam, "Modelling the Supply of Wood Fuel in Ancient Rome," in *Environment and Society in the Long Late Antiquity*, ed. A. Izdebski and M. Mulryan (Leiden, 2019), 148–59.

38 C. Morrisson, "Trading in Wood in Byzantium: Exchange and Regulations," in *Trade in Byzantium*, ed. P. Magdalino and N. Necipoğlu (Istanbul, 2016), 105–27.

39 J. Koder, "*Stew and Salted Meat*: Opulent Normality in the Diet of Every Day?" in *Eat, Drink, and Be Merry*, 59–72.

40 Michael Psellus, *Chron.* 2.7.

41 Nicetas Choniates, *Hist.* 3.4, ed. van Dieten, 114.

42 A. F. Stone, "Eustathios and the Wedding Banquet for Alexios Porphyrogennetos," in *Feast, Fast or Famine: Food and Drink in Byzantium*, ed. W. Mayer and S. Trzcionka (Brisbane, 2005), 33–42.

43 Constantine VII, *De ceremoniis* 2.44.

44 John Cinnamus, *Epitome*, ed. Meineke, 199, 299.

45 Nicephorus Gregoras, *Byzantina historia*, ed. Schopen and Bekker, 1:43.

46 A. Laiou, "The Provisioning of Constantinople during the Winter of 1306–1307," *Byzantion* 37 (1967): 91–113.

47 Manuel Chrysoloras, *Ep.* 1, PG 156.44B.

48 Ducas, *Hist.* 13.7; N. Necipoğlu, "Economic Conditions in Constantinople during the Siege of Bayezid I (1394–1402)," in *Constantinople and Its Hinterland*, 157–67.

49 Ducas, *Hist.* 34.10, 42.1.

50 Van Dam, *Rome and Constantinople*, 55, 59.

51 R. Murphey, "Provisioning Istanbul: The State and Subsistence in the Early Modern Middle East," *Food and Foodways* 2 (1988): 217–63; S. Ağir, "The Evolution of Grain Policy: The Ottoman Experience," *Journal of Interdisciplinary History* 43 (2013): 571–98.

# 6: Constantinople: Building and Maintenance

## Enrico Zanini

### A Subject of Study, a Point of View, and a Method

As with any city, Constantinople developed from the complex inter-action between people and the natural environment. On the one hand, its population shaped the city's physical living space. On the other hand, these same spaces conditioned the lives of its residents, who, in turn, adapted to the urban environment inherited from their predecessors.

As an urban organism, Constantinople stands out because of its uninterrupted, centuries-long duration.[1] During this long life the city wore many hats, some simultaneously, others in sequence. Before Constantine (306–37) it was an "average" Greco-Roman city. At the time of its refoundation in the early fourth century it became the largest of Late Antiquity's many "new cities."[2] Between the late fourth and the fifth centuries it emerged as a dynastic capital for Constantine's successors and the Theodosian family, joining Antioch, Alexandria, Jerusalem, and Thessalonike as one of the great cities of the late antique Mediterranean. Then, for more than a millennium, it was the capital of the enduring but ever-changing Byzantine Empire, whose profound territorial transformations affected the city's supply lines and networks. Moreover, throughout its life Constantinople was a Christian city and a cosmopolitan, multicultural megalopolis; it was the ideal "New Rome," but also a medieval and late medieval city, which bore no resemblance to the actual Rome.[3] It represents, there-fore, the quintessence of complexity, especially in terms of its material aspect:[4] each image of the city had its expression in urban space because of the work of the architects and masons who responded to changes in building techniques, customer demand, and legal administration.

Constantinople is even more interesting for archaeologists. Although its history and structure are known, its physical remains are fragmentary. Basic infrastructure elements such as defensive walls and features of the water supply system still mark modern Istanbul's urban landscape, as do religious monuments, many of which have been transformed into mosques. In addition, myriad scattered elements await systematic reconnaissance.[5] Rather than describe this archaeological material aseptically, this contribution approaches the topic of building as if it were a complex thermodynamic system.[6] It examines the city as a living organism, considering the ongoing construction and deconstruction of its urban fabric as the product of three interacting processes: construction "engines," objective conditions, and socio-economic factors.

Construction engines, which may be natural or manmade, are the forces driving the construction and transformation of urban space. Earthquakes and fires, catastrophes resulting first in destruction and then in reconstruction, qualify as primary construction engines, as does the need for necessities such as food and water, a mandate requiring the construction of such infrastructure elements as ports, warehouses, and aqueducts. Finally, institutional transformations drive building and restoration.

Objective conditions facilitate the realization of theoretical building projects. These conditions may include the availability of building materials and workforces, supply structures, and economic support. Context influences these conditions. For example, public buildings tend to be built with more durable materials and greater professionalism, conditions that guarantee longer survival in the urban landscape and so condition subsequent choices.

Finally, social and economic factors play a role. Housing models may vary according to social class, or the patronage activities of social elites may change over time in response to new cultural conditions. The real estate market, difficult to study for want of documentation, may also fall into this category.

These considerations must also be seen in the context of later conservation. Preservation of medieval Constantinople's material aspect has depended not only on the quality of building materials and the technical skills of Byzantium's master builders, but also on the value accorded those buildings and spaces in Ottoman Constantinople and modern Istanbul. Such evaluations contributed to the transformation of churches into mosques or the maintenance of cisterns and public baths during the Ottoman period.

## Infrastructure Projects, Public Monuments, Vernacular Architecture

Three categories structure Constantinople's material aspect: urban infrastructures, public monuments, and private building. Archeologically, urban infrastructure represents the most well- known aspect of the Constantinopolitan built environment.[7] Such projects – roads, ports, warehouses, aqueducts, cisterns, defensive walls - stand apart from other building ventures by virtue of scale and cost. As large-scale, state-funded enterprises, these public projects require huge financial investment, large building sites, a host of specialized crafts-men, and the acquisition or manufacture of specific building materials. Designed for longevity, they also emphasize structural solidity and ease of maintenance: as such, they do not represent the full range of urban building experience.

In addition, infrastructure projects permanently transform the urban landscape and with it the "urban ecosystem." In Constantinople, city walls, aqueducts, cisterns, and harbors stood as elements of continuity in the urban setting, gradually assuming the character of "natural" landscape components, their anthropic origin notwithstanding. For example, the fifth-century construction of the Theodosian walls created new urban territory, the space between the fourth-century Constantinian wall and the new defensive circuit. Neither urban nor rural, this newly enclosed area enjoyed an intermediate status between town and country, which led to a new legal status by the sixth century, one allowing for the burial of human remains. This intermediate status also resulted in the establish-ment of the monastic complexes and prestige residences that came to define the region's landscape.[8]

The aqueduct attributed to Valens played a similar role. Attracted by access to drinking water, members of the late antique urban aristoc-racy built their residences in its shadow.[9] Throughout the city's history, the water system represented an effective substitute for the natural water resources the city lacked; a sort of artificial river, accompanied by a network of small lakes and springs (cisterns and fountains), created at a moment when Byzantine society and its economy were particularly strong. Between the seventh and ninth centuries, when the city's population and inhabited area contracted dramatically, this system con-tinued to function as if it were a natural resource. In the middle and late Byzantine periods it is possible to imagine water features as elements around which population nuclei coalesced[10] on the model of other Mediterranean urban contexts.[11]

Public monuments represent the second category. Excluding monuments such as honorific columns, these are mostly churches. In many ways these monuments resemble large infrastructures, but with significant distinctions. Late antique and early Byzantine church patronage was mainly public, although there are cases of important private projects; among them two sixth-century churches, Anicia Juliana's Hagios Polyeuktos,[12] and Justinian's Saints Sergios and Bakchos.[13] After the sixth century, private projects became the norm: society's elites increasingly saw the financing of church building as a powerful tool for self-presentation in this world, and insurance for the afterlife in the world to come. In the middle and late Byzantine periods the number of private ecclesiastical foundations exploded, increasing from approximately fifty churches at the time of Justinian (526–65) to nearly 300 four centuries later.[14] A significant reduction in architectural scale accompanied the increase in building numbers, resulting in smaller, more manageable building sites. Building techniques became standardized and more simplified, while patrons concentrated their economic resources on interior decoration.

Despite differences in size and social function from infrastructure projects, religious buildings share at least two characteristics with them: an expectation of longevity and the potential to transform the urban ecosystem. This transformative potential was often limited, however: churches may fall more easily into ruin, and their presence does not necessarily contribute to the functional redefinition of urban space. Nevertheless, ecclesiastical building could still have an impact. Hagia Sophia remained a pole of attraction throughout the city's life, while the sanctuary of the Virgin in the Blachernai district drew the imperial residence to that area in the late Byzantine period. Similarly, the church of the Holy Apostles attracted several high-status dwellings to its neighborhood, probably in synergy with the nearby aqueduct.

With respect to infrastructures and monuments, a sense of saturation characterizes Constantinople's urban morphology. Between the fourth and the sixth centuries the city realized virtually all of its infrastructure needs and constructed many of its main ecclesiastical monuments. This relatively rapid development essentially satisfied urban requirements for the remainder of its history. Thus, the celebrated sixth-century Justinianic "Golden Age" should be understood as the culmination of an already established process. External events precipitated the two major building projects, Hagia Sophia and Holy Apostles: the Nika Rebellion of 532 for the former, and the decay wrought by time for the latter. Similarly, the series of cisterns attributed to Justinian represented the completion and revitalization of the water system inaugurated in previous centuries.

Private building, the third category, follows different rules than those of infrastructure and monument projects. Here, practical concerns prevail. Building materials and techniques vary and there is often recourse to recycled materials and non-specialized techniques; the average life of such buildings tends to be low, and, as they are frequently replaced by other structures, the impact on urban morphology is temporary.

Nevertheless, private construction is interesting. Ideally, archaeological research into the spaces of everyday life should allow a more balanced view of Constantinople by offering an alternative to the stereotypical paradigms of "luxury and decadence" that have previously colored its study, but such archaeological knowledge is practically non-existent; however, theoretical reconstruction based on models derived from other late antique and Byzantine Mediterranean cities is possible.[15] In addition, written sources, especially legal texts, compensate for the lack of archaeological data.

## LEGISLATION

When Constantinople was refounded, its new design complemented that of the preexisting Graeco-Roman city, whose functions were only partially incorporated into the new organism. The brief initial construction phase (324–30) suggests that the plan was conceived as a sketch that would be completed over time. In this ongoing process, established monuments and infrastructures came to dictate aspects of the new layout. Monumental areas shared space with private buildings, and sources testify to the private use – both authorized and unauthorized – of public monuments and spaces.

In the Theodosian code, laws introduced between 380 and 410 address illegal building practices.[16] At least three laws (*CTh.* 15.1.25 and 15.1.39, from 389; 15.1.46, from 406) refer to "public decorum," prohibit construction of private houses close to public buildings, and require that temporary structures attached to public monuments or their spaces be removed. A law of 409 (*CTh.* 15.1.47) prohibited these installations within the imperial palace or its vicinity, indicating that the practice was active even there.

By the time of Theodosios II (402–50), policy had changed. Private use of public spaces and monuments was no longer prohibited, nor was the removal of precarious structures imposed. A new law (*CTh.* 15.1.51, from 413) allowed landowners on whose property the new city walls had been built the use of towers, in exchange for a commitment to maintain them. Another law (15.1.52, from 424) refers to residences with attached shops in the portico of the Baths of Zeuxippos, but does not require their removal as long as owners provide for the bath's lighting and the repair of its roofs.

A law issued by Zeno (474–91) in 482 (*CIC*, VIII.10.12), establishing new rules for the private use of the porticoes along the Mese between the Augusteion and the Forum of Constantine, makes the controlled removal of restrictions regarding access to public space even more explicit.[17] It allows private shops occupying no more than four intercolumniations to operate in the porticoes, requiring that they limit their depth, so as not to hinder pedestrian traffic, and that wooden structures be dressed with marble slabs in conformity with the avenue's overall décor. Requirements for the Mese's other sections would have been less rigid, depending on the distance from the center and the provisions of the *Praefectus Urbi* (city prefect).

The picture changes in the following centuries: sources suggest that there was a rapid loss of public control over urban landscape management.[18] After the crisis that started in the second half of the sixth century and deepened in the seventh and eighth centuries, the urban fabric appears to have been in ruinous condition, with many of the city's earlier monuments semi-abandoned, co-opted for different uses, or transformed into quarries for the recovery of building materials.

Until the mid-sixth century, however, urban planning legislation guaranteed sufficient control of public building management. Theodosios II, Leo (457–74), Zeno, Anastasios (491–518), and Justinian all introduced laws addressing the maintenance of urban decorum together with rules for fire prevention, illicit construction in the aftermath of natural disasters, and the protection of landscape.

With respect to urban decorum, basic Roman legislation seems to have remained in force. Removal of statues and valuable decorative materials from ruined public buildings was outlawed, as was their transport to other cities. These laws, referred to in Justinianic urban legislation (*CIC. VIII, 10*), must have been respected, because eighth- and ninth-century sources describe an urban landscape still populated by ancient statues. Archaeological evidence from other early Byzantine urban centers confirms this picture. The voluntary concealment of ancient statues in these cities from what was probably the same period[19] suggests that such sculpture had remained visible until that time.

Fires constituted the primary risk and were among the main drivers of construction activity, more so even than earthquakes, which also played an important role in redefining the Constantinopolitan cityscape. Decrees aimed at fire prevention set maximum building heights, required a minimum distance between buildings, and limited the number and size of balconies, which, being wood, acted as bridges that facilitated the spread of fire from one building to another.

Nevertheless, large-scale fires were a constant scourge, following one another with impressive frequency. Between the second half of the fifth century and the beginning of the seventh century, sources report at least thirteen major fires (465, 475, 498, 509, 510, 532, 548, 559, 560, 561, 563, 583, 603). The fire of 465 burned for four days, devastating an area of approximately 2.5 km² in the districts overlooking the Sea of Marmara. After this disaster Leo issued a law aimed at preventing illegal reconstruction by speculators. Zeno reiterated this same law a little more than a decade later.[20]

Zeno's law also contains the first reference to landscape, in particular the importance of sea views. It forbids newly reconstructed buildings from blocking older structures' views. Eventually Justinian developed this idea more fully, issuing a new law (*CIC, Nov.* 43) against speculators who had sought to circumvent Zeno's ruling. His legislation highlights the value given to quality of life considerations.

Taken together these legal provisions suggest that some neighborhoods, especially those within the circuit of the Constantinian walls, were densely populated. Only the residential structures along the main streets were limited to a height of two or three stories:[21] buildings in less prominent locations may have risen to heights of nine or ten floors, reaching and perhaps exceeding the maximum limit of 100 feet (*c*.30 m) set by the Leo's law (*CIC*, VIII, 10, 12.4). These structures probably used brick in the lower stories, relying on wood for construction of the upper floors. Analogy to Julian of Ascalon's mid-sixth-century urban-planning treatise from Palestine suggests that this "vernacular architecture," together with imperial laws regulating building practice, followed the rules of customary law in dealing with issues of land use, views, housing, drainage, and landscape.[22] That said, it is unclear how some of the treatise's basic precepts such as the restriction of activities carrying fire risks to the periphery were implemented in a megalopolis such as Constantinople. The most credible hypothesis is to imagine a "nucleated" urban fabric; that is, a model in which artisanal activities are located in sparsely inhabited areas surrounding nodal, thickly settled points.[23]

Urban space would have been used differently in the less densely populated neighborhoods of the urban aristocracy. Here buildings enjoyed a large footprint, and upper floors were limited or absent.[24] In the early Byzantine period, these neighborhoods were adjacent to the imperial palace, where the remains of the "palaces" of Lausos and Antiochos survive today, on the hills overlooking the Bosporos, where aristocratic *oikoi* (houses) linked to members of the imperial family were located,[25] and the minimally urbanized area between the Constantinian and Theodosian walls.[26] It is no coincidence that in the middle and late Byzantine periods urban elites identified these last two areas as the preferred places for church building.

## CONSTRUCTION

The material body of Constantinople was made possible by a well-established and ongoing production chain that allowed patrons to realize their architectural visions in physical form.[27] This chain began with planning and continued with the construction site's preparation and the acquisition and installation of building materials at the hands of qualified technicians. In the case of infrastructure projects or large public monuments, the chain was longer, more clearly articulated, and specialized. For the vernacular architecture that constituted the greater mass of the urban fabric, it was shorter.

Design, the transcription of a patron's ideas into concrete form, required execution of and responsibility for specific competencies, and represented the first step in the case of large-scale works. The *mechanikos*, a professional figure who combined the aesthetic skills of the architect (in some cases the term *architekton* is used with the same meaning) and the technical skills of the engineer, met these requirements. Sources recording the names and activities of these professionals allow an understanding of their work.[28] The two architects of Justinianic Hagia Sophia, Anthemios of Tralles and Isidore of Miletus, are universally known from Prokopios of Caesarea's report of the building project (*De Aed.* I, I, 24–5), which describes them as direct and authoritative interlocutors for the emperor himself. Also known is the professional career of Isidore the Younger (*De Aed.*, II, viii, 25), who was charged with the reconstruction of Hagia Sophia's dome after the original construction's collapse (Agathias, *Hist.*, 5, ix, 4).[29]

Architects and engineers of this level not only had to propose and implement bold architectural solutions such as those used in the great monuments of the Justinianic age, but also to manage the huge construction sites that such buildings required. The tenth-century *Narratio* of the construction of Hagia Sophia provides a vivid image of these sites. Although not entirely consistent with reality, the *Narratio* nevertheless preserves several credible details, among them the building site's dimension, the pyramidal, almost military organization of the workforce, and the complexity of a building process requiring many different specialists. Concrete evidence of the site's complexity survives in the masons' marks inscribed at various points in the church's marble furnishings. These archaeological traces demonstrate that different groups of artisans worked simultaneously on different parts of the building.[30]

Management of smaller construction sites was obviously much simpler. Literary sources offer no specific information; however, Constantinopolitan projects were probably not too different from those in other regions of the late antique period in which architects and masons from different regions came together to create "consortiums" for managing the phases of a building project from start to finish.[31]

All buildings, even small- and medium-scale private projects, were required to follow the same legal and practical rules for design and construction. In the absence of direct sources it is again possible to argue by analogy. Inscriptions from Belus in Syria testify to the presence of specialized technicians (sometimes referred to as *architektonikes*, but more commonly known as *technites*) who sign off on the construction of medium- and small-size buildings.[32]

This archaeological and epigraphical data fit well with the laws outlining the responsibilities of architects and engineers regarding building quality (*CTh.* 15. 1.24, dated to 385). The same is also true for the aforementioned laws of Zeno, which imposed heavy financial penalties on architects and engineers found evading laws during construction and reconstruction. Other legislation (*CIC*, XII.19.12) indicates the existence of state architects connected to the office of *Praefectus Urbi*, who specialized in the treatment of construction-related conflicts.

The set of laws, competencies, and economic practices regulating urban construction in Constantinople was transformed into physical building with the use of different materials and techniques. As always, literary and archaeological information skews in favor of larger infrastructure projects and public monuments. Five chronologically overlapping construction typologies characterize these projects between the fourth and fifteenth centuries.

Information about fourth-century techniques is scant. Isolated monuments, largely of marble, constitute the main evidence.[33]

Sections of brick or mixed brick and limestone masonry walls generally assigned to this epoch are visible in the curved foundational structure of the Hippodrome known as the *sphendone* and along the main sides of the racetrack.[34] However, these fragments cannot be inserted into a definite typology as they are too small, isolated, and without detailed study. By contrast, the most important infrastructure project from this early period, the Valens aqueduct, conforms to established Greco-Roman construction traditions, using a double curtain technique with a cement conglomerate covered with medium-sized (20–8 cm high) limestone blocks.[35]

A mixed technique, associated with the fifth and sixth centuries, in which irregular, friable layers of cement covered with small to medium limestone blocks alternate with brick courses characterizes the second typology. The brick courses, which are four or five bricks high and bound with a tenacious mortar, extend the full depth of the wall and connect the curtain walls at regular height intervals. This technique was probably developed for the construction of the Theodosian land walls (405–13) in response to the need for speed and economy, and appears in other buildings of the same period: the *propylaeum* of the Theodosian Hagia Sophia, the church of Saint John of Studios, the cisterns of Aetios and Aspar, and the Palace of Antiochos.

The technique is not chronologically bound, and continued to be used throughout the city's life. It appears in the sixth-century walls of the church of Hagia Irene, and in eleventh- and twelfth- century buildings such as the Fethiye Camii where the blocks are framed by thin bricks. It also appears in fourteenth-century examples, among them the Kariye Camii's *parekklesion* and the palace known as Tekfur Saray.

A third typology characterizes the great building projects of the late fifth and early sixth centuries. In it, brick masonry courses alternate with a single leveling band of limestone blocks at intervals of approximately twenty rows of brick. This technique appears for the first time in the church of the Theotokos in Chalkoprateia. It then is used in the church of Saints Sergios and Bakchos, the Justinianic Hagia Sophia, the Baths of Zeuxippos, and the north church of the Kalenderhane Camii complex.[36] This technique also appears in the eleventh and twelfth centuries (Aykapı Church, Fethiye Camii, St. George of the Mangana) using thinner bricks to square the individual limestone blocks, following a technique attested in Greece and in the Balkans.

A fourth technique, entirely of brick, appears in many eleventh- and twelfth-century churches, among them the buildings now known as the Bodrum Camii, the Eski Imaret Camii, the Fenari Isa Camii, and the Zeyrek Kilise Camii, formerly the Church and the Monastery of Christ Pantokrator. Known as the "recessed brick" or "concealed course" technique in which beds of mortar between two rows of bricks appear to be particularly thick, this construction method conceals an additional row of brick within the mortar course by setting it back from the plane of the façade and covering it with mortar.[37]

Finally, late Byzantine buildings use many different techniques. The prevalent typology is that of alternating bands of brick and stone blocks; with the difference that the number of rows constituting the alternation may vary considerably, often with the aim of creating decorative effects.[38] For example, an elegant masonry in which four rows of blocks alternate with two to three rows of brick characterizes some of the finest buildings of the fourteenth and fifteenth centuries, among them Bogdan Saray, Kariye Camii, Manastır Mescidi, Sancaktar Mescidi, Sinan Paşa Mescidi, and Tekfur Saray.[39]

While laying techniques varied, the basic materials of Constantinopolitan building remained constant. Three basic materials were used: small and medium-sized stone blocks, most of which were limestone, brick, and mortar. Bricks were normally square, with well-standardized measures. These measures varied over time: $31 \times 31 \times 5.5$ cm in the age of Constantine, $37 \times 37 \times 4.5$ at the beginning of the sixth century, and $33.5 \times 33.5 \times 4$ from the late sixth century onward.[40] Most of the bricks – and probably also the stone blocks – used in subsequent centuries were recovered from large buildings that had fallen into disrepair, a fact that may explain the spread of less regular walls, such as those with recessed brick technique or with blocks of limestone framed by thin bricks.

To bind small blocks and bricks together a good quality mortar was used, at least until the time of Justinian: it was rich in lime and made more tenacious by the addition of small aggregates (small stones, brick fragments) and brick dust, which gave it a distinctive pink color. In all buildings mortar beds tend to be higher than those used in the earlier Roman period. This practice may indicate a tendency to use bricks and cut stone with parsimony, perhaps because of supply problems.

The *Narratio* of Hagia Sophia's construction (chapter 8)[41] lingers on the peculiar qualities of this mortar, which hardened very quickly, making it possible to speed up the construction process. Construction times, which in the particular case of Hagia Sophia (532–7) appear to have been exceptionally fast, seem to confirm this quality. That said, technical analyses have not identified any trace of the components, which in some cases are very imaginative (boiled barley and soft pieces of elm) to which the *Narratio* credits this extraordinary performance.[42]

Whatever the case, Constantinople was a giant building site for almost two centuries after its foundation. Its construction in such a relatively short period implies the existence of large supply sources for cut stone and brick, which had to be produced in extraordinary numbers. For example, construction of the Theodosian land-walls alone[43] required at least fifteen million bricks: according to current estimates,[44] manufacture of this amount of brick would have required 1,500 working cycles of a standard furnace, operated by a workforce equivalent to approximately 300,000 man-days. Brick stamps testify to well-organized production, subject at all phases to quality control and producers' accreditation. Very large building sites requested custom-made products, as evidenced by the brick-marks relating to Hagia Sophia.[45]

Equally abundant supply sources must be assumed for the prestige materials, marble in particular, used for wall revetments, columns, capitals, and other furnishings. The vast majority of the marble used in Constantinople was from nearby quarries at Prokonnesos in the Sea of Marmora. The workshops produced a surplus, as the extensive use of semi-finished or finished capitals in contexts without particular aesthetic pretensions, such as the large underground cisterns from the Justinian period, indicates.[46] By contrast the most valuable colored marbles arrived from the empire's far-flung regions, offering concrete testimony to the extent of the territory controlled by Constantinople.

## CONCLUSIONS

It is possible to see the story of Constantinopolitan construction in the city's first 200 years as a single undertaking. The concentration of political will, economic capacity, and logistic conditions combined to facilitate the influx of the necessary building materials, specialized knowledge, and technological skills from a pan-Mediterranean architectural catchment. The enormity of this enterprise led to a radical change in the urban ecosystem, transforming what had been a minimally urbanized territory into a concentrated urban center.

In the following centuries this concentration of buildings determined the survival of the urban organism. Materials recovered from abandoned buildings supplied the raw material for new construction and restoration. More importantly, it provided Constantinople with the infrastructures necessary to the survival and operation of a city of its dimensions, a concentration of buildings that offered its inhabitants the necessary resources for urban living and created the administrative center so essential to the functioning of the complex state that was the Byzantine Empire.

It was this concentration of building that attracted first the admiration and then the destructive lust of western medieval observers that resulted in the debacle of the Fourth Crusade (1204). It also put Constantinople in the sights of Mehmed II the Conqueror (1441–6/ 1451–81) as he searched for an established and reusable administrative center for his new complex state organization.

## FURTHER READING

Bardill, J., Brickstamps of Constantinople, 2 vols. (Oxford, 2004).

Crow, J., "The Infrastructure of a Great City: Earth, Walls and Water in Late Antique Constantinople," in Technology in transition A.D. 300–650, ed. L. Lavan, E. Zanini, and A. Sarantis (Leiden and Boston, 2007), 251–85.

Dark, K. R. and F. Özgümüş. Constantinople: Archaeology of a Byzantine Megapolis (Oxford, 2013).

Ousterhout, R., Master Builders of Byzantium (Princeton, 2000).

Saliou, C., "Construire en capitale: la loi de Zénon sur la construction privée à Constantinople (CJ VIII, 10, 12), une relecture," in Constantinople réelle et imaginaire: autour de l'oeuvre de Gilbert Dagron (TM 22.1), ed. C. Morrisson and J.-P. Sodini (Paris, 2018), 79–102.

Zanini, E., "Materiali e tecniche costruttive degli edifici costantinopolitani in età paleologa: un approccio archeologico," in L'arte di Bisanzio e l'Italia al tempo dei Paleologi 1261–1453, ed. A. Iacobini and M. della Valle (Rome, 1999), 301–20.

## NOTES

1 D. Kuban, Istanbul, an Urban History: Byzantion, Constantinopolis, Istanbul (Istanbul, 1996); R. Ousterhout, "Building Medieval Constantinople," Proceedings of the PMR Conference 19/20 (1994–6): 35–67; V. Franchetti Pardo, "Da Bisanzio a Costantinopoli: profilo storico-urbanistico della capitale imperiale; dalle origini a Giustiniano," in Bisanzio, Costantinopoli, Istanbul, ed. T. Velmans (Milan, 2008), 13–38.

2 E. Rizos, ed. New Cities in Late Antiquity: Documents and Archaeology (Turnhout, 2017).

3 R. Janin, Constantinople byzantine: Développement urbain et répertoire topographique (Paris, 1964); C. Mango, Le développement urbain de Constantinople (IVe–VIIe siècles) (Paris, 1985); P. Magdalino, Constantinople Médiévale: Études sur l'évolution des structures urbaines (Paris, 1996); Magdalino, "Medieval Constantinople: Built Environment and Urban Development," in EHB 2: 529–37.

4 F. A. Bauer "Urban Space and Ritual: Constantinople in Late Antiquity," ActaIRNov 15 (2001): 27–61; S. Bassett, The Urban Image of Late Antique Constantinople (Cambridge and New York,

2004); R. Ousterhout, "Constantinople and the Construction of a Medieval Urban Identity," in *The Byzantine World*, ed. P. Stephenson (London and New York, 2010), 334–51.

5 W. Müller-Wiener, *Bildlexikon zur Topographie Istanbuls: Byzantion, Konstantinupolis, Istanbul bis zum Beginn d. 17. Jh.* (Tübingen, 1977); H. Maguire and R. Ousterhout, "Introduction. Constantinople: The Fabric of the City," *DOP* 54 (2000): 157–9; J. Freely and A. Çakmak, *Byzantine Monuments of Istanbul* (Cambridge, 2004); K. R. Dark and F. Özgümüş, *Constantinople: Archaeology of a Byzantine Megapolis* (Oxford, 2013).

6 B. Trigger, "Monumental Architecture: A Thermodynamic Explanation of Symbolic Behaviour," *World Archaeology* 22.2 (1990): 119–32; J. L. Bintliff, "The Paradoxes of Late Antiquity: A Thermodynamic Solution," *AntTard* 20 (2012): 69–73.

7 J. Crow, "The Infrastructure of a Great City: Earth, Walls and Water in Late Antique Constantinople," in *Technology in Transition (A.D. 300–650)*, ed. L. Lavan, E. Zanini, and A. Sarantis (Leiden and Boston, 2007), 251–85.

8 Dark and Özgümüş, *Constantinople*, 98–104.

9 A. Berger, "Streets and Public Spaces in Constantinople," *DOP* 54 (2000): 161–72.

10 V. Kidonopoulos, "The Urban Physiognomy of Constantinople from the Latin Conquest through the Palaiologan Era," in *Byzantium: Faith, and Power (1261–1557): Perspectives on Late Byzantine Art and Culture*, ed. S. T. Brooks (New York, 2006): 98–117.

11 E. Giorgi, *Archeologia dell'acqua a Gortina di Creta in età protobizantina* (Oxford, 2016).

12 R. M. Harrison and M. Harrison, *A Temple for Byzantium: The Discovery and Excavation of Anicia Juliana's Palace-Church in Istanbul* (Austin, 1989).

13 T. F. Mathews, "The Palace Church of Sts. Sergius and Bacchus in Constantinople," in *Archaeology in Architecture. Studies in Honor of Cecil L. Striker*, ed. J. Emerick and D. Deliyannis (Mainz, 2005), 137–41.

14 C. L. Striker, J. M. Russell, and J. C. Russell "Quantitative Indications about Church Building in Constantinople, 325–1453 AD," *Architectura* 38 (2008): 1–12.

15 O. Dally and C. J. Ratté, eds., *Archaeology and the Cities of Asia Minor in Late Antiquity* (Ann Arbor, 2011)

16 I. Baldini Lippolis, "Private Space in Late Antique Cities: Laws and Building Procedures," in *Housing in Late Antiquity: From Palaces to Shops*, ed. L. Lavan, L. Özgenel, and A. Sarantis (Leiden and Boston, 2007), 197–237.

17 C. Saliou, "Construire en capitale: la loi de Zénon sur la construction privée à Constantinople (CJ VIII, 10, 12), une relecture," *TM* 22/1 (Paris, 2018), 79–102.

18 G. Dagron, *Constantinople imaginaire: Etudes sur le recueil des Patria* (Paris, 1984); Av. Cameron and J. Herrin. *Constantinople in the Eighth Century: The Parastaseis Syntomoi Chronikai: Introduction, Translation, And commentary* (Leiden, 1984).

19 H. Saradi, "The Use of Ancient Spolia in Byzantine Monuments: The Archaeological and Literary Evidence," *International Journal of the Classical Tradition* 3.4 (1997): 395–423.

20 Saliou, "Costruire en capitale."

21 Dagron, *Constantinople imaginaire*, 529.

22 C. Saliou, *Le traité d'urbanisme de Julien d'Ascalon. Droit et architecture en Palestine au VIᵉ siècle* (Paris, 1996).

23 P. Magdalino, "The Maritime Neighborhoods of Constantinople: Commercial and Residential Functions, Sixth to Twelfth Centuries," *DOP* 54 (2000): 209–26

24 C. Machado, "Aristocratic Houses and the Making of Late Antique Rome and Constantinople," in *Two Romes: Rome and Constantinople in Late Antiquity*, ed. L. Grig and G. Kelly (Oxford, 2012), 136–60.

25 P. Magdalino, "Aristocratic Oikoi in the Tenth and Eleventh Regions of Constantinople," in *Byzantine Constantinople: Monuments, Topography and Everyday Life*, ed. N. Necipoğlu (Leiden, 2001), 53–69.

26 Dark and Özgümüş, *Constantinople*, 98–104.

27 R. Ousterhout, *Master Builders of Byzantium* (Princeton, 1999).

28 E. Zanini, "Technology and Ideas: Architects and Master-Builders in Early Byzantine World," in *Technology in Transition*, 381–405.

29 Dagron, *Constantinople imaginaire*, 191–314; see also C. Mango, "Byzantine Writers on the Fabric of Hagia Sophia," in *Hagia Sophia from the Age of Justinian to the Present*, ed. R. Mark and A. Ş. Çakmak (Cambridge, 1992), 41–56.

30 A. Paribeni, "Le sigle dei marmorari e l'organizzazione del cantiere," in *S. Sofia di Costantinopoli: L'arredo marmoreo della Grande Chiesa giustinianea*, ed. A. Guiglia Guidobaldi and C. Barsanti (Città del Vaticano, 2004), 651–734.

31 Zanini, "Technology and Ideas," 394–7.

32 G. Tate, "Les métiers dans les villages de la Syrie du Nord," *Ktema* 16 (1991): 73–8.

33 C. Barsanti, "Costantinopoli: testimonianze archaeologiche di età costaniniana," in *Costantino il grande, dall'antichità all umanesimo: colloquio sul Cristianesimo nel mondo antico, Macerata 18-20 Dicembre 1990*, ed. G. Bonamente and F. Fusco (Macerata, 1992), 115–50.

34 J. B. Ward-Perkins, "Notes on the Structure and Building Methods of Early Byzantine Architecture," in *The Great Palace of the Byzantine Emperors: Second Report*, ed. D. Talbot Rice (Edinburgh, 1958), 52–104, esp. 62–6.

35 K. O. Dalman, *Der Valens-Aquäduct in Konstantinopel* (Bamberg, 1933).

36 J. Bardill, *Brickstamps of Constantinople*, 2 vols. (Oxford, 2004), 1, 52–3.

37 P. L. Vocotopoulos, "The Concealed Course Technique: Further Examples and a Few Remarks," *JÖB* 28 (1979): 247–60.

38 R. Ousterhout, "Observations on the 'Recessed Brick' Technique during the Palaeologan Period," *Archaiologikon Deltion* 39 (1984): 163–70.

39 E. Zanini, "Materiali e tecniche costruttive degli edifici costantinopolitani in età paleologa: un approccio archeologico," in *L'arte di Bisanzio e l'Italia al tempo deli Paleologi, 1261–1453*, ed. A. Iacobini and M. della Valle (Rome, 1999), 301–20.

40 Bardill, *Brickstamps*, 1:339.

41 Chapter 8. For translation into French see: Dagron, *Constantinople imaginaire*, 200.

42 R. A. Livingston, "Material Analysis of the Masonry of the Hagia Sophia Basilica, Istanbul," in *Soil Dynamics and Earthquake Engineering VI: WIT Transactions on the Built Environment 3*, ed. A. Ş. Çakmak and C. A. Brebbia (Southampton/Boston, 1993), 849–65, www.witpress.com/elibrary/wit-transactions-on-the-built-environment/3/13470.

43 M. Ahunbay and Z. Ahunbay "Recent Work on the Land Walls of Istanbul: Tower 2 to Tower 5," *DOP* 54 (2000): 227–39. N. Asutay-Effenberger, *Die Landmauer von Konstantinopel-Istanbul: Historisch- topographische und baugeschichtliche Untersuchungen* (Berlin and Boston, 2007).

44 J. DeLaine, *The Baths of Caracalla: A Study in the Design, Construction, and Economics of Large-Scale Building Projects in Imperial Rome* (Portsmouth, RI, 1997): 114–18.

45 Bardill, *Brickstamps*, 312–14, 965–71.

46 J.-P. Sodini, "Le commerce des marbres à l'époque protobizantine, I: IV^e–VII^e siècle," in *Hommes et richesses dans l'Empire byzantine, IVe–VIIesiècle*, 2 vols. (Paris, 1989), 1: 163–86; N. Asgari, "The Proconnesian Production of Architectural Elements in Late Antiquity, Based on the Evidence from the Marble Quarries," in *Constantinople and Its hinterland*, ed. C.A. Mango and G. Dagron (Aldershot, 1995), 263–88.

# 7: THE DEFENCE OF CONSTANTINOPLE

## Eric McGeer

T he effect of the wars and invasions of the sixth and seventh
centuries was, to adapt Cyril Mango's summation, to transform
the Byzantine Empire into a world of one city. That that world
endured for over a thousand years was in no small measure owing to the
massive land walls constructed in the early fifth century which, save for
one interruption, safeguarded Constantinople in its role as the New
Rome, the imperial capital of a centralised monarchical state and the
spiritual capital of Orthodox Christianity. The factors at play in the
defence of Constantinople – geography, fortifications, land and naval
forces, adequate supply of water and provisions,[1] and, most importantly
in the eyes of its inhabitants, the miraculous tutelary powers resident in
the God-guarded City[2] – contributed in different ways, at different
times, to the longevity not just of the city but of the distinct political
and cultural entity that began with its dedication in 330 and ended with
its capture in 1453. As long as Constantinople survived, so did the
identity, inheritance and purpose of the empire. We would be contem-
plating a very different historical landscape today had Constantinople
succumbed, along with the other major cities of the Roman and
Christian east, to the Persians and Avars in the early seventh century
or to the Arabs in the late seventh and early eighth centuries.[3] For the
Byzantines, these and other deliverances, celebrated in annual liturgies
and lodged in historical memory, furnished proof of Constantinople's
pre-eminence as the Queen of Cities and of their own unique place and
mission within God's design for humanity.

The city's location at the eastern tip of the Thracian peninsula
determined the means and priorities of its defence; in turn, the alluring
wealth and prestige of Constantinople necessitated the construction and
maintenance of fortifications capable of resisting assault by land and sea.
The latter posed the lesser threat, since the prevailing winds and currents, not to mention the adverse conditions and winter storms that

restricted the sailing season, worked against enemy vessels attacking the city from the Bosporos or the Sea of Marmora or attempting to maintain a blockade long enough to starve out the defenders. It was also no easy task to coordinate land and sea forces operating from the European and Asian sides of the Bosporos. As long as the enemy could be kept out of the Golden Horn, the city was relatively secure on its seaward sides. It was on the western, landward side where no natural obstacle impeded invaders that the city was susceptible to attack. During the fifth and again in the sixth century attempts were made to block invaders by means of man-made barriers. One such, known as the Long Wall (or Wall of Anastasios), spanned the Thracian peninsula from the Black Sea to the Sea of Marmora some sixty-five kilometres west of Constantinople. Another shorter wall blocked access to the city's hinterland across the narrow neck of the Thracian Chersonese. At such a distance from the city, however, neither wall could be consistently manned or maintained as an effective barrier and both fell into disuse by the seventh century.[4] The promontory along which the invaders had to make their approach, however, tapered enough that the city itself could be cordoned off by fortifications reaching from the Sea of Marmora to the Golden Horn, which if strong enough would allow even a patchwork garrison to withstand an enemy many times its size. Once enclosed by a circuit of walls, Byzantine Constantinople might best be pictured as an impenetrable island fortress which in a pre-gunpowder age could be taken only through the negligence or connivance of the city's inhabitants.

The series of attested fortifications charts the stages of the city's development from a small settlement to the second capital of the Roman empire. Literary evidence indicates that the ancient city was walled and that the fortifications in place at the end of the second century AD withstood the siege undertaken by the army of Septimius Severus (192–211) for three years. This emperor is said to have ordered the demolition of the walls in punishment for the city's support of his rival Pescennius Niger, but whether the so-called Severan wall represents a new fortification later built at his command or the reconstruction of the original wall is uncertain.[5] There may also have been another rampart added to bolster the defences against the threat posed by the Goths in the mid-third century, but the reference to this outer structure is too meagre to propose a location.

With Constantine the Great's (306–37) selection of the site as an imperial residence and capital in the fourth century, however, the placement and effectiveness of the city's defences assumed even greater importance. Integral to his ambitious building programme was the

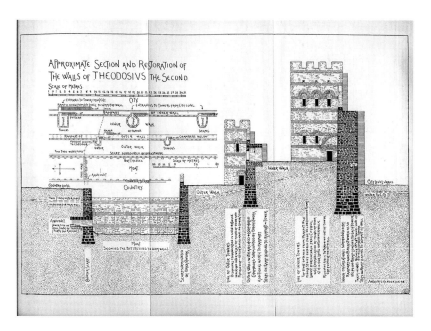

7.1 Map of Constantinople with defensive walls. (After van Millingen, *Byzantine Constantinople*)

construction of a new circuit laid out in an arc nearly three kilometres from the existing wall to accommodate the intended expansion of the urban precinct and to demonstrate the permanence of his projected New Rome. Of this Constantinian wall nothing remains today, although its course has been plausibly retraced from topographic and literary evidence and three of its gates identified (Fig. 7.1). It appears to have been modelled on the Aurelian wall in Rome, consisting of a single wall and towers, and it was to serve its purpose in 378 when the Goths who had annihilated the emperor Valens' army at Adrianople proved unequal to the task of breaching the city's defences. Redundant after the construction of the fifth-century circuit, the 'old wall' was still standing in the middle of the eighth century. The last mention in the sources records the collapse of a section during an earthquake in 860, after which the Constantinian wall crumbled into disrepair or was dismantled for use in other buildings. One of its gates survived until the early sixteenth century, another until the nineteenth.[6]

The need to secure the capital became all the more acute in view of the Gothic incursions of the late fourth century and the growing menace of the Huns. Work on the most imposing and complex defences girding any city in the Roman world may have begun with the construction of the Golden Gate about the year 390 but was concentrated between 405 and 413 when the new fortifications were laid out on a line two kilometres west of the Constantinian wall[7] (Figs. 7.1 and 7.2). Built under the supervision of the praetorian prefect of the East Anthemios, yet known ever afterwards as the Theodosian Walls (from the emperor Theodosios II (402–50) during whose reign they assumed their lasting form), the fortifications stretched for nearly six kilometres from the Sea of Marmora to the Golden Horn. Made up of three walls fronted by a wide ditch, they were executed on such an unprecedented scale to compensate for the lack of commanding topographical advantages. What few advantages of natural elevation the builders could incorporate were compromised by a serious liability where the terrain dipped with the Lykos river valley, giving attackers one place where they enjoyed the advantage of height over the defenders. The site of the walls, however, appears to have been dictated by considerations of food and water supply, since the new circuit now enclosed the three large cisterns that lay outside the Constantinian wall, as well as the then largely empty interval that offered room for cultivation, storage and pasturage for domestic animals.[8] Only a few years after

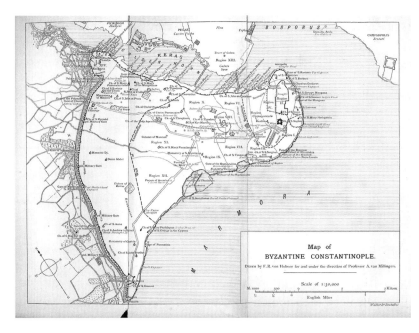

7.2 Landwalls of Theodosios II, section. (After van Millingen, *Byzantine Constantinople*)

their completion, the Theodosian Walls suffered major damage from an earthquake in 447, which brought down whole sections along with fifty-seven towers. The haste with which they were rebuilt, prompted by fear of Attila the Hun's descent upon the vulnerable city, was recorded in two inscriptions boasting that the reconstruction had taken just sixty days, 'an achievement even Pallas Athene could scarcely have matched'. Out of this historical event grew the edifying fable that lived on in urban lore, which had the two chariot factions, Blues and Greens, channelling their rivalry into a joint undertaking to repair the walls in a time of crisis. Both contributed teams of labourers who worked from each end of the circuit, thus restoring the integrity of the city's defences and symbolising the unity of the city's population.[9]

The inner wall, the mainstay of the system, was all but insurmountable to attackers and invulnerable to the siege technology and tactics of the Late Antique and mediaeval eras.[10] It loomed over the outer defences, standing roughly twelve metres high and built to a thickness of nearly five metres. Its hard, outer facings were made of limestone blocks precisely cut and set. The inner core was filled with mortared rubble. Horizontal bands of brick running through the wall acted as a kind of skeletal structure, bonding the facings with the inner core and making each section of the wall more compact. Ninety-six towers, nearly twenty metres high and placed fifty to seventy metres apart according to the lay of the land, gave the inner wall even greater dominance over the approaches. The upper chamber in each tower could house arrow-launching devices (*ballistae*) positioned to shoot through openings on the front and sides; platforms on the top of the towers supported defensive artillery that could rain projectiles down upon attackers or their siege equipment. Resting on a bedrock foundation, the inner wall could not be undermined. Ten gates allowed access into and out of the city, while smaller postern gates allowed soldiers to move to one part of the fortifications from another. The main gates were flanked by high towers set forward from the wall to form a narrow passageway over which the defenders had full view. The most famous of these entrances was the Golden Gate (a fortress unto itself), the imperial passageway and a sacred site on the route followed by the city's religious processions and military triumphs.

Twenty metres or so in front of the inner wall ran another wall, eight metres high along its front face. Although less thick than the inner wall, it too consisted of a hard facing of limestone blocks bonded with the core of mortared rubble by brick banding. The space between the two walls was filled with the earth excavated from the moat and packed in behind the outer wall to provide a solid embankment that cushioned the impact of battering rams and obviated mining operations. The outer wall was built with two levels of defence, the lower consisting of a series of small chambers with loopholes for archers, the upper of a battlement with crenellations allowing archers and slingers to shoot from cover. Finally, this outer wall was likewise reinforced by ninety-six towers projecting five metres forward to enable archers and *ballistae* to shoot at attackers directly or from the flank if they reached the wall. The placement of the towers in the inner and outer walls alternated (rear–front–rear) along the circuit so that each tower of the outer wall was overlooked by two flanking higher towers along the inner wall. The gates in this outer wall lined up with those in the inner wall to allow direct passage into the city, but here again high flanking towers and walls stood over these entry points.

Before attackers could even reach the walls they had first to contend with the moat that ran parallel to the fortifications, twelve to fifteen metres in front of the outer wall. Whether dry or filled with water, the moat was an intractable impediment, with a depth of over seven metres and a width of eighteen – in other words, too deep and wide for besiegers to bridge or fill in. The rear retaining wall of the moat was capped by a crenellated balustrade serving as the outermost of the triple walls. Two metres in height, it could shelter slingers and archers shooting across or down into the moat. Even if attackers got past this ditch and rampart, they had to cross the wide, empty expanse spread before the second wall, fully exposed to the defenders manning the towers and battlements above. The layout of the Theodosian Walls thus forced attackers to fight their way through a triple set of fortified terraces, more than sixty metres from beginning to end, that rose successively with each level to a height of twenty-five metres. It was to many attackers even more a psychological than a physical barrier.

In a system designed to keep attackers well away from the main wall, defenders had little to fear from the tactics and technology of contemporary siege warfare. Logistics weighed heavily in favour of the defenders, since attackers required a great number of soldiers, and an accompanying fleet, to conduct a siege with any hope of success. Whereas Constantinople could be provisioned and reinforced by sea, the severity of the winter season placed limits on the supplies and time necessary to the besiegers. Hence the most effective methods in siege warfare, starving out the garrison and undermining the walls, were too laborious and too time-consuming for the attackers.[11] Given the range of the archers and defensive artillery on the walls, it was also very difficult to construct siege towers close to the fortifications, much less advance them across the moat up to the outer wall. Siege artillery presented little threat, since few attackers possessed the capacity to bring heavy catapults to bear on the walls. In view of the range from which such catapults would have operated, and the size of the stones they could hurl, any enemy projectiles striking the walls would have done negligible damage. In the contest between defensive and offensive technology, the scales tipped decidedly in favour of the defenders throughout the city's history. Even in 1453, the Turkish cannon and bombards, for all their sound and fury, had greater effect on the defenders' morale than on the land walls themselves. Despite the damage they inflicted on the outer walls they never created a breach that the attackers could exploit.[12]

The Theodosian Walls did not traverse the full length between the Sea of Marmora and the Golden Horn. In the north-west corner of the city, in the district of Blachernai, the walls merged with an already existing citadel that made a distinct bulge in the defences. Over the centuries the Blachernai section was extended or reinforced a number of times, most importantly by the emperor Herakleios (610–41) who after the Persian-Avar siege built a wall to protect the Church of the Blachernai and to strengthen the juncture of the land and sea defences by the Golden Horn; by Leo V (813–20), who added an outer wall near the same juncture; and Manuel I Komnenos (1143–80), who had a high, sturdy rampart bolstered by towers constructed to enclose the Blachernai Palace, by then the principal imperial residence in the city.[13]

The origins of the sea walls are less clear, and uncertainties remain as to their extent (or very existence) until the late seventh century.[14] The seaward defences were a secondary concern as long as the Mediterranean remained a Roman lake. In the same year that a Vandal fleet captured Carthage (439), however, the first efforts to fortify the city's shoreline are attested in an edict calling for the sea walls to be carried as far as the new land walls to form a complete circuit.[15] Built on a simpler scale but at much greater length, the fortifications along the Sea of Marmara and the Golden Horn, contoured to the city's littoral and harbours, consisted of a single wall punctuated by as many as 188 towers along the Sea of Marmora and 110 along the Golden Horn. It would appear that the initial defences along the Golden Horn were incomplete or perceived as the weakest section in the entire circuit, since at the height of the siege in 626 the Avars' Slav allies attempted a landing on the shoreline near the Blachernai quarter that was repulsed by a Byzantine flotilla assigned to the defence of that particular section.[16] The strength of the Theodosian Walls compelled attackers to try their luck against the seemingly weaker fortifications in the Blachernai section. Other besiegers, such as the rebel Thomas the Slav in 821, the Bulgar khan Symeon in 921, the rebel Leo Tornikios in 1047, and the men of the Fourth Crusade in 1203–4 also marshalled their forces opposite the Blachernai–Golden Horn juncture of the land and sea walls.[17]

The improvement or repair of the sea walls receive attention in the sources when the threat of naval attack appeared imminent. Faced with the rise of Arab sea power in the latter seventh century, a series of emperors, particularly Tiberios III (698–705) and Anastasios II (713–15), are reported to have strengthened the sea wall in anticipation of the armada which eventually arrived in 717 and carried on a siege for over a year. This is also the first time we hear of the famous chain stretched across the mouth of the Golden Horn to deny enemy vessels access to that critical waterway. Following the near-run victory over the afore-mentioned Thomas the Slav, whose fleet broke into the Golden Horn and enabled him to make a dangerous assault on the Blachernai quarter, the emperors Michael II (820–29) and Theophilos (829–42) embarked on an ambitious programme to reinforce the sea walls, especially the vulnerable section along the Golden Horn. As was the case with the civic restoration undertaken by Constantine V (741–75), made necessary by a succession of calamities (earthquakes, plague, civil unrest), the steps taken by Michael II and Theophilos were intended both to make the capital more secure after the Arab capture of Crete, and to restore the harbour facilities along the Golden Horn which had long since fallen into decay.[18] 'Theophilos, having renewed the city' begins one of the many inscriptions engraved upon the walls and towers that proclaim the fulfillment of the emperor's duty to augment or restore the city's defences that should also be understood in con-nection with the recovery and renewal of Constantinople at various stages in its history.[19] The coin struck by Michael VIII Palaiologos (1261–82) soon after he regained the city in 1261 to commemorate his restoration of the walls is perhaps the most distinctive proclamation of this type of imperial initiative.[20] What the inscriptions show most clearly is that it was not just the effect of invasions and sieges that took their toll on the walls, but wear and tear, and the 'earthquakes, fissures, and the damage wrought by the passage of time' which are often cited as the chief cause of repairs to the walls throughout the city's history:[21]

The outer rampart of the Theodosian Wall was rebuilt
during the reign of our most pious sovereigns Justin and
Sophia by the servants of the most pious sovereigns, the most
illustrious spatharios and sakellarios Narses and Stephen who
took charge of the work.

Leo with Constantine, holders of the sceptre, raised up this
tower which had fallen down.

Possessing Thee, O Christ, an unbreakable wall, the
sovereign and pious emperor Theophilos raised this wall on
new foundations; protect it, Lord of All, with Thy might and
display it to the end of time standing unshaken
and unmoved.

In the year 1024, the pious sovereign Basil built up from the
foundations this tower which over a long time the force of
the sea, battering it with wave upon violent wave, caused
to collapse.

To all Romans: The great emperor Romanos raised up this
new and immense tower from the foundations.

This God-guarded gate of the life-giving source was
restored with the assistance and outlay of Manuel Bryennios
Leontaris during the reign of the pious sovereigns John and
Maria Palaiologos.

Although the funds and labour to maintain the walls required
special taxes and levies (as is recorded of Leo III's extensive repairs in
740), sound fortifications reduced other burdens. Sheltered behind
forbidding defences that even a scratch force could man effectively,
Constantinople had no need of a large, permanent garrison which was
both an expense and potential source of insurrection which prudent
emperors sought to minimise.[22] Quartering soldiers in the capital and
increasing taxes to support a military that already consumed the lion's
share of state revenues did not endear the rulers to the ruled. The most
telling example of such disaffection was Nikephoros II Phokas (963–9),
whose unruly soldiers and scouring taxation earned him the hatred of
the populace despite his successes on the battlefield.[23] The lesson that
his fate taught was not lost on later emperors, such as Isaac I Komnenos
(1057–9) who after securing the throne was quick to reward and disperse
his army before the soldiers could get out of hand as they wandered

about the city.[24] A few years later, however, Alexios Komnenos (1081–118) was unable to control his troops after they broke into the city and never quite cleansed his reputation of the stain of the looting spree that accompanied his accession to power. It was yet another reminder that the inhabitants of Constantinople often had more to fear from the city's nominal protectors than from foreign enemies.

The defence of Constantinople by land and naval forces began at the empire's frontiers. As long as these remained stable and distant, and with sufficient warning, the palace regiments and imperial bodyguards (*Exkoubitores* and *Scholai*), members of the chariot factions and other citizens capable of bearing arms could be mobilised and reinforced by troops from the regional armies stationed near the capital. The availability of these armies was another matter, as in 626 when the emperor Herakleios, placing his hopes in the strength of the walls and the armed citizenry, could spare only a detachment of his army on campaign to aid the city against the Avars and Persians. The retraction of the empire's frontiers in the seventh century, caused by the Muslim conquests in the east and the establishment of the Bulgar khanate to the northwest, brought the threat of attack on Constantinople much closer. The reorganisation of the army into territorial units (*themata*) first placed the capital under the protection of the Opsikion, the elite corps stationed in the region across the Bosporos; and a new fleet, the *Karabisianoi*, was created to defend the approaches to the city through the Aegean Sea and Hellespont. The danger these units posed to invaders, however, proved to be far less than the danger they posed to the sovereign, since the commanders of such overly strong forces rarely resisted the temptation to seize power and were a greater threat to the capital than were the empire's enemies. The *Karabisianoi* were broken up into smaller fleets (the maritime themata of Samos, Aegean Sea, and the *Kibyrrhaiotai*) which patrolled their home waters and when necessary lent assistance to the imperial navy based in Constantinople. The latter was more an offensive than a defensive force, however, and was often on campaign in foreign waters, leaving the capital and its outskirts vulnerable to attack.

The land forces were similarly restructured. Following the brief usurpation of Artavasdos in 742–43, the emperor Constantine V subdivided the Opsikion (along with the other large themata) and raised new regiments, known as the *tagmata*, to serve as the emperor's mobile field force. Recruited as an elite, they were never large in number, and were stationed in Constantinople or close by in Thrace and Bithynia; but their primary use was offensive and opportunistic enemies sought to attack the capital when these forces were away on campaign, as in 860 when the Rhos (Rus') descended on the city unopposed and went on a terrifying rampage through the surrounding areas – one occasion when the absence of military resistance left the outcome, in the minds of contemporaries, to the intervention of the city's supernatural protectors.[25] On other occasions, however, both the land and naval forces reacted quickly and effectively, the best examples of their ability to coordinate their efforts coming in 941 and 1043 when they combined to inflict crushing defeats on the Rhos.[26]

There were never any regular garrison troops in Constantinople throughout the city's history. The city walls were the only constant. They bought time for the emperor, or in his absence the Eparch of the City and the Patriarch, to cobble together a defensive force made up of any ships and soldiers on hand, able-bodied citizens pressed into service and those simply described as rabble. The only permanent military presence in the capital were the palace guard regiments, almost always composed of foreigners (such as the famous Varangian Guard), which were charged with protecting the person of the emperor, a duty closely entwined with the defence of the capital. It is important to note that two of these palatine units, the *Noumera* and *Teichistai* (or Walls), kept watch over the walls of the palace, not of the city, although these and any other guardsmen on hand would of course be used in defence of the city if attacked.[27] Yet even the palace guards were in constant flux, coming and going with the ebb and flow of emperors, recruits and money, and by the time of the Turkish siege in 1453 there seem to have been none worthy of mention.[28]

The sieges of Constantinople rank among the most dramatic events in the city's history. Some grew with the telling, but the accounts in the sources preserve details about the defence of the city that show the combination of factors that determined the outcome. Not least of these was the contest of morale between attackers and defenders. The inhabitants of the city, braced by the display of the Virgin's robe or reports of Her miraculous apparition, united in the defence of the city when attacked by foreign enemies; but it was one thing to defend the city against external foes, quite another to defend an unpopular emperor against an internal rival. Usurpers failed to enter the city by force or stealth when the citizenry rallied to the emperor, often through the political influence of the Patriarch, and they gained entry when the emperor could not count on either populace or Patriarch. Leo Tornikios very nearly succeeded in breaking into the capital in 1047, but in the end had to watch his army camped before the walls lose heart and melt away when the Patriarch Michael Keroularios and the rather motley garrison refused to abandon Constantine IX Monomachos (1042–55). Ten years later it was the same Patriarch whose machinations against Michael VI Stratiotikos (1056–7) forced the emperor to abdicate and permitted the rebel Isaac Komnenos to enter the city without a siege.[29]

Amid the stories of stubborn resistance and miraculous deliverances, there are others showing how surprisingly easy it could be to get through the defences if one knew the right places or had the right connections inside the city. In 705, after three days of huffing and puffing outside the capital in a bid to regain the throne, Justinian II (685–95/705–11) and a few of his men wriggled along a forgotten water duct beneath the walls and joined with his partisans within the city to depose his rival Tiberios III.[30] According to the chronicler John Zonaras, in 1081 Alexios Komnenos persuaded a detachment of *Nemitzoi* (Germans) guarding a tower near the Charisios (Adrianople) Gate to turn against the soldiers manning the walls in that section, which opened the way for his forces and enabled him to seize the throne from Nikephoros III Botaneiates (1078–81).[31] The most egregious instance of heedless defenders and opportunistic insiders is the Byzantine recapture of Constantinople from the Latins in 1261. While reconnoitring with a small force near the city, Alexios Strategopoulos (d. 1271) discovered that the Venetian fleet and garrison were absent on campaign. With the assistance of local Greeks who mounted the walls from inside and eliminated the few sentinels keeping watch, he had his men rush through the gate the locals had forced open, taking the Latin inhabitants completely by surprise and panicking them into evacuating the city.[32]

The siege of 1453 that ended with the capture of Constantinople and the extinction of the Byzantine Empire nevertheless reveals the strength of the city's defences and resolve of its defenders. Only by the extraordinary transport of the Sultan's ships into the Golden Horn, the demoralising and wearing effect of the cannons, and the sheer weight of numbers did a besieging army of perhaps 60,000 soldiers finally overcome a garrison numbering 8,000 at most. And it was the infelicitous combination of the panic sown by the wounding and evacuation of the stalwart Genoese ally Giovanni Giustiniani and the defenders' neglect of a small postern gate that permitted the Turks to breach the walls after seven weeks of assaults, bombardments and mining. The extensive repairs to the fortifications in the years before the final siege and the gallant defence may only have delayed the inevitable, but the thousand-year-old walls very nearly prolonged the life of the empire and its slender hopes of survival.

## FURTHER READING

Asutay-Effenberger, N., *Die Landmauer von Konstantinopel-İstanbul. Historisch- topographische und baugeschichtliche Untersuchungen* (Berlin and Boston, 2007).

Crow, J. G., 'The Long Walls of Thrace', in *Constantinople and Its Hinterland*, ed. C. Mango and G. Dagron (Aldershot, 1995), 109–24.

Crow, J. G., 'The Infrastructure of a Great City: Earth, Walls and Water in Late Antique Constantinople', in *Technology in Transition A.D. 300–650*, ed. L. Lavan, E. Zanini, and A. Sarantis (Leiden and Boston, 2007), 251–85.

Crow, J. G., 'Recent Research on the Anastasian Wall in Thrace and Late Antique Linear Barriers Around the Black Sea', in *Roman Frontier Studies 2009*, ed. N. Hodgson, P. Bidwell and J. Schachtmann (Oxford, 2017), 131–8.

Foss, C. and D. Winfield, *Byzantine Fortifications: An Introduction* (Pretoria, 1986).

Greatrex, G., 'Procopius and Agathias on the Defences of the Thracian Chersonese', in *Constantinople and Its Hinterland*, ed. C. Mango and G. Dagron (Aldershot, 1995), 125–9.

Haldon, J. F., 'Strategies of Defence, Problems of Security: The Garrisons of Constantinople in the Middle Byzantine Period', in *Constantinople and Its Hinterland*, ed. C. Mango and G. Dagron (Aldershot, 1994), 143–55.

Janin, R., *Constantinople byzantine: Développement urbain et répertoire topographique* (Paris, 1964).

Mango, C., *Le développement urbain de Constantinople (IVe–VII siècles)* (Paris, 1985).

Müller-Wiener, W., *Bildlexikon zur Topopgraphie Istanbuls: Byzantion, Konstantinupolis, Istanbul bis zum Beginn d. 17. Jh.* (Tübingen, 1977).

Philippides, M. and W. Hanak, *The Siege and the Fall of Constantinople in 1453: Historiography, Topography and Military Studies* (Abingdon and New York, 2011).

Van Millingen, A., *Byzantine Constantinople: The Walls of the City and Adjoining Historical Sites* (London, 1899).

## NOTES

1 For the importance of the food and water supply in matters of defence, see Chapters 4 and 5 in this volume and J. G. Crow, 'The Infrastructure of a Great City: Earth, Walls and Water in Late Antique Constantinople', in *Technology in Transition A.D. 300–650*, ed. L. Lavan, E. Zanini and A. Sarantis (Leiden and Boston, 2007), 251–85.

2 N. Baynes, 'The Supernatural Defenders of Constantinople', in *Byzantine Studies and Other Essays* (London, 1960), 248–60.

3 See J. D. Howard-Johnston, *Witnesses to a World Crisis: Historians and Histories of the Middle East in the Seventh Century* (Oxford, 2010), and M. Jankowiak, 'The First Arab Siege of Constantinople', *TM* 17 (2013): 237–320.

4 J. G. Crow, 'Recent Research on the Anastasian Wall in Thrace and Late Antique Linear Barriers Around the Black Sea', in *Roman Frontier Studies 2009*, ed. N. Hodgson, P. Bidwell and J. Schachtmann (Oxford, 2017), 131–8, and Crow, 'The Long Walls of Thrace', in *Constantinople and Its Hinterland*, ed. C. Mango and G. Dagron (Aldershot, 1995), 109–24;

G. Greatrex, 'Procopius and Agathias on the Defences of the Thracian Chersonese', in *Constantinople and Its Hinterland*, 125–9.

5  C. Mango, *Le développement urbain de Constantinople (IVe–VII siècles)* (Paris, 1985), 13–15; G. Dagron, *Constantinople imaginaire: études sur le recueil des Patria* (Paris, 1984), 63–5.

6  A. van Millingen, *Byzantine Constantinople: The Walls of the City and Adjoining Historical Sites* (London, 1899), 15–33; T. Preger, 'Studien zur Topographie Konstantinopels. III. Die Konstantinsmauer', *BZ* 19 (1910): 450–61; R. Janin, *Constantinople byzantine: Développement urbain et répertoire topographique*, 2nd ed. (Paris, 1964), 26–31, 263–5; Mango, *Développement urbain*, 24–5, 32–3.

7  There is no consensus on the chronology of the walls' construction. The most sensible discussions are: Crow, 'Infrastructure of a Great City', 262–8, and J. Bardill, *Brickstamps of Constantinople*, 2 vols. (Oxford, 2004), vol. 1, 122–5, whose arguments that the system was built according to a single plan are accepted here.

8  Mango, *Développement urbain*, 46–50.

9  See van Millingen, *Byzantine Constantinople*, 44–51 (for Greek and Latin inscriptions); Dagron, *Constantinople imaginaire*, 182–5.

10  The study of the Theodosian Walls begins with van Millingen, *Byzantine Constantinople*, 40–153; Janin, *Constantinople byzantine*, 261–86; C. Foss and D. Winfield, *Byzantine Fortifications: An Introduction* (Pretoria, 1986), 41–70, who give a thorough summary incorporating the two-volume *Die Landmauer von Konstantinopel*, by F. Krischen and T. von Lüpke (Berlin, 1938), and B. Meyer-Plath and A. M. Schneider (Berlin 1943; reprint 1974); W. Müller-Wiener, *Bildlexikon zur Topopgraphie Istanbuls: Byzantion, Konstantinupolis, Istanbul bis zum Beginn d. 17. Jh.* (Tübingen, 1977), 286–95, with a chronological overview of the construction and repairs in Byzantine and Ottoman periods. M. Philippides and W. Hanak review the state of the walls shortly before the siege of 1453, in *The Siege and the Fall of Constantinople in 1453: Historiography, Topography and Military Studies* (Abingdon and New York, 2011), 297–357. The most recent archaeological analysis of the walls is by N. Asutay-Effenberger, *Die Landmauer von Konstantinopel-İstanbul: Historisch- topographische und baugeschichtliche Untersuchungen* (Berlin and Boston, 2007). For an accessible introduction with good illustrations, see S. Turnbull, *The Walls of Constantinople AD 324–1453* (Oxford, 2004).

11  On the methods of attack and defence in Byzantine sieges, see E. McGeer, *Sowing the Dragon's Teeth: Byzantine Warfare in the Tenth Century* (Washington, DC, 1995), 152–63; and D. Sullivan, 'A Byzantine Instructional Manual on Siege Defense: The *De obsidione toleranda*. Introduction, English Translation and Annotations', in *Byzantine Authors: Literary Activities and Preoccupations*, ed. J. W. Nesbitt (Leiden, 2003), 139–266.

12  Philippides and Hanak, *The Siege and the Fall of Constantinople in 1453*, 475–505.

13  The complex development of the walls in this area is reviewed by van Millingen, *Byzantine Constantinople*, 109–53; Foss and Winfield, *Byzantine Fortifications*, 47–52; Asutay-Effenberger, *Die Landmauer von Konstantinopel-İstanbul*, 13–27, 118–27.

14  C. Mango, 'The Shoreline of Constantinople in the Fourth Century', in *Byzantine Constantinople. Monuments, Topography and Everyday Life*, ed. N. Necipoğlu (Leiden, 2001), 17–28, esp. 24–5.

15  Janin, *Constantinople byzantine*, 287–300; Müller-Wiener, *Bildlexikon*, 308–19, outlines the chronology of the sea walls; see also van Millingen, *Byzantine Constantinople*, 178–267; Foss and Winfield, *Byzantine Fortifications*, 70–3.

16  J. D. Howard-Johnston, 'The Siege of Constantinople in 626', in *Constantinople and Its Hinterland*, 131–42.

17  J. Skylitzes, *A Synopsis of Byzantine History 811–1057*, trans. John Wortley (Cambridge, 2010), 36–43, 211–12, 414.

18  P. Magdalino, 'The Maritime Neighborhoods of Constantinople: Commercial and Residential Functions, Sixth to Twelfth Centuries', *DOP* 54 (2000): 209–26.

19  P. Magdalino, 'Renaissances d'une capitale: l'urbanisme constantinopolitain des dynasties impériales', *TM* 22.1 (2018): 55–77 and 'Constantine V and the Middle Age of Constantinople', in *Studies on the History and Topography of Byzantine Constantinople*, ed. P. Magdalino (Aldershot, 2007), no. IV.

20  A.-M. Talbot, 'The restoration of Constantinople under Michael VIII', *DOP* 47 (1993): 243–61, esp. 249.

21 These examples are drawn from the inscriptions recorded in Janin, *Constantinople byzantine*, 261–300.

22 J. F. Haldon, 'Strategies of Defence, Problems of Security: The Garrisons of Constantinople in the Middle Byzantine Period', in *Constantinople and Its Hinterland*, 143–55.

23 *The History of Leo the Deacon: Byzantine Military Expansion in the Tenth Century*, trans. A.-M. Talbot and D. Sullivan (Washington, DC, 2005), 112–13.

24 J. Zonaras, *Epitomae historiarum*, ed. M. Pinder and Th. Büttner, 3 vols. (Bonn, 1841–97), vol. 3: 666.

25 See *The Homilies of the Patriarch Photius*, trans. by C. Mango (Cambridge MA, 1958), 74–110.

26 Skylitzes, trans. Wortley, 221–2, 404–7.

27 J. F. Haldon, *Byzantine Praetorians: An Administrative, Institutional and Social Survey of the Opsikion and Tagmata, c. 580–900* (Bonn, 1984), 191–256, 258–75; H. Ahrweiler, *Byzance et la mer: La marine de guerre, la politique et les institutions maritimes de Byzance aux VIIe–XIVe siècles* (Paris, 1966), 19–35, 102–7.

28 M. C. Bartusis, *The Late Byzantine Army: Arms and Society, 1204–1453* (Philadelphia, 1992), 271–86.

29 Skylitzes, tr. Wortley, 413–16, 462–5.

30 *Nikephoros Patriarch of Constantinople: Short History*, trans. C. Mango (Washington, 1990), 102–3.

31 Zonaras, *Epitomae historiarum*, vol. 3, 727–8.

32 Bartusis, *Late Byzantine Army*, 38–42.

# PART III

# URBAN EXPERIENCES

# 8: IMPERIAL CONSTANTINOPLE

## Paul Magdalino

Eusebius of Caesarea refers to Constantinople as 'the emperor's city', reserving the title of 'reigning city' to Rome.[1] Yet by the end of the fourth century Constantinople too was known as such, just as it had come to be designated 'New Rome'. By the sixth century it was the only recognised 'reigning city' in the Roman world, and so it remained in the standard usage of Greek and Latin authors throughout the Middle Ages. Whether in the obvious sense that Constantinople housed the emperor's residence and the seat of government, or in the implied sense that the city itself was sovereign – an implication reinforced by the variant expression 'queen of cities' – the term expressed the reality that Constantine's foundation was first and foremost an imperial capital, whose civic status and urban character depended on its political function. Constantinople quickly became an economic and demographic hub, a religious metropolis, a centre of Greek and Latin learning, and a magnificent showcase of architecture and décor, with provision of social services on a massive scale. These functions were ancillary to and consequent on the presence of the emperor and his court. For the city's first fifty years that presence was intermittent. It subsequently became permanent and pervasive. Constantinople thus marked an important new development in the evolution of the Greco-Roman city. On the one hand, Constantine (306–37) and his successors wanted their capital to compete with every previous *polis* in the traditional terms of civic amenities and public monuments; on the other hand, they aspired to the ideal expressed by John Chrysostom's description of the City of God: 'For that city is most royal and splendid; it is not like our cities, which are divided into market place and palace, but there all is palace.'[2] This chapter maps the imperial presence in Constantinople's urban and suburban space during its lifetime as a Roman capital, looking at the space reserved to the emperor and the court hierarchy, at satellite residences of the imperial hub and at the use and politicisation of public space.

# IMPERIAL PALACES
## The Great Palace

Two of the main accounts of Constantinople's foundation list the imperial palace first among Constantine's intramural constructions.[3] Two other accounts place the Palace after the Hippodrome, emphasising the connection between the two by the spiral staircase that led from the Palace to the imperial box in the spectator stands of the circus.[4] All four accounts confirm that both constructions deliberately reproduced the arrangement at Rome, where the imperial palace on the Palatine Hill communicated directly with the Circus Maximus in the valley below, an arrangement copied in provincial capitals of the Tetrarchy, most of which Constantine knew well. Whether inspired by Rome or recent experience of the Tetrarchic capitals at Thessalonike and Nicomedia, the creation of a hippodrome-palace complex had to be his priority in planning his new capital. Whether he completed and enlarged an existing hippodrome, as some sources state, or built it anew, the suitability and availability of the terrain determined the site, which in turn established the palace's location on its south-eastern side.[5]

In Istanbul, a large open space, the At Meïdanı ('Horse Square'), marks the Hippodrome's site, but the Great Palace has disappeared from the modern cityscape, apart from the remains of its ninth-century seaside façade.[6] The kernel of Constantine's palace was in the area now occupied by the Sultan Ahmet (Blue) Mosque; however, the exact topography and identity of its individual structures remain hypothetical, and distinctions between Constantine's building programme and the additions and modifications introduced by his successors are impossible to distinguish in the written record. Documentation of the palace's expansion between the fourth and tenth centuries to cover the area between the Hippodrome and the seashore is patchy, particularly for the Theodosian emperors (379–50) who are known to have been prolific builders. Only in the tenth century does the irregular early evidence yield to more systematic descriptions in works commissioned by the emperor Constantine VII Porphyrogennetos (913–59) between 945 and 959: the Continuation of the Chronicle of Theophanes,[7] the biography of the emperor's grandfather Basil I,[8] and the *Book of Ceremonies*, a compilation of documents recording and prescribing the procedures of court ceremonial.[9] The first two texts offer detailed accounts of palace buildings erected by the emperors Theophilos (829–42) and Basil I (867–86).[10] The third gives stage directions for receptions and processions in all ceremonies in which the emperor participated inside and outside the Palace. Sporadic references, mainly in historical sources, document the palace's post-tenth-century additions.[11]

Since the majority of ceremonial venues were within the Palace, the *Book of Ceremonies* is in effect an animated map of the imperial court. It is the main source for the buildings where the emperor and his entourage were on show, and it is almost the only source for the connections between them. It is also frustratingly opaque. Although its component texts date from different periods, each shows only one, present moment in the existence of the spaces mentioned. Interested only in ceremonial venues, it mentions living quarters, government offices and service areas only in passing, if at all, although these made up a large part of the complex. It often refers to a single building by different names. Its directions are for users familiar with the setting, who need neither the architecture nor the distances explained. The differences in the hypothetical plans of the Palace drawn by modern scholars on its basis underscore the information's imprecision.[12]

Thus, 150 years after chance finds during the construction of an Istanbul railway line first stimulated research, the exact topography of this 'vast and irregular agglomeration of reception and banqueting halls, pavilions, churches and chapels, residential quarters, baths, colonnades, sporting grounds and gardens, all enclosed within a strong wall'[13] remains elusive. It will be so as long as the area is closed to systematic archaeological investigation. Yet progress has been made. Although buildings excavated in the 1930s and 1950s, the Peristyle courtyard (now the Mosaic Museum) and Apsed Hall, continue to defy identification,[14] structures uncovered by rescue excavations east of Hagia Sophia from 1997 to 2008 have plausibly been matched with buildings mentioned in texts; among them the Chalke gate, the Palace's monumental front entrance.[15] Moreover, the realisation that the Palace was built on a series of terraces, at 32 m, 26 m and 16 m above sea level and at sea level itself, has aided visualisation of its development and helped to make sense of the *Book of Ceremonies*' descriptions.[16] Thus the speculation generated by the source and the site has not been in vain. Despite disagreements and dead ends, the trial and error of research has constructed a plausible history of the imperial hub of the imperial city.[17]

Until the sixth century emperors, when in town, inhabited the Palace of Constantine, a complex of buildings mainly at the 32 m level. Here their official appearances were centred on the main reception hall, the Consistorium, and the banqueting hall known as the Hall of the

Nineteen Couches, from the couches, set in semi-circular recesses, on which guests reclined to dine at official banquets.[18] One source credits Theodosios II (405–50) with laying out the imperial polo ground, the Tzykanisterion, at sea level, and building the neighbouring complex at 16 m that came to be known as the Boukoleon Palace.[19] However, the Boukoleon's hub, the octagonal Chrysotriklinos ('Golden Hall') is reliably attributed to Justin II (565–78) and his successor Tiberios II (578–82). They and their successors did not vacate the upper palace, but they undoubtedly initiated the situation reflected in the *Book of Ceremonies*, where the Chrysotriklinos functions as the default throne room and the emperor's ceremonial movements begin and end in his apartments on the building's south side.[20]

All subsequent additions and alterations were on the 16 m terrace and at sea level. A seventh-century emperor, probably Constans II (641–68), ordered construction of the Palace harbour of Boukoleon, which communicated by a monumental staircase with the Chrysotriklinos and eventually gave its name to the complex.[21] Justinian II in his first reign (685–95) built two large ceremonial halls, the Ioustinianeios and the Lausiakos, between the Hippodrome and the Chrysotriklinos.[22] Either Justinian II or, more likely, Constantine V (741–75) built the church of the Pharos on the terrace east of the throne room; later the church, rebuilt by Michael III (843–67), became a shrine of Christianity's most precious relics.[23] Reception areas, chapels, pavilions and apartments added by Theophilos filled the space between the Chrysotriklinos and the upper Palace on the eastern side, probably incorporating constructions of Tiberios II.[24] An even more ambitious building programme of Basil I concentrated on the lower levels, including an extension at sea level to which his son Leo VI (886–912) also contributed. Nikephoros II Phokas (963–9) capped this activity with a wall fortifying the Boukoleon complex against the threat of urban riots.[25] Like the *Book of Ceremonies*, which was completed around the same time, the wall marked the end of a long period of investment in the culture and environment of the Great Palace. It was another century before Constantine X Doukas (1059–67) felt the need to provide a new reception hall and living quarters east of the Boukoleon,[26] and two centuries before Manuel I (1143–80) made the last substantial additions to the Boukoleon ensemble, a reception hall overlooking the western wall and a Seljukid-style pavilion, the Mouchroutas, west of the Chrysotriklinos.[27]

When the French crusader Robert de Clari visited the conquered city in 1204, the Boukoleon Palace impressed him as an ensemble of 'five hundred rooms, all connected with each other and all made of gold mosaic, and there were a good thirty chapels, both great and small'.[28] This is as good a description as possible in so few words, not least because of its evocation of the labyrinthine itineraries described in the *Book of Ceremonies*. The figures are realistic considering that the description applies to the whole of the Great Palace, and not just to the Boukoleon. The main upper Palace structures mentioned in the *Book of Ceremonies* were probably still visible in 1204, given that buildings continued in use long after the tenth century. Thus, well into the eleventh century, the staff of the imperial bureaucracy were still forced to recline on couches, Roman style, at ceremonial banquets.[29] The Oaton or Trullan hall, where the Sixth Ecumenical Council had convened in 680–1, served in the twelfth century as a financial archive that was converted into a formal reception area to celebrate an imperial betrothal in 1181, on the 500th anniversary of the Council.[30] In 1200, the Palace guards units occupied the premises where their predecessors had been quartered since the time of Constantine.[31]

Robert of Clari's compressed description gives the impression of a uniform, homogeneous space, undifferentiated by age, function and stages of accretion. It ignores service areas, government offices, recreational spaces and sub-groupings of 'rooms' and 'chapels', together with internal zoning and the external boundaries of the Palace. While the architectural variety that Robert missed eludes us, we do have some idea of the access restrictions that probably did not affect him as a foreign tourist with an occupying army. Eleventh- and twelfth-century sources indicate that Nikephoros Phokas' wall was not the only barrier between Palace and city, and that those wishing to enter had to pass – or break – through gates in an outer circuit, probably the wall attributed to Justinian II.[32] At the same time, earlier sources indicate that parts of the Palace had always been accessible, at least by appointment, to people outside the court hierarchy. Thus, Nikephoros II's wall seems to have hardened and redrawn the line between 'public' and 'private', 'inner' and 'outer' areas; between the halls where the emperor held court on a daily basis, and those that were opened on special occasions; between the sealed space that shut out common people, and the porous space where non-titled commoners could penetrate on authorised business.[33]

The Great Palace's golden age, as reflected in the *Book of Ceremonies*, saw the expansion of the imperial urban sector, from the sixth to the ninth century, at the expense of the public, civic sector. This growth, which involved the incorporation of public institutions into the palatine fabric, meant an increase in the liminal space between palace and city. The Blue and Green circus factions, representing the urban populace, were brought into the Palace to cheer the emperor on his way to church, and, on his wedding day, to serenade him and his bride as they proceeded to the nuptial chamber. Justinian II and Theophilos created special fountain-courtyards for the factions to perform. With the demise of public ministries in the Praetorian Prefecture, their functions migrated to financial offices and judicial tribunals at the edges of the palace precinct. Finally, in the ninth and tenth centuries, two important sanctuaries, the Nea and the Chalke, built at opposite ends of the Palace, were neither public churches nor palace chapels, but independent foundations with their own dedicated clergy and endowments. Three units in this peripheral zone stand out for their liminal, polyvalent status: the Chalke gatehouse, the Magnaura and the Nea Ekklesia. As the front entrance to the Palace, the Chalke gatehouse displayed pictorial propaganda, both in its inner mosaic decoration and as 'posters' affixed to the outer façade. It also served as a law court and a prison. In the tenth century, the Chalke church of Christ was built either on top of or beside it. Originally a small chapel built by Romanos I Lekapenos (920–44), the church was reconstructed by John I Tzimiskes (969–76) to house important relics and his burial. By the twelfth century a school was attached to it.[34]

The Magnaura, north-east of the Chalke, was a large, fourth-century basilica. It may have originated as a Senate House; after renovation by Justinian and Herakleios (610–41), it functioned as a 'parliament hall', where the sovereign held public audiences, publicised constitutional decisions, and pronounced his annual *silention*, an address to the nation, at the beginning of Lent. Here, at the reception of foreign ambassadors, the emperor's throne was mechanically raised in the air. At different moments in the ninth century the Magnaura briefly housed a law court and a school of higher education.[35]

The Nea Ekklesia (New Church), built by Basil I between 876 and 880, was the largest church built in Constantinople for two and a half centuries. The five-domed structure occupied the site of the former Tzykanisterion, on the level below the Boukoleon complex's 16 m terrace, and was thus considered to be near, but not in, the Palace. Annexes enhanced its liminal status: a school and a garden flanked by porticoes extended as far as the new Tzykanisterion; the church's financial office, contiguous with a formerly detached administrative unit, the Palace of Marina, which Basil restored as the Neos Oikos and his son Leo VI embellished with the addition of an antique-style bath-house. The Nea thus launched a new, emphatically dynastic peripheral ensemble. Constantine X Doukas renewed the dynastic emphasis by adding – or restoring – buildings that made the Tzykanisterion the centre of a new imperial family residence.[36]

After 1204 the Great Palace went into a long decline punctuated by moments of reuse that did not reverse the slow and occasionally sudden dilapidation of its ancient structures.

## The Blachernai Palace

The palace of the Blachernai, in the northern corner of the intramural area, was the only other imperial residence to become a permanent governmental seat.[37] The preferred residence of the twelfth-century emperors, it was the sole seat of government for both the Latin empire of Constantinople (1204–61) and the empire of the Palaiologoi (1261–1453). Robert of Clari describes it in 1204 in similar terms to the Great Palace: 'a good twenty chapels, and a good two to three hundred rooms, all connected to each other and all decorated with mosaics'.[38] Yet its beginnings had been modest, its importance slow to develop. It was first established by Anastasios I (491–518) as an annexe of the recently built sanctuary of the Virgin Mary, where the emperor could dine and rest when he worshipped at the church and bathed at the adjacent ritual bath. The complex remained outside the city wall until the seventh century, and continued thereafter to be on the front line against besieging armies. It was outside the Blachernai Palace that Patriarch Nicholas I appeased Tsar Symeon of Bulgaria with a form of coronation in 914,[39] and that Constantine IX Monomachos (1042–55) in 1047 showed himself to the army of the rebel Leo Tornikes.[40] This detail shows that the Palace was no longer confined to low ground near the church, but had expanded up the hill. However, the decisive expansion came later with the building programme of the Komnenos dynasty: Alexios I (1057–9) and Manuel I Komnenos' (1143–80) reception halls, the apartment buildings added by John II (1118–43), Manuel and Isaac II Angelos (1185–95/ 1203–4), and the chapels constructed following the lead of Isaac I (1057–9), who had restored the ninth-century church of St Thekla. The bulging line of the new section of city wall that Manuel erected documents the Komnenian expansion. Manuel's buildings probably formed the palace's centrepiece and remained its nucleus. They were then inhabited by the Latin emperors (1204–61) and Michael VIII Palaiologos (1258–82) after the expulsion of the Latin regime. The Palaiologoi undoubtedly made their mark on the ensemble, although it is impossible to determine whether constructions attributed to Andronikos II (1282–1328) – a major throne room and a raised outdoor platform for the performance of court ceremonial – were new additions or renovations of existing structures.[41] Equally difficult to identify and date is the one substantial remaining building, the elevated three-storey hall built over the city wall at the top of the hill.[42] Known to Istanbul's inhabitants as a 'royal residence' (Tekfur Baladi/Saray), it was probably the only part of the Blachernai Palace complex that remained functional in the final decades before 1453.

## Other Imperial Palaces in the City and Suburbs

Other imperial palaces in and around Constantinople varied according to origin and function. Like the Blachernai, the churches of Holy Apostles and the Virgin of the Source (Pege) had palace annexes that the emperor used during religious feasts.[43] In exceptional circumstances, emperors and their families moved into aristocratic palaces that had become crown property and had come, in some cases, to accommodate monastic communities. Such were the Palace of Eleutheriou, the power base of the empress Eirene,[44] the palace of the Myrelaion monastery, where the widow of Isaac I Komnenos lived after his abdication (1059),[45] and the palace attached to the Mangana monastery, where Alexios I died in 1118.[46] The only regular alternatives to the Great Palace and the Blachernai were the purpose-built 'holiday homes' where emperors went, mainly in summer, for a change of scene. Some were within the city, like the Palace of Bonus and the other 'splendid palaces' built by Romanos I,[47] but otherwise all known examples were outside the walls.[48] Initially the most important resorts were on the European side, at the Hebdomon (Bakırköy) on the Sea of Marmara, and St Mamas (near Beşiktaş) on the Bosporos, In the sixth century Justinian I and his successors built and frequented new palaces on the Bosphoros's eastern side, at Hiereia (Fenerbahçe), Sophianai (Çengelköy) and Damatrys (Palamud Tepe). Theophilos followed around 830 with the Palace of Bryas, which is said to have imitated palace buildings in Baghdad. The European suburbs subsequently returned to favour with the construction of a palace at Pegai (Kasımpaşa), north of the Golden Horn, and the palaces of the Aretai and the Philopation in parkland west of the city.[49] The last important suburban palace, Damalis or Skoutari, was built, probably by John II or

Manuel I, at Chrysopolis (Üsküdar), the Bosporos's main Asian crossing point.[50]

Although suburban palaces served mainly as summer residences for recreation, especially hunting, each was the seat of government while the emperor was in residence. Newsworthy political events took place in them. Like the tents of the imperial headquarters when the emperor was on campaign, they were stations in a reduced circuit of itinerant rulership, substitutes for the Great Palace and the Blachernai Palace, and, as such, centres, not satellites, of power.

## Urban Outposts of Imperial Power

### The Prefectures

All central imperial government departments were in principle located within the Palace, with two notable exceptions: the urban Prefecture and the Praetorian Prefecture of the East. The prefect (*eparchos*) of Constantinople had full responsibility for law, order and the regulation of trade. His praetorium was effectively the 'town hall'; it included the main city prison, and stood on the central avenue (Mese) close to the Forum of Constantine.[51] The Praetorian Prefect of the East was, until the seventh century, the highest judicial and financial authority under the emperor in the Roman Empire's eastern provinces. In the late fourth century his office was transferred from Antioch to Constantinople and housed on the Acropolis of ancient Byzantion. The Prefecture consisted of two basilican halls and other buildings; it had a large staff and dealt with streams of litigants.[52] By the eighth century it disappears from the sources and we assume that its judicial and financial functions had relocated to 'ministries' in the Great Palace's liminal area.

### The Houses of the Imperial Aristocracy

Just as the Palace was divided between the emperor's private, domestic space and reception areas where he and his officials conducted the ritual and administrative business of government, so was court society divided between the emperor's family and household staff. While family and staff lived in the Palace, the officials and dignitaries of the Senate commuted daily from homes in the city, thus extending the imperial presence throughout the urban environment. The *Book of Ceremonies* illustrates the satellite status of these houses in descriptions of promotion ceremonies that end with the newly promoted dignitary being escorted from the Palace to his house by a cortège reminiscent of an imperial procession.[53] The eleventh-century historian Michael Psellos reveals, from personal experience, the imperial concern that imperial officials have houses appropriate to their rank.[54] Imperial input was evident from the foundation of the city, when Constantine is said to have provided houses for the senatorial aristocracy.[55] The importance of such elite houses as units of urban development is clear from Themistios's description of the expansion that took place fifty years later, under Theodosios I (379–80), when the imperial court and central bureaucracy 'settled down' in Constantinople:

> It is not the case that the public sector advances while the private sector falls behind, but the city grows like a living thing, and it is as if everything is seized by a common inspiration from the emperor's enthusiasm that affects both officials and private citizens alike. One man erects a vestibule, another a bedchamber, another a reception hall, another a dining hall with seven or nine couches.[56]

In this way, houses of the imperial elite became the defining points of neighbourhoods throughout the city and suburbs, as locations and addresses commonly referred to by the formula 'the buildings of X' long after X's death.[57]

As Themistios makes clear, many elite houses resulted from private initiative and were, theoretically, private property. It is equally clear, however, that elite housing, especially at the top end of the range, was ultimately a political resource that remained at the emperor's disposal for constant reallocation to his dependents. Imperial relatives, including mistresses, government officials, foreign ambassadors and exiled foreign princes, all needed to be housed in accordance with their status, as did provincial governors, generals and bishops when in Constantinople on duty. Only twenty years after Themistios wrote, Synesios of Cyrene recalled 'the royal house' behind the Great Palace, which had been built for Ablabius, a close associate of Constantine the Great, and now belonged to Placidia, half-sister of the ruling emperor Arkadios (395–408).[58] Further west was a palace belonging to Arkadios's daughter Pulcheria, which reappears in 565 as the residence of Justinian's successor, in 963 as the home of the then emperor's father and in the twelfth century as the house of an imperial brother.[59] To the north, overlooking the Golden Horn, stood the house of the fifth-century general Aspar. It reappears in the tenth century, first as the temporary urban residence of visiting Armenian princes, and then as the home of another influential power-broker, the 'prime minister' Basil the Parakoimomenos. It probably housed an imperial brother in the twelfth century, and its location identifies it as the palace of one of the last Byzantine magnates, Loukas Notaras.[60]

The houses of the senatorial aristocracy formed a dense network throughout the city, with many doubles in the suburbs, more or less replicating the prestige elements of the imperial palace. The known examples showed astounding durability of status and location, even though they rarely remained within the possession of one family for more than a generation.

### A Civic Theatre of Imperial Power

The civic space of imperial Constantinople was created by emperors and served to advertise their presence and power. The Hippodrome, theatres and great public baths that functioned until the sixth century, the streets and squares lined with porticoes: these were sites of public entertainment, cultural activity, social gathering and commercial exchange. As in other Roman cities, they also served as permanent showcases for imperial statues and triumphal monuments, and in the imperial capital they doubled as backdrops for the emperor's public appearances. When he moved through the city in procession, or presided over public events, notably the races at the Hippodrome, the open spaces, gateways and colonnades of Constantinople were transformed into a theatre of power stretching from the Palace to the walls. The most splendid gateway in the walls, the Golden Gate, was reserved for the emperor's triumphal homecoming.[61] No hard division between imperial space and public or civic space existed, just a political hierarchy of spaces, all more or less imperial.

### Imperial and Sacred Space

The relationship of imperial to sacred space is different in that the church insisted on a distinction between imperial and priestly functions.[62] Thus, consecrated churches were places where the emperor's writ did not run and his usual supremacy was reversed. Although allowed limited access to the sanctuary, he received the sacraments following rules established for laymen, and his agents were prohibited from arresting asylum seekers.[63] Yet, given the emperor's role in providing the city with sacred capital, he also had a major share in its sacred real estate. Imperial palaces were full of chapels, and in addition to the major monasteries that came under imperial jurisdiction and patronage, important city churches, like the earliest Constantinopolitan church of the Virgin, had imperial status. Sacred and imperial institutions increasingly converged: the advent of a sacred relic had the style of an imperial parade, while the imperial triumph came to incorporate elements of ecclesiastical processions. Just as the emperor was not quite a priest but more than the chief layman, imperial space in the imperial city was not entirely secular, and became less so with time.

## FURTHER READING

Bauer, F. A., ed., *Visualisierung von Herrschaft: Frühmittelalterliche Residenzen – Gestalt und Zeremoniell* (Istanbul, 2006).

Constantine Porphyrogennetos, *Book of Ceremonies*, ed. with French translation and commentary by G. Dagron, D. Feissel, B. Flusin, *Constantin VII Porphyrogénète, Le Livre des cérémonies*, 5 vols (Paris 2020); ed J. J. Reiske (Bonn, 1829), reproduced with English translation and same pagination by A. Moffatt and M. Tall, 2 vols. (Canberra, 2012).

Dagron, G. *Emperor and Priest: The Imperial Office in Byzantium* (Cambridge, 2003).

Ebersolt, J. *Le Grand Palais de Constantinople et le Livre des Cérémonies* (Paris, 1910).

Featherstone, M., J.-M. Spieser, G. Tanman, and U. Wulf-Rheidt, eds., *The Emperor's House. Palaces from Augustus to the Age of Absolutism* (Berlin-Boston, 2015).

Guilland, R. *Études de topographie de Constantinople byzantine*, 2 vols (Amsterdam, 1969).

Macrides, R., J. A., Munitiz, D., Angelov, *Pseudo-Kodinos and the Constantinopolitan Court: Offices and Ceremonies* (Farnham, 2013).

Magdalino, P. 'Court Society and Aristocracy', in *Social History of Byzantium*, ed. J. Haldon (Chichester, 2009), 212–33.

Mango, C. *The Brazen House: A Study of the Vestibule of the Imperial Palace of Constantinople* (Copenhagen, 1959).

Mango, C. 'The Palace of the Boukoleon', *CahArch* 45 (1997): 41–50.

Mullett, M. and R. Ousterhout, eds., *The Holy Apostles: A Lost Monument, a Forgotten Project, and the Presentness of the Past* (Washington, DC, 2020).

Ödekan, A., E. Akyürek, and N. Necipoğlu, eds., *The Byzantine Court: Source of Power and Culture* (Istanbul, 2013).

Pitarakis, B., ed., Hippodrom/Atmeydanı: İstanbul'un Tarih Sahnesi *[Hippodrome/ Atmeydani: A Stage for Istanbul's History]*, 2 vols. (Istanbul, 2010).

## NOTES

1 Eusebius, *VC*, I. 26, 33, 39, 40: III. 7, 47, 48; IV. 61, 63, 69.
2 *PG* 57–8, col. 23.
3 Zosimos, II.31, 1; *Patria*, I. 59.
4 Malalas, *Chronographia*, XIII. 7; *Chronicon Paschale*, ed. Dindorf, 528, tr. Whitby, 18.
5 See G. Dagron, 'From One Rome to the Other', C. Mango, 'A History of the Hippodrome of Constantinople' and J. Bardill 'Archaeologists and Excavations in the Hippodrome', in *Hippodrome/Atmeydani*, 2 vols, ed. B. Pitarakis (Istanbul, 2010), vol. 1, 29–35, 36–44, 83–90; U. Wulf-Rheidt, 'The Palace of the Roman Emperors on the Palatine', in *The Emperor's House, palaces from Augustus to the Age of Absolutism*, ed. M. Featherstone, et al. (Berlin-Boston, 2015), 3–18 at 13.

6  C. Mango, 'Ancient Spolia in the Great Palace of Constantinople', in *Byzantine East, Latin West: Art-Historical Studies in Honor of Kurt Weitzmann*, ed. C. Moss and K. Kiefer (Princeton, 1995), 645–9.

7  Ed. and tr. M. Featherstone and J. Signes Codoñer, *Theophanis Continuati libri I–IV*, CFHB 53 (Boston and Berlin, 2015).

8  Ed. and tr. I. Ševčenko, *Theophanis Continuati liber V, Vita Basilii imperatoris*, CFHB 42 (Boston and Berlin, 2011).

9  Constantine Porphyrogennetos, *Book of Ceremonies*, Constantine Porphyrogennetos, *Book of Ceremonies*, ed. with French translation and commentary by G. Dagron, D. Feissel, B. Flusin, *Constantin VII Porphyrogénète, Le Livre des cérémonies*, 5 vols (Paris 2020; ed. J. J. Reiske, tr. A. Moffatt and M. Tall (Canberra, 2012).

10  *Theophanes Continuatus*, III. 42–4; *Vita Basilii*, 87–90.

11  P. Magdalino, 'Manuel Komnenos and the Great Palace', *BMGS* 4/1 (1978): 101–14, and Magdalino, 'Power Building and Power Space in Byzantine Constantinople: the Ethics and Dynamics of Construction and Conservation', in *The Byzantine Court, Source of Power and Culture*, ed. A. Ödekan et. al. (Istanbul, 2013), 55–62 at 62.

12  For reconstructions up to the 1950s, see C. Mango, *The Brazen House* (Copenhagen, 1959), 14–17; for later attempts, and the methodological challenges, W. Müller-Wiener, *Bildlexikon zur Topographies Istanbuls* (Tübingen, 1977), 229–37; J. Bardill, 'Visualizing the Great Palace of the Byzantine Emperors at Constantinople', in *Visualisierungen von Herrschaft, Frühmittelalterliche Residenzen – Gestalt und Zeremoniell*, ed. F. A. Bauer (Istanbul, 2006), 5–45; and M. Featherstone, 'The Great Palace as Reflected in the *De Ceremoniis*', in *Visualisierungen von Herrschaft*, 47–61; A. Berger, 'The Byzantine Court as a Physical Space', in *The Byzantine Court*, 3–12.

13  Mango, *Brazen House*, 12.

14  K. R. Dark, 'Roman Architecture in the Great Palace of the Byzantine Emperors at Constantinople during the Sixth to Ninth Centuries', *Byzantion* 77 (2008): 87–105; M. Featherstone, 'Theophilus's Margarites: The "Apsed Hall" of the Walker Trust', in *Di Bisanzio dirai ciò che è passato, ciò che passa e che sarà. Scritti in onore de Alessandra Guiglia*, ed. S. Pedone and A. Paribeni (Rome, 2018), 173–86.

15  A. Denker, 'Excavations at the Byzantine Great Palace (*Palatium Magnum*) in the Area of the Old Sultanahmet Jail', in *The Byzantine Court*, 13–18.

16  E. Bolognesi Recchi-Franceschini, 'The Great Palace of Constantinople', in *Neue Forschungen und Restaurierungen im byzantinischen Kaiserpalast von Istanbul*, ed. W. Jobst, R. Kastler and V. Scheibelreiter (Vienna 1999), 9–16.

17  M. Featherstone, 'Space and Ceremony in the Great Palace of Constantinople under the Macedonian Dynasty', *Settimana di studio della Fondazione centro italiano di studi sull'Alto Medioevo LXII – Le Corti nell'Alto Medioevo, Spoleto 24–9 aprile* 2014 (Spoleto 2015): 587–610.

18  S. Malmberg, 'Dazzling Dining: Banquets as an Expression of Imperial Legitimacy', in *Eat, Drink and Be Merry*, ed. L. Brubaker, 75–91, at 83-8.

19  C. Mango, 'The Palace of the Boukoleon', *CahArch* 45 (1997): 41–50.

20  M. Featherstone, 'The Chrysotriklinos as Seen through the *De Cerimoniis*', in *Zwischen Polis, Provinz und Peripherie. Beiträge zur byzantinschen Kulturgeschichte*, ed. A. Monchizadeh and L. M. Hoffmann (Wiesbaden, 2005), 845–52; M. Featherstone, 'The Everyday Palace in the Tenth Century', in *The Emperor's House*, 149–58.

21  D. Heher, 'Der Palasthafen des Bukoleon', in *Die byzantinischen Häfen Konstantinopels*, ed. F. Daim (Mainz, 2016), 67–90 ; P. Magdalino, 'Renaissances d'une capitale: l'urbanisme constantinopolitain des dynasties impériales', *TM* 22/1 (2018): 55–77, esp. 65–6.

22  *Patria*, III. 130; Magdalino, 'Renaissances'.

23  P. Magdalino, 'L'église du Phare et les reliques de la Passion à Constantinople (VIIe/VIIIe–XIIIe s.)', in *Byzance et les reliques du Christ*, ed. J. Durand and B. Flusin (Paris, 2004), 15–30.

24  Featherstone, 'Theophilus's Margarites'.

25  Mango, 'Boukoleon'.

26  *Patria*, III. 25; Magdalino, 'Power Building and Power Space', 62.

27  Magdalino, 'Manuel Komnenos and the Great Palace'. For the Mouchroutas, see also S. Redford, 'Constantinople, Konya, Conical Kiosks, Cultural Confluence', in *The Byzantine Court*, 41–7, esp. 41–2.

28  Robert of Clari, *La conquête de Constantinople*, 82.

29 Michael Psellos, *Michaelis Pselli oratoria minora*, ed. A.R. Littlewood, (Leipzig, 1985), 46.

30 Magdalino 'Power Building and Power Space', 60–2.

31 Magdalino, 'Manuel Komnenos and the Great Palace', 111, n. 47.

32 The three entry and exit points in the revolts of 1042 and 1200 were the Chalke Gate, the gate under the imperial box in the Hippodrome and a gate at the Tzykanisterion : John Skylitzes, *Ioannis Scylitzae Synopsis Historiarum*, CFHB 5, ed. H. Thurn (Berlin and New York, 1973), 419; Nicholas Mesarites, *Die Palastrevolution von Johannes Komnenos*, ed. A. Heisenberg (Würzburg, 1907).

33 P. Magdalino, 'The People and the Palace', in *The Emperor's House*, 169–80.

34 Mango, *Brazen House*, 149–69; Denker, 'Excavations', 15–16.

35 Magdalino, 'Renaissances', 67–8.

36 P. Magdalino, 'Observations on the Nea Ekklesia of Basil I', *JÖB* 37 (1987): 51–64; P. Magdalino, 'The Culture of Water in the "Macedonian Renaissance"', in *Fountains and Water Culture in Byzantium*, ed. B. Shilling and P. Stephenson (Cambridge, 2016), 130–44, esp. 138–41; P. Magdalino, 'Modes of Reconstruction in Byzantine Constantinople', in *Reconstruire les villes: temps et espaces réappropriés*, ed. E. Capet, et. al. (Turnhout, 2019), 255–68.

37 Müller-Wiener, *Bildlexikon*, 223–4; N. Asutay-Effenberger, 'The Blachernae Palace and its Defense', in *Cities and Citadels in Turkey: From the Iron Age to the Seljuks*, ed. S. Redford and N. Ergin (Leuven, 2013), 253–76; R. Macrides, 'The Citadel of Constantinople', in *Cities and Citadels*, 277–304; Macrides et al., *Pseudo-Kodinos*, 367–70.

38 Robert of Clari, 82; Macrides, 'Citadel', 279–80.

39 Symeon Logothete, *Chronicle*, 135.11, ed. S. Wahlgren, *Symeonis Magistri et Logothetae chronicon*, CFHB 44/1 (Berlin and New York, 2006), 301.

40 M. Psellos, *Chronographia*, VI.21; Asutay-Effenberger, 'Blachernae Palace', 258–60.

41 P. Magdalino, 'Pseudo-Kodinos' Constantinople', in *Studies on the History and Topography of Byzantine Constantinople* (Aldershot and Burlington, 2007), no. XII, esp. 3–5, 13–14.

42 Müller-Wiener, *Bildlexikon*, 244–7; N. Asutay-Effenberger, *Die Landmauer von Konstantinopel* (Berlin and Boston, 2007), 134–42.

43 'God-guarded palace' at Holy Apostles: P. Magdalino, 'Around and About the Holy Apostles', in *The Holy Apostles* ed. M. Mullett and R. Ousterhout (Washington, DC, 2020), 131–42; dining hall and apartment at the Pege: *Book of Ceremonies*, 108–14.

44 Magdalino, 'Modes of Reconstruction'.

45 Skylitzes Continuatus, ed. E. Tsolakes, tr. with introduction and commentary E. McGeer and J. Nesbitt, *Byzantium in the Time of Troubles. The Continuation of the Chronicle of John Skylitzes (1057-1070)*.(Leiden and Boston, 2020), 50–51.

46 Anna Komnene, *Alexiad*, XV. 11, 9; John Zonaras, *Epoitomae historiarum*, vol. 3, ed. Th. Büttner-Wobst (Bonn, 1897), 759. Cf. F. Spingou, 'Snapshots from the Eleventh Century: The Lombards from Bari, a Chartularios from Petra, and the Complex of the Mangana', *BMGS* 39 (2015): 50–65, esp. 61–5.

47 *Theophanes Continuatus*, ed. Bekker, 431; Skylitzes, ed. Thurn, 252; *Book of Ceremonies*, II.6, (Reiske/Moffatt-Tall p., 532).

48 H. Hellenkemper, 'Politische Orte? Kaisersommerpaläste in Konstantinopel', in *The Emperor's House*, 243–56.

49 H. Maguire, 'Gardens and Parks in Constantinople', *DOP* 54 (2000): 251–64.

50 Hellenkemper, 'Politische Orte?', 251; K. Belke, 'Tore nach Kleinasien : die Konstantinopel gegenüberliegenden Häfen Chalkedon, Chrysopolis, Hiereia und Eutropiu Limen', in *Die byzantinischen Häfen*, 161–71, esp. 166–7.

51 Evident from the context of its mention in *Book of Ceremonies*, II.19 (Reiske/Moffatt-Tall, p. 609).

52 C. Mango, *Studies on Constantinople* (Aldershot, 1993), addenda, I.

53 *Book of Ceremonies*, I.55, 56, 57, 61, 63 (Reiske/Moffatt-Tall, pp. 236, 241, 242, 244, 251, 254, 255, 268, 271).

54 Michael Psellos, *Chronographia*, VII.99 (a 6).

55 Sozomenos, *Church History*, II.3, 4.

56 Themistios, *Orations*, XVIII, 222d–223a, *Themistii orationes quae supersunt*, vol. 1, ed. H. Schenkel.and G. Downey (Leipzig, 1965), 321–2.

57 P. Magdalino, 'Neighbourhoods in Byzantine Constantinople', in *Hinter den Mauern und auf dem offenen Land: Neue Forschungen zum Leben im byzantinischen Reich*, ed. F. Daim and

J. Drauschke (Mainz, 2016), 23–30 at 26–7; A. Berger, *Untersuchungen zu den Patria Konstantinupoleos* (Bonn, 1988), 173–5.

58  Synesios of Cyrene, *Letters*, no. 61, ed. A. Garzya (Rome, 1979), 176.

59  Magdalino, 'Modes of Reconstruction'.

60  P. Magdalino, 'The House of Basil the Parakoimomenos', in *Le saint, le moine et le paysan: Mélanges d'histoire byzantine offerts à Michel Kaplan*, ed. O. Delouis, S. Métivier and P. Pagès (Paris, 2016), 323–8; Th. Ganchou, 'La tour d'Irène' (Eirene Kulesi) à Istanbul: le palais de Loukas Notaras?', *Travaux et Mémoires* 21/1 (2017): 169–256.

61  G. Kazan, 'What's in a Name? Constantinople's Lost "Golden Gate" Reconsidered', in *Discipuli Dona Ferentes: Glimpses of Byzantium in Honour of Marlia Mundell Mango*, ed. T. Papacostas and M. Parani (Turnhout, 2017), 291–320.

62  See generally, G. Dagron, *Emperor and Priest: The Imperial Office in Byzantium* (Cambridge, 2003).

63  R. J. Macrides, 'Killing, Asylum and the Law in Byzantium', *Speculum* 63 (1988): 509–38.

# 9: RESIDENTIAL CONSTANTINOPLE

## Albrecht Berger and Philipp Niewöhner

This chapter considers Constantinopolitan domestic architecture by examining written sources and material remains. It discusses the evidence chronologically and according to social group, distinguishing between the early Byzantine period and the middle and late Byzantine periods to demonstrate that, institutional continuity notwithstanding, the makeup of the residential city and its components changed over time.

## LITERARY SOURCES

### Terminology

In Greek, *oikos* or its derivative designations *oikia* and *oikema* may refer to almost any residential building. Oikos denotes anything from a simple house on a square ground plan to a big tenement or an aristocratic palace. In a wider sense, *oikos* also included a household's members: the landlord, his family, servants and slaves.[1] *Domos*, in contrast, is mostly associated with the imperial sphere.

Latin terminology was more differentiated. *Domus* corresponds to *oikos*, while *insula* originally denoted a city block on which a *domus* was built. When, in the Imperial period, multi-storied tenement buildings partially replaced the houses of Rome, *insula* was applied to each floor.[2] In Rome, a *vicus* was a residential quarter or the street leading through it. This terminology is partially adopted in the only Latin document referring to Constantinople, the *Notitia urbis Constantinopolitanae* (*c*.425).[3]

The *Notitia*[4] is the basic source for early Byzantine Constantinople's topography. It describes the city's fourteen regions, enumerating houses, monuments, public buildings and officials. Comparison between regions and the numbers of houses, guild members and public baths in each shows that elite residences clustered around the main urban arteries, and along the shores of the Bosporos and the Sea of Marmara, while non-elite residences occupied the slopes above the Golden Horn.[5] The numbers also demonstrate that more than half of the city's housing stood on less than 30 per cent of its surface in the commercial regions facing the Golden Horn.

Because the *Notitia* lists 4,388 *domus*, but no *insulae*, we must assume that *domus* refers to both types of residences. The text also lists 322 *vici sive angiportus*, 'streets or alleys'.[6] Most belonged to the prestigious regions along the main street, the Mese, and were probably high-class residential building compounds that should not be counted with the houses.[7]

Finally, the *Notitia* also lists five palaces, six 'divine houses' (*domus divinae*), and three 'most noble houses' (*domus nobilissimae*). Not all are identifiable, but the owners named are female members of the Theodosian dynasty (379–457). Except for the houses of Marina and Pulcheria, later sources do not mention these residences again. Judging by the number of houses in the *Notitia*, Constantinople's population around 425 was probably no more than 150,000–200,000 people. Thereafter, it seems to have steadily increased, until plague hit the city in 542, at which time the population may have numbered between 300,000 and 400,000.[8]

In later periods the social life of common people mostly took place in smaller neighbourhoods centred on old aristocratic houses (*oikoi*), many of which had been converted to social welfare institutions such as hospitals or old people's homes, often with a public bath.[9] No fixed terminology exists for these neighbourhoods, and the word *geitonia*, from *geiton* (neighbour), is used throughout the Byzantine age for units of different size and character.[10]

## Imperial Residences

The main imperial residence from the fourth to the eleventh centuries was the Great Palace. Located at the eastern end of the Constantinopolitan peninsula, its oldest part,[11] planned and partially built in the time of Constantine (306–37), lay on the southeast flank of the Hippodrome. Now concealed by the seventeenth-century mosque of Sultan Ahmed, its reconstruction is based on literary evidence, mainly the tenth-century *Book of Ceremonies*.[12]

The palace was accessible from the north-east through the court of the Tribunal and a colonnaded marble portal. A smaller horseshoe-shaped court stood behind it, giving access to an assembly hall on the left and a dining hall on the right. The inner palace with the coronation hall and emperor's private apartments followed in a straight line to the south-west. The shape of individual buildings is unknown, except for that of the elongated dining hall which had nine niches on either side and one at the end, all equipped with dining couches.

Additions expanded the complex. Around 500, a new monumental entrance was built, the Chalke or Brazen Gate.[13] Administrative buildings and barracks were added on the terraced eastern slopes, and a ceremonial space, the Chrysotriklinos (Golden Hall), built under Justin II (565–78), extended the palace towards the Sea of Marmora.[14] Justinian II (first reign 685–95) added two reception halls; Constantine V (741–75) the Pharos Chapel.[15] Later, Theophilos (829–42) built several small pavilions, and Basil I (867–86) added the New Church and the Kainourgion (New Palace),[16] while simultaneously restoring abandoned older buildings.[17] In 965 Nikephoros II Phokas (963–9) built a fortification wall.[18] The last known addition is the Mouchroutas, a Seljuq-style pavilion from around 1170.

From the late eleventh century, the Blachernai Palace in the city's north-west corner was used increasingly for official purposes. Originally a complex of reception halls and residential buildings used by emperors visiting the nearby Blachernai church, it was expanded under Alexios I (1081–1118) and Manuel I (1143–80).[19] By the mid-twelfth century it was the main imperial residence, and the old palace was used for ceremonial purposes.

The Latin emperors after 1204, and the Byzantine emperors after 1261, alternated residence between the Great Palace and the Blachernai Palace. Both complexes were slowly decaying, and the Great Palace lay almost completely in ruins at the time of the Ottoman conquest in 1453.

## Elite Residences

In the early Byzantine period imperial family members and high-ranking aristocrats built luxurious residences. Concentrated along main streets such as the Mese, the Long Portico and the road leading to the church of Holy Apostles, they often were built on hilltops or elevated terraces with substructures. Most early houses fell into ruin during the seventh and eighth centuries, and, as with churches and palaces, the new aristocratic houses built after that time were smaller than their predecessors. A twelfth-century description of an aristocratic house from the middle Byzantine period, which was probably once owned by Nikephoros III Botaneiates (1078–81),[20] indicates that it was actually a complex of buildings including two churches on several terraces with extensive substructures.

## Non-elite Residences

Little is known about the residences of ordinary people. When the population increased rapidly after c.380, tenement houses must have become common. With the seventh- and eighth-century population decrease, big tenements disappear from the records. Later sources mention no houses of more than two or three storeys.

## Monasteries

Monks, who first appeared in the city around 340, were part of the resident population. Initially they were not much more than beggars, often supported by aristocratic sponsors. After 381 they began to settle outside the Constantinian walls. The first monastery was that founded by the Syrian monk Isaakios (d. 416).[21] Constantinopolitan synod subscription lists indicate that the number of monasteries rose from twenty-three in 448 to seventy-three in 536. Most early communities were between the Constantinian and Theodosian walls or in the less densely settled western part of the Constantinian city.

When Constantinople's population declined during the seventh and eighth centuries, many monasteries perished too. Few old houses were restored during the ninth-century recovery. Instead monks began to invade the central residential areas, often taking over older structures. Monasteries were created by adding residential buildings to churches. Conversely, palaces were converted into monasteries or charitable institutions by building a new church onto a restored oikos. Thus, a Theodosian palace became the Myrelaion monastery, and the house of Hilara was turned first into a hospital and then into the Pantokrator monastery.[22]

In the middle Byzantine period, new monasteries typically sprang up in peripheral areas. The Hodegon monastery, a foundation of unclear date, the ninth-century Lazaros monastery, the eleventh-century Mangana monastery, attached to a new imperial palace, and the twelfth-century monastery of Christ Philanthropos all followed this pattern.

Hostels and welfare institutions such as hospitals, old age homes and orphanages were associated with these communities and made up an important element of the residential cityscape in the early and middle Byzantine periods. Many were established in former aristocratic houses, and were often connected to a public bath.

In the late period, when the city again lost inhabitants, some monasteries extended their possessions, such as the fourteenth-century Bebaia Elpis (Sure Hope) monastery. Its walls eventually enclosed between fifteen and twenty hectares in in what once had been the most congested area of Constantinople.[23]

## Jewish Residences

Jews lived in Constantinople from the fourth century;[24] however, there is no evidence that they were required to live separately before the eleventh century, when Constantine Monomachos (1042–55) expelled them in 1044.[25] Most settled just outside the sea walls on the Constantinopolitan side of the Golden Horn,[26] before being forced out again in 1061 when they relocated to Pera on the opposite side.[27] In 1165 about 2,500 Jews are reported to have lived there.[28] Expelled by the Crusaders after 1204, they returned in 1261, living outside the walls in the southern Vlanga region.[29]

## Merchant Quarters

At least since the tenth century, when the Rhos (Russians) were installed in an abandoned imperial residence on the Bosporos, foreign merchants were accommodated in separate housing.[30] From the late eleventh century 'concessions', special zones near the harbours on the Golden Horn, were granted to Italian merchants. The first was given to the Venetians in 1082 or 1092; it extended uphill from the 'old Jewish wharf' and included three wharves, a church and an administrative building.[31] It was not walled, and a public road, the Long Portico, ran across it.[32] Enlarged after 1204, the concession eventually included three-eighths of the city.[33]

The Pisans founded a concession in 1111,[34] the Genoese in 1169. Originally across the Golden Horn in Galata/Pera, the Genoese concession eventually moved to Constantinople proper where it consisted of a wharf, an area near the water, and a separate complex, the 'Palace of Botaneiates'. Having been expelled from Constantinople after 1204, the Genoese returned in 1267 and were granted the entire suburb of Galata/Pera. Although a treaty of 1303 defined the concession's limits and prohibited fortification, the Genoese soon built a city wall, extending it in 1348 to the Galata Tower on the hill above the settlement.[35] Galata/Pera was quickly and densely built up and survived the end of Byzantine rule.

## ARCHAEOLOGICAL EVIDENCE

### Elite Residences

Numerous early Byzantine elite residences survive, albeit as ruins. The Theodosian period provides the earliest archaeological evidence. Surviving residences manifest the same architectural features that signal elevated living in other cities: porticoes, peristyle courts, vestibules, reception and dining halls, floor mosaics, marble wall revetment, vaults, domes and private baths.

Sigma-shaped porticoes lined the approaches to many residences: the building that belonged to the Theodosian chamberlain Antiochos,[36] its neighbour, the palace of Lausos,[37] a residence in the Mangana quarter[38] and the palace that became the Myrelaion church and monastery (Fig. 9.1).[39]

At the palace of Lausos, the sigma-shaped portico opened onto a domed vestibule with eight lateral niches that in turn led to a reception and dining room. The Myrelaion palace showed a similar arrangement; a sigma-shaped portico preceded a rotunda with six lateral niches. Décor included a floor mosaic with personifications and hunting themes, and marble wall revetment from Docimium in Phrygia.[40] The Myrelaion rotunda may have served as a vestibule, but except for some porticoes and a smaller, second rotunda that appears to have housed a private bath, the rest of the palace is unknown.[41]

Reception and dining halls had either central or longitudinal plans, with at least one apse for seating the landlord. Both the palace of Antiochos and the Mangana-quarter building had hexagonal halls, probably domed, that included four lateral conchs for accommodating dinner guests. The palace of Lausos had an apsed longitudinal hall with six smaller conchs. Another apsed hall appears to have been part of an extensive complex overlooking the Golden Horn on the peninsula's northern side. Although sometimes identified with the later palace of Botaneiates,[42] the apsed hall makes an early Byzantine date more likely.[43]

A large Theodosian hall with a mosaic floor and surrounding porticoes north-west of Hagia Sophia may also have been a palace,[44] and the Walker Trust Peristyle,[45] a sixth- or seventh-century court, may

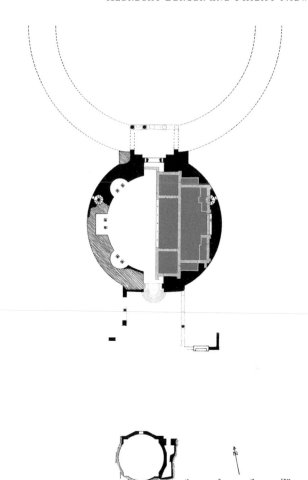

9.1 The Myrelaion Rotunda (black) and Palace (superimposed grey outline to right), Istanbul, early and middle Byzantine periods. (Plan courtesy of R. Naumann and P. Niewöhner)

have formed part of an elite residence on the imperial palace's southern flank. Its mosaic floor with a potpourri of hunting, outdoor and gaming scenes conforms to the common repertoire of elite representation seen throughout the empire. A mosaic floor from what appears to have been another large, vaulted, possibly domed, dining hall depicts the Triumph of Dionysus, probably dates from the second half of the fifth century, and occupies the centre of what may have been a sigma-shaped dining area.[46] The Walker Trust Peristyle gave onto an apsed hall, whose marble entablature blocks indicate opulent wall revetment (Fig. 9.2).[47]

9.2 Early Byzantine cornice block associated with the wall revetment of the apsed hall next to the Walker Trust peristyle, Istanbul Archaeological Museum Inv. 2320. (Photo courtesy of P. Niewöhner)

This early Byzantine tradition was discontinued,[48] and early palaces were often reconfigured. The Antiochos palace became the church of St Euphemia no later than the seventh century,[49] and by the eighth century the main hall of the palace of Lausos was turned into an open-air cistern that was partially built over by a mausoleum annexed to St Euphemia.[50] The apsed hall north-west of Hagia Sophia also became a cistern,[51] and the hexagonal hall in the Mangana quarter was altered, possibly as a bath.[52] The Walker Trust peristyle was walled off, its mosaic floor covered.[53] The complex was in ruins by the mid-twelfth century.[54]

The Myrelaion rotunda was repurposed for use both as a cistern and as a middle Byzantine palace substructure (Fig. 9.1).[55] Location aside, the later palace had nothing in common with its early Byzantine predecessor. It was smaller, with thinner walls, and, in contrast to the horizontal footprint of earlier residences, it was probably a lofty, multi-storied, tower-like block. As with some earlier residences, the Myrelaion complex also became church property: its last secular resident, Romanos I Lekapenos (920–44), converted it into a monastery.

As the Myrelaion indicates, a new kind of elite residence emerged in middle Byzantine Constantinople. While some early residences may not have been remodelled,[56] new building suggests that the idea and

9.3 South façade of the late Byzantine Tekfur Saray, the former palace of the Porphyrogennetos Constantine. (Photo courtesy of P. Niewöhner)

ideal of elite housing had essentially changed, and that later replace-ments were smaller and less substantial. Tower-like residences similar to the Myrelaion palace became the norm, as the thirteenth-century Tekfur Sarayı suggests. Identified with the palace of the Porphyrogennetos Constantine, the third son of Michael VIII (1259–82),[57] its southern façade combines a tall, unapproachable lower zone of massive ashlar masonry with a lofty top storey of colourful brickwork and panoramic windows affording splendid views across the city (Fig. 9.3).[58] The north elevation gives onto a walled yard and displays a rhythmical arrangement of arched openings and brickwork on three storeys, moderating the building's defensive character. The city walls attach to the complex and form part of the yard enclosure.

Similar features characterize Mermerkule, the remains of a fifteenth-century residence,[59] and the Tower of Eirene in mid-town Constantinople that was later integrated into Ottoman structures.[60] These Constantinopolitan palaces share their blocky, tower-like configuration, ground floor defensive walls and panoramic upper windows with elite middle Byzantine provincial residences at Syllaion in Pamphylia,[61] Nymphaeum in Asia[62] and Eskihisar in Bithynia.[63] Similarly, at Syllaion and at Eskihisar upper storeys were built on top of and overlooked city or fortress walls. These middle and late Byzantine palaces stand in a tradition of rural elite houses that started to replace urban residences in the fifth century.[64] The landed aristocracy appears to have brought this tradition to Constantinople when, beginning in the middle Byzantine period, it became increasingly involved in the capital and court.[65]

## IMPERIAL RESIDENCES

The Great Palace survives only in tantalizing fragments,[66] for example the partially excavated Chalke gate.[67] Located next to the hippodrome and connected to it by an imperial viewing box (*kathisma*), the palace's general design and structure echoed the relationship between the Palatine and Circus Maximus at Rome or the design of palace-hippodrome complexes in the Tetrarchic capitals of Milan, Trier, Sirmium, Thessalonike and Antioch.[68]

Over time emperors absorbed neighbouring elite residences and extended the palace east and south to the city walls and the seashore. Suites with panoramic windows were eventually built on top of and overlooking the maritime fortifications.[69] Some may have been from the early Byzantine period and were thus comparable to the sea façade of Diocletian's fourth-century palace at Split.[70] Others were from middle Byzantine times.[71] One part had its own landing and was known as *Boukoleon*, which is attested as the name of a mid-seventh century courtier who may have been responsible for the building work.[72]

The middle Byzantine period brought changes. While the Constantinian palace appears to have served ceremonial functions until at least the tenth century,[73] the actual residence seems to have shifted to adjacent areas within the complex whose more recent buildings would have been smaller and easier to maintain.[74] Any remaining early

9.4 Middle Byzantine Tower of Isaac Angelos (1185–1195, 1203–1204) from the southwest. (Photo courtesy of P. Niewöhner)

traditions were further weakened, when, in the twelfth century, emperors took up residence and started to conduct business in the Blachernai palace,[75] substantially remodelling it.[76] One of the few remaining buildings, the tower of Isaac Angelos (1185–95, 1203–4), forms a single room perched on top of and overlooking the land walls (Fig. 9.4) in a manner similar to the residences at Syllaion and Eskihisar/ Niketiaton. Thus, in contrast to the Roman and early Byzantine periods, imperial palaces of the middle and late Byzantine age emulated those of the landed aristocracy.

Emperors also maintained country residences near Constantinople.[77] During the reigns of Theodosios I (379–95) and Justinian I (527–65), a villa southwest of the city at Rhegion[78] occupied an elevated position above the Sea of Marmara. There it formed an extensive complex of colonnades, courtyards and rooms comparable to Hadrian's villa at Tivoli or the Tetrarchic country residence near Piazza Armerina on Sicily, including apsidal halls that may have been used for audiences and dining, and a bath building.[79]

Byzantine authors refer occasionally to buildings in an oriental, or foreign, style, thus confirming the native Byzantine character[80] of all other imperial palace architecture. The ninth-century extra-urban palace in Bryas, on the Bosporos's Asiatic side, was built when John the Grammarian returned from an embassy to the Abbasid court in Syria and provided a description of an Arab model.[81] Around 1200 Nicholas Mesarites elaborated on the strange features of a palace hall that he calls Mouchroutas that was allegedly the work of 'a Persian hand'.[82] These references would hardly make sense if other palace buildings were also of foreign origin.

## FURTHER READING

Anderson, B., 'Social Clustering in 5th-c. Constantinople: The Evidence of the Notitia', *JRA* 29 (2016): 494–508.

Bardill, J., 'Visualizing the Great Palace of the Byzantine Emperors at Constantinople: Archaeology, Text, and Topography', in *Visualisierungen von Herrschaft. Frühmittelalterliche Residenzen – Gestalt und Zeremoniell*, ed. F. A. Bauer (Istanbul, 2006), 5–45.

Berger, A., 'The Byzantine Court as a Physical Space', in *The Byzantine Court: Source of Power and Culture*, ed. A. Ödekan, E. Akyürek and N. Necipoğlu (Istanbul, 2013), 3–12.

Berger, A., *The Byzantine Neighborhood: Urban Space and Political Action*, ed. B. Anderson and F. Kondyli, 2022.

Magdalino, P., 'Neighbourhoods in Byzantine Constantinople', in *Hinter den Mauern und auf dem offenen Land: Neue Forschungen zum Leben im byzantinischen Reich*, ed. F. Daim and J. Drauschke (Mainz, 2016), 23–30.

Niewöhner, P., 'The late Late Antique Origins of Byzantine Palace Architecture', in *The Emperor's House: Palaces from Augustus to the Age of Absolutism*, ed. M. Featherstone, J.-M. Spieser, G. Tanman, and U. Wulf-Rheidt (Berlin and Boston, 2015), 31–52.

Rice, D. T., ed., *The Great Palace of the Byzantine Emperors: Second Report* (Edinburgh, 1958).

## NOTES

1 P. Magdalino, 'The Byzantine Aristocratic *Oikos*', in *The Byzantine Aristocracy IX to XII Centuries*, ed. M. Angold (Oxford, 1984), 92–111.

2 L. P. Homo, *Rome impériale et l'urbanisme dans l'antiquité* (Paris, 1951); J.-P. Guilhembet, 'La densité des domus et des insulae dans les XIV régions de Rome selon les Régionnaires: représentations cartographiques', *MEFRA* 108 (1996): 7–26.

3 C. Strube, 'Der Begriff Domus in der Notitia Urbis Constantinopolitana', in *Studien zur Frühgeschichte Konstantinopels*, ed. H.-G. Beck (Munich, 1973), 121–34.

4 J. Matthews, *Notitia Urbis Constantinopolitanae*, in *Two Romes. Rome and Constantinople in Late Antiquity*, ed. L. Grig and G. Kelly (Oxford, 2012), 81–115; A. Berger, 'Regionen und Straßen im frühen Konstantinopel', *IstMitt* 47 (1997): 349–414, esp. 350–6.

5 B. Anderson, 'Social Clustering in 5th-c. Constantinople: The Evidence of the Notitia', *JRA* 29 (2016): 494–508, esp. 505.

6 Matthews, '*Notitia*', 87.

7 A. Berger, 'The View from Byzantine Texts', in *Byzantine Neighborhoods*, ed. B. Anderson and F. Kondyli (forthcoming).

8 A. E. Müller, 'Getreide für Konstantinopel: Überlegungen zu Justinians Edikt XIII als Grundlage für Aussagen zur Einwohnerzahl Konstantinopels im 6. Jahrhundert', *JÖB* 43 (1993): 1–20.

9 P. Magdalino, 'The House of Basil the Parakoimomenos', in *Le saint, le moine et le paysan, Mélanges d'histoire byzantine offerts à Michel Kaplan*, ed. O. Delouis, S. Métivier, and P. Pagès (Paris, 2016), 323–8.

10 Berger, 'The View', and Magdalino, 'House of Basil', 23–30.

11 J. Kostenec, 'The Heart of the Empire: The Great Palace of the Byzantine Emperors Reconsidered', in *Secular Buildings and the Archaeology of Everyday Life in the Byzantine Empire*, ed. K. Dark (Oxford, 2004), 4–36.

12 Constantine Porphyrogennetos, *The Book of Ceremonies*, ed. and trans. A. Moffatt and M. Tall (Canberra, 2012). Includes the Greek text of I. I. Reiske's edition (Bonn, 1829).

13 C. Mango, *The Brazen House: A Study of the Vestibule of the Imperial Palace of Constantinople* (Copenhagen, 1959).

14 M. Featherstone, 'The Chrysotriklinos as Seen through *De Cerimoniis*', in *Zwischen Polis, Provinz und Peripherie: Beiträge zur byzantinischen Geschichte und Kultur*, ed. A. Monchizadeh and L. M. Hoffmann (Wiesbaden, 2005), 845–52.

15 H. Klein, 'Sacred Relics and Imperial Ceremonies at the Great Palace of Constantinople', in *Visualisierung von Herrschaft. Frühmittelalterliche Residenzen: Gestalt und Zeremoniell*, ed. F. A. Bauer (Istanbul, 2006), 79–99.

16 J. Bardill, 'Visualizing the Great Palace of the Byzantine Emperors at Constantinople: Archaeology, Text, and Topography', in *Visualisierungen von Herrschaft*, 5–45.

17 M. Featherstone, 'Der Große Palast von Konstantinopel: Tradition oder Erfindung?', *BZ* 106 (2013): 119–38.

18 C. Mango, 'The Palace of the Boukoleon', *CahArch* 45 (1997): 41–50.

19 N. Asutay-Effenberger, 'The Blachernai Palace and Its Defense', in *Cities and Citadels in Turkey from the Iron Age to the Seljuks*, ed. S. Redford and N. Ergin (Leuven, 2013), 253–76.

20 M. Angold, 'Inventory of the So-called Palace of Botaneiates', in *The Byzantine Aristocracy*, 254–66.

21 G. Dagron, 'Les moines et la ville: Le monachisme à Constantinople jusqu'au concile de Chalcédoine (451)', *TM* 4 (1970): 227–76.

22 P. Magdalino, 'Medieval Constantinople', in Magdalino, *Studies on the History and Topography of Byzantine Constantinople* (London, 2007), no. I, esp. 50–2.

23 A. Effenberger, 'Die Klöster der beiden Kyrai Martha und die Kirche des Bebaia Elpis- Klosters in Konstantinopel', *Millennium* 3 (2006): 255–94.

24 D. Jacoby, 'The Jews of Constantinople and Their Demographic Hinterland', in *Constantinople and Its Hinterland*, ed. C. Mango and G. Dagron (Aldershot, 1995), 221–32, esp. 221–2.

25 D. Jacoby, 'Les quartiers juifs de Constantinople à l'époque byzantine', *Byzantion* 37 (1967): 167–227, esp. 168–75.

26 As suggested by *Annae Comnenae Alexias*, 6. 5. 10.

27 Jacoby, 'Quartiers juifs', 175–89.

28 Benjamin of Tudela, *The Itinerary of Benjamin of Tudela* (Malibu, 1983), 72.

29 Benjamin of Tudela, *The Itinerary of Benjamin of Tudela*, 189–96.

30 J. Pargoire, 'Saint-Mamas, le quartier des Russes à Constantinople', *Échos d'Orient* 11, no. 71 (1908): 203–310; A. Berger, *Untersuchungen zu den Patria Konstantinupoleos* (Bonn, 1988), 697.

31 D. M. Nicol, *Byzantium and Venice: A Study in Diplomatic and Cultural Relations* (Cambridge, 1988); T. F. Madden, 'The Chrysobull of Alexius I Comnenus to the Venetians: The Date and the Debate', *JMedHist* 28/2 (2002): 199–204; P. Frankopan, 'Byzantine Trade Privileges to Venice in the Eleventh Century: The Chrysobull of 1092', *JMedHist* 30/2 (2004): 135–60; P. Magdalino, 'The Maritime Neighborhoods of Constantinople: Commercial and Residential Functions, Sixth to Twelfth Centuries', *DOP* 54 (2000): 209–26, esp. 222–6; D. Jacoby, 'The Venetian Quarter of Constantinople from 1082 to 1261: Topographical Considerations', in *Novum Millennium: Studies on Byzantine History and Culture Dedicated to Paul Speck*, ed. C. Sode and S. Takács (Aldershot, 2001), 153–70, esp. 155–7.

32 Berger, *Untersuchungen*, 442–4.

33 Berger, *Untersuchungen*, 160–7; D. Jacoby, 'The Venetian Government and Administration in Latin Constantinople, 1204–1261: A State within a State', in *Quarta crociata: Venezia – Bisanzio – Impero Latino*, ed. G. Ortalli, G. Ravegnani and P. Schreiner, 2 vols (Venice, 2006), 1: 19–79, esp. 36–42.

34 S. Borsari, 'Pisani a Bisanzio nel XII secolo', *Bollettino Storico Pisano* 60 (1991): 59–75; D. Jacoby, 'Pisan Presence and Trade in Late Byzantium', in *Koinotaton Doron: Das späte Byzanz zwischen Machtlosigkeit und kultureller Blüte*, ed. A. Berger, S. Mariev, G. Prinzing and A. Riehle (Berlin, 2016), 47–59.

35 A. M. Schneider and M. I. Nomidis, *Galata, topographisch-archäologischer Plan* (Istanbul, 1944).

36 H. Belting and R. Naumann, *Die Euphemia-Kirche am Hippodrom zu Istanbul und ihre Fresken* (Berlin, 1966), 13–23, 34–44.

37 R. Naumann, 'Vorbericht über die Ausgrabungen zwischen Mese und Antiochus-Palast 1964 in Istanbul', *IstMitt* 15 (1965): 135–48; J. Bardill, 'The Palace of Lausus and Nearby Monuments in Constantinople', *AJA* 101 (1997): 67–95; M. Alexaki, Icons as Punishers. Two Narrations from the Vaticanus gr. 1587 Manuscript (BHG 1390 f)', *BZ* 114 (2021): 35–64.

38 R. Demangel and E. Mamboury, *Le quartier des Manganes et la première région de Constantinople* (Paris, 1939), 81–93; S. Ćurčić, *Architecture in the Balkans: From Diocletian to Süleyman the Magnificent* (New Haven, 2010), 87–9; D. Daffara, 'L'edificio di Gülhane a Costantinopoli', *Thiasos* 5 (2016): 69–88.

39 R. Naumann, 'Der antike Rundbau beim Myrelaion und der Palast Romanos I. Lekapenos', *IstMitt* 16 (1966): 199–216.

40 P. Niewöhner, 'The Rotunda at the Myrelaion in Constantinople: Pilaster Capitals, Mosaics, and Brick Stamps', in *The Byzantine Court: Source of Power and Culture*, ed. A. Ödekan, E. Akyürek and N. Necipoğlu (Istanbul, 2013), 25–36.

41 D. T. Rice, 'Excavations at Bodrum Camii, 1930', *Byzantion* 8 (1933): 151–74, esp. 158–62; S. Ćurčić, 'Design and Structural Innovation in Byzantine Architecture before Hagia Sophia', in *Hagia Sophia from the Age of Justinian to the Present*, ed. R. Mark and A. Ş. Çakmak (Cambridge, 1992), 16–38, esp. 29–31, figs 26–7.

42 C. Wulzinger, 'Byzantinische Substruktionsbauten Konstantinopels', *JDAI* 28 (1913): 370–95, esp. 376–82.

43 The original masonry of pure brickwork conforms to an early Byzantine date. The mixed masonry is later: P. Verzone, *Palazzi e domus: dalla tetrarchia al VII secolo* (Rome, 2011), 85–8.

44 R. Duyuran, 'Mosaiques découvertes près de la prefecture d'Istanbul', *Istanbul Arkeoloji Müzesi Yıllığı* 9 (1960): 70–2; Ö. Dalgiç, 'Early Floor Mosaics in Istanbul', in *Mosaics of Anatolia*, ed. G. Sözen (Istanbul, 2011), 101–12, esp. 103–5, figs 2–3; P. Niewöhner, 'The Decline and Afterlife of the Roman Entablature: The Collection of the Archaeological Museum Istanbul and other Byzantine Epistyles and Cornices from Constantinople', *IstMitt* 67 (2017): 237–328, esp. 271–4, figs 70–6.

45 D. T. Rice (ed.), *The Great Palace of the Byzantine Emperors: Second Report* (Edinburgh, 1958); W. Jobst, R. Kastler and V. Scheibelreiter, *Neue Forschungen und Restaurierungen im byzantinischen Kaiserpalast von Istanbul* (Vienna, 1999). J. Bardill, 'Visualizing the Great Palace', 12–20.

46 Ö. Dalgic, 'The Triumph of Dionysus in Constantinople: A Late Fifth-Century Mosaic in Context', *DOP* 69 (2015): 15–47.

47 Niewöhner, 'Decline and Afterlife', 286–91, figs 111–21.

48 K. R. Dark, 'Houses, Streets, and Shops in Byzantine Constantinople from the Fifth to the Twelfth Centuries', *JMedHist* 30/2 (2004): 83–107, esp. 97–8; R. Ousterhout, 'Constantinople and the Construction of Medieval Urban Identity', in *The Byzantine World*, ed. P. Stephenson (London, 2010), 334–51.

49 A. Berger, 'Die Reliquien der heiligen Euphemia und ihre erste Translation nach Konstantinopel', *Hellenika* 39 (1988): 311–22.

50 One of the mausolea appears to have been depicted on the Trier Ivory in 796: P. Niewöhner, 'Historisch-topographische Überlegungen zum Trierer Prozessionselfenbein, dem Christusbild an der Chalke, Kaiserin Irenes Triumph im Bilderstreit und der Euphemiakirche am Hippodrom', *Millennium* 11 (2014): 261–88 at 280.

51 M. Harrison and G. R. J. Lawson, 'The Mosaics in Front of the Vilayet Building in Istanbul', *Istanbul Arkeoloji Müzesi Yıllığı* 13/14 (1966): 216–18, esp. 216 suggest a sixth-century date for the cistern, because the bricks, mortar and masonry looked early to them.

52 See note 38.

53  G. Brett, W. J. Macaulay and R. B. K. Stevenson, *The Great Palace of the Byzantine Emperors: First Report* (Oxford, 1947), 16, 33–5; D. T. Rice (ed.), *The Great Palace of the Byzantine Emperors: Second Report* (Edinburgh, 1958), 9. Cf. M. Featherstone, 'Theophilus's Margarites: The "Apsed Hall" of the Walker Trust?' in *Di Bisanzio dirai ciò che è passato, ciò che passa e che sarà. Scritti in onore die Alessandra Guiglia*, ed. S. Pedone and A. Paribeni (Rome, 2018), 173–86.

54  Rice, *Second Report*, 44.

55  K. Wulzinger, *Byzantinische Baudenkmäler zu Konstantinopel auf der Seraispitze, die Nea, das Tekfur-Serai und das Zisternenproblem* (Hannover, 1925), 98–108; Naumann, *Euphemia- Kirche*.

56  Magdalino, 'House of Basil', 323–8; P. Magdalino, 'Constantinople in the Age of Constantine VII Porphyrogennetos', in *Center, Province and Periphery in the Age of Constantine VII Porphyrogennetos*, ed. N. Gaul, V. Menze and C. Bálint (Wiesbaden, 2018), 39–54, esp. 45–8; P. Magdalino, 'Modes of Reconstruction in Byzantine Constantinople', in *Reconstruire les villes: temps et espaces réappropriés*, ed. E. Capet et al. (Turnhout, 2019), 255–67.

57  C. Mango, 'Constantinopolitana', *JDAI* 80 (1965): 305–36, esp. 334–6.

58  A. Van Millingen, *Byzantine Constantinople: The Walls of the City and Adjoining Historical Sites* (London, 1899), 109–14; Wulzinger, *Byzantinische Baudenkmäler*, 63–89; B. Meyer-Plath and A. M. Schneider, *Die Landmauer von Konstantinopel*, 2 vols (Berlin, 1943), 2: 95–100; N. Asutay-Effenberger, *Die Landmauer von Konstantinopel-Istanbul* (Berlin, 2007), 135–42; F. Yenişehirlioğlu, 'Les fours et la production des céramiques du palais de Tekfur à Istanbul', in *Actas del VIII Congreso Internacional de Cerámica Medieval*, 2 vols. (Ciudad Real, 2009), 2: 617–32 ; S. Ćurčić, *Architecture*, 528–30.

59  U. Peschlow, 'Die befestigte Residenz von Mermerkule', *JÖB* 51 (2001): 385–401; Asutay-Effenberger, *Landmauer*, 110–17; S. Ćurčić, 'Georgios Palaiologos Kantakouzenos (1390–c. 1459): An Unknown Late Byzantine Architect', in *Ἥρως Κτίστης. Μνήμη Χαράλαμπου Μπούρα*, ed. M. Korres et al. (Athens, 2018), 139–52, esp. 144–8.

60  A. Berger, 'Zur Topographie der Ufergegend am Goldenen Horn in der byzantinischen Zeit', *IstMit* 45 (1995): 149–65, esp. 158; T. Ganchou, '"La tour d'Irène" (Eirene Kulesi) à Istanbul: le palais de Loukas Notaras?', in *Οὗ δῶρόν εἰμι τὰς γραφὰς βλέπων νόει: Mélanges Jean-Claude Cheynet*, ed. B. Caseau, V. Prigent and A. Sopracasa (Paris, 2017), 169–256.

61  C. Foss, 'The Cities of Pamphylia in the Byzantine Age', in C. Foss, *Cities, Fortresses, and Villages of Byzantine Asia Minor* (London, 1996), no. II, esp. 20–1; P. Niewöhner, 'The Late Late Antique Origins of Byzantine Palace Architecture', in *The Emperor's House*, 31–52, esp. 41–2, figs 9–10.

62  H. Buchwald, 'Lascarid Architecture', *JÖB* 28 (1979): 261–96, esp. 263–8; S. Çağaptay, 'How Western Is It? The Palace at Nymphaion and Its Architecture', in *Change in the Byzantine World in the Twelfth and Thirteenth Centuries*, ed. E. Akyürek, N. Necipoğlu and A. Ödekan (Istanbul, 2010), 357–62; Niewöhner, 'Late Antique Origins', 42–3, figs 12–13.

63  Foss, 'Cities of Pamphylia', 50–8; Niewöhner, 'Late Antique Origins', 40–1, fig. 8.

64  Niewöhner, 'Late Antique Origins'; Niewöhner, 'Houses', in *The Archaeology of Byzantine Anatolia*, ed. P. Niewöhner (New York, 2017), 39–59.

65  Angold, 'Inventory', 236–53; P. Stephenson, 'The Rise of the Middle Byzantine Aristocracy and the Decline of the Imperial State', in *The Byzantine World*, 22–33; P. Schreiner, 'The Architecture of Aristocratic Palaces in Constantinople in Written Sources', in *The Byzantine Court*, 53–6; A. Berger, 'Städtische Eliten im byzantinischen Raum', in *Städte im lateinischen Westen und im griechischen Osten zwischen Spätantike und Früher Neuzeit*, ed. E. Gruber, M. Popović, M. Scheutz and H. Weigl (Vienna, 2016), 165–75, esp. 169–71; L. Andriollo and S. Métivier, 'Quel rôle pour les provinces dans la domination aristocratique au X^{ie} siècle?', in *Autour du premier humanisme byzantin & des Cinq études sur le XI^{e} siècle, quarante ans après Paul Lemerle*, ed. B. Flusin and J.-C. Cheynet (Paris, 2017), 505–29.

66  J. Kostenec, 'The Heart of the Empire. The Great Palace of the Byzantine Emperors Reconsidered', in *Secular Buildings and the Archaeology of Everyday Life*, 4–36; Bardill, 'Visualizing the Great Palace'; C. Barsanti, 'Le chiese del Grande Palazzo di Costantinopoli', in *Medioevo: La chiesa e il palazzo*, ed. A. C. Quintavalle (Milano, 2007), 87–100; F. Tülek, 'A Fifth Century Floor Mosaic and a Mural of Virgin of Pege in Constantinople', *CahArch* 52 (2005–2008): 23–30; A. Berger, 'The Byzantine Court as a Physical Space', in *The Byzantine Court*, 3–12; N. Westbrook, *The Great Palace in Constantinople* (Turnhout, 2019).

67  Ç. Girgin, 'La porte monumentale trouvée dans les fouilles près de l'ancienne prison de Sultanahmet', *Anatolia antiqua* 16 (2008): 259–90; A. Denker, 'The Great Palace', in *Byzantine*

*Palaces in Istanbul*, ed. G. Baran Çelik et al. (Istanbul, 2011), 11–69, esp. 16–17; A. Cutler and P. Niewöhner, 'Towards a History of Byzantine Ivory Carving from the Late Sixth to the Late Ninth Century', in *Mélanges Catherine Jolivet-Lévy*, ed. B. Pitarakis et al. (Paris, 2016), 89–108, esp. 93–8.

68 D. Chatzilazarou, 'Le centre monumental de Constantinople, espace de synthèse des traditions urbaines gréco-romaines', in *Constantinople réelle et imaginaire autour de l'œuvre de Gilbert Dagron* (*TM* 21.1), ed. C. Morrisson and J.-P. Sodini (Paris, 2018), 35–54; L. Mulvin and N. Westbrook (ed.), *Late Antique Palatine Architecture* (Turnhout, 2018).

69 E. Mamboury and T. Wiegand, *Die Kaiserpaläste von Konstantinopel zwischen Hippodrom und Marmara-Meer* (Berlin, 1934), 1–25.

70 Ćurčić, *Architecture*, 86.

71 Rice, *Second Report*, 168–93; Bardill, 'Visualizing the Great Palace', 35–9; Ćurčić, *Architecture*, 270.

72 C. Mango, 'The Palace of the Boukoleon', *CahArch* 45 (1997): 41–50; C. Barsanti, 'Un inedito disegno delle rovine del complesso costantinopolitano del Boukoléon', in *Forme e storia: scritti di arte medievale e moderna per Francesco Gandolfo*, ed. W. Angelelli and F. Pomarici (Rome, 2011), 45–58; D. Heher, 'Der Palasthafen des Bukoleon', in *Die byzantinischen Häfen Konstantinopels*, ed. F. Daim (Mainz, 2016), 67–88; P. Magdalion, 'Renaissances d'une capitale', in: *Constantinople réelle et imaginaire, autour de l'œuvre de Gilbert Dagron* (*TM* 21.1), ed. C. Morrisson and J.-P. Sodini (Paris, 2018), 55–77, at 65 f.

73 M. Featherstone, 'Space and Ceremony in the Great Palace of Constantinople under the Macedonian Emperors', in *Le corti nell'alto Medioevo*, 2 vols. (Spoleto, 2015), 2: 587–610.

74 M. Featherstone, 'The Everyday Palace in the Tenth Century', in *The Emperor's House*, 149–58.

75 F. Tinnefeld, 'Der Blachernenpalast in Schriftquellen der Palaiologenzeit', in *Lithostroton: Studien zur byzantinischen Kunst und Geschichte. Festschrift für Marcell Restle*, ed. B. Borkopp and T. Steppan (Stuttgart, 2000), 277–85; R. Macrides, 'The "Other" Palace in Constantinople: The Blachernai', in *The Emperor's House*, 159–68.

76 A. M. Schneider, 'Die Blachernen', *Oriens* 4 (1951): 82–120; N. Asutay-Effenberger, 'The Blachernai Palace and Its Defense', in *Cities and Citadels in Turkey from the Iron Age to the Seljuks*, ed. S. Redford and N. Ergin (Leuven, 2013), 253–76; H. F. Yılmaz, U. M. Ermiş and F. Özgümüş, 'Report of the New Findings from Byzantine Istanbul', *IstMitt* 67 (2017): 329–56, esp. 339–42.

77 S. Runciman, 'The Country and Suburban Palaces of the Emperors', in *Charanis Studies: Essays in Honor of Peter Charanis*, ed. A. E. Laiou-Thomadakis (New Brunswick, 1980), 219–28; H. Hellenkemper, 'Politische Orte? Kaiserliche Sommerpaläste in Konstantinopel', in *The Emperor's House*, 243–56.

78 A. M. Mansel, 'Les fouilles de Rhegion près d'Istanbul', in *Actes du Ve Congrès International d'Etudes Byzantines*, 2 vols (Paris, 1951), 2: 256–60; Verzone, *Palazzi e domus*, 169–81.

79 Ćurčić, *Architecture*, 91, figs 83–4.

80 T. F. Mathews and A.-C. Daskalakis-Mathews, 'Islamic-Style Mansions in Byzantine Cappadocia and the Development of the Inverted T-Plan', *JSAH* 56/3 (1997): 294–315; C. Bouras, 'The Impact of Frankish Architecture on Thirteenth-Century Byzantine Architecture', in *The Crusades from the Perspective of Byzantium and the Muslim World*, ed. A. E. Laiou and R. P. Mottahedeh (Washington, DC, 2001), 247–62; N. Asutay-Effenberger, 'Spuren seldschukischen Lebensstils in der imperialen Architektur Konstantinopels im 12. Jahrhundert', in *Grenzgänge im östlichen Mittelmeerraum*, ed. U. Koenen and M. Müller-Wiener (Wiesbaden, 2008), 169–87; Çağaptay, 'How Western Is It?'; Ćurčić, *Architecture*, 271, 353–4, 528–31.

81 *Chronographiae quae Theophanis Continuati nomine fertur. Libri I–IV*, ed. M. Featherstone and J. Signes-Codoñer (Berlin, 2015), 142 (book 3, chapter 9). Cf. S. Eyice, 'Un palais byzantin construit d'après les plans des palais abbasides: Le palais de Bryas', *Belleten* 23 (1959): 79–104; A. Walker, *The Emperor and the World* (Cambridge, 2012), 41–4.

82 N. Mesarites, *Die Palastrevolution des Johannes Komnenos*, ed. A. Heisenberg (Würzburg, 1907), 44–6. Cf. N. Asutay-Effenberger, '"Muchrutas": Der seldschukische Palastpavillon im Großen Palast von Konstantinopel', *Byzantion* 74 (2004): 313–29; Walker, *Emperor and the World*, 175–6; S. Redford, 'Constantinople, Konya, Conical Kiosks, Cultural Confluence', in *The Byzantine Court*, 41–7.

## 10: COMMERCIAL CONSTANTINOPLE

### Koray Durak

From the fourth century, when the Gothic King Athanaric expressed his astonishment at the bustle of ships in Constantinople's harbors,[1] until its fall to the Ottoman Turks in 1453, Constantinople was the commercial capital of the Byzantine Empire. In this long period, two major turning points are identifiable: the seventh century, which saw the end of the capital's late antique development; and the Crusader invasion of 1204, which interrupted an economic expansion that had started in the ninth century and left the city subservient to European commercial dominance. This chapter examines the commercial development of Constantinople, concentrating on the city's commercial topography, its provisioning, trade networks, merchant class, and manufacturing industries as well as government control over them.

### LATE ANTIQUITY, FOURTH THROUGH SEVENTH CENTURIES

With commercial and harbor facilities on the Golden Horn, pre-Constantinopolitan Byzantion was an emporium that prospered from tolls imposed on boats traveling between the Black Sea and the Mediterranean.[2] It was not, however, a match for Alexandria or Antioch until Constantine (306–37) transformed it into the seat of his empire. From that moment, Constantinople grew richer together with the eastern Mediterranean region.[3] A large population rich with consumer potential made late antique Constantinople an enormous market. Grain, olive oil, and wine, the quintessential needs of every Mediterranean metropolis, arrived predominantly from the empire's southern provinces. Egypt, North Africa, Macedonia, Thrace, Bithynia, and western Asia Minor provided grain.[4] Oil and wine came from Syria, Palestine, Cilicia, Cyprus, and Asia Minor's Aegean coast, as amphorae from the Saraçhane and Yenikapı harbor excavations

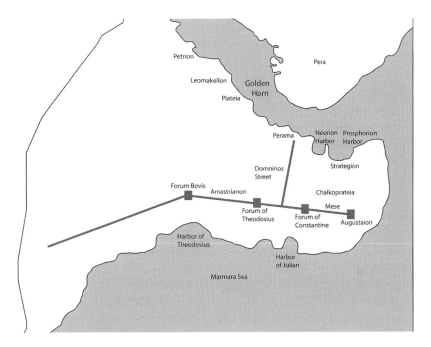

10.1 Map of Constantinople showing commercial areas. (Map courtesy of K. Durak)

indicate.[5] The state's role in provisioning is debated, but current scholarship favors a free-trade model. For instance, *Annona civica* – the system for requisitioning wheat, wine, oil, dried legumes, and lard for provisioning Constantinople – met the demands of only 27 percent of the city's population. Other foods such as meat, fish, and vegetables were outside the system. Moreover, the vessels of the ship-owners' guild and the contract transporters that carried *annona* grain to Constantinople filled their ships with commercial goods for their return voyages.[6]

Imperial warehouses (*horrea*) for storing *annona* shipments were close to the city's harbors (Fig. 10.1). The late antique Julian and Theodosian ports on the Marmara coast had two grain *horrea*, which also may have stored building materials for the expanding city. More important were three *horrea* and an oil storehouse at the Prosphorion and the Neorion harbors on the Golden Horn. The location of private provisioning storage facilities is unknown, but probably was close to the harbors. Most bread was sold in private bakeries throughout the city. *Macella* (fish and meat markets) were concentrated around the Theodosian Forum (modern Beyazıt) and the Strategion (Eminönü). There were, therefore, two areas of commercial activity for foodstuffs:

the section between the Prosphorion harbor and the Strategion, and the area between the Julian and Theodosian harbors and the Theodosian Forum.[7]

The market for manufactured goods was also lively, sustained by imports and local production. Syrian silk found customers, as did glass from the Syrio-Palestinian coast. African red slip tableware followed the main sea route connecting the coast of central North Africa with Constantinople via the Peloponnesos, and competed in the city's markets with Phocaean red slip ware.[8] Constantinople had its own industries and merchants too. In the sixth and seventh centuries the city exported goods around the Mediterranean: copper objects went everywhere, metal buckles to Sardis, marble architectural elements to Italy, building tiles to Mesembria, cloth to Carthage.[9] The raw materials needed for the city's manufacturing industries were metal (especially silver and copper), wood, raw silk, textiles, papyrus, skin/fur, and ingredients for perfume. Regarding the commercial topography, workshops, many of which acted as shops selling finished goods, were concentrated around the main avenue, the Mese, which was crossed by Domninos Street, a commercial thoroughfare, and the road connecting the Augustaion (Sultanahmet) to the Strategion. Booksellers were in the Basilica and coppersmiths in the Chalkoprateia district, both of which were close to the Augustaion. Skin-dressers/furriers and goldsmiths clustered between the Augustaion and the Forum of Constantine (Fig. 10.1).[10]

Although sixth-century records indicate that there were some local importers, most appear to have been provincials until the seventh century when more Constantinopolitan merchants ventured abroad.[11] Constantinopolitan bankers supported merchants with loans. Interest rates depended on the lender's status and the type of commercial activity undertaken. In Justinianic law, interest rates for aristocrats were 4 percent per year, 8 percent for commercial establishments. Maritime loans could reach 12 percent because of the risk involved. Copper coins (follis) were better for daily transactions than gold (solidus), especially after Anastasios' (491–518) reforms ended inflation in smaller denominations.[12] Some commercial activity was taxed. For example, charges were collected from ship-owners sailing toward Constantinople at Hieron at the northern mouth of the Bosporos and at Abydos in the Hellespont. Justinian turned these checkpoints into customs stations, where officials collected the duty known as the octava (12.5 percent). Anastasios' abolition of chrysargyron/collatio lustralis, a tax on artisans and merchants instituted by Constantine, brought relief for many.[13] State jurisdiction over credit mechanisms, coinage, and taxation extended to guilds, which the city prefect supervised. Guilds, especially those less vital to state interests, probably enjoyed more freedom from state control than once thought.[14] In brief, from trade routes and goods, to legal infrastructures and ideology, Constantinople's commerce was bound to late Roman Mediterranean production and exchange systems within an economic structure that was responsive, but not tied to the state's needs.

## AN ECONOMIC POWERHOUSE, SEVENTH THROUGH TWELFTH CENTURIES

The seventh century saw the loss of some of the empire's richest provinces to political actors such as Arabs, and the introduction of a new administrative system limiting the role for cities. In Constantinople the population fell below 100,000 after the sixth-century plague and the termination of *annona*. Only one imperial warehouse remained: Lamia, near the Theodosian harbor. With the transfer of commercial facilities to the Julian harbor in the sixth century and the navy's later removal to the Neorion, southern harbors and neighborhoods grew in commercial significance,[15] and Constantinople continued to act as a magnet for commerce, albeit on a diminished scale.[16] Grain now came from nearby regions, with occasional supplies from North Africa and Sicily, at least until the late seventh-century Islamic conquests.[17] Long-distance trade in ceramics persisted into the late seventh century, as deposits of African red slip ware and Syro-Palestinian amphorae from Saraçhane indicate. By the eighth century, however, more localized networks predominated, as eighth-century levels in the Yenikapı excavations suggest.[18] A new Constantinopolitan product, glazed white ware I, replaced older wares, but distribution was limited to the Aegean, Cyprus, and Cherson.[19] Shrinking trade networks confirm this regionalization. As a social group, Constantinopolitan artisans were important; however, they were small-scale operators compared to the merchant-officials who controlled the production and sale of commodities, like silk, slaves, and provisions.[20]

## *Controlled Development, Ninth and Tenth Centuries*

Byzantium's ninth- and tenth-century political and economic expansion benefited the Byzantine capital. Constantinople received grain from Thrace, Bithynia, Macedonia, Thessaly, western Asia Minor, and Bulgaria. The baker's guild bought grain and made bread, which was sold at bakeries in the Artopoleia district between the Constantinian and Theodosian fora and shops throughout the city.[21] Wine came from the Aegean islands, Bithynia, Thrace, and coastal Bulgaria; local production *intra muros* or in nearby Chalcedon was also considerable. Most wine must have arrived via sea: the late tenth-/early eleventh-century Yenikapı Shipwreck I shows that wine was shipped in amphorae from the Marmora Sea's northern shore. Once arrived, taverners sold it throughout the city.[22] Shepherds and swineherds supplied meat, driving animals on hoof from hinterlands such as Nikomedia, while some butchers went as far as the river Sangarios to meet sellers of flocks from the Anatolia plateau. Animal markets were in the Forum of Theodosios, the Strategion, and the Amastrianon.[23] Apart from the gourmet needs of the few, produce grown in the Constantinopolitan hinterland and gardens around the Theodosian walls met the demand for fresh fruits and vegetables. Fishermen tended nets in the Bosporos and the Marmara Sea. Although they occasionally sold fish themselves in the city, fishmongers, permitted to sell only at *macella* and markets on the Golden Horn, were required to buy from fishermen at wharves or on the beach.[24]

Constantinople had a developed manufacturing industry.[25] A large construction industry employed builders, stonemasons, gypsum workers, locksmiths, carpenters, and painters. Pottery workshops produced glazed white wares and polychrome ware, while a glass a workshop close to the Strategion indicates the existence of glass production. The textile industry (predominantly silk and linen) was also significant. Raw silk and silk from the Near East was sold on the Mese and at the Forum of Constantine, as was linen. Tanners prepared and cut skins for harnesses, saddles, and shoes, and skin-dressers/furriers operated in the Forum of Constantine. Goldsmiths/jewelers occupied a section of the Mese between the Forum of Constantine and the Augustaion, coppersmiths the Chalkoprateia. Perfumers, soap makers, and chandlers catered to personal and domestic needs. Candle-makers were in many neighborhoods, the Forum of Constantine, Domninos Street, and the Hagia Sophia area included. Perfumers were strategically located in the Augustaion so that the sweet smells could reach the Great Palace.[26] In sum, foodstuffs and animals were marketed in an outer band stretching from the Strategion and its harbor Prosphorion to the Forum of Theodosios and the Amastrianon, which had access to the Julian and Theodosian harbors. Manufactured goods were sold in an inner band, with luxury goods concentrated on the strip between the Great Palace and the Constantinian forum (Fig. 10.1).[27]

Until the eleventh century Byzantium traded with three major international economic zones. It maintained close relations with Umayyads, Abbasids, and Fatimids, especially after the early tenth century. Islamic merchants bought silk, rarer items such as books and hunting birds, and high-end products in Constantinople, selling textiles and aromatics in return. The city was also a transit point for trade between the Slavic and Islamic worlds (linen and walrus tusk for Mediterranean markets; silk and pepper for Bulgarian and Russian markets).[28] Merchants from the Near East stored their merchandise in the *mitaton* (inn), located toward the Golden Horn, possibly in Perama (Eminönü). Some stayed for only a few months, others for years. Arab merchants in traditional garb ("black garment and brick-colored shoes") could be seen in the Forum Bovis (modern Aksaray) in the 950s.[29]

The Black Sea, especially its western and northern coasts, constituted a second zone. Bulgaria was an important partner. Wine amphorae, ceramics, cups, and plates from Constantinople were discovered in shops in the Bulgarian capital, Preslav. Silk and fruits from Byzantium were also traded. In exchange, Bulgarian merchants brought honey and linen to Constantinople.[30] After treaties of 911 and 944, the Rhoss (Rus') brought slaves, furs, wax, and honey to the capital. They stayed outside the walls, near St. Mamas, and were only allowed to enter the city in small, unarmed groups to buy limited amounts of silk. The northern Black Sea region was also a source of salted fish, caviar, and naphtha, and a market for painted glass vessels, bracelets, and beads.[31] Ceramic finds and amphorae excavated on the western and northern Black Sea coast connect these regions to Constantinople.[32] Finally, Italian cities, especially Venice and Amalfi, linked Constantinople to Western Europe. Venetians carried slaves, iron, wood, weapons, and cloth to the empire, and imported silk and spices from Byzantium and furs from the Black Sea.[33] In short, Constantinople imported raw materials and cheaper commodities from northern and western neighbors, engaged in a highly developed commerce with the Islamic south, exported its finished products in all directions, and was a transit center for Black Sea–Mediterranean trade.

Constantinopolitan artisans and merchants worked under a mixed regime of free market and state intervention in the ninth and tenth centuries. The state-controlled guild system prevented monopolies, protected consumers, ensured the supply of provisions, and supported the government's strategic concerns. The state did not determine prices, but contributed to their formation via mechanisms such as just price and just profit. Entrepreneurs secured capital through loans or partnerships.

Goldsmiths and money-changers located in the commercial districts, the Mese especially, loaned money using Justinianic interest rates. Partnership typically involved a two-person contract in which one party supplied capital, the other labor, and both shared the profit. A simple trimetallic exchange system used one denomination for each metal without fractions: a gold *nomisma*, silver *miliaresion*, and copper *follis*. Artisans and merchants, who usually did not own their workshops, paid tax on property they rented. They met obligations to guilds and the city eparch through payment and corvée, and paid commercial taxes, especially *kommerkion*, a 10 percent charge on goods entering Constantinople.[34] To sum up, Constantinople and its hinterland was an economic region protected by the state. The city eparch monitored foreign merchants, controlled their commercial activities, and limited their stays. Moreover, although all imports were welcome, export of metals, arms, and top-quality silk was forbidden. These arrangements would change in the coming centuries.[35]

## An Expanding Market, Eleventh and Twelfth Centuries

Amid empire-wide economic growth in the eleventh and twelfth centuries Constantinople again became a cosmopolitan city with a huge consumer base and a powerful artisan and merchant class.[36] The rising middle class and the elite selected from commodities arriving from the provinces and foreign countries: consumers favored Thracian Ganos wine over that of Varna, and many customers preferred Seljuk pottery to local wares.[37] Constantinopolitan merchants began journeying to Egypt, and the wealth of merchants and bankers attracted imperial attention as a source of income.[38] Merchants and artisans took on important roles in city politics, were instrumental in expressing the people's will, and briefly obtained the right to become senators, a privilege normally reserved for the landed/administrative elite.[39]

From the ninth to the twelfth centuries, Constantinople was a center for local, regional, interregional, and international commerce. Local partners included suburbs west to Selymbria and those on the Bosporos's Asian shore. Regional trade extended to Thrace and Bithynia, with the ports of Rhaidestos, Abydos, Kyzikos, and Pylai connected directly to the capital.[40] Inter-regionally, the southern Black Sea coast furnished linen (Pontos and Kerasous), and was a transit center for the spice trade (Trebizond). In the eleventh and twelfth centuries the empire's southwestern reaches supplied murex (Peloponnesos), silk (Thebes, Andros), raw silk (Calabria), olive oil (Sparta), cheese, and sweet wine (Crete). Amphorae from shipwrecks and pottery distribution indicate that between the ninth and thirteenth centuries there were two major sea routes to the capital, one running from southern Greece along the west Aegean coast, and another from the eastern Mediterranean following the east coast of Asia Minor.[41]

In this period Constantinopolitan merchants found new partners and faced competitors from abroad. Ayyubid and Seljuk merchants frequented the city regularly. Italians, however, represented the fastest-growing group. In 1082, Alexios I Komnenos (1081–1118) allowed Venetians to establish a quarter in Constantinople and to trade tax-free in most Byzantine ports. To balance Venetian power, similar privileges were given to Pisans in 1111 and the Genoese in 1155.[42] Nevertheless, Venetians became the protagonists in Byzantium's foreign trade, importing wood, metals, arms, and cloth from the Mediterranean and western Europe. They also gained some control over internal trade, carrying Theban silk and provisions such as Spartan olive oil to Constantinople. This competitive edge and other Italians' entry into the city's retail market angered Constantinople's productive classes, as government action against Venetians (1171) and an anti-Latin pogrom (1182) confirm.[43]

Although the commercial center moved toward the Marmara coast in the middle Byzantine period, the lower Golden Horn was still bustling with artisans' shops. The Islamic *mitaton* and the Leomakellon retail market (near Unkapanı) contributed to its commercial life, and the establishment of Italian quarters between the Neorion and Perama aided the area's resurgence as the main trading center by the twelfth century (Fig. 10.1).[44] A more liberal trade environment existed in the eleventh and twelfth centuries. Both landlords and peasants used market mechanisms to provision Constantinople, with the state intervening in times of crisis. Increased investment resulted in higher interest rates, an incentive to releasing captive capital. Small wonder that clerics and aristocrats became involved in lending and trading activities from this period onward. Sources reveal a more positive attitude toward profit seeking. The guild system became more liberal, allowing room for the "free professions" of law and money-changing. By the twelfth century Constantinopolitan merchants used an articulated monetary system: a gold *hyperpyron*, a *trachy aspron* of 30 percent gold, a copper–silver alloyed *stamenon*, and a copper *tetarteron*. It is true that Italian merchants stimulated commercial exchange, but their privileges harmed the economically protected status of Constantinople. Finally, seizure of the Queen of Cities in 1204 completed their penetration of the market.[45]

## PART OF A LARGER WHOLE, THIRTEENTH THROUGH FIFTEENTH CENTURIES

The Fourth Crusade and the subsequent Latin rule (1204–61) had a negative impact on the Constantinopolitan economy. The court fled to areas under Byzantine rule along with a significant portion of the population, artisans included. Although fires in 1203 and 1204 destroyed commercial districts, the Venetian quarter was repaired and some Venetians grew rich during the Latin rule.[46] The Byzantine capture of the city in 1261 and the following two centuries witnessed the evolution of Constantinople's commercial organization. Its diminishing population and the loss of the hinterland to Turks and Serbs led to a decline in demand, while a flood of western goods and Italian domination negatively affected Constantinople's industries and merchant class. For example, by the mid-fourteenth century annual customs revenues of the Genoese in Pera were approximately six times higher than those of Constantinople.[47]

Italians provisioned the city with grain, oil, wine, dried fruits, and cheese from the Aegean, the Black Sea, Italy, and Spain. Merchants from Constantinople and Monemvasia in southern Greece were also involved, but their networks were limited to the Aegean and the Black Sea coasts. Venetians and the Genoese dominated the luxury market, leaving Byzantine merchants the trade in raw materials, food, and textiles. Constantinopolitan merchants thus played an active but subsidiary role.[48] However, retail traders and artisans in Constantinople were mostly local, although Venetians and Greek speakers with Venetian citizenship also participated in the workforce. For instance, in 1350 Byzantine authorities protested the number of taverns owned by Venetian traders. Next to provisioning, textiles, clothing, construction, and transportation represented the major trades. Italians now imported textiles, arms, and glass to Byzantium. Italian and Islamic fine wares fully penetrated the market, and the production of Constantinopolitan glazed white ware did not resume after 1204. The remaining artisans manufacturing luxury goods served a small circle. Overall, manufacturing and exchange declined in comparison to the Comnenian period.[49]

Despite these negative developments, opportunities remained. Constantinople's role as a transit center between Mediterranean and

Black Sea networks increased. Venetians and Genoese imported Mediterranean alimentary products and textiles for distribution to Ottoman Asia Minor and the Black Sea region, while they exported grain, slaves, and silk from the Black Sea to the Mediterranean and Europe. Muslim and Christian Greek merchants from Ottoman territories visited Constantinople regularly, while Byzantine merchants traded with Bursa. Other European communities – Florentines, Anconitans, Ragusans, and Catalans – were established in the capital by the fifteenth century.[50] Enterprising Constantinopolitan sailors, merchants, and bankers gained from cooperation with the Italians. As governmental and ideological barriers against commercial entrepreneurship disappeared, artisans joined guilds that were more independent of state control, and aristocrats, who had fewer opportunities for investing in land, turned increasingly to trade.[51]

Topographic development followed earlier patterns. The Golden Horn, with its docks and warehouses, became the city's commercial hub. Aristocratic and merchant houses and workshops clustered in the northwest section of town. The main food market stretched from Petrion to Plateia, along the central and upper Golden Horn (Fig. 10.1). Save for the Genoese in Pera, European merchants occupied the lower Golden Horn. The area around the Mese maintained its commercial identity, but vineyards also grew there. As the Castilian envoy Clavijo remarked, Constantinople was underpopulated, with fields and orchards in its midst. A thousand years had passed since the historian Zosimos' (460–520) claim that crowding made streets impassable.[52] In the intervening millennium, Constantine's city both retained its character and changed. Although the degree of governmental control and the profile of local and foreign merchants varied, it remained a coveted consumer market, a center of manufacturing, and a transit point between major economic zones. Throughout its history, streets connected its coastal commercial centers to the Mese, the main stage of the theater named Constantinople. That same avenue was to become the main axis of another capital, Ottoman Konstantiniyye.

## FURTHER READING

Balard, M. and A. Ducellier, eds., *Constantinople 1054–1261, tête de la chrétienté, proie des latins, capitale grecque* (Paris, 1996).

Kaplan, M., "Les artisans dans la société de Constantinople aux VIIe–XIe siècles," in *Byzantine Constantinople; Monuments, Topography and Everyday Life*, ed. N. Necipoğlu (Leiden, 2001), 245–60.

Magdalino, P., "Medieval Constantinople," in *Studies on the History and Topography of Byzantine Constantinople* (Aldershot, 2007), no. I.

Mango, M. M., "The Commercial Map of Constantinople," *DOP* 54 (2000): 189–207.

# NOTES

1 Jordanes, *Iordanis Romana et Getica*, ed. T. Mommsen (Berlin, 1882), 95.

2 "Byzantion," *RE* 3/1: 1123, 1137, 1143.

3 J.-P. Sodini, "Productions et échanges dans le monde protobyzantin (IV^e–VII^e siècle): le cas de la céramique," in *Byzanz als Raum*, ed. K. Belke, F. Hild, J. Koder, and P. Soustal (Vienna, 2000), 193; S. T. Loseby, "The Mediterranean Economy," in *NCMH:1, c.500–c.700*, ed. P. Fouracre (Cambridge, 2005), 616.

4 J. L. Teall, "The Grain Supply of the Byzantine Empire, 330–1025," *DOP* 13 (1959): 87–139, esp. 135–6; J. Durliat, "L'approvisionnement de Constantinople," in *Constantinople and Its Hinterland*, ed. C. Mango and G. Dagron (Aldershot, 1995), 19–33 at 24.

5 C. Wickham, *Framing the Early Middle Ages: Europe and the Mediterranean, 400–800* (Oxford, 2005), 708, 715, 781–2; C. Morrisson and J.-P. Sodini, "The Sixth-Century Economy," in *EHB* 1: 165–220 at 210; E. Öncü and S. Çömlekçi, "Yenikapı Kazıları ve Bizans Dönemi Amphora Buluntuları," in *XIth Congress Aiecm3 on Medieval And Modern Period Mediterranean Ceramics Proceedings*, ed. F. Yenişehirlioğlu, 2 vols. (Ankara, 2018) 1: 15–28, esp. 19–22.

6 S. Kingsley and M. Decker, "New Rome, New Theories on Inter-regional Exchange: An Introduction to the East Mediterranean Economy in Late Antiquity," in *Economy and Exchange in the East Mediterranean during the Late Antiquity*, ed. S. Kingsley and M. Decker (Oxford, 2001), 1–27 at 13; J.-M. Carrié, "Were Late Roman and Byzantine Economies Market Economies? A Comparative Look at Historiography," in *Trade and Markets in Byzantium*, ed. C. Morrisson (Washington, 2012), 13–26 at 20; A. D. Lee, *From Rome to Byzantium AD 363 to 565* (Edinburgh, 2013), 237.

7 J. Matthews, *Notitia Urbis Constantinopolitanae*, in *Two Romes, Rome and Constantinople in Late Antiquity*, ed. L. Grig and G. Kelly (Oxford, 2012), 81–115 at 104, 107; P. Magdalino, "The Maritime Neighborhoods of Constantinople: Commercial and Residential Functions, Sixth to Twelfth Centuries," *DOP* 54 (2000): 209–26, esp. 211–12; M. M. Mango, "The Commercial Map of Constantinople," *DOP* 54 (2000): 187–209 at 190, 193, 198.

8 Prokopios, *The Anecdota or Secret History*, ed. and trans. H. B. Dewing (London, 1954), 296; Ş. Atik, "Late Roman/Early Byzantine Glass from the Marmaray Rescue Excavations at Yenikapı in Istanbul," in *Late Antique/Early Byzantine Glass in the Eastern Mediterranean*, ed. E. Laflı (Izmir, 2009), 1–16 at 3; C. Abadie-Reynal, "Céramique et commerce dans le bassin Égéen du IV^e au VII^e siècle," in *Hommes et richesses dans l'Empire Byzantin I. IV–VII siècle* (Paris, 1989), 143–59, esp. 150, 156–7; Wickham, *Framing*, 714, 781; J. W. Hayes, *Excavations at Saraçhane in Istanbul*, 2 vols. (Princeton, 1992), 2: 5–6; for African red slip ware finds in Yenikapı, see R. Asal, "Commerce in Istanbul and the Port of Theodosius," in *Istanbul: 8000 Years, brought to Daylight – Marmaray, Metro, Sultanahmet Excavations*, ed. A. Karamani- Pekin and S. Kangal (Istanbul, 2007), 180–9 at 184.

9 A. H. M. Jones *The Later Roman Empire, 284–602: A Social, Economic and Administrative Survey*, 3 vols. (Oxford, 1964), 2: 688, 857; M. M. Mango, "Beyond the Amphora: Non-Ceramic Evidence for Late Antique Industry and Trade," in *Economy and Exchange*, 87–106 at 95–6; C. Foss and J. A. Scott "Sardis," in *EHB* 2: 615–22 at 616; J.-P. Sodini, "Marble and Stoneworking in Byzantium, Seventh- Fifteenth Centuries," in *EHB* 1: 129–46 at 133; A. Poulter, "The Use and Abuse of Urbanism in the Danubian Provinces during the Later Roman Empire," in *The City in Late Antiquity*, ed. J. Rich (London, 2001), 99–135 at 131; H. Magoulias, "The Lives of the Saints as Sources of Data for the History of Commerce in the Byzantine Empire in the VIth and VIIth Cent.," *Kleronomia* 4 (1971): 303–30 at 309–10.

10 Agathias, *Agathiae Myrinaei Historiarum libri quinque*, ed. B. G. Niebuhr (Bonn, 1828), 128; *Chronicon Paschale*, ed. L. Dindorf, 2 vols. (Bonn, 1832) 1: 622–3; *CIC CI*, iv.59.2; *The Miracles of St. Artemius*, ed. and trans. V. S. Crisafulli and J. W. Nesbitt (Leiden, 1997), 91, 129, 159; Magoulias, "The Lives," 306–7; Mango, "Commercial Map," 197.

11 Constantine Porphyrogennetos, *Three Treatises on Imperial Military Expeditions*, ed. J. F. Haldon (Vienna, 1990), 140; Prokopios, *The Anecdota*, 296; P. Magdalino, "The Merchant of Constantinople," in *Trade in Byzantium*, ed. P. Magdalino and N. Necipoğlu (Istanbul, 2016), 181–91 at 182–4.

12 *CIC Nov*, 106; D. Gofas, "The Byzantine Law of Interest," in *EHB* 3: 1095–104 at 1096–8; Morrisson and Sodini, "The Sixth Century Economy," in *EHB* 1: 212.

13 H. Antoniadis-Bibicou, *Recherches sur les douanes à Byzance: l'Octava, le Kommerkion et les commerciaires* (Paris, 1963), 76–8; Jones, *The Later Roman Empire*, 1: 110, 237, 2: 826–7, 3: 271; Prokopios, *The Anecdota*, 290, 292.

14 P. Garnsey and C. Whittaker, "Trade, Industry, and the Urban Economy," in *CAH*, 13, ed. Av. Cameron and P. Garnsey (Cambridge, 2007), 312–37 at 318–20, 325; L. Cracco Ruggini, "Collegium e corpus: la politica economica nella legislazione e nella prassi," in *Istituzioni giuridiche e realtà politiche nel tardo impero (III–IV sec. d. c)*, ed. G. G. Archi (Milan, 1976), 63–94; C. Morrisson, ed., *Le monde byzantin I: L'Empire romain d'Orient (330–641)* (Paris, 2004), 211.

15 C. Mango, *Le développement urbain de Constantinople (IVe–VIIe siècles)* (Paris, 1985), 53–60; P. Magdalino, "The Harbors of Byzantine Constantinople," in *Stories from the Hidden Harbor, Shipwrecks of Yenikapı*, ed. Z. Kızıltan (Istanbul, 2013), 11–15 at 14.

16 For a positive view, R. S. Lopez, "The Role of Trade in the Economic Readjustment of Byzantium in the Seventh Century," *DOP* 13 (1959): 67–85. N. Oikonomides describes C. Mango's description of Constantinople in the early Middle Ages in *Le développement urbain* as "a much too pessimistic view," in "The Economic Region of Constantinople: From Directed Economy to Free Economy, and the Role of the Italians," in *Europa medievale e mondo bizantino*, ed. G. Arnaldi and G. Cavallo (Rome, 1997), 199–238 at 221. For a less optimistic view, see J. Haldon, *Byzantium in the Seventh Century* (Cambridge, 1990), 114–24.

17 Teall, "The Grain Supply," 97, 117, 122; Wickham, *Framing*, 125–6.

18 C. Abadie-Reynal, "Les échanges interrégionaux de céramiques en Méditerranée orientale entre le IVe et le VIIIe siècle," in *Handelsgüter und Verkehrswege*, ed. E. Kislinger et al. (Vienna, 2010), 25–44 at 27–8; Asal, "Commerce in Istanbul," 185.

19 Wickham, *Framing*, 716–17, 782–3; J. Haldon, "Production, Distribution and Demand in the Byzantine world, c. 660–840," in *The Long Eighth Century: Production, Distribution and Demand*, ed. I. L. Hansen and C. Wickham (Leiden, 2000), 225–64 at 244–5, 249–51; Hayes, *Excavations*, 2: 4, 7, 12–18.

20 A. E. Laiou, "Exchange and Trade, Seventh–Twelfth Centuries," in *EHB* 2: 697–770 at 707–8; P. Schreiner, "Die Organisation byzantinischer Kaufleute und Handwerker," in *Untersuchungen zu Handel und Verkehr der vor- und frühgeschichtlichen Zeit in Mittel- und Nordeuropa*, ed. H. Jankuhn and E. Ebel (Göttingen, 1989), 44–61 at 47; N. Oikonomides, "Entrepreneurs," in *The Byzantines*, ed. G. Cavallo (Chicago, 1997), 144–71 at 147–8.

21 Teall, "The Grain Supply," 118–26; P. Magdalino, "The Grain Supply of Constantinople, Ninth-Twelfth Centuries," in *Constantinople and Its Hinterland*, 35–47; M. Kaplan, "Le ventre de l'Empire," in *Constantinople 1054–1261, tête de la chrétienté, proie des latins, capitale grecque*, ed. M. Balard and A. Ducellier (Paris 1996), 86–103; J. Koder, ed., *Das Eparchenbuch Leons des Weisen*, CFHB, 33 (Vienna, 1991), 128–30; Nikephoras, *The Life of St Andrew the Fool*, ed. L. Rydén, 2 vols. (Uppsala, 1995), 2:28, 92–4.

22 M. F. Hendy, *Studies in the Byzantine Monetary Economy c. 300–1450* (Cambridge, 1985), 49–51; J. Lefort, "The Rural Economy, Seventh–Twelfth Centuries," in *EHB* 1: 231–311 at 249; Teall, "Grain Supply," 125; N. Günsenin, "Ganos Wine and Its Circulation in the 11th century," in *Byzantine Trade, 4th–12th Centuries*, ed. M. M. Mango (Farnham, 2009), 145–53 at 149–50; *Eparchenbuch*, 131.

23 *Eparchenbuch*, 122–7, 134–7; Hendy, *Studies*, 562–4; Leo, Metropolitan of Synada, *The Correspondence of Leo, Metropolitan of Synada and Syncellus*, ed. M. P. Vinson (Washington, 1985), 86.

24 J. Koder, "Fresh Vegetables for the Capital," in *Constantinople and Its Hinterland*, 49–56 at 53–4; G. Dagron, "The Urban Economy, Seventh–Twelfth Centuries," in *EHB* 2: 393–462 at 447, 458; J. Koder, "Maritime Trade and the Food Supply of Constantinople in the Middle Ages," in *Travel in the Byzantine World*, ed. R. Macrides (Burlington, 2002), 109–24; G. Dagron, "Poissons, pêcheurs et poissonniers de Constantinople," in *Constantinople and Its Hinterland*, 57–73.

25 For the Constantinopolitan artisans, see M. Kaplan, "Les artisans dans la société de Constantinople aux VIIe–XIe siècles," in *Byzantine Constantinople: Monuments, Topography and Everyday Life*, ed. N. Necipoğlu (Leiden, 2001), 245–60.

26 R. Janin, *Constantinople byzantine* (Paris, 1950), 90–6; T. Thomov and A. Ilieva, "The Shape of the Market: Mapping the Book of the Eparch," *BMGS* 22, no. 1 (1998): 105–16; Mango, "Commercial Map," 202. For saleswomen selling expensive embellishments at the Forum of Constantine, see *The Life of St Andrew the Fool*, 2:140; for the fruit-seller, see 102. For glass production, see A.-M. Talbot, "The Posthumous Miracles of St. Photeine," *AB* 112 (1994): 85–104 at 101. For ceramic production and workshops, see Hayes, *Excavations*, 2: 12, 18–21, 30, 35 and K. Dark, *Byzantine Pottery* (Charleston, 2001), 85. For the shops of the skindressers/furriers and candlemakers, see *Theophanes Continuatus*, ed. I. Bekker (Bonn, 1838), 420. For the linen and silk shops at the Mese and the Forum of Constantine, see *Eparchenbuch*, 94–101 and N. Oikonomides, "Quelques boutiques de Constantinople au X$^E$ s.: prix, loyers, imposition (Cod. Patmiacus 171)," *DOP* 26 (1972): 345–56 at 347.

27 Mango, "Commercial Map," 204.

28 K. Durak, "Commerce and Networks of Exchange between the Byzantine Empire and the Islamic Near East from the Early Ninth Century to the Arrival of the Crusaders" (PhD dissertation, Harvard University, 2008), 51–169, 424–36; D. Jacoby, "Byzantine Trade with Egypt from the Mid-Tenth Century to the Fourth Crusade," *Thesaurismata* 30 (2000): 25–77.

29 Durak, "Commerce and Networks," 338–413; *Eparchenbuch*, 94; S. V. Reinert, "The Muslim Presence in Constantinople, 9th–15th Centuries: Some Preliminary Observations," in *Studies on the Internal Diaspora of the Byzantine Empire*, ed. H. Ahrweiler and A. E. Laiou (Washington, DC, 1998), 125–50 at 131–40.

30 Laiou, "Exchange and Trade," in *EHB* 2: 704; I. Jordanov, "Preslav," in *EHB* 2: 667–71 at 667–69; *Eparchenbuch*, 108.

31 J. Shepard, "Constantinople, Gateway to the North," in *Constantinople and Its Hinterland*, 253–60; I. Sorlin, "Les traités de Byzance avec la Russie au Xe siècle (I)," *Cahiers du monde russe et soviétique* 2 (1961): 313–60 at 329–37; N. Ristovska, "Distribution Patterns of Middle Byzantine Painted Glass," in *Byzantine Trade*, 199–220 at 204–7. J. Shepard, "'Mists and Portals': The Black Sea's North Coast," in *Byzantine Trade*, 421–41 at 426–27 and 435–7.

32 V. François, "A Distribution Atlas of Byzantine Ceramics: A New Approach to the Pottery Trade in Byzantium," in *Trade in Byzantium*, 143–56 at 146; N. Günsenin, "La typologie des amphores Günsenin: Une mise au point nouvelle," *Anatolia Antiqua* 26 (2018): 89–124 at 89–99.

33 D. Jacoby, "Venetian Commercial Expansion in the Eastern Mediterranean, 8th–11th Centuries," in *Byzantine Trade*, 371–91 at 372; D. Jacoby, "Silk Crosses the Mediterranean," in *Le vie del Mediterraneo; Idee, uomini, oggetti (secoli XI–XVI)*, ed. G. Airaldi (Genoa, 1997), 35–79 at 55–79; W. Heyd, *Histoire du commerce du Levant au moyen-âge*, 2 vols. (Leipzig, 1885) 1: 94, 100, 107; M. E. Martin, "The Venetians in the Byzantine Empire before 1204," *ByzF* 13 (1988): 201–14 at 212.

34 N. Oikonomides, "Un vaste atelier: artisans et marchands," in *Constantinople 1054–1261*, 104–35 at 112–17; O. Maridaki-Karatza, "Legal Aspects of the Financing of Trade," in *EHB* 3: 1105–20 at 1106–16; G. Dagron, "Urban Economy," in *EHB* 2: 423–5, 432–8; Gofas, "The Byzantine Law of Interest," in *EHB* 3: 1099–102; Laiou, "Exchange and Trade, Seventh–Twelfth Centuries," in *EHB* 2: 718, 734–5.

35 Oikonomides, "Economic Region," 221–38.

36 P. Lemerle, *Cinq études sur le XI$^e$ siècle byzantin* (Paris, 1977); M. F. Hendy, "'Byzantium, 1081–1204': The Economy Revisited Twenty Years on," in M. F. Hendy, *The Economy, Fiscal Administration and Coinage of Byzantium* (Aldershot, 1989), no. III.

37 D.-C. Hesseling and H. Pernot, eds., *Poèmes prodromiques en grec vulgaire* (Amsterdam, 1910), poem 3, 48–71; Jacoby, "Venetian Commercial Expansion," 377–8; J. Dimopoulos, "Trade of Byzantine Red Wares, from the 11th–13th Centuries," in *Byzantine Trade*, 179–90 at 183.

38 S. D. Goitein, *Mediterranean Society: The Jewish Communities of the Arab World as Portrayed in the Documents of the Cairo Geniza*, 6 vols. (Berkeley, 1967), 1: 44–6; Dagron, "Urban Economy," in *EHB* 2: 417.

39 Hendy, *Studies*, 570–90; S. Vryonis, "Byzantine Dēmokratia and the Guilds in the Eleventh Century," *DOP* 17 (1963): 287–314 at 314.

40 Dagron, "Urban Economy," in *EHB* 2: 403–4. For the effects of economic relationships between the capital and the provinces, see M. Angold, "The Shaping of the Medieval Byzantine City," *ByzF* 10 (1985): 1–38.

41 *EB*, 106–12; D. Jacoby, "Silk in Western Byzantium before the Fourth Crusade," *BZ* 84.2 (1992): 452–500 at 495–6; Jacoby, "Venetian Commercial Expansion," in *Byzantine Trade*, 377–78; François, "A Distribution Atlas," 146l J. Vroom, "Byzantine Sea Trade in Ceramics: Some Case Studies in the Eastern Mediterranean (ca. Seventh–Fourteenth Centuries)," in *Trade in Byzantium*, 157–79 at 170; Dimopoulos "Trade of Byzantine Red Wares," 181.

42 Reinert, "Muslim Presence," 140–3; M. Balard, "Un marché à prendre: l'invasion occidentale," in *Constantinople 1054–1261*, 184–201 at 184–6; D. Jacoby, "Italian Privileges and Trade in Byzantium before the Fourth Crusade: A Reconsideration," *Anuario de estudios medievales* 24 (1994): 349–68.

43 R.-J. Lilie, *Handel und Politik zwischen dem byzantinischen Reich und den italienischen Kommunen Venedig, Pisa und Genua in der Epoche der Komnenen und der Angeloi (1081–1204)* (Amsterdam, 1984), 222–41, 264–70; Oikonomides, "Un vaste atelier," 100; Jacoby. "Venetian Commercial Expansion," 377–8; D. Jacoby, "Mediterranean Food and Wine for Constantinople: The Long-Distance Trade, Eleventh to Mid-fifteenth Century," in *Handelsgüter und Verkehrswege*, 127–47 at 129–32.

44 P. Magdalino, "Medieval Constantinople," in *Studies on the History and Topography of Byzantine Constantinople* (Aldershot, 2007), no. I: 86–102; Magdalino, "Maritime Neighborhoods," 221–3.

45 M. Attaliates, *Michaelis Attaliotae Historia*, ed. I. Bekker (Bonn, 1853), 201–4; A. E. Laiou and C. Morrisson, *The Byzantine Economy* (Cambridge, 2007), 138–55, 160–2; D. Jacoby, "Byzantine Outsider in Trade," in *Strangers to Themselves: The Byzantine Outsider*, ed. D. Smythe (Aldershot, 2000), 129–47 at 131; Oikonomides, "Economic Region," 232–4.

46 L. B. Robbert, "Rialto Businessmen and Constantinople, 1204–1261," *DOP* 49 (1995): 43–58; D. Jacoby, "Venetian Settlers in Latin Constantinople (1204–1261): Rich or Poor?" in D. Jacoby, *Byzantium, Latin Romania and the Mediterranean* (Aldershot, 2001), no. VII; D. Jacoby, "Urban Evolution of Latin Constantinople (1204–1261)," in *Byzantine Constantinople*, 277–97 at 294–5.

47 N. Gregoras, *Nicephori Gregorae Byzantina Historia*, ed. L. Schopen (Bonn, 1830), 2: 841–2.

48 J. Chrysostomides, "Venetian Commercial Privileges under the Palaeologi," *Studi veneziani* 12 (1970): 267–356 at 267–89; A. E. Laiou, "The Byzantine Economy in the Mediterranean Trade System: 13th–15th Centuries," *DOP* 34 (1980): 177–222; K.-P. Matschke, "Commerce, Trade, Markets, and Money, Thirteenth–Fifteenth Centuries," in *EHB* 2: 771–806; N. Oikonomides, *Hommes d'affaires grecs et latins à Constantinople: XIIIe–XVe siècles* (Montreal, 1979), 83–92; Jacoby, "Mediterranean Food and Wine," 128–43.

49 Oikonomides, *Hommes d'affaires*, 92–105; Chrysostomides, "Venetian Commercial Privileges," 298–302; Dark, *Byzantine Pottery*, 73–5; K.-P. Matschke, "Late Byzantine Urban Economy," in *EHB* 2: 489–93; Matschke, "Commerce, Trade, Markets," in *EHB* 2: 771–2; E. Kislinger, "Gewerbe im späten Byzanz," in *Handwerk und Sachkultur im Spätmittelalter* (Vienna, 1988), 103–26 at 122–3.

50 D. Jacoby, "Constantinople as Commercial Transit Center, Tenth to Mid-fifteenth Century," in *Trade in Byzantium*, 193–210; N. Necipoğlu, "Ottoman Merchants in Constantinople during the First Half of the Fifteenth Century," *BMGS* 16 (1992): 158–69; M. Balard, "L'organisation des colonies etrangères dans l'empire byzantin (XIIe–XVe siècle)," in *Hommes et richesses dans l'Empire byzantin, II. VIIIe–XVe siècle*, ed. V. Kravari, J. Lefort, and C. Morrisson (Paris, 1991), 261–76 at 265–7.

51 A. E. Laiou-Thomadakis, "The Greek Merchant of the Palaeologan Period: A Collective Portrait," *Praktika tes Akademias Athenon* 57 (1982), 96–132; Oikonomides, *Hommes d'affaires*, 108–23; N. Necipoğlu, *Byzantium between the Ottomans and the Latins: Politics and Society in the Late Empire* (Cambridge, 2009), 193–6, 228.

52 Oikomides, *Hommes d'affaires*, 97–106; V. Kidonopoulos, *Bauten in Konstantinopel 1204–1328: Verfall und Zerstörung, Restaurierung, Umbau und Neubau von Profan- und Sakralbauten* (Wiesbaden, 1994), 203–12, 230–7; R. G. Clavijo, *Embassy to Tamerlane* (Oxon, 2005), 48; Zosimos, *Histoire nouvelle*, 3 vols., ed. and trans. F. Paschoud (Paris, 1971), 1: 108.

# II: SACRED DIMENSIONS: CHURCH BUILDING AND ECCLESIASTICAL PRACTICE

## Vasileios Marinis

All these marvels which I have recounted to you here and still a great many more than we could recount, the French found in Constantinople after they had captured it, nor do I think, for my part, that any man on earth could number all the abbeys of the city, so many there were, both of monks and nuns, aside from the other churches outside the city.[1]

Robert de Clari (d. after 1216)

The king [of Jerusalem, Amalric, d. 1174] was escorted throughout the whole city both within the walls and without. He visited the churches and monasteries of which there was an almost infinite number.[2]

William of Tyre (d. 1186)

Medieval Constantinople was a city of churches and monasteries; so many that visitors, especially foreigners, often resorted to hyperbolic description. They did so with justification. Sources provide evidence for about 500 churches of various types between the fourth and fifteenth centuries.[3] Admittedly, not all existed at the same time, and name changes over time may have led to the occasional duplication, but it is also likely that some religious establishments are not mentioned, thus evening the score. Tenth-century sources list 159 churches inside the city walls, with dozens more in the suburbs.[4] In short, ecclesiastical buildings featured prominently in Constantinople's urban landscape for most of its history. We get a sense of this presence even in contemporary Istanbul. Hagia Sophia's graceful masses still dominate Sultanahmet; the Pantokrator complex (Zeyrek Camii), between the third and the fourth hills, remains imposing, visible from many parts of the old city; and the Fatih Camii, on the highest point inside the walls, suggests the lost magnificence of Holy Apostles, whose site it occupies.

This chapter examines the relationship between church building and ecclesiastical practice in Byzantine Constantinople. The former requires no explanation. The latter refers mostly to prescribed rituals that took place inside these churches; the celebration of the Divine Liturgy and other services of the Byzantine rite.[5] It outlines the ways in which architecture accommodates and responds to the exigencies of ritual both on a practical, and on a symbolic level. Dedicatory inscriptions, liturgical commentaries, and other theological texts, although unconcerned with the interaction between architecture and liturgy, reveal how church buildings were understood symbolically as worship spaces, manifestations of piety, wealth, power, and prestige, and places of perpetual commemoration, reminding us that a Byzantine church is more than the material context for the Divine Liturgy's celebration.

## CHURCH ARCHITECTURE IN CONSTANTINOPLE

There were different types of churches in Constantinople. Justinian's legislation offers four categories, based mostly on financial status: (1) Hagia Sophia, the Great Church; (2) three churches – Hagia Eirene, Chalkoprateia, and Saint Theodore *en tois Sphorakiou* – that were attached to Hagia Sophia and served by its clergy; (3) churches with their own clergy that were financially dependent on Hagia Sophia; and (4) independent churches.[6] The last were the most numerous. For simplicity, these ecclesiastical foundations may be divided into two groups: "public" churches – *katholikai ekklesiai*, lit. "catholic churches" – and private foundations.[7] The latter encompasses a variety of structures, from small chapels attached to residences to large churches and monasteries. Because Constantinople never had an administrative division into parishes, these private foundations served the spiritual needs of the population's majority.

Churches and monasteries were slow to appear in the urban fabric. Only four ecclesiastical buildings can be attributed to the emperor Constantine (306–37).[8] About a century later, the *Notitia urbis Constantinopolitanae*, a Latin description of the city composed between 425 and 427, includes fourteen churches. There were probably more.[9] Building activity increased in the second half of the fifth century and during the reign of Justinian I (527–65).[10] According to the historian Prokopios, Justinian built or restored over thirty churches in Constantinople and its hinterland.

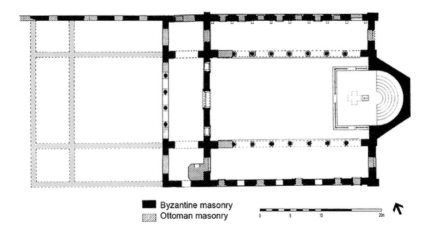

■ Byzantine masonry
▨ Ottoman masonry

11.1 Saint John Stoudios, plan, fifth century. (After R. Ousterhout)

The main church of the Stoudios monastery, from the mid-fifth century, exemplifies the city's pre-Justinianic ecclesiastical architecture (Fig. 11.1).[11] Stoudios is also significant because it was originally built as a *katholike ekklesia* before being turned into a monastery, something that was not uncommon.[12] It is a three-aisled basilica, measuring *c.*27 by 26 meters, which was originally covered by a wooden trussed roof. An atrium lay before the church to the west. A three-sided apse projects from the eastern wall. A gallery, now lost, extended over the narthex and the side aisles. Stoudios is remarkably open: there are five doors on the basilica's west wall, with further doorways, now blocked, on all sides of the naos (nave), including four on the east side. Comparable arrangements existed in and were characteristic of other early Constantinopolitan churches.[13]

Sixth-century ecclesiastical architecture is better known, owing to the surviving monuments and the abundant written record.[14] The variety of plans, dimensions, and vaulting solutions is remarkable. Saint Polyeuktos, built by Anicia Juliana between 517/18 and 520/1, was a five-aisled basilica, measuring about 58 by 52 meters (Fig. 11.2) with a coffered wood ceiling.[15] Saints Sergios and Bakchos, built in the late 520s by Justinian before his ascent to the throne, is a double-shell domed construction, measuring less than 30 meters square (Fig. 11.3).[16] Known only from descriptions, the church of the Holy Apostles as rebuilt by Justinian *c.*536–50 to replace an earlier construction by Constantius II (337–61) was a substantial cruciform building with five domes, one over each arm of the cross and a larger dome surmounting the crossing.[17] But the pinnacle of late antique ecclesiastical architecture

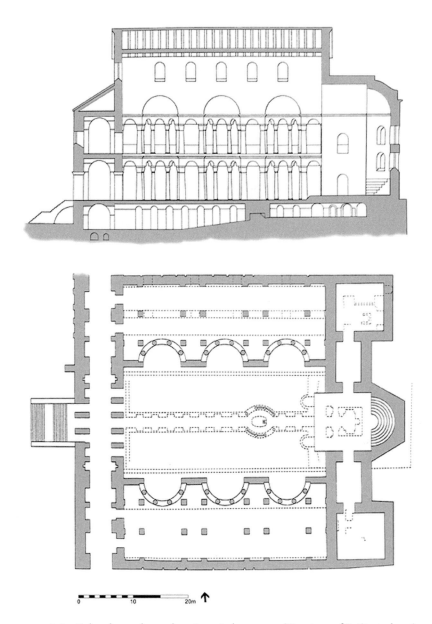

11.2 Saint Polyeuktos, plan and section, sixth century. (Courtesy of R. Ousterhout)

was Justinian's Hagia Sophia (Figs. 11.4 and 11.5).[18] Completed in the five years from 532 to 537, it remains a feat of imagination, ingenuity, and design, and a forceful statement of power and status. With interior dimensions of c.70 by 76 meters, it is a three-aisled basilica, but, in

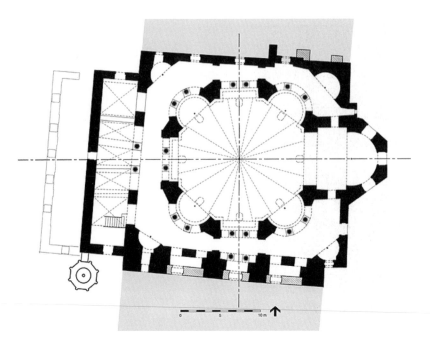

11.3 Sergios and Bakchos, plan, sixth century. (Courtesy of R. Ousterhout)

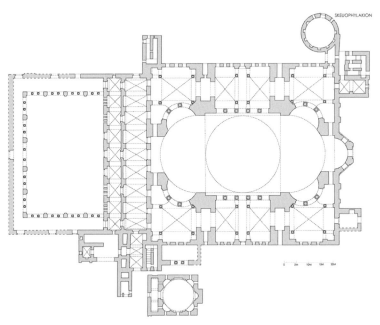

CONSTANTINOPLE/ ISTANBUL - HAGHIA SOPHIA   REPRESENTATION   PLAN   SCALE 1:500

11.4 Hagia Sophia, Constantinople, plan, sixth century (redrawn after R. Krautheimer, *Early Christian and Byzantine Architecture*. (New Haven and London, 1984), fig. 164)

11.5 Hagia Sophia, view toward the dome. (Photo courtesy of Vasileios Marinis)

contrast to fifth-century examples, vaulted throughout. The most prominent element is the enormous dome on pendentives – c.31 meters in diameter – over the center bay. The result is a unified and breathtaking interior, a magnificent stage for imperial and religious rituals.

In some churches, inter-columnar parapets, some of which may have been of considerable height, closed off side aisles.[19] Such divisions may imply a separation of congregants, perhaps between men and women, although evidence for such practice is ambiguous.[20] In the late antique Constantinopolitan churches a sanctuary barrier separated the bema, single-apsed and without pastophoria, from the naos. This barrier could be π-shaped or straight, a low parapet or a high structure with columns and an architrave.[21] The congregation probably had visual access to the bema most of the time. Inside the bema was the altar, the epicenter of liturgical activity, often surmounted by a ciborium. Some basilicas, such as Stoudios, had crypts, accessed through a staircase and perhaps for housing relics, in front of the main apses.[22]

The city's first cathedral, Hagia Eirene, stands north of Hagia Sophia and is closely associated with it. The original Constantinian structure was destroyed in the Nika riot (532) and rebuilt as a domed basilica with a dome 16 meters in diameter, a narthex, and an atrium. The sixth-century building was in turn damaged in an earthquake of 740 and rebuilt, probably during the reign of empress Eirene

(797–802).[23] The dimensions and plan of the Justinianic building were maintained, but a cross-domed unit was introduced in the gallery level. In its present form Hagia Eirene is the only surviving church from the Transitional Period (seventh to mid-ninth centuries).

Surviving Middle Byzantine (842–1204) monuments show considerable variety, from small domed tetraconchs, such as the early eleventh-century church of Theotokos Mouchliotissa, which measures *c*.12 by 12 meters,[24] to the late twelfth-/early thirteenth-century cross-domed Theotokos Kyriotissa (Kalenderhane Camii), whose dome has a diameter of *c*.8 meters.[25] The most common type (in Constantinople and elsewhere) is the cross-in-square, also known as quincunx, inscribed cross plan, or four-column plan. The naos is divided into nine bays, with the central one capped by a dome on a drum supported (usually) by four columns as at the church of Myrelaion (Bodrum Camii) (Fig. 11.6).[26] Originally part of an urban palace, the Myrelaion was built *c*.920 by emperor Romanos I Lekapenos (920–44). The complex was eventually converted into a nunnery.[27] Constructed of brick, it measures roughly 10 by 17 meters, and has a tripartite bema and a narthex.

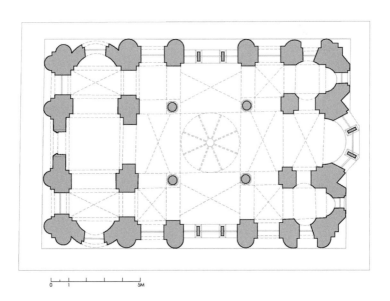

CONSTANTINOPLE / ISTANBUL - MYRELAION  REPRESENTATION  PLAN B  SCALE 1:75

11.6 Myrelaion Church, Constantinople, plan. (Redrawn after C. L. Striker, *The Myrelaion (Bodrum Camii) in Istanbul* (Princeton, 1981), fig.19)

The absence of interior divisions and the naos's compact dimensions make the cross-in-square type appropriate for small, single-gendered monastic communities.[28] The type's earliest examples are found in eighth-century monasteries in nearby Bithynia, and may have been imported to Constantinople from there.[29] Several of the city's cross-in-square churches, such as the north church *tou Libos* (Fenari İsa Camii, from 907) and those in the twelfth-century Pantokrator complex, belonged to monasteries. The type also appeared in secular buildings.[30]

Middle Byzantine churches differ significantly from their late antique counterparts: the naos, a continuous unified space, emphasizes the vertical rather than the horizontal axis; a tripartite bema replaces a single apse; and there are fewer egresses. These differences signal changes in ritual practices and the symbolic understanding of the church building.

Many of these trends continue in the Late Byzantine period (1204/61–1453), although a new aesthetic also emerged.[31] Michael VIII Palaiologos (1259–82), who was responsible for the recovery of Constantinople from the Latins (1261), launched an ambitious restoration program, focusing on infrastructure such as walls and harbors, together with churches and monasteries.[32] Further restoration of ecclesiastical buildings took place during the reign of Andronikos II (1282–1328), often at aristocratic initiative. The Theotokos Pammakaristos complex (Fethiye Camii), on the fifth hill in Istanbul's Çarşamba neighborhood (Fig. 11.7), is typical.[33] The main church, from the late eleventh or early twelfth century, was constructed by John Komnenos and his wife Anna Doukaina. It is a variant of the cross-domed church with an inner ambulatory, which was used for the burial of John's family. After 1261 the monastery came into the possession of the court official Michael Glabas Tarchaneiotes (b. *c.*1235, d. after 1304) and his wife Maria. Glabas was probably responsible for the addition of the north arm of the outer ambulatory, which originally terminated in a domed chapel to the east. In *c.*1310, after Glabas' death, Maria added to the south side of the main church an elegant cross-in-square chapel to house her husband's tomb, which she eventually shared. The outer ambulatory's western and southern arms, probably from the second quarter of the fourteenth century, postdate the chapel.

The Pammakaristos complex exemplifies a situation common after 1261. A wealthy patron acquires an earlier ecclesiastical foundation, abandoned or needing repair, and restores it, adding subsidiary spaces – chapels or outer ambulatories – to accommodate family tombs. These later additions envelop and preserve the older church, but also

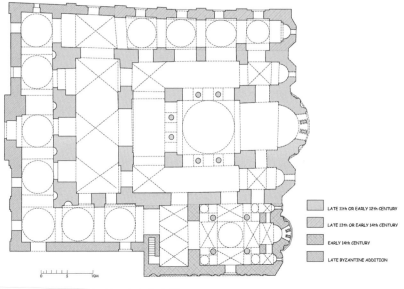

LATE 11th OR EARLY 12th CENTURY

LATE 13th OR EARLY 14th CENTURY

EARLY 14th CENTURY

LATE BYZANTINE ADDITION

0      5      10M

CONSTANTINOPLE / ISTANBUL - PAMMAKARISTOS    REPRESENTATION    PLAN    SCALE 1:100

11.7  Theotokos Pammakaristos, Constantinople, plan. (Redrawn after R. Anderson in H. Belting, C. Mango, and D. Mouriki, *The Mosaics and Frescoes of Saint Mary Pammakaristos (Fetiye Camii)* (Washington, DC, 1978), fig. A)

disrupt its harmony and symmetry, creating a "manneristic" effect.[34] This process occurs time and again in Late Byzantine Constantinople. In *c.*1280, Theodora Palaiologina, wife of Michael VIII, added a church dedicated to Saint John the Forerunner alongside the tenth-century church of Theotokos *tou Libos* (Fig. 11.8).[35] Surrounding the center bay on three sides, an inner ambulatory housed tombs, as in the main church of Pammakaristos. An outer ambulatory along the two churches' west and south sides was constructed shortly after the completion of Saint John. Another case is the Chora monastery (Kariye Müzesi/Museum).[36] The present naos, an atrophied Greek cross plan, dates to the early twelfth century. The monastery fell into disrepair during the Latin occupation. Around 1315 Theodore Metochites, a court official of Andronikos II, took over the foundation, restoring the main church and making several additions: a two-story annex on the naos's north side, two narthexes to the west, and a funerary chapel to the south. He also redecorated the interior with marble revetments, mosaics, and frescoes, creating an agglomeration of spaces without clear relation to one another.

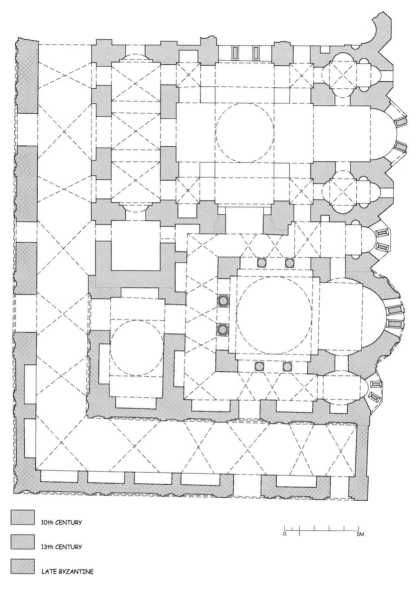

10th CENTURY

13th CENTURY

LATE BYZANTINE

0    1                        5M

CONSTANTINOPLE / ISTANBUL - LIPS MONASTERY   ACTUAL STATE   PLAN A   SCALE 1:100

11.8  Monastery *tou Libos*, Constantinople, plan. (Courtesy of Vasileios Marinis)

189

## Architecture and Liturgy in Late Antique Constantinople

A lack of direct sources necessitates reconstruction of Constantinople's early liturgy from circumstantial evidence and retrojection from later developments. Nevertheless, the ritual's form is reasonably well understood.[37] Outdoor processions of the faithful, headed by the bishop and the clergy, and occasionally members of an imperial party, preceded the city's main liturgical celebration in the cathedral (initially Hagia Eirene, subsequently Hagia Sophia). Those not participating in this procession awaited clerics and officials outside the church in its atrium, west of the narthex. Once the procession arrived, clergy and laity entered the building. The multiple entrances in early Constantinopolitan churches offered easy access for the faithful, who entered with the clergy. Preparation of the First Entrance, with which the first part of the service, the Liturgy of the Word, began, took place in the narthexes.[38] After clergy and laity entered the church, the celebrant bishop took his place on the throne behind the altar in the center of the apse, the clergy surrounding him. The congregation made its way into the naos. The pronounced horizontal axis of early basilicas accommodated these processional movements.

The Liturgy of the Word included readings from the Old Testament, the Acts or the Epistles, and the Gospels. These texts were proclaimed from the ambo, a platform accessed by a staircase and connected to the bema through an elevated corridor called the *solea*. After the readings the bishop preached the sermon and then dismissed the catechumens. Second-floor galleries, which communicated directly with the outside, may have permitted catechumens, who were relegated there, to leave without disturbing the congregation.[39] Women also used galleries, and, on occasion, imperial parties.[40]

The liturgy proper began with the Great Entrance, when deacons transferred the Eucharistic gifts, bread and wine, from the *skeuophylakion* (lit. "the place to keep the vessels") to the main altar. In Constantinople the *skeuophylakion* was often a detached building,[41] although evidence suggests that an internal *skeuophylakion* near the altar also existed.[42] After the clergy's reading of the Eucharistic prayers and consecration of the gifts, people received communion. The liturgy concluded with a clerical procession from inside the church to the *skeuophylakion*, where the clergy consumed leftover Eucharistic elements and removed liturgical vestments.[43]

## MEDIEVAL DEVELOPMENTS

If the Divine Liturgy in early Christian Constantinople was public, corporate, and open, in the Middle Byzantine period it became introverted and compressed.[44] This change happened in tandem with the transformation of Constantinople's urban character, which included the obliteration of public, open space, one of the hallmarks of late antique cities.[45] This development affected the public nature of early Christian worship and ecclesiastical architecture. At the same time, monasteries became increasingly powerful. The monasticization of urban space and church architecture reflected a similar process in liturgical life. Worship practices in monasteries were self-contained and with few exceptions took place inside the foundation. Outdoor processions, reduced in number, largely pertained to the cathedral rather than the monastic rite. Elements of the outdoor stational liturgy simply were affixed to the beginning of the service. The two entrances became truncated appearances of the clergy: at the First Entrance, the Gospel book was processed from the altar into the nave and back. In the Great Entrance, the Eucharistic elements were transferred from their place of preparation (now the north room of the tripartite bema) to the altar.

Constantinopolitan church architecture reflects these changes in ritual practice. For example, because the community congregated directly inside the church, multiple doors no longer were needed. The unified naos was particularly apt for the short, circular processions, but the most notable planning adjustment was the tripartite bema – a significant departure from the single-apse sanctuary of earlier basilicas. The north room was used for preparation of the Eucharistic elements, which grew from a single short prayer read by the bishop in the *skeuophylakion* to a progressively complicated and symbolically laden ritual called the *prothesis*.[46] The use of the corresponding south room, now called *diakonikon*, is not always easy to determine; it probably was used to store liturgical vessels and vestments.[47]

The form and function of the sanctuary barrier, commonly designated the *templon* in Middle Byzantine sources, also changes. No Constantinopolitan example has survived but elsewhere it consisted of low parapets surmounted by columns carrying an architrave. As early as the eleventh century, veils and curtains hung from the *templon* concealed ritual activities in the bema from the laity in the naos.[48] By the end of the thirteenth century, inter-columnar icons had become common, lending an air of permanence to the visual separation of clergy and laity, which persists today.[49] Simultaneously, a progressively heightened sense of sacredness attached to the Eucharistic elements and the act of consecration; laypeople were deemed unworthy of casting their impure gaze on the sacrament.[50]

## BURIALS AND COMMEMORATIONS

The desire for privileged burials and perpetual commemoration that would secure a blissful afterlife constituted a powerful force behind church building. A privileged burial was inside a church, as close as possible to the altar. Internal burial was an ancient custom, despite prohibitions in imperial and ecclesiastical law. Such tombs were most often located in areas of secondary liturgical importance, such as narthexes, chapels, and outer ambulatories in order to circumvent imperial and canonical prohibitions.

Patrons of ecclesiastical foundations often left detailed instructions pertaining to their commemoration, which was to take place at least annually, but often daily. The *typikon* (Foundation Document) of the Kosmosoteira monastery in Pherrai, written by the *sebastokrator* Isaac Komnenos (son of Emperor Alexios I, d. after 1152), sums up the transactional relationship between patrons and beneficiaries:

> I want the monks to recite the *Kyrie eleison* forty times for my sake during every one of the said vigils, after the dismissal. I wish their prayers to be [performed] in good conscience and not unwillingly, inasmuch as I did assign my own possessions and properties to the monastery and to them.[51]

The *typikon* of the convent of Theotokos *tes Bebaias Elpidos* in Constantinople, founded by Theodora Synadene in the first half of the fourteenth century, clarifies that the monastery was established for the glory of God and the honor of the Theotokos, and for the nuns to commemorate the foundress's extended family "with all zeal and diligence."[52] The document outlines the elaborate commemoration of Theodora, her parents, husband, children, and their descendants. The monastery's main church was to be decorated and appropriately lit with six candelabra. The nuns were to prepare *kollyba*, the boiled wheat used in liturgical celebrations of the dead. Eleven external priests, who were also responsible for the evening commemorative service, were to join the monastery's resident priest.[53]

Several medieval churches in Constantinople housed burials in subsidiary spaces and the naos.[54] There were twenty-nine tombs and four ossuaries in the two churches in the monastery *tou Libos* (Fig. 11.8).[55] Nowadays, barren church interiors obscure the prominence of tombs. Only in the Chora parekklesion is there a sense, however fragmentary, of such spaces' visual clamor. Luxuriously appointed tombs, with portraits of the deceased and lengthy laudatory inscriptions, vied with each other for the prayerful attention of monastics and visitors.

## BEYOND ARCHITECTURE AND LITURGY

A church's main function is the accommodation of liturgy. On a practical level this purpose implies a degree of liturgical planning reflecting the form and exigencies of ritual. However, beyond the essential requirement that a church have a bema and a naos, the ways in which architecture accommodates ritual have little impact on a building's overall appearance, as evident in the late antique churches of Constantinople, where the interaction between architecture and ritual is demonstrably stronger than in later periods. Although there is variety in plan, dimension, elevation, and vaulting, these churches have several common elements: multiple doors, galleries with direct external connection, and ample atria.

Non-liturgical considerations also affect appearance. The dome of Saints Sergios and Bakchos, composed of flat and scalloped segments, recalls the half-dome of the Serapeum at Hadrian's Villa, indicating a transference to Constantinople of innovative, second-century architectural forms; or the conscious imitation of an imperial Roman past.[56] Either way, this most prominent architectural element has nothing to do with liturgical need. Similarly, the scale of Hagia Sophia's dome and its daring support system should be understood as a competitor to the Pantheon in Rome.[57]

With respect to the symbolic understanding of church buildings, other kinds of symbolism predominate. Two epigrams from the church of Saint Polyeuktos offer an example.[58] The first, carved "all round inside the naos," celebrates Juliana's illustrious ancestry, her orthodoxy, and her fame as a patron. It further claims that her many ecclesiastical foundations will save her from oblivion and that the saints she has thus served will protect her family. The second, inscribed on a series of plaques "at the entrance of the church, outside the narthex," compares Juliana to the emperors Constantine and Theodosios, both great imperial builders, and praises, among other things, the church's foundations, columns, marble revetments, and gilded ceiling. In short, Saint Polyeuktos was a visible and enduring manifesto of Anicia Juliana's wealth, power, and ancestry.[59] Thus the important aspects of the building – its size, form, and decoration – related not to liturgical planning, but to Juliana's desire to advertise her family, her affluence, and her piety.

Moreover, both the church's dimensions and its sculptural decoration have been seen as deliberate echoes of biblical descriptions of the Temples of Solomon and Ezekiel.[60] The second epigram states that Juliana has "alone overpowered time and surpassed the wisdom of the celebrated Solomon, raising a temple to receive God, the richly wrought and gracious splendor of which a great epoch cannot celebrate" (I.10.47–50), a claim suggesting not simply an improvement on Solomon's Temple, but a surpassing representation of an eschatological heavenly temple.[61] The implications for those assembled for the Liturgy in Saint Polyeuktos are significant. The material context of their ritual was not simply a building with doors, atrium, apse, and ambo. Rather, the church offered a foretaste of heavenly and eschatological worship; a place where notions of time and space, earthly and celestial, collapsed.

A tenth-century poem on the Stoudios basilica by John Geometres offers a different interpretation of a church building: it is an imitation of the cosmos, heaven and earth.[62] The translucent smoothness of the floor stones is like a tranquil sea, and columns shine "like some limpid stream from melting snow." The visitor beholds "the earth itself and the things of the earth in the variety of their colors and the beauty of their depiction." The main apse, with a now-lost mosaic of Christ in glory, represents heaven. The church building as a microcosm recalls Jewish interpretations of the Tabernacle and the Temple.[63] Its most forceful Christian articulation is the seventh-century *Mystagogia* by Maximos Confessor, which describes the church as an image of the world, with the nave symbolizing earth and the visible things, the sanctuary heaven.[64] This *topos* becomes one of Byzantium's most popular and enduring ideas. As late as the fifteenth century, Symeon, bishop of Thessalonike (d. 1429), divides the church into three parts: the narthex is earth, the nave the heavens, the sanctuary those things beyond the heavens.[65]

## THE CHURCH BUILDING AS A THEOLOGICAL ABSTRACTION

Liturgical commentaries, such as those by Maximos and Symeon of Thessalonike, articulated an explicit understanding of churches as liturgical spaces.[66] It should be noted, however, that these commentaries are primarily (and sometimes exclusively) concerned with interpretation of the Divine Liturgy; material context is secondary to a wider symbolic system. Liturgical commentaries follow roughly two interpretive methods, both fashioned after patristic scriptural exegesis: a spiritual interpretation whereby anagogical contemplation of the ritual uncovers heavenly realities (*theoria*); and a historical explication in which the Liturgy is a mimesis of Christ's redemptive work on earth (*historia*). The *Historia Ekklesiastike and Mystike Theoria*, attributed to Germanos I, patriarch of Constantinople (d. 730), combines both models.[67] It also offers the most extensive treatment of the Divine Liturgy's architectural context and a symbolic interpretation of a church building:

> The church is the temple of God, a holy precinct, a house of prayer, a gathering of people, the body of Christ . . . The church is earthly heaven, where the heavenly God dwells and walks about. It represents symbolically the crucifixion and burial and the resurrection of Christ. It is glorified more than Moses's tent of witness, in which were the mercy seat and the Holy of Holies.[68]

This passage conflates the building with the assembly of the faithful (*ekklesia*), implying that the structure has no meaning outside the *ekklesia* and the services performed. Furthermore, it understands the church as an earthly reflection of heaven, God's dwelling place, as were the Tabernacle and the Temple before it. However, the idea that the church represents Christ's passion through the celebration of the Divine Liturgy is more eminent.[69]

Subsequent chapters focus on the church's specific parts, especially those in and around the bema, assigning one or multiple symbolic associations to each. These associations fall into three categories: memorials of Christ's death and resurrection, reflections of the heavenly liturgy and anticipations of times to come, and fulfillments of Old Testament pre-figurations.

Because the Divine Liturgy reenacts Christ's redemptive work on earth, different parts of the building become topographical markers associated with important events. The central apse symbolizes the cave where Jesus was buried (ch. 3), the altar marks the place where his body was laid (ch. 4), and the ambo manifests the stone that sealed his tomb (ch. 10). The assignment of meaning relates to architectural form and spatial relationships. The main apse symbolizes the caves of Christ's birth and burial because of its semicircular shape and crowning half dome.

The north room symbolizes Golgotha. In accordance with biblical narrative (John 19:41–2), it is close to the tomb/apse.

Parts of the building also reflect the heavenly realm. Most obvious is the connection between the heavenly and the earthly sanctuary (*thysiasterion*), in which the clergy represent the heavenly powers that worship God (ch. 6). The synthronon with the bishop's centrally placed cathedra signifies the throne where Christ the King of All sits with the apostles in anticipation of the Last Judgment (ch. 7).

Finally, parts of the church constitute Old Testament prefigurations. The altar was prefigured by the table upon which the manna descended from heaven (ch. 4), while the ciborium corresponds to the Ark of the Covenant (ch. 5).

Thus, for the author of the *Historia*, the church operates on several symbolic levels. It is God's abode, much like the Tabernacle and the Temple, but it surpasses the Jewish sanctuaries. It fulfills a host of Old Testament prefigurations. As heaven on earth it reflects heavenly realities, especially the angelic worship offered to God. Above all the church recreates a holy topography onto which the ritual acts of the Divine Liturgy are grafted.

The complex sign system that liturgical commentaries showcase is indifferent to the architectural particularities of size, plan, and building material. The building becomes an abstraction, a shell within which Christ's incarnation and his salvific dispensation are reenacted. Certainly, the commentaries needed to be applicable to all churches. However, the most significant reason for this indifference was the malleability and adaptability of the Divine Liturgy, which could be (and still is) celebrated in buildings of extraordinary variety without losing any of its efficacy and only some of its magnificence.

CONCLUSION

Constantinopolitan church architecture was intrinsically linked to ecclesiastical practice. On a basic level, aspects of the building corresponded to the requirements of ritual; modification of such aspects reflected changes in ritual's form. Thus the multiple doors of the early basilicas, necessary for the joint entrance of people and clergy at the beginning of the Divine Liturgy, are found nowhere in medieval churches, because the Liturgy began inside. That said, a direct correspondence between architecture and ritual cannot account either for the buildings' overall forms and types or for congregants' perception of them. The size and opulent decoration of Saint Polyeuktos and Hagia Sophia were above all statements of the power, prestige, and wealth of their donors. In the Late Byzantine period, the proliferation of narthexes and outer ambulatories reflects both a new aesthetic and, in its provision of burial space, a preoccupation with commemoration and remembrance. Symbolically, too, churches were understood in a variety of ways: as a new and better Temple, the house of God, heaven on earth, imitations of the universe, and reflections of Holy Land topography. When we take these considerations together, we better grasp the Byzantine worshipper's experience.

## FURTHER READING

Janin, R., *La géographie ecclésiastique de l'empire byzantin, I: Le siège Constantinople et le patriarcat oecuménique, 3: Les églises et les monastères*, 2nd ed. (Paris, 1969).

Marinis, V., *Architecture and Ritual in the Churches of Constantinople: Ninth to Fifteenth Centuries* (Cambridge and New York, 2014).

Mathews, T. F., *The Early Churches of Constantinople: Architecture and Liturgy* (University Park, 1971).

Ousterhout, R., *Eastern Medieval Architecture: The Building Traditions of Byzantium and Neighboring Lands* (Oxford, 2019).

Taft, R. F., *The Byzantine Rite: A Short History* (Collegeville, 1992).

## NOTES

1 R. de Clari, *The Conquest of Constantinople*, trans. E. H. McNeal (New York, 1964), 111–12.

2 William of Tyre, *A History of the Deeds Done Beyond the Sea by William, Archbishop of Tyre*, 2 vols., trans. and annotated by E. A. Babcock and A. C. Krey (New York, 1943), 2:382.

3 R. Janin, *La géographie ecclésiastique de l'empire byzantin, I: Le siège Constantinople et le patriarcat oecuménique, 3: Les églises et les monastères*, 2nd ed. (Paris, 1969).

4 C. Mango, "The Relics of St. Euphemia and the Synaxarion of Constantinople," *BollGrott* 53 (1999): 79–87, esp. 79; P. Magdalino, "Medieval Constantinople," in *Studies on the History and Topography of Byzantine Constantinople*, ed. P. Magdalino (Aldershot, 2007), no. I: 1–111, esp. 27–31.

5 For an overview, see R. F. Taft, *The Byzantine Rite: A Short History* (Collegeville, 1992).

6 G. Dagron, "Constantinople: Les sanctuaires et l'organisation de la vie religieuse," in *Actes du XIe congrès international d'archéologie chrétienne* (Paris, 1989), 1069–85, esp. 1079–80.

7 E. Herman, "The Secular Church," in *CMH* 4, *The Byzantine Empire, Part II: Government, Church and Civilization*, ed. J. M. Hussey (Cambridge, 1967), 105–34, esp. 117–18; H. G. Beck, *Kirche und theologische Literatur im byzantinischen Reich* (Munich, 1977), 83–6; Dagron, "Constantinople: Les sanctuaires et l'organisation de la vie religieuse," 1080–3.

8 G. Dagron, *Naissance d'une capitale: Constantinople et ses institutions, 330–451* (Paris, 1974), 388–409.

9 M. Havaux, "Théodose II, Constantinople et l'Empire: une nouvelle lecture de la Notitia Urbis Constantinopolitanae," *RH* 681 (2017): 3–54, esp. 18–19.

10 P. Magdalino, "Medieval Constantinople: Built Environment and Urban Development," in *EHB* 2: 529–37, esp. 529–30.

11 Janin, *La géographie ecclésiastique*, 430–40; T. F. Mathews, *The Early Churches of Constantinople: Architecture and Liturgy* (University Park, 1971), 19–27.

12  C. Mango, "The Date of the Studius Basilica at Istanbul," *BMGS* 4 (1978): 115–22, esp. 117, 120.

13  Mathews, *Early Churches*, 28–38.

14  R. Ousterhout, *Eastern Medieval Architecture: The Building Traditions of Byzantium and Neighboring Lands* (Oxford, 2019), 175–96; R. Ousterhout, "Aesthetics and Politics in the Architecture of Justinian," *TM* 22.1 (2018): 103–20.

15  J. Bardill, "A New Temple for Byzantium: Anicia Juliana, King Solomon, and the Gilded Ceiling of the Church of St. Polyeuktos in Constantinople," in *Social and Political Life in Late Antiquity*, ed. W. Bowden et al. (Leiden and Boston, 2006), 339–70; J. Bardill, " Église Saint-Polyeucte à Constantinople: Nouvelle solution pour l'énigme de sa reconstitution," in *Architecture paléochrétienne*, ed. J.-M. Spieser (Gollion, 2011), 77–103.

16  J. Bardill, "The Church of Sts. Sergius and Bacchus in Constantinople and the Monophysite Refugees." *DOP* 54 (2000): 1–11.

17  N. Karydis, "Justinian's Church of the Holy Apostles: A New Reconstruction Proposal," in *The Holy Apostles: A Lost Monument, a Forgotten Project, and the Presentness of the Past*, eds. M. Mullett and R. G. Ousterhout (Washington, DC, 2020), 99–130.

18  R. J. Mainstone, *Hagia Sophia: Architecture, Structure, and Liturgy of Justinian's Great Church* (New York, 1988); N. Schibille, *Hagia Sophia and the Byzantine Aesthetic Experience* (Farnham and Burlington, 2014); B. V. Pentcheva, *Hagia Sophia: Sound, Space, and Spirit in Byzantium* (University Park, 2017); Ousterhout, *Eastern Medieval Architecture*, 199–216.

19  U. Peschlow, "Dividing Interior Space in Early Byzantine Churches: The Barriers between the Nave and Aisles," in *Thresholds of the Sacred: Architectural, Art Historical, Liturgical, and Theological Perspectives on Religious Screens, East and West*, ed. S. E. J. Gerstel (Washington, DC, 2006), 53–71, esp. 54–5, 62–5.

20  R. F. Taft, "Women at Church in Byzantium: Where, When – and Why?" *DOP* 52 (1998): 27–87.

21  Mathews, *Early Churches*, 109–10.

22  Mathews, *Early Churches*, 27, 32–3.

23  S. Feist, *Die byzantinische Sakralarchitektur der Dunklen Jahrhunderte* (Wiesbaden, 2019), 25–46; U. Peschlow, *Die Irenenkirche in Istanbul* (Tübingen, 1977), 206–14.

24  V. Marinis, *Architecture and Ritual in the Churches of Constantinople, Ninth–Fifteenth Centuries* (Cambridge, 2014), 199–200.

25  C. L. Striker and D. Kuban, *Kalenderhane in Istanbul*, 2 vols. (Mainz, 1997–2007), 1: 23–100.

26  C. L. Striker, *The Myrelaion (Bodrum Camii) in Istanbul* (Princeton, 1981).

27  Janin, *La géographie ecclésiastique*, 351–4.

28  C. Mango, *Byzantine Architecture* (New York, 1976), 178–80; P. Charanis, "The Monk as an Element in Byzantine Society," *DOP* 25 (1971): 61–84, esp. 69–73 (community size).

29  Marinis, *Architecture and Ritual*, 50–1.

30  S. Ćurčić, *Architecture in the Balkans from Diocletian to Süleyman the Magnificent* (New Haven, 2010), 271–2.

31  Ousterhout, *Eastern Medieval Architecture*, 595–618; V. Kidonopoulos, "The Urban Physiognomy of Constantinople from the Latin Conquest through the Palaiologan Era," in *Byzantium, Faith and Power (1261–1557): Perspectives on Late Byzantine Art and Culture*, ed. S. T. Brooks (New York, 2006), 98–117.

32  A.-M. Talbot, "The Restoration of Constantinople under Michael VIII," *DOP* 47 (1993): 243–61.

33  H. Hallensleben, "Untersuchungen zur Baugeschichte der ehemaligen Pammakaristoskirche der heutigen Fethiye Camii in Istanbul," *IstMitt* 13.14 (1963–4): 128–93; C. Mango, D. Mouriki, and H. Belting, *The Mosaics and Frescoes of St. Mary Pammakaristos (Fethiye Camii) at Istanbul* (Washington, DC, 1978); Janin, *Géographie ecclésiastique*, 208–13.

34  Ousterhout, *Eastern Medieval Architecture*, 607.

35  Marinis, *Architecture and Ritual*, 182–4.

36  R. Ousterhout, *The Architecture of the Kariye Camii in Istanbul* (Washington, DC, 1987).

37  Mathews, *Early Churches*, 111–15; J. F. Baldovin, *The Urban Character of Christian Worship: The Origins, Development, and Meaning of Stational Liturgy* (Rome, 1987), 167–226; Taft, *The Byzantine Rite*, 22–41; Marinis, *Architecture and Ritual*, 15–16.

38  J. Mateos, *The Liturgy of the Word* (Fairfax, VA, 2016).

39  Mathews, *The Early Churches*, 125–30.

40  Taft, "Women at Church."
41  R. F. Taft and S. Parenti, *Il Grande Ingresso* (Grottaferrata, 2014), 353–9.
42  V. Marinis, "The *Historia Ekklesiastike kai Mystike Theoria*: A Symbolic Understanding of the Byzantine Church Building," *BZ* 108 (2015): 753–70 at 764–7.
43  R. F. Taft, *The Communion, Thanksgiving, and Concluding Rites* (Rome, 2008), 583–8.
44  Marinis, *Architecture and Ritual*, 16–19.
45  H. Saradi, "Space in Byzantine Thought," in *Architecture as Icon: Perception and Representation of Architecture in Byzantine Art*, ed. S. Ćurčić and E. Chatzetryphonos (Princeton, 2010), 73–105, esp. 87; Magdalino, "Medieval Constantinople," 17–55.
46  T. Pott, *Byzantine Liturgical Reform* (Crestwood, NY, 2010), 197–228.
47  Marinis, *Architecture and Ritual*, 37–8.
48  Marinis, *Architecture and Ritual*, 48.
49  S. E. J. Gerstel, "An Alternate View of the Late Byzantine Sanctuary Screen," in *Thresholds of the Sacred*, 135–61.
50  Marinis, *Architecture and Ritual*, 47–8.
51  *BMFD*, 804.
52  *BMFD*, 1563; Janin, *Géographie ecclésiastique*, 158–60.
53  *BMFD*, 1555–6, 1561.
54  V. Marinis, "Tombs and Burials in the Monastery *tou Libos* in Constantinople," *DOP* 63 (2009): 147–66, esp. 150–2.
55  Marinis, "Tombs and Burials."
56  Ousterhout, "Aesthetics," 103–6.
57  Ousterhout, "Aesthetics," 106–9.
58  W. R. Paton, trans., *Anthologia Graeca* I.10 (Cambridge, MA, 1916), 6–11; M. Whitby, "The St. Polyeuktos Epigram (AP I.10): A Literary Perspective," in *Greek Literature in Late Antiquity: Dynamism, Didacticism, Classicism*, ed. S. F. Johnson (Aldershot and Burlington, 2006), 159–87.
59  Whitby, "Epigram," 165.
60  R. M. Harrison, *A Temple for Byzantium: The Discovery and Excavation of Anicia Juliana's Palace-Church in Istanbul* (Austin, 1989), 137–44.
61  Bardill, "New Temple," 342–4.
62  W. T. Woodfin, "A Majestas Domini in Middle-Byzantine Constantinople," *CahArch* 51 (2003–4): 45–53.
63  K. E. McVey, "Spirit Embodied: The Emergence of Symbolic Interpretations of Early Christian and Byzantine Architecture," in *Architecture as Icon*, 41–2.
64  P. Mueller-Jourdan, *Typologie spatio-temporelle de l'ecclesia byzantine: la mystagogie de Maxime le Confesseur dans la culture philosophique de l'antiquité tardive* (Leiden and Boston, 2005), 99–192.
65  S. Hawkes-Teeples, ed. and trans., *St. Symeon of Thessalonika: The Liturgical Commentaries* (Toronto, 2010), 240.
66  R. Bornert, *Les commentaires byzantins de la divine liturgie du VIIe au XVe siècle* (Paris, 1966).
67  R. F. Taft, "The Liturgy of the Great Church: An Initial Synthesis of Structure and Interpretation on the Eve of Iconoclasm," *DOP* 34–5 (1980–1): 45–75; for text and translation, P. Meyendorff, *St. Germanus of Constantinople: On the Divine Liturgy* (Crestwood, 1984).
68  Marinis, "*Historia Ekklesiastike*," 755.
69  Marinis, "*Historia Ekkesiastike*," 753–62.

# 12: Sacred Dimensions: Constantinopolitan Monasticism

## Dirk Krausmüller

C hristian monasticism, which originated in the third century as a retreat into the Egyptian desert, became an urban phenomenon as early as the fourth century, when Basil the Great (330–79) composed a set of rules which favoured communal (coenobitic, from *koinos* = common, and *bios* = life) living over solitary (eremitical, from *eremos* = desert) experience. Monasteries began to appear in and around Constantinople within a century of its foundation. By the mid-sixth century the city was home to nearly seventy houses. Once established, monasticism was integral to the city's identity. It was a multiform phenomenon that encompassed both the extreme ascetic practices of the 'holy men',[1] and the communal living of the coenobitic tradition, which put a premium on moderation and conformity, declaring that a good monk should in no way differ from his fellows or weaken his body unduly through fasts and vigils.[2]

### Early Period: Fourth through Sixth Centuries

After shadowy beginnings the outline of Constantinopolitan monasticism gains clearer contours in the fifth and early sixth centuries. Saints' lives (hagiography) provide the bulk of the documentation, focusing on individual monastic heroes who pursued the ascetic ideal. The first important figure in this tradition was Isaac, a charismatic from Syria who prophesied that the emperor Valens (364–78) would die in battle if he did not renounce his heretical Arian beliefs. When the prophecy materialized the eparch of the city was so impressed that he built Isaac a monastery. These episodes, however, represent only one part of the picture.[3] Monks were also political activists. Isaac opposed the Constantinopolitan bishop John Chrysostom, and worked to secure his deposition. Dalmatus, Isaac's successor as abbot, followed his example by engineering the removal of the patriarch Nestorius. A few decades later Daniel, a Syrian monk who lived on top of a column, also meddled in politics, coming to the rescue of the patriarch who was pressured by a 'heretical' emperor.[4]

Although holy men continued to flock to the city, no lives of contemporary monks were written in the sixth century.[5] This demands an explanation. Legal texts from Justinian's reign (527–65) help us to understand what may have happened.[6] They not only address questions of monastic property but intervene in the inner workings of monasteries, stipulating that abbots be chosen by the patriarch and that monks sleep in common dormitories instead of private cells. In other words, they favour strict coenobiticism. This monastic ideal rarely finds expression in hagiographical texts, which may account for the decline in hagiography.

## SEVENTH THROUGH NINTH CENTURIES

After Justinian's rule, Constantinopolitan monastic life is poorly documented. That said, it is clear that the monastic population changed between the reigns of Justin II (565–74) and Leo III (717–41).[7] On the one hand, Anatolian communities migrated to Constantinople during the Persian wars (602–28). On the other hand, the influx of monks from Syria came to an end when the Eastern provinces were lost to the Arabs (638). Since the city's population declined radically in this period, it is likely that some monasteries disappeared. At the same time, the existence of ruined buildings provided new habitats for hermits. Whatever their numbers, monks appear to have played only a marginal role in ecclesiastical politics, and emperors tended to choose their episcopal candidates from the clergy of Hagia Sophia rather than monastic communities.

The evidence only improves again with the reign of the Iconoclast emperor Constantine V (741–75). Later sources record that in the latter part of his reign Constantine turned against the monastic estate. He is said to have closed monasteries, confiscated monastic property and forced a great number of monks to marry in a spectacular ceremony that took place in the Hippodrome. There is no doubt some exaggeration but on the whole the accounts appear to be credible. Less clear are the emperor's motives. Sources give the impression that he took these steps because the monks were defenders of icon veneration and therefore opposed his religious policy. Yet there is very little evidence to support this claim. Even Stephen the Younger, a hermit on Mt Auxentius near the capital, who in his life is presented as the archetypal

Iconophile seems to have been punished because of his connections with members of the elite who were opposed to Constantine.[8] This raises the question: why did the emperor turn against monasticism?[9] It seems that he rejected the traditional view that monks were the Christian elite because they remained celibate, and instead thought that good Christians should marry and have children. With this stance he followed an existing trend. Already two decades earlier the monk John of Damascus had inveighed against people who claimed that 'he who does not raise a seed for Israel' was cursed by God. Indeed, from the Second Iconoclasm (814–43) we have evidence that monks had lost their monopoly on sainthood. Lives were produced of laymen who were husbands and fathers and yet became wonderworkers. The evidence comes from Asia Minor but there seems little doubt that proponents of this new view were also found in the capital.

After the end of the Second Iconoclasm such texts were no longer composed. By this point, however, matters had already changed considerably. From the reign of Constantine's son Leo IV (886–912) onwards monks became increasingly assertive. Abbots attended the Second Council of Nicaea (787) in unprecedented numbers and played a more prominent role than at previous ecumenical councils.[10] The same years also saw a stunning monastic revival. Scions of Constantinopolitan elite families had themselves tonsured and founded monasteries in Bithynia. The most important of these figures was Theodore, abbot of Sakkoudion (759–826), whom Empress Irene (797–802) later entrusted with the leadership of the ancient Constantinopolitan monastery of Stoudios.

The Monastery of John Prodromos (John the Baptist) of Stoudios (ton Stoudiou/en tois Stoudiou) was founded in the fifth century by the Senator Stoudios from whom it took its name. It was located in the southern end of the green belt between the old Constantinian wall and the Theodosian wall. Once Theodore had become its abbot it became the foremost monastery in the capital. His sermons (catecheses) permit us an insight into the workings of the community.[11] The large monastic population, which some number as high as 700, was designed to be independent and self-sustaining. To that end monks worked, both manually and intellectually, performing tasks as varied as farming and manuscript production. The scale of the monastery mandated an elaborate hierarchy, with overseers reporting to Theodore on the flock's behaviour. Communal activities were paramount as they forged a feeling of togetherness. In the morning monks gathered to celebrate

Matins. The Divine Liturgy (the counterpart of the Western mass) came later, followed by a midday meal, Vespers (the evening prayer), an evening meal and Compline (the night prayer). During Lenten periods only one meal was served, and the minor prayer hours Prime, Tierce, Sext and None were performed in church. Yet Theodore did not demand total conformity: the diet of each monk varied according to his needs.

As these details indicate, Theodore was a proponent of the coenobitic life. He took this stance at a period in which coenobitic monasticism was regarded as inferior to eremitism, and monks were expected to learn the ropes in a community before striking out on their own as hermits. Theodore challenged this view, arguing that all monastic experiences were of equal value and that monks should adhere to their chosen path. Further, he was adamant that no one engage in ascetic practice without his knowledge, observing that a daily meal was not counter to saintly status. To make his point he appealed to a late antique ethos that prized moderate behaviour as the 'royal highway' and considered extreme asceticism as the equivalent of sloth because it weakened the body, gave the practitioner airs and provoked feelings of resentment in his fellow monks. Only during Lenten periods were monks permitted to go for whole days without food. Significantly, he expressed this view in a hagiographical text, the life of Theophanes of Agros, declaring, in opposition to the hagiographic traditions that viewed extreme fasting as a hallmark of saintly status, that the true saint's practice was moderate.[12]

The catecheses also addressed the concerns of Theodore's community, especially the monks' sorrow that they did not perform miracles. Theodore consoled them, arguing that harmonious communal living is as miraculous a feat as healing and the control of nature, and insisted that monks who liberate themselves from lust and greed are the equals of those who drive out demons.

Theodore's catecheses focus firmly on *praxis*, particularly the war against the passions.[13] He has little to say about the contemplation of nature and the vision of God, the next stages in the traditional model of spiritual ascent. Although he tells his monks to imagine the splendour of heaven, such activity falls well short of true mystical experience. This approach is not merely a matter of personal preference but reflects a broader suspicion of mysticism.

Theodore's promotion of the moderate, coenobitic life over that of the solitary put him at odds with provincial monastics, who stressed the inspired, prophetic aspects of monastic experience. The lives of the Anatolian holy men Joannicius and Peter of Atroa contain episodes in which the saints look into the minds of their followers and read their thoughts. By contrast, Theodore declares that he can only know his monks' inner states by making inferences from their appearance and behaviour.[14] Observing that no one can know the mind of God, he also denies the human ability to prophesy death,[15] again in contrast to the claims of Joannicius and Peter. In short, there raged a full-blown culture war, which pitted representatives of the Constantinopolitan elite such as Theodore against holy men from the provinces who were of much lower social status.

Theodore was a hardliner, who often ran afoul of emperor and patriarch, suffering periods of exile in consequence.[16] The result of his tenacious rule was the creation of a monastic community that was able to resist coercion from emperor and patriarch alike. In the ninth century this independence was challenged. Sources document tensions between the monastic house and the lay church as abbots clashed repeatedly with the patriarch.[17] At one period, during the patriarchate of Photios (877–86), abbots selected by the patriarch governed the monastery. A period of decline ensued, and the Stoudios monastery only regained its status as the capital's foremost house during the long tenure of Anatolius who commissioned several saints' lives and what was probably the first monastic rule, the so-called Stoudite *Hypotyposis*, which proudly announces that the Stoudite way of life is the best possible one for a monk.[18]

The Stoudite *Hypotyposis* signals a return to the monastic vision of Theodore after a breakdown in coenobitic discipline. Two surviving late ninth-century lives show that extreme asceticism had become acceptable in Constantinopolitan monasticism: Joseph the Hymnographer is said to have fasted more than all other members of the community, and his colleague, Euarestus of Kokorobion, is praised for his strenuous asceticism, which almost killed him. The hagiographers relate that both men later became abbots, but never portray them as spiritual directors. Texts from tenth-century Stoudios are cut from a different cloth, suggesting a return to the values of the previous era. *Vita C* of Theodore claims that in his youth Theodore ate from all dishes served in the refectory because he did not want to be different from other monks.

## Tenth through Twelfth Centuries

These texts inaugurate a new era, which lasted until the year 1204 when Constantinople was conquered by the Crusaders. In this period momentous changes took place in monastic organization, religious practice and the conception of the monastic ideal. The crucial years were in the late eleventh and early twelfth centuries. By the later twelfth century a new status quo had gained almost universal acceptance. The debates that accompanied the changes found their expression in a broad range of texts: lives, catecheses, treatises and letters. Yet the most important genre was undoubtedly that of the 'extended' monastic rule or *typikon*. These texts differ from the Stoudite *Hypotyposis* not only in length but also in content: passages of a technical nature are complemented by ideological statements, which express their authors' monastic visions. The oldest rule is the Stoudios typikon, which probably dates to the late tenth century, and was intended as a replacement for the *Hypotyposis*. The typikon of the Panagios monastery, a new foundation by monks from Mt Athos, followed in the early eleventh century. Both texts are lost but their contents can be reconstructed from later adaptations. In the later eleventh century two further texts were produced, the rules of the Evergetis and the Petra monasteries. All were composed by monks, usually abbots. From the later eleventh century onwards typika written by or for lay people begin to appear. Only the first, the *Diataxis* of the state official Michael Attaleiates (1021–80), seems to be an ad hoc creation. All the others are based on the existing rules of the Evergetis and Stoudios monasteries.[19] Yet they add new elements that were dear to the heart of the lay founders; commemorations of themselves, their families and their associates, which were to be celebrated in great splendour, so as to ensure the salvation of their souls.[20]

The extended rules provide insight into the organisation of monastic communities.[21] At Stoudios there existed a three-part hierarchy: officials responsible for the administration of the monastery who were led by the steward, priests and deacons with the protopresbyter at their head who took charge of worship, and the wearers of the small and great habit, two different types of monastic garb, one for beginners and one for the advanced. It seems that the three hierarchies were separated from each other but that an effort was made to correlate them in order to avoid conflict. The officials were at least deacons, and no monk could be ordained priest or deacon if he had not previously been clad in the great habit. The Stoudios typikon emphasised the role of ordained monks. Only priests were allowed to give blessings. Even the steward had to rely on their services if he were a layman. Moreover, in the church, and possibly also in the refectory, the order of precedence followed the ecclesiastical hierarchy rather than the hierarchy of the monastic offices, with the sole exception of the steward. This practice is in stark contrast to the Evergetis typikon, which recognises only one hierarchy, that of monastic officials, and never refers to a pecking order. Unlike Stoudios, the Evergetis monastery was a recent foundation and the community was much smaller. Yet there can be no doubt that the two texts also reflect different monastic visions. In the Evergetis typikon the abbot is portrayed as a father figure whereas in the Stoudios typikon he is a great lord before whom the monks prostrate themselves. Thus it is not surprising that informal relationships played an important role at Stoudios. The *Ascetic Chapters* of the Stoudite monk Symeon, which date to the same period, show that the monks visited each other in their cells in order to create a network of friends. Even though such activities were strictly forbidden in the Stoudios typikon, it is doubtful that they were ever stamped out.

The extended rules also cast light on the economic aspect of the monasteries for which whey were written.[22] The texts and their appendices list estates and properties whose income ensured the communities' material well-being. Such lists were drawn up both by monastic and by lay founders. For a long time the motivation of lay benefactors was straightforward. Property endowments to ecclesiastical institutions were inalienable, which guaranteed that their descendants would retain control over them. In the last decades of the eleventh century, however, the situation changed radically. The Evergetis typikon, which was composed by the first two abbots, stipulates that the monastery be autonomous and self-governing. Subsequently, lay founders began to adopt similar arrangements. At the same time the institution of *charistike* (*charistike dorea* = gift of grace) became a contentious issue. The charistike was a system of giving administrative control of monasteries to private persons or institutions for a restricted period, commonly a lifetime or several generations. Originally established to assist failed monasteries, the idea was to entrust laymen with administration on the ground that they would use their resources and expertise to restore a community's fortunes. But as time went on the system became corrupted, and charistike was seen by emperors as a means to remunerate loyal servants, so that even rich communities were all but dispossessed. Matters came to a head when the monk and former patriarch of Antioch, John of Oxia, berated emperor Alexios I (1081–1118) for having permitted such misuse. This incident does not, however, mean that the charistike disappeared altogether.[23] In the second half of the twelfth century, metropolitan Eustathius of Salonika, a former patriarchal deacon, criticised Athonite monks for being all too interested in the acquisition and management of landed property. He emphasised that the monks of Constantinople focused exclusively on spiritual matters and left the administration of their lands to laypeople. Even where this was not the case, there was a growing consensus in Constantinople that at least the monastic elite should steer clear of worldly matters. The Pantokrator typikon, drawn up at the behest of emperor John II (1118–43), distinguishes between monks responsible for the running of the monastery and monks tasked with celebrating services. Even more interesting is the case of the Petra monastery, which had no landed property at all and was funded by gifts from aristocrats and emperors. Petra then served as a model for emperor Manuel I's (1118–80) foundation of Kataskepe, which drew its income from the fisc.[24]

The authors of typika engaged in a debate about what constitutes the proper monastic life. They stressed coenobitic conformity, ascetic moderation and worldly withdrawal. Yet not everybody was prepared to subject themselves to this ideal. Two notable exceptions were Symeon the New Theologian (949–1022) and his self-proclaimed disciple, Nicetas Stethatos (c.1005–90), who both received their monastic formation at Stoudios. Symeon stands out as a mystic, the first in the Chalcedonian churches since Late Antiquity, and the first one ever in Constantinople. He wrote about his visions of divine light in verse and prose.[25] When he became abbot of the Mamas monastery in Constantinople he addressed his flock with catecheses which encapsulated his monastic vision. Symeon was convinced that anyone who showed the requisite contrition could become a mystic. He emphasised the personal relationship between a novice and his spiritual father, a stance that was becoming unusual. When he began to venerate his own spiritual father, another Symeon, the author of the *Ascetic Chapters*, he fell foul of the ecclesiastical authorities and was banished to the provinces, where he founded a new monastery. Nicetas, deeply impressed by Symeon's writings, took care to edit them and bring them into circulation. He spent most of his life at Stoudios, eventually becoming its abbot. In his *chef d'œuvre*, the *Centuries*, a treatise on spiritual practice, he claimed that as a mystic he had privileged knowledge from God, which he could pass on to the faithful. To make this point he reduced traditional notions of spiritual ascent to the appropriation of teachable knowledge, thus transforming the idea of mystical experience. His aim was to speak as an instructor of the people in Hagia Sophia. Yet he faced vicious opposition from lay intellectuals who made fun of his rustic language and his allegorical approach to Scriptural exegesis. What made his position even more precarious was the fact that his vision of the monastic calling was not shared by the majority of monks in the capital.[26]

Despite Symeon's claims, mystical experiences were always the preserve of the few. The rules never allude to this aspect of the monastic life. Indeed, it seems that claims to visionary experiences were seen ever more critically. In the twelfth century the monk Constantine Chrysomallos was posthumously excommunicated and his writings banned, although his views do not seem to have differed greatly from those of Symeon.[27] Much more widely debated were ascetic activities, especially fasting.[28] The Stoudite elite continued to propagate strict coenobiticism. The authors of the typikon make it clear that in the refectory all must eat the same food, regardless of their personal preferences, which goes even beyond what Theodore had demanded. The Panagios typikon inveighs against those who fast for several days, claiming that asceticism is no virtue because it is visible and only for show. No monk, it admonishes, should be different from his brethren. The Petra typikon also follows this trend. Indeed, the only exception is the Evergetis typikon, which allows monks who wish to fast to stay away from communal meals. That said, one of its adaptations follows the mainstream view by demanding that every monk attend every meal and eat from all dishes. Significantly, the topos of conformity also finds expression in hagiography, which had previously been wedded to the ideal of the 'holy man'.

The monastic elite's legalistic mindset is particularly evident in a related debate: the question of what one should eat on Wednesdays and Fridays.[29] Although these had been the traditional weekly fast days since the time of the early church, they were barely considered in early rules. In the eleventh century, however, stipulations were successively tightened until only a single meal of dry food was considered acceptable. Henceforth, a new kind of text appears, dietary typika, which explain how this basic regime is to be relaxed on feast days and during festal periods. However, hardliners were dissatisfied with this solution. At the end of the eleventh century, Patriarch Nicholas Grammatikos, a former Constantinopolitan abbot, claimed that on Wednesdays and Fridays fasting always took precedence, even in the case of Christmas. In this debate 'proof texts' played an important role. Treatises by Nicetas Stethatos and John of Oxia support each demand with quotations from Patristic authors. Claims to charismatic authority had no relevance, and if the dietary stipulations of saintly founders contradicted the new standard they were declared uncanonical and invalid. Another significant development was an obsession with the pre-Lenten fast of

Aracavor observed by the Monophysite Armenians,[30] in which all monks were required to eat cheese in the 'Cheesefare' week to demonstrate that they were not heretics. Even aspiring holy men were subject to this rule.

The trend towards ever greater regimentation is also visible in monastic worship.[31] The old regime is reflected in the Stoudite *Hypotyposis*. It records that Matins, Vespers and Compline were celebrated in the *katholikon* (main church) throughout the year, as had been the case in Theodore's time. It is not as forthcoming about the minor hours, Prime, Tierce, Sext and None. Yet we can gather that these prayer times were observed during the three Lenten periods but not during festal periods after Christmas and Easter. Moreover, it appears that they were performed by the monks in their cells.

In this case the Stoudios typikon does not introduce any changes. Yet change did come. It is first attested in a rule by Nicon of the Black Mountain, dated to the 1050s, which stipulates that monks are to gather daily in the church, feasts included, to perform the minor hours. Moreover, the rule introduces a new liturgical component, the so-called inter-hours, which followed the minor hours and were also performed in the *katholikon* at Nicon's monastery. This regime had considerable impact on the monks' lives. With it they could no longer decide how and to what extent they wished to worship.

Nicon lived near Antioch but there is no doubt that the innovations he introduced originated in the capital. The impact of the new regime on Constantinopolitan monastic settings is seen in the *Concise Hypotyposis* of Nicetas Stethatos, which offers a detailed explanation of the inter-hours protocol which leaves little doubt that this observance was new at Stoudios. Indeed, according to Nicetas both minor hours and inter-hours were performed in cells and not in the katholikon as Nicon had stipulated. There can be no doubt that the text was written in order to demonstrate that the community of Stoudios passed muster in a changed environment. This initiative is in stark contrast to the Evergetis monastery, where the typikon makes no mention of inter-hours and stipulates that minor hours be celebrated in cells. Only during the Lenten periods was the situation different. The *synxarium*, a text regulating daily worship, indicates that minor hours were celebrated in church and inter-hours in cells. This regulation was doubtless a conscious decision to give monks the opportunity to worship in private. Such a stance, however, was difficult to maintain. Adaptations of the Evergetis typikon state regularly that minor hours and inter-hours should be celebrated in the church all year round.

The reform movement also had an impact on another important aspect of the monastic life: almsgiving.[32] Symeon's *Ascetic Chapters* indicate that tenth-century Stoudios monks had funds of their own, which they distributed to the poor. In the course of the eleventh century private property came to be outlawed as it ran counter to the coenobitic ideology. Yet this does not mean that private almsgiving had disappeared. Monks gave away part of the food they were given in the refectory and some of the clothes they received from the monastery's stores. In due course, however, this practice was also forbidden as authors of monastic rules insisted that alms be given by the community as a whole. This stipulation met with fierce resistance since monks believed that personal distribution of alms was necessary to attain salvation. This conflict is reflected in the Panagios typikon, which rails against disobedient members of the community.

The eleventh century also saw important changes in the relation between monasteries and the patriarchate.[33] Canon law stipulated that the patriarch install the abbots of the capital. Yet in the late tenth century he could only discharge this duty in monasteries that were directly under his control. In 'imperial' monasteries such as Stoudios it was the emperor who fulfilled this task, choosing from three candidates selected by the monks and presenting the new abbot with the staff that was the sign of his office. In the middle of the eleventh century, however, a new concept came into existence. An illumination in a Stoudite manuscript depicts the abbot receiving his staff from Christ. The ritual corresponding to this scenario is described in the Evergetis typikon. In it the abbot-elect takes the staff from the altar, a placeholder for Christ. One reason for this change may have been the growing assertiveness of the patriarchs who demanded that installation be performed by bishops. The monasteries sought to counter this claim by appealing directly to God as the source of all ecclesiastical authority. In the long run, however, this ingenious strategy was not successful. By the end of the century the patriarchs had made sure that all abbots received their office from them. This change seems to have been connected to a promise of patriarchal help against the *charistikarioi*. Monks of the early twelfth century accepted without demur that abbots who had not received confirmation from a bishop were imposters. The Pantokrator typikon shows how difficult it was to find elbow room in this changed environment. It stipulated that the installation be performed by a foreign bishop who was forbidden by canon law to meddle in the internal affairs of another diocese, but accepted that this arrangement required special patriarchal dispensation.

Another contentious issue was confession.[34] Canon law stipulated that only priests could perform this duty, and determined the appropriate penance for individual sins. Yet for a long time this mandate remained a dead letter. Monks were confessors, whether they were ordained or not, and they used their own judgement when they imposed penances. The Stoudios typikon demanded that abbots hear confession but did not require them to be priests. The same stipulation can be found in the Evergetis typikon. By then, however, change was already afoot. Patriarch Nicholas Grammatikos declared that only priest-monks could hear confession, and that even they needed a special permission. Later rules accepted this position. In the late twelfth century the patriarch and his synod even forced an abbot of Evergetis to step down because he was not ordained and therefore could not hear confession.

The emphasis on moderation and conformity, the downgrading of charismatic authority in favour of book learning and the subjection to the patriarchate set Constantinopolitan monasticism apart from its counterparts in the provinces where traditional notions of monastic life based on the ideal of the inspired holy man persisted. This dichotomy came to a sudden end in 1204 when the Crusaders conquered Constantinople. Monasteries continued to exist, but they were now under the control of the Latin patriarch. When in 1261 the city was reconquered by the Byzantines the status quo had changed completely. In a monastic rule drawn up for Michael VIII (1261–82) it is again the emperor who installs the abbot. Moreover, the practice of performing inter-hours, whether privately or communally, appears to have been discontinued. In the fourteenth century, Constantinopolitan communities were under the sway of Mt Athos, which had become the undisputed centre of Byzantine monasticism.[35] It was there that the hesychastic method was developed. This method consisted of the so-called Jesus prayer, a short formula that was endlessly repeated, and breathing exercises. Its aim was to give the practitioner visions of light, which were considered to be an outflow of the divine. Such a lifestyle militated against community life since it required monks to stay in their cells. This led to the rise of the so-called *idiorrhythmia*, where monasteries were turned into loose confederations of individuals and the office of abbot was eventually replaced by a committee.[36]

## Further Reading

Hatlie, P., *The Monks and Monasteries of Constantinople, ca. 350–850* (Cambridge, 2007).
Talbot, A.-M., *Varieties of Monastic Experience in Byzantium, 800–1453* (Notre Dame, 2019).

# Notes

1 On the holy man see the seminal article of P. Brown, 'The Rise and Function of the Holy Man in Late Antiquity', *JRS* 61 (1971): 80–101.
2 See P. Rousseau, 'Eccentrics and Coenobites in the Late Roman East', *ByzF* 24 (1997): 35–50.
3 For the following see G. Dagron, 'Les moines et la ville: Le monachisme à Constantinople jusqu'au concile de Chalcédoine (451)', *TM* 4 (1970): 227–76.
4 On Daniel see M. Raub Vivian, 'The World of Daniel the Stylite: Rhetoric, Religion, and Relationships in the Life of the Pillar Saint', in *The Rhetoric of Power in Late Antiquity: Religion and Politics in Byzantium, Europe and the Early Islamic World*, ed. E. De Palma Digeser, R. M. Frakes and J. Stephens (London, 2010), 147–66.
5 See P. Hatlie, *Monks and Monasteries of Constantinople, 350–850* (Cambridge, 2007), 133–71.
6 See A. Hasse-Ungeheuer, *Das Mönchtum in der Religionspolitik Kaiser Justinians I: Die Engel des Himmels und der Stellvertreter Gottes auf Erden* (Berlin, 2016), 110–57.
7 For the following see Hatlie, *Monks and Monasteries*, 212–53.
8 See M.-F. Auzépy, *La Vie d'Étienne le Jeune par Étienne le Diacre* (Aldershot, 1997), 34–40.
9 For the following see D. Krausmüller, 'Chastity or Procreation? Models of Sanctity for Byzantine Laymen During the Iconoclastic and Post-iconoclastic Period', *Journal for Late Antique Religion and Culture*, 7 (2013): 51–71, esp. 49–68.
10 See M.-F. Auzépy, 'La place des moines à Nicée II (787)', *Byzantion* 58 (1988): 5–21.
11 For the following see J. Leroy, 'La vie quotidienne du moine studite', *Irénikon* 27 (1954): 21–50; and J. Leroy, *Studitisches Mönchtum: Spiritualität und Lebensform* (Graz, 1969).
12 See S. Efthymiadis, 'Le panégyrique de Théophane le Chronographe par S. Théodore Studite (BHG 1792b)', *AB* 31 (1993): 259–90, esp. 274.
13 For the following see D. Krausmüller, 'Nobody Has Ever Seen God: The Denial of the Possibility of Mystical Experiences in Eighth- and Eleventh-Century Byzantium', *Journal of Late Antique Religion and Culture* 11 (2017): 65–73.
14 For the following see D. Krausmüller, 'Diorasis Denied: Opposition to Clairvoyance in Byzantium from Late Antiquity to the Eleventh Century', *JÖB* 65 (2015): 111–28.
15 For the following see D. Krausmüller, 'Can Human Beings Know the Hour of Their Own Death or of the Death of Others? A Ninth-Century Controversy and Its Historical Context', *ZRIV* 53 (2016): 63–82.
16 For the following see Hatlie, *Monks and Monasteries*, 365–99.
17 See E. von Dobschütz, 'Methodios und die Studiten: Strömungen und Gegenströmungen in der Hagiographie des 9. Jahrhunderts', *BZ* 18 (1909): 41–105.
18 See O. Delouis, 'Écriture et réécriture au monastère de Stoudios à Constantinople (IXᵉ-Xᵉ s.): quelques remarques', in *Remanier, métaphraser: Fonctions et techniques de la réécriture dans le monde byzantin*, ed. S. Marjanovich-Dushanich (Belgrad, 2011), 101–10.
19 See R. Jordan and R. Morris, *The Hypotyposis of the Monastery of the Theotokos Evergetis, Constantinople (11th–12th Centuries)* (Farnham and Burlington, 2012); and D. Krausmüller and O. Grinchenko, 'The Tenth-Century Stoudios *Typikon* and Its Impact on Eleventh- and Twelfth-Century Byzantine Monasticism', *JÖB* 63 (2013): 153–75.
20 See E. A. Congdon, 'Imperial Commemoration and Ritual in the Monastery of Christ Pantokrator', *RÉB* 54 (1996): 161–99.
21 For the following see D. Krausmüller, 'Multiple Hierarchies: Servants and Masters, Monastic Officers, Ordained Monks, and Wearers of the Great and the Small Habit at the Stoudios Monastery (10th–11th Centuries)', *BSl* 74 (2016): 92–114.
22 For the following see J. P. Thomas, *Private Religious Foundations in the Byzantine Empire* (Washington, DC, 1987), 133–6.
23 For the following see P. Magdalino, *The Empire of Manuel I Komnenos, 1143–1180* (Cambridge, 1993), 270–2, 299.
24 See D. Krausmüller, 'Take No Care for the Morrow! The Rejection of Landed Property in Eleventh- and Twelfth-Century Byzantine Monasticism', *BMGS* 42 (2018): 45–57.
25 For the following see H. J. M. Turner, *St. Symeon the New Theologian and Spiritual Fatherhood* (Leiden, New York and Cologne, 1990).
26 See D. Krausmüller, 'An Embattled Charismatic: Assertiveness and Invective in Nicetas Stethatos' *Spiritual Centuries*', *BMGS* 44 (2020): 1–18.

27  See J. Gouillard, 'Quatre procès de mystiques à Byzance (vers 960–1143). Inspiration et autorité', *RÉB* 36 (1978): 5–81, esp. 29–35.
28  For the following see D. Krausmüller, 'From Competition to Conformity: Saints' Lives, Typika, and the Byzantine Monastic Discourse of the Eleventh Century', in *Byzantium in the Eleventh Century: Being In-Between*, ed. M. D. Lauxtermann and M. Whittow (Abingdon and New York, 2017), 199–215.
29  For the following see D. Krausmüller, 'The Athonite Monastic Tradition during the Eleventh and Early Twelfth Centuries', in *Mount Athos and Byzantine Monasticism*, ed. A. Bryer and M. Cunningham (Aldershot, 1996), 57–65.
30  See P. Ermilov, '"Satanic Heresy": On One Topic in Anti-Armenian Polemic', in *Orthodoxy and Heresy in Byzantium. The Definition and the Notion of Orthodoxy and Some Other Studies on the Heresies and the Non-Christian Religions*, ed. A. Rigo and P. Ermilov (Rome, 2010), 79–90.
31  For the following see D. Krausmüller, 'Liturgical Innovation in Eleventh- and Twelfth-Century Constantinople: Hours and Inter-hours in the Evergetis *Typikon*, Its 'Daughters' and its 'Grand-daughters'', *RÉB* 71 (2013): 149–72.
32  For the following see D. Krausmüller, 'From Individual Almsgiving to Communal Charity: The Impact of the Middle Byzantine Monastic Reform Movement on the Life of Monks', *JÖB* 66 (2016), 111–26.
33  For the following see D. Krausmüller, 'Decoding Monastic Ritual: Auto-installation and the Struggle for the Spiritual Autonomy of Byzantine Monasteries in the Eleventh and Twelfth Centuries', *JÖB* 58 (2008): 75–86.
34  For the following see D. Krausmüller, '"Monks Who Are Not Priests Do Not Have the Power to Bind and to Loose": The Debate about Confession in Eleventh- and Twelfth-Century Byzantium', *BZ* 109 (2016): 703–32.
35  See D. Krausmüller, 'The Triumph of Hesychasm', in *The Cambridge History of Christianity 5: Eastern Christianity*, ed. M. Angold (Cambridge, 2006), 101–26.
36  See A.-M. Talbot, *Varieties of Monastic Experience in Byzantium, 800–1453* (Notre Dame, 2019), 39–43.

# 13: SACRED DIMENSIONS: DEATH AND BURIAL

## Mark J. Johnson

Burial practices in Constantinople largely echoed those found in the Greek and Roman worlds and then in other Christian communities from the fourth to the fifteenth century. Laws and practices used in the late antique period continued customs established in Roman law, but evolved as Christian customs changed in later centuries, favoring church burials. As the capital, the city also was home to imperial tombs and those of other high officials, which were naturally more elaborate than those ordinary citizens. Unfortunately, for a city of this size and importance relatively little material evidence of these practices remain.

The most basic burial law of the Romans and the Greeks before them was that burials were to take place outside of the boundaries of the city, separating the dead and their space from the living and theirs. Only a few exceptions to this law were permitted, including emperors, certain dignitaries of the religion such as the Vestal Virgins, and founders of cities. All Roman cities had cemeteries outside of their walls, with larger tombs and mausolea lining suburban roads.[1]

Burial in extramural cemeteries was the practice in ancient Byzantium as well, with cemeteries located outside of the ancient city walls located along the roads leading west to Thrace. Numerous finds between the Çemberlitaş and Beyazıt districts west of Hagia Sophia demonstrate the presence of a cemetery in this area, a necropolis that served the ancient city from the fifth century BCE on.[2] A new cemetery was established outside of the expanded city of Constantine in the area of the church of Hagios Mokios.[3] Attributed in some sources to Constantine (306–37), the church was a large basilica with side aisles and an atrium, which seems to have fulfilled a role similar to the great cemetery basilicas that he had built in the suburbs of Rome. In an unusual move, Constantine organized the gravediggers and burial providers and put them under control of the Church, donating money so that burials would be free to the capital city's inhabitants.[4]

The expansion of the city with a new set of walls in the fourth century led to the enclosure of the old cemeteries within the new urban space and the formation of new ones outside the new city gates. This turn of events raised the question of what to do about the old burials in the newly enclosed cemeteries. A law issued in 381 may have been intended to deal with this issue. In it, the Emperors Gratian, Valentinian, and Theodosios order that any burials in sarcophagi and urns above ground be moved to a location outside the city, while burials below ground be left intact.[5]

When the city was expanded and yet another new city wall built under Theodosios II (401–50) in the early fifth century, the cemeteries established during the fourth century similarly found themselves in a planned urban area. In this case, however, these necropolei continued to flourish for centuries. The old Constantinian wall, therefore, marked and continued to mark the sacred boundary of the city, and the area to its west continued to serve this function as well as accommodate some urban growth. Indeed, new tombs, including hypogea, or underground chambers, dating to the fifth century, were built inside the Theodosian wall, including some built against the inner side of the wall and decorated with Christian-themed frescoes.[6]

The most significant burial monument in the city was the church of the Holy Apostles, begun a few years before Constantine died in 337.[7] In planning his eventual final resting place the emperor had the example of other late Roman imperial mausolea, which were largely domed rotundas, but the added consideration that his would be the first such monument for a Christian ruler. His solution was to adopt the basic architectural form of the mausolea of his immediate predecessors and combine it with the emerging idea of the Christian commemorative structure, such as that seen in another of his buildings, the Church of the Holy Sepulcher in Jerusalem. As described by his biographer Eusebius, Constantine ordered that his sarcophagus be placed in the church that was not only dedicated to the Apostles but also possessed memorials to the Twelve, perhaps intended from the beginning to contain their relics. In so doing, he expressed the desire to share the benefit of services and the prayers that offered there.[8] Although the form of the building has been debated, there is enough in Eusebius' description to permit the building to be interpreted as a domed rotunda, like other imperial mausolea. It is probable that it was a double-shell structure with a tall domed core surrounded by an ambulatory with niches, similar to the design of Constantine's daughter Constantina's slightly later monument in Rome.[9]

At some point in the 350s, Constantine's son and heir, Constantius II (337–61), made changes to the church of the Holy Apostles, separating its two functions. A cruciform building was added to the west of the rotunda and became both the church proper and the focal point for the veneration of the apostles, a structure dedicated only in 370. The rotunda remained intact but became a dynastic mausoleum at this point; memorials to the apostles were removed, and Constantius was later interred there. He was followed by many of the later heirs to the throne through the fifth century, including Theodosios, Marcian (450–7), Leo (457–74), Zeno (474–91), and Anastasios (491–518). These emperors were buried in massive porphyry sarcophagi, a few of which survive (Fig. 13.1).[10] A number of later emperors starting with Michael III (842–67) and ending with Constantine VIII (962–1028) were also interred in the structure, making a total of at least twenty imperial burials.

Over time satellite structures were added to the complex. The so-called "North Stoa" held the sarcophagi of a few late fourth-century emperors, probably Julian (361–3), Jovian (363–4), and Valentinian (375–92). The "South Stoa" seems to have been built by Arkadios

13.1 Imperial porphyry sarcophagi, fourth and fifth centuries, from the Mausoleum of Constantine, Archaeological Museum, Istanbul. (Photo courtesy of Mark J. Johnson)

(377–408) and contained his sarcophagus, along with those of his wife Eudoxia (d. 404) and their son Theodosios II (408–50).

Justinian (527–65) rebuilt the cruciform church in the sixth century, replacing it with another building of the same plan but covering its crossing and each arm with domes. He also added his own mausoleum in the sixth century, a cruciform structure attached to the north arm of the church, where he, his wife Theodora (d. 548), and many of their successors were interred. The church and the rotunda mausoleum remained standing until a few years after the Turkish conquest when both were razed and replaced with the Fatih mosque and Mehmed the Conqueror's tomb.[11]

At least two bishops of Constantinople were buried in the church itself. Theodosios II had the remains of John Chrysostomos (d. 407) transferred there in 437, and his sister Pulcheria (d. 453) and her husband Marcian, the new emperor, ordered the remains of the Archbishop Flavian (d. 449) brought to Constantinople and placed inside the church.[12]

The complex of the Church of the Holy Apostles was located inside the city walls built by Constantine, but intra-urban burials of emperors and important religious figures were exceptions to the general proscription against such burials under Roman law. The complex simply represents the Christianization of this practice. All other burials remained under the ban of urban burials, a point reemphasized in the law of 381 referred to above, which added that no one should assume that resting places of the apostles and martyrs within the city were suitable places of burial; ordinary citizens were excluded from burial in those places just as they were from burial in the rest of the city.

As time went on, the prohibition against intra-urban burials evaporated. During the plague that hit Constantinople in 747 so many people died that, as the ninth-century chronicler Theophanes notes, "all of the cemeteries both in the city and the suburbs were filled" causing the living to resort to using dry cisterns and pools as well as vineyards and "the orchards within the old [Constantinian] walls" as additional places for burials.[13] The proscription was officially repealed under Leo VI (886–912), but this was more of a recognition of how burial customs had changed than a "new" policy.[14] Some evidence of urban burials during the seventh and subsequent centuries has been found in the form of a marble sarcophagus carved with crosses, reused early Christian sarcophagi, and burial inscriptions.[15]

Another development in funerary practices in Constantinople was the use of churches as places of burial, a practice that came to be followed throughout the empire and mirrored developing customs in the medieval west. The practice started in Constantinople with the Church of the Holy Apostles, as noted, but already in 527 Justin I (518–27) and his wife Euphemia (d. 523/24) were buried in another church at the Monastery of the Augusta. Their remains were later transferred to the Holy Apostles but numerous subsequent emperors were buried in other churches in the capital: Maurice (582–602) and his family in St. Mamas, Constantine VI (780–97) and his family in St. Euphrosyne, John Tzimiskes (969–76) in the Chapel of the Savior at the Chalke, and Basil II (976–1025) in the church of St. John the Baptist in the city's suburb of Hebdoman.[16]

This custom was adopted by the non-imperial elites of city, in particular by those who had the means to found new churches and monasteries. At the north church of the Lips monastery (Fenari Isa Camii), dedicated to the Theotokos and built in the early ninth century, excavations revealed five marble sarcophagi under the floor of the narthex, aligned to the doors leading into the naos, with additional tombs in the north and south side aisles of the naos. These most likely belonged to the founder of the monastery, the admiral Constantine Lips (d. 917), and his family.[17] Clergy were also buried inside the city walls. For example, the remains of Theodore of Stoudios (d. 826) and those of his brother Joseph of Thessalonike (d. 830) were brought to the church of St. John Studios and placed in the same tomb as their uncle, Plato (d. 814), in a chapel dedicated to the martyrs located to the east of the main church.[18]

Although some emperors continued to be buried at the church of the Holy Apostles, from Michael III to Constantine VIII, others were not only buried in other churches as noted but founded their own monasteries and churches to become dynastic burial monuments. Romanos I Lekapenos (920–44, d. 948) built the Myrelaion, a palace and small church that became the burial place for himself and his family. Romanos III Argyros (1028–34) built the monastery of the Peribleptos and was buried there. Nikephoros III Botaneiates (1078–81) restored the church a few decades later and it became his place of burial. Constantine IX Monomachos (1042–55) built the church of St. George Mangana and buried his mistress Maria there in 1044; he was buried next to her upon his death. Alexios I Komnenos (1081–1118) built the church of Christ Philanthropos where he was buried after his death.[19]

None of these burials survived the Turkish conquest of the city, so literary accounts provide the best evidence as to their placement within the churches and their architectural settings. The design of Byzantine churches had evolved into more compact structures such as the cross-in-square type and similar buildings that possessed a tripartite sanctuary on the east, a nave with a central dome flanked by side aisles defined by columns or piers holding the structure of the drum and dome, and a pronaos or narthex on the west. The central apse and the space immediately in front of it constituted the bema or sanctuary. Burials in the form of tombs placed either under the floor or above the floor in sarcophagi or marble enclosures were situated in the narthex or along the side aisles, but not in the space of the bema or the area immediately in front of it.[20]

The reason for the siting of burials in churches in some places but not in others is explained in part by the fifteenth-century theologian, Symeon of Thessaloniki, who in describing the theological concept of the church building divides it into three parts: the pronaos, naos (nave), and sanctuary. The pronaos represents the earth, the naos represents heaven, and the sanctuary the things "beyond heaven," noting that the last was a space reserved for the clergy.[21] Therefore, burials in the narthex or lateral spaces of the naos were acceptable, but could not be placed in the sanctuary.

Why did people seek burial in churches? One thought is that as the remains of the martyrs and other important saints had been moved by this time from their original locations in cemeteries to urban churches. People still wanted to be buried near them (burial *ad sanctos*, near the saint) in hopes of establishing a relationship with the saint that might benefit them in the afterlife.[22]

Many of the church burials in Constantinople that are known were connected to the founders of those churches. The founders hoped that their demonstration of faith and desire to glorify God through building churches would help in their own salvation. As the Presbyter Alexios Tesaites wrote in 1232: "Those who erect churches, they do it for three reasons: first to praise God; second to pray on behalf of the emperor's rule; third to commemorate those who are buried there and orthodox everywhere."[23] The *typika*, or foundation documents, of the monasteries make this point clear, as well. Having a burial church connected with a monastery also provided the benefit of having the monks pray for the founders' salvation. Being in the presence of the relics of saints also offered the benefit of a shared blessing of the prayers of the faithful and the church services in the same way that Constantine had expressed a desire to share in the honor accorded the apostles in his original church of the Holy Apostles.

Many of these ideas were implemented in the dynastic burial chapel of the Komnenian dynasty of the twelfth century at the Pantokrator monastery, founded in 1118 by Empress Irene (d. 1134). A second church was later built to the north of the first one and in the 1130s Irene's husband, John II Komnenos (1118–43), added a chapel, locating it in the narrow space between the two existing churches. Given the available space, it has a single nave with an apse on its east end, the naos itself covered by two domes of unequal size. A door on the west connects to the narthex shared by all three churches.[24] The chapel was dedicated to St. Michael, the archangel whose trumpet blast will initiate the resurrection of the dead. The surviving *typikon* for the monastery was written in 1136 and explains that the east end of the chapel contained the *templon* and bema, and that the dome covering this area was called that "of the Incorporeal." The western part of the chapel, covered by its own dome, was identified as the "heroon of the exterior," reviving an ancient term meaning a monument for heroes that had previously been used for the Mausoleum of Constantine at the Holy Apostles. A tomb against the west wall was used for John and Irene's son Alexios who died in 1142, and then shared with John who died the following year. John's son Manuel I (1143–80) became the next emperor and buried his first wife in the chapel at her death in 1160. Manuel himself followed his body placed in a tomb made of dark stone and covered by a lid with seven spires or dome-like extensions, the whole of which may have stood under the western dome.[25]

Although the building remains intact, none of the tombs or its decoration survive. Information about the furnishings of the chapel is found in the *typikon* and other sources. Manuel had ordered a pinkish stone slab brought to Constantinople from Ephesus earlier in his reign. This was the "Stone of Unction" believed to be the marble slab on which the body of Christ was prepared for burial.[26] First kept in the church of the Pharos, Manuel had it transferred to the Heroon, where it was placed in proximity to his and the other imperial tombs. The chapel was decorated in fresco, or more likely mosaic, on the lateral arches of the space, including scenes of Christ's Crucifixion, the Resurrection, the Tomb of Christ, and one of Christ appearing to the Marys at the tomb on Easter morning.[27] The Stone of Unction and this decoration were all meant to tie the Savior's death and resurrection to the deaths and hoped for resurrections of members of the imperial family. In addition, candles and lamps were to be continually lit near each tomb and in the center of the Heroon. On the days of the commemorations of John, Irene, and Alexios, one of the most important icons in the

Byzantine world, the Hodegetria icon, was to be brought from its chapel to the Pantokrator and placed in the eastern part of the chapel, but still near the imperial tombs, in what can be seen an attempt to invoke the intercessory powers of the Virgin.[28]

From the same period and with similar attention to detail is the description of the tomb that John II Komnenos' brother Isaac (d. after 1152) designed for himself in the church of the Chora monastery. He later founded a church at Pherrai and decided to move his planned tomb there and it is from the *typikon* of that church that we know that the monument he had made in the Chora was transferred to Pherrai. The items he mentions are the stone slabs making up the coffin, a cast bronze railing, portraits of his parents, and a stand for a mosaic icon of the Mother of God, all to be sent to his new church, leaving behind only a portrait of himself, made while he was young.[29]

Three important funerary churches of the Palaiologan period survive, two of them with at least some part of their decoration intact. Late in the thirteenth century, Theodora Palaiologina (d. 1303), the widow of Emperor Michael VIII Palaiologos (1259–82), had a new church dedicated to St. John the Forerunner built to the south of the church of the Theotokos in the monastery of Constantine Lips discussed above.[30] The new church was intended to serve as an imperial mausoleum, with the *typikon* of the monastery including specific instructions for burials in the new church.[31] In it, Theodora stated that the body of her daughter, probably Anna, was buried to the right of the entrance of the church and then instructed that her tomb and that of her mother should be "built after the intervening door," apparently in the south aisle of the church where two tombs with *arcosolia*, or arched niches, are still present. She then stated that any of her children or sons-in-law, as well as grandchildren and their spouses, could be buried in the church in the future if they so desired. Theodora lived as a nun in her own foundation during her last years and when she died in 1303 was entombed in the church, as she had instructed. Her sons, Emperor Andronikos II (1282–1328, d. 1332) and Constantine (d. 1306), were also buried there.

The arcosolium tomb type came to be common during the Palaiologan era, but its origins are much earlier, going back to early Christian times where it was often employed in catacomb tombs in which the barrel vault over the tomb was a symbol of heaven. As a tomb feature, the arcosolium reappeared in Constantinople in the twelfth century.[32] In essence it is a kind of canopy and canopies over important sarcophagi were found in the Crusader Holy Land, Norman Sicily and Rome during the twelfth century.[33]

In Palaiologan Constantinople, *arcosolia* were sometimes given a marble arched entablature, carved with figures and perhaps with an inscription as well. An arch carved with busts of the apostles now in the archaeological Museum of Istanbul may have come from the tomb of Theodora.[34] The tomb proper within the niche was composed of a slab of marble for the front and another for the lid. The wall above the tomb was often decorated with frescoes or mosaic; those in the church of St. John at the Lips monastery have a few remnants of mosaic.

The monastery church of St. Mary Pammakaristos was remodeled at the end of the thirteenth/beginning of the fourteenth century by Michael Tarchaneiotes Glabas and his wife, Maria.[35] After he died in about 1304 she had a parekklesion, or side chapel, constructed on the south flank of the main church to be a monument for her husband and her own eventual mausoleum. This structure took the form of a small cross-in-square church with a central core. Four columns rose to support a drum and dome. There was a tripartite sanctuary on the east and a small narthex on the west. Against the north wall of the naos is an arcosolium that presumably held the tomb of the Michael and Maria. Three other *arcosolia* in the narthex held tombs for other family members and additional tombs were found in the main church and its added exonarthex.

Mosaics decorated the interior of the parekklesion, with a depiction of Christ Pantokrator in the dome and various saints on the vaults of the surrounding spaces. In the main apse, where a depiction of the Virgin Mary is normally found in a Byzantine church, is a seated figure of Christ. The reason for this anomaly is clear when one sees that the conches of the flanking side apses contain standing figures of the Virgin on the north and of John the Baptist on the south, both in poses of supplication. Together, the three images form a depiction of the Deesis, with Mary and John acting as intercessors, a subject strongly tied to the funerary function of the chapel.

A contemporary church provides the most complete example of a late Byzantine burial church and is the best preserved of all such buildings from the whole of Byzantine Constantinople. The Church of Christ in Chora, also known as the Kariye Camii or Kariye Museum, is a middle Byzantine church that was restored and enlarged by the Sebastokrator Theodore Metochites in 1316–21.[36] The modifications included the addition of an ambulatory hall on the north side of the church, an exonarthex on the west and a parekklesion on the south flank, the latter intended as the funerary chapel for Theodore and some of his colleagues.

New decoration, consisting of mosaics in the church and narthexes and frescoes in the parekklesion completed the remodeling.

Eight *arcosolia* tombs are found in the church, one in the inner narthex, three in the outer narthex, and four in the parekklesion. The first was built into the north end of the inner narthex. As is the case with all eight, the coffin and remains that would have been contained in the lower part of the niche have been removed. Above the burial, the wall was painted with a fresco of which the lower half remains. On the left, a seated Virgin Mary holds the Christ child; on the right, the drapery of two figures is visible. An inscription identifies one of the figures as Demetrios, who was of royal lineage, perhaps the youngest son of Emperor Andronikos II.[37] The three tombs in the outer narthex were created by filling in the arches of what were originally windows. Tomb E has portraits of a man, woman, and a child. The central figure has a dress with monograms of the Asanaioi-Palaiologoi families and portraits of a nun and a monk. This can be identified as the tomb of Irene Raoulaina Palaiologina, widow of Constantine Palaiologos, the brother of Emperor Andronikos II, and mother-in-law of Irene, the daughter of Theodore Metochites. Tomb F also belonged to a member of the Palaiologan family, but the identity of the occupant of Tomb G is unknown.

The parekklesion remains a spectacular display of late Byzantine art and funerary ideology. It is entered through a triple arcade resting on two columns on the west. Built with a single nave, it terminates in a semicircular apse at its eastern end and has four *arcosolia* tombs, two each on the north and south walls. An arch divides the space into two bays; that on the west is covered by a pumpkin dome, frescoed with an image of the Virgin at its apex. On the east, the bay is covered with a sail vault, also frescoed, as is the apse and its conch.

Tomb A, located on the northern side of the western bay, is the largest of the tombs and thought to have belonged to Theodore (Fig. 13.2). Unfortunately it has lost its original fresco decoration, but still possesses its large, intricately carved marble arch, bearing angels on either end of its front. To the east, on the north wall, Tomb B has lost every bit of its decoration. On the south wall, Tomb C, in the eastern bay, has its decoration relatively intact, depicting four full length figures. The central couple is dressed in princely attire, but nothing remains to help identify them.

Tomb D, in the western part of the south wall, sits across from the arcosolium of Theodore's tomb, and is the only one with a surviving inscription. Carved into its marble archway, the inscription identifies the occupants of the tomb as the Grand Constable Michael Tornikes, a

13.2 Arcosolium tomb niche of Theodore Metochites, Christ of the Chora Church (Kariye Museum), Istanbul. (Photo courtesy of Mark J. Johnson)

friend of Theodore's, and his wife of royal lineage (Fig. 13.3). The couple is depicted twice: on the back wall in aristocratic dress and on the side walls of the niche as monastics with an inscription informing the viewer that these are the "same people" as those on the back wall.

The fresco decoration of the chapel as a whole is based on its funerary function.[38] In the vault of the apse is a scene of the Anastasis, in which Christ, having broken the gates of Hell, begins the Resurrection by lifting Adam and Eve from their tombs. The vault in front of the apse contains a scene of the Last Judgement, a subject common in Western religious art but rare in Byzantine art. Even rarer is its placement not on a wall but on the surface of a vault.

The decoration of the dome covering the western bay depicts the Virgin Mary, as noted. In this context she is there in her role as intercessor, and her prominence suggests that the chapel may have been dedicated to her. The fact that this depiction covers the bay where Theodore's tomb is located is significant and her importance as intercessor is emphasized in the decoration of the northeast pendentive. Close to the

13.3 Arcosolium tomb niche of Michael Tornikes, Christ of the Chora Church (Kariye Museum), Istanbul. (Photo courtesy of Mark J. Johnson)

arcosolium of Theodore, it shows a nude male figure representing Theodore's soul ascending from the tomb toward the Virgin in the dome. Death, intercession, judgment, and resurrection are the themes of the afterlife that awaited those whose tombs were here.

It is reflective of the transformation of Constantinople following the Turkish conquest and its growth into a major modern city that not a single one of the tombs discussed here has remained intact. It is also noteworthy that so few places of burial have survived in a condition to even be studied. The possibility exists that additional burials may be found in the area of former cemeteries, and perhaps others under the floors of surviving churches, but the few surviving remains of the monumental tombs of the elites will of necessity represent the many others that have disappeared with time. Enough examples have survived that permit an understanding of evolving burial practices in Constantinople – from traditional burials in extra-urban cemeteries, to their transformation into Christian cemeteries and the move to burials in churches. With some customs particular to Byzantine Orthodox traditions, they are practices that matched those established in other cities of the Roman and medieval Christian world.

## FURTHER READING

Johnson, M. J., *The Roman Imperial Mausoleum in Late Antiquity* (Cambridge, 2009).
Marinis, V., "Tombs and Burials in the Monastery *tou Libos* in Constantinople," *DOP* 63 (2009): 147–66.

Mullett, M. and R. G. Ousterhout, eds., *The Holy Apostles: A Lost Monument, a Forgotten Project, and the Presentness of the Past* (Washington, DC, 2020).

Ousterhout, R., "Temporal Structuring in the Chora Parekklesion," *Gesta* 34 (1995): 63–76.

Ousterhout, R., *Eastern Medieval Architecture: The Building Traditions of Byzantium and Neighboring Lands* (Oxford, 2019).

# NOTES

1 J. M. C. Toynbee, *Death and Burial in the Roman World* (Ithaca, NY, 1971), 48–9; exceptions, M. J. Johnson, *The Roman Imperial Mausoleum in Late Antiquity* (Cambridge, 2009), 25, with references.

2 W. Müller-Wiener, *Bildlexikon zur Topographie Istanbuls: Byzantion, Konstantinupolis, Istanbul bis zum Beginn d. 17. Jh.* (Tübingen, 1977), 219–22; K. Dark and F. Özgümüş, *Constantinople: Archaeology of a Byzantine Megapolis – Final Report on the Istanbul Rescue Archaeology Project 1998–2004* (Oxford, 2013), 42–4, 63.

3 A. Berger, "Mokios und Konstantin der Große: Zu den Anfängen des Märtyrerkults in Konstantinopel," in *Antecessor Festschrift für Spyros N. Troianos zum 80. Geburtstag*, ed. V. A. Leontaritou, K. A. Bourdara, and E. S. Papagianni (Athens, 2013), 165–85, especially 176–85.

4 S. E. Bond, "Mortuary Workers, the Church, and the Funeral Trade in Late Antiquity," *JLA* 6 (2013): 135–51.

5 *CTh* 9.17.6; G. Dagron, "Le christianisme dans la ville," *DOP* 31 (1977): 1–25, esp. 15–16.

6 J. Deckers and Ü. Serdaroğlu, "Das Hypogäum beim Silivri-Kapi in Istanbul," *JbAC* 36 (1993): 140–63; M. I. Tunay, "Byzantine Archaeological Findings in Istanbul during the Last Decade," in *Byzantine Constantinople: Monuments, Topography and Everyday Life*, ed. N. Necipoğlu (Leiden, 2001), 217–31.

7 Johnson, *Mausoleum*, 119–29; M. J. Johnson, "Constantine's Apostoleion: A Reappraisal," in *The Holy Apostles: A Lost Monument, a Forgotten Project, and the Presentness of the Past*, ed. M. Mullett and R. G. Ousterhout (Washington, DC, 2020), 79–98; J. Bardill, *Constantine, Divine Emperor of the Christian Golden Age* (Cambridge, 2012), 367–84; for the imperial burials in the complex see P. Grierson, "The Tombs and Obits of the Byzantine Emperors (337–1042)," *DOP* 16 (1962): 3–63.

8 Eusebius of Caesarea, *Life of Constantine*, 4:58–60, ed. and trans. Av. Cameron and S. Hall (Oxford, 1999), 176–77; C. Mango, "Constantine's Mausoleum and the Translation of Relics," *BZ* 83 (1990): 51–61; reprinted in his *Studies on Constantinople* (Aldershot, 1993), no. V, with addendum, was the first to develop the theory that Constantine's Apostoleion was a domed rotunda and not a basilica or cross shaped building.

9 Johnson, *Mausoleum*, 139–56.

10 N. Asutay-Effenberger and A. Effenberger, *Die Porphyrsarkophage der oströmischen Kaiser* (Wiesbaden, 2006).

11 See Dark and Özgümüş, *Constantinople*, 83–96; and additional contributions in Mullett and Ousterhout, *Holy Apostles.*

12 Grierson, "Tombs and Obits," 6.

13 Theophanes, *Chronicle*, A.M. 6238, trans. H. Turtledove (Philadelphia, 1982), 11.

14 *Novella* 53 in *Les novelles de Léon VI le Sage*, ed. and trans. P. Noailles and A. Dain (Paris, 1944), 202–5.

15 Dark and Özgümüş, *Constantinople*, 42–4.

16 For imperial burials outside of the Holy Apostles, see Grierson, "Tombs," 45–60; A. Carile, "Funerali e sepolture imperiali a Costantinopoli fra realtà e leggenda," *Nea Rhome, rivista di ricerche bizantinistiche* 9 (2012): 43–57.

17 V. Marinis, "Tombs and Burials in the Monastery *tou Libos* in Constantinople," *DOP* 63 (2009): 147–66, esp. 156–61.

18 V. Marinis, *Architecture and Ritual in the Churches of Constantinople, Ninth–Fifteenth Centuries* (Cambridge, 2014), 85–6.

19 Carile, "Funerali," 55–6; Marinis, *Architecture*; and R. Ousterhout, *Eastern Medieval Architecture: The Building Traditions of Byzantium and Neighboring Lands* (Oxford, 2019) for the churches.

20 For the locations of burials within churches see Marinis, *Architecture*, 59–63 and 73–5.

21 PG 155: 704; discussed in Marinis, "Tombs," 153.

22 E. Dyggve, "The Origin of the Urban Churchyard," *ClMed* 13 (1952): 147–58. Marinis, *Architecture*, 60–3, explaining that there were other possible factors.

23 F. Miklosich and I. Müller, eds., *Acta et diplomata graeca medii aevi sacra et profana*, 6 vols. (Vienna, 1860–90; reprint Athens 1961), 4: 58; Marinis, "Tombs," 158.

24 For the church of St. Michael at the Pantokrator Monastery and its decoration and furnishings see R. Ousterhout, "Architecture, Art, and Komnenian Ideology at the Pantokrator Monastery," in *Byzantine Constantinople*, ed. Necipoğlu, 133–50; R. Ousterhout, "Byzantine Funerary Architecture of the Twelfth Century," in *Drevnerusskoe iskustvo: Rusi i stranii byzantinskogo mira XII vek* (St. Petersburg, 2002), 9–17.

25 For Manuel's unusual tomb see N. Ševčenko, "The Tomb of Manuel I Komnenos, Again," in *First International Byzantine Studies Symposium*, ed. A. Ödekan, E. Akyürek, and N. Necipoğlu (Istanbul, 2010), 609–16.

26 I. Drpić, "Manual I Komnenos and the Stone of Unction," *BMGS* 43 (2019): 60–82.

27 Typikon of Emperor John II Komnenos for the Monastery of Christ Pantokrator in *Constantinople*, chapter 29, trans. R. Jordan, *BMFD* 2: 754.

28 Typikon of Emperor John II Komnenos for the Monastery of Christ Pantokrator in *Constantinople*, chapter 29, trans. R. Jordan, chapters 34–5, 2: 756.

29 Typikon of the Sebastokrator Isaac Komnenos for the Monastery of the Mother of God Kosmosoteira near Bera, chapter 89, trans. N. P. Ševčenko, *BMFD* 2: 838.

30 Marinis, "Tombs," 161–4; Marinis, *Architecture*, 182–91.

31 Typikon of Theodora Palaiologina for the Convent of Lips in *Constantinople*, chapter 18, trans. A.-M. Talbot, BMFD, 3: 1278–9.

32 Marinis, *Architecture*, 73–4.

33 I. Herklotz, *"Sepulcra" e "Monumenta" del medioevo*, 2nd edition (Rome, 1990), 49–84.

34 H. Belting, "Skulptur aus der Zeit um 1300 in Konstantinopel," *MünchJb* 23 (1972): 63–100, on 67–70.

35 H. Belting, C. Mango, and D. Mouriki, *The Mosaics and Frescoes of St. Mary Pammakaristos (Fethiye Camii) at Istanbul* (Washington, DC, 1978); A. Effenberger, "Zu den Gräbern in der Pammakaristoskirche," *Byzantion* 77 (2007): 170–96.

36 R. Ousterhout, *The Architecture of the Kariye Camii in Istanbul* (Washington, 1987); R. Ousterhout, *The Art of the Kariye Camii* (London, 2002); P. Underwood, *The Kariye Djami*, Vol. 1, *Historical Introduction and Description of the Mosaics and Frescoes* (New York, 1966).

37 For detailed descriptions of the decoration of each tomb and possible identifications see Underwood, *Kariye Djami*, 269–99.

38 R. Ousterhout, "Temporal Structuring in the Chora Parekklesion," *Gesta* 34 (1995): 63–76; E. Akyürek, "Funeral Ritual in the Parekklesion of the Chora Church," in *Byzantine Constantinople*, 89–104.

# Part IV

# Institutions and Activities

# 14: THE ADMINISTRATION OF CONSTANTINOPLE

## Andreas Gkoutzioukostas

From its establishment as the new imperial base of Constantine the Great (306–37) Constantinople enjoyed a unique administrative regime. From 359 on, this administration centred on the official known in Latin as Prefect of the City of Constantinople (*praefectus urbi*), and in Greek as the Eparch of the City (*eparchos*). An imperially appointed governor, the Prefect/Eparch was the city's chief operating officer. As such he presided over an army of civil servants and had oversight of a range of administrative activity, some of which changed over time. This chapter examines the history of this office, its administrative structure and administrative responsibilities between the fourth and the fifteenth centuries.

### BEGINNINGS: FROM *ANTHYPATOS* (PROCONSUL) TO EPARCH OF THE CITY

Unlike other urban centres in the later Roman Empire, the administrative status of Constantinople was independent of the provincial system and, more specifically, of the jurisdiction of the governor of the province of Europe to which it had originally belonged. Initially an official known as the anthypatos was placed in charge of the city.[1] The first attested governors of Constantinople, however, are referred to by the generic Greek term *archon* (ruler). The archon's main duties involved policing and surveillance of foreigners, including control of residence permits.[2]

In 359, Constantius II (337–61) terminated the position of the anthypatos and introduced the office of the Prefect or Eparch of Constantinople.[3] The new office was modelled on that of the Prefect of the City of Rome (*praefectus urbis Romae*), both in terms of its operations and in terms of its jurisdictional range.[4] This self-conscious reflection of the institutions of the old capital had the effect of equating

Constantinople institutionally with Rome.[5] From the fourth century on, the city's administration was synonymous with the office of the eparch.[6]

The prefect was aided in his efforts by numerous officials working both at the neighbourhood level and in the central offices of his administration. The seat of his office, the *Praitorion*, was located in the city centre near the Forum of Constantine, on the Mese, the capital's principle thoroughfare.[7]

EARLY ADMINISTRATION: FOURTH THROUGH
SEVENTH CENTURIES

The first prefect was an experienced official, Honoratus, a former praetorian prefect of Gaul who also had served in other provincial posts.[8] From the time of Honoratus on the duties of the eparch expanded beyond the initial policing mandate of the anthypatos. The prefect came to oversee matters related to law enforcement: the examination of civil and criminal cases, the judgment of appeals from neighbouring provinces and legal proceedings pertinent to guardianship and wills. In addition, he was responsible for the oversight of public services such as landscaping, ornamentation and urban planning, and the operations of the water supply, sanitation and night lighting. His office also maintained the senatorial census. Finally, he became president of the Senate,[9] which Constantius II elevated and equated with the Senate of Rome.[10] Individual citizens of the capital, together with group organizations such as the circus factions (*demoi*) and guilds all were subject to the prefect.[11] Eventually his office took charge of almost every aspect of the city's operation. With the emergence of Constantinople as the permanent seat of emperors, and the city's population growth and geographical expansion, the importance of the eparch of the city only increased. He became the highest authority in the capital, representing the emperor by whom he was appointed and to whom he was accountable.[12]

We lack specific information about the number and duties of the eparch's subordinates. There is, however, evidence from the office on which his was modelled, the praefectus urbis Romae.[13] Analogy to the Roman prefecture makes it possible to reconstruct aspects of the organization of the Constantinopolitan service. That said, only three of the fifteen officials who served under the Roman prefect are mentioned in the sources concerning the prefect of Constantinople:[14] the prefect of the *annona* (grain supply), an office probably introduced during the reign of Anastasios (491–518),[15] the master of tax assessment (*magister census*) who first appears in 472[16] and who was responsible with his subordinates (*censuales*) for the valuation of property and the taxation of senators,[17] and the prefect of the night watch (*prefectus vigilum/nykteparchos*), first mentioned around 385–9.[18]

As far as the Constantinopolitan prefect's bureau (*officium urbanum*) is concerned, it is also assumed to have been similar to that of the prefect of Rome, although we are ignorant of its exact composition.[19] Sources refer only to the following functionaries: the *princeps*, the head of the officium, who had mainly judicial duties, particularly the arrest and prosecution of criminals; the *cornicularius*, who certified the prefect's acts by signing off on them; the *adjutor* (assistant), who was head of the group known as the *officiales* and who had initially policing and then judicial duties; the *commentariensis* and his subordinates, the *adiutores*, who ran the goals and guarded the Praitorion, the seat of the prefect and the city's main prison, at the same time that they were responsible for the implementation of verdicts and torture; the *ab actis* and his assistants, who oversaw civil court cases; the *numerarius* or *primiscrinius* and his subordinates, who dealt with issues such as funding for public works projects and the organization of the food supply; and the *censuales* who interacted with the Senate, keeping the minutes of their meetings and maintaining the tax rolls.[20]

With time, the number of officials (*officiales*) who worked in the prefect's bureau came to number in the thousands. Those up to the rank of cornicularius became permanent members of the eparch's officium, and enjoyed relative independence. At the same time, the princep who belonged to the men (*agentes in rebus*) of *magister officiorum* (master of offices), played a special role. Among his duties was the supervision of state officers and the submission of relevant reports to the emperor. He kept an eye on the prefect and could step in, if necessary, to allow the intervention of the imperial guard (*scholae palatinae*), who were under the authority of the magister officiorum.[21]

Although the eparch was responsible for maintaining order and security in Constantinople, it appears that he did not possess notable military forces, a fact explained by the presence of imperial military units in the capital.[22] Other officials who contributed to the policing of the city were the public servants known as *curatores*, one for each of its fourteen administrative districts (*regiones*), each of whom was accompanied by a state slave (*vernaculus*), who was also a crier, and the *vicomagistri*, the heads of the subdivisions (*vici*) of the regiones, who supervised the night watch, while the *collegiati*, recruited from the guilds (*collegia*),[23] were responsible for fire-fighting.[24]

## JUSTINIAN I (527–65) AND THE SIXTH CENTURY

Justinian I, aiming to ensure safety in the capital, especially after an uprising against his rule known as the Nika Riot (532), introduced a number of changes to the administrative structure. In 535 he reorganized the office of the praefectus vigilum or nykteparchos. Formerly a subordinate of the eparch of the city, the praefectus vigilum/nykteparchos now became an independent official, the *praetor plebis* (magistrate of the people), who was directly accountable to the emperor. With the aim of relieving the burden on the eparch of the city, his duties were not limited only to the nocturnal hours, as in the case of nykteparchos, but were extended to cover the daylight hours as well. The *praetor* helped to maintain order, fight fires and safeguard citizen's property in cases of arson. He had twenty soldiers at his command, and thirty *matricarii*, who were probably fire-fighters. He also heard civil and criminal cases with the aid of a legal advisor (*assessor*) and his department was organised like that of the prefect of the city. The praetor plebis could also enforce penalties imposed by the eparch's tribunal. Justinian's statement that the new official should refrain from cooperating with known criminals deserves special attention; it indicates that public authorities exploited a network of underworld informants to maintain order and to arrest dealers in stolen goods and other criminals, a practice Justinian attempted to end.[25] The praetor did not command substantial forces: with the men available to him it would have been difficult to supervise all the districts of Constantinople. We should keep in mind, however, that the praetor did not replace the prefect of the city, but had a subsidiary role. Most probably his area of focus was around the Hippodrome, where disturbances regularly took place. That said, the praetor is never mentioned in the context of the few incidents which are reported to have occurred in Constantinople after 535, although there is evidence for the office until the seventh century.[26] From the seventh century onwards sources no longer attest the position, suggesting that the eparch's office probably absorbed its duties. References to a praetor plebis in legal sources postdating the seventh century should therefore be understood as anachronistic, and do not indicate that the office survived. Similarly, later sources mentioning night-prefects, do not describe this office, but other officials charged with maintaining order after dark.[27]

Justinian I's interest in order and security led to the creation of a second new position in 539, that of the *quaesitor* (*koiaisitor*). The quaesitor tracked provincial visitors to the capital, identifying and verifying the reasons for their visits. He expedited the hearing of these visitors' court cases, and when trials were delayed or postponed he even adjudicated cases himself. He also questioned unemployed men or slaves loitering in the city, returning provincials to their towns and slaves to their masters, assigning able-bodied Constantinopolitans to manual labour and deporting those who refused. The quaesitor also investigated complaints against civil servants by provincials or citizens of Constantinople. When necessary he imposed the prescribed penalties. Finally, he also investigated forgery cases,[28] and, if the sixth-century historian Prokopios is to be believed,[29] punished pederasts and prosecuted those engaged in illicit sexual relations with women, as well as Christians remiss in their religious duties.

This office did not survive for long.[30] In later legal sources the term *koiaistor* (*quaestor*) replaces that of koiaisitor (quaesitor), and the duties of the quaesitor were divided. The quaestor appears to have assumed responsibility for forgery cases,[31] while the eparch, in all probability, took over the monitoring of provincials.[32]

## SEVENTH THROUGH TENTH CENTURIES: THE EPARCH AS 'PATER POLEOS'

Justinian's innovations, which appear to have been short lived, built upon the extant administrative structure without fundamentally changing it. The structure developed in the fourth century continued to be the basis of Constantinopolitan administration for the next several centuries. During this time the eparch continued as city governor, although there were changes in the titles assigned to personnel. In the seventh century his subordinates are attested to have been the *subadiuva*, who seems to correspond to the earlier *primiscrinius*, the *commentariensis* and the *secretarius* or *protosecretarius*, who appears to have been the counterpart of what was originally the *princeps* and the later *logothetes of the praitorion*, who was responsible for the seat of eparch.[33]

The eparch of the city, also referred to as 'politarches' (ruler of the city or citizens), continued to maintain order and security, arrest criminals and enforce imperial decrees in Constantinople.[34] The *vigla* or *kerketon*, which was apparently a night watch patrol under his jurisdiction, enforced the curfew, and punished offenders with lashing and imprisonment until their public trial.[35]

In the ninth century, in addition to being the highest-ranking city official responsible for order and security and second only to the emperor, the eparch became the supreme judicial officer. He had civil and criminal jurisdiction over the city,[36] and was responsible for the imposition of exile and other restrictive measures. While he heard appeals, his own verdicts were final. He adjudicated cases related to the emancipation of slaves, betrothal and guardianship, as well as lawsuits against *argyropratai* (jewellers). He ensured that slaves did not engage in public prostitution and that money brokers refrained from illegal conduct and exchanged money fairly. In addition he punished freed slaves who disrespected or insulted their patrons, wives or children, and could 'forbid any person in the city or in a part of it trade, spectacles, activities and advocacy in the Forum, namely the market, for a limited or an unlimited time'.[37] He was also responsible for regulating the price of certain goods, such as meat.[38] What is more, members of the trading and craft guilds of Constantinople, Byzantine and foreign, remained under his jurisdiction: in particular, the eparch monitored their activities to ensure the capital's food supply.[39] Finally, it seems that he could settle disputes between professors in Constantinople.[40]

With respect to judicial activities, a list of court precedence known as the *Kletorologion* of Philotheos (899) records the eparch among the *kritai*, along with the koiaistor, the most prominent member of the imperial chancery, and the *epi ton deeseon*, who was in charge of receiving and answering petitions addressed to the emperor.[41]

To exercise his various duties the eparch had at his disposal a number of subordinates, enumerated in the same source.[42] The *symponos* (assessor) assisted the eparch in trade-related matters and the adjudication of cases.[43] The logothetes of the praitorion oversaw, as mentioned, the seat of the eparch's administration, the Praitorion, which also housed Constantinople's most important prison.[44] His duties were mainly policing, but he may also have had judicial responsibilities. District judges (*kritai of the regions*) heard minor cases arising between the residents of the capital in each of its fourteen administrative regions. There were also two assistants to the eparch (*protokankellarioi*), who had their own assistants (*kankellarioi*) as subordinates. One probably served with the symponos, the other with the logothetes of the praitorion. The *kentyrion* (centurion) commanded the troops assigned to the eparch for maintaining order. Four inspectors (*epoptai*) reviewed the capital's tax lists. The eparch's office also controlled commercial activity. Officials included guild heads (*exarchoi, prostatai*), notaries (*nomikoi* or *taboullarioi*), heads of the city's neighbourhoods (*geitoniarchai*),[45] inspectors (*boullotai*) who affixed the eparch's seal on goods once they had been inspected, and a port administrator (*parathalassites*) who examined merchandise arriving at the city's ports.[46] Other officials included those who controlled foreign merchants in Constantinople (*legatarioi*), who probably worked with the symponos,[47] and inspectors of (silk) thread (*mitotes*).[48]

The eparch continued to oversee services related to sanitation and the maintenance of public spaces. As occasion required, he also saw to the decoration of the city and the imperial palace. For example, after a victorious military campaign he adorned the road between the entrance to the city at the Golden Gate and the palace with ornamental plants, flowers, fabrics and chandeliers to welcome the triumphant emperor.[49]

When the emperor was on campaign, the eparch was among the officials who remained in the capital to replace him. Together with the holder of the title of *magistros*, he 'had charge of state affairs and the day-to-day administration respectively'.[50]

Because the eparch and his department oversaw every aspect of the capital's daily life, he was designated 'father of the city'.[51] Contemporary sources confirm the significance of this administrative and judicial office. Emperors provided for it by ensuring that it was staffed by individuals known for their legal experience and moral integrity.[52]

## EVOLUTION AND CHANGE: THE ELEVENTH AND TWELFTH CENTURIES

Before becoming emperor himself, Romanos III Argyros (1028–32) was appointed eparch of Constantinople. On the occasion the scholar Michael Psellos observed that the office was almost identical to that of the emperor, a remark that indicates the significance of the position.[53]

In the eleventh century, however, the eparch's office underwent changes. Specifically, the parathalassites, previously a subordinate of the eparch, emerged as an independent high-ranking officer who controlled maritime traffic and the transport of goods in the ports of Constantinople. He had judicial authority over disputes arising between mariners reaching those ports[54] as well as taxation duties. By the late twelfth century there is evidence for the simultaneous existence of more than one parathalassites.[55]

The emergence of a new office, that of the *praitor of Constantinople*, which appears in the eleventh century, should probably be connected with the changes in the eparch's office. The praitor's precise duties are unknown; however, it seems probable that he was invested at the very least with judicial authority, since the duties of officers with the terms praitor or krites in their title were mainly juridical, and the eleventh-century textbook, the *Peira* (51.29), mentions a praitor, who may be identified with the praitor of Constantinople, as a judge.[56]

Other changes also had an impact on the eparch's position in the judicial hierarchy. In the second half of the eleventh century the *droungarios of the vigla*, who previously had commanded the regiment (*tagma*) of vigla (watch) or *arithmos* (number) which guarded the emperor and the palace, became the empire's supreme judge, a position that evolved to become a kind of minister of justice. From the time of Michael VII (1071–8) he was known as the *megas droungarios*.[57]

Consequently, although the eparch of the city continued to be responsible for Constantinopolitan administration and policing, as well as for the monitoring of guilds,[58] he relinquished part of his authority, and by the end of the eleventh century he had lost his status as supreme judge of the empire. Nevertheless, he remained an important officer and judge.[59] He was among the 'supreme judges' who had 'authority and power'. He heard the civil and criminal cases of private citizens and continued to be solely competent for the examination of cases concerning members of guilds, for their arrest, if need be, and for the imposition of the relevant penalties.[60]

## THE PALAIOLOGAN ERA: THIRTEENTH THROUGH FIFTEENTH CENTURIES

In 1204, when the empire was dissolved in the aftermath of the capture of Constantinople by the army of the Fourth Crusade, the office of eparch of the city ceased to exist. Later, in 1261, the city was recaptured by Alexios Strategopoulos and the empire restored. At that time Alexios became the city's de facto governor and was commissioned by the emperor Michael VIII Palaiologos (1261–82) to adorn the palaces and to prepare Constantinople for his reception and installation. Alexios also took measures to ensure the security and orderliness of the city both by day and by night.[61]

Subsequently the office of the eparch of the city appears to have been formally revived,[62] although there is some thought that the duties relating to the capital's administration were assumed not by a specific institution but by various civil servants.[63] It is certainly a fact that various terms referring to the head and governor of the capital appear in sources as early as the thirteenth and fourteenth centuries, among them archaizing references to the anthypatos, the city's initial administrative governor.[64] In 1264 the *sebastokrator* Constantine Tornikes was appointed the first official governor of the city since the restoration of Byzantine rule.[65] Subsequently, Constantine Chadenos became the first governor to be designated by the term 'eparch'.[66]

Although this office was not as high ranking as it was in the previous centuries, it appears that the eparch, who can probably be identified with the *Capitaneus Constantinopolis/in Constantinopoli* (Captain of Constantinople/in Constantinople) attested in Genovese documents,[67] continued to be responsible for maintaining order in Constantinople, making arrests, executing imperial orders and supplying the city. He also performed an auditing role regarding markets and commercial activity at the capital's ports, and adjudicated cases concerning commercial transactions.[68] To carry out his duties the prefect had at his disposal subordinates who are referred to as being associated with the eparch and his office.[69] Unfortunately nothing more is known about them. Judging by the exhortations of the patriarch Gregory of Cyprus (1284), who advised the emperor to dispatch troops to the eparch, it appears that the latter did not always have enough forces available to enforce his decisions.[70]

In the early fourteenth century (1304/5), two eparchs are attested for the first time. It is unclear whether they performed actual duties, as Andronikos II (1282–1328), the emperor under whom they appear, is known to have removed the insignia granting the eparch his authority.[71] Other fourteenth-century sources confirm the demotion of the office. The fourteenth-century lists of court precedence assign the eparch a low rank,[72] and a treatise on court ceremonial states that he no longer performed any duties.[73]

Thus, by the fourteenth century, the office of the eparch did not come with actual duties, but was rather a court title. Thereafter the administration of Constantinople was taken over by other trusted imperial officers, such as the *parakoimomenos* (court official, literally 'the one who sleeps at the side [of the emperor]') Alexios Apokaukos or the *prostrator* ('the first of the imperial grooms', a court and military officer) Theodoros Synadenos.[74]

The city governors, who did not bear any specific name or title, played an enhanced political role especially in times of political crisis and civil strife, as for example in the case of Alexios Apokaukos, who, when put in charge of the city and its suburbs during the civil war (1341–7) between John V Palaiologos (1341–91) and John VI Kantakuzenos (1347–54), persecuted the supporters of Kantakuzenos.[75]

In such turbulent times other officials called *demarchoi* (mayors), who probably constituted the revival of the Middle Byzantine geitoniarchai and were, it seems, initially under the orders of the prefect and then of each governor of the city, also assumed an important role.[76] The demarchoi were responsible for policing, order and just conduct, supervision of the taboullarioi and the organization of militias in the district of their jurisdiction.[77]

Two other officials related to the administration of Constantinople were the *hetaireiarches* and the *megas hetaireiarches* (court and military officer, initially the commander of a unit of emperor's bodyguard called *hetaireia*). These officials were responsible for refugees,[78] most of whom came from Asia Minor as a result of Turkish conquests. Their mandate was to protect them from the arbitrary behaviour of civil servants. Finally, the praetor plebis, who reappears in the fourteenth century, does not seem to have performed any duties.[79]

CONCLUSION

From the fourth century on the administration of Constantinople was identified with the office of the prefect of the city, a position that came to carry a broad mandate. Eventually the long arm of the eparch stretched into virtually every aspect of Constantinopolitan pubic life. As changing historical conditions made their impact on his office, the eparch saw this power modified until, in the last centuries of the city, his title was essentially ceremonial, its functions having been distributed among other officials. Yet, even in this last phase of the city's history, when the urban administration appears to have lost cohesion, its overriding concern remained consistent with the initial mandate given to the fourth-century urban prefect: the maintenance of the social order, the oversight of foreign visitors, the regulation of supply systems and the control of commercial markets.

FURTHER READING

Agoritsas, D., Κωνσταντινούπολη. Η πόλη και η κοινωνία της στα χρόνια των πρώτων Παλαιολόγων (1261–1328) (Thessaloniki, 2016).
Bury, J. B., *The Imperial Administrative System in the Ninth Century. With a Revised Text of the Kletorologion of Philotheos* (London, 1911) (reprint: New York 1958).

Chastagnol, A., *La Préfecture Urbaine à Rome Sous le Bas-Empire* (Paris, 1960).
Dagron, G., *Naissance d'une capitale: Constantinople et ses institutions de 330 à 451* (Paris, 1984).
Franciosi, E., *Riforme istituzionali e funzioni giurisdizionali nelle novelle di Giustiniano: Studi su Nov. 13 e Nov. 80* (Milan, 1998).
Gkoutzioukostas, A., *Η απονομή δικαιοσύνης στο Βυζάντιο. Τα κοσμικά δικαιοδοτικά όργανα και δικαστήρια της πρωτεύουσας (9ος–12ος αι.)* (Thessaloniki, 2004).
Gkoutzioukostas, A., 'Ο πραίτωρ του δήμου/των δήμων', *Βυζαντινά* 24 (2004): 133–66.
Gkoutzioukostas, A., 'The Praitor Mentioned in the History of Leo the Deacon and the Praitor of Constantinople: Previous and Recent Considerations', *Βυζαντιακά* 25 (2005–6): 103–15.
Guilland, R., 'Études sur l'histoire administrative de l'empire byzantin. L'Éparque. I. L'éparque de la ville – 'Ο ἔπαρχος τῆς πόλεως', *BSl* 41 (1980): 17–32 and 145–80.
Koder, J., The Authority of the Eparchos in the Markets of Constantinople (according to the Book of the Eparch)', in *Authority in Byzantium*, ed. Pamela Armstrong (Abingdon and New York, 2011), 83–110.
Magdalino, P., *The Empire of Manuel I Komnenos, 1143–1180* (Cambridge, 1993).
Matschke, K.-P., 'Rolle und Aufgaben der Demarchen in der spätbyzantinischen Hauptstadt', Jahrbuch für Geschichte des Feudalismus 1 (1977): 211–31 (=*Das spätbyzanische Konstantinopel*, 153–87).
Matschke, K.-P., 'Rolle und Aufgaben des Gouverneurs von Konstantinopel in der Palaiologenzeit', *Byzantinobulgarica* 3 (1969): 81–101 (=Kl.-P. Matschke *Das spätbyzantinische Konstantinopel. Alte und neue Beiträge zur Stadtgeschichte zwischen 1261 und 1453* (Hamburg, 2008).
Oikonomidès, N., *Les listes de préséance byzantines des IXe et Xe siècles* (Paris, 1972).
Sinnigen, W. G., *The Officium of Urban Prefecture during the Later Roman Empire* (Rome, 1957).

# NOTES

1 Socrates, *Historia ecclesiastica* II.41.1, ed. G. C. Hansen (Berlin, 1995).
2 Libanius, *Orationes*, 1.44–5 and 80, ed. R. Foerster, *Libanii opera*, vol. 1 (Leipzig, 1903).
3 See n. 1; Sozomenus, *Historia ecclesiastica*, ed. J. Bidez and G. C. Hansen (Berlin, 1960), IV.23.3.
4 For Rome see A. Chastagnol, *La Préfecture Urbaine à Rome sous le Bas-Empire* (Paris, 1960), 21–183.
5 See below for the establishment of the Senate in Constantinople.
6 See G. Dagron, *Naissance d'une capitale: Constantinople et ses institutions de 330 à 451*, 2nd ed. (Paris, 1984), 215–26, the most thorough study concerning the administration of Constantinople in the fourth and fifth centuries on which my analysis is based; R. Guilland, 'Études sur l'histoire administrative de l'empire byzantin. L'Éparque. I. L'éparque de la ville – 'Ο ἔπαρχος τῆς πόλεως', *BSl* 41 (1980): 17–32 and 145–80; R. Guilland, 'Études sur l'histoire administrative de l'empire byzantin. L'Éparque. III. L'Apoeparque – ἀπὸ ἐπάρχων', *BSl* 43 (1982): 30–44. Cf. J-Cl. Cheynet, 'L'Éparque: Correctifs et Additifs', *BSl* 45 (1984]) 50–4.
7 See G. Dagron, *Naissance*, 239. Cf. R. Janin, *Constantinople Byzantine*, 2nd ed. (Paris, 1964), 165–9; N. Westbrook, 'The Account of the Nika Riot as Evidence for Sixth-Century Constantinopolitan Topography', *Journal of the Australian Early Medieval Association* 7 (2011): 33–54.
8 *PLRE* 1, Honoratus 2; Dagron, *Naissance*, 240–2.

9 See Dagron, *Naissance*, 226–32 and 278–82 for discussion of the sources and a table outlining the prefect's duties.

10 Dagron, *Naissance*, 124–35.

11 *CIC CI* 1.28.4.

12 Dagron, *Naissance*, 230.

13 *Notitia Dignitatum*, Occ. IV, ed. C. Neira Faleiro (Madrid 2004).

14 See Dagron, *Naissance*, 233, on the officials mentioned below.

15 *CIC CI* 12.19.12.1.

16 *CIC CI* 1.3.31.

17 Ioannes Lydus, *Des magistratures de l'État romain/De magistratibus populi Romani*, II.30, ed. M. Dubuisson and J. Schamp, 2 vols (Paris, 2006).

18 *CIC CI* 1.43.1.

19 For the civil servants mentioned below see W. G. Sinnigen, *The Officium of the Urban Prefecture during the Later Roman Empire* (Rome, 1957), for Constantinople in particular, 116, with a list of the officiales. See also Chastagnol, *Préfecture urbaine*, 214–39; Dagron, *Naissance*, 234–7.

20 For the censuales see also Dagron, *Naissance*, 149–50.

21 Dagron, *Naissance*, 237–8.

22 Dagron, *Naissance*, 238–9.

23 See also *CIC CI* 4.63.5 (420), where their number amounts to 563.

24 Ed. O. Seeck, *Notitia Dignitatum* (Berlin, 1876), 230–43. See also A. H. M. Jones, *The Later Roman Empire 284–602*, 3 vols (Oxford, 1964), 2: 694–5; Dagron, *Naissance*, 233–4.

25 *CIC Nov* 13 (535). See also E. Franciosi, *Riforme istituzionali e funzioni giurisdizionali nelle novelle di Giustiniano: Studi su Nov. 13 e Nov. 80* (Milan, 1998), 57–102; A. Gkoutzioukostas, 'Ο πραίτωρ του δήμου/των δήμων', *Βυζαντινά* 24 (2004): 133–66.

26 *PLRE* 3, Comitas qui et Dipundiaristes 3 (547–51); Theophylaktos Simokattes, *Historiae*, ed. C. de Boor, revised P. Wirth (Stuttgart, 1974), VI.10.6.

27 Gkoutzioukostas, 'Ο πραίτωρ του δήμου', 153–62.

28 *CIC Nov* 80 [539]. For this office see Franciosi, *Riforme istituzionali*, 103–34; A. Gkoutzioukostas, *Ο θεσμός του κοιαίστωρα του ιερού παλατίου: Η γένεση, οι αρμοδιότητες και η εξέλιξή του* (Thessalonike, 2001), 106–12, with older bibliography; A. Laniado, *Ethnos et droit dans le monde protobyzantin, Ve–VIe siècle. Fédérés, paysans et provinciaux à la lumière d'une scholie juridique de l'époque de Justinien* (Geneva, 2015), 215–54.

29 Prokopios, *Historia Arcana*, 20, 9–10, ed. J. Haury, G. Wirth, Procopii Caesariensis *opera omnia*, 3 vols (Leipzig, 1963). See also Gkoutzioukostas, *Ο θεσμός του κοιαίστωρα*, 111–12.

30 Laniado, *Ethnos et droit*, 237–8, argues that it disappeared before 617.

31 Gkoutzioukostas, *Ο θεσμός του κοιαίστωρα*, 113–18.

32 Laniado, *Ethnos et droit*, 238–42.

33 J. F. Haldon, *Byzantium in the Seventh Century* (Cambridge, 1990), 273–4.

34 See, for example, A. Gkoutzioukostas, 'Πολιτάρχης και πολιταρχία στα Θαύματα του Αγίου Δημητρίου και σε άλλες βυζαντινές πηγές', *Βυζαντινά* 27 (2007): 165–85; R. Guilland, 'L'Éparque', 19–20; A. Gkoutzioukostas, *Η απονομή δικαιοσύνης στο Βυζάντιο. Τα κοσμικά δικαιοδοτικά όργανα και δικαστήρια της πρωτεύουσας (9ος-12ος αι.)* (Thessalonike, 2004), 38, n. 146; J. Koder, 'The Authority of the Eparchos in the Markets of Constantinople (according to the Book of the Eparch)', in *Authority in Byzantium*, ed. Pamela Armstrong (Abingdon and New York, 2013), 83–110, here 84.

35 Nikephoros, Life of St Andrew the Fool, ed. L. Rydén, II (Upsala, 1995), lines 245–9

36 According to the Eisagoge 4.4 (see note 38) the eparch also prosecuted crimes committed within a radius of hundred miles of Constantinople, as had the prefect of Rome (see also Peira 51.9, in J. and P. Zepos, eds., *Jus graecoromanum*, 8 vols (Athens, 1931; reprint Aalen, 1962), 4, 1–260). This extended jurisdiction was a later addition. See Dagron, *Naissance*, 230 and n. 2, who rejects any jurisdiction for the eparch beyond the city. By contrast, see J. Koder, 'The Authority', 86–7.

37 Translated by J. Koder, 'The Authority', 99–101.

38 For the above eparch's duties see Eisagoge 4.1–11, 11.7 and Procheiros Nomos 1.13 and 4.24, in Zepos, *Jus*, 2, 236–368 and 107–228. Cf. Basilicorum Libri LX.], vols 1–8, ed. H. J. Scheltema, N. van der Wal and D. Holwerda (Groningen 1955–88), 6.4.2 (Digest 1.12.1 and 3). For an English translation of this text as well as of the fourth title of Eisagoge, see J. Koder, 'The Authority', 99–101. See also Gkoutzioukostas, *Η απονομή δικαιοσύνης*, 103–5.

THE ADMINISTRATION OF CONSTANTINOPLE

39  J. Koder, ed., Das Eparchenbuch Leons des Weisen, CFHB 33 (Vienna, 1991). For the prefect and the functioning of markets see J. Koder, 'The Authority', 87–8 and 104–8, with English translation of the relevant excerpts from the Book of the Eparch.

40  *Anonymi Professoris Epistulae*, ed. A. Markopoulos, CFHB 37 (Berlin, 2000), no 68.8–11, p. 1.

41  N. Oikonomidès, *Les listes de préséance byzantines des IXe et Xe siècles* (Paris, 1972), 107.4–7.

42  Oikonomidès, *Les listes*, 113. 8–22.

43  Cf. also Koder, 'The Authority', 89–90, who speaks of more than one symponos.

44  R. Guilland, 'Le Prétoire. Tὸ πραιτώριον', *Ελληνικά* 17 (1962): 100–4 (= R. Guilland, *Études de topographie de Constantinople Byzantine*, 2 vols (Berlin and Amsterdam, 1969), 2 : 36–9.

45  P. Magdalino, 'Neighbourhoods in Byzantine Constantinople', in *Hinter den Mauern und auf dem offenen Land: Leben im Byzantinischen Reich*, ed. F. Daim and J. Drauschke (Mainz, 2016), 23–30.

46  For these officials see J. B. Bury, *The Imperial Administrative System in the Ninth Century: With a Revised Text of the Kletorologion of Philotheos* (London, 1911; reprint New York 1958), 70–3; R. Guilland, 'L'Éparque', 22–6; Oikonomidès, *Les Listes*, 320–1.

47  See *ODB* 1:704; Koder, 'The Authority', 90–1.

48  Koder, 'The Authority', 91.

49  See for example Constantine Porphyrogennetos, *Three Treatises of Imperial Military Expeditions*, ed. J. Haldon (Vienna, 1990), 140.737–41, 144,795–6, 146.831–148.834. See also Guilland, 'L'Éparque', 19–20.

50  Constantine Porphyrogennetos, *Three Treatises*, 144.799–146.807 and 147 (English translation). See also Koder, 'The Authority', 84.

51  Constantine Porphyrogennetos, *De cerimoniis* in *Le Livre des cérémonies*, ed. Vogt, 2 vols (Paris, 1939), 70.6; Theophanes Continuatus, ed. I. Bekker (Bonn, 1838), 461. See also Guilland, 'L'Éparque', 19. It has been argued that in the reign of Nicephorus II Phocas (963–9) another high-ranking official was introduced, the *praitor*, who was the prefect's equal and had judicial and policing duties. However, this officer was not created, and in the tenth century the eparch remained the only high-ranking governor of Constantinople with judicial and policing duties. See A. Gkoutzioukostas, 'The Praitor Mentioned in the History of Leo the Deacon and the Praitor of Constantinople: Previous and Recent Considerations', *Βυζαντιακά* 25 (2005–6): 103–15.

52  See Gkoutzioukostas, *Η απονομή δικαιοσύνης*, 74; Koder, 'The Authority', 84.

53  Michael Psellos, *Chronographia*, ed. D.-R. Reinsch, vol. 1, *Millenium Studies* 51 (Berlin and Boston, 2014), II, 10.2–3, p. 29.

54  Ed. Zepos, *Jus* 4, 1–260.

55  For the parathalassites and the evolution of his office see Gkoutzioukostas, *Η απονομή δικαιοσύνης*, 193–4, with bibliography. See also K. Smrylis, 'Trade Regulation and Taxation in Byzantium, Eleventh-Twelfth Centuries', in *Trade in Byzantium*, ed. N. Necipoğlu and P. Magdalino, with the assistance of I. Jevtić (Istanbul, 2016), 65–87, here 81–5.

56  Gkoutzioukostas, 'The Praitor', 111–14, with the relevant sources.

57  Gkoutzioukostas, *Η απονομή δικαιοσύνης*, 130–8.

58  Cecaumenus, *Strategikon*, ed. M. D. Spadaro, 'Raccomandazioni e consigli di un galantuomo', *Ελληνικά* 2 (1998): 44–242, ch. 1.10; See also Gkoutzioukostas, *Η απονομή δικαιοσύνης* 260, n. 1184.

59  See also P. Magdalino, *The Empire of Manuel I Komnenos, 1143–1180* (Cambridge, 1993), 229–30.

60  Gkoutzioukostas, *Η απονομή δικαιοσύνης*, 234–6 and n. 1072 and 1077.

61  Georgius Pachymeres, ed. A. Failler, *Relation Historiques*, 5 vols CFHB 24.1–5 (Paris 1984–2000), 1: 215.6–29.

62  R. Guilland, 'L'Éparque', 31–2; D. Kyritses, 'The Byzantine Aristocracy in the Thirteenth and Early Fourteenth Centuries' (PhD thesis, Harvard University, 1997), 43–4, 401; A. Laiou, 'Constantinople sous les Paléologues', in *Le monde byzantin*, vol. 3: *Byzance et ses voisins 1204–1453*, ed. A. Laiou and C. Morrisson (Paris, 2011), 131–43, here 141–2; D. Agoritsas, *Κωνσταντινούπολη. Η πόλη και η κοινωνία της στα χρόνια των πρώτων Παλαιολόγων (1261–1328)* (Thessalonike, 2016), 223–6.

63  K.-P. Matschke, 'Rolle und Aufgaben des Gouverneurs von Konstantinopel in der Palaiologenzeit', *Byzantinobulgarica* 3 (1969): 81–101, here 82 and 100 (= K.-P. Matschke, *Das spätbyzantinische Konstantinopel. Alte und neue Beiträge zur Stadtgeschichte zwischen 1261 und 1453* (Hamburg, 2008), 117 and 149). See also *ODB* 1:704; A. Kontogiannopoulou, *Η εσωτερική*

πολιτική τοῦ Ἀνδρονίκου Β´ Παλαιολόγου (1282–1328): Διοίκηση – Οἰκονομία (Thessalonike, 2004), 128–9.

64 For a full list see Agoritsas, Κωνσταντινούπολη, 224–5 with the relevant sources.

65 Georgius Pachymeres vol. 1, 297.27–8; PLP 29219.

66 Georgius Pachymeres vol. 1, 31.29; PLP 30346.

67 This identification is not generally accepted. See for example A. Laiou, Constantinople and the Latins: The Foreign Policy of Andronicus II, 1281–1328 (Cambridge, MA, 1972), 72, 277.

68 See Agoritsas, Κωνσταντινούπολη, 226–8. Cf. also Matschke, 'Rolle', 85–97 (123–43); Kontogiannopoulou, 129–30.

69 Gregorius II patriarcha, Epistulae, ed. S. Eustratiades (Alexandria, 1910), no. 126.

70 Gregorius II patriarcha, no. 132. See also Agoritsas, Κωνσταντινούπολη 228–9.

71 Georgius Pachymeres, vol. 4, 565.8–15. See also Pseudo-Kodinos, Traité des offices, ed. J. Verpeaux (Paris, 1966), 135.12–18.

72 See Agoritsas, Κωνσταντινούπολη, 226. See also Pseudo-Kodinos and the Constantinopolitan Court: Offices and Ceremonies, ed. R. Macrides, J. A. Munitiz D. Angelov (Farnham, 2013), 455–7.

73 Pseudo-Kodinos 138.4, 178.7–11.

74 See Matschke, 'Rolle', 82, 100 (117, 149–50); L. Maksimović, The Byzantine Provincial Administration under the Palaiologoi (Amsterdam, 1988), 94–5, n. 199; Kyritses, The Byzantine Aristocracy, 44.

75 Matschke, 'Rolle', 88, 95–7 (127–8, 140–4); see also Laiou, 'Constantinople', 141.

76 For other civil servants related to the function of the markets or the taxation of the residents of Constantinople see Matschke, 'Rolle', 94 (138); Agoritsas, Κωνσταντινούπολη, 233.

77 K. Sathas, Mesaionike Bibliotheke/Μεσαιωνικὴ Βιβλιοθήκη, 7 vols (Venice, Athens and Paris, 1872–1894; reprinted Athens, 1972), 6: 643–4; K.-P. Matschke, 'Rolle und Aufgaben der Demarchen in der spätbyzantinischen Hauptstadt', Jahrbuch für Geschichte des Feudalismus 1 (1977): 211–31 (= Matschke, Das spätbyzanische Konstantinopel, 153–87; Agoritsas, Κωνσταντινούπολη, 231–2.)

78 Pseudo-Codinus, 186.24–7 and 178.16–23.

79 Gkoutzioukostas, 'Ὁ πραίτωρ δήμου', 162–5.

## 15: PHILANTHROPIC INSTITUTIONS

## Timothy S. Miller

I n mourning the Turkish conquest of Constantinople, the Greek scholar Andronikos Kallistos recalled this city's impregnable walls, its vibrant intellectual life, and its thriving markets. After praising Constantinople's beautiful harbor, Andronikos listed its many philanthropic institutions – hospitals, old-age homes, asylums for the poor – facilities that the city zealously supported.[1] Almost 200 years earlier Gregory of Cyprus had considered Constantinople's welfare institutions essential elements of the capital's urban life. According to Gregory, when Michael VIII (1258–82) recaptured Constantinople he restored the walls and churches and then repaired the city's hospitals, hospices, and orphanages.[2]

In describing Constantine's (306–37) foundation of Constantinople in the 320s, however, the fifth-century historian Sozomenos omitted any mention of welfare institutions. Instead, he described the city's fortifications, the Senate House, and the grain supply for the new capital's growing population. In the place of specific charitable institutions he emphasized the philanthropic spirit of the city's inhabitants toward the needy, a virtue which made the new capital a worthy rival of Old Rome.[3]

Besides building Constantinople, Constantine also converted to Christianity, a decision which introduced a new worldview requiring individual believers, church leaders, and local city councils to assist those in need. As a result prosperous Christians, emperors included, began to establish welfare institutions in Constantinople after 350.[4]

### TERMINOLOGY

By 550 Constantinople had acquired many social welfare institutions, supported by bishops, monastic leaders, wealthy laymen, and the imperial government, facilities which sources describe with new terms, which are important to define.

*Orphanotropheion* identified a group home for orphans. In Constantinople, the oldest and most prestigious philanthropic institution was the Great Orphanotropheion, located on the city's citadel overlooking the Bosporos.[5] In addition to this central facility, many monasteries maintained small orphanotropheia.[6]

Etymologically, *ptochotropheion* or *ptocheion* meant an institution to feed and house the poor, but before the tenth century sources universally used these terms to designate leprosaria. Eustathios, bishop of Sabasteia, and Basil of Caesarea called the leprosaria they opened in Asia Minor ptochotropheia.[7] In his sermon condemning Christians' disdain for lepers, Gregory of Nazianzos referred to lepers as the poorest of the poor because they had lost the capacity to help themselves.[8] Thus, the fifth-century historian Sokrates referred to Constantinople's principal leprosarium as an asylum for the poor while the tenth-century Typikon of the Great Church, collating earlier sources, called this same institution a ptocheion.[9] Only once did a Byzantine writer call the leprosarium in Constantinople a *lobotropheion* (a more precise word for leprosarium), but not before the twelfth century.[10]

*Nosokomeion* designated a place to treat people suffering from diseases, and by 400 the staff of such institutions usually included salaried physicians. Thus, nosokomeion may be translated as a hospital for the sick.[11] A more difficult term, often replacing nosokomeion in popular use, was xenon. The sixth-century historian Prokopios used xenon in its classical meaning – a guest house or hospice for visitors.[12] A less classicizing text of the same century, the *Miracles of Kosmas and Damian*, however, selected xenon to identify an institution with surgeons, operating room, and a locked storage cabinet for medicines.[13]

The tenth-century *Suda* encyclopedia provided two definitions for xenon. One defined xenon as a house for receiving strangers and the sick, a definition applicable to both a hospital and a hospice. The second definition is more specific: "Nosokomeion: a xenon where disease is treated, not a permanent disability or a permanent condition since disease is not understood as either of these."[14] According to this definition, a xenon treated what modern medicine calls acute illnesses. Two sources, contemporary with the Suda, used xenon in this second sense. Theophanes Continuatus' compendium described the xenon, built by Emperor Theophilos (829–40), as a place open to fresh breezes, perfect for restoring health, a facility which the emperor stocked with life-saving pharmaceuticals.[15]

The second source is a vicious poem by Symeon the Logothete, attacking an enemy who had been appointed a provincial judge.

At one time when you were constipated,
You ran around everywhere in the xenones
And were fed by the enema clysters.[16]

Clearly, the xenones that this future judge frequented were not simple guest houses, but medical facilities offering out-patient services. Moreover, they were located throughout the city, "everywhere."[17]

The word xenon should not be confused with *xenodocheion*, a term always indicating a simple hospice in Byzantine Greek.[18] Xenodocheia had opened in Constantinople by the end of Constantius II's reign (337–61).[19] Christian bishops and monastic communities in the Eastern provinces had established xenodocheia a generation earlier to offer pious travelers safer places, both spiritually and physically, than the Greco-Roman world's raucous commercial inns (*pandocheia*).[20]

*Gerokomeia* were originally founded as asylums for the aged. According to urban tradition in Constantinople, several aristocrats opened such homes during the fifth century.[21] Soon, however, gerokomeia began to accept patients who suffered from chronic diseases.[22]

Finally, *diakoniai* differed from all other philanthropic facilities. They were founded by sixth-century Monophysite communities to offer charitable assistance to their own flock so that believers did not have to seek help from Calcedonians.[23] After the defeat of the Monophysite movement in Constantinople in 565, these diakoniai were taken over by the Orthodox church. As they evolved, they focused on providing free baths for the poor. They played a key role in transferring Constantinople's bathing practices from the monumental Greco-Roman bath houses with open pools to modest hamams where bathers washed in small tubs in semiprivate alcoves.[24]

## ORIGINS

Sozomenos' account of fourth-century ecclesiastical politics identified a man named Marathonios as the spirit behind the city's earliest welfare institutions. A former military official who left government service to become a deacon in the Constantinopolitan church, Marathonios was best known for having introduced a form of monasticism to Constantinople. He also used his private fortune to organize houses for the sick and poor. Influenced by Eustathios, a monastic leader from

Anatolian Sebasteia, Marathonios united these philanthropic houses to his monastic communities, which he called *synoikiai*.[25]

Sozomenos' account indicates that Marathonios' monks worked without pay in these communities tending the sick or assisting the poor, who may have joined the ascetics in governing these synoikiai. The first evidence of salaried professionals working in synoikiai comes from John Chrysostom's tenure as bishop of Constantinople (398–405). According to his biographer, Palladios, Chrysostom's frugality was such that he could reassign resources originally earmarked for the episcopal palace to fund an existing nosokomeion and open additional ones, for which he hired physicians, professional cooks, and salaried attendants from among the unmarried.[26] These celibate nurses may have been monks from Marathonios' original communities.

## FROM ARIANISM TO ORTHODOXY

The city's first organized charities developed in an Arian Christian context. Deacon Marathonios was an Arian, as was his superior, Makedonios, bishop of Constantinople (342–6; 350–60), and the reigning emperor Constantius II. Marathonios' monastic communities and their philanthropic services won for Bishop Makedonios support among Constantinople's lower classes. Despite Constantius' hostility to Makedonios (he deposed him twice), the bishop retained his see for ten years, and when the emperor finally banished him in 360 a crowd accompanied their shepherd to the city gates, praising him as a lover of the poor.[27]

Makedonios' movement, however, did not vanish after 360. Makedonios withdrew to Bithynia with some of his followers. Communities of Marathonian monks survived there to the end of the fourth century and reemerged in Constantinople after 400, where they again took up philanthropic work, laying the foundations for what would become Nicaean charitable endeavors.[28] One such Marathonian was a woman named Nikaretē.

Born into an aristocratic Bithynian family, Nikaretē came to Constantinople around 400. Using her considerable wealth she provided free medical care to the poor and to aristocratic friends whom professional physicians had failed to heal. By this time Nikaretē had rejoined the official Nicaean Church, but she had not abandoned the philanthropic practices of Marathonios. Sozomenos referred to Nikaretē as a *spoudaia* (zealous one), a word identifying people leading a celibate life devoted to acts of charity, the life which Marathonian monks had espoused decades earlier.[29]

A similar case was that of Auxentios. Like Nikaretē he grew up in a Bithynian Makedonian community before converting to Nicaean orthodoxy. His close spiritual companion and fellow spoudaios, Markianos, followed the same path and became important in Nicaean circles.[30] Patriarch Gennadios (458–71) appointed Markianos *oikonomos* (administrative overseer) of the Great Church from which post Markianos profoundly influenced the future development of Constantinopolitan welfare institutions by separating them legally from the episcopal (Patriarchal) Church and allowing them to administer their endowments independently.[31]

Marathonian communities also survived within Constantinople's walls under the two Arian bishops Eudoxios (360–70) and Demophilos (370–80), both opponents of Makedonios, and under the Nicaean bishops, Gregory of Nazianzos (380–81) and Nektarios (381–97).[32] One of these Marathonian communities evolved into Constantinople's greatest philanthropic institution, the Orphanotropheion.

## THE ORPHANAGE OF CONSTANTINOPLE

Constantinopolitans always considered the Orphanotropheion their premier charitable institution. Its directors (*orphanotrophoi*) wielded considerable influence in the capital's church. The fifth-century orphanotrophos, Akakios, secured the election of his friend Gennadios as patriarch in 458 and himself became patriarch in 471.[33] In subsequent centuries orphanotrophoi continued to exercise power in the Constantinopolitan church, and under Emperor Nikephoros I (802–12) they began serving as government officials.[34] One orphanage director, John the Paphlagonian, was prime minister under Michael IV (1034–41).[35]

The primacy of the Orphanotropheion resulted from its status as the capital's oldest social welfare institution and from its relationship with Hagia Sophia: not only was it located close to the cathedral, it also shared the episcopal church's legal and fiscal privileges. In 472 Emperor Leo I (457–74) guaranteed that all privileges, past and future, bestowed on Hagia Sophia would apply also to the Orphanotropheion.[36] This arrangement resulted from Markianos' reorganization of Constantinopolitan philanthropies. Once the Orphanotropheion became independent of Hagia Sophia, its privileges as an episcopal agency were threatened.

When, in 471, the orphanotrophos Akakios became patriarch he requested that Leo guarantee the orphan home's continued enjoyment of the Great Church's privileges.[37]

Leo's constitution also identified the orphanage's first director, Saint Zotikos.[38] Beyond Leo's statement little evidence survives concerning Zotikos. Legends, however, grew up around his name, stories preserved in three hagiographical texts. Although all postdate 1000, these short biographies contain valuable information.[39] First, all claim that Zotikos lived when Constantius ruled, at the same time that Marathonian ascetics flourished. Second, the oldest version of the Zotikos vita portrays him as living a life of perfect chastity, wearing humble clothing, and assisting the poor – all attributes of Marathonian monks.

In a second constitution Leo stipulated that the orphanotrophos was obligated "to sustain destitute minors and be solicitous for their education."[40] No evidence survives to reveal how the Orphanotropheion housed and fed its wards, but sources do describe an educational program, especially regarding training in music. A Syriac chronicle revealed that, in the mid-fifth century, the brother of the orphanotrophos Akakios composed hymns for an orphan choir and that the people of Constantinople flocked to the orphanage to hear the children sing.[41]

Singing remained an important aspect of the orphans' education. By the early ninth century the Orphanotropheion was known for a distinctive style of chanting.[42] Descriptions of court ceremonies mention orphans singing for the emperor on Epiphany and other feasts.[43] Significantly, singing had also been a central aspect of worship for Marathonios' monks and their heirs, the spoudaioi community of Auxentios and Markianos.[44]

The impact of the music program at the Constantinopolitan orphanage becomes clearer if we examine the orphanotrophium at Rome. Latin documents first mention this institution when a pope, probably Sergius I (687–701), refurbished it to provide for the children in its care, and to ensure "that the order of singers not die out, and the disgrace of the house of God not ensue."[45] So important was singing at this papal orphanage that, by the ninth century, Romans referred to it as the *schola cantorum* (school for singers).[46]

The Byzantine origin of the papal orphanotrophium (a Greek loanword) is proven by the survival of songs in Greek, which the children continued to sing at a time when the Greek language had vanished in central Italy. A twelfth-century Latin manuscript transliterated one of the chants into Latin characters.[47] In it the children saluted Christ and implored Him and God to grant Romania (the Byzantine state) victory over its enemies.[48] The orphans in Constantinople chanted hymns similar to this in Hagia Sophia or perhaps in the Great Palace.

The evolution of the Roman orphanotrophium into a renowned music school stimulated similar developments in other Italian cities. By the sixteenth century music had become so important in educating orphans that the Italian synonym for orphanage, *conservatorio*, implied a music school.[49] Antonio Vivaldi, a priest and composer who spent his entire life as music director in a Venetian orphanage, made this tradition famous.[50] Zotikos' orphanage in Constantinople thus exercised lasting influence on Western music.

Although we have no direct evidence of training in Greek grammar at the orphanage before 1100, we can infer the existence of such a program from Leo's stipulation that the orphans receive an education. Moreover, smaller orphan schools, run by monasteries, all provided lessons in grammar along with training in singing.[51] After Emperor Alexios I Komnenos (1081–1116) reorganized the Orphanotropheion, its grammar school became one of the best in the capital.[52] During the twelfth century three men –Stephen Skylitzes, Leo of Rhodes, and Basil Pediades – all taught there, became well-known literary figures, and subsequently received metropolitan sees in the empire.[53] Theodore Prodromos, Komnenian Constantinople's most famous literary figure, spent his life teaching in the school.[54] In addition to his many poems and a romance, Prodromos composed *schede*, grammar and orthography exercises for his students. Pupils at the orphanage and in other Constantinopolitan schools engaged in schede contests and quizzes on fine points of classical Greek grammar.[55] On important occasions Emperor Manuel I Komnenos (1140–1180) himself attended these contests.[56]

The twelfth-century Orphanotropheion evolved into such a prestigious school that one wonders how many destitute orphans actually went there. From the fifth century on some orphans were wealthy enough that the orphanotrophos had to assume guardianship to protect their property.[57] It may be that these well-off orphans eventually filled most of the Orphanotropheion's places.

The best description of the orphan school comes from Anna Komnene's history of her father Alexios' reign. Anna mentioned students from France, Italy, and barbarous Scythia, all learning classical Greek together with native Byzantines.[58] Theodore Prodromos praised the Orphanotropheion for introducing Hellenes and barbarians to the wonders of ancient Greek.[59] By contrast, Cyril Phileotes valued

Constantinople's orphanage for teaching Christian doctrine. According to Cyril, many Greek children, fleeing Turkish raids in Anatolia, would have lost the faith if the Orphanotropheion had not prepared them for the saving waters of Baptism.[60] Moreover, earlier evidence reveals that the Orphanotropheion had been preparing orphans and adults for Baptism for centuries.[61]

Exactly how the Orphanotropheion fit into the child welfare program in Constantinople is uncertain. Most true orphans, children who had no living parents, were entrusted to uncles, older brothers, or other adult relatives. Constantinopolitan monasteries accepted many other orphans without relatives willing to serve as guardians.[62] The Orphanotropheion seems to have been responsible for foreign children and displaced Greeks from Asia Minor.

Besides its primary function as a home and school for displaced children, the Orphanotropheion also helped in feeding Constantinople, especially during shortages. Repeatedly Byzantine authors compared orphanotrophoi to Joseph, Jacob's son whose advice spared Pharaoh's Egypt from famine.[63] In praising Alexios Aristenos, a twelfth-century Orphanage director, Nikephoros Basilakes addressed him as a new Joseph who had saved Constantinople from starvation. Basilakes also called Aristenos *sitodotes*, an official supervising grain supplies in Greco-Roman cities.[64]

How orphanotrophoi organized the capital's grain supply is unknown. Two lead tokens, issued by a seventh-century diakonia, identified recipients of a grain dole.[65] Since Emperor Herakleios (610–41) cancelled the government annona system it is tempting to suggest that Christian diakoniai had taken over the annona in Constantinople as was the case in contemporary Rome.[66]

By the eleventh century, however, other ecclesiastical institutions – xenodocheia, ptocheia, and monasteries – were importing grain to the capital.[67] The twelfth-century scholar, John Tzetzes, always short of cash, insisted on his right to receive food for himself and his mule from the oikonomoi of the Pantokrator Monastery.[68] Bread tokens also reveal that, from the tenth century on, prominent Constantinopolitan aristocrats were helping to feed the needy from their private resources.[69] In some fashion the Orphanage directors coordinated these efforts while maintaining a special granary to cover any shortfalls in a complex system.

The Orphanotropheion exercised another philanthropic function, supervising the city's only leprosarium across the Golden Horn on the Galata Hill.[70]

## THE LEPROSARIUM AND PTOCHEIA

All versions of the Zotikos Legend associate this saint not with the Orphanotropheion, but with Constantinople's leprosarium by fashioning a fantastic narrative about Zotikos' martyrdom at the hands of the Arian Emperor Constantius to explain why the saint was buried outside the city walls at his leprosarium and not at his primary foundation, the Orphanotropheion.[71] The true account would have revealed Zotikos to be an associate of Marathonios and Makedonios, men opposed to the Nicene Creed. Because of this association, Zotikos was forced to leave the Orphanotropheion in the heart of Constantinople sometime after Constantius deposed Makedonios (360), and to live and die at his leprosarium in Galata. According to the Zotikos Legend he was buried near a spring, which had gushed forth at his death.[72]

During Chrysostom's episcopacy, Arians still controlled the Zotikos leprosarium in Galata.[73] By 427, however, the Zotikos leprosarium had rejoined the official Nicaean community because its director Sissinios was chosen as patriarch of Constantinople, yet another indication of how much the clergy and people of Constantinople respected Zotikos' philanthropic legacy and that of Marathonios.[74]

Leo I's legislation states that the orphanotrophos administered other charitable institutions and monasteries besides the Orphanotropheion;[75] but it does not mention the leprosarium. We know, however, that the leper asylum remained open and connected to the Orphanotropheion because, when Justin II (565–78) built a church dedicated to Saints Paul within the orphanage precinct, he required that the orphanotrophos make a yearly payment to the leprosarium.[76]

In the following centuries emperors supported the leprosarium and expanded its facilities. After Slavs and Avars destroyed the institution, Maurice (586–602) rebuilt it on a larger scale.[77] More than 300 years later Constantine VII (945–59) substantially enlarged the facility and initiated a tradition of imperial visits to distribute gold coins to the lepers and treat their sores with soothing oils.[78]

John I Tzimiskes (969–79) increased the size of the leprosarium again and continued anointing patients himself.[79] Romanos III (1028–34) added a dormitory after an earthquake had damaged both the Orphanotropheion and the leprosarium.[80] Subsequent emperors continued visiting patients, personally treating their sores and bathing them in the pool filled by waters from Zotikos' spring. The renowned scholar Michael Psellos portrayed the visit of Constantine IX (1042–55) as a liturgical service accompanied by music.[81]

John II Komnenos (1118–43) recommenced expansion. Initially he had planned to build a leper home next to his Pantokrator Monastery, but local residents blocked his plans, forcing John to add facilities to the Zotikos leprosarium.[82]

A twelfth-century seal from Zotikos' leprosarium, or ptocheion, has puzzled some historians because the reverse inscription, "Seal of the brothers of Saint Zotikos," implies that the lepers exercised some rights as a legal corporation.[83] Two laws, one issued by Anastasios (491–518), the other by Justinian (527–65), explain these rights.

Anastasios' constitution required that all legal actions (sales, rentals, mortgaging, etc.) be conducted before the ptocheion's staff and in the presence of the residents.[84] Moreover, Anastasios added "that whatever is pleasing to the majority shall prevail."[85] Thus, in a large ptocheion (i.e., leprosarium) such as the Zotikos, Anastasios' law allowed lepers to control the institution's endowment. Justinian added that donors could make gifts to the ptocheion or to those who lived there. In other words, the lepers formed a legal personality that could accept gifts as a corporation, distinct from the leprosarium, as well as approve legal acts binding on the institution.[86]

Although the seal of the brothers of Saint Zotikos provides the only hard evidence that lepers exercised legal rights, the laws of Anastasios and Justinian suggest that lepers in Constantinople wielded significant power in governing their institutions. Latin sources from the medieval west not only support such a conclusion, but also reveal that these sixth-century laws from Byzantium inspired remarkable experiments in self-governance.

A document from thirteenth-century France preserves rules for a leper community in Brives, a constitution guaranteeing leper residents the right to elect their master, to approve land transfers, to audit accounts, and even to remove their master for incompetence or moral failure.[87]

Another document from the leprosarium at Verona dated 1235 records a dispute between the institution's director, a leper apparently appointed by the bishop, and the residents who were furious that this director had ignored their rights to approve property decisions. One of the leaders of the opposition was a woman named Briana who dominated the debate.[88]

## HOSPITALS (XENONES AND GEROKOMEIA)

Byzantine sources agree that a man named Sampson founded the first hospital in Constantinople, an institution located next to Hagia Sophia.[89] Like the Orphanotropheion, the Sampson hospital enjoyed the privileges of Hagia Sophia.[90] Moreover, Sampson himself resembled the orphanage founder, Zotikos, in that he, like Zotikos, was buried outside the city, at Saint Mokios's church. In 380 the Nicaean emperor Theodosios I (347–95) expelled the Arians from Constantinople, but allowed them to take possession of Saint Mokios since it lay beyond the walls.[91] Later Constantinopolitan legends located many Arian graves there, the tomb of Saint Sampson among them.[92]

Sampson's vita offers several indications that Sampson, like Zotikos, was a Marathonian monk who supported Bishop Makedonios. Sampson lived in a humble house in the center of town, wore simple clothing, and pursued the angelic life of celibacy.[93] Moreover, he engaged in Marathonian charity by providing beds in his house for poor patients while they received medical treatment, setting an example for that other Makedonian-Marathonian spoudaia, Nikaretē.[94]

After the Nike Fire of 532, Justinian (527–65) not only rebuilt Hagia Sophia but also the Sampson Xenon, adding several upper stories to the hospital. By the reign of Maurice, *archiatroi*, the leading physicians of Constantinople, were treating patients there.[95] In fact, from Justinian's reign the capital's archiatroi were always associated with the city's hospitals.[96]

The *Miracles of Saint Artemios* include a story from the reign of Herakleios (610–41) which provides a snapshot of the medical staff at the Christodotos Xenon, an institution similar to the Sampson in having ties to the Patriarchal church. Thus, a close associate of the patriarch held the post of chief administrator (xenodochos) while archiatroi and medical assistants (*hypourgoi*) treated patients. The archiatroi made morning and evening rounds and worked in monthly shifts. There was also a reduced night staff consisting of at least one trained hypourgos and several non-medical assistants (*hyperetai*).[97]

Shortly after 800 Theodore of Stoudios described the well-ordered ranks of hospital caregivers and contrasted this successful organization with the disorder within the church resulting from Iconoclasm. According to Theodore the xenodochos, medical supervisors (*protarchoi*), archiatroi, regular physicians (*mesoi*), and hypourgoi all worked together to achieve the philanthropic goal of healing. Theodore's use of this well-ordered hospital to illustrate how the church should function indicates that such elaborate medical facilities were common.[98]

Ninth-century court ceremony also revealed archiatroi associated with Constantinople's hospitals. On the tenth day of the Christmas season the emperor dined with the xenodochoi of the capital's leading hospitals together with the archiatroi, dressed in their distinctive blue robes.[99]

In the twelfth century, John II Komnenos (1118–43) drafted the Pantokrator Typikon, a document presenting the most complete picture of a functioning hospital. These regulations required that the Pantokrator Monastery maintain a xenon of five wards for fifty patients, each ward served by two physicians, hypourgoi, and hyperetai.[100] None of these features was unusual; even its system of monthly rotations for the physicians existed in earlier institutions, as at the Christodotos hospital.[101]

Besides treatment for patients in the wards, Constantinopolitan xenones provided free medical services to the population at large, as Symeon the Logothete's depiction of his enemy's visits to hospital clinics for constipation indicated. Evidence from eleventh-century legal commentaries reveals that hospitals had also become the principal suppliers of medicines. In defining the Latin word *pementarius* (pharmacist), the commentary reads: "Pementarioi are those who are dedicated to collecting plants and storing them in the xenones and those who are concerned with these remedies."[102] Another entry defines pementarioi as those entrusted with the supervision of medicines at the xenones, or those who sell medicines and perfumes. Five such pementarioi staffed the Pantokrator xenon.[103]

According to these legal commentaries, commercial pharmacies took second place to xenon clinics in providing medicines to the people of Constantinople. When the twelfth-century historian Kinnamos praised Emperor Manuel I (1143–80) for inventing new remedies, he added that the capital's citizens could obtain the emperor's remedies in the hospitals; Kinnamos did not even mention commercial pharmacies.[104]

Byzantine xenones were not facilities only for the poor. About 640, Stephen, a deacon of Hagia Sophia and an active official in the capital's Blue Faction, a man with a home and loving parents to care for him, entered the Sampson Xenon for what we would call today elective surgery. He did this not because poverty drove him to seek rudimentary nursing care, but for a specific medical procedure.[105] In the tenth century, Bardas, a member of the emperor's personal retinue, fell ill with a lung infection. He was given a bed in the Sampson, but the physicians declared him incurable. On the night of Sampson's feast day, while the physicians were commemorating the founder's death at Saint Mokios, the saint healed Bardas miraculously in a dream.[106] During the twelfth century, the reigning emperor Manuel I's sister-in-law Eirene entered the Pantokorator Xenon for medical care. An anonymous poem described her examination by a hospital physician accompanied by two medical students.[107]

One wonders whether these elite patients monopolized the beds at Constantinople's best xenones. Several sources, however, demonstrate that people without resources also received hospital care. A tenth-century story recounts the fate of Sergios who, beaten almost to death by robbers, was later found on the street and taken to the Euboulos Xenon. Here physicians treated him for seven days but finally determined that his case was hopeless. They ordered his transfer from the xenon to a "holy house" dedicated to the Martyr Nicholas.[108] Although imperial princesses were occasionally patients at the Pantokrator hospital, John II Komnenos required that the xenon supply at least fifteen sets of nightclothes for poorer patients who could not afford their own.[109]

Sergios' story raises a new problem regarding welfare institutions. What sort of facility was the Holy House of Saint Nicholas where poor Sergios was taken to die? Some might answer a xenodocheion, but I have found no example of a Constantinopolitan hospice accepting a debilitated or dying patient. As noted above, ninth-century court ceremonial required the emperor to invite hospital directors with the city's archiatroi to the banquet on the tenth day of Christmas. The emperor, however, also invited the directors of the city's gerokomeia.[110]

Originally, gerokomeia housed the elderly (*gerontes*), but sources depict gerokomeia as providing for people suffering from problems besides old age. In describing Theodore Prodromos' last days, his friend Eugenianos mentioned that Prodromos was living in a gerokomeion, "not because of old age, but because of a chronic disease."[111] Isaak, the brother of Emperor John II Komnenos, attached to his monastery in Thrace a gerokomeion for thirty-six patients, requiring that the monks maintain a physician and ten hypourgoi for these patients, whom he never called elderly but "those who are sick."[112] Moreover, if patients in the gerokomeion regained their health they were free to leave.[113] Obviously patients never recovered from old age. Finally, if a resident did recover but wished to remain in the gerokomeion he or she could do so.[114] As in the case of Sergios, physicians did not allow patients to occupy hospital beds if they had no hope of recovery; similarly, it is unlikely that xenon patients could remain in a ward if they had recovered.

Bearing in mind the *Suda*'s definition of xenon as a place to treat acute illnesses and Eugenianos' comment that Prodromos entered a gerokomeion because of a chronic condition, gerokomeia may have evolved from old-age homes into medical facilities for people suffering from chronic conditions. Thus, emperors invited gerokomeia supervisors along with the xenon directors on the tenth day of Christmas because both institutions provided for the health care needs of Constantinople's population.[115]

## Conclusion

Constantinople's social welfare institutions were extraordinary for the range of their services: homes for orphans, lepers, and the poor; free baths at the diakoniai; food provided in emergencies; and medical care for acute and chronic diseases. Like nobles in Western Europe, the wealthy supported these institutions through personal giving and by encouraging rulers to establish and sustain welfare facilities. In Constantinople, however, the wealthy also planned to use these institutions if they or their close relatives had need of their services. For this reason we can be reasonably certain that no one in a Byzantine hospital had to share a bed with one or two other patients as occasionally happened at the Hôtel Dieu in Paris, nor did orphans in Constantinople receive only training in artisanal crafts. Indeed, the twelfth-century Orphanotropheion hired leading intellectuals of the empire for its students.

Because both rich and poor benefitted from the Orphanotropheion, the leprosarium, and the many xenones, gerokomeia, and diakoniai, the quality of service was better than in the West. Byzantine writers – Gregory of Cyprus, Andronikos Kallistos, and others – viewed these institutions as unique to Constantinople, almost as impressive as the city's famous walls and the great dome of Hagia Sophia.[116]

### Further Reading

Bennett, D., *Medicine and Pharmacy in Byzantine Hospitals* (Leiden, 2017).
Brown, P., *Poverty and Leadership in the Late Roman Empire* (Hanover and London, 2002).
Constantelos, D., *Byzantine Philanthropy and Social Welfare*, 2nd ed. (New Rochelle, 1991).
Dagron, G., "Les moines et la ville," *TM* 4 (1970): 227–76.
Holman, S., ed., *Wealth and Poverty in Early Church and Society* (Grand Rapids, 2008).
Miller, T., *Birth of the Hospital in the Byzantine Empire*, rev. ed. (Baltimore, 1997).
   *Orphans of Byzantium: Child Welfare in the Christian Empire* (Washington, DC, 2003)
Miller, T. and J. Nesbitt, *Walking Corpses: Leprosy in Byzantium and the Medieval West* (Ithaca, NY, 2014).

### Notes

1 A. Kallistos, *Monodia de Constantinopoli capta*, PG 161: 1132–42 at 1135.
2 Gregory of Cyprus, *Laudatio Michaelis Palaeologi*, PG 142: 345–86 at 377–8.
3 Sozomenos 2.3.1. See *Sozomenos: Kirchengeschichte*, ed. J. Bidez (Berlin, 1960), 51–3.
4 T. S. Miller, *The Birth of the Hospital in the Byzantine Empire* (Baltimore, 1997), 69–76; P. Brown, *Poverty and Leadership in the Later Roman Empire* (Hanover and London, 2002), 26–44.
5 Genesios, 1.9 in *Regnum Libri quattuor*, ed. A. Lesmüller-Wiener and H. Thurn (Berlin and New York, 1978), 9.

6  T. S. Miller, *The Orphans of Byzantium: Child Welfare in the Christian Empire* (Washington, DC, 2003), 61–2.

7  T. S. Miller and J. Nesbitt, *Walking Corpses: Leprosy in Byzantium and the Medieval West* (Ithaca, NY, 2014), 74.

8  Gregory of Nazianzos, *De pauperum amore (Oratio XIV)*, PG 35: 857–909, cols. 865–7. English translation in *The Sunday Sermons of the Great Fathers*, 4 vols., trans. M. F. Toul (Chicago, 1963), 43–64.

9  Sokrates 7.26.3 in *Sokrates: Kirchengeschichte*, ed. G. C. Hansen (Berlin,1995), 375 and J. Mateos, ed., *Le typicon de la Grande Église. MS Sainte-Croix no. 40, Xe siècle*, Vol. 1, *Le cycle des douze mois* (Rome, 1962), 190 (January 8).

10  Kedrenos, 2: 504 in *Georgius Cedrenus*, ed. I. Bekker, 2 vols. (Bonn, 1838–9).

11  Palladios 5: 133–6 in *Dialogue sur la vie de Jean Chrysostome: Introduction, texte critique, traduction française, et notes*, 2 vols., ed. and trans. A.-M. Malingrey with P. Leclercq (Paris, 1988), 1: 122.

12  Prokopios, *De aedificiis*, 1.11.23–7.

13  *Kosmas und Damianos*, miracle 30, ed. L. Deubner (Leipzig and Berlin, 1907), 173–6.

14  *Suda, sub voce*, "xenon"; cf. "nosokomeion" in *Suidae Lexicon*, 5 vols., ed. A. Adler (Leipzig, 1928–38).

15  Theophanes Continuatus 3.8 in *Theophanes Continuatus*, ed. I. Bekker (Bonn, 1838).

16  Symeon Logothetes, 578 in V. Vasiljevskij, "Dva nadgrobuykh stikhothorenija Simeona Logofeta," *Vizantijskij Vremmenik* 3 (1896): 574–8.

17  Contrast P. Horden, "How Medicalized Were Byzantine Hospitals?" in *Sozialgeschichte Mittelalterischer Hospitäler*, ed. N. Bulst and K.-H. Spieß (Ostefildern, 2007), 213–35.

18  Miller, *Birth of the Hospital*, 26–9.

19  "Fragmente eines arianischen Historigraphen" in Philostorgios, *Philostorgios: Kirchengeschichte*, ed. J. Bidez (Berlin, 1981), 202–41, at 225.

20  E. Kislinger, "Taverne, alberghi, e filantropia ecclesiastica a Bizanzio," *Atti della Accademia delle Scienze di Torino* 120 (1986): 83–96.

21  *Patria* III, 251 (paras. 105 and 106) in *Scriptores originum Constantinopolitanarum*, 2 vols., ed. T. Preger (Leipzig, 1907), 2: 251.

22  Constantine Manasses, *Constantini Manassis Brevarium*, lines 3481–4 (p. 150), ed. I. Bekker, CSHB (Bonn, 1837).

23  D. Caner, "Charitable Ministrations (Diakoniai), Monasticism, and the Social Aesthetic of Sixth-Century Byzantium," in *Charity and Giving in Monotheistic Religions*, ed. M. Frenkel and Y. Lev (Berlin and New York, 2009), 45–73, at 45–7; Miller, *Birth of the Hospital*, 129–32.

24  P. Magdalino, "Church, Bath, and Diakonia in Medieval Byzantium," *Church and People in Byzantium*, ed. R. Morris (Birmingham, 1990), 165–88.

25  Sozomenos, 4.20.1–2 (pp. 169–70); 4.27.1–7 (pp. 183–5); G. Dagron, "Les moines et la ville: Le monachisme à Constantinople jusqu'au concile de Chalcédoine (451)," *TM* 4 (1970): 229–76, esp. 245–53; S. Elm, *Virgins of God: The Making of Asceticism in Late Antiquity* (Oxford, 1994), 111–12.

26  Palladios, chapter 5, lines 128–39 (1: 122).

27  Markianos and Martyrios, 170 in P. Franchi di Cavalieri, "Una pagina di storia bizantina del secolo IV: il martirio dei santi notari," *AB* 64 (1946): 132–75.

28  Sozomenos, 4.27.3–7 (pp. 184); Dagron, "Moines," 246–8.

29  Sozomenos, 8.23.1–6 (pp. 379–81).

30  *Vita Auxentii*, in PG 114: 1377–436, at 1380.

31  Theodoros Anagnostes, *Theodoros Anagonostes: Kirchengeschichte*, ed. G. Hansen (Berlin, 1971), 106; M. Wallraff, "Markianos-Ein prominenter Konvertit vom Novatianismus zur Orthodoxie," *Vigilae Christianae* 52 (1998): 1–29.

32  Dagron, "Moines," 246–7.

33  Miller, *Orphans*, 178.

34  Miller, *Orphans*, 179 (Andrew of Crete); 185 (government official).

35  J. Nesbitt, "The Orphanotrophos: Some Observations on the History of the Office in Light of Seals," *SBS* 8, ed. J.-C. Cheynet and C. Soda (Munich and Leipzig, 2003), 51–62, especially 59–60.

36  *CIC* 1.3.34 (35).

37  Miller, *Orphans*, 182.

38  *CIC* 1.3.34 (35) line 11.

39 *Vita Zotici* II, 339–45 in T. S. Miller, "The Legend of Saint Zotikos according to Constantine Akropolites," *AB* 112 (1994): 339–76.

40 *CIC* 1.3.31 (32).

41 Zachariah of Mitylene, 4.11 in Zachariah of Mitylene, *The Syriac Chronicle*, trans. J. F. Hamilton and E. W. Brooks (London, 1899), 80.

42 Vita Antonii junioris, 211–12 in A. Papadopoulos-Kerameus, "Vita Antonii junioris," *Provoslavnij Palestinskij Sbornik*, 19 (1907): 186–216.

43 Miller, *Orphans*, 213.

44 Sozomenos, 7.21.6–8 (p. 334); Gregory of Nazianzos, *In Pentecosten*, PG 36: 428–52 at 440; *Vita Auxentii*, 1380.

45 Liber Diurnus V.97 in *Liber Diurnus Romanorum Pontificum*, ed. H. Foerster (Bern, 1958), 177; J. Smits van Waesberghe, "Neues über die Schola Cantorum zum Rom," in *Zweiter internationaler Kongress für katholische Kirchenmusik (Wien 4–10 Oktober 1954)* (Vienna, 1955), 111–19, esp. 114.

46 '*Liber Pontificalis: texte, introduction, et commentaire*, 3 vols., ed L. Duchesne (Paris, 1886–1957) 2: 92.

47 Z. Patala, "Les chants grecs du *Liber Politicus* du chanoine Benoît," *Byzantion* 66 (1996): 512–30.

48 Patala, "Les chants," 519–23; Miller, *Orphans*, 217–18 for evidence that the boys came from the *schola cantorum*.

49 *OED*, sub voce 'conservatory,' no. 6; S. Di Giacomo, *Il Conservatorio dei poveri di Gesù Cristo e quello di S. M. di Loreto* (Naples, 1928).

50 M. Pincherle, *Vivaldi: Genius of the Baroque*, trans. C. Hatch (New York, 1957).

51 Miller, *Orphans*, 226; *Vita Petri Argivorum*, 7–8, ed. A. Mai in *Patrum nova bibliotheca*, 10 vols. (Rome, 1844–1905), 9.3: 1–17.

52 Anna Komnene, 15.7.9 in *Anna Comnène: Alexiade*, 3 vols., ed. B. Leib (Paris, 1934–45), 3: 218, trans. E. W. Sewter (Baltimore, 1969).

53 Miller, *Orphans*, 232–7.

54 Prodromos, *Eisiterios orphanotropho Alexio Aristeno*, PG 133: 1268–74 at 1269; Miller, *Orphans*, 242–5.

55 Mlller, *Orphans*, 228–9; T. S. Miller, "Two Teaching Texts from the Twelfth-Century Orphanotropheion," in *Byzantine Authors, Literary Activities and Preoccupations: Texts and Translations Dedicated to the Memory of Nicolas Oikonomides*, ed. J. Nesbitt (Leiden and Boston, 2003), 9–20.

56 K. Horna, "Eine unedierte Rede des Konstantin Manasses," *Wiener Studien*, 28 (1906): 171–204, at 181 lines 264–9.

57 *CIC* 1.3.31 (32).

58 Anna Komnene, 15.7.9 (3: 218).

59 Prodromos, "Monodie," 7 in L. Petit, "Monodie de Theodore Prodrome sur Étienne Skylitzès métropolitain de Trébizonde," *Bulletin d'Institut archéologique russe à Constantinople/, Izvestija Russkogo Arheologiçeskogo Instituta v Konstantinopole* 6 (1903): 1–13.

60 Vita Cyrilli, in *Vie de Saint Cyrille le Philéote, Moine Byzantin: Introduction, téxte critique, traduction et notes*, ed. É. Sargolos (Brussels, 1964), 230.

61 Miller, *Orphans*, 223–4.

62 Anna Komnene, 15.7.3 (3:214). See commentary, Miller, *Orphans*, 1–2 and note 3.

63 Miller, *Orphans*, 199–202.

64 Basilakes, 25 in *Nicephori Basilacae orationes et epistolae*, ed. A. Garzya (Leipzig, 1984); for the *sitodotes*, see Miller, *Orphans*, 200 and note 100.

65 J. Nesbitt, "Byzantine Copper Tokens," in *SBS* 1, ed. N. Oikonomides (Washington, DC, 1987), 67–75.

66 O. Bertolini, "Per la storia delle diaconie romane nell' alto medio evo sino alla fine del secolo VIII," *Archvio della Società Romana di Storia Patria* 70 (1947): 1–146, esp. 140–1.

67 P. Magdalino, "The Grain Supply of Constantinople, Ninth–Twelfth Centuries," in *Constantinople and Its Hinterland*, ed. C. Mango and G. Dagron (Aldershot, 1995), 35–47.

68 I. Tzetzes, letters 98–9 in *Ioannis Tzetzae epistolae*, ed. P. A. M. Leone (Leipzig, 1972), 142–6.

69 B. Caseau, "L'exercise de la charité à Byzance d'après les sceaux et les tessères (Ve – XIIe siècles)," *TM* 21.1 (2017): 31–52, esp. 47–52.

70 *Kletorologion of Philotheos*, 123 and 319 in *Les listes de préséance byzantines des IXe et Xc siècles: Introduction, téxte, traduction et commentaire*, ed. N. Oikonomides (Paris, 1972), 67–235.

71  G. Sidéris, "Lèpre et lépreux à Constantinople: Maladie, épidémie et idéologie impériale à Byzance," in *La Paléodémographie: Mémoire d'os, mémoire d'hommes,* ed. L. Buchet, C. Dauphin, and I. Séguy (Antibes, 2006), 187–207, esp. 196–8.

72  Vita Zotici I, 80 in M. Aubineau, "Zoticos de Constantinople, nouricier des pauvres et serviteur des lépreux," *AB* 93 (1975): 67–108.

73  Pseudo-Martyrios, chapters 62–6 in *Oratio funebris in laudem Sancti Ioannis Chrysostomi: Epitaffio attribuito a Martirio di Antiochia,* ed. M. Wallraff, Italian trans. C. Ricci (Spoleto, 2007), 116–22.

74  Sokrates, 7.26.1–5 (p. 375).

75  *CIC* 1.3.34 (35). *Ptocheiis* would include the Zotikos Leprosarium.

76  Vita Zotici I, 82.

77  Vita Zotici I, 82.

78  Theophanes Continuatus, 6.18 (p. 449).

79  Leo Diaconus, 6.5 in *Leonis diaconi Caloënnis historia libri decem et liber de Velitatione Bellica,* *CSHB* (Bonn, 1828), 99–100.

80  E. Kislinger, "Zur Lage der Leproserie des Pantokrator-Typikon," *JÖB* 42 (1992): 171–5, esp. 174, n. 24.

81  M. Psellos, 73–4 in *Michael Psellus: Orationes Panegyricae,* ed. G. Dennis (Stuttgart and Leipzig, 1994).

82  Typikon Pantokrator, 111–13 in P. Gautier, "Le typikon du Christ Sauveur Pantocrator," *REB* 32 (1974): 1–145. English trans. R. Jordan in *BMFD* 725–81; Kislinger, "Leprosie," 171–5.

83  Nesbitt, *Byzantine Authors,* 420, n. 6; J. Nesbitt, "St. Zotikos and the Early History of the Office of Orphnaotrophos," in *Byzantine State and Society: In Memory of Nikos Oikonomides,* ed. A. Avramea, A. Laiou, and E. Chrysos (Athens, 2003), 417–22, at 420, note 6; for illustration see Miller and Nesbitt, *Walking Corpses,* 87.

84  *CIC* 1.2.17.

85  *CIC* 1.2.17 (2).

86  *CIC* 1.2.19.

87  Brives Statutes, 204–14 in *Statuts d'Hôtels-Dieu et de léproseries; recueil de textes du XIIe au XIVe siècle,* ed. L. Le Grand (Paris, 1901).

88  Carte di Verona, 146–50. For her testimony see *Le carte dei lebbrosi di Verona tra XII e XIII secolo,* ed. A. Rossi Saccomani with introduction by G. De Sandra Gasparini (Padua, 1989), 146–50.

89  T. S. Miller, "The Sampson Xenon," *ByzF* 15 (1990): 101–35.

90  *CICNov* 131.15.

91  *Vita Sampsonis I,* 15, in F. Halkin, "Saint Sampson le xénodoque de Constantinople," *Rivista di studi bizantini e neoellenici,* n.s. 14–16 (1977–9): 6–17; *Parastaseis syntomoi chronikai,* 1 in *Constantinople in the Early Eighth Century: The Parastaseis Syntomoi Chronikai,* ed. A. Cameron and J. Herrin (Leiden, 1984), 56–7; Sozomenos, 7.5.5–7.

92  Parastaseis, 1; 5d (p. 62).

93  *Vita Sampsonis I,* 8–10.

94  *Vita Sampsonis I,* 10; cf. Sozomenos, 8.23.1–6.

95  *Vita Sampsonis I,* 13–15; *Oratio Anastasii in psalmam VI,* PG: 89: 1077–116.

96  Miller, *Birth of the Hospital,* 47–9; 153–5; P. van Minnen, "Medical Care in Late Antiquity," *Cleo Medica* 27 (1995): 153–69, esp.,164–7. *Pace* V. Nutton, "Essay Review," *Medical History* 30 (1986): 218–21. Regarding Nutton's argument, see A. Kaldellis, *Procopius of Caesarea: Tyranny, History, and Philosophy at the End of Antiquity* (Philadelphia, 2004), 150–9 and 223–8, esp. 226.

97  Miracle 22 in *The Miracles of Saint Artemios,* ed. and trans. V. Crisafulli and J. Nesbitt (Leiden, 1997).

98  Theodore Studites, Letter 477 in *Theodori Studitae epistulae,* ed. G. Fatouros (Berlin and New York, 1992), 690–1.

99  *Kletorologion,* 183.

100  Typikon Pantokrator, 82–7.

101  Typikon Pantokrator, 87, lines 955–64; cf. *Miracles Artemios,* miracle 22 (p. 134, lines 18–19).

102  *Scholia,* 60.39.3.7 in *Basilicorum libri LX. Series B Volumen IX, Scholia in librum LX, 17–69* (Groningen, 1985), 3748.

103  *Scholia,* 60.39.3.12 (p. 3748); cf. Typikon Pantokrator, 101, lines 1205–18; Typikon Paantokrator, 89, lines 996–8.

104  J. Kinnamos, *Ioannis Cinnami epitome rerum ab Ioanne et Alexio Comnenis gestarum,* ed. A. Meineke, CSHB (Bonn, 1836), 190.

105  *Miracles Artemios*, miracle 21 (pp. 124–9).
106  *Vita Sampsonis* II, PG 115: 277–308 at 301–6.
107  T. Miller, "Medical Thought and Practice," in *The Cambridge Intellectual History of Byzantium*, ed. A. Kaldellis and N. Siniossoglou (Cambridge, 2017), 265–6.
108  *Vita Sancti Lucae Stylitae*, 218 in H. Delehaye, ed., *Les Saints Stylites* (Paris and Brussels, 1923).
109  Typikon Pantokrator, 85, lines 925–30.
110  *Kletorologion*, 183.
111  Eugenianos, 460 in L. Petit, "Monodie de Nicétas Eugénianos sur Théodore Prodrome," *Vizantinijskij Vremennik* 9 (1902): 446–63.
112  Typikon Kosmosoteira, chapter 61 in L. Petit, "Typikon du monastère de la Kosmosotira près d'Ainos (1152)," *Bulletin d'Institut archéologique russe à Constantinople/Izvestija Russkogo Arheologiçeskogo Instituta v Konstantinopole* 11 (1908): 17–75. English trans. N. Ševčenko *BMFD* 2, 782–858.
113  Typikon Kosmosoteira, chapter 70 (54, lines 7–10).
114  Typikon Kosmosoteira, chapter 70 (55, lines 28–35).
115  *Kletorologion*, 183.
116  E. Fenster, *Laudes Constantinopolitanae* (Munich, 1968), 155, 187, 198, 343–6.

# 16: SCHOOLS AND LEARNING

## Niels Gaul

I n 384, the sophist Themistios, close to retirement after a distinguished career in the still young Constantinopolitan court and
senate, proclaimed that even though Homer knew only nine
Muses, no fewer than twice this number would do justice to the New
Rome![1] His wish was to come true: at the city's zenith in the twelfth
century hundreds of students memorized grammar, puzzled over schedography (riddles consisting of homophone but not homograph syl-
lables) and learnt to extemporize in prose and verse.[2] Scores of rhetors
praised God and emperor in lofty words and frequented literary salons
in the houses of aristocratic patrons or their friends.[3] They argued
theological matters in public debates, and discussed philosophy and
astronomy in private circles.[4] On feast days, discussions of medicine,
geometry and music filled the courtyards of the city's ancient churches.[5]
Medieval Constantinople's 30,000 hectares brimmed with learning.

Learning on the Bosporos did not begin with the emperors' arrival
in the fourth century: ancient Byzantium had produced its modest share
of poets and orators.[6] It was, however, the imperial pull that made the
new capital an attractive place to teach and study, and that allowed
Constantinople to rival the ancient, venerable centres of learning at
Antioch, Gaza (rhetoric), Athens, Alexandria, Aphrodisias, Apameia
(philosophy), Berytus (law) or, indeed, Rome itself. Once the school
in Athens closed in 529 and the other cities had fallen out of the imperial
sphere in the seventh and eighth centuries,[7] Constantinople remained
the empire's unrivalled learning centre.

In February 357, legislation addressing qualifications of would-be
administrators introduced by Constantine's heir Constantius II (337–61)
stipulated, 'by no means shall any person obtain a place of the first order,
unless it is established that he excels in the practice and training of the
liberal studies and that he is so polished in the use of letters that words
proceed from him without the offence of imperfections'. Further, more

honourable ranks were promised to those 'worthy of the first place on account of [their] studies and [their] skills in the use of words'.[8] Anyone hoping to enter and climb the bureaucratic ranks was thus expected to possess an education in grammar and basic rhetoric, a 'universal education' (enkyklios paideia), and to express himself in the classicizing, or Atticizing, sociolect that first had become popular in the second century during the period of the second sophistic, and remained the bedrock of public discourse in medieval Byzantium. This practice of recruiting and promoting civil servants – or 'civil savants', as they have been called[9] – remained in place throughout the Byzantine millennium.[10] The famous Choniates brothers, Michael and Niketas, are a case in point. Sent to Constantinople by their godfather, Niketas, the metropolitan of Chonai, and trained by the foremost rhetorician of the time, Eustathios (later metropolitan of Thessalonike), Michael subsequently pursued a career in the church and became metropolitan of Athens. His younger brother Niketas became a minister at the imperial court, and a celebrated rhetor. Learning was thus a social currency,[11] a means of acquiring distinction, at least for those families affluent enough to send their sons to Constantinople and pay for tuition, or for those lucky enough to find a patron. It facilitated upward social mobility and centre–province cohesion.[12]

Learning was closely intertwined with the emperor's presence in Constantinople, not only in practical but also in ideological terms. The imperial role in reviving and fostering education became a topos of late Roman[13] and Byzantine imperial ideology (whether accurate or not). Themistios praised Constantius II; George the Monk gave credit to Michael III (842–67) and his mother, Theodora. The Scriptores post Theophanem commended the kaisar Bardas (d. 866), John Skylitzes, Constantine VII Porphyrogennetos (913/945–59). Michael Psellos praised Constantine IX Monomachos (1042–55) while Anna Komnene (1083–c.1153) described her father's school in the Orphanotropheion. In the thirteenth century George Kyprios hailed George Akropolites, and Nikephoros Choumnos and Nikephoros Gregoras lauded Kyprios, and, through them, Michael VIII Palaiologos (1259–82), the conqueror of Constantinople.[14]

## SCHOOLS AND TEACHERS

A web of semi-public and private grammar schools blanketed medieval Constantinople. These schools offered universal instruction in the disciplines roughly corresponding to the medieval trivium (grammar, rhetoric, logic/elementary philosophy). Occasionally they were joined with institutions of primary learning, as was the case with the school near the Holy Apostles.[15] By contrast, the advanced disciplines of the quadrivium, especially arithmetic, geometry and astronomy, were either confined to imperial foundations (when such existed) or left to private initiative.

On the one hand, the famous fourth-century sophist Libanios, who spent two brief stints in Constantinople, reports that competition for teaching posts followed the same rules as in any city of the eastern empire. Public and private teachers taught in public spaces, eager to demonstrate their social connections and attract a large following of students: if a private teacher's student entourage superseded a salaried colleague's, he could hope to replace the latter. Lessons seem to have taken place mostly in the imperial Basilica, opposite Hagia Sophia, and the colonnades surrounding its courtyard. On the other hand, imperial presence made a difference. In other cities it fell to the council to appoint teachers. In Constantinople the emperor himself made the appointments. At his second tenure Libanios had to seek Constantius II's (337–61) permission to be relieved of his duties and return to Antioch.[16] Around the time of his departure, in 355, the emperor promoted one of Libanios's colleagues, the philosopher Themistios, to the senate:[17] he went on to become *praefectus urbi* (prefect of the city) and the confidant and porte-parole of four successive Christian emperors. His trajectory epitomizes the career a man of learning could hope to make in the imperial system. The pagan Themistios set the model for later Byzantine literati.[18] His account of Constantius's foundation of a scriptorium-cum-library in 357 formulated a first vision of Constantinople as a universal centre of learning:

> for now is the time to export and traffic from you not, by Zeus, gold, timber, and porphyry-dye ... but the trading-station which the emperor has established for you just now, the goods from there are virtue and wisdom. And for such merchandise will come to us not from retailers, sailors, and the lowly rubble, but the eminent, those most eager after knowledge, and the bloom of the Greeks; learning (*logoi*) and education (*paideia*) are the merchandise.[19]

Only in February 425, did Theodosios II (401–50) regulate Constantinopolitan teaching more firmly and establish an imperial school.[20] The school's size reflected imperial prestige: with fifteen *magistri* (teachers) for Greek, thirteen for Latin, two for law and one for philosophy, it was one of the largest in the empire. However, it is unclear whether all thirty-one posts were always filled. Above all, Theodosios drew a clear distinction between imperially appointed magistri, whose position now became far more secure, and private teachers who were henceforth banned from public venues.

Theodosios relocated instruction from the Basilica to the splendidly refurbished Capitol, but it is unclear how long teaching continued there, and whether the Basilica ever fell completely out of use. The latest appointments at the Capitol are attested under Justinian I (527–65).[21] At the same time the Basilica neighbourhood was busy with book merchants and scribes for hire, and it remained a place of vivid public debate.[22] By the middle Byzantine period teaching was once again, or still, associated with the area around the Basilica. According to an iconophile legend, the iconoclast emperor Leo III (r. 717–41) put an end to learning in Constantinople by burning the 'universal teacher' with his twelve disciples in the latter's palace there.[23]

For the early ninth century, in the absence of other evidence for the functioning of schools, treatises such as John the later (?) metropolitan of Sardis's commentary on Aphthonios's *Progymnasmata* suggest the ongoing teaching of rhetoric.[24] Only in the later ninth and tenth centuries do we get a firmer grasp on schools again. No longer associated with public institutions such as the Basilica or the Capitol, they now were located in or near churches and monasteries.[25] At least three of these schools, those affiliated with the Forty Martyrs, St Theodore *ta Sphorakiou* and the Theotokos *ton Chalkoprateion* may have functioned continuously from the sixth century.[26] If so, proximity of the latter two to the Basilica may not be coincidental.[27] Over the following centuries one finds schools operating, in addition to these three, in the precincts of the churches of St Peter, the Theotokos *tes Diakonisses*, the Holy Apostles and the New Church.

Such grammar schools lasted at least into the later eleventh century, and seem to have provided universal education for future courtiers, bureaucrats and bishops.[28] The schoolmaster was now known as *maïstor* or, more rarely, *magistor*, the Graecized form of the Latin term *magister*. Although their schools were located in ecclesial and monastic precincts, most maïstores seem to have been laymen; it would thus be misleading to imagine these schools in the same vein as the monastic or cathedral schools that dominated the Latin Middle Ages.[29]

While already in late antiquity the size of a student entourage often proved crucial, by the middle Byzantine period the 'student vote' had been formalized: new maïstores were elected by their advanced students[30] and only afterwards received imperial approval.[31] Such was the case with Abraamios-Athanasios, the later founder of the Lavra on Mt Athos, in the early tenth century, or Michael Psellos's elevation to a chair in 'philosophy' in 1047.[32] The emperor could override the system, as Theophilos (827–42) seems to have done when installing Leo the Philosopher as a public teacher at the Forty Martyrs.[33]

Every grammar school seems to have evolved around one maïstor. Only occasional and usually rather short-lived imperial initiatives afforded more than one chair. Shortly after 843, Bardas founded a school that was headed by the very Leo whom Emperor Theophilos had previously appointed to the Forty Martyrs (in between lay a brief stint at the last iconoclast metropolitan of Thessalonike). It had four professors (there is no evidence that these were known as maïstores):

> Leo the Philosopher took charge of the philosophical school at the Magnaura,[34] and his disciple Theodore was at the head of the room of geometry; Theodegios that of astronomy, and Kometas that of grammar, which Hellenizes speech. Helping these latter in abundant wise and often attending out of his love of learning, Bardas strengthened the pupils' natural disposition and caused them to grow plumage and progress forward with appropriate time, as if giving feathers to words.[35]

Similarly, at Constantine VII's tenth-century foundation (inspired by Bardas's),[36] four teachers taught the disciplines of philosophy (Constantine, the emperor's private secretary), rhetoric/grammar (Alexander the ex-metropolitan of Nicaea), geometry (Nikephoros the patrician) and astronomy (the imperial secretary Gregorios).[37] Constantine VII's teachers were of higher social status than Bardas's, yet their ranks do not seem to depend on their teaching activities to the same degree as Themistios's above or Psellos and Xiphilinos's below.

By contrast, maïstores who taught in the churches and monasteries of Constantinople were assisted by senior students. British Library ms Add. 36749, which preserves the collected letters of an anonymous tenth-century schoolmaster, informs us of these arrangements.[38] Such assistant teachers were afforded a say in the school's fortunes and probably were in charge of teaching younger students while the master himself, as he informed Nikephoros the chamberlain and imperial clergyman who enquired about his nephew, examined their progress twice weekly via oral exams.[39] By the eleventh century, grammar-schools usually had a deputy master.[40]

Whatever rights of oversight the senate possessed in late antiquity seem to have moved to the patriarch in middle Byzantine times. The anonymous schoolmaster mentions the patriarch's right to redistribute students across the schools of Constantinople.[41] Another two of his letters refer to a patriarchal *artidion* (literally, a small loaf of bread; here an allowance), that had been withheld for six months, and an *eulogia* (gift, stipend) respectively, though their exact purpose remains unclear.[42]

Anonymous depicts himself in fierce competition over students: he accused the maïstor Michael of poaching his students and was subjected to similar accusations by another maïstor, the priest Philaretos.[43] He also complained to the patriarch about a neighbouring schoolmaster, perhaps identical with Michael, who poached his students.[44] By the eleventh century such rivalry among schools and their masters was channelled into schedography contests, as attested in the poems of Christopher Mitylenaios.[45]

Anonymous's 'placement record' defined his value in this market of learning – hence his constant lobbying for his students to obtain a salaried position in the patriarchate or the bureaucracy.[46] Several letters show him addressing the imperial *mystikos* (private secretary): one is a straightforward recommendation for one of his students, while in the other Anonymous 'threatens' that his students would plaster the thoroughfares of Constantinople with iambic poems praising the mystikos unless he agreed to meet Anonymous (so that the latter could lobby in person).[47] He expressed regret that the metropolitan of Sardis had chosen not to employ one of these alumni as secretary, and stated that at times he felt that his students were overlooked for appointments.[48] His letters to two court officials, the '*protospatharios* and disciple', Stephen, or the '*bestetor* and disciple', Constantine, open the possibility that members of the court hierarchy reckoned among his students. Yet one of his letters to Stephen makes the latter's father responsible for settling tuition fees, which implies that either Stephen held the senatorial dignity of protospatharios at a relatively young age or, more likely, that his title was added to the heading only at a later stage, when the letters were prepared for circulation.[49]

Placement record and connections mattered as they helped – as in late antiquity – to attract students, on whose fees the anonymous schoolmaster depended for his livelihood (the patriarchal stipend notwithstanding).[50] Intriguingly, fees were not fixed:

We, brother, have left not only you but almost all of our students to their own conscience, so that everyone display the befitting kindliness in accordance with what [financial] capacity he might have, but have not forced anybody [to pay a specific amount], and may God grant not to force anyone. While we are of such disposition, the many who show themselves ungrateful to us not for want of means but for their own meanness, shall receive their just reward at their own time.[51]

Generally, ad hoc arrangements were possible: in one letter the anonymous schoolmaster implies that one ought not to charge students from one's hometown. Elsewhere he seems content to offer instruction in exchange for manual service.[52]

From the mid-eleventh century imperial involvement increased. In 1047, Constantine IX Monomachos appointed the polymath Michael Psellos and his friend, John Xiphilinos, to newly created chairs. He appointed Psellos *hypatos* (consul) of the philosophers, apparently attaching a second chair to the school at St Peter's to accommodate that position, and made Xiphilinos *nomophylax* (guardian of the law), perhaps at his own splendid foundation of St George at Mangana.[53] The nomophylax received an annual salary of four pounds of gold and a silk garment; as well as a ceremonial staff and senatorial rank.[54] This arrangement may have applied to the hypatos, too:[55] if so Psellos and Xiphilinos were the first literati to achieve senatorial rank as a direct result of their learning and teaching activity since Themistios in the fourth century. As with previous imperial appointments, the nomophylax taught publicly without collecting fees. He was allowed, however, to accept donations from any student 'hailing from a privileged household'.[56]

The arrival of the Komnenoi fundamentally transformed the system. By 1107, Alexios I Komnenos (1081–1118) and his patriarch, Nicholas III Grammatikos, created a number of *didaskaleia* (teaching positions)[57] which seem to have formed, certainly later in the century, a college of twelve and a clear hierarchy.[58] These *didaskaloi* (teachers) should be understood as public orators instructing the faithful rather than 'teachers'.[59] During his visit to Constantinople in 1136, Anselm bishop of Havelberg (d. 1158) testified that these twelve teachers were dispersed to churches across the city.[60] They were all deacons or priests, and the three highest-ranking salaried members of the patriarchal diaconate at Hagia Sophia. These were the didaskaloi of the Psalter, of the Apostles and of the Gospels, joined by the master of rhetors as fourth in rank, an office held by prominent rhetoricians such as Theophylaktos, the later archbishop of Ohrid, or Eustathios, the later metropolitan of Thessalonike.[61]

By this time the maïstores seem to have disappeared or rather been transformed into didaskaloi. Perhaps in consequence private schoolmasters – known as *grammatikoi* – become more visible: the notorious John Tzetzes is an example.[62] (Private teaching was by no means unprecedented, as seen above: it existed in late antique Constantinople, and Leo the Philosopher allegedly taught in his run-down lodgings before being appointed to the school at the church of the Forty Martyrs.)

After 1261, Michael VIII Palaiologos initially hastened to restore teaching to the city that had once again become the empire's capital. In keeping with the general early Palaiologan imitation of Komnenian precedent, he breathed new life into Alexios I's foundation, in the Orphanotropheion, and ordered his chief minister, the *megas logothetes* George Akropolites, to offer instruction in rhetoric.[63] Yet any efforts to maintain public education petered out during the long rule of Palaiologos's son, Andronikos II (1282–1328). On the one hand, the seeds planted by his father blossomed and Andronikos presided over a court of learning and rhetorical display.[64] Gentlemen scholars such as George Kyprios and Maximos Planoudes were given lodging in the imperial Christ Akataleptos monastery, where they presided over a learned circle rather than a formal school.[65] On the other hand, the emperor's coffers were empty. The last mention of teachers receiving imperial salaries comes in a letter of Theodore Hyrtakenos, a *grammatikos* who, though well connected, appears to have been unsuccessful in his own campaign for an imperial stipend.[66]

## AFTER SCHOOL

Those who had completed their education were ready to enter the job market. In the tenth century personal networks were all-important: we saw the anonymous schoolmaster lobby directly with various members of the bureaucracy or bishops. As had Bardas, Constantine VII spent much time with the students in his palace school:

> The emperor showed particular interest in and care for the students, whom he invited almost every day to dine with him, whom he supported with stipends and with whom he conversed in a most friendly manner. A short time elapsed and, with the emperor's help and prudence, these important

arts and sciences were restored; thus choosing among the students, he appointed them judges, notaries, and metropolitan bishops. In this way, he adorned and enriched the polity of the Romans with wisdom.[67]

The passage shows how closely learning and empire had become intertwined. Contact with the powerful motivated students. At the same time the emperor could foster personal bonds, possibly over years, and ultimately choose those he trusted.

From the eleventh century onward, while personal connections continued to matter, an ostensibly meritocratic system of examinations emerged which, by the twelfth century, seems to have operated in two tiers. On the lower level, students were quizzed in schedography. Every summer[68] they gathered in the palace where they were examined by a learned courtier. Tellingly, this happened in the presence of the emperor:

> The occasion had arrived, at which boys come together in order to wrestle with each other, whom grammar, that has given birth to them and has made them suckle the breast of schedographic forethought, sends to the palace in order to wrestle over *logoi* before the emperor as judge of the contest and gymnasiarch. And on that occasion, the emperor appointed [Nikephoros] Komnenos to examine the children: and the children in their oral boxing match watched the latter's tongue, as it was the examiner of their prowess (with words). What wisdom he brought to this task! How sweet were his words! What a labyrinth of baits he put into words: as beautiful as the surface of his examination, as graceful was its deeper layer, too; and the bait on the surface was attractive and the hidden fish-hook strong. Once a youngster beguiled by the apparent [layer of the exercise] opened his mouth, the trap immediately ensnared him.[69]

School-leaving examinations, on the other hand, became tied into veritable 'theatres of state'. They coincided with a major annual court event, the encomium on the emperor performed by the master of rhetors on Epiphany (6 January). Psellos's students accompanied him while he delivered his encomium in praise of Constantine IX Monomachos.[70] While we do not know whether his disciples performed after their master on this occasion, Theophylaktos of Ohrid, in his oration to Alexios Komnenos in 1088, hints that his did. Towards the very end he turned to his disciples saying, 'I have passed on to you the secrets of the trade, in order that the tapestry may be more perfect and varied',[71] a phrase suggesting that they added their shorter praises to his long one. Similarly, Nicholas Mesarites indicates that his brother John performed after the master of rhetors under whom he had studied, and was subsequently offered a post in the bureaucracy.[72]

In the late Byzantine period such formalized displays were replaced with more informal interviews, such as in the case of young Gregory Palamas, the future champion of hesychasm, who was examined by Andronikos II's chief minister, Theodore Metochites. After interrogating young Palamas, Metochites was so impressed,

> that he could not restrain himself and could not conceal his wonder, but turning to the emperor he said, full of marvel: 'Even Aristotle himself, I believe, if he had been seated here in our presence listening to this young man, would have bestowed more than moderate praise on him . . . ' Therefore the emperor took, as it were, pride in the noble young man, and was full of joy and imagined great things for the youth, and formed plans on that behalf.[73]

Such an interview is probably also what Theodore Hyrtakenos had in mind when he said that young Alexios Apokaukos, his former student, 'went to the imperial court only to become known by the emperors, even then with a dignified and solemn appearance'.[74]

Many of those appointed kept up their scholarly pursuits while in public life. The protospatharios and protasekretis Photios, before his elevation to the patriarchate, taught his own 'choir' of students, who were eagerly awaiting his return from the palace.[75] Theodore Metochites, Andronikos II's chief minister in the early fourteenth century, found time for his learned passions in candlelight as his days were busy with running the state. It was in such figures then that education turned into scholarship.[76]

## FURTHER READING

Agapitos, P. A., 'Teachers, Pupils and Imperial Power in Eleventh-Century Byzantium', in *Pedagogy and Power: Rhetorics of Classical Learning*, ed. Y. L. Too and N. Livingstone (Cambridge, 1998), 170–91.

Agapitos, P. A., '"Middle-Class" Ideology of Education and Language, and the 'Bookish' Identity of John Tzetzes', in *Ideologies and Identities in the Medieval Byzantine World*, ed. Y. Stouraitis (Edinburgh, forthcoming).

Bernard, F., 'Educational Networks in the Letters of Michael Psellos', in *The Letters of Psellos*, ed. M. Lauxtermann and M. Jeffreys (Oxford, 2017), 13–41.

Browning, R., 'Teachers', in *The Byzantines*, ed. G. Cavallo (Chicago, 1997), 95–116.

Lemerle, P., 'Le gouvernement de philosophes', in *Cinq études sur le XI<sup>e</sup> siècle byzantine*, P. Lemerle (Paris, 1977), 193–248.

Lemerle, P., *Byzantine Humanism: The First Phase* (Canberra, 1986).

Markopoulos, A., 'Education', in *The Oxford Handbook of Byzantine Studies*, ed. E. Jeffrey, J. Haldon and R. Cormack (Oxford, 2008), 785–95.

Schlange-Schöningen, H., *Kaisertum und Bildungswesen im spätantiken Konstantinopel* (Stuttgart, 1995).

Speck, P., *Die Kaiserliche Universität von Konstantinopel* (Berlin, 1974).

Steckel, S., N. Gaul and M. Grünbart (eds), *Networks of Learning: Perspectives on Scholars in Byzantine East and Latin West, c. 1000–1200* (Berlin, 2015), 235–80.

Wilson, N., *Scholars of Byzantium*, rev. ed. (London, 1996).

# NOTES

This chapter was completed with funding from the European Research Council (ERC) under the European Union's Horizon 2020 research and innovation programme (grant agreement no. 726371, PAIXUE).

1 Themistios, *or.* 31.355a–b, *Themistii orationes qui supersunt*, ed. G. Downey and A. F. Norman (Leipzig, 1965), 2:191.24–192.2.

2 P. A. Agapitos, 'Grammar, Genre and Patronage in the Twelfth Century', *JÖB* 64 (2014): 1–22, on schedography. On verse, F. Bernard, *Writing and Reading Secular Poetry in Byzantium, 1025–1081* (Oxford, 2014), 209–51, and W. Hörandner, A. Rhoby and N. Zagklas, eds, *A Companion to Byzantine Poetry* (Leiden, 2019).

3 P. Magdalino, *The Empire of Manuel I Komnenos, 1143–1180* (Cambridge, 1993), 413–88; M. Mullett, 'Aristocracy and Patronage', in *The Byzantine Aristocracy, IX–XIII Centuries*, ed. M. Angold (Oxford, 1984), 173–201.

4 Av. Cameron, *Arguing It Out* (Budapest, 2016); for the philosophical work in Anna Komnene's circle, e.g. C. Barber and D. Jenkins, eds, *Medieval Greek Commentaries on the Nicomachean Ethics* (Leiden, 2009); on astronomy, P. Magdalino, *L'Orthodoxie des astrologues* (Paris, 2007), 91–132.

5 Nicholas Mesarites, 'Description of the Church of the Holy Apostles', § 42, *Grabeskir-che und Apostelkirche*, ed. A. Heisenberg (Leipzig, 1908), 2: 90–4; *Nicholas Mesarites: His Life and Works*, trans. M. Angold (Liverpool, 2017), 129–31.

6 See *RE* III 1 (1897): 1149; Philostratos *V.Soph.* 1.24 (Marcus) and 2.11 (Chrestos).

7 A. Markopoulos, 'In Search for "Higher Education" in Byzantium', *ZRVI* 50 (2013): 30–2; R. Cribiore, *The School of Libanius* (Princeton, 2007), 42–82. On Athens, E. Watts, 'Justinian, Malalas, and the End of Athenian Philosophical Teaching in A.D. 529', *JRS* 94 (2004): 168–82. For political background J. Haldon, *The Empire That Would Not Die* (Cambridge, MA, 2016).

8 *CTh* 14.1.1.

9 M. Maas, *John Lydus and the Roman Past* (London, 1992), 29.

10 F. Bernard, 'Educational Networks in the Letters of Michael Psellos', in *The Letters of Psellos*, ed. M. Lauxtermann and M. Jeffreys (Oxford, 2017), 13–41 at 13.

11 E.g. P. Bourdieu, *Distinction* (London, 1984).

12 C. Rapp, 'Literary Culture in the Age of Justinian', in *The Cambridge Companion to the Age of Justinian*, ed. M. Maas (Cambridge, 2005), 379–82; N. Gaul, 'Rising Elites and Institutionalization – *Ethos/Mores* – "Debts" and Drafts', in *Networks of Learning*, ed. S. Steckel, N. Gaul and M. Grünbart (Berlin, 2015), 235–80 at 251–3.

13 H. Schlange-Schöningen, *Kaisertum und Bildungswesen im spätantiken Konstantinopel* (Stuttgart, 1995), 10–39.

14 Themistios, *or.* 4.59b–61c, ed. Downey, 1:84.15–87.17; George the Monk, *Chronicle, Georgi Monachi Chronicon*, ed. C. de Boor (Leipzig, 1904), 2:742.19–22; *Theoph. Cont.* 4.26.12–16,

*Chronographiae quae Theophanis Continuati nomine fertur Libri I–IV*, ed. and trans. J. Signes Codoñer and M. Featherstone (Berlin, 2015), 262–3 and *Theoph. Cont.* 6, *Theophanes Continuatus*, ed. I. Bekker (Bonn, 1838), 446.1–9; John Skylitzes, 237.23–238.30, ed. J. Thurn (Berlin, 1973); John Skylitzes, *A Synopsis of Byzantine History*, trans. J. Wortley (Cambridge, 2010), 229; *Funeral Oration for John Xiphilinos*, § 10, *Michael Psellus: Orationes funebres*, ed. I. Polemis (Berlin, 2014), 127–8; *Psellos and the Patriarchs*, trans. I. Polemis (Notre Dame, 2015), 190–1; *Alexiad* 15.7.9; Anna Komnene, *Annae Comnenae Alexias*, ed. D. R. Reinsch and A. Kambylis (Berlin, 2001),1:484–5; Anna Komnene, *The Alexiad*, trans. E. R. A. Sewter and P. Frankopan (London, 2009), 454–5; *PG* 142.380D–381D; N. Gaul, *Thomas Magistros und die spätbyzantinische Sophistik* (Mainz, 2011), 272–4.

15  The grammar school was north-east of the church: Mesarites, 'Church of the Holy Apostles', §§7–11, ed. Heisenberg, 17–22; tr. Angold, 87–90.

16  G. Dagron, *Naissance d'une capitale*, 2nd ed. (Paris, 1984), 220–1; Cribiore, *School of Libanius*, 60–1; Schlange-Schöningen, *Kaisertum und Bildungswesen*, 91–111.

17  Heather and Moncur, *Politics, Philosophy, and Empire*, 101.

18  P. Heather, 'Themistius: A Political Philosopher', in *The Propaganda of Power*, ed. M. Whitby (Leiden, 1998), 125–50; A. Kaldellis, *The Argument of Psellos' Chronographia* (Leiden, 1999), 169–70 n. 349.

19  *Or.* 4.61a–b, ed. Downey, 1:86.20–87.6; P. Lemerle, *Byzantine Humanism: The First Phase* (Canberra, 1986), 55–9; J. Vanderspoel, *Themistius and the Imperial Court* (Ann Arbor, 1995), 96–100.

20  *CTh* 14.9.3.

21  John Lydos described his appointment in *De mag.* 3.28.4–29.4, *Jean le Lydien: Des magistratures de l'état romain*, 2 vols, ed. M. Dubuisson and J. Schamp (Paris, 2006), 2:78–80: see Maas, *John Lydus*, 34–5 and Schlange-Schöningen, *Kaisertum und Bildungswesen*, 135–8.

22  Rapp, 'Literary Culture in the Age of Justinian', 378.

23  George the Monk, *Chron.*, ed. de Boor, 2:742.1–22; *Patria* 3.31, *Accounts of Medieval Constantinople*, ed. and trans. A. Berger (Cambridge, MA, 2013), 154–7. The legend seems to derive from Theophanes year 726/AM 6218, *The Chronicle of Theophanes Confessor*, trans. C. Mango and R. Scott (Oxford, 1997), 560. On the 'universal teacher', Lemerle, *Byzantine Humanism*, 93–8; P. Speck, *Die Kaiserliche Universität von Konstantinopel* (Berlin, 1974), 65 and 74–91; E. Kountoura-Galake, 'Legend and Reality: The Case of Oikoumenikos Didaskalos in the Early Palaiologan Period', in *Hypermachos*, ed. C. Stavrakos, A.-K. Wassiliou and M. K. Krikorian (Wiesbaden, 2008), 173–86.

24  K. Alpers, *Untersuchungen zu Johannes Sardianos und seinem Kommentar zu den Progymnasmata des Aphthonios* (Braunschweig, 2009).

25  Speck, *Kaiserliche Universität*, 67–73.

26  For a different opinion Speck, *Kaiserliche Universität*, 67 n. 3.

27  Magdalino, 'Medieval Constantinople', 39–40; see map in Speck, *Kaiserliche Universität*, 106.

28  Cf. Lemerle, *Byzantine Humanism*, 250: 'secondary school'.

29  Gaul, 'Rising Elites and Institutionalization'. Rich Constantinopolitan monasteries may have owned dormitories/schools, such as the Stoudite monastery's καταγώγιον τῶν παίδων (children's lodging). There is no other evidence of any special school infrastructure. See N. M. Kalogeras, 'Byzantine Childhood Education and Its Social Role from the Sixth Century until the End of Iconoclasm' (PhD thesis, University of Chicago, 2000), 150–7.

30  Compare John Mauropous's letter of endorsement for Michael Psellos: Lauxtermann, 'Michael Psellos and John Mauropous', 125.

31  Speck, *Kaiserliche Universität*, 36–9. Speck thinks the city eparch dispensed imperial approval.

32  M. Lauxtermann, 'The Intertwined Lives of Michael Psellos and John Mauropous', in *Letters of Psellos*, ed. M. Lauxtermann and M. Jeffreys (Oxford, 2017), 89–127 at 121–2.

33  *Theoph. Cont.* 4.27.83–6. Whether Leo became a 'regular' maïstor or was known by a different title remains unknown.

34  Skyl. 101.75–6 qualifies that not the whole school, but only Leo's chair, was located in the Magnaura.

35  *Theoph. Cont.* 4.29.14–22, ed. Signes Codoñer and Featherstone, 272, tr., 273.

36  Speck, *Kaiserliche Universität*, 22–8 proved that there was no continuity from Bardas's foundation.

37  *Theoph. Cont.* 6, ed. Bekker, 446.10–14.

38  A. Markopoulos, *Anonymi professoris epistulae* (Berlin, 2000), 4. On the Anonymous and his school: R. Browning, 'The Correspondence of a Tenth-Century Byzantine Scholar', *Byzantion*

24 (1954), 397–452; Lemerle, *Byzantine Humanism*, 286–98; A. Steiner, *Untersuchungen zu einem anonymen byzantinischen Briefcorpus des 10. Jahrhunderts* (Frankfurt, 1987).

39 *Ep.* 110.13–19.

40 In Anonymous's school, this post may de facto have been held by Ephraim (cf. *ep.* 20.13–14) and Ioannikios (*ep.* 96.26–7); however, the title is not mentioned.

41 Anonymous schoolmaster, *ep.* 47.62–5 (cf. n38). In the specific context of a letter against a rival *maïstor*, Philarethos, Anonymous says he is not afraid of intervention by patriarch, emperor or eparch of Constantinople in an unspecified matter (*ep.* 68.11–14).

42 *Epp.* 1 and 54. Michael Psellos's (?) letter Π 399.12–18 (*Michael Psellus: Epistulae*, ed. S. Papaioannou (Leipzig, 2019), 2:820–1), written on behalf of the *maïstor* of *tes Diakonisses*, states that teaching space (παιδευτήριον) was provided free of charge, but no salary was paid.

43 For Michael, *epp.* 36 and 51; for Philaretos, *ep.* 68.

44 *Ep.* 47.29–37.

45 Christopher Mitylenaios, *carm.* 9–11, *The Poems of Christopher of Mytilene and John Mauropous*, ed. and trans. F. Bernard and C. Livanos (Cambridge, MA, 2018), 14–21, cf. Bernard, *Writing and Reading Secular Poetry*, 253–90.

46 On his addressees see Lemerle, *Byzantine Humanism*, 296–8 and Markopoulos, *Anonymi professoris epistulae*, 17*–18*.

47 *Epp.* 40 and 94; the latter translated in Gaul, 'Rising Elites and Institutionalization', 273.

48 *Ep.* 85.48–56; *ep.* 47.7–19.

49 To Stephen, *epp.* 9 and 11; to Constantine, *epp.* 37 and 58. Cf. also *ep.* 6.

50 Again *epp.* 9, 11, 37 and 58; or *ep.* 39, to Christopher, the *chartoularios* of the New Church.

51 *Ep.* 58.17–22, to Constantine the *bestetor*. *Ep.* 109 suggests that payment in kind might also be acceptable (in this case a pot).

52 Anonymous schoolmaster: *ep.* 78.1–3 and *ep.* 29.8–10; similar arrangements are attested in the Palaiologan period, see Gaul, *Thomas Magistros*, 237–9.

53 See Lauxtermann, 'Michael Psellos and John Mauropous', 112–23 and, previously, P. A. Agapitos, 'Teachers, Pupils and Imperial Power in Eleventh-Century Byzantium', in *Pedagogy and Power*, ed. Y. L. Too and N. Livingstone (Cambridge, 1998), 170–91.

54 John Mauropous, 'Novel', §11, *Novella constitutio saec. XI medii*, ed. A. Salač (Prague, 1954), 25; see Z. Chitwood, *Byzantine Legal Culture and the Roman Legal Tradition, 867–1056* (Cambridge, 2017), 167–78.

55 Certainly according to Psellos: W. Wolska-Conus, 'Les écoles de Psellos et Xiphilin sous Constantin IX Monomaque', *TM* 6 (1976): 224–8.

56 Mauropous, 'Novel', §14, ed. Salač, 27.

57 P. Gautier, 'L'édit d'Alexis Iᵉʳ Comnène sur la réforme du clergé', *REB* 31 (1973): 165–201; P. Magdalino, 'The Reform Edict of 1107', in *Alexios I Komnenos*, ed. M. Mullett and D. C. Smythe (Belfast, 1996), 199–218; M. Angold, *Church and Society in Byzantium under the Comneni* (Cambridge, 1995), 91–5.

58 A hierarchy emerged already in the eleventh century when a chair at St Peter's was more prestigious than at the Theotokos *tes Diakonisses*, see Psellos's letter Π 399.31–8 (cf. n42). Already the *Life of Athanasios of Athos* speaks of a *prokathemenos* (president) of schools but the evidence is too isolated to infer much from it.

59 Magdalino, *Empire of Manuel I*, 327.

60 See Magdalino, *Empire of Manuel I*, 325–6 regarding the possible composition of this 'college'. Contrast Angold, *Church and Society*, 93.

61 The first mention of the master comes in a letter by Psellos addressed to the 'metropolitan of Thessalonike and one-time *maïstor* of the rhetors', but this may be a later conflation with Eustathios: cf. *Michael Psellus: Epistulae*, ed. S. Papaionnou (Berlin, 2019), 2:785 app. (Π 376); see also Magdalino, *Empire of Manuel I*, 326n32. On Eustathios, see Eustathios of Thessalonike: *Commentary on Homer's Odyssey*, vol. 1, ed. E. Cullhed (Uppsala, 2016) and B. van den Berg, 'Homer and the Good Ruler in the "Age of Rhetoric": Eustathios of Thessalonike on Excellent Oratory', in *Homer and the Good Ruler in Antiquity and Beyond*, ed. J. J. H. Klooster and B. van den Berg (Leiden 2018), 219–38.

62 On Tzetzes, who failed to obtain a public teaching post, see P. A. Agapitos, '"Middle-class" Ideology of Education and Language, and the "Book-ish" Identity of John Tzetzes', in *Ideologies and Identities in the Medieval Byzantine World*, ed. Y. Stouraitis (Edinburgh, forthcoming);

E. Cullhed, 'The Blind Bard and "I": Homeric Biography and Authorial Personas in the Twelfth Century,' *BMGS* 38 (2014): 49–67.

63  S. Mergiali, *L'enseignement et les lettrés pendant l'époque des Paléologues (1261–1453)* (Athens, 1996), 15–29. Akropolites was joined by Manuel Holobolos: Pachymeres, *Histories*, 4.14; Georges Pachymérès, *Rélations Historiques*, ed. A. Failler (Paris, 1984), 2:369.5–371.5; cf. I. Pérez Martín, 'Le conflit de l'union des églises (1274) et son reflet dans l'enseignement supérieur de Constantinople', *BSl* 56 (1995): 411–22.

64  N. Gaul, 'All the Emperor's Men (and His Nephews)', *DOP* 70 (2017): 245–70.

65  For 'gentlemen scholars' see R. Browning, 'Teachers', in G. Cavallo (ed.), *The Byzantines* (Chicago, 1997), 105–6.

66  Theodore Hyrtakenos, *ep.* 77.19–26, *The Letters of Theodoros Hyrtakenos*, ed. A. Karpozilos and G. Fatouros (Athens, 2017), 272–4. Cf. A. Karpozilos, 'The Correspondence of Theodore Hyrtakenos', *JÖB* 40 (1990): 275–84.

67  *Theoph. Cont.* 6.446.14–22.

68  Gaul, 'Rising Elites and Institutionalization', 276–7.

69  Constantine Manasses, 'Encomium on Nikephoros Komnenos', ed. E. Kurtz, *VizVrem* 17 (1910): 302–22.

70  Psellos, *or. pan.* 6.261–91, 341–45, *Michaelis Pselli: Orationes Panegyricae*, ed. G. T. Dennis (Stuttgart, 1994), 98–9, 101. Cf. P. Lemerle, 'Le gouvernement de philosophes', in Lemerle, *Cinq études*, 218–19.

71  Theophylaktos, *or.* 5, ed. P. Gautier, *Théophylacte d'Achrida: Discours, Traités, Poésies* (Thessalonike, 1980), 243.13–14.

72  Mesarites, 'Funeral Oration for his Brother John', §§16–17, ed. A. Heisenberg, trans. Angold, 154–6.

73  Philotheos Kokkinos, 'Life of Gregory Palamas', §11, Φιλοθέου τοῦ Κοκκίνου Ἁγιολογικὰ ἔργα, ed. D. G. Tzames (Thessalonike, 1985), 438.11–22.

74  Hyrtakenos, *ep.* 69.34–6, ed. and trans. Karpozilos and Fatouros, 250–2.

75  Speck, *Kaiserliche Universität*, 14–18.

76  N. Wilson, *Scholars of Byzantium*, rev. ed. (London, 1996).

# 17: ENTERTAINMENT

## Marcus Rautman

L ike any great city, Constantinople was a nexus of social space, civic ceremony, commercial entertainment, and endless diversion. Medieval observers saw a busy urban environment where streets and plazas were regularly taken over by processions, churches and monasteries were filled with clergy and worshipers, and competitive games and performances took place in the open-air hippodrome. Public celebrations reached their greatest number and most elaborate form during the fifth and sixth centuries, but continued in varied ways into the late Middle Ages. Many of these local pastimes were still known in Ottoman times.

Popular entertainment and events of mass spectacle belong to the larger sphere of culturally contingent leisure activities. Leisure in premodern societies generally concerned time and activity spent apart from the sustaining obligations of daily life. For most people unstructured time was shaped mainly by the passing seasons, with observances of distant agricultural origin offering predictable opportunities for shared relaxation. Processions, games, and feasting were common ways of gathering members of a community to observe and participate in occasions of public visibility. The increasingly routinized staging of festivals in classical Mediterranean cities provided long days of organized socializing that implicitly reinforced cultural values and political order.[1]

Within the sociology of leisure, the study of entertainment generally focuses on cooperative activities in urban environments. A broad understanding of entertainment encompasses non-utilitarian activities that temporarily hold the attention of participants. Theoretical approaches distinguish levels of subjective engagement. Unstructured, self-directed, and small-group activities within the home can be seen as characteristic of casual leisure or folk culture. Diversions undertaken outside the household gain complexity with repetition and coordination of expectations in games and performance, with temporary differentiation of participants as entertainers and audience. More elaborate spectacles held in public, purpose-built settings involve organizers, performers, and supporting staff, with an increasingly commercial role serving observers of varying degrees of personal investment. As a consumer-oriented product, conceived and managed for an objectified mass audience, such occasions belong to the sphere of popular culture.[2]

Written sources for understanding entertainment in Byzantine Constantinople range from the prescriptive protocols of church and palace to the proscriptive harangues of religious leaders. Saints' lives, chronicles, and narrative histories describe festivals, and medieval authors mention the involvement of residents in preparing, staging, and watching these events. The unruly intensity of enthusiastic crowds could also have unforeseen consequences, and on occasion violence and riots flared. John Chrysostom and other guardians of public decorum warned that attending mass spectacles could lead to laughter, immodest and licentious behavior, impulsiveness, and loss of responsible identity. While theatrical shows were generally improvisational, their potential to critique and undermine social order was clear to officials like Justinian (527–65), who suppressed Christological mimes and withdrew funding for their public performance.[3] Some of the most negative views came from bishops attending the late seventh-century Council in Trullo, whose canons discouraged clergy and monks from attending the hippodrome and condemned exhibitions of mimes, wild animals, and public dancing.[4] Yet other sources make clear that organized spectacles were inseparable from the intensity of city life, with state-sponsored processions, games, and performances growing out of playful, demonstrative interactions experienced every day in street, market, and home. Writing of Antioch in the later fourth century, Libanios explains how urban festivals enabled people to play, eat, and live "as agreeably as possible." Leo the Deacon claims that spectacles were more popular among residents of tenth-century Constantinople than anywhere else.[5]

## Rhythms of Urban Life

The founding of New Rome brought from Italy a number of festive civic traditions that were observed with public parades, services, and games, as well as private gatherings of family and friends for sharing meals and exchanging gifts. As in centuries past, the festival of *Calends* (*Kalendae Ianuariae*) opened the new year with the hanging of laurel wreaths on doors, costumed parades, and gift-giving. The associated feast of *Vota* was of similar antiquity and is known as late as the tenth century in the form of street revels, hippodrome races, and banquets in the imperial palace. The mid-winter *Lupercalia* recalled Rome's legendary origins with acclamations, feasting, and a famous footrace, all part of a month-long palace festival preceding Lent. The ancient harvest festival of *Bruma* or *Brumalia*, once tied to Dionysus, continued to be celebrated with processions, dancing, and nightly bonfires taking place from November 24 through the winter solstice. Constantinople's anniversary on May 11 was marked by processions and worship services throughout the Middle Ages, with a gilded statue of Constantine brought in a chariot to the hippodrome to be recognized by his reigning successor.[6]

As for the liturgical calendar, the tenth-century *typikon* (regulatory document) of Hagia Sophia and *Synaxarion* (calendar of feast days) of Constantinople preserve feast cycles that ran from the annunciation of the Virgin's birth (*Evangelismos tou Theotokou*) on September 8 to her ascension into heaven (*Koimesis*) on August 15. The Triumph of Orthodoxy marked the beginning of Lent by recalling the restoration of icons in the mid-ninth century; critical victories over the Arabs and other foes were observed throughout the year. Local martyrs and saints were commemorated in a growing number of minor feasts. The *Book of Ceremonies* describes ancient and enduring customs of the tenth-century palace. Imperial birthdays, anniversaries, and military triumphs added further excitement to the civic calendar.[7]

## PROCESSIONS

The staging of processions through Constantinople's porticoed streets and secondary roads was an opportunity to present civic, religious, and military elites to residents and visitors. As multidimensional public rituals, parades express status hierarchies while reinforcing the social integration of community members. The progressive, carefully managed unfolding of processions through space and time heightens the emotional engagement of spectators as well as participants, and can blur the distinction between secular and religious occasions.[8] Urban topography was well suited to such occasions. Two major streets led from the Golden Gate and Adrianople Gate in the land walls as far as the Capitol and the Philadelphion, where they merged and continued east as the central thoroughfare known as the Mese. The route took advantage of high, level ground and passed through several plazas along the way to the palace: open squares with freestanding columns set up by Arkadios (395–408) and Marcian (450–57), the expansive Theodosian Forum with triumphal arches and columns, and the circular Forum of Constantine with its towering porphyry shaft supporting a colossal statue of the emperor. Paved with marble and framed by porticoes, this ceremonial path culminated in the Regia and surrounding buildings like the Augusteion and Baths of Zeuxippos, the cathedral of Hagia Sophia, and residences of patriarch and emperor. The most important processions began at Hagia Sophia or the Great Palace and invariably included the Constantinian forum. Accounts mention extensive preparations for such events as well as the noisy crowds that hailed dignitaries passing through the streets – freshly swept and washed, populated with statues, decorated with banners and garlands, and lit by hanging lamps and torches – on solemn and festive occasions.[9]

The enduring traditions of the Roman triumph marked the return from campaign of the victorious emperor and his generals. Received by city leaders at the Golden Gate, the mounted ruler led his army down the Mese, stopping in each forum to be cheered by residents. At the Forum of Constantine the emperor dismounted and walked with the patriarch to the cathedral for special services of thanks. The final site of acclamation was the hippodrome, the city's premier public space, where the emperor oversaw the display of prisoners and weapons and distributed spoils of victory to the public. The exhilarating, day-long sequence of events, which began outside the walls and wound through the city's heart, continued the ritualized festivities of classical Rome with their reassuring messages of order, tradition, and divine sanction.[10]

## HIPPODROME

Apart from street processions and worship in Hagia Sophia, the highlights of Byzantine public spectacle took place in the hippodrome. The location survives in the plaza known today as *At Meydanı*. The sprawling open-air racetrack lay along the landward flank of the imperial palace near the eastern terminus of the Mese, and formed a grand performative space between the emperor and his urban public. A busy schedule of state-sponsored events promised entertainment throughout the year, and in this way established the capital's prestige among cities. The large crowds reflected Constantinople's diverse population, as area residents joined visiting merchants and tradesmen, cultural tourists, religious pilgrims, and dignitaries from abroad. Spectators created further diversion in the form of audience interaction and response, which ranged from informal mingling to coordinated acclamations of the emperor, to unpredictable outbursts of violence. The hippodrome's lingering place in the urban imagination is clear from its use for assemblies, processions, and exhibitions into the Ottoman period.[11]

The hippodrome was clearly integral to Constantine's city, and from its foundation served as the primary venue for public gatherings and traditional Roman entertainments. Gladiatorial events were not among these: imperial concern and oppressive expense brought such crowd pleasers to an end in the fourth century. No less brutalizing were staged hunts of exotic animals (venationes), which were held in the amphitheater known as the Kynegion and hippodrome into the sixth century, and were continued later by parades and exhibitions. Performances of mimes, acrobats, and jugglers provided interludes between other events.[12]

Chariot races were among antiquity's most popular forms of mass spectacle, having originated in funerary commemorations and religious festivals to claim a key place in Mediterranean urban life.[13] The earliest games in Rome took place in the Circus Maximus, whose location at the base of the Palatine hill combined public assembly with political engagement. The creation of an equally impressive if slightly smaller facility in Constantinople, the hippodrome, continued this tradition. Evidence suggests that the hippodrome was about 120 m wide and had a length exceeding 400 m, from the two-storied starting gate (carceres) near the Mese to the curved end (sphendone) to the south. Vaulted substructures at the south end supported a level racing surface that was enclosed by long rows of tiered seats. Spectators entered the hippodrome by multiple gates and sat on unsheltered embankments of earth, wooden benches, or marble seats. The imperial loge (kathisma), located near the middle of the structure's east side, was directly accessible from the Great Palace. A platform (stama) below the kathisma was used for making announcements and incidental performances between races. Estimates of seating capacity have ranged from 30,000 to 80,000 spectators, a significant share of the city's population whatever the case.[14]

Spectators beheld a multilayered view of the hippodrome: the gravel racetrack, monuments lining the central barrier, and the facing crowd with city rooftops and sea beyond. The euripos or spina, a low barrier between turning posts that allowed a clear view of the action, divided the racetrack. A parade of monuments set up on the euripos brought visitors into dialogue with the past. Freestanding columns, pyramids, and obelisks evoked a sense of ancient monumentality. Sources describe statues of historical and mythological figures and animals gathered by Constantine (306–37) to enhance his new capital.[15] Three monuments survive: a tall obelisk of coursed limestone masonry, perhaps set up by Constantine and given a new coating of bronze plates in the tenth century; the three-headed serpent column from Delphi, originally dedicated to commemorate the Greek victory at Plataea (479 BC); and the granite obelisk of Thutmose III (1479–1425 BC), brought from Karnak and set atop a massive, two-tiered marble base around 390. Reliefs on the northeast side of the obelisk's lower base record the excitement of its month-long installation, as teams of laborers strain to drag the monolith into the hippodrome in what must have been a spectacular display of engineering prowess. The obelisk appears with other monuments amid chariots and racing officials on the southwest side of the upper base. Other reliefs depict Theodosios I (379–95) and colleagues in the kathisma, along with dignitaries, soldiers, and spectators watching acrobats or dancers perform to wind pipes and water organs.[16]

Survivors of the hippodrome's glory days also include four life-size gilt bronze horses, now in Venice, which may once have stood atop the carceres. Victorious chariot drivers were memorialized by painted portraits displayed on the kathisma and freestanding statues on inscribed bases on the euripos.[17] These were the most famous of all Byzantine performers, men whose celebrity was enhanced by competing for rival factions at racetracks across the empire. The best-known was Porphyrios, who enjoyed a successful career in the sixth century. Two surviving statue bases represent Porphyrios with chariots, horses, and attendants, and holding variously a whip, palm, or crown. Inscribed texts and images articulated the connection between athletic and imperial victory.[18]

Chariot drivers were the most visible of hippodrome personnel. For centuries racing logistics were overseen by competitive factions or teams of supporters (demes). During the late republic members of the four main teams distinguished themselves by wearing colors that could be recognized wherever races took place. In Constantinople the Blue and Green teams were instrumental in recruiting drivers, procuring horses, supplying equipment, and managing events. The empress Theodora (d.548) was a lifelong supporter of the Blues, even though her father had trained performing bears for the Greens. Porphyrios raced on behalf of both factions during his long career. Factions and allies occupied separate parts of the hippodrome, and team leaders, acclaimers, and hecklers were organized by rows. One of the surviving Porphyrios monuments depicts supporters or entertainers dressed in short tunics, playing pipes, and waving banners in triumph. Heated rivalries between teams offered fertile ground for sorcery, and lead curse tablets were deployed against opposing drivers and horses. For many young men the cultivated antagonism between factions was entertainment in itself. The immersive intensity of boisterous, freewheeling demonstrations often led to violent clashes that spread into city streets, seen most dramatically in the Nika riots of 532. The reduced scale of racing after the seventh century eroded the power of these partisan organizations, which continued as largely ceremonial teams that worked with imperial officials to organize games. As late as the tenth century the factions appeared in carefully organized scenes of acclamation and response in support of the emperor.[19]

The inauguration of the new consul in early January brought days of festivities to the hippodrome. By the early sixth century the consulship had become a largely honorary post, responsible mainly for staging lavish public entertainments. Sources describe a formal procession to the hippodrome, where the consul was presented to the crowd with trappings of office. Ivory diptychs carved for Areobindus (506) and Anastasios (517) depict the consul as he wanted to be seen: splendidly attired, seated in his box amid imperial images and attributes of rank, presiding with ceremonial staff and raised flag (mappa) to begin seven days of games. The figure's imposing image contrasts with small but energetic scenes of acrobats, dancers, and horses, as well as hapless animals hunted in the arena.[20]

Festivals continued over several days and included competitions featuring people and animals. Full days devoted to chariot racing typically opened and closed each occasion; others were given over to staged hunts and theatrical displays. The sixth century saw as many as twenty-five races in the morning with again as many in the afternoon. Ballots drawn from a spherical urna (tumbler) determined the order of events. A designated starter signaled the beginning of each race, which normally consisted of seven counterclockwise circuits, with the winner completing a victory lap on his way to receive palm and crown. The Berlin "Kugelspiel," a carved marble ballgame device whose reliefs feature racing officials and competitors, preserves glimpses of the races.[21] Egyptian papyri of the later fifth or sixth century record the sequence of events with acrobats, jugglers, tightrope walkers, and mimes appearing between the display of trophies, processions, and races. The many professionals attracted to Constantinople provided a rich menu of fast-paced diversions.[22]

Church leaders were suspicious of all hippodrome occasions. While the kaleidoscopic, carnival-like atmosphere clearly appealed to local crowds, it attracted from an early date the reproach of Tertullian, Lactantius, and Chrysostom. Imperial edicts from the fourth to sixth centuries reflect the growing weight of clerical opprobrium, and led to the Council in Trullo's exclusion of clergy and monks from races and staged amusements, even those accompanying weddings.[23]

Yet chariot races never lost their social and political value. For audience members they provided varied, day-long spectacles at minimal cost, along with unlimited opportunity for expressive interaction. For the state, races offered a way to demonstrate generosity and authority in a controlled, hierarchically structured setting. Inscribed and visual acclamations on the charioteer monuments echo the language of imperial monuments, and broaden the idea of shared triumph that connected the individual supporter with a sense of generalized victory.

Racing's decline after the seventh century reflects wider changes in Byzantium brought about by economic and military pressures accompanying a reduced population and territory. Crowds continued to gather in the hippodrome, but less often and for events that took place mainly as imperial pageant. The *Book of Ceremonies* makes clear the highly ritualized nature of racing in the tenth century, now largely limited to the celebration of *Lupercalia* and similar festivals.[24] On other occasions, races and mock battles might be staged to honor an important military victory or the transfer of imperial power.[25] The continuing renown of the hippodrome as Constantinople's signature entertainment venue survives in a series of frescoes in the eleventh-century cathedral of St. Sophia in Kiev, where the detailed treatment of a courtly procession, musical performances with dancers, musicians, a pipe organ, and other entertainments express the power of public amusement.[26] Western-style jousting events (*tornemen* and *dzoustra*) seem to have been introduced during the city's Latin occupation.

## ON STAGE

Theatrical entertainments were another popular spectacle inherited from classical times. Roman citizens had long been in the habit of attending public performances and several open-air theaters are known in early Constantinople. Unlike classical drama, stage productions in late antiquity aimed at visual rather than literary appeal, and ranged from choreographed group performances to individual displays of acrobatic and illusionist skill. One of the most elaborate forms of stage performance was pantomime (*pantomimos*), a ballet-like retelling of familiar mythological tales known in the third century BC. Commanding public stage or private dining room, a single interpretive dancer assumed well-known character roles by wearing distinctive costumes and trappings. The expressive eloquence of non-verbal performance was reinforced by instrumental or sung musical accompaniment.[27] By contrast, the less decorous antics of mimes and mummers offered broadly comedic diversion in the tradition of burlesque and slapstick. Expressive mime (*mimos*) performances had an equally long history, with plots drawn from easily recognized, often transgressive aspects of everyday life: family dramas, mistaken identities, infidelities, crime, violence. Requiring no scenery and few props, mimes moved freely from stage to street corners and taverns, delivering lively action supported by flutes, pipes, lyres, singing, and drums.[28] Acrobats and jugglers appear in different media and are mentioned by late medieval authors. The depiction of small, costumed, and sometimes nude figures on carved ivory boxes of the tenth–twelfth centuries suggests the broad parody and implicit social commentary of playful display.[29]

Like other forms of mass entertainment the theater was viewed by authorities with suspicious tolerance. Chrysostom and others saw the manipulative inauthenticity of dramatic roleplaying (*hypocrisis*) as inherently blasphemous.[30] Naturally the unpredictable and emotional response to public performance contributed to immorality and political subversion. Performers were seen as inhabiting the social margin; foreigners, slaves, and especially women were regarded as morally irresponsible, even as they were invited to play in the palace itself. Prokopios' overheated account of Theodora's stage career likely drew on widespread prejudices about the moral fluidity of the entertainment community as much as its enduring popular acclaim.[31]

## DIVERSIONS OF DAILY LIFE

Constantinople's inhabitants spent much of their time outside, in the unstructured middle ground between ordered spectacle and easy domesticity. The locations and routines of productive labor ranged from tending urban gardens and orchards to bringing commodities to neighborhood markets, with light industry and retail often sharing the same space. Distinctions between purposeful work and leisurely pastime changed constantly in urban plazas and streets, where shops, restaurants, taverns, schools, baths, and personal services allowed casual and transactional socializing among women as well as men.[32]

Broad, porticoed streets were among Constantinople's most characteristic urban features. While major processions stuck to these primary routes, secondary streets in peripheral quarters saw myriad local celebrations. Neighborhood churches and shrines hosted small festivals and occasional markets. Clerical students and their teachers observed the October 25 feast of their patrons, the martyrs Markianos and Martyrios, by wearing crowns, masks, and costumes while processing through the Forum of Constantine to the church of the Holy Notaries. Some craft workers and guild members arranged their own celebrations. Michael Psellos writes how women involved in the textile trades held their festival of Agathe on March 12, noting weaving competitions and displays of artistry by wool carders, spinners, and weavers, as well as a street procession with merrymaking, dancing, and singing.[33] Depending on the occasion and local temperament, panegyric markets might include banquets, rhetorical contests, parades, masquerades, animal displays, and general carousing.

Streets were busy throughout the day. Carts and wagons kept to the main roads, with porters carrying their loads through uneven, winding alleys. Food vendors, scribes, and moneychangers lined the porticoes, which were good places to meet people and pass time with friends. Keeping passages clear of debris and lit by torches at night was up to shopkeepers, who might briefly expand their domain by setting benches and tables for customers outside their doors. Floor mosaics, graffiti, and game boards carved into the paving of porticoes reflect the attractions of recreational leisure. Observers note the boisterous conviviality of restaurants, taverns, and baths, where acrobats, illusionists, and jugglers shared their talent at close range. Trained bears, birds, and dogs were always reliable attractions. Mime-like performers and storytellers continued to play back streets and tavernas.

## AT HOME

Houses were a valued refuge within Constantinople and the place where residents spent much of their time, finding respite from the demands of city life. Domestic entertainments for aristocratic families were arranged by household staff or hired performers, and resembled events seen in the imperial palace and hippodrome. Animal games and managed hunts in park-like enclosures involved exotic animals as well as trained dogs and falcons. Formal dining continued to be the best way to display status through setting, furnishings, menu, and service. Echoing state banquets at the palace and entertainments in the hippodrome, elite dinner parties featured acrobats, dancers, jugglers, and musicians. The Kiev frescoes underscore the prestige of large instrumental ensembles that might include bells, drums, organ, harp, lute, horns, pipes, and cymbals.[34]

Literature claimed a significant place on the entertaining spectrum of aristocratic households during late antiquity and again in the eleventh through thirteenth centuries. For many authors, writing allowed respite from workaday toil in administration, teaching, or law. Letters and poems were composed, exchanged, and collected among friends, apparently for reading aloud before small groups. Homeric texts continued to be taught and read for entertainment, along with classical and Byzantine texts of a philosophical, scientific, and technical nature. Works of classicizing history were typically modeled on Thucydides or Xenophon and suggest interest in oral recitation, perhaps as serialized readings over multiple evenings. Elite households were the main venues for such literary and rhetorical *theatra*, which might have taken place in purpose-built halls.[35] Oral readings of saints' lives and universal chronicles could have provided a kind of uplifting entertainment in urban monasteries as well. The emergence in the twelfth century of works of heroic epic and fictional romance, such as the narrative of *Digenes Akrites*, suggests an expanding taste for different levels of literary entertainment in late medieval families.[36]

A final stratum of entertainment ran through ordinary households. Family members and friends gathered in the home to observe social milestones from birth to burial. The arrival and christening of a child were opportunities for gifts and feasting. The exchange of wedding vows in church was followed by a reception and meal at the house of the groom. Typically held in the evening, these banquets were accompanied by drinking, dancing, and singing through the night, and in leisured, aristocratic circles might continue for days.

Children would have been a constant presence in streets, markets, and homes. Little remarked by medieval writers, the restless pastimes of childhood can be glimpsed in objects from burials and late medieval paintings. Toys were made of bone, clay, metal, textile, wicker, and wood; acorns, flowers, pebbles, and pinecones served as imaginative playthings as well. Wheeled pull-toys took the form of domestic animals, chariots, and wagons. Lessons in language, socializing, and roleplaying came within the family, with early distractions including mold-made ceramic rattles and whistles, drinking vessels and twittering cups, and dolls made of rags or carved of wood. Younger children devised their own amusements, with knucklebones, spinning disks, and balancing tops offering hours of solitary play. Older boys and girls threw fabric and leather balls, played with hoops and sticks of metal and wood, rode on carts and swings, and shared imagined meals served on tiny clay vessels.[37] The sixth-century mosaics of the Great Palace show children interacting with companions and domestic animals, who must have been a familiar sight in city streets. Imitative games were based on parental routines and grew in complexity by observing adults in street processions, shops, taverns, and churches. The pervasive presence of clergy and monks inspired playful baptisms and liturgies, which could be seen as the roleplaying of future ecclesiastics. City officials, soldiers, and foreigners offered promising fodder for imitative play.[38]

Simple games combining chance and skill called for tossing pebbles, pinecones, knucklebones, and carved bone dice (*kyboi*). Games with mutually agreed rules offered lessons in friendly competition, with the appearance of gaming boards in everyday places making clear they were used as casual diversions outside the home. Variants of checkers (*petteia*) and backgammon (*tabli*) were played on surfaces scratched on tiles or paved courtyards. Games of three-in-a-row required only a square surface with nine holes or an incised nine-spot. Merels was played on a pattern of inscribed squares with players moving markers along nested squares joined by radiating lines. The game of *zatrikion* or chess seems to have come from Persia; Anna Komnene recalls her father Alexios I playing this in the early twelfth century. No less than children's playthings, the enduring concerns and entertainments of adults can be seen underlying the world of Byzantine toys and imagination.[39]

## FURTHER READING

Boeck, E., "The Power of Amusement and the Amusement of Power: The Princely Frescoes of St Sophia, Kiev, and their Connections to the Byzantine World," in *Greek Laughter and Tears: Antiquity and After*, ed. M. Alexiou and D. Cairns (Edinburgh, 2017), 243–62.

Cameron, A., *Porphyrius the Charioteer* (Oxford, 1973).

Cameron, A., *Circus Factions: Blues and Greens at Rome and Byzantium* (Oxford, 1976).

Dagron, G., *L'hippodrome de Constantinople: Jeux, peuple et politique* (Paris, 2011).

Pitarakis, B., ed., *Hippodrom/Atmeydanı: İstanbul'un Tarih Sahnesi [Hippodrome/Atmeydani: A Stage for Istanbul's History]* (Istanbul, 2010).

Puchner, W., "Acting in the Byzantine Theater: Evidence and Problems," in *Greek and Roman Actors: Aspects of an Ancient Profession*, ed. P. Easterling and E. Hall (Cambridge, 2002), 304–24.

Puk, A., *Das römische Spielewesen in der Spätantike* (Berlin, 2014).
Roueché, Ch., "Entertainments, Theatre, and Hippodrome," in *Oxford Handbook of Byzantine Studies*, ed. E. Jeffreys, J. Haldon, and R. Cormack (Oxford, 2008), 677–84.

# NOTES

1  C. Rojek, *Leisure and Culture* (New York, 2000); Z. Papakonstantinou, "Work and Leisure," in *A Cultural History of Work in Antiquity*, ed. E. Lytle (London, 2018), 159–71.
2  G. H. Lewis, "The Sociology of Popular Culture," *Current Sociology* 26 (1978): 3–64; R. Stebbins, "The Sociology of Entertainment," in *21st Century Sociology: A Reference Handbook*, ed. C. D. Bryant and D. L. Peck (Thousand Oaks, 2007), 178–85; B. Bergmann, "Introduction," in *The Art of Ancient Spectacle*, ed. B. Bergmann and C. Kondoleon (Washington, DC, 1999), 9–35.
3  CIC Nov. 123, 44; in W. Puchner, *Greek Theatre between Antiquity and Independence* (Cambridge, 2017), 72.
4  G. Nedungatt and M. Featherstone eds., *The Council in Trullo Revisited* (Rome, 1995), 45–185, especially 99, 132–33, 142–44, Canons 24, 51, 62.
5  Libanios, *Progymnasmata* 12.5.1, in F. Graf, *Roman Festivals in the Greek East from the Early Empire to the Middle Byzantine Era* (Cambridge, 2015), 129; M. Mullett, "No Drama, No Poetry, No Fiction, No Readership, No Literature," in *A Companion to Byzantium*, ed. L. James (Marden, 2010), 227–38, esp. 227–9; S. Tougher, "Having Fun in Byzantium," in *A Companion to Byzantium*, 135–45; P. Marciniak, "The Byzantine Performative Turn," in *Within the Circle of Ancient Ideas and Virtues: Studies in Honour of Professor Maria Dzielska*, ed. K. Twardowska, et al. (Krakow, 2014), 423–30.
6  Graf, *Roman Festivals*, 175–83, 208–24; Av. Cameron and J. Herrin, *Constantinople in the Eighth Century: The Parastaseis Syntomoi Chronikai* (Leiden, 1984), 131–3.
7  For palace festivals, H. A. Klein, "Sacred Relics and Imperial Ceremonies at the Great Palace of Constantinople," in *Visualisierungen von Herrschaft: Frühmittelalterliche Residenzen – Gestalt und Zweremoniell* ed. F. A. Bauer (Istanbul, 2006), 79–99; Constantine Porphyrogennetos, *The Book of Ceremonies*, ed. A. Moffatt (Canberra, 2012).
8  I. Östenberg, S. Malmberg, and J. Bjørnebye, *The Moving City: Processions, Passages and Promenades in Ancient Rome* (London, 2015); V. Manolopoulou, "Processing Emotion: Litanies in Byzantine Constantinople," in *Experiencing Byzantium*, ed. C. Nesbitt and M. Jackson (Farnham, 2013), 153–71.
9  A. Berger, "Imperial and Ecclesiastical Processions in Constantinople," in *Byzantine Constantinople: Monuments, Topography and Everyday Life*, ed. N. Necipoğlu (Leiden, 2001), 73–87; F. A. Bauer, "Urban Space and Ritual: Constantinople in Late Antiquity," *Acta ad Archaeologiam et Historiam Artium Pertinentia* 15 (2001): 27–59; H. W. Dey, *The Afterlife of the Roman City: Architecture and Ceremony in Late Antiquity and the Early Middle Ages* (Cambridge, 2015), 77–84.
10  Bauer, "Urban Space and Ritual"; Dey, *Afterlife of the Roman City*.
11  B. Pitarakis, ed., *Hippodrom/Atmeydanı: İstanbul'un Tarih Sahnesi* [Hippodrome/Atmeydani: A Stage for Istanbul's History], 2 vols. (Istanbul, 2010).
12  A. Cameron, *Porphyrius the Charioteer* (Oxford, 1973), 228–30; C. Mango, "Daily Life in Byzantium," *JÖB* 31/1 (1982): 337–53, esp. 345–53; C. Roueché, "Entertainments, Theatre, and Hippodrome," in *OHBS*, 677–84.
13  F. Meijer, *Chariot Racing in the Roman Empire: spectacles in Rome and Constantinople* (Baltimore, 2010); D. A. Parnell, "Spectacle and Sport in Constantinople in the Sixth Century CE," in *A Companion to Sport and Spectacle in Greek and Roman Antiquity*, ed. P. Christesen and D. G. Kyle (London, 2013), 633–45; A. Puk, *Das römische Spielewesen in der Spätantike* (Berlin, 2014), 180–5.
14  J.-C. Golvin and F. Fauquet, "L'hippodrome de Constantinople: Essai de restitution architecturale du dernier état du monument," *AntTard* 15 (2007): 181–214. For a recent survey of sources and monuments, J. Bardill, "The Architecture and Archaeology of the Hippodrome in Constantinople," in *Hippodrom/Atmeydanı*, 1: 91–148.

MARCUS RAUTMAN

15 For the monuments, mostly lost, C. Mango, "Antique Statuary and the Byzantine Beholder,"
DOP 17 (1963): 55–75; S. Bassett, The Urban Image of Late Antique Constantinople (Cambridge
and New York, 2004), 212–32.
16 J. Bardill, "Monuments and Decoration of the Hippodrome in Constantinople," in Hippodrom/
Atmeydanı, 1: 149–84; P. Stephenson, The Serpent Column (Oxford, 2016).
17 For epigrams, Pal. Anth. 15.41–50 and Anth. Plan. 35–87; Cameron, Porphyrius, 96–116.
18 Cameron, Porphyrius, 4–95; Bardill, "Monuments and Decoration of the Hippodrome," 171–9.
19 S. G. Giatsis, "The Organization of Chariot-Racing in the Great Hippodrome of Byzantine
Constantinople," International Journal of the History of Sport 17 (2000): 36–68; C. Roueché, "The
Factions and Entertainment," in Hippodrom/Atmeydanı, 1: 50–64.
20 Novellae Constitutiones 105.1; discussed by A. Eastmond, "Consular Diptychs, Rhetoric and the
Languages of Art in Sixth-Century Constantinople," AH 33 (2010): 742–65, esp. 742.
21 A. Effenberger, "Das Berliner 'Kugelspiel'," JbBM 49 (2007): 27–56.
22 A. Cameron, Circus Factions: Blues and Greens at Rome and Byzantium (Oxford, 1976), 213–14;
C. Roueché, "Spectacles in Late Antiquity: Some Observations," AntTard 15 (2007): 59–64,
esp. 62.
23 Tertullian, De spectaculis 4–13, 30; Lactantius, Divinae institutiones 6.20; Chrysostom, Homily
against those who have abandoned the church and deserted it for games and theaters; Canon 24,
Nedungat and Featherstone, Council in Trullo, 99. In general, R. Lim, "Consensus and
Dissensus on Public Spectacles in Early Byzantium," ByzF 24 (1997): 159–79.
24 Book of Ceremonies 1.77–82; G. Dagron, "L'organisation et le déroulement des courses d'après le
Livre de Cérémonies," TM 13 (2000): 3–200; Graf, Roman Festivals, 175–83.
25 Leo Diaconus, The History of Leo the Deacon: Byzantine Military Expansion in the Tenth Century,
trans. A. M. Talbot ad D. F. Sullivan (Washington, DC, 2005), 47–50. For a day at the races in
the eleventh century, Christopher of Mytilene and John Mauropus, The Poems of Christopher of
Mytilene and John Mauropous, ed. F. Bernard and C. Livanos (Cambridge, MA, 2018), 180–9,
poem 90.
26 E. Boeck, "The Power of Amusement and the Amusement of Power: The Princely Frescoes of
St Sophia, Kiev, and their Connections to the Byzantine World," in Greek Laughter and Tears:
Antiquity and After, ed. M. Alexiou and D. Cairns (Edinburgh, 2017), 243–62.
27 E. Hall, "Introduction: Pantomime, a Lost Chord of Ancient Culture," in New Directions in
Ancient Pantomime, ed. E. Hall and R. Wyles (Oxford, 2008), 1–40; Puk, Das römische
Spielewesen, 289–300; Puchner, Greek Theatre between Antiquity and Independence, 30–4.
28 F. Tinnefeld, "Zum profanen Mimos in Byzanz nach dem Verdikt des Trullanums," Byzantina
6 (1974): 321–43; P. Marciniak, "How to Entertain the Byzantines: Some Remarks on Mimes
and Jesters in Byzantium," in Medieval and Early Modern Performance in the Eastern Mediterranean,
ed. A. Öztürkmen and E. Birge Vitz (Turnhout 2014), 125–48; T. Palágyi, "Between
Admiration, Anxiety, and Anger: Views on Mimes and Performers in the Byzantine World,"
in Medieval and Early Modern Performance, 149–65; A. Foka, "Gender Subversion and the Early
Christian East: Reconstructing the Byzantine Comic Mime," in Laughter, Humor, and the (Un)
Making of Gender: Historical and Cultural Perspectives, ed. A. Foka and J. Liliequist (New York,
2015), 65–83.
29 E. D. Maguire and H. Maguire, Other Icons: Art and Power in Byzantine Secular Culture
(Princeton, 2007), 145–53; V. Kepetzi, "Scenes of Performers in Byzantine Art, Iconography,
Social and Cultural Milieu: The Case of Acrobats," in Medieval and Early Modern Performance,
345–8.
30 R. Webb, "Mime and the Dangers of Laughter in Late Antiquity," in Greek Laughter and Tears,
219–31.
31 Prokopios, Anecdota 9; R. Webb, "Female Entertainers in Late Antiquity," in Greek and Roman
Actors: Aspects of an Ancient Profession (Cambridge, 2002), 282–303; Palágyi, "Between
Admiration, Anxiety, and Anger," 149–55.
32 A. E. Laiou, "Women in the Marketplace of Constantinople (10th–14th Centuries)," in
Necipoğlu, Byzantine Constantinople, 261–73; L. Garland, "Street-Life in Constantinople:
Women and the Carnivalesque," in Byzantine Women: Varieties of Experience 800–1200, ed.
L. Garland (Aldershot, 2006), 163–76.
33 The Poems of Christopher of Mytilene, 286–303, poem 136; A. E. Laiou, "The Festival of 'Agathe':
Comments on the Life of Constantinopolitan Women," in Byzantium: Tribute to Andreas
N. Stratos, ed. N. A. Stratos (Athens, 1986), 111–22).

34 S. Malmberg, "Dazzling Dining: Banquets as an Expression of Imperial Legitimacy," in *Eat, Drink, and Be Merry (Luke 12:19): Food and Wine in Byzantium*, ed. L. Brubaker and K. Linardou (Aldershot, 2007), 75–91; Boeck, "Power of Amusement," 256–61.

35 N. Gaul, "Performative Reading in the Late Byzantine *Theatron*," in *Reading in the Byzantine Empire and Beyond*, ed. T. Shawcross and I. Toth (Cambridge, 2018), 215–34.

36 B. Croke, "Uncovering Byzantium's Historiographical Audience," in *History as Literature in Byzantium*, ed. R. Macrides (Farnham and Burlington, 2010), 25–53; Puchner, *Greek Theatre*, 52–111; E. Jeffreys, *Digenis Akritis: The Grottaferrata and Escorial Versions* (Cambridge, 1998); E. Jeffreys, trans., *Four Byzantine Novels* (Liverpool, 2012).

37 For a few examples, D. Papanikola-Bakirtzis, ed., *Daily Life in Byzantium* (Athens, 2002), 206–11; B. Pitarakis, "The Material Culture of Childhood in Byzantium," in *Becoming Byzantine: Children and Childhood in Byzantium*, ed. A. Papaconstantinou and A.-M. Talbot (Washington, DC, 2009), 167–251, for toys, 218–51.

38 C. Hennessy, "Young People in Byzantium," in *A Companion to Byzantium*, ed. L. James (Malden, MA, 2010), 81–92, for games, 87–8.

39 Pitarakis, "Material Culture of Childhood," 233–8; Anna Komnene, *The Alexiad*, trans. E. R. A. Sewter (London, 1969; rev. ed., P. Frankopan, London, 2009), 12.6.

PART V

ENCOUNTERING CONSTANTINOPLE

# 18: Medieval Travellers to Constantinople

## Wonders and Wonder

### Nike Koutrakou

From its very beginnings, in the 330s, Constantinople attracted visitors from around the empire and the territories beyond its borders. So great was the influx that historians commented on the overpopulated city's strained conditions. In the late fifth or early sixth century, Zosimos commented on its great size, maintaining that no other urban centre was comparable to it in size and prosperity.[1] Thereafter and throughout the middle ages Constantinople saw a steady flow of visitors, travellers who arrived from the cardinal points to experience the city from various stations in life and in myriad ways.[2] Their interactions with Constantinople are the subject of this chapter, which offers an overview of the people who came to the city, their motives for travel and their perceptions of the capital and the empire of which it was a hub for more than a millennium.

## Sources

Evidence for these visits derives from literary sources, which fall into two categories: those written by the Byzantines and those written by the visitors themselves. The Byzantine sources are of two kinds. Histories, chronicles, official texts and hagiographies, together with the more personal genres of poems and letters, observe travellers from a local point of view, injecting casual observations into discussions, often in response to a specific traveller or episode that spurred a writer's interest. Others, such as geographical notices, maps and patriographies convey information about the place and may have been directed towards travellers.

Within this second group, patriographies, narratives outlining urban histories and their lore, constitute an especially valuable resource. The fifth-century *Notitia Urbis Constantinopolitanae*, an anonymously authored text, which may have been the work of a retired Constantinopolitan official, states that its purpose is to record the attributes of Constantinople for its admirers. To that end, it catalogues the city's fourteen administrative regions, listing major monuments, officials and institutions.[3]

Later patriographies expand upon this information. The eighth-century *Parastaseis syntomoi chronikai*[4] (*Brief Historical Notices*) dispenses information about the location of buildings and monuments, the ways in which they were understood and their significance to locals. Interpretations could vary. A statue's subject might be forgotten or reinterpreted over time. For example, the *Parastaseis* records uncertainty about the identity of a statue that some identified as Verina, wife of Leo I (457–74), others the goddess Athena.[5] Such controversies help to explain the multiple identifications of monuments and sculptures in foreigners' tales, such as the attribution of Justinian's sixth-century column to both Herakleios (610–41) and Constantine (306–37).[6]

Most important are the travellers' own statements. These eyewitness accounts, written by Western, Arab and Slav visitors, include a variety of genres: ambassadorial reports, travel journals, pilgrims' accounts and liberated prisoners' observations. As documents, they record motives for individual travel, the monuments people saw and the impressions they generated. In addition, they demonstrate the role of status and reception in the response to the city, and the ways in which limited language skills or a surfeit of contradictory information might colour the understanding of places and people.[7] They reveal that visitors, with the possible exception of mercenaries and visiting military officials, were not trained observers. While they may have been impressed by Constantinople's massive walls and defensive towers or by the number and dimensions of its churches, they rarely remarked upon detail.[8] Indeed, their narrations were often recollections written after the fact, sometimes years after a traveller's return home. As a result these testimonies sometimes offer only the most general of impressions; a perception of Constantinople rather than a detailed accounting of its sights and sounds. The selective, often biased nature of these reports is revealing, for in them we glimpse the fascination Constantinople and its inhabitants held for outsiders.

## VISITORS

Absence of specific data makes it impossible to calculate the number of people visiting or passing through Constantinople at any given moment.[9] However, sources do offer a view of the types of people who came, the motives for their travel and their responses to their urban encounter. With the exception of diplomatic envoys, refugees, hostages and prisoners of war, people who travelled due to circumstances beyond their control, most visitors arrived of their own volition and for specific purposes. Whether from the provinces or abroad for short-term or long-term stays, a variety of administrative, personal and economic reasons motivated their journeys. Some travelled because they were summoned to address legal affairs, others to present a petition to the emperor. Some, such as the Arab and Western students who sought instruction from the renowned eleventh-century scholar Michael Psellos came to study.[10] Still others came for trade, or, as was the case with foreign mercenaries, to make a living.

There were also special classes of visitors, among them heads of state, princes and foreign potentates, and the occasional pope. They rated special receptions by the emperor, as was the case with the Russian princess Olga in 946/957.[11] Ecclesiastics, papal envoys, bishops, abbots and monks participating in Church councils, men who often served as envoys and were treated as such, constitute another group. These visitors were often received at the highest level. In 530, Justinian I (527–65) welcomed the monk Sabas on his arrival from Palestine, receiving him with honours similar to those due to a head of state. The emperor sent imperial ships and church officials to welcome him and escort him into the city,[12] thus underscoring the monk's emblematic status as a holy leader. In fact, Sabas was offered the hospitality of the Palace and direct access to the emperor at any time.

As it turns out, Sabas came with specific requests, Church tax exemptions and the request to build monasteries and a hospice in Jerusalem among them.[13] Other religious figures had no such purpose, and often did so under duress, as was the case with Pope Vigilius (537–55) who was summoned by Justinian,[14] or Pope Martin II (653–4) who was brought to trial under Constans II (641–68).[15]

Among these reluctant travellers there were refugees, exiles seeking protection and hostages exchanged in the framework of diplomatic relations. Their treatment was usually an honourable one, as in the case of the noble young Goths taken in the aftermath of Justinian's conquest of Ravenna. Sometimes it was even a regal one, as the golden retirement on a Bosporos estate offered to the Vandal King Gelimer attests. These hostages had a role to play. They could be displayed as part of a process of 'romanisation' and used for the purposes of imperial policy abroad. Their presence at imperial ceremonies and functions was part of the court ceremonial and used to impress official guests and visitors,[16] and to promote the image to foreigners of a city secure from enemies.

Muslim Arabs, arriving in Constantinople as prisoners of war, offer particular descriptions. Although these texts vary according to individual experience, they share common concerns: an interest in the city's prisons, especially the praetorian goal; a focus on the imperial court, at which they customarily were received in ceremonial banquets, and on the Hippodrome, where they were participants in the emperor's triumphal processions and spectators at the accompanying celebratory races.[17] They were impressed by the Hippodrome's monumental character although they often misinterpreted its significance as theatre for the display of imperial authority.[18]

Needless to say, the reception of these individuals and, consequently, their impressions of the Byzantine capital often depended upon the circumstances of their visit. There was a difference between what an ambassador was shown or hoped to be shown, and the experience of a hostage or a travelling pilgrim. Thus, ambassadors lodged sumptuously in the palace complex or in a patriarchal/palatial residence and were granted access to the emperor, while common visitors admired such structures only from the outside.

*On Sending and Receiving Ambassadors*, a small text prefacing Constantine VII's (913–59) compilation *De Legationibus*, is eloquent on the subject of foreign envoys and their reception. It advises that if they come from distant nations, or weaker ones, they are to be shown sights suitable for the empire's purposes. In this way the empire might impress or intimidate them. If, however, they are from populous nations with military strength, the text warns that they should not be shown the capital's riches, but its strong walls and well-equipped army.[19]

## MOTIVES

Diplomacy was a major impetus for travel to Constantinople. Yet diplomatic records, instructions to envoys and ambassadorial reports have not been well preserved since by their very nature they were not intended for public consumption.[20] Moreover, those that do survive often have little if anything to say about the city and its inhabitants: ambassadorial instructions and reports from envoys of the Italian republics of Genoa[21] and Pisa[22] focus on the negotiation of loans and other economic and commercial issues.

Nevertheless, some diplomatic experiences and their related dispatches provide a goldmine of information, as in the case of the two texts written by Liutprand of Cremona (*c*.920–72/73), the *Antapodosis* and the *Relatio de Legatione Constantinopolitana*.[23] Liutprand, bishop of Cremona, was an experienced diplomat, envoy to the pope in Rome and two-time ambassador to Constantinople in the tenth century.[24] His accounts document his experiences at the courts of Constantine VII Porphyrogennetos (908–59) between 949 and 950, and Nikephoros II Phokas (963–9) in 968. Rich in detail about Constantinopolitan life in general and imperial life in particular, they demonstrate clearly the extent to which an envoy's reception matters. Liutprand's warm reception in 949–50 led to a positive description of Constantinople in the *Antapodosis*. However, *Relatio*, Liutprand's account of his mission to the emperor Nikephoros II Phocas (963–9) in 968 on behalf of the Holy Roman Emperor Otto I (962–73) to negotiate a marriage alliance between the emperor's son and a Byzantine princess, tells a completely different story. The embassy was unsuccessful; consequently the *Relatio* offers a wholly negative view of Constantinople, probably with an eye to justifying the ambassador's failure.

Liutprand complained about everything: the emperor was ugly, the marble palace to which he was assigned was 'hateful, cold and waterless', offering no protection against cold, heat or rain.[25] In describing the imperial procession from the palace to Hagia Sophia, he emphasized the participants' old, threadbare garments and the impoverished, bare-footed Constantinopolitan mob acclaiming the emperor. He thought the prices in the market, where he needed three gold pieces to buy a day's worth of food for his twenty-five-person retinue and the four guards assigned to him, were exorbitant,[26] and that the wild assess in a royal park outside Constantinople where he attended imperial entertainment were nothing more than donkeys. Liutprand also rails against his warden, calling him his 'persecutor',[27] a man who kept him incommunicado, allowing only his cook to go out without an interpreter for provisioning, with the result that he bought foodstuffs at inflated prices. He also complains that some of his purchases were confiscated, presumably purple fabrics whose export was prohibited.[28]

Liutprand's reaction was not isolated. Treatment of envoys could be as significant as political events in determining the tenor of a report, as happened when Fredrick Barbarossa's representative, the bishop of Münster, was imprisoned by Isaac II Angelos (1185–1204).[29] Thus, the author of the *Gesta Regis Ricardi* describes hate and fear on one side, indignation and contempt on the other.[30]

As Byzantine sources indicate, these feelings could be mutual, and some envoys were less than welcome. Patriarch Athanasios (1289–93/1303–10) resented Muslim envoys, complaining to Andronikos II

(1282–1328) that they are 'good for nothing, being sent of no better masters'.[31] He also rails against the fact that, in contrast to the situation of Christians in Islamic lands, Muslims in Constantinople were allowed to 'openly climb up on high, as is the custom in their land, and shout forth' public prayers.[32]

While the Bishops of Cremona and Münster lamented their receptions, others clearly fared better. In some cases, emperors themselves acted as guides to the city's marvels, tailoring their tours to a visitor's interests. Leo I escorted Goubazios, king of the Lazes, to visit the pillar saint Daniel the Stylite,[33] and Alexios I (1081–1118), as part of a stratagem that allowed him to gain time to build fortifications, offered the visiting Turkish emir Abdul Ghasim personalized tours emphasising the city's baths and colonnades together with the horse races and hunts in which his guest was known to participate,[34] as if following the advice of *On Sending and Receiving Ambassadors*. Clavijo, the Spanish ambassador to Tamerlane's court, visited Constantinople in 1403 where he rated a tour with the emperor's son-in-law by claiming a distant family relation to the emperor. Clavijo's descriptions focus on churches and monasteries; however, he also notes the ubiquitous existence of ruins and vegetable gardens inside the walls, confirming the fifteenth-century city's decay.[35] In 1420 the emperor himself showed the city's relics to Ghillebert de Lannoy, the joint envoy of France and England to Constantinople.[36]

Pilgrimage was also a potent motivation for travel, and pilgrims' accounts, which focus largely on churches and relics, offer different insights. They often report legends, reflecting differing levels of education and credulity.[37] Sometimes their information appears garbled, as if derived from sketchy understandings attendant upon poor language skills. Their information also depended on the sights to which they were able to gain access, and access itself depended on social and financial status. As Stephen of Novgorod complained in the fourteenth century, Constantinople was an expensive city, in which one would encounter no relics without spending lavishly for a good guide.[38]

Benjamin of Tudela, a Spanish Rabbi and experienced traveller who visited between 1160 and 1173, described Constantinople as a 'busy city' noting 'merchants come to it from every country by sea or land'. In his estimation no other city was comparable, save Baghdad.[39] However, a merchant's impression also depended on the time at his disposal and his ability to circulate. Regulations governing foreign merchants from the late ninth-/early tenth-century *Book of the Eparch* were strict, specifying the areas in which they might take up residence and the duration of their stays. Syrian merchants were allotted no more than three months.[40] For the Russians whose delegations often included both envoys and merchants,[41] the limit was six. From the eleventh century on, when commercial privileges were granted to the Italian maritime republics, Venetian and Genoese merchants formed their own Constantinopolitan colonies, hosting a continuous stream of visitors.[42]

Another factor driving travel was the search for knowledge, either through study with famous teachers, including visits to venerable elders for guidance and counsel,[43] or through the acquisition of manuscripts. Benjamin of Tudela mentions 'men learned in all the books of the Greeks', implying knowledge of Constantinople as an academic centre.[44] The patriarchal and imperial libraries attracted scholars from East and West. Around 1167, William Medicus, abbot of St Denis, together with another monk brought Greek Patristic texts to France from Constantinople.[45] Incidental visitors, people passing through on the way to or from Palestine, were a common phenomenon, especially in the fourth and fifth centuries. Some travellers took advantage of pilgrimages to other centres to make side trips to Constantinople. The mid-ninth-century *Life of St. Ioannikios* recounts how the saint, originally a member of the mounted guard known as the *excubitores*, and a veteran of the battle of Markellai (796) against the Bulgarians, was induced by a vision to embrace monastic life upon returning to Byzantine territory. Before taking up his calling he passed through Constantinople, where 'he offered prayers in all the churches'.[46]

Mercenaries and soldiers brought a different kind of appreciation to the city. Odo of Deuil (1110–62) arrived in Constantinople in 1147, following the armies of the second Crusade. He was one of the rare visitors to comment on civilian architecture.[47] Odo visited the imperial residence at the Blachernai Palace, describing it with an eye for its defensive position. He praised the excellence of its substructure despite its location on low ground, and its height, which afforded a view 'upon sea, fields and the city'.[48]

Whatever their motives, all visitors appeared interested in the city's past and the legends surrounding its monuments. This fascination often gave birth to distinctive interpretations, which had more to do with the visitors' preconceptions than with actual Constantinopolitan legends. Arab travellers offered imaginative interpretations of statues on the hippodrome's central barrier,[49] and of the city's churches. Russian accounts are full of legends from the Constantinopolitan past, focussing on the healing accomplished by icons and relics and other miraculous Christian occurrences. For example, the fourteenth-century 'Russian

Anonymous' relates Michael the Archangel's role in guarding Hagia Sophia during its construction. [50]

## THE SITES

Visitors regularly commented on two things: Constantinople's size and its architecture. Already in the fourth century it was admired for its 'walls and theatres and race courses and palaces, and the beautiful great porticoes and that marvellous work the underground and overhead river [i.e. aqueduct] and the splendid and admired column [i.e. the column of Constantine] and the crowded marketplace and restless people'.[51] Later, Byzantine writers continued to promote the idea of Constantinople as a large, populous, famous city, even when their texts, such as the tenth-century version of the so-called 'Tale of the Agarene', which describes Constantinople as a 'famous megalopolis' and New Rome,[52] were only loosely connected with it. The historian Niketas Choniates (c.1155–1217), recounting a popular triumph procession of Manuel I Komnenos (1118–80), also described twelfth-century Constantinople as a populous and capacious 'megalopolis',[53] and in the fourteenth century the chronicler Ephraim of Ainos called the city the 'wonder and glory of the universe'.[54]

Outsiders echoed these sentiments in their general observations of the urban fabric, remarks about individual monuments and fascination with the imperial house. When the Frankish Bishop Arculf visited on his return from Jerusalem sometime between 675 and 680, he commented on building materials. Coming from a place poor in stone, he was impressed by the prevalence of stone construction, which he compared with that of Rome. He also admired the strong city walls and the Great Church, Hagia Sophia.[55]

Apart from the city's infrastructure, the imperial city's major attraction was the emperor. Although only privileged visitors such as Liutprand were given audiences, travellers were able to see the imperials at public processions. Many described them, paying particular attention to dress. Already in the fourth century, at the time of Theodosios I (379–95), imperial vestments and other dignitaries' dress was seen to enhance the prestige of the ceremony.[56] These costumes were commented upon either with admiration for or a critical eye to their 'vintage' quality. Benjamin of Tudela noted garments of silk with gold embroidery and precious stones.[57] At the sack of Constantinople in 1204, crusaders looted Justinian's regalia, decorated in gold and precious stones.[58] Although the crusaders found his body uncorrupted and proclaimed it a miracle, they nevertheless emptied his tomb and those of the other emperors in search of precious gems and jewels.[59] As a fourteenth-century hagiographical text put it, the crusaders stripped everything of value from the city's churches, imperial palaces and aristocratic residences.[60] Manuel I's (1143–80) richly ornamented purple dress, embroidered with precious gems 'as bright as red coals', bears witness to the impression the emperor made both in life and in death. According to a late thirteenth-century miracle story,[61] the garment, which had been made for ambassadorial receptions, was deposited on his coffin at his death. It is also indicative of the kinds of treasure found in 1204. Long after the crusader sack, when Constantinople was a shadow of its previous self, the impression of a wondrous city persisted. Stephen of Novgorod, who visited during Easter week in 1348 or 1349,[62] emphasized that 'there was much that amazed [the visitor] and that the human mind cannot express'.[63]

A number of the city's architectural masterpieces were on every visitor's agenda: the Great Palace complex, Hagia Sophia, the Hippodrome, the city's walls and, in later centuries, the Blachernai palace. Benjamin of Tudela, described the precious lamps in Hagia Sophia and Hippodrome entertainments. He also mentioned the Great Palace as the palace of emperor Manuel I's forefathers, while concentrating his description on Manuel's own renovated Blachernai Palace.[64] The impressive equestrian statue of Justinian I near Hagia Sophia is a regular feature in accounts: Harun ibn Yahya mentions it in the late ninth or early tenth century[65] as does Stephen of Novgorod in the mid-fourteenth.[66]

Numerous churches, 'according to the number of days of the year' as one visitor put it,[67] also claimed travellers' attention. Admired for their lavish marble, gold and silver decorations,[68] these churches were also home to relics. Ever since Constantine's mother, Helena, sent a piece of the True Cross from Jerusalem,[69] Constantinople was known as a special abode of relics. It housed the relics of Christ's Passion: pieces of the True Cross, the crown of thorns, the nails with which he had been fixed to the cross, the sponge with which he had been offered vinegar and the spear that had pierced his side.[70] There were also relics of the Virgin Mary: her Robe, brought to Constantinople by Leo I in 473 and still seen by Ignatius of Smolensk in the fourteenth century,[71] and her Girdle. These precious objects, together with the relics of numerous saints and martyrs, attracted visitors and pilgrims and transformed the imperial city into a New Jerusalem.[72] Constantinople claimed this title early. In the fifth-century *Life of Daniel the Stylite*, Daniel has a vision in which Symeon Stylites advises him against visiting the Holy Land because of Saracen raids, recommending instead that he go to Constantinople, the New Jerusalem.[73] Thereafter, references to Constantinople as the New Jerusalem increased steadily.[74]

Several relevant legends echoed the Constantinopolitan policy of relic acquisition: a later text, an account of the martyrdom of saints Adrian and Natalia, ascribes the presence of their relics in Constantinople to the saints' intervention. In that pious tale Adrian suffered martyrdom in Nicomedia. Subsequently, Natalia, guided by a vision of her husband, brought his remains (his hand) to Constantinople.[75]

Secondary relics, such as fabrics which had been deposited on saints' tombs or reliquaries, were also created and spread throughout the city's churches and monasteries. Pope Gregory the Great (590–604) sent fabric which had been deposited on St Paul's tomb to Constantinople at the request of the wife of emperor Maurice (582–602).[76] The number of relics multiplied in later centuries as the faithful fled to Constantinople, precious remains in hand, before the Persian and Arab conquests of eastern Byzantine territory. According to some calculations the city housed more than 3,700 relics from 476 different saints.[77]

As a major Constantinopolitan attraction, relics are often mentioned. The Saxon Willibaldus, later bishop of Eichstadt, visited Nicaea and Constantinople around 724, on his return from Palestine. Of his visit to Constantinople he mentioned only one thing: his ability to view the relics of Andrew, Luke and Timothy, at the church of the Holy Apostles, every day.[78] After 1204, when the city fell to the crusaders, many of its relics and their precious reliquaries found their way to the West. Many remained, however, and, according to the testimony of Russian pilgrims,[79] were venerated until the last days of the empire.

Hagia Sophia, where the Relics of the Passion were venerated during the Easter week, was the main attraction, but the Blachernai church, where the Virgin's Robe was exhibited, was also an important centre along with several other churches and monasteries.

Miraculous icons and the relics of novel saints also attracted pilgrims from the Eastern countries. The eleventh-century historian Kedrenos[80] mentions the remains of a new saint-confessor that appeared during Iconoclasm, St Joseph the Hymnographer. His body, which was buried in the Monastery *tou Krataiou*, was recognized anew in the mid-thirteenth century. Russian pilgrims also mention the remains of the patriarch Athanasios. Writing at the end of the fourteenth century,

Ignatius of Smolensk recalled visiting Athanasios's monastery and kissing his remains,[81] whose display became an event about 1330.[82] Ironically, a Venetian merchant operating under the erroneous assumption that the relics represented the remains of the early church father Athanasios of Alexandria, brought this staunch anti-unionist figure's bodily parts, to Venice after 1453.[83]

## CONCLUSION

Visitors to Constantinople were dazzled by the city's reputation. They were prepared to admire its wonders, and did so. Their perceptions of Constantinople were more idealistic than realistic, and their reports often amount to a statement of intent. By and large they describe a desire to participate in the Byzantine enterprise, to be close to the centre of power that was both secular and spiritual. The stories that circulated about the city's wealth, mentioning precious stones, gold and silver, are repeated almost verbatim from one account to another. They not only enhanced the image of a wonderful city but also provoked a desire to partake of those treasures. In no small measure this kind of storytelling must have contributed to the considerations that resulted in the deviation of the fourth crusade to Constantinople and the eventual sack of 1204.

Constantinople was not perfection, but its defects went largely unremarked by its visitors. There were rich and poor as in every megalopolis, but only an occasional visitor, one motivated by less than benign sentiments as in the case of Liutprand, remarked on the city's indigent. With the obvious exception of the crusader stories written in the aftermath of 1204 in which the desire to justify the city's conquest is overwhelming, only some of the city's visitors report on events in times of crisis. For its visitors Constantinople was as a city outside of time, a city of dreams, where everything was marvellous. It appeared as if it were an open-air museum with monuments and a population of mannequins, which participated only in imperial processions and hippodrome entertainments. Only during the city's fourteenth- and fifteenth-century decline did visitors, still marvelling at monuments and relics, see and report on the real, impoverished Constantinople, its inhabitants and the refugees from the surrounding countryside who flocked together in the streets.

Everyone saw Constantinople according to his own preconceptions and knowledge base. In addition to the city's fabled wealth,

Westerners had a fair knowledge of its churches, the learning to be found in manuscripts and its works of art. Russians saw Constantinople as a Christian city, the birthplace of their faith. Its monuments stood as the embodiment of legends they knew from Byzantine texts in translation. They were familiar with the legends generated by the city's history and its monuments, and for them coming to Constantinople was a return to the source, a search for origins. Muslim visitors, with limited knowledge of Christian precepts, also interpreted what they saw according to their own concepts. Arab visitors saw the races and the monuments in the Hippodrome according to Muslim tradition, mentally 'appropriating' the city. Like their Western counterparts, these visitors understood the city in a manner commensurate with their knowledge and aspirations. In short, visitors mostly remarked upon legends not history. Constantinople was a legend itself. As such, it generated legends – on jewels, riches beyond count, relics. It was a mental treasure trove for everyone.

## FURTHER READING

Cantino-Wataghin, G. and J-P Caillet, eds, 'Le voyage dans l'Antiquité Tardive: réalités et images', *AntTard* 24 (2016).

Ciggaar, K. N., *Western Travellers to Constantinople: The West and Byzantium, 962–1204 – Cultural and Political Relations* (Leiden, New York, and Cologne, 1996).

Drocourt, N., *Diplomatie sur le Bosphore. Les ambassadeurs étrangers à Constantinople*, 2 vols (Paris, 2015).

Erdeljan, J., *Chosen Places: Constructing New Jerusalems in Slavia Orthodoxa* (Leiden and Boston, 2017).

Lidov, A., ed., *New Jerusalems: The Translation of Sacred Spaces* (Moscow, 2006).

Macrides R., ed., *Travel in the Byzantine World* (Aldershot, 2002).

Majeska, G., *Russian Travelers to Constantinople in the Fourteenth and Fifteenth Centuries* (Washington, DC, 1984).

Morrisson, C. and J.-P. Sodini, eds, *Constantinople réelle et imaginaire: autour de l'œuvre de Gilbert Dagron* (Paris, 2018).

Vin, J. P. A. van der, *Travellers to Greece and Constantinople* (Istanbul, 1980).

## NOTES

1  Zosimus, II 35–6, ed. I. Bekker (Bonn, 1887), 101.

2  J. P. A. Van der Vin, *Travellers to Greece and Constantinople* (Istanbul, 1980); G. Majeska, *Russian Travelers to Constantinople in the Fourteenth and Fifteenth Centuries* (Washington, DC, 1984); K. N. Ciggaar, *Western Travellers to Constantinople: The West and Byzantium, 962–1204 – Cultural and Political Relations* (Leiden, New York and Cologne, 1996); N. Drocourt, *Diplomatie sur le Bosphore: Les ambassadeurs étrangers à Constantinople*, 2 vols (Paris, 2015).

3 J. Matthews, 'The Notitia Urbis Constantinopolitanae', in *Two Romes: Rome and Constantinople in Late Antiquity*, ed. L. Grig and G. Kelly (Oxford, 2012), 81–115.

4 Th. Preger, *Scriptores Originum Constantinopolitanum*, Leipzig 1901–1907, 1–73; Av. Cameron and J. Herrin, eds, *Constantinople in the Eighth Century: The Parastaseis Syntomoi Chronikai* (Leiden, 1984), 17–29 for dating.

5 Preger, *Scriptores*, 60.

6 R. Macrides, 'Constantinople: The Crusaders' Gaze', in *Travel in the Byzantine World*, ed. R. Macrides (Aldershot, 2002), 193–212, esp. 201–2.

7 On language, K. Ciggaar, 'Bilingual Word Lists and Phrase Lists: For Teaching or for Travelling?', in Macrides, *Travel in the Byzantine World*, 165–8.

8 E.g. Cristoforo Buondelmonti, *Description des iles de l'Archipel par Christophe Buondelmonti*, trans. E. Legrand (Paris 1897), 241–43; Cristoforo Buondelmonti, *Liber Insularum archipelagi*, ed. I. Siebert and M. Plassmann (Wiesbaden, 2005); Cristoforo Buondelmonti, *Description of the Aegean and Other Islands*, ed. and trans. E. Edson (New York, 2018).

9 J. Haldon, 'Commodities and Traffic Routes: Results and Prospects, Current Problems and Current Research', in *Handelsgütter und Verkehrswege: Aspekte der Warenversorgung im östlichen Mittelmeer (4. bis 15. Jahrhundert)*, ed. E. Kislinger, J. Koder and A. Külzer (Vienna, 2010), 289–94.

10 M. Psellos, *Michele Psello, Epistola a Michele Cerulario*, ed. U. Criscuolo (Naples, 1973), 25.

11 *De Cerimoniis Aulae Byzantinae*, ed. J. J. Reiske (Bonn, 1829–1830), II 15, 597–8. English translation: Constantine Porphyrogennetos, *The Book of Ceremonies*, ed. A. Moffat and M. Tall (Canberra, 2012).

12 *Life of Sabas*, ed. E. Schwartz, *Kyrillos von Skythopolis* (Leipzig, 1939), 86–200, esp. 173.

13 *Life of Sabas*, ed. E. Schwartz, *Kyrillos von Skythopolis*, 175.

14 The pope was still there in 547–8 on the issue of the three chapters. Cf. A. Christophilopoulou, *Βυζαντινή Ἱστορία*, 2nd ed., 3 vols (Thessalonica, 1996), 1: 295.

15 B. Neil, *Seventh-Century Popes and Martyrs: The Political Hagiography of Anastasius Bibliothecarius* (Turnhout, 2006), 246–7 and 190–3 for translation of the pope's process, *Narrationes de exilio sancti papae Martini*.

16 J. Herrin, 'Constantinople and the Treatment of Hostages, Refugees and Exiles During Late Antiquity', in *Constantinople réelle et imaginaire: autour de l'œuvre de Gilbert Dagron*, ed. C. Morrisson and J.-P. Sodini (Paris, 2018), 739–56, esp. 751–2.

17 A. Berger, 'Sightseeing in Constantinople: Arab Travellers c. 900–1300', in Macrides, *Travel in the Byzantine World*, 179–91.

18 S. Metivier, 'Note sur l'hippodrome de Constantinople vu par les Arabes', *TM* 13 (2000), 175–80.

19 PG 113, 636D.

20 Such reports are usually surmised, as those by embassies between Constantinople and Damascus: cf. A. Kaplony, *Konstantinopel und Damascus: Gesandschaften und Vertägen zwischen Kaisern und Khalifen 639–750* (Berlin, 1996), 373, 385, 405.

21 G. Bertolotto, 'Nuova Serie di documenti sulle relazioni di Genova con l'Impero bizantino', *Atti della Societa Ligure di Storia Patria* 28 (1898): 343–570, esp. 347, 368–405.

22 G. Müller, ed., *Documenti sulle relazioni delle città toscane coll'Oriente cristiano e coi Turchi fino all'anno 1531* (Florence, 1879), 71–3.

23 Liutprand of Cremona, *Liutprandi Cremonensis Opera omnia. Relatio de legatione Constantinopolitana*, ed. P. Chiesa (Turnhout, 1998), 1–150 (Antapodosis), 187–218 (Relatio de legatione Constantinopolitana); English translation: Liutprand of Cremona, *Complete Works of Liutprand of Cremona*, ed. and trans. P. Squatriti (Washington, DC, 2007).

24 J.-M Moeglin, and A. Péquinot, *Diplomatie et 'Relations Internationales' au Moyen Age (IXe-XVe siècle)* (Paris, 2017), 412–13 ; Squatrini, *Complete Works of Liutprand*, 3–37.

25 Liutprandi Relatio, chap. 13.

26 Liutprandi Relatio, chap. 34.

27 Liutprandi Relatio, chap. 13.

28 J. Koder, ed., *Das Eparchenbuch Leons der Weisen*, CFHB, 33 (Vienna, 1991), 4, 8.

29 *Itinerarium Peregrinorum et Gesta regis Richardi*, ed. W. Stubbs (London, 1864), 46.

30 *Itinerarium Peregrinorum et Gesta regis Richardi*, ed. W. Stubbs, 45.

31 A. M. Talbot, *The Correspondence of Athanasios I Patriarch of Constantinople* (Washington, DC, 1975), 84/24–5, letter 41

32 Talbot, *The Correspondence of Athanasios I Patriarch of Constantinople*, 84/25–6, letter 41.
33 *Vita Danielis Stylitae*, ed. H. Delehaye, *Les Saints Stylites* (Brussels, 1923), 49, §51.
34 Anna Komnene, *Annae Comnenae Alexias*, VI, x, 10, ed. D. Reinsch and A. Kambylis (Berlin, 2001), 192.
35 Ruy Gonzalez de Clavijo, *Embajada a Tamorlan, estudio y edición de un manuscrito del siglo XV*, ed. F. Lopez Estrada (Madrid, 1943); Ruy Gonzalez de Clavijo, *Clavijo Embassy to Tamerlane 1403–1406*, trans. G. le Strange (New York and London, 1928) 40.
36 M. Angold, 'The Decline of Byzantium Seen through the Eyes of Western Travelers', in Macrides, *Travel in the Byzantine World*, 221–2.
37 Vin, *Travellers*, 10–11
38 Majeska, *Russian Travelers*, 44–6.
39 Benjamin of Tudela, *The Itinerary of Benjamin of Tudela, Critical text, Translation and Commentary*, ed. M. N. Adler (London, 1907), 12.
40 *Das Eparchenbuch Leons der Weisen*, 5.5, 96; A. Laiou et al., *The Economic History of Byzantium from the Seventh through the Fifteenth Century*, 3 vols (Washington, 2002), 2: 507–9.
41 I. Sorlin, 'Les traités de Byzance avec la Russie au Xe siècle (I)', *Cahiers du monde russe et soviétique* 2 (1961): 313–60 and 447–75, esp. 447–9.
42 Ciggaar, *Western Travellers*, 24.
43 As attested in the fourteenth-century *Vita Dionysii Athonitae*, ed. B. Laourdas (Athens, 1956), 47.
44 Benjamin of Tudela, 13.
45 Ciggaar, *Western Travellers*, 97, n. 49
46 Vita S. Ioannicii, auctore Petro monacho, *Acta SS, Novembris* II/1 (Brussels, 1894), 384–405, esp. §7, 387C.
47 N. Asutay-Effenberger, 'The Blachernae Palace and its Defense', in *Cities and Citadels in Turkey from the Iron Age to the Seljuks*, ed. S. Redford and N. Ergin (Leuven, 2013), 253–76; R. Macrides, 'The Citadel of Byzantine Constantinople', in *Cities and Citadels*, 277–304, esp. 284.
48 Odo of Deuil, *De Profectione Ludovici VII in Orientem*, ed. and trans. V. G. Berry (New York, 1948), 64; Macrides, 'Constantinople: The Crusaders' Gaze', 196
49 Metivier, 'Note sur l'hippodrome de Constantinople', 178.
50 Majeska, *Russian Travelers*, 128–9
51 Themistios, *Orationes*, 33.6; B. Croke, 'Reinventing Constantinople: Theodosius I's Imprint on the Imperial city', in *From the Tetrarchs to the Theodosians: Later Roman History and Culture, 284–350*, ed. S. McGill, C. Sogno and E. Watts (Cambridge, 2010), 241–64, esp. 245, 257.
52 B. Flusin and Marina Detoraki, 'Les histoires édifiantes de Constantinople', in *Constantinople réelle et imaginaire*, 509–65, esp. 520.
53 N. Choniates, *Nicetae Choniatae, Historia*, ed. I. A. van Dieten (Berlin, 1975), 157.
54 Ephraim of Ainos, *Ephraem Aenii, Historia Chronaca*, ed. O. Lampsides (Athens, 1990), 337, v. 9554.
55 Vin, *Travellers*, 14.
56 Croke, 'Reinventing Constantinople', 256.
57 Benjamin of Tudela, 12–13.
58 Corripus described Justinian's funeral vestment. Cf. Av. Cameron, 'Old and New Rome, Roman Studies in Sixth-Century Constantinople', in *Transformations of Late Antiquity*, ed. P. Rousseau and M. Papoutsakis (Aldershot, 2009), 15–36, esp. 18–19.
59 Choniates, 647–8.
60 Philotheos of Selymbria, *Speech on St Agathonikos*, in PG 154: 1230–40 at 1237, accessed through Byzhadb.eie.gr.
61 Stavrakios Chartophylax, *Speech on the Miracles of St Demetrios*, ed. I. Iberitis, *Makedonika*, 1 (1940): 334–76, here at 368, accessed through Byzhadv.eie.gr.
62 Majeska, *Russian Travelers*, 17.
63 Majeska, *Russian Travelers*, 28.
64 Benjamin of Tudela, 12–13.
65 A. Vasiliev, 'Harun ibn Yahya and His Description of Constantinople', *Seminarium Kondakovium*, 5 (1932): 149–64 at 160. C. Mango, 'Justinian's Equestrian Statue', in C. Mango, *Studies on Constantinople* (Aldershot, 1993), no. 11; Berger, 'Sightseeing in Constantinople', 184.
66 Majeska, *Russsian Travelers*, 34.

67  Benjamin of Tudela, 12.
68  *Theophanes Continuatus*, ed. I. Bekker (Bonn, 1888) 325–6 and 332.
69  H. Klein, 'Constantine, Helena and the Cult of the True Cross in Constantinople', in *Byzance et les réliques du Christ*, ed. B. Flusin and J. Durand (Paris, 2004), 31–59, esp. 35.
70  P. Magdalino, 'L'eglise du Phare et les réliques de la passion à Constantinople (VIIe/VIIIe–XIIIe siècles)', in *Byzance et les réliques du Christ*, 15–30, esp. 27.
71  Majeska, *Russian Travelers*, 92–3.
72  P. Guran, 'The Byzantine "New Jerusalem"', in *New Jerusalems: The Translation of Sacred Spaces*, ed. A. Lidov (Moscow, 2006) 17–23; B. Flusin, 'Construire une nouvelle Jerusalem: Constantinople et les reliques', in *L'Orient dans l'Histoire religieuse de l'Europe. L'invention des Origines*, ed. M. A. Amir-Moezzi and J. Scheid (Turnhout, 2000), 51–70.
73  *Vita Stylitae*, 11–12, §10.
74  J. Erdeljan, *Chosen Places: Constructing New Jerusalems in Slavia Orthodoxa* (Leiden and Boston, 2017), 54, n. 12; P. Guran, 'The Byzantine "New Jerusalem"', 17–19; Flusin, 'Construire une nouvelle Jerusalem', 66–8.
75  'Une Passion des saints Adrien et Natalie', in *Hagiologie Byzantine*, ed. F. Halkin (Brussels, 1986), 47–55, esp. 51.
76  C. Metzger, 'Tissus et culte des reliques', *AntTard* 12 (2004): 183–6 at 184.
77  I. Kalavrezou, 'Helping Hands for the Empire. Imperial Ceremonies and the Cult of the Relics at the Byzantine Court', in *Byzantine court culture from 829 to 1204*, ed. H. Maguire (Washington, DC, 1997), 53–79, esp. 53.
78  Vin, *Travellers*, 15 and n. 8
79  Majeska, *Russian Travelers*, passim.
80  G. Kedrenos, *Georgius Cedrenus*, ed. I. Bekker (Bonn, 1838), III 244.
81  Majeska, *Russian Travelers*, 95–7.
82  Talbot, *The Correspondence of Athanasios I*, xxvii.
83  D. Stiernon, 'Le quartier de Xérolophos à Constantinople et les reliques vénitiennes du Saint Athanase', *REB* 19 (1961): 165–88.

# 19: Pilgrimage to Constantinople

## Annemarie Weyl Carr

Throughout the Middle Ages pilgrims came to Constantinople.[1] Most traveled unrecorded, but some recorded their experiences. Their accounts form the core of this survey.[2] For few of these people was Constantinople the sole destination; it was part of the journey to Jerusalem. For few, too, was "pilgrim" their only identifier; they were diplomats, secular or ecclesiastical emissaries, merchants, mercenaries, crusaders, scholars, and missionaries. Diverse as they were, two factors unite them: their accounts center on the visitation of holy relics, and all are from outside Byzantium. This signals their major pitfall: recorded journeys are long-distance ones. For medieval *Rhomaioi* (Romans = Byzantines), Constantinople was not continents away, nor did pilgrimage assume the expectation of arduous distance that it did for Europeans and Russians.[3] Thus the travel account did not become a literary genre in Greek as it did in the medieval West and Russia. Yet Rhomaioi certainly came to Constantinople. The centuries-long life of Constantinople's many churches makes it clear, that their religious life was sustained not by foreign visitation, but by Orthodox believers themselves.[4] Though information about Constantinople's holy sites is conveyed, above all, by foreigners, their texts must be read to reveal the Byzantines themselves.

Constantinopolitan pilgrimage was bound to Jerusalem by geography, but also by an ideological bond, as seen in an episode of 446 in which Daniel the Stylite (d. 493) was admonished to go not to Jerusalem, but to Byzantium, where he would find a new Jerusalem, with martyrs' shrines and places of prayer.[5] What this meant would evolve over centuries, engaging at least two different conceptions of what it was to be a new Jerusalem. Neither was in any concrete sense mimetic.[6] One was based on possession of Holy Land relics, above all those of Christ himself.[7] Having within its walls the material witnesses to Christ's own life and death transformed Constantinople into a site of their abiding presence. Rooted by legend in the retrieval of Christ's cross and nails by Helena, the mother of Constantine (d. 330–6), and Constantine's (306–37) interment of the Apostles Andrew, Luke, and Timothy in his burial church of the Holy Apostles, this identity was realized only gradually, in later historical contexts.[8] Emperors accomplished it, often fighting infidel aggressors of Jerusalem itself, and it consolidated both their own and their city's status as chosen guardians of God's place and people. But the relics assembled in Constantinople were not confined to those of Christ, or even to those of his associates and biblical events. Holy relics of every source and sort were gathered there, and Christ was not alone in making it his abode.[9] A whole heavenly court – the Virgin, the Baptist, the Apostles, martyrs, and holy bishops – took up residence in the in many mansions of the city's churches. The idea of a new Jerusalem thus intersected with that of a heavenly Jerusalem. A new Jerusalem of Christ joined a heavenly Jerusalem of his saints, gathered from Christendom in "the city protected by God." These two conceptions evolved and interacted slowly over the centuries, assuming shifting forms in pilgrims' eyes.

Constantinople emerged slowly as a pilgrim destination, as seen in Holy Land pilgrim accounts from 300 to 800 CE. While many pilgrims did pass through Constantinople, few wrote about it and only briefly.[10] The nun Egeria, who arrived in about 385 from western Europe, appreciated its size but departed at once, seeking the biblical sites.[11] The one relic she revered, that of St. Euphemia, was in Chalcedon, not Constantinople; Constantine and Helena's Holy Land relics go unremarked. Three centuries pass before the next account, by the Frankish Holy Land pilgrim Arculf, who arrived shortly before 683.[12] His account is brief, but each element is striking. He opens with a myth about the city's founding, in which Constantine is prompted by mysterious displacements of his military equipment to select its present triangular site. Variations on this myth of divine guidance would haunt Europeans' accounts. Arculf also tells about a small panel painting of the Virgin and Child, which was thrown by a Jew into a latrine, rescued by a Christian, and then miraculously secreted droplets of oil.[13] Both his own, European curiosity about Byzantium's holy images and the tale itself would live on. Finally, Arculf details the veneration of the Wood of the Lord's Cross in the "round church" of Hagia Sophia.[14] This, of course, is Justinian's Great Church, which epitomized Constantinople's grandeur. The Cross relic is not Helena's, but the one that the emperor Herakleios (610–41) had won from Chosroes II (590–628), restored triumphantly to Jerusalem in 630, and then translated to the security of Constantinople as the Holy Land fell to the Arabs in 636. He had already brought the Lance and Sponge of the Crucifixion. Wood, Lance, and Sponge would become the core of Constantinople's new Jerusalem. Arculf says the relic emitted sweet smells and healing fluid, anticipating Constantinople's later sensualized spectacles. The ritual that Arculf describes also anticipates the Middle Byzantine ceremony of the Elevation of the Cross in Hagia Sophia, one of the great rituals uniting Cross and empire.[15]

Between Egeria and Arculf lay Constantinople's aggrandizement under Justinian, and Byzantium's loss of the Holy Land under Herakleios. Both were formative for Constantinople's self-image as a holy city. It was still tentative, though, as seen in the account of Bishop Willibald, who arrived at Easter in 727.[16] He dwelt for two years in a cell overlooking Holy Apostles, and is the first to report on its most famous relics: the three Apostles interred in the altar, and John Chrysostom entombed before it. The city itself claims no attention from him. Passion relics, holy icons, even the Holy Apostles itself, pass unnoticed.

Christian pilgrimage, curtailed by the Persian and Arab conquests of Jerusalem, revived in the tenth century.[17] Major conversions – Russians in 988, Scandinavians in around 1000, and Hungary under King Stephen in the 1030s – brought vast new populations into contact with the lure of Holy Land pilgrimage, and spurred overland travel.[18] Harald Hardrada, king of Norway, had been chief of the Varangian guard in Constantinople and a Jerusalem pilgrim before his coronation in 1046;[19] Anthony, hegumen of Monastery of Caves in Kiev, journeyed to Constantinople and Mount Athos the early eleventh century; his later successor Varlaam went to Constantinople and Jerusalem in 1062;[20] Raoul Glaber wrote of Europeans crowding Jerusalem;[21] and the ensuing decades saw veritable mass pilgrimages from Europe,[22] of which one, reputedly of 7,000, did pass through Constantinople in 1064, though with no record of its sojourn.[23] Specific information on pilgrimage in Constantinople remains indirect, however, until the remarkable text known as the *Mercati Anonymous*.

*Mercati Anonymous*, a late eleventh-century Latin translation from an earlier Greek original, presents a topographically ordered roster of sixty churches in Constantinople with their major relics and miracle stories.[24] It must have been created and translated for the use of pilgrims to the city. A description of Jerusalem follows it, showing the two cities' bond as pilgrimage destinations. Late Antique buildings – Hagia Sophia and Holy Apostles, St. John Stoudion, Ss. Sergius and Bacchus, the

Marian churches of Chalkoprateia and Blachernai, the Hippodrome, the columns of Justinian (527–565) and Constantine – are joined by brilliant new ones – the palace churches of the Nea and St. Mary of the Pharos, Leo VI's (870–912) St. Lazarus, Romanos III's (1028–34) Peribleptos, Constantine IX's (1042–55) St. George Mangana, the Hodegon with its great Lucan icon. The text opens with St. Mary of the Pharos, home of the Passion relics.[25] It lists forty-eight relics, a quarter of its total number and double those in Hagia Sophia.[26] Twenty were relics of Christ, including the Mandylion, Kerameion, and Christ's letter to Abgar.[27] The Pharos' relics represented three centuries of calculated imperial acquisition.[28] Gained especially during the tenth-century wars of expansion, they were intended to consolidate and consecrate realm and rulers alike as a city and people of God.

The Pharos was not a public church; it was in the imperial palace. Yet pilgrims did gain access. The monk Joseph from Canterbury of c.1090 is an example.[29] He stayed with friends known to the imperial family, perhaps Varagians from England, and they arranged his access. He was so rapt by the experience that he offered to buy a relic of St. Andrew on the spot. Whether he succeeded is unknown, but acquiring relics was a major goal of Constantinople pilgrims.[30] More observant was a French pilgrim of much the same date, known from a manuscript in Tarragona.[31] Ravished by the beauty and gold of the city, he signed up to study Greek at Hagia Sophia, and eagerly absorbed not only sights but stories. His account opens at Hagia Sophia, but he was more awed by the Passion relics at the Pharos. An enthusiast of the Virgin Mary, he introduces her into the myth of Constantine's choice of Constantinople's site,[32] provides a valuable account of the Hodegetria icon's procession,[33] and makes a fascinating comparison between the "usual miracle" at Blachernai and Jerusalem's miracle of the Holy Fire.[34] Two texts intimate that pilgrim access to the Passion relics was not only possible, but encouraged and even exploited by the Komnenian emperors. Nikolaos Mesarites' impassioned recitation about them from 1201[35] conjures a "decalogue" of ten relics gleaming, supple, and instinct with the vitality of Christ's life. They literally make Constantinople a Jerusalem: "[T]his church," he says, "is another Sinai, another Bethlehem, another Jordan, Jerusalem, Nazareth, Bethany, Galilee." His exhortative cadence suggests he presented his decalogue publicly. One early twelfth-century English pilgrim may even echo his words.[36] The other suggestive text is the spurious letter of Alexios I (1081–1118) to Robert of Flanders,[37] inventorying the

Passion relics and inviting Europeans to come defend them. As crusaders, they came.

Twelfth-century pilgrims can be divided into two groups, civilians and crusaders, though the distinction may be blurred by the Norwegian warrior kings like Eric, welcomed with his wife Bothilda by Alexios I (1081–1118) on their way to Jerusalem in 1103,[38] and Sigurd Magnusson "the Crusader," who astonished John II (1118–43) with his wealth and eloquent Greek on his way back from the Holy Land around 1111.[39] Among civilians, neither the Englishman Saewulf who passed Constantinople on his way home from the Holy Land in 1103,[40] nor the Russian Abbot Daniel who traversed it going to and from Jerusalem in 1106,[41] wrote anything about it. But four accounts – an early twelfth-century English text later translated into Greek,[42] another of around 1150,[43] a third description of 1157 by the Islandic monk and future abbot Nicolaus Thingeyrarensis,[44] and a fourth by an unidentified author of around 1190[45] – offer a strikingly convergent picture of the European pilgrim experience in Constantinople. All focus on relics, omitting stories and ceremonies, listing them copiously but without order, often omitting the names of churches. Nonetheless, it seems clear that none visited more than five of a very limited inventory of shrines. All cited Hagia Sophia, the Pharos, and Holy Apostles; three visited the Chalkoprateia and St. George Mangana; and one saw the Pantokrator Monastery. None ventured as far as Blachernai, as the pilgrim of the Tarragona manuscript had, or spoke of the Hodegetria, though Danes who visited the city in the 1190s left a different description of its procession from his.[46] They focused on biblical and dominical relics, and hugged the eastern tip of the city near Hagia Sophia and the Pharos. The profusion of Byzantine saints included by the *Mercati Anonymous* does not figure in their accounts. Contrasting theirs to the *Mercati* text reveals two distinct if overlapping Jerusalems, one focused on Christ's life and death, the other evoking a citywide veil of protective sanctity cast by the confluence of countless saints. Often understood as a western European text for western European pilgrimage, the *Mercati* text goes far beyond the uses to which known western pilgrims might have put it. It was initially in Greek, and like the crowded public performances at Blachernai and the Hodegon, it must reflect – and plausibly originated in – the Byzantine reality of pilgrimage to Constantinople.

Akin to the *Mercati Anonymous* is the *Pilgrim Book* of Dobrinja Jadrejkovič, later Archbishop Anthony of Novgorod, who came to Constantinople as a layperson on church business in 1200.[47] His is the richest and most actively engaged of all accounts, including half again as many churches and relics as the *Mercati Anonymous*. He greets relics with a kiss, describes feast days and distinctive rituals, points out healing and miracle-working sites, and – in Hagia Sophia – details the singing of the Great Entrance and Matins services.[48] He narrates icon stories with relish, repeating some from the *Mercati*, like the icon wounded by a Jew and thrown in the well at Hagia Sophia (echoing Arculf's), but adding new ones, like the four- fingered Christ in Hagia Sophia.[49] His list of Hagia Sophia's relics overlaps enough with those of the *Mercati* to assure congruence, omitting some things but adding others, above all what must have been local lore – Anna who gave her house for Hagia Sophia, St. Theophanides who guarded Hagia Sophia's keys, St. Athenogenes whose death was delayed till his father finished the mass[50] – and living events.[51] Pilgrimage emerges for him as a participative immersion in his own faith and its traditions. The sites to which he devotes the most extensive attention – Hagia Sophia, the Pharos, the Holy Apostles, the Mangana, the Chalkoprateia – are those on which European pilgrims had focused, too. To this extent, he and the European pilgrims shared a common pilgrimage experience,[52] but these sites are embedded for Anthony in a much thicker surround of local rather than scriptural knowledge. Quite as much as he journeyed to a new Jerusalem of Christ's life, he came into a vast but familiar community of saints.

Anthony's is the last of the civilian accounts before 1204. The crusaders, too, were pilgrims, but their access to the city's sacred marvels was severely limited. As Fulcher of Chartres explained, they were allowed to enter the city only at the rate of five or six each hour to pray in the churches.[53] He does not say if this meant prayer in one of Constantinople's Latin-rite churches, or in the great pilgrimage destinations. Fulcher himself, Robert the Monk of Reims,[54] and Bartolf of Nangis,[55] all in the First Crusade (1095–9), do not recount visits to the great relics and may not have seen them. Nonetheless, they are extravagant in their admiration for Constantinople's size, site, walls, polyglot crowds, and profusion of marble and bronze. For them as for Arculf the city's magnificence certified divine favor. "Let no one doubt that this city was founded with God's favor,"[56] wrote Robert. He included a version of Arculf's myth of the city's siting, now with a mysterious woman (not Mary, as for his close contemporary of the Tarragona manuscript) who promised Constantine great things. Thus, he concludes, the most holy relics find refuge here, and Constantinople is their very safe home.[57]

Robert's sense of protective grace did not last. Odo of Deuil, historian of the Second Crusade (1147–9), did see the Pharos relics, but left a bitter critique of Constantinople's squalid underbelly.[58] William of Tyre, subjected to the full imperial sight-seeing tour laid on for King Amaury of Jerusalem in 1171, reported seeing not only the Passion relics but "churches and monasteries, of which there was an almost infinite number."[59] Only with Robert of Clari do we hear the impressions of a crusader able to wander the city at will.[60]

Robert participated in the Fourth Crusade (1202–4),[61] but his impressions of Constantinople were formed like those of Anthony of Novgorod in the days before its fall. They counterbalance Anthony's. Though Robert gives a methodical résumé of the Pharos' major relics,[62] prowls dazzled amid the miracle-working columns and glittering gems of Hagia Sophia,[63] visits the column of the Flagellation and imperial tombs at the Holy Apostles,[64] and – like Anthony – inspects the tears of Mary on the Stone of Unction at the Pantokrator,[65] his real admiration is for the city's secular wonders: Justinian's column (for all the ten herons' nests on its top),[66] the Hippodrome, its masterful animal sculptures,[67] the Golden Gate flanked by elephants,[68] the Theodosian columns and paired female statues with their prognosticating imagery.[69] Robert must have absorbed from residents the current lore about these antiquities.[70] His interest anticipates that of pilgrims in the Palaiologan centuries. So, too, does a fascinating episode at the Blachernai palace, where he encountered the coal-black king of Nubia, on pilgrimage from Jerusalem and residing in the palace at the emperor's invitation.[71] Though East Christians certainly knew Constantinople,[72] their accounts survive only from the Palaiologan period.

Unlike Robert's, Gunther of Pairis' narrative authenticating the relics acquired by his abbot during the sack of Constantinople,[73] the Anonymous *Rituale seu mandatum insignis ecclesiae Suessionesis* doing the same for those of Soissons,[74] and the section on Bishop Conrad of Halberstadt's pilgrimage to Greece in the *Gesta Episcoporum Halberstadtensium*,[75] belong fully to the thirteenth century. Under the rubric of crusade, moreover, they belong to the genre of pilgrimage literature; however, the rapacity with which they treat Constantinople's relics precludes seeing them as devotional.

One thirteenth-century text remains. The Nestorian monk, Rabban Ṣauma, on pilgrimage from Beijing to Jerusalem, made his way through Constantinople in 1281.[76] The emperor welcomed him, lodged him in a palace, and gave him guides to the saints' relics. Thus, Rabban Ṣauma became the first pilgrim to document what relics remained after 1204. In Hagia Sophia he recorded the relics of Lazarus, the Magdalene, and the Hodegetria nearby.[77] He saw the right hand of John the Baptist: used in imperial ritual and seen still by Anthony of Novgorod in the Pharos, this clearly survived 1204.[78] The Stone of Unction with the tears of Mary remained at the Pantokrator, as did a jug from Christ's miracle at Cana which Rabban Ṣauma is the first to record. In the Holy Apostles, though John Chrysostom's body had been taken to Venice, Rabban Ṣauma venerated his tomb, and again is the first to record, along with the Column of the Flagellation, the stone where Peter lamented bitterly.[79] If many relics were gone, then, others were emerging. Whether Rabban Ṣauma saw the Passion relics is not said.

The fifty years after Rabban Ṣauma yield no descriptions of Constantinople, but the century from the 1332 to the 1437 offers an unprecedented fourteen, one by an anonymous Armenian, five Russian, and eight by continental Europeans. The earliest were by two Saxons: the knight, Wilhelm von Boldensele, in 1332,[80] and the parish priest, Ludolph von Suchem, in 1336–41,[81] both on pilgrimage to Sinai. Their accounts, both influential, are closely intermingled: Ludolph appropriated large portions of Wilhelm's text, including his passage on Constantinople.[82] After a vivid description of the city's site and extravagant praise for Hagia Sophia, this reports that Wilhelm was able, on the emperor's order, to see the Passion relics – the Cross, tunic, sponge, reed, and one nail – as well as the body of John Chrysostom and many other venerable relics.[83] Clearly the Passion relics had reconstituted themselves.

Wilhelm and Ludolph are the last Europeans who wrote about Constantinople as pilgrims. The remaining six, all in Constantinople between 1403 and 1437, were more truly travelers. They not only came on secular missions, but also encountered the city's sacred heritage through the lens of cultural rather than devotional interest. Ruy Gonzalez de Clavijo,[84] Ghillebert de Lannoy,[85] and Pero Tafur[86] were diplomats; Bertrandon de Broquière, though traveling as a pilgrim, was a spy;[87] Cristoforo Buondelmonti was a monk and humanist scholar;[88] and Johann Schildberger was a mercenary knight escaping Turkish captivity.[89] Their accounts are invaluable: Clavijo's refined descriptions of art and architecture, Buondelmonti's maps, Schildberger's anthropological curiosity, and Pero Tafur's engaged archaeological perceptiveness give documentary clarity to our understanding of the city, but their testimony assumes devotional cogency only when seen in conjunction with that offered by pilgrims from the east.

The Armenian pilgrim must have been in Constantinople near or soon after 1400;[90] the five Russians between 1349 and 1422.[91] They, too, came on varied professional tasks. Stephen of Novgorod[92] and Ignatius of Smolensk[93] were on church business, Alexander the Clerk was a business man,[94] Zosima was a monk escorting an imperial bride,[95] and the Anonymous may have written his text as a travel guide rather than to record a journey.[96] Nonetheless, their accounts have a striking homogeneity.[97] All emulate Anthony of Novgorod in organizing their texts by church rather than by relic. All are long, engaging the whole city, and although each followed his own path they often stopped at the same destinations. As in the period before 1204, major monuments were the core sites favored also by western Europeans: Hagia Sophia, of course, the Hodegetria, Holy Apostles, the Pantokrator, the Virgin's church at Blachernai, and the monastery of St. John at Petra.[98] This suggests, again, that Constantinople offered a devotional experience common to all pilgrims regardless of origin or creed. Beyond this core, however, lay a far larger group of churches visited consistently by the Russian and East Christian pilgrims but rarely by Europeans. These sites honored saints and hierarchs dear to the Church of Constantinople. They included points of living sanctity: ceremonial liturgies, sites with curative powers, miracle-working icons. Steady inclusion of the church of the prophet Daniel may be illuminated by the assertion of both Ignatius and Zosima that one could obtain one's pilgrim seal there: a surviving seal with the prophet Daniel may exemplify such objects.[99] Especially notable in his adherence to much the same itinerary is the Armenian pilgrim. His Armenian identity is clear in his veneration of Armenian saints,[100] use of Armenian names for others,[101] and awareness of the Armenian Church's relation to the Peribleptos church.[102] But his itinerary also embraces the sites favored by the pilgrims from the east.

The contrast of east and west must not be overemphasized, for interests are often concurrent. Stephen of Novgorod, Clavijo, and Tafur all give observant descriptions of the Hodegetria's ever-evolving per-formance.[103] Both Ignatius of Smolensk and Bertrandon de Broquière write of the performance at Hagia Sophia of a play about Nebuchadnezzar and the Three Hebrews.[104] Both groups are informa-tive concerning the surviving Passion relics. Stephen of Novgorod arrived on Holy Thursday, 1349, and as in Arculf's day the Passion relics, on display in Hagia Sophia,[105] were swarmed by ardent devotees. Their exposure was rare enough to draw heaving crowds. Forty years later the Russian Anonymous writes that they are on the altar at St. George Mangana, in boxes inside a box, and except on Holy

Thursday, one venerated the box .[106] By 1400 they were in the monastery of St. John in Petra at the far western end of Constantinople near the imperial residence at Blachernai.[107] They must have been moved closer to emperor and court. Clavijo, who saw them there, provides the most detailed extant description of the items, their grouping, and their packaging.[108] He also notes that only the emperor had the key. The last to see them was Pero Tafur, in a private showing at Hagia Sophia with the emperor and empress.[109] Constantinople was a small community by then. The emperor might with his one key have been able to expose the Passion relics to much of the population. But it seems that these relics, which the Komnenian emperors had publicized so freely, were intimately bound now to the emperor himself.

The Passion relics had always been central to the concept and experience of Constantinople for European pilgrims. Theirs were journeys of distance, to places far away and events long ago. The ceremonies and miracles of the present paled for them beside things from the past. They sought a new Jerusalem of Christ and his accomplices. The Passion relics never assumed the same centrality in the pilgrimage accounts of the Russian and eastern pilgrims. For them, the whole city was a site of living sanctity, reverberant with wondrous events and saints familiar from the liturgy's yearly round. Theirs were pilgrimages of arrival, in a city whose sanctity foreshadowed that of heaven.

## FURTHER READING

Ciggaar, K. N. *Western Travellers to Constantinople: The West and Byzantium, 962–2404: Cultural and Political Relations* (Leiden, New York, and Cologne, 1996).

Majeska, G. P., *Russian Travelers to Constantinople in the Fourteenth and Fifteenth Centuries* (Washington, DC, 1984).

Majeska, G. P., "Russian Pilgrims in Constantinople," *DOP* 56 (2002): 93–108.

Vin, J. P. A. Van der, *Travellers to Greece and Constantinople: Ancient Monuments and Old Traditions in Medieval Travellers' Tales*, 2 vols. (Istanbul, 1980).

Wilkinson, J., *Jerusalem Pilgrims before the Crusade* (Warminster, 2002).

Wilkinson, J., *Egeria's Travels*, 3rd ed. (Warminster, 1999).

Wilkinson, J., *Jerusalem Pilgrimage 1099–1185* (London, 1988).

## NOTES

1 K. N. Ciggaar, *Western Travellers to Constantinople: The West and Byzantium, 962–2404: Cultural and Political Relations* (Leiden, New York, and Cologne, 1996); J. P. A. van der Vin, *Travellers to Greece and Constantinople: Ancient Monuments and Old Traditions in Medieval Travellers' Tales*, 2 vols. (Istanbul, 1980).

2 Women, though known to have been pilgrims, vanish as authors after late antiquity: see A. M. Talbot, "Introduction," *DOP* 56 (2002): 59–61 at 60.

3 Talbot, "Introduction," 61, summarizing a conclusion drawn by several papers in the same volume.

4 P. Magdalino, "Medieval Constantinople," in *Studies on the History and Topography of Byzantine Constantinople*, ed. P. Magdalino (Aldershot, 2007), no. I, 29–30.

5 H. Delehaye, "La vie de Daniel le stylite," *Les saints stylites*, Subsidia hagiographica 14 (Brussels, 1923), 11–13.

6 R. Ousterhout, "Constantinople and the Construction of a Medieval Urban Identity," in *The Byzantine World*, ed. P. Stephenson (London and New York, 2010), 334–51.

7 See especially B. Flusin, "Construire une nouvelle Jérusalem: Constantinople et ses reliques," in *Orient dans l'histoire religieuse de l'Europe*, ed. M.A. Amir-Moezzi and J. Scheid (Turnhout, 2000), 51–70.

8 Excellently summed up in P. Maraval, *Lieux saints et pèlerinages d'Orient. Histoire et géographie des origins à la conquête arabe* (Paris, 1985), 92–8.

9 P. Guran, "The Constantinople: New Jerusalem at the Crossing of Sacred Space and Political Theology," in *Новы Иерусалимы: Иеротолу и Иконография* [New Jerusalems: Hierotopy and Iconography], ed. A. Lidov (Moscow, 2009), 35–55 at 48.

10 J. Wilkinson, *Jerusalem Pilgrims before the Crusades* (Warminster, 2002); J. Wilkinson, *Egeria's Travels*, 3rd edition (Warminster, 1999); J. Wilkinson, *Jerusalem Pilgrimage 1099–1185* (London, 1988); *Palestine Pilgrims Text Society*, 15 vols. (London, 1887–97), building on the publications of the Palestine Pilgrims Text Society.

11 Wilkinson, *Egeria's Travels*, 142.

12 Adomnan, "The Holy Places: The Third Book", in Wilkinson, *Jerusalem Pilgrims*, 201–6.

13 Adomnan, "The Holy Places," 205–6.

14 Adomnan, "The Holy Places," 202.

15 B. Flusin, "Les cérémonies de l'exaltation de la Croix à Constantinople au XIe siècle d'après la *Dresdensis* A 104," in *Byzance et les reliques du Christ*, ed. J. Durand and B. Flusin (Paris, 2004), 61–89.

16 Hugeburc, "Life of St. Willibald," in Wilkinson, *Jerusalem Pilgrims*, 233–51.

17 L. Bréhier, *L'Église et l'Orient au Moyen Age: Les Croisades* (Paris, 1928), 32.

18 Though maritime travel remained the dominant mode. On travel routes, see Vin, *Travellers to Greece and Constantinople*, 1: 9–16; J. Richard, "Le transport outre-mer des croisés et des pélerins," in *Maritime Aspects of Migration*, ed. K. Friedland (Cologne and Vienna, 1989), 27–44.

19 S. Sturluson, *Heimskringla, Part Two: Sagas of the Norse Kings*, trans. S.Laing, revised with introduction and notes by P. Foote (London, 1961), 169–71; K. Ciggaar, "Visitors from North-Western Europe to Byzantium. Vernacular Sources: Problems and Perspectives," *ProcBrAc* 132 (2007): 123–55 at 127–29.

20 J.-P. Arrignon, "Un pèlerin russe à Constantinople: Antoine de Novgorod," in *Toutes les routes mènent à Byzance*, *Médiévales* 12 (1987): 33–41 at 33.

21 Bréhier, *L'Église et l'Orient*, 32, 43.

22 Bréhier, *L'Église et l'Orient*, 43–5.

23 E. Joranson, "The Great German Pilgrimage of 1064–1065," in *The Crusades and Other Essays Presented to Dana C. Munro by His Former Students*, ed. Louis J. Paetow (New York, 1928), 3–43.

24 K. N. Ciggaar, "Description de Constantinople par un pèlerin anglais," *REB* 34 (1976): 211–68; S. G. Mercati, "Santuari de reliquie costantinopolitane secondo il codice Ottoboniano Latino 169 prima della conquista Latina (1204)," *RendPontAcc*, ser. 3, 12 (1936): 133–56.

25 P. Magdalino, "L'Église du Phare et les reliques de la Passion à Constantinople (VIIe/VIIe – XIIIe siècles)," in *Byzance et les reliques du Christ*, ed. J. Durand and B. Flusin (Paris, 2004), 15–30.

26 On the relics of Hagia Sophia, see J. Wortley, "Relics and the Great Church," *BZ* 99 (2006): 631–47.

27 A comparison of all medieval lists of the Pharos' Passion relics is in M. Bacci, "Relics of the Pharos Chapel: A View from the Latin West," in *Восточнохристианские Реликвии, Eastern Christian Relics*, ed. A. Lidov (Moscow, 2003), 234–48 at 243–5.

28 Listed by Flusin, "Construire une nouvelle Jérusalem," 54–5.

29 C. H. Haskins, "A Canterbury Monk at Constantinople, c. 1090," *EHR* 25 (1910): 293–95.

30 C. Mango, "Introduction," in *Byzance et les reliques du Christ*, 11–14 at 13.

31 Krijnie N. Ciggaar, "Une description de Constantinople dans le *Tarragonensis 55*," *REB* 53 (1995): 117–40.

32 Ciggaar, "Une description de Constantinople," 128.

33 Ciggaar, "Une description de Constantinople," 127; in English translation in B. N. Pentcheva, *Icons and Power: The Mother of God in Byzantium* (University Park, 2006), 135–6.

34 Ciggaar, "Une description de Constantinople," 121–2.

35 A. Heisenberg, *Nikolaos Mesarites Die Palastrevolution des Johannes Komnenos* (Würzburg, 1907), 29, paras. 12–31, 13; French translation by B. Flusin, "Les reliques de la Sainte-Chapelle, et leur passé imperial à Constantinople," in *Le trésor de la Sainte-Chapelle*, ed. J. Durand, M.-P. Laffitte, and D. Giovannoni (Paris, 2001), 29–30.

36 Ciggaar, "Une description anonyme de Constantinople du XIIe siècle," *REB* 31 (1973): 335–54 at 340: "et spineam coronam adhuc virentem et floridam," compared with Heisenberg, *Nicholas Mesarites'* "ἔτι χλοάζων καὶ ἐξανθῶν καὶ μένων ἀκήρατος" on 29, para. 13.

37 In English by C. Sweetenham, trans., *Robert the Monk's History of the First Crusade, Historia Iherosolimitana* (Aldershot, 2005), 219–22; E. Joranson, "The Problem of the Spurious Letter of Emperor Alexius to the Count of Flanders," *AHR* 55 (1950): 811–32.

38 Ciggaar, *Western Travellers to Constantinople*, 111.

39 Ciggaar, *Western Travellers to Constantinople*, 112; Sturluson, *Heimskringla*, part II, 282–6.

40 Saewulf, "Pilgrimage of Saewulf to Jerusalem and the Holy Land," in Wilkinson, *Jerusalem Pilgrimage*, 94–116.

41 Daniel the Abbot, "The Life and Journey of Daniel, Abbot of the Russian Land," in Wilkinson, *Jerusalem Pilgrimage*, 120–71.

42 Ciggaar, "Une description anonyme," 335–54.

43 P. E. D. Riant, *Exuviae sacrae constantinopolitanae. Fasciculus documentorum ecclesiasticorum, ad byzantine lipsana in Occidentem saeculo XIIIe translate, spectantium*, 3 vols. (Paris and Leipzig, 1877–1904), 2: 211–12.

44 Riant, *Exuviae sacrae constantinopolitanae*, 2: 213–16.

45 Riant, *Exuviae sacrae constantinopolitanae*, 2: 216–17.

46 Ciggaar, "Une description de Constantinople," 140; English translation in A. Lidov, "Spatial Icons: The Miraculous Performance with the Hodegetria of Constantinople," in *Иеротопиа: Создание Сакралых Простанств в Византии и Древней Руси* [Hierotopy: The Creation of Sacred Spaces in Byzantium and Medieval Russia], ed. A. Lidov (Moscow, 2006), 349–71 at 352.

47 The most recent translation is M. Ehrhard, "Le Livre du pèlerin d'Antoine de Novgorod," *Romania* 58 (1932): 44–65. See also Mme. B. de [Sofiia Petrovna] Khitrowo, "Antoine, Archevêque de Novgorod, Le Livre du pèlerin," in *Itinéraires russe in Orient, I, 1* (Geneva, 1889; repr. Osnabrück, 1966), 87–111. George Majeska is preparing a new edition and translation.

48 Ehrhard, "Le Livre du pèlerin d'Antoine," 53, 56.

49 Ehrhard, "Le Livre du pèlerin d'Antoine," 48, 51.

50 Ehrhard, "Le Livre du pèlerin d'Antoine," 50.

51 Ehrhard, "Le Livre du pèlerin d'Antoine," 55.

52 G. Majeska, "Russian Pilgrims in Constantinople," *DOP* 56 (2002): 93–101.

53 Fulcher of Chartres, *A History of the Expedition to Jerusalem, 1095–1127*, trans. Frances Rita Ryan (Sisters of St. Joseph), ed. with an introduction by Harold S. Fink (Knoxville, TN, 1969), 78, paragraphs 8 and 9 .

54 Robertus Monachus, "Historia Iherosolimitana," *RHC HOcc* 3 (1866): 719–882 at 750–1.

55 Bartolfus de Nangeio, "Gesta Francorum Expugnantium Iherusalem," *RHC HOcc* 3 (1866): 490–543 at 490–4.

56 Robertus Monachus, "Historia Iherosolimitana," 750–51; English translation by Vin, *Travellers to Greece and Constantinople*, 2: 509.

57 Robertus Monachus, "Historia Iherosolimitana," 750–51; English translation by Vin, *Travellers to Greece and Constantinople*, 2: 509.

58 Odo of Deuil, *De profectione Ludovici VII in orientem: The Journey of Louis VII to the East*, ed. and trans. V. G. Berry (New York, 1948), 63–7.

59 William of Tyre, *A History of Deeds Done beyond the Sea by William, Archbishop of Tyre*, 2 vols., trans. and annotated by E. A. Babcock and A. C. Krey (New York, 1943), 2: 382.

60 Robert of Clari, *The Conquest of Constantinople*, trans. with introduction and notes by E. H. McNeal (Toronto, 1996).

61 He even came home with relics: Robert of Clari, *The Conquest of Constantinople* 5–6.

62 Robert of Clari, *The Conquest of Constantinople*, 103.

63 Robert of Clari, *The Conquest of Constantinople*, 106–7.

64 Robert of Clari, *The Conquest of Constantinople*, 108.

65 Robert of Clari, *The Conquest of Constantinople*, 112–13.

66 Robert of Clari, *The Conquest of Constantinople*, 106.

67 Robert of Clari, *The Conquest of Constantinople*, 110.

68 Robert of Clari, *The Conquest of Constantinople*, 108.

69 Robert of Clari, *The Conquest of Constantinople*, 110.

70 R. Macrides, "Constantinople: The Crusaders' Gaze," in *Travel in the Byzantine World*. ed. R. Macrides (Aldershot, 2002), 193–212.

71 Robert of Clari, *The Conquest of Constantinople*, 79–80 and n. 79.

72 Like the Georgian painter-monk Ioane Tokha discussed by Z. Skhirtladze, "The Image of the Virgin on the Sinai Hexaptych and the Apse Mosaic of Hagia Sophia, Constantinople," *DOP* 68 (2014): 369–86.

73 A. J. Andrea, ed. and trans., *The Capture of Constantinople: The Hystoria Constantinopolitana of Gunther of Pairis* (Philadelphia, 1997); edited text in Gunther of Pairis, *Hystoria Constantinopolitana: Untersuchung und kritische Ausgabe*, ed. Peter Orth (Hildesheim, 1994).

74 A. J. Andrea, *Contemporary Sources for the Fourth Crusade*, revised edition (Leiden, 2008), 230–5; edited text in A. J. Andrea and Paul I. Rachlin, "Holy War, Holy Relics, Holy Theft: The Anonymous of Soissons's *De Terra Iherosolimitana* – An Analysis, Edition, and Translation," *Historical Reflections* 18 (1992): 157–63.

75 Andrea, *Contemporary Sources*, 239–64.

76 S. Brock, "Rabban Ṣauma à Constantinople," in *Mémorial Mgr Gabriel Khouri-Sarkis (1898–1968)* (Louvain, 1969), 245–53.

77 Brock, "Rabban Ṣauma à Constantinople," 246.

78 Brock, "Rabban Ṣauma à Constantinople"; I. Kalavrezou, "Helping Hands for the Empire: Imperial Ceremonies and the Cult of Relics at the Byzantine Court," in *Byzantine Court Culture from 829 to 1204*, ed. H. Maguire (Washington, DC, 1997), 53–79, esp. 67–79.

79 Brock, "Rabban Ṣauma à Constantinople," 247.

80 *Itinerarius Guilielmi de Boldensele*, in C. L. Grotesend, "Die Edelherren von Boldensele oder Boldensen," *Zeitschrift des historischen Vereins für Niedersachsen* 1852 (1855): 211–86, esp. 237–86.

81 Ludolph von Suchem, *Description of the Holy Land, and of the Way Thither, Written in 1350*, trans. Aubrey Stewart (London, 1895); G. A. Neuman, "Ludolphus de Sudheim, *De Itinere Terre Sancte*," *AOL* 2 (1882): *Voyages*, III, pp. 322–77.

82 G. Schnath, "Drei niedersächsische Sinaipilger um 1330," in *Festschrift Percy Ernst Schramm*, 2 vols., ed. P. Classen (Wiesbaden, 1964), 1: 464–71. Schnath, 469–70, cites twenty-nine known manuscripts of Ludolph's text, circulated in both German and Latin, while Wilhelm's helped inspire John de Mandeville.

83 Grotesend, "Die Edelherren von Boldensele," 238.

84 R. G. Clavijo, *Clavijo Embassy to Tamerlane 1403–1406*, trans. Guy le Strange (New York and London, 1928).

85 G. Lannoy, *Oeuvres de Ghillebert de Lannoy, voyageur, diplomate et moraliste*, ed. C. Potvin (Louvain, 1878).

86 P. Tafur, *Pero Tafur, Travels and Adventures 1435–1439*, ed. and trans. M. Letts (New York and London, 1926).

87 G. R. Kline, *The Voyage d'Outremer by Bertrandon de la Broquière, Translated, Edited, and Annotated with an Introduction and Maps* (New York, Bern, and Frankfurt am Main, 1988).

88 G. Gerola, "Le vedute di Costantinopoli di Cristoforo Buondelmonti," *SBN* 3 (1931): 247–79.

89 J. Schiltberger, *The Bondage and Travels of Johann Schiltberger in Europe, Asia, and Africa 1396–1427*, ed. and trans. J. Buchan Telfer (New York, 1970).

90 S. Brock, "A Medieval Armenian Pilgrim's Description of Constantinople," *REArm* 4 (1967): 81–102.

91 G. P. Majeska, *Russian Travelers to Constantinople in the Fourteenth and Fifteenth Centuries* (Washington, DC, 1984).

92 Majeska, *Russian Travelers to Constantinople*, 16–47 text of the "Wanderer of Stephen of Novgorod," 28–47.

93 Majeska, *Russian Travelers to Constantinople*, 48–113; text of "Journey to Constantinople" of Ignatius of Smolensk, 76–113.

94 Majeska, *Russian Travelers to Constantinople*, 156–6, text of Alexander the Clerk's "On Constantinople," 160–65.

95 Majeska, *Russian Travelers to Constantinople*, 166–93, text of the "*Xenos*" (Wanderer) of Zosima the Deacon, 176–93.

96 Majeska, *Russian Travelers to Constantinople*, 114–54, text of "Anonymous Description of Constantinople," 128–54.

97 Majeska, "Russian Pilgrims in Constantinople," 101.

98 Majeska, "Russian Pilgrims in Constantinople," 99, lists churches prominent in Russian texts with the number of western pilgrims who visited each.

99 G. Majeska, "A Medallion of the Prophet Daniel in the Dumbarton Oaks Collection," *DOP* 28 (1974): 361–66.

100 Brock, "A Medieval Armenian Pilgrim's Description," 85, Gregory the Illuminator; 87, two Armenian Saints.

101 Brock, "A Medieval Armenian Pilgrim's Description," 96, Yakovik for James the Persian; 97, Apirindos for Spyridon.

102 Brock, "A Medieval Armenian Pilgrim's Description," 81.

103 Majeska, Russian Travelers, 36; Clavijo, Clavijo Embassy to Tamerlane, 83; Tafur, *Pero Tafur, Travels*, 141–2.

104 Majeska, *Russian Travelers to Constantinople*, 100; Kline, *The Voyage d'Outremer*, 100.

105 Majeska, *Russian Travelers to Constantinople*, 30.

106 Majeska, *Russian Travelers to Constantinople*, 140.

107 Brock, "A Medieval Armenian Pilgrim's Description," 88; Clavijo, *Clavijo Embassy to Tamerlane*, 81–3.

108 Clavijo, *Clavijo Embassy to Tamerlane*.

109 Tafur, *Pero Tafur, Travels*, 140.

## 20: ENCOUNTERING AND INVENTING CONSTANTINOPLE IN EARLY MODERN EUROPE

### Sean Roberts

Among the world's cities, Constantinople loomed especially large in late medieval and early modern European imagination. In illuminated manuscripts, on the walls of villas and townhouses, and increasingly in printed books, cycles of the world's greatest cities conveyed history, geography, and myth.[1] As a second and emphatically Christian Rome, the Byzantine capital found itself included in these lists and compendia. In the early fifteenth century the city's walls were a kind of apotropaic shield against the Ottoman advance. Then, following Mehmed II's conquest in 1453, Constantinople became a lost jewel to be reclaimed, a cautionary tale of Christian unity's failure, a sign of God's judgment. None of these images or descriptions, of course, bore much resemblance to the real city on the Bosporos whether before or after 1453. Indeed, comparison of Constantinople's conventional image in the west to what is known about the city at the time of the conquest reveals the fundamentally invented character of this reputation.

Before the Ottoman siege, walls which may once have housed more than half-a-million residents and which drew upon the resources of a vast empire now sheltered perhaps 50,000 or fewer. By all reliable accounts the city within was little more than a series of building complexes and monuments separated by abandoned green space.[2] In contrast, many of the maps, views, and descriptions familiar to viewers in Paris, Florence, or Nuremberg presented a dense urban fabric of ancient buildings, above all Hagia Sophia, encircled by the walls, towers, and gatehouses of the impenetrable ancient polis. This is how the city appeared in the woodcut accompanying Hartman Schedel's *World Chronicle* of 1493. In other cases, like the manuscript and printed versions of Ptolemy's *Geography*, painters and printmakers recreated discrete architectural vignettes of the city's best-known sites, the hippodrome and its monuments, columns like that of Arkadios and the imperial palace.[3]

Discrepancies between Constantinople's true state and its representation were inevitable. Both the ebb and flow of information in the pre-modern Mediterranean and the historical resonance of the capital ensured that artists and writers in France, Italy, or Germany could bend their representations to local needs and concerns. A common thread, however, in nearly every fifteenth- and sixteenth-century description is the reconstruction of an ideal, ancient vision of the city. Constantinople's outsized and enduring prominence was due, in no small part, to Western Europeans' developing antiquarian interests. Their posture toward the city was part of a larger, shifting constellation of attitudes toward Byzantium in particular and the past more generally.[4] Admiration for a lost, supposedly authentic antiquity came to be juxtaposed against not only the present inhabitants of Greece, but equally against the products of a more recent past.

Late medieval and early modern writers frequently pitted the texts, buildings, and material culture of the ancient world against those which were merely old. Byzantine culture was often in the latter category.[5] In his foundational set of artists' lives, the Tuscan painter Giorgio Vasari (1511–74) described the Byzantine-style paintings and mosaics common in Italy during the later middle ages as pale echoes of the arts of the ancient Greeks. Such works were stylistically "rude," populated by awkward figures with "bug-eyes, arms outstretched, standing on tiptoe." For Vasari, the Greeks and their art were the wrong kind of old.[6] In other cases, writers ignored contemporary Greeks in favor of the classical past's history and myths. When the Florentine Francesco Berlinghieri (1440–1501) described Greece he did so with ancient place names drawn from writers like Pliny and Strabo. He recorded events from the Trojan war, the transformations recounted by Ovid, and the location of Praxiteles' most famous sculptures. He passed almost without comment over contemporary inhabitants, Ottoman and Greek alike. In short, Greece found itself fossilized in Western European descriptions, presented as the remnant of something rather than as the thing itself.[7] So powerful was this desire to fix the classical past in place that even the momentous changes brought about by Ottoman rule and unprecedented urban reconstruction by architects like Sinan were soft-pedaled in humanist accounts well into the sixteenth century.[8]

Rather than push Constantinople away from contemporary consciousness, antiquarian prejudices kindled a hunt for the city's pristine classical conditions, missions to salvage its antique remains from supposedly negligent caretakers, and, when this proved impossible, imaginative reconstruction of this ideal past. Conflicts and confluences between the poles of invention and discovery preoccupied early modern inquiries into the natural world and human history alike.[9] Those who sought Constantinople's past were no exception. Travel allowed a select group of scholars, diplomats, merchants, writers, and artists to "discover" the city. Their accounts inevitably mix fresh observations with preconceptions drawn from common attitudes and specialized education. These accounts, in turn, invented the capital anew for readers and viewers, even those with professional interest, who lacked the opportunity or desire to embark on the long and potentially hazardous journeys to the city. In most meaningful senses, what a reader or viewer in Antwerp or Venice understood as Constantinople was invented (and often persistently reinvented) by writers, artists, and their interlocutors over the course of the period. This chapter examines a few travelers and the comprehensive if contradictory vision of the city that emerged both from their direct encounters with its people and spaces and from the reframing of their vision by those at home in Western Europe.

Early modern attention to archaeological accuracy contributed to shifting attitudes toward the Byzantine capital. Artists increasingly sought to make the settings of myth, history, and scripture convincing for viewers through direct emulation of the buildings, costume, and art of the ancient world. Wealthy patrons drove the development of a market for the material remains of antiquity – gems, cameos, and sculpture especially – as a culture of collecting emerged. The *studiolo* and *kunstkammer* provided dedicated spaces for the display of precious objects indexing a lost, golden age.[10] By the fifteenth century this interest was driven by the resurgent knowledge of the Greek language among Western European scholars. A growing market for Greek texts and for their translation into Latin and European vernaculars spurred searches for classical works unknown in the west. The arrival in Italy of Claudius Ptolemy's previously "lost" second-century *Geography* at the advent of the fifteenth century was all the proof that many intellectuals needed that troves of such riches awaited discovery. Recovered from Constantinople's Chora monastery, rapidly translated into Latin, and almost as quickly paraphrased in Tuscan, Venetian, French, and German, Ptolemy rapidly assumed the status of a leading authority on all matters geographic for scholars eager to ground their knowledge in an unimpeachable pedigree.[11]

The tantalizing possibility that more such treasures might be unearthed in Constantinople sparked the imagination of literati and their patrons. And while funding and potential financial rewards were usually born by patrons, travel itself fell to antiquarians since it was these specialized scholars who possessed the philological skills to recognize new texts.[12] The emerging early modern printing industry also provided incentives for the rediscovery and revelation of "lost" texts. Claims for the immediate or revolutionary development of print culture in the fifteenth century are exaggerated. Many of the travelogues discussed here found their way into print only in the succeeding centuries, and the widespread scribal and illumination industries of the later middle ages were more than adequate to spread works like Cristoforo Buondelmonti's *Book of Islands* far and wide. Still, increasing literacy in Greek demanded a supply of books and printing operations like that of Aldo Manuzio rose to meet demand.[13] Likewise, an entrepreneurial hope for profit drove large-scale printed projects and sparked artistic and authorial interest in Constantinople.

Western and Central Europeans traveled to the Byzantine – and later Ottoman – capital as a waypoint for pilgrimage, as part of diplomatic envoys, in the service of trade, and frequently in the hope of securing patronage and personal profit. Often these motives can be difficult to separate; a devout pilgrim might well be on the lookout for lucrative wares, and a seasoned diplomat might find himself awed by the city's churches and shrines. The Ottoman conquest changed the contours of these journeys, yet it was hardly a point of definitive rupture for travel to the former Byzantine territories. Venetian galleys continued to make their way east laden with textiles and to return with the wares the Ottoman entrepôt provided. When hostilities interrupted this Venetian–Ottoman pipeline, other powers swooped in to seize the opportunity. Florentine merchants, for example, initiated numerous attempts to corner the market for woolen fabrics in the late fifteenth and sixteenth centuries. Travel did, to be sure, become more difficult and less certain as the political and military balance of Mediterranean power shifted in favor of the Ottomans. Far from curtail interest, however, the increasing, if exaggerated, risks to travel piqued the curiosity and aroused the fantasies of would-be visitors.[14] Above all, the common thread of burgeoning antiquarian interest and expertise characterized those who would shape the city's image for readers and viewers in Europe.

The Florentine Cristoforo Buondelmonti (1386–c.1430) was an early such visitor.[15] Ordained as a priest and trained in the increasingly fashionable classical literature of the day, Buondelmonti departed his native city in 1415. His purpose, at least at the outset, was the acquisition of previously unknown manuscripts for patrons in Florence. From his home base on the island of Rhodes he spent the next dozen years traveling throughout the Aegean, recording what he saw and what he learned from those he encountered. In the process Buondelmonti produced the most influential example of what would become a hugely popular genre, the "Book of Islands" or *isolario*.[16] Along with notes on their location and physical geography, his isolario included maps of each island along with brief historical events and significant myths said to have transpired there. These anecdotes were mostly drawn from familiar sources like Pliny, Ovid, and their popular offshoots, especially Pierre Bersuire's moralized version of the *Metamorphoses*. The conventional nature of this information did nothing to discourage Buondelmonti's insistence that his book represented "not what I have learned by hearsay but what I have seen in the past six years with my own eyes after much reflection."[17]

Though the islands were his primary concern, Buondelmonti clearly felt that a comprehensive account of the region and its ancient past could not omit Constantinople. Hardly an encomium, the isolario presents instead a vision of a "ruined city" in which there remained "few inhabitants." The focus is nearly entirely upon the city's antiquities and especially upon buildings and monuments which Buondelmonti assigned to the construction campaigns of the emperors Justinian and Theodosios. The churches of Hagia Sophia and Holy Apostles occupy a significant portion of this short account and emphasize the ruined state of the former.[18] If these descriptions are concerned primarily with the past, they are not purely "classicizing" in the conventional sense. Buondelmonti was a priest and in contrast to some modern expectations he was, like many fifteenth-century intellectuals, more invested in the recovery of an explicitly Christian antiquity than with a pre-Christian past.[19] It would be hard, for example, to overestimate the significance of fifteenth-century interest in the original, Greek gospels in encouraging antiquarian adventures.[20] Constantinople's significance in this context was rivaled only by Rome and the Holy Land. As the purpose-chosen capital of the Christian Emperor Constantine, the city occupied a place of paramount importance for narratives both of late antiquity's transformation and for the eventual loss of the faith's Eastern sites to "Saracen" and ultimately Ottoman incursion.

Buondelmonti visited Constantinople and its environs decades before the Ottoman conquest. His account, in that sense, provides a control for later visitors, whose impressions were colored by their attitudes toward the city's new lords, the Turks. Indeed, Buondelmonti blames contemporary Byzantines for the poor state of Greece's antiquities and makes a clear distinction between the ancient Greeks and their present-day descendants. The fifteenth-century Greeks he encountered were "enemies of the Latins, who never obtain a secure peace with them. If they promise something, they do not keep their promises." They had "fallen to ignorance and rigidity in [their] ancient opinions." The failed attempts to unify the churches and the bad blood generated during the crusades had never really been forgotten, and Buondelmonti rarely missed an opportunity to reopen these wounds. He recounts, for example, a spurious claim that the Greeks had murdered 50,000 Latin crusaders with poisoned bread outside the Vlanga Gate during the second crusade. [21] The isolario's polemic tone demonstrates that, for humanist observers, Constantinople did not have to be lost to the Turks to be lost. Buondelmonti was aware, of course, of escalating Turkish incursions and he recognized their contribution to the empire's political decay. Yet visitors in the coming century would say little worse of the Turks than the Florentine of the Greeks. The tenor of these critiques and even the vocabulary of "barbarism" would bear remarkable similarities.

The city map included in many of the isolario manuscripts amplified the antiquarian concerns of the description. In Buondelmonti's earliest examples and the influential mid-fifteenth-century copy produced by Henricus Germanus, Constantinople appears not as a ruin but as a heavily fortified perimeter enclosing discrete and clearly reconstructed monuments.[22] In contrast to Buondelmonti's descriptions of decay, Hagia Sophia, Holy Apostles, and the Imperial Palace appear in their pristine and ancient glory. Such antiquarian views would be among the most influential sources for later European images of the city. They served as ubiquitous models for the next half-century in manuscripts of Ptolemy, inspired printed views of the city, like the now lost prospect of Francesco Rosselli, and cemented Constantinople's place in collections of the world's cities.[23] The tendency of such views to freeze the city in its ancient state would take on greater resonance in the decades following the Ottoman conquest, substituting a more comfortable past for a politically uncertain present.

Like Buondelmonti, the French humanist Pierre Gilles (1490–1555) was drawn to Constantinople by the lure of its past, and specifically by the hope of acquiring rare bibliographic treasures.[24] Gilles possessed a wide-ranging and first-rate humanist education along with a diverse set of professional interests. He is frequently called the founder of French zoology because of his natural philosophical works, especially his taxonomic treatise on marine life. Yet he was, first and foremost, devoted to the collection and editing of ancient texts.[25] He rose to prominence under the patronage of bishop (later Cardinal) Georges d'Armagnac, himself a voracious book collector. Gilles eventually attracted the attention of François I (1515–47), and it was in the monarch's employ that he set off for the east in 1544. He would remain in Constantinople for three years and would return briefly in 1550 after further travels in the region. Though his mission was to purchase books for François' library, the king's death shortly after Gilles' arrival in Constantinople meant that funding earmarked for the library never arrived and that the humanist's own priorities shifted to those of securing new patronage and employment. He traveled widely, eventually entering the employ of the Ottoman military and accompanying Suleyman's campaign against the Safavids in 1548.[26] These misadventures underscore the practical exigencies that often shaped the lives of these travelers yet which tend to be overshadowed by their imaginative antiquarian reconstructions.

Despite his frustrated efforts to track down lost manuscripts, Gilles' sojourn was hardly unproductive. Instead these years of observation laid the groundwork for his *On the Topography of Constantinople and Its Antiquities*, ultimately among the most influential descriptions of the city. The title itself proclaims the work's emphasis, the ancient core of the city. A significantly more substantial text than that of Buondelmonti, the bulk of Gilles' *Antiquities* was devoted to the city's physical geography, the history of its founding, and especially to the location and dimensions of ancient buildings. While it draws on a range of conventional sources, especially the *Notitia Urbis Constantinopolis*, it is important in its own right as what is arguably the most detailed and significant early modern account of the city. Indeed, the text suggests that Gilles had access to Greek works unknown to Western European scholars.[27] The Ottoman capital he encountered does occasionally rear its head. The need to pin down discrepancies between the contemporary state of monuments and their original condition inadvertently introduces such observations. Gilles sometimes displays a practical, nononsense approach to Ottoman construction, as in his extensive description of the Topkapı palace and its surroundings. Describing the sultan's dais, he wrote of "a small marble structure, gleaming with gold and silver and precious stones . . . surrounded by a portico supported with spiraled columns of rare marble, their capitals and bases entirely gilded."[28] That same willingness to engage the present also offers insight into the scholar's ambition to look past the visible present for an invisible past hiding beneath its surface.

For all its precision the tone of the *Antiquities* remains consistent with the isolario. As for Buondelmonti, the city's modern inhabitants were, for Gilles, "Barbarous men" who had "toppled and buried in barbarous buildings these ancient, heroic works of the city's art." Of course, for the latter traveler these were not only the later Byzantine Greeks but also Constantinople's current custodians, the Ottomans, "who in the last century have not ceased utterly destroying the vestiges of the ancient city."[29] He passes entirely without comment on the Byzantine art and material culture of recent centuries. His own written reconstruction of the ancient city was necessitated by a populace that was "daily demolishing, effacing, and utterly destroying the small remains of antiquity."[30] That said, Gilles' hostility betrays an important truth; he relied heavily on these "barbarous" inhabitants for information. Clearly some sixteenth-century Greek and Ottoman Constantinopolitans were familiar enough with the city's monuments to provide the previously unreported information which appears in the *Antiquities*. Such obviations are part and parcel of many such travelogues as is the apparent ignorance of Ottoman patrons, artists, and intellectuals of developing antiquarian attitudes toward the city's past.[31]

Gilles' tendency to denigrate the modern city and its denizens is hardly unique, nor is the privilege he bestows on the past at the present's expense confined to treatments of Constantinople. Since the time of Petrarch, the condition of ancient buildings and sites had been lamented; Buondelmonti wrote of Crete's ancient port that, "by the humble houses of peasants we found sepulchers of the most white marble; swine were fed in them and were scratching the magnificent sculptures that decorated their perimeter."[32] Humanists like Flavio Biondo admonished contemporaries to halt the decay of Rome's ancient monuments.[33] Such exhortations and laments only intensified during the first half of the sixteenth century, particularly in Rome where the city's cinquecento print makers and publishers spawned an industry dedicated to antiquarian and reconstructive maps and views of the eternal city.[34] As in the works of Buondelmonti and Gilles, derision of contemporary and recent overseers and inhabitants as ignorant and negligent pervades many such publications. These pejorative attitudes toward the present were, in part, self-serving. They vouched for the indispensable expertise of antiquarian scholars, artists, and publishers while safely exaggerating the grandeur of an always partially lost, but endlessly reconstructible past.

Gilles wrote the majority of his *Antiquities* in Rome where he spent the final five years of his life. These contemporary Roman conversations and the texts and images they generated undoubtedly influenced the shape Constantinople would take in his finished account. Yet unlike Rome, whose material past was a troubled mix of pre-Christian temples, idols, sites of martyrdom, and paleo-Christian shrines, Constantinople offered exceptionally fertile and comfortingly clear ground for Gilles' imaginative acts of reconstruction, while the city's geographic distance, along with the confessional and linguistic differences dividing Western Europeans from Greeks, authorized the *Antiquities'* invective tone. Most importantly, while humanist writers considering Rome necessarily contended with the ambivalence generated by the papacy's own transformation of the city, Gilles faced a less controversial task. Constantinople's urban renaissance under architects like Sinan could be safely consigned to the category barbarism. The conflation of Ottomans with barbarians was not invariable as later fifteenth-century antiquarian debates regarding their Scythian or Trojan origins indicate.[35] Nonetheless, it was a common-enough construction as to require no significant justification by Gilles. Similarly, the perceived absence of pre-Christian architecture in Constantinople inoculated antiquarians against the criticisms that sometimes faced those who sought to preserve Rome's ancient monuments from Christian spoliation.

Melchior Lorck (1526/7–88?), who traveled to and resided in Constantinople between 1555 and 1559, offers a contrast to book hunters like Buondelmonti and Gilles. Though he possessed a first-rate humanist education, Lorck was not a professional antiquarian but an artist, above all a painter, draftsman, and print maker. Trained, like so many prominent artisans, as a goldsmith, he hailed from a family of significant means. A diligent self-promoter who even wrote a short autobiography, Lorck quickly found himself imbricated within networks of patronage and politics that spread from his native to Denmark throughout the German lands. His prominence as a painter attracted the attention of Karel Van Mander, who discussed Lorck in his *Het Schilderboek*.[36] In the service of Danish King Christian III (1534–59) and later Holy Roman Emperors Charles V (1519–58) and Ferdinand I (1556–64), Lorck traveled widely throughout Europe, and was dispatched by the Hapsburg emperor to Constantinople as part of Ogier Ghiselin de Busbecq's peace envoy in 1555. Artists were not unusual inclusions among diplomatic missions; the Venetian painter Gentile Bellini's sojourn at Mehmed II's court is only the most famous example.[37] Their proficiency with military engineering and cartography along with drawing's vital significance as an information technology in the pre-photographic age meant that artists offered more than those talents we conventionally associate with their profession.[38]

Lorck's duties on Busbecq's mission are not clear, though he did produce portraits of the ambassador and other prominent members of the embassy.[39] Whatever his official role, the artist's encounter with the city laid the groundwork for projects that would occupy him for the remainder of his life. Like his predecessors, Lorck was fascinated by the ancient city and its monuments. Though not a scholar like Buondelmonti or Gilles, he possessed a solid, humanist education alongside his apprenticeship. Lorck's drawings of relief sculpture around the city, including those of several column and obelisk pedestals, remain invaluable sources for destroyed works. Like Gilles, Lorck had spent time in Italy, steeped in the antiquarian conversations of his day, by the time he was working in earnest on his graphic compendia of Constantinople.[40]

More so than Gilles before him, Lorck arrived to encounter a thriving Ottoman metropolis. Bustling with trade, teeming with new construction, and swollen to a population rivaling its ancient height, this was a city different in nearly every way from the ruin that had greeted Buondelmonti. Unlike his predecessors, Lorck leaned into these unfamiliar surroundings, seeking to capture some sense of the city that lay atop the ruins of the ancient one. This engagement ultimately took the form of two ambitious projects, neither of which made their way into print during his lifetime. The first, the *Turkish Publication*, was an encyclopedic collection of images of the city's Ottoman inhabitants, buildings, and military. Printed in 1626 some forty years after Lorck's death, the relationship between that edition and the artist's intentions remains unclear and provides only partial insight into his ambitions.[41] The second undertaking fared even worse. A massive, panoramic view of Constantinople, Lorck's *Prospect* was undoubtedly intended as a series of woodcuts, but survives only as seventeen drawings on paper.[42] Other works published during his lifetime give little sense of his attitudes toward the Ottomans and their capital; a largely panegyric description of Suleyman on the one hand, a polemic tract on the Turks as a sign of the coming apocalypse on the other.[43]

Whatever his personal feelings there could be little doubt by Lorck's day that the Ottoman city was a force in and of itself, one which could only be uneasily elided with the past. His own artisanal outlook, the inclination of someone invested in capturing the visible world through observation, must partially explain the refreshingly descriptive character of many of his works. A pen and ink drawing of rooftops and chimneys looking toward the Sea of Marmara presents a hastily captured glimpse at a living city. Though less spontaneous, woodcuts of the Atik Ali Pasha and Suleymaniye mosques in the *Turkish Publication* offered many early modern Europeans their first real images of Ottoman buildings.[44] Even more directly, Lorck's *Prospect* emphasizes an almost documentary sense of observational naturalism, presenting the city's buildings as if from a fixed vantage point. This impression is, of course, illusory. The panorama was produced from sketches made at diverse viewpoints, over a period of years, and was brought to fruition only after Lorck's return to Western Europe. Nevertheless, the preponderance of seemingly irrelevant detail, and the inclusion of a self-portrait of the artist as observer, insists upon facticity and presence.[45]

This shift was not solely the product of the artist's own outlook and training. The range of Lorck's projects, the seeming eclecticism of the *Turkish Publication*, the *horror vacui* of the panorama, point to the ways that European curiosity about Constantinople and its inhabitants was turned from a set of limited antiquarian interests to an embrace of the Ottoman character of the city. Ottoman customs and culture came to take their place within an expanding European market for books of costumes encompassing a wide world of ethnographic difference.[46] Increasingly in the seventeenth century a thirst for the exotic came to characterize the publishing industries of Amsterdam, London, and Antwerp. Volumes combining reportage of the sort suggested by Lorck's ostensibly first-hand observations mixed increasingly with the emerging fantasies of the day.[47]

Travelers like Buondelmonti, Gilles, and Lorck were hardly the norm, even among those with a professional interest in the former Byzantine capital. Voyages to the east, whether by land, river, sea, or some combination of these, were at best long and risky. Unpredictable relations between the Venetians and the Ottoman state, whose navy controlled the Mediterranean from the fifteenth through later sixteenth centuries, meant that any such journey might end in frustration or catastrophe. The sculptor Matteo de' Pasti, for example, was bound for Constantinople on a diplomatic mission for the lord of Rimini when he was arrested by Venetian authorities on Crete on suspicion of espionage in the sultan's service.[48] Artists and antiquarians alike, then, mostly stayed at home. Even those who did visit frequently found themselves at arm's length from the sites and people they hoped to learn about and describe. Barriers of language and creed, along with the geographic segregation of the Latin community and embassies under

Byzantine rule, tended to mitigate direct encounters with the capital. Such barriers accelerated under the Ottoman regime. Access to some of the spaces associated most intimately with the city – including the then mosque of Hagia Sophia and most of the Topkapı Palace – was forbidden to nearly all European visitors. Indeed, the Hapsburg embassy was under house arrest for a significant part of their stay in the city. Such enclosure was not uncommon for diplomatic visitors, who were always under suspicion as spies.[49]

Most Western Europeans encountered Constantinople through the imaginative representations of travelers like Buondelmonti, Gilles, and Lorck. Despite the eyewitness rhetoric – verbal and visual – employed by nearly all such travelers, even these encounters were, as we have seen, often strictly limited. The accounts and images that most readers and viewers relied upon were themselves the products of mitigation, not only by obvious circumstances like Lorck's confinement, but also by cultural barriers confronting these travelers. Perhaps even more importantly, the antiquarian expertise that so many visitors brought to Constantinople acted not only as a spur to discovery but as the most potent template limiting the inventions such discoveries generated. Though such templates were showing significant cracks by Lorck's day, they would only truly be supplanted once the power dynamic of the Mediterranean was transformed. The political decline of Ottoman hegemony, and with it the rise of European colonialism, would usher in a model that would transform the image of the city. Orientalism would ultimately provide both a spark to new discoveries and an even tighter, vice-like grip on the Western European imagination of Constantinople.

## FURTHER READING

Clark, L. R. and N. Um, "The Art of Embassy: Situating Objects and Images in the Early Modern Diplomatic Encounter," *Journal of Early Modern History* 20 (2016): 2–18.

Buondelmonti, C., *Cristoforo Buondelmonti: Description of the Aegean and Other Islands,* ed. and trans. E. Edson (New York, 2018).

Fischer, E. H., *Melchior Lorck,* 4 vols. (Copenhagen, 2009–2015).

Gilles, P. *Pierre Gilles' Constantinople: A Modern English Translation with Commentary,* ed. and trans. K. Byrd (New York, 2009).

Hetherington, P. "Vecchi e non antichi: Differing Responses to Byzantine Culture in Fifteenth-Century Tuscany," *Rinascimento* 32 (1992): 203–11.

Kafescioğlu, Ç., *Constantinopolis/Istanbul: Cultural Encounter, Imperial Vision, and the Construction of the Ottoman Capital* (University Park, 2009).

Maier, J., *Rome Measured and Imagined* (Chicago, 2015).

Necipoğlu, G., "Visual Cosmopolitanism and Creative Translation: Artistic Conversations with Renaissance Italy in Mehmed II's Constantinople," *Muqarnas* 29 (2012): 1–81.

Nelson, R., "Byzantium and the Rebirth of Art and Learning in Italy and France," in *Byzantium: Faith and Power (1261–1557)*, ed. H. Evans (New York, 2004): 515–44.

Roberts, S., *Printing a Mediterranean World: Florence, Constantinople, and the Renaissance of Geography* (Cambridge, MA, 2013).

# NOTES

1 M. Bourne, "Francesco II Gonzaga and Maps as Palace Decoration in Renaissance Mantua," *Imago Mundi* 51 (1999): 51–82; N. Miller, *Mapping the City: The Language and Culture of Cartography in the Renaissance* (London, 2003).

2 Ç. Kafescioğlu, *Constantinopolis/Istanbul: Cultural Encounter, Imperial Vision, and the Construction of the Ottoman Capital* (University Park, 2009): 2–23.

3 In addition to further references below see to start I. R. Manners, "Constructing the Image of a City: The Representation of Constantinople in Christopher Buondelmonti's *Liber Insularum Archipelagi*," *Annals of the Association of American Geographers* 87 (1997): 72–102.

4 A. Nagel and C. Wood, *Anachronic Renaissance* (Cambridge, MA, 2010).

5 P. Hetherington, "Vecchi e non antichi: Differing Responses to Byzantine Culture in Fifteenth-Century Tuscany," *Rinascimento* 32 (1992): 203–11; and R. Nelson, "Byzantine Art in the Italian Renaissance," in *Heaven and Earth: Art of Byzantium in Greek Collections*, ed. A. Drandaki, D. Papanikola-Bakirtzi, and A. Tourta (Los Angeles, 2014), 327–35.

6 G. Vasari, *Le vite de più eccellenti pittori scultori e architettori, nelle redazioni del 1550 e 1568*, Vol. 2, ed. R. Bettarini (Florence, 1966), 29–36.

7 S. Roberts, *Printing a Mediterranean World: Florence, Constantinople, and the Renaissance of Geography* (Cambridge, MA, 2013), 148.

8 On the Ottoman transformation of the city during the later fifteenth and early sixteenth century see esp. Kafescioğlu, *Constantinopolis/Istanbul*; and G. Necipoğlu, *The Age of Sinan: Architectural Culture in the Ottoman Empire* (London, 2005).

9 See esp. J. D. Fleming, "Introduction," in *The Invention of Discovery 1500–1700*, ed. J. D. Fleming (Burlington, 2011), 1–14.

10 A. Cutler, "From Loot to Scholarship: Changing Modes in the Italian Response to Byzantine Artifacts, 1200–1750," *DOP* 49 (1995): 237–67; M. Ruvoldt, "Sacred to Secular, East to West: The Renaissance Study and Strategies of Display," *Renaissance Studies* 20 (2006): 640–57.

11 G. Dalché, "The Reception of Ptolemy's Geography," in *The History of Cartography*, 3 vols., ed. D. Woodward (Chicago, 2007), 3: 285–364; and Roberts, *Printing a Mediterranean World*, 22–5.

12 See esp. A. Diller, "The Greek Codices of Palla Strozzi and Guarino Veronese," *JWarb* 24 (1961): 313–21; and R. Nelson, "Byzantium and the Rebirth of Art and Learning in Italy and France," in *Byzantium: Faith and Power (1261–1557)*, ed. H. Evans (New York, 2004): 515–23.

13 See, to start, N. Wilson's introduction to A. Manuzio, *The Greek Classics*, ed. and trans. N. Wilson (Cambridge, MA, 2016); also O. Margolis, *Aldus Manutius: A Cultural History* (forthcoming).

14 B. Wilson, "Assembling the Archipelago: *Isolarii* and the Horizons of Early Modern Public Making," in *Making Space Public in Early Modern Europe*, ed. Angela Vanhaelen and J. P. Ward (New York, 2013), 101–26; P. Brummett, *Mapping the Ottomans: Sovereignty, Territory, and Identity in the Early Modern Mediterranean* (Cambridge, 2015), 277–324.

15 See to start B. Bessi, "Cristoforo Buondelmonti: Greek Antiquities in Florentine Humanism," *The Historical Review* 9 (2012): 63–76; and C. Buondelmonti, *Description of the Aegean and Other Islands*, ed. and trans. E. Edson (New York, 2018).

16 G. Tolias, "*Isolarii*, Fifteenth to Seventeenth Century," in *The History of Cartography*, 3 vols., ed. D. Woodward (Chicago, 2007), 3: 263–84 at 265–7.

17 Buondelmonti, *Description*, 95.

18 Buondelmonti, *Description*, 147–50.

19 Nagel and Wood, *Anachronic Renaissance*, esp. 65–70.
20 Diller, "The Greek Codices of Palla Strozzi and Guarino Veronese," 314–21; and Roberts, *Printing a Mediterranean World*, 70–1.
21 Buondelmonti, *Description*, 150.
22 Manners, "Constructing the Image of a City"; Tolias, "*Isolarii*, Fifteenth to Seventeenth Century," 265–7; and Buondelmonti, *Description*, 6–10.
23 Miller, *Mapping the City*, 25–40; and J. Maier, "Francesco Rosselli's Lost View of Rome," *ArtB* 94 (2012): 395–411.
24 P. Gilles, *The Antiquities of Constantinople, based on the translation by John Ball*, ed. R. G. Musto (New York, 1988); and P. Gilles, *Pierre Gilles's Constantinople: A Modern English Translation with Commentary*, ed. and trans. K. Byrd (New York, 2009).
25 M.-F. Auzépy and J.-P. Grélois, eds. *Byzance retrouvée: Érudits et voyageurs français (XVIᵉ-XVIIᵉ siècles)* (Paris, 2001), 30–1; Nelson, "Byzantium and the Rebirth of Art and Learning," 543.
26 Musto, "Introduction," in Gilles, *Antiquities*, xi–xxx at xxiii; and Byrd, "Introduction," in Gilles, *Pierre Gilles' Constantinople*, xx.
27 Nelson, "Byzantium and the Rebirth of Art and Learning," 543; and P. Gilles, *De topographia Constantinopoleos et de illius antiquitatibus libri quattuor* (Lyon, 1561). For observations about access to texts see editor's comments in Gilles, *Pierre Gilles' Constantinople*, xx.
28 Gilles, *Pierre Gilles' Constantinople*, 17–18. See also, the similar translation in Gilles, *Antiquities*, 22.
29 Gilles, *Pierre Gilles' Constantinople*, 47 and Gilles, *Antiquities*, 51 for a similarly worded, but different translation.
30 Gilles, *Antiquities*, 222. See also Gilles, *Pierre Gilles' Constantinople*, 225 for a similarly worded, but different translation.
31 G. Necipoğlu, "Visual Cosmopolitanism and Creative Translation: Artistic Conversations with Renaissance Italy in Mehmed II's Constantinople," *Muqarnas* 29 (2012): 1–81; Roberts, *Printing a Mediterranean World*, 130–2; G. Casale, "Did Alexander the Great Discover America? Debating Space and Time in Renaissance Istanbul," *Renaissance Quarterly* 72 (2019): 863–909.
32 C. Buondelmonti, *Descriptio insulae Cretae*, ed M.-A. van Spitael (Herakleion, 1981) 251–6 as cited by Bessi, "Cristoforo Buondelmonti," 65.
33 H. Günther, "L'idea di Roma antica nella 'Roma instaurata' di Flavio Biondo," in *Le due Rome del Quattrocento*, ed. Sergio Rossi (Rome, 1997), 380–93; I am also grateful to R. J. Clines for sharing thoughts from his forthcoming *Ancient Others: Barbarians in the Italian Renaissance*.
34 J. Maier, *Rome Measured and Imagined, Early Modern Maps of the Eternal City* (Chicago, 2015). On evolving attitudes towards antiquity in Rome see, L. Barkan, *Unearthing the Past: Archaeology and Aesthetics in the Making of Renaissance Culture* (New Haven, 1999).
35 N. Bisaha, *Creating East and West: Renaissance Humanists and the Ottoman Turks* (Philadelphia, 2006), 43–93; and M. Meserve, *Empires of Islam in Renaissance Historical Thought* (Cambridge, MA, 2008).
36 E. H. Fischer, *Melchior Lorck*, 4 vols. (Copenhagen, 2009), 1: 63–8.
37 For Bellini's trip to Constantinople see esp. E. Rodini, "The Sultan's True Face," in *The Image of the Turk and Islam in the Western Eye*, ed. J. Harper (Burlington, 2011), 21–40; and D. Y. Kim, "Gentile in Red," *I Tatti Studies* 18 (2015): 157–92.
38 On artists as ambassadors see T. McCall and S. Roberts, "Art and the Material Culture of Diplomacy," in *Italian Renaissance Diplomacy*, ed. M. Azzolini and I. Lazarini (Toronto, 2017), 214–33; and L. R. Clark and N. Um, "The Art of Embassy: Situating Objects and Images in the Early Modern Diplomatic Encounter," *Journal of Early Modern History* 20 (2016), 2–18.
39 Fischer, *Melchior Lorck*, 1: 87–97.
40 Fischer, *Melchior Lorck*, 1: 69–72.
41 Fischer, *Melchior Lorck*, 3: 7–20 for the printing history.
42 M. Iuliano, "Melchior Lorck's Constantinople in the European Context," in Fischer, *Melchior Lorck*, 4: 25–62.
43 Fischer, *Melchior Lorck*, 3: 13–16.
44 Fischer, *Melchior Lorck*, 1: 95–101.
45 Iuliano, "Melchior Lorck's Constantinople in the European Context," 42–50.
46 A. R. Jones and M. Rosenthal, *The Clothing of the Renaissance World: Europe, Asia, Africa, the Americas; Cesare Vecellio's Habiti Antichi et Moderni* (London, 2008).

47 See B. Schmidt, *Inventing Exoticism: Geography, Globalism, and Europe's Early Modern World* (Philadelphia, 2015).

48 For Matteo's aborted journey see McCall and Roberts, "Art and the Material Culture of Diplomacy," 218–23; S. Roberts, "The Lost Map of Matteo de' Pasti," *Journal of Early Modern History* 20 (2016): 19–38; and A. G. Cevizli, "Mehmed II, Malatesta, and Matteo De' Pasti," *Renaissance Studies* 31 (2017): 43–65.

49 See, for example, the seventeenth-century case of the Venetian Niccolò Guidalotto: N. B.-A. Debby, "Crusade Propaganda in Word and Image in Early Modern Italy," *Renaissance Quarterly* 67 (2014): 503–43.

## 21: BYZANTIUM IN EARLY MODERN ISTANBUL

### Çiğdem Kafescioğlu

I n Constantinople there was not one, unitary Byzantium that newcomers encountered; not one, unitary "Ottoman" subject to respond to the city's ancient, late antique, and medieval legacies. Understanding perspectives on Byzantium in early modern Istanbul requires rendering visible the city's multiple temporalities, the ways in which they were understood by Ottoman subjects, the means by which places and images played into imagining the Constantinopolitan past, and the shifting significance of Byzantium's remaining buildings, monuments, and fragments. Changes in historical thinking, redefinitions of confessional and cultural boundaries, and the growth of the city into a metropolis informed perceptions of and responses to the Byzantine legacy (Fig. 21.1). In an effort to highlight the multiple ways in which the past was present in and had bearing on the lives and imaginations of Istanbulites, this chapter explores Byzantium in the post-Byzantine city within the framework of four topics: rupture and ruin, structures of *longue durée*, translation and notions of antiquarianism, and, finally, the lives and the reflections of Byzantine monuments and spolia.[1]

### 1455: RUPTURE AND RUIN PORTRAYED

Surveys of Constantinople and Galata, dated 1455, are rare documents from the early years of Ottoman rule.[2] The Galata document surveys houses, tax-paying residents, and their level of wealth; the Constantinople document includes properties that had come into the possession of the court, describing them and identifying their inhabitants. They provide a snapshot of the city two and a half years after its fall, beyond the conquering army's siege and sack and before Mehmed II's (1444–6/1451–81) conclusive move of the Ottoman capital from Edirne (ancient Adrianopolis) to Constantinople, in 1459.[3]

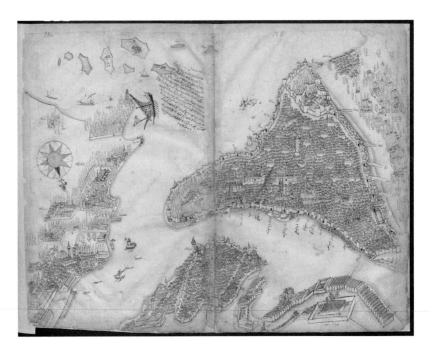

21.1 View of Istanbul, Piri Reis' *Kitāb-ı Baḥriye*, second half of the seventeenth century, Staatsbibliothek zu Berlin, Preußischer Kulturbesitz, Orientabteilung, Diez A. Fol. 57, folio. 28a–28b. (Photo courtesy of Staatsbibliothek zu Berlin)

Ordered according to an Ottoman conceptualization of urban space, the Constantinople survey divides the city into neighborhoods (*maḥalle*), many named for churches, monasteries, or Byzantine elites. Starting from the Blachernai area, it covers the Golden Horn's western shores and slopes, the districts along the land walls, the Golden Gate, and Psamatia, before proceeding inland where it cuts off at the incomplete section on *Maḥalle-i Ayasofya*, the Hagia Sophia neighborhood. The 1455 survey presents a picture consistent with late Byzantine descriptions of the city as largely empty and dotted with village-like settlements around monasteries. The Studios Monastery register suggests one such site: a hospital; several double-storey structures with multiple rooms and partitions; a larger building with twenty-two rooms above and ten below; ten buildings registered as "houses of the Tekvur"; two churches, one of them the church of St. John the Baptist; a refectory; five wineries; and stables stood within a walled enclosure entered through a stone gate. At the gate and nearby were a number of shops, confirming the impression that these were largely self-sufficient areas within the city.[4] Gennadios Scholarios, the first Greek patriarch of the Ottoman era, described one such monastery in 1454 as "trampled under foot [plundered] and stripped of everything."[5]

Capturing aspects of an urban fabric which largely disappeared in the following centuries, the 1455 document presents a picture of destitution and ruin: deserted residences, empty churches falling into ruin, houses lacking doors, a church robbed of its lead roof covering, other buildings covered with reeds, and many structures "in a ruinous state" (*ḫarāba mütevecciḥ*, literally, "turning to ruin"). Some inhabitants of these buildings were Constantinopolitans who had returned after the city's fall; most were new arrivals from western Anatolia and Thrace. Prior to the late fifteenth-century systematic deportations that constituted the Ottomans' largest effort to repopulate the city, few people agreed to accept the ruler's invitation to move here and promises of freehold property.[6] The city's unstable and difficult conditions are evident in the population's mobility: many new residents returned home in the two years between 1453 and the completion of the survey, leaving their places to other newcomers. Alongside them lived those abandoned in the tumult following the city's fall: widowers, the disabled, and the elderly. Other records corroborate these glimpses of involuntary mobility and deserted houses and churches, allowing us to imagine life in the fallen city for those who remained, for those who came (or returned) of their own will, and for those who would be deported there in the following decades.

Beyond the monasteries the survey presents a picture of sparse settlements of one- and two-story houses, some within courts or gardens, and a smaller number of shops. Few churches survived: the majority were abandoned and a small number were used as workshops or shops. Four small mosques (*masjid*) are recorded, one adjacent to an empty church, another converted from a monastery refectory, indicators that, with the important exception of Hagia Sophia, Islamization of churches was not a priority during these years.[7]

The survey excludes the districts that were most densely settled in the earlier part of the century, the areas adjacent to the Neorion port and the slopes connecting it to the Mese. Foundation and survey documents from the following decades indicate something of this area's fabric. Residences were more lavish than those registered in the 1455 survey, among them palaces of later fifteenth-century statesmen incorporating such structures as a Byzantine tower, or an audience hall reached by a double staircase. A "house with the lion," perhaps originally a Venetian building in the trading colony near the Neorion port, gave its name to one of the city's quarters; the palace of the Venetian *bailo* (ambassador), in the court's possession until the turn of the sixteenth century, was given to the keeper of the royal treasury and became his residence. Houses represented in Matrakçı Nasuh's *Mecmū'-i Menāzil*, stone, brick, and composite masonry structures with sunroofs supported by elegant columns, may have incorporated such elite residences.[8]

Another gap in the survey is the Church of Holy Apostles. Given to the Orthodox Patriarchate shortly following the city's conquest, it was abandoned in the autumn of 1454 when the Patriarch Gennadios allegedly asked that the patriarchate be moved to the Pammakaristos monastery.[9] Possibly excluded from the survey because it was considered sultanic property, the church was pulled down some years later to open space for Mehmed II's mosque complex. This project was one step in a city-wide push for monumentalization, infrastructure building, and repopulation that Mehmed II undertook to rebuild Constantinople as the seat of his throne in conjunction with newly empowered elites of Byzantine and Balkan background.

## STRUCTURES OF SPACE AND THOUGHT

Observers of 1453 have rightly emphasized rupture, noting the Byzantine fabric's gradual disappearance, due to church conversions, voluntary and involuntary changes in housing stock (whose othering was denoted in official documents from the 1470s onwards by the terms *kāfirī* or *kāfiriyyü'l-bina'*, infidel, or "infidel-built"),[10] spoliation, and shifts in cultural and religious dispositions. However, rupture and continuity constitute two conjoined facets of Constantinopolitan history beyond that date. Constantinople's long-term attributes, particularly its location at a major Eurasian crossroad, sealed its centrality to premodern regional and interregional political, economic, and cultural dynamics; the site's shortcomings, too, continued to shape the acts and visions of those who ruled and its inhabitants' lives.

The natural resources available to the eastern Mediterranean's foremost urban center were at most times incommensurate with its population. For grain Constantinople depended on an expansive hinterland, which incorporated Thrace and lands around the Aegean, the larger expanses of the Roman and the Ottoman empires, including Egypt.[11] Other staples arrived from shorter distances. Whether Byzantine or Ottoman, the court city continued to attract and to demand luxury items. Land and sea ports were integral to the city's provisioning, and their links with the city predetermined, to a degree, the organization of transport, storage, and distribution throughout the Ottoman era.[12]

The city's Roman layout, marked by the Mese connecting the city center at the east to the walls, gates, and the lands beyond to the west, and the north–south axes linking the Golden Horn and Propontis shores to the center, survived in basic outline; however, the shape of the urban armature changed. The transformation of the Byzantine city's Macros Embolos, the avenue connecting the Neorion port to the Mese, into Istanbul's Uzun Çarşı (Long Market), and the location of the main market for luxury goods (*bedestān*) close to these two axes captures the spatial continuity.

The intersection of the Macros Embolos and the Mese, possibly the site of the Tetrapylon, came to house a set of public monuments that marked this node of city-wide circulation.[13] Topography determined water use, which in turn played a role in siting major edifices, as with the Hürrem Sultan baths that took over the location of the late antique Zeuxippos baths near Hagia Sophia.[14] From the initial restoration of Istanbul's waterways by Mehmed II to Süleyman's (1520–66) expansion of the system in the 1560s to provide water to an exploding population, the Byzantine system provided the basis for the water infrastructure. The restoration of the Valens aqueduct, an icon of the emperor's ability to provide water, and the system's ancient pedigree were signified through an informed manner of architectural referencing in the nearby fountain from which the restored system's waters poured: the Kırkçeşme ("forty fountains"), a composition of alternating round and pointed arches, displayed a Byzantine double peacock relief among other spolia (Fig. 21.2). The "ancient" (*kadīm*) water sources and conduits, and names of particular water structures, remained a powerful presence not only in literary and historical works addressing Ottoman Istanbul's water distribution, but also in technical and official documentation pertinent to supervision, repair, and construction processes.[15]

To consider the long-term, structural aspects of the Constantinopolitan past is not to reduce the city's millennial history to one of undifferentiated sameness. Neither should focus on the long term obscure the fact that revivals had an important role in the resignification of the city's imperial heritage. Revival, as the final section of this chapter suggests, was indeed a long-term attribute. If the requirements of topography, availability, and distribution technology resulted in significant overlaps between the Byzantine and Ottoman water systems, Ottoman projects also involved the revival of late antique models.

21.2 The Kırkçeşme fountain, 1935. (Photo Nicholas V. Artamonoff, Nicholas V. Artamonoff photographs of Istanbul and Turkey, 1935–1945, ICFA.NA.0015, Dumbarton Oaks, Trustees for Harvard University, Washington, DC)

Mehmed II, whose desire to restore the city to its former grandeur is noted repeatedly in period sources, realized a Roman feat in restoring the system that had been out of use for several hundred years.[16] At the same time earlier Ottoman practices informed the building of Istanbul's public baths, sites of sexually segregated socialization, often built close to mosques and answering also to ritual requirements predicated in Islamic practice.[17]

Long-term attributes informed long-term structures of thought, whereby notions of rulership and symbolic presence overlapped with the structural constraints of provisioning, urban circulation, and water use.[18]

Imperial representation endured in the visible remains of the palace, church, and circus complex that made up Constantinople's symbolic center. In the heart of the Ottoman capital, Hagia Sophia, the city's primary imperial mosque until the empire's demise, the Topkapı Palace, the seat of rule until 1850, and the Hippodrome, the major public square into the twentieth century, articulated imperial power and public presence, however differently enacted compared to late antique and medieval times.[19]

The Church of the Holy Apostles crowning the city's fourth hill, the monument of Constantine (306–37) and Justinian (527–65) that housed the relics of the apostles and tombs of Byzantine emperors, may be the ultimate sign of Ottoman rulers' claims on the Constantinopolitan past. The demolition of the church and the imperial mausolea to open space for the mosque and mausoleum of Mehmed II is a reminder that intimate connection to the past involved destruction as much as it did revival and resignification. Mehmed II's mosque preserved the footprint of the Holy Apostles in its layout, the sultan "burying" the church and Constantine's mausoleum under his own dynastic mosque.[20] References to Constantine in period sources indicate that the choice of site, the building's iconography, which emulated and revived the dome configuration of Hagia Sophia, the placement of Mehmed II's mausoleum in response to the emperor's tomb, and, finally, the transportation of Byzantine imperial sarcophagi to the sultan's palace were far from accidental.[21] Nor were such references short lived. When the court historiographer Seyyid Lokman (d. after 1601) narrated Süleyman's restoration and expansion of the water distribution system in the northern forested hinterland in the 1560s, he started with Constantine, describing him as the system's first builder, noting that the emperor had spoliated Üsküdar's city wall to build his aqueduct.[22] Lokman transposed to the city's hinterland a notion of imperial continuity, predicated on the trope of the emperor/sultan battling with, and in the case of Süleyman eventually reining in, the city's sources of cyclical disaster: earthquakes, fires, floods, and plague.

## TRANSLATION, MYTH MAKING, AND FACETS OF ANTIQUARIAN THOUGHT

In the years following the decision to make Constantinople the seat of the Ottoman throne (a process that evolved in the decade following 1453), authors differently positioned vis-à-vis Ottoman authority and the city, and addressing distinct audiences, created two narrative strands recounting the foundation of Constantinople and the creation of its primary monument, Hagia Sophia.[23] One strand derives directly from the *Patria*, a tenth-century compilation of Constantinopolitan narratives. A partial copy was added to Mehmed II's book collection in 1474, followed by translations/adaptations into Persian and Turkish, which include the *Diegesis* section of the *Patria* on Hagia Sophia and shorter sections on stages of the city's foundation by Byzas and by Constantine.[24] The second strand, also partly based on the *Patria*, begins the city's history with a founder figure unknown to any Byzantine author: one Yanko bin (son of) Madyan, who is presented as the father (in some versions an ancestor) of Byzas and who boasts a familial or symbolic connection to Solomon.[25] An amalgamation of narrative strands that culled episodes of the city's legendary past from Arabic, Turkish, and Greek sources, the text is most striking in its master narrative that locates the city within an inescapable cycle of construction and ruination. Founded at the wrong hour, Constantinople was bound to be destroyed by plague, earthquakes, fires, and other disasters, each a portent of its ultimate ruination at the End of Time.

Several themes emerge from these two strands. The conquest of Constantinople as a portent of the Last Hour, a shared trope in Byzantine, Latin, and Islamic traditions alike, was worked into several Ottoman texts from the 1460s onwards; that is, after the Ottoman court's decision to move into and rebuild the city.[26] Apocalyptic and messianic imagery, reintroduced into the intellectual and political worlds of western Eurasia in the fifteenth century, and resonating with earlier Byzantine apocalyptic thought, captured the desires, fears, and disappointments of Constantinople's new denizens. In foundation tales it was evoked both to reinforce and to condemn the emerging imperial vision.[27] Apocalyptic narratives captured social and moral criticism. (One description of the Last Hour read, "urbanites became lords and the vile and the lowly came to rule."[28]) They inscribed in the city's conquest the beginning of the End. Absorbed into the burgeoning historiographic tradition, these narratives remained, through the following century, integral to imperial imagery, imbuing Ottoman sultans with messianic power and apocalyptic agency.[29]

"After us, gaze at our works Verily, our works point to us," the historian Mustafa Âli (d. 1600) quoted in his late sixteenth-century version of the foundation myth, commenting on the monumental columns of the Hippodrome.[30] Drawing upon earlier Ottoman foundation narratives, Âli turned to the medieval Arabic couplet to appraise

Constantinople's ancient past, and to situate the city's builders within a shared temporal space that included the Byzantine past and the Ottoman present. Earlier renderings of the *Patria* and its interpretations were integrated into dynastic histories. Starting with Idris-i Bidlisi (d. 1520) who wrote in Persian, and Ibn Kemal (d. 1534) who wrote in Turkish, the city's past was reconfigured to suggest the predestined and inevitable ascendance of the house of Osman to the Constantinopolitan throne.[31] The anticipated Islamization of Justinian's Hagia Sophia, a trope of medieval Arabic writing on Byzantium, was integral to these narratives, which featured such motifs as the destruction wrought on the ancient world's monuments at the moment of the prophet Muhammad's birth, whose intervention, moreover, saved the dome of Hagia Sophia from collapsing.[32]

The foundation tales were a medium through which medieval understandings of Constantinople's Roman legacy continued to circulate among the city's early modern denizens. Inherited from written and possibly oral traditions, stories attributing all manner of protective and some destructive power to the city's ancient heritage were alive and well at the time Evliya Çelebi compiled a comprehensive list of the city's talismans in the later 1600s. They survived, with few changes, into the nineteenth century.[33]

The ineluctable presence of the ancient past in Constantinople is encountered in each variant of the foundation narratives, not only in references to mythic and historic beginnings, but also in antiquarian and aesthetic sensibilities, and the attention to ancient materiality manifest in commentaries on Hagia Sophia. Ibn Kemal's preface to his rendering of the *Patria* epitomizes the response. His paean to the unique and eternal building, its multitude of arches and half domes crowned by the heavenly dome, its vast space, and its ornamented surfaces ends with a comment on the silvery Prokonnesian marble pavement noting, "the one who glances at its pure marble floor would think it pure water, flowing in waves." Here is a distant echo of the sixth century, when Paul the Silentiary likened these same marbles to the waves of the sea.[34]

Authors who transmitted and embellished the Hagia Sophia stories wrote with keen awareness and intimate knowledge of the materials and their procurement. The ancient sites that were the sources of Hagia Sophia's marbles and stones, Ephesus, Miletopolis, and Kyzikos among them, were the same sites that furnished the stones and marbles of the Süleymaniye in the 1550s, highlighting the mobility of building images and materials, a common trait of premodern monumental iconographies.[35] It would be wrong, however, to attribute Ottoman writing on ancient monuments and sites, and their architectural and sculptural remains, to translations of and inspiration from the *Patria* alone. Architectural descriptions in Firdevsi-i Rumi's (1453–d. after 1512) *Book of Solomon* presented to Bayezid II (1481–1512) make no reference to the *Patria*, but are nevertheless replete with the sense of antiquarian admiration, emotive engagement, and keen attention to materiality.[36]

*Patria* translations and adaptations continued to be a vital part of commentary on the dynasty and its capital city. As a set of templates and images located within diverse genres (history, geography, political commentary, and prognosticative texts), they expressed different authorial intentions.[37] Narrative paths forked once more in the middle decades of the seventeenth century, when translations from Greek and Latin, paralleled by and integrated into a novel encyclopedist trend, brought new knowledge into Ottoman letters. In stark contrast to the tales that had circulated for nearly 200 years, translations by Katib Çelebi (d. 1657) introduced the perspectives of other Byzantine voices such as Ioannes Zonaras, Niketas Choniates, Nikophoros Gregoras, and Laonikos Chalcocondyles,[38] alongside histories of western Europe and the Roman Empire.[39] Translation and novel modes of intellectual production may have informed new approaches to the ancient past. Describing each of the city's ancient columns that had survived to his day, Hezarfen Hüseyin Efendi (d. 1691) alerted his reader, "Do not imagine that there is anything buried under or hidden atop this column." Regarding the Column of Arkadios he added, "it was erected only to manifest the power of the reign and for fame and commemoration," displaying a studied effort to rid the monuments of their talismanic associations and to highlight their imperial symbolism. Similarly, Hezarfen's relation of Justinian's construction of the Hagia Sophia makes no reference to legendary founders. The monument's Islamization was not an event preordained in the era of the Prophet, but the feat of Sultan Mehmed.[40] Less attentive to materiality and without the aesthetic tropes that had shaped writing on Hagia Sophia and the city's Ottoman monuments, Hezarfen's work attests to the burgeoning of a historical sensibility keen on documenting, dating, and transmitting what he deemed authentic knowledge based on Greek and Latin texts.[41]

## TANGIBLE PAST: MONUMENT, SPOLIA, REPLICA

In one of the more than 200 paintings in the *Sūrnāme-ı Humāyūn*, the *Book of Imperial Festivities* (1588), a heretofore overlooked drawing of the

Theodosian obelisk base preserves the trace of a sixteenth-century gaze on this monument (Fig. 21.3).[42] Showing the *kathisma* (viewing box) linked to the Great Palace with its royal occupants, the painting also offers an interpretation of the obelisk base, combining reliefs from different sides in a single face. An image of Theodosios I (379–95) and his court from the south side appears above within a triple-arched portico, while a depiction of the obelisk's erection from the east side appears below. The event narrated in the festival book, the forty-eight-day celebration that took place in the Hippodrome in the spring of 1582, was watched by Murad III (r. 1574–95) from his imperial loggia attached to the Ibrahim Pasha Palace, across from the site where the *kathisma* was once located. The cultural translation at work was now captured in a painting destined for the imperial treasury, in which Emperor Theodosios and Sultan Murad shared the same picture frame, both simultaneously partaking in urban spectacle.

Awareness of the Hippodrome's imperial associations are also conveyed in a revivalist gesture of the influential grand vizier of Sultan Süleyman's early reign, Ibrahim Pasha. For a decade between the Ottomans' Hungarian campaign in 1526 and the execution of Ibrahim in 1536, the Hippodrome was home to a group of three classicizing statues of Apollo, Diana, and Hercules, which the vizier had brought as trophies from Buda and exhibited on the circus in a manner resonant of the site's late antique use (Fig. 21.4).[43] The statues, produced at the order of King Matthias Corvinus (r. 1458–90) by the Italian-educated sculptor Giovanni Dalmata to stand at the gate of his new palace were, in turn, products of another revivalist act, highlighting shared predilections beyond the core geographies of the Renaissance.[44]

While Byzantine statuary and Ottoman attitudes toward it other than the talismanic are difficult to pinpoint in early modern Istanbul, the architectural legacy presents a different situation. Earlier Ottoman responses to Byzantine architecture in Bythinia and Thrace, and attitudes toward the imperial legacy subsequent to the fall/conquest of Constantinople, have been explored from different perspectives.[45] The history of Ottoman interventions to the fabric of the Hagia Sophia, and Ottoman architects' responses to its architectural iconography and formal and spatial configuration, occupy a central place in this discussion.[46] Competitive responses to, reinterpretations of, and direct quotations from the building are readable in Ottoman architectural works, starting from the first major intervention of Mehmed II that brought down Holy Apostles, and continuing in increasingly elaborate fashion in the architecture of Sinan.

(a)

(b)

21.3 Intizami, *Sūrnāme-i Humāyūn*, (a) procession of cooks with sugar figures at the Hippodrome and (b) detail of the obelisk base, 1588. Topkapı Palace Museum Library H. 1344, y.24b–25a. (Photo courtesy of Topkapı Palace Museum Library)

(a)

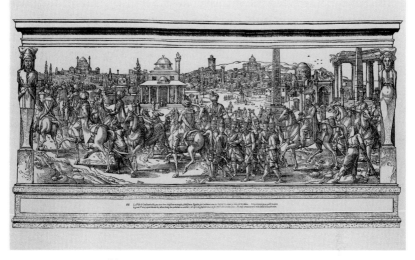

(b)

21.4 Pietr Coecke van Aelst, "Procession of Sultan Süleyman through the Hippodrome," part of the seven-part series *Ces Moeurs et fachons de faire de Turcz*, *c.*1553, Antwerp, (a) Süleyman's procession and (b) detail of the Dalmata statues. (Photo public domain, courtesy of the Metropolitan Museum of Art, New York, Harris Brisbane Dick Fund, 1928, 28.85.7 a–b)

Numerous interventions to the Hagia Sophia signified the building's Islamization and its inclusion among Ottoman dynastic monuments, the minarets being the most conspicuous among them. Two additions to the edges of the building in the later sixteenth century highlight less often explored perspectives on Byzantium (Fig. 21.5).[47] In 1577 Sinan constructed the mausoleum of Selim II south of the building, within an area recently cleared of squatter housing and ringed by a new enclosure wall. With its dome supported on a square mass and a structural and spatial configuration that connected the octagonal baldachin to the surrounding wall system through deep exedrae projecting from the dome base, the mausoleum is an eloquent response to the late antique architectural aesthetic of the monument in whose shadow it was built. The Prokonnesian marble facing the exterior, an unusual choice in Ottoman dynastic and elite tombs, also bespeaks a desire to respect, and to submit to, the monument's late antique aesthetic.[48] Conformity to Hagia Sophia's architectural language extends to the contemporaneous gate connecting the building's southeastern vestibule to the newly created enclosure wall, an architectural composition made up of spoliated sixth-century fragments of porphyry columns and two-zone basket capitals featuring doves.[49] Defying utilitarian or triumphalist interpretations of spoliation, these two additions highlight the antiquarian sensibility informing some of the interventions to the monument, whose past remained, through changing modes of interpretation and historical thinking, integral to the mental worlds of Istanbulite patrons, designers, and denizens.

Concentrating on the Ottoman response to Hagia Sophia alone ignores the larger late antique and medieval legacy embodied in the city's early modern monuments. The range of fifteenth-century buildings once mistaken for Byzantine structures in an earlier era of scholarship, among them the Sheikh Vefa convent and mosque, the central market hall (*bedestān*) of today's Covered Bazaar, and the Kırkçeşme fountain, underline the continuation of sensibilities that shaped the Byzantine–Ottoman "overlap architecture" of late medieval Bythinia, even as a revivalist gaze focused mainly on the Hagia Sophia-shaped religious architecture of the elites.[50] Quotations from Constantinople's late antique and medieval monuments, among them undulating drums, window-pierced curtain walls, and tympanum arches, remained part of the architect's vocabulary through the later sixteenth century. Spoliated materials, especially porphyry and other colored marbles that had been recycled since the medieval era, remained in use, while a medieval aesthetic favoring variety transformed, through the 1500s, into one prioritizing uniformity, even as it showcased prized fragments.[51] The mid-sixteenth century bespeaks increasing sophistication in Ottoman architectural interpretations of the antique, as observed, for example, in the complex double-shell designs of sanctuaries and funerary structures

(a)

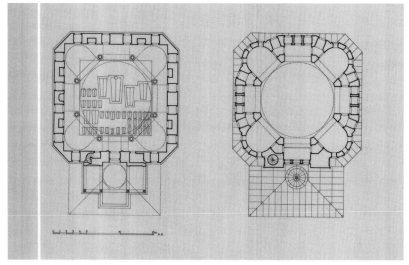

(b)

21.5 Sinan, Hagia Sophia, (a) mausoleum of Selim II plan and (b) external view, Istanbul, 1574 (photos courtesy of Boğaziçi University Aptullah Kuran Archive), and (c) entrance to the south-western vestibule. (Photo courtesy of Alessandra Gu'gl'a)

that resonate with structural and spatial configurations of ancient Mediterranean monuments from Split to Jerusalem. It is in fact difficult to analyze the polygonal support systems and double-shell designs of some of Sinan's most striking works, such as the Selimiye in Edirne, or the Sokollu mosque in Azapkapı, Istanbul, without considering the Justinianic church of Ss. Sergios and Bakchos and its late antique cognates.[52]

That responses to the city's past changed with shifts in Ottoman cultural and intellectual predilections and political rearrangements is perhaps best captured by a set of eighteenth-century references to Constantinople's Byzantine monuments. In the 1720s, when the new Sa'dabad palace in Kağıthane, a favored excursion spot north of the Golden Horn, was constructed, a canal redirecting water from the Kağıthane river included a replica of the Hippodrome's Serpent Column.[53] The canal's white marble floor, arranged in small cascades for visual and aural effect, featured undulating decoration modeled after the carved marble columns in the Basilica cistern. These replicas of the ancient city center brought to the new elite abode outside the city wall partook of a minor Byzantine revival, visible also in a number of intramural monuments such as the Byzantinizing public library built next to the mosque of Mehmed II in 1742, and architectural quotations in the Zeynep Sultan and Laleli mosques of 1760.[54] Such allusions to the past were meaningful for eighteenth-century elites who sought to expand the temporal and geographic bounds of their cultural references, and engaged in novel manners with visual cultures of contemporary Iran and Europe, and with the Byzantine and the Timurid past.

An expanded range of actors, among them members of the newly visible bureaucracy who regarded architectural connoisseurship as part of their urbane identity, and Greek intellectuals with multiple connections to the Ottoman court, to Istanbul's salons, and to European academic and intellectual currents, were part of the cultural environment in which these edifices were designed and used.[55] It is likely that more widespread references to the Byzantine past in the architecture of the city's multiple communities have not survived. This new turn in architectural culture marked the final step in the continuous but shifting attentiveness to Byzantium in early modern Istanbul where Ottoman elites, designers, and a multilingual intelligentsia participated in the memorialization and reuse of the past. The emergent mode of historicism that reshaped antiquarian predilections in the 1800s and left its traces in the letters and the spaces of a modernizing Constantinople would be articulated within the confines of hardening ethno-religious boundaries, whereby Byzantium came to be associated exclusively with Greek communal identity, and ruling elites turned their gaze more attentively to the Islamic past.

## FURTHER READING

Hamadeh, S. and Ç. Kafescioğlu, eds., *A Companion to Early Modern Istanbul* (Leiden, 2021).

Kafescioğlu, Ç., *Constantinopolis/Istanbul: Cultural Encounter, Imperial Vision, and the Construction of the Ottoman Capital* (University Park, 2009).

Magdalino, P. and N. Ergin, *Istanbul and Water* (Leuven, 2015).

Necipoğlu, G., "The Life of an Imperial Monument: Hagia Sophia after Byzantium," in *Hagia Sophia from the Age of Justinian to the Present*, ed. R. Mark and A. S. Çakmak (Cambridge, 1992), 195–225.

## NOTES

1 Kostantiniyye, the Arabicized form of Constantinople, remained the city's official name through the Ottoman period. It is most frequently encountered in literary and historical texts of the early modern era, alongside Istanbul, in use at least since the thirteenth century. On the city between the later fifteenth and eighteenth centuries, S. Hamadeh and Ç. Kafescioğlu, eds., *A Companion to Early Modern Istanbul* (Leiden, 2021).

2 Topkapı Palace Museum Archives D. 2203; H. İnalcık, *The Survey of Istanbul 1455: The Text, English Translation, Analysis of the Text, Documents* (Istanbul, 2012); F. Emecen, "1455 Tarihli Istanbul ve Galata Tahririnin Kayıp Sayfaları," *The Journal of Ottoman Studies* 56 (2020): 287–317.

3 A. Pertusi, *La Caduta Di Costantinopoli* (Rome, 1976).

4 İnalcık, *Survey*, 81, 351–2.

5 N. Necipoğlu, "Gennadios Scholarios and the Patriarchate: A Reluctant Patriarch on the 'Unhappy Throne'," in *The Holy Apostles: A Lost Monument, a Forgotten Project, and the Presentness of the Past*, ed. M. Mullet and R. G. Ousterhout (Washington, DC, 2020), 237–46 at 243.

6 İnalcık, *Survey*, 61–87; on deportations, S. Yerasimos, "La fondation d'Istanbul ottomane," in *7 Centuries of Ottoman Architecture: A Supra National Heritage* (Istanbul, 1999), 205–24.

7 On church conversions, Ç. Kafescioğlu, *Constantinopolis/Istanbul: Cultural Encounter, Imperial Vision, and the Construction of the Ottoman Capital* (University Park, 2009), 21–2, 99–100, 223–5.

8 Kafescioğlu, *Constantinopolis/Istanbul*, 199–205.

9 Necipoğlu, "Gennadios Scholarios," 242.

10 O. Ergin, ed., *Fatih Sultan Mehmed'in vakfiyeleri* (Istanbul, 1945); Kafescioğlu, *Constantinopolis/Istanbul*, 202–3.

11 C. Mango, "The Development of Constantinople as an Urban Centre," in *Studies on Constantinople*, C. Mango (Aldershot, 1993), no. I; A. Shopov, "Urban Agriculture," in Hamadeh and Kafescioğlu, *A Companion to Early Modern Istanbul*.

12 P. Magdalino, "The Grain Supply of Constantinople, Ninth–Twelfth Centuries," in *Studies on the History and Topography of Byzantine Constantinople* (Aldershot, 2007), no. IX; C. Mango, "Development;" Kafescioğlu, *Constantinopolis/Istanbul*, 28–45.

13 M. Cerasi, "The Urban and Architectural Evolution of the Istanbul Divanyolu: Urban Aesthetics and Ideology in Ottoman Town Planning," *Muqarnas* 22 (2005): 204–6.

14 Kafescioğlu, *Constantinopolis/Istanbul*, 82, 85–6.

15 M. Akkuş, ed. Eyyubî, Menâkıb-ı Sultan Süleyman (Risâle-i Pâdişâh-Nâme) (Ankara, 1991); K. Çeçen, *Sinan's Water Supply System in Istanbul* (Istanbul, 1996), 46–7.

16 Kafescioğlu, *Constantinopolis/Istanbul*, 103–9.

17 N. Macaraig, *Çemberlitaş Hamami in Istanbul: The Biographical Memoir of a Turkish Bath* (Edinburgh, 2018), chap. 4.

18 S. Vryonis, "Byzantine Constantinople and Ottoman Istanbul: Evolution in a Millennial Imperial Iconography," in *The Ottoman City and Its Parts: Urban Structure and Social Order*, ed. I. Bierman, R. A. Abou-El-Haj, and D. Preziosi (New Rochelle, 1991), 13–52; Kafescioğlu, *Constantinopolis/Istanbul*, 130–42.

19 G. Necipoğlu, "Visual Cosmopolitanism and Creative Translation: Artistic Conversations with Renaissance Italy in Mehmed II's Constantinople," *Muqarnas* 29 (2012): 1–81 at 22–35; Kafescioğlu, *Constantinopolis/Istanbul*, 53–142.

20 J. Raby, "From the Founder of Constantinople to the Founder of Istanbul: Mehmed the Conqueror, Fatih Camii, and the Church of the Holy Apostles," in Mullet and Ousterhout, *The Holy Apostles*, 247–85 at n. 4.

21 Reviewed in Raby, "From the Founder."

22 *Seyyid Lokman, Tārīḫ-i Sulṭān Süleymān*, T413, Chester Beatty Library, Dublin fol. 16r–24r. Possibly a reference to Valens' spoliation of Chalcedon's city walls.

23 On the conflicted process, S. Yerasimos, *La fondation de Constantinople et de Sainte-Sophie dans les traditions turques: Légendes d'empire* (Istanbul and Paris, 1990), 99–159; C. Kafadar, *Between Two Worlds: The Construction of the Ottoman State* (Berkeley, 1995), 138–54.

24 On the Topkapı Palace *Patria* manuscript (TSMK, G.İ. 6), J. Raby, "Mehmed the Conqueror's Greek Scriptorium," *DOP* 37 (1983): 15–34 at 18–19; and A. Akışık- Karakullukçu, "Mehmed II's *Patria*, Byzas' Palace, and the Topkapı Palace: Ottoman Classicizing in the Fifteenth Century," in *The Post-1204 Byzantine World: Novel Approaches and New Directions*, ed. N. Gaul (Abingdon, forthcoming).

25 Yerasimos, *La Fondation*, 62–96; for the connection to Solomon; also M. Âli, *Künhü'l Ahbâr*, vol. 2, ed. M. Hüdai Şentürk (Ankara, 2003), 20.

26 K. Şahin, "Constantinople and the End Time: The Ottoman Conquest as a Portent of the Last Hour," *Journal of Early Modern History* 14 (2010): 317–54; F. M. Emecen, *Fetih Ve Kıyamet, 1453: İstanbul'un Fethi Ve Kıyamet Senaryolan* (Istanbul, 2012); C. H. Fleischer, "A Mediterranean Apocalypse: Prophecies of Empire in the Fifteenth and Sixteenth Centuries," *JESHO* 61 (2018): 18–90.

27 Yerasimos, *La Fondation*; Şahin, "Constantinople"; Fleischer, "Mediterranean Apocalypse."

28 A. Bican Yazıcıoğlu, *Dürr-i Meknun = Saklı İnciler*, ed. N. Sakaoğlu (Istanbul, 1999).

29 Fleischer, "Mediterranean Apocalypse."

30 Âli, *Künhü'l Ahbâr*, 50.

31 Ibn Kemal, *Tevârih-i Âl-i Osman, VII. Defter*, ed. Ş. Turan (Ankara, 1957), 76–89; I. Bitlisi, Heşt Behişt, *VII. Ketibe: Fatih Sultan Mehmed Devri 1451–1481*, ed. and trans. M. I. Yıldırım (Ankara, 2013), 56–66.

32 N. M. El-Cheikh, *Byzantium Viewed by the Arabs* (Cambridge, MA, 2004), 66–8.

33 A. Berger, "Magical Constantinople: Statues, Legends, and the End of Time," *Scandinavian Journal of Byzantine and Modern Greek Studies* 2 (2016): 9–29; Evliya Çelebi, *Evliya Çelebi Seyahatnâmesi*, ed. R. Dankoff, S.A. Kahraman, and Y. Dağlı (Istanbul, 2006), 26–8; H. Carnoy and J. Nicolaïdès, eds., *Folklore de Constantinople* (Paris, 1894), 15–62.

34 Ibn Kemal, *Tevârih*, 78–80; on Byzantine discourses on the marbles, F. Barry, "Walking on Water: Cosmic Floors in Antiquity and the Middle Ages," *ArtB* 89 (2017): 627–56; B. V. Pentcheva, *Hagia Sophia: Sound, Space, and Spirit in Byzantium* (University Park, 2017).

35 G. Necipoğlu, "Connectivity, Mobility, and Mediterranean 'Portable Archaeology': Pashas from the Dalmatian Hinterland as Cultural Mediators," in *Dalmatia and the Mediterranean: Portable Archeology and the Poetics of Influence*, ed. A. Payne (Leiden, 2013), 369–73.

36 Firdevsi, *Süleymânnâme*, vol. 1, T 406, Chester Beatty Library, Dublin, fols. 7r–8v.

37 In addition to histories and chronicles catalogued by Yerasimos, *La fondation*, 252–6, variations of the foundation narrative are found in different writing genres, among them al-Bistami's prognosticative text, *Tercüme-i Miftah-ı Cifrü'l-Cāmi'*, Istanbul University Library, T.6624, fols. 222v–225r; Aşık Mehmed's geography, *Menāzırü'l 'Avālim*, ed. M. Ak (Ankara, 2007), 2: 1054–1078; and Hezarfen Hüseyin's political commentary, *Telhîsü'l-beyân Fî Kavânîn-i Âl-i Osmân*, ed. S. İlgürel (Ankara, 1998), 45–8.

38  Katib Çelebi, *Târih-i Kostantiniyye ve Kayâsire*, ed. İ. Solak (Konya, 2009); Katib Çelebi, *Katip Çelebi'nin Yunan Roma ve Hristiyan tarihi hakkındaki risalesi: (İrşâdü'l-Hayârâ ilâ Târîhi'l- Yûnân ve'r-Rûm ve'n-Nasârâ)*, ed. B. Yurtoğlu (Ankara, 2012).

39  Traces of this "translation movement" with reference to Constantinopolitan history, though obscure, are found also in Çelebi, *Seyahatnâme*, 35.

40  Hezarfen, *Telhîs*, 45–8; Hüseyin Hezarfen, *Tenkīhü't-Tevārīh*, Paris, Bibliothèque nationale de France, Supplément turc 136, 167r–173v. The single prognosticative motif in the latter foundation account is an astrologer warning Constantine that the end of the city would come when ships were transported through land, 165v.

41  "As I did not find reliable (*dürüst*) accounts, I translated from Greek and Latin," Hezarfen, *Tenkīhü't-Tevārīh*, 164v. Eusebios and Kedrenos were among Hezarfen's sources; C. Bekar, "Hezarfen Hüseyin'in Evrensel Tarihinde Yeni Bir Bizans ve Konstantinopolis Algısı," *XVII. Türk Tarih Kongresi, 15–17 Eylül 2014* (Ankara, 2018), 4:17–38.

42  On the *Sûrnâme*, Ç. Kafescioğlu, "Picturing the Square, the Streets, and Denizens of Early Modern Istanbul: Practices of Urban Space and Shifts in Visuality," *Muqarnas*, 37 (2020): 139–77; and S. Tansuğ, *Şenlikname Düzeni* (Istanbul, 2018 [first ed. 1961]).

43  F. Yenişehirlioğlu, "İbrahim Pasha and Sculpture as Subversion in Art," in *Hippodrom/ Atmeydanı: A Stage for Istanbul's History*, ed. B. Pitarakis (Istanbul, 2010), 111–27. On statuary in the Byzantine Hippodrome, S. Bassett, *The Urban Image of Late Antique Constantinople* (Cambridge and New York, 2004), 50–1, 85–9, 212–32.

44  On connections and parallels beyond the core areas of the Renaissance, P. Burke, *The European Renaissance: Centers and Peripheries* (London, 1998).

45  R. G. Ousterhout, *Eastern Medieval Architecture: The Building Traditions of Byzantium and Neighboring Lands* (Oxford, 2019), 679–90.

46  G. Necipoğlu, "The Life of an Imperial Monument: Hagia Sophia after Byzantium," in *Hagia Sophia from the Age of Justinian to the Present*, ed. R. Mark and A. Çakmak (Cambridge, 1992), 195–225.

47  Necipoğlu, "The Life," 205–11.

48  U. Tanyeli, "Sinan ve Antik Dünyanın Mirası," *Uluslararası Mimar Sinan Sempozyumu Bildirileri*, ed. A. Aktaş-Yasa (Ankara, 1996), 87–98; A. Kuran, *Sinan: The Grand Old Master of Ottoman Architecture* (Istanbul, 1987), 86–91.

49  C. Barsanti and A. Guiglia, "*Spolia* in Constantinople's Hagia Sophia from the Age of Justinian to the Ottoman Period: The Phenomenon of Multilayered Reuse," in *Spolia Reincarnated: Afterlives of Objects Materials, and Spaces in Anatolia from Antiquity to the Ottoman Era*, ed. I. Jevtić and S. Yalman (Istanbul, 2018), 113–15.

50  R. G. Ousterhout, "The East, the West, and the Appropriation of the Past in Early Ottoman Architecture," *Gesta* 43 (2004): 165–76; Kafescioglu, *Constantinopolis/Istanbul*, 66–70, 109–25.

51  Necipoğlu, "Connectivity, Mobility," 354–73.

52  Tanyeli, "Antik Dünyanın"; G. Necipoğlu, *The Age of Sinan: Architectural Culture in the Ottoman Empire* (London, 2005), 82–103; Necipoğlu, "Connectivity, Mobility," 345–53.

53  Ü. Rüstem, "*Spolia* and the Invocation of History in Eighteenth-Century Istanbul," in *Spolia Reincarnated*, 292–6.

54  Y. Sezer, "The Architecture of Bibliophilia: Eighteenth-Century Ottoman Libraries" (PhD dissertation, Massachusetts Institute of Technology, 2016), 152–67; Rüstem, "*Spolia*," 303–6.

55  Sezer, "The Architecture," 51–3; K. A. Leal, "The Ottoman State and the Greek Orthodox of Istanbul: Sovereignty and Identity at the Turn of the Eighteenth Century" (PhD dissertation, Harvard University, 2003), 398–445.

# BIBLIOGRAPHY

Abadie-Reynal, C., "Céramique et commerce dans le bassin Égéen du IV<sup>e</sup> au VII<sup>e</sup> siècle," in *Hommes et richesses dans l'Empire Byzantin I. IV–VII siècle*, ed. Abadie-Reynal, G. Dagron, C. Morrisson, and J. Lefort (Paris, 1989), 143–59.

Abadie-Reynal, C., "Les échanges interrégionaux de céramiques en Méditerranée orientale entre le IV<sup>e</sup> et le VIII<sup>e</sup> siècle," in *Handelsgüter und Verkehrswege*, ed. E. Kislinger et al. (Vienna, 2010), 25–44.

Aberth, J. *An Environmental History of the Middle Ages: The Crucible of Nature* (London, 2013).

*Acta et diplomata graeca medii aevi sacra et profana*, 6 vols., ed. F. Milosich and I. Müller (Vienna, 1860–90; reprint Athens, 1961).

Agapitos, P. A., "Teachers, Pupils and Imperial Power in Eleventh-Century Byzantium," in *Pedagogy and Power: Rhetorics of Classical Learning*, ed. Y. L. Too and N. Livingstone (Cambridge, 1998), 170–91.

Agapitos, P. A., "Grammar, Genre and Patronage in the Twelfth Century," *JÖB* 64 (2014): 1–22.

Agapitos, P. A., "'Middle-Class' Ideology of Education and Language and the 'Bookish' Identity of John Tzetzes," in *Ideologies and Identities in the Medieval Byzantine World*, ed. Y. Stouraitis (Edinburgh, forthcoming).

Agathias, *Agathiae Myrinaei Historiarum libri quinque*, ed. B. G. Niebuhr (Bonn, 1828).

Ağir, S., "The Evolution of Grain Policy: The Ottoman Experience," *Journal of Interdisciplinary History* 43 (2013): 571–98.

Agoritsas, D. *Κωνσταντινούπολη. Η πόλη και η κοινωνία της στα χρόνια των πρώτων Παλαιολόγων (1261–1328)* (Thessalonike, 2016).

Ahrweiler, H., *Byzance et la mer: La marine de guerre, la politique et les institutions maritimes de Byzance aux VIIe–XIVe siècles* (Paris, 1966).

Ahrweiler, H. and A. Laiou, *Studies in the Internal Diaspora of the Byzantine Empire* (Washington, DC, 1998).

Ahunbay, M. and Z. Ahunbay, "Recent Work on the Land Walls of Istanbul: Tower 2 to Tower 5," *DOP* 54 (2000): 227–39.

Akışık Karakullukçu, A., "Mehmed II's Patria, Byzas' Palace, and the Topkapı Palace: Ottoman Classicizing in the Fifteenth Century," in *The Post-1204 Byzantine World: Novel Approaches and New Directions*, ed. N. Gaul (Abingdon, forthcoming).

Akkuş, M., ed. *Eyyubî, Menâkıb-ı Sultan Süleyman (Risâle-i Pâdişâh-Nâme)* (Ankara, 1991).

Akyürek, E., "Funeral Ritual in the Parekklesion of the Chora Church," in *Byzantine Constantinople: Monuments, Topography and Everyday Life*, ed. N. Necipoğlu (Leiden, Boston, and Cologne, 2001), 89–104.

Al-Bistami, ʿA.-R., *Tercüme-i Miftāḥ-ı Cifrü ʾl-Cāmiʿ*, T6624, Istanbul University Library.

Alchermes, J., "Spolia in Roman Cities of the Late Empire: Legislative Rationales and Architectural Reuse," *DOP* 48 (1994): 167–78.

Âli, M., *Künhü'l Ahbâr*, 2 vols., ed. M. Hüdai Şentürk (Ankara, 2003).

Alpers, K., *Untersuchungen zu Johannes Sardianos und seinem Kommentar zu den Progymnasmata des Aphthonios* (Braunschweig, 2009).

Altuğ, K., "Planlama İlkeleri ve Yapım Teknikleri Açısından, Tarihi Yarımada'daki Bizans Dönemi Sarnıçları (Notes on planning and construction techniques of Byzantine cisterns in the historical peninsula of Istanbul)," *Restorasyon/Konservasyon* 15 (2012): 3–22.

Altuğ, K., "Reconsidering the Use of Spolia in Byzantine Constantinople," in *Di Bisanzio dirai ciò che è passato, ciò che passa e che sarà: Scritti in onore di Alessandra Guiglia*, ed. S. Pedone and A. Paribeni (Rome, 2018): 3–16.

Anastasius, *Oratio Anastasii in psalmam VI*, PG: 89: 1077–116.

Anderson, B., "Leo III and the Anemodoulion," *BZ* 104 (2011): 41–54.

Anderson, B., "Social Clustering in 5th-c. Constantinople: The Evidence of the Notitia," *JRA* 29 (2016): 494–508.

Anderson, G., "Islamic Spaces and Diplomacy in Constantinople: (Tenth to Thirteenth Centuries C.E.)," *Medieval Encounters* 15 (2009): 86–113.

Ando, C., "The Palladium and the Pentateuch," *Phoenix* 55 (2001): 369–410.

Andrea, A. J., *Contemporary Sources for the Fourth Crusade*, revised edition (Leiden, 2008).

Andrea, A. J. and P. I. Rachlin, "Holy War, Holy Relics, Holy Theft: The Anonymous of Soissons's *De Terra Iherosolimitana* – An Analysis, Edition, and Translation," *Historical Reflections* 18 (1992): 157–75.

Andrea, A. J., ed. and trans., *The Capture of Constantinople: The Hystoria Constantinopolitana of Gunther of Pairis* (Philadelphia, 1997).

Andriollo, L. and S. Métivier, "Quel rôle pour les provinces dans la domination aristocratique au Xie siècle?" in *Autour du premier humanisme byzantin & des Cinq études sur le XIe siècle, quarante ans après Paul Lemerle*, ed. B. Flusin and J.-C. Cheynet (Paris, 2017), 505–29.

Angold, M., "Archons and Dynasts: Local Aristocracies and the Cities of the Later Byzantine Empire," in *The Byzantine Aristocracy: IX to XIII Centuries*, ed. M. Angold (Oxford, 1984), 236–53.

Angold, M., "Inventory of the So-called Palace of Botaneiates," in *The Byzantine Aristocracy: IX to XIII Centuries*, ed. M. Angold (Oxford, 1984), 254–66.

Angold, M., "The Shaping of the Medieval Byzantine City," *ByzF* 10 (1985): 1–38.

Angold, M., *Church and Society in Byzantium under the Comneni* (Cambridge, 1995).

Angold, M., "The Decline of Byzantium Seen through the Eyes of Western Travelers," in *Travel in the Byzantine World*, ed. R. Macrides (Aldershot, 2002), 213–32.

Angold, M., *The Fourth Crusade: Event and Context* (Harlow, 2003).

Angold, M., *Nicholas Mesarites: His Life and Works* (Liverpool, 2017).

*Anonymi Professoris Epistulae*, ed. A. Markopoulos, CFHB 37 (Berlin, 2000).

Antoniadis-Bibicou, H., *Recherches sur les douanes à Byzance: L'"octava," le "kommerkion" et les commerciaires* (Paris, 1963).

Arioğlu, E. and K. Anadol, "Galata Tower Restoration Project," *International Association for Bridge and Structural Engineering Congress Report* 11 (1980): 951–6.

Armstrong, P. and M. Trapp, eds., *Authority in Byzantium* (Farnham, 2013).

Arrignon, J.-P., "Un pèlerin russe à Constantinople: Antoine de Novgorod," in *Toutes les routes mènent à Byzance*, *Médiévales* 12(1987): 33–41.

Asal, R., "Commerce in Istanbul and the Port of Theodosius," in *Istanbul: 8000 Years Brought to Daylight – Marmaray, Metro, Sultanahmet Excavations*, ed. A. Karamani-Pekin and S. Kangal (Istanbul, 2007), 180–9.

Asgari, N., "The Proconnesian Production of Architectural Elements in Late Antiquity, Based on the Evidence from the Marble Quarries," in *Constantinople and Its Hinterland*, ed. C. Mango and G. Dagron (Aldershot, 1995), 263–88.

Aşık Mehmed, *Menāzırü'l ʿAvālim*, ed. M. Ak (Ankara, 2007).

Asutay-Effenberger, N., "'Muchrutas': Der seldschukische Palastpavillon im Großen Palast von Konstantinopel," *Byzantion* 74 (2004): 313–29.

Asutay-Effenberger, N., *Die Landmauer von Konstantinopel-İstanbul: Historisch- topographische und baugeschichtliche Untersuchungen* (Berlin and Boston, 2007).

Asutay-Effenberger, N., "Spuren seldschukischen Lebensstils in der imperialen Architektur Konstantinopels im 12. Jahrhundert," in *Grenzgänge im östlichen Mittelmeerraum*, ed. U. Koenen and M. Müller-Wiener (Wiesbaden, 2008), 169–87.

Asutay-Effenberger, N., "The Blachernai Palace and Its Defense," in *Cities and Citadels in Turkey from the Iron Age to the Seljuks*, ed. S. Redford and N. Ergin (Leuven, 2013), 253–76.

Asutay-Effenberger, N. and A. Effenberger, *Die Porhyrsarkophage der oströmischen Kaiser* (Wiesbaden, 2006).

Atik, Ş., "Late Roman/Early Byzantine Glass from the Marmaray Rescue Excavations at Yenikapı in Istanbul," in *Late Antique/Early Byzantine Glass in the Eastern Mediterranean*, ed. E. Laflı (Izmir, 2009), 1–16.

Attaliates, M., *Historia*, ed. I. Bekker (Bonn, 1853).

Attaliates, M. *Michaelis Attaliate Historia*, ed. I. Bekker (Bonn, 1853).

Aubineau, M., "Zoticos de Constantinople, nouricier des pauvres et serviteur des lépreux," *AB* 93 (1975): 67–108.

Auzépy, M.-F., "La place des moines à Nicée II (787)," *Byzantion* 58 (1988): 5–21.

Auzépy, M.-F., *La Vie d'Étienne le Jeune par Étienne le Diacre* (Aldershot, 1997).

Auzépy, M.-F. and J.-P. Grélois, eds. *Byzance retrouvée: Érudits et voyageurs français (XVIᵉ-XVIIᵉ siècles)* (Paris, 2001).

Avram, A. and C. P. Jones, "An Actor from Byzantium in a New Epigram from Tomis," *ZPapEpig* 178 (2011): 126–34.

Aydingün, S. G., "Some Remarkable Prehistoric Finds at Istanbul-Kucukcekmece," in *SOMA 2008: Proceedings of the XII Symposium in Mediterranean Archaeology, Eastern Mediterranean University, Famagusta, North Cyprus, 5–8 March, 2008*, ed. H. Oniz (2009), 154–7.

Bacci, M., "Relics of the Pharos Chapel: A View from the Latin West," in *Восточнохристианские Реликвии, Eastern Christian Relics*, ed. A. Lidov (Moscow, 2003), 234–45.

Bakirzis, C., "The Urban Continuity and Size of Late Byzantine Thessaloniki," *DOP* 57 (2003): 35–64.

Balard, M., "L'organisation des colonies étrangères dans l'empire byzantin (XIIᵉ–XVᵉ siècle)," in *Hommes et richesses dans l'Empire byzantine, II. VIIIᵉ–XVᵉ siècle*, ed. V. Kravari, J. Lefort, and C. Morrisson (Paris, 1991), 261–76.

Balard, M., "Un marché à prendre: l'invasion occidentale," in *Constantinople 1054–1261: tête de la chrétienté, proie des latins, capitale grecque* ed. A. Ducellier and M. Balard (Paris, 1996), 184–201.

Balard, M. and A. Ducellier, eds. *Constantinople 1054–1261, tête de la chrétienté ; proie des latins; capitale grecque* (Paris, 1996).

Baldini Lippolis, I. "Private Space in Late Antique Cities: Laws and Building Procedures," in *Housing in Late Antiquity: From Palaces to Shops*, ed. L. Lavan, L. Özgenel, and A. Sarantis (Leiden and Boston, 2007), 197–238.

Baldovin, J. F., *The Urban Character of Christian Worship: The Origins, Development, and Meaning of Stational Liturgy* (Rome, 1987).

Barber, C. and D. Jenkins, eds., *Medieval Greek Commentaries on the Nicomachean Ethics* (Leiden, 2009).

Bardill, J., "The Palace of Lausus and Nearby Monuments in Constantinople," *AJA* 101 (1997): 67–95.

Bardill, J., "The Church of Sts. Sergius and Bacchus in Constantinople and the Monophysite Refugees," *DOP* 54 (2000): 1–11.

Bardill, J., *Brickstamps of Constantinople*, 2 vols. (Oxford, 2004).

Bardill, J., "A New Temple for Byzantium: Anicia Juliana, King Solomon, and the Gilded Ceiling of the Church of St. Polyeuktos in Constantinople," in *Social and Political Life in Late Antiquity*, ed. W. Bowden et al. (Leiden and Boston, 2006), 339–70.

Bardill, J., "Visualizing the Great Palace of the Byzantine Emperors at Constantinople: Archaeology, Text, and Topography," in *Visualisierungen von Herrschaft: Frühmittelalterliche Residenzen – Gestalt und Zeremoniell*, ed. F. A. Bauer (Istanbul, 2006), 5–45.

Bardill, J., "Archaeologists and Excavations in the Hippodrome," in *Hippodrome/Atmeydanı*, 2 vols., ed. B. Pitarakis (Istanbul, 2010), vol. 1, 83–90.

Bardill, J., "The Architecture and Archaeology of the Hippodrome in Constantinople," in *Hippodrom/Atmeydanı: İstanbul'un Tarih Sahnesi = Hippodrome/Atmeydani: A Stage for Istanbul's History*, 2 vols., ed. B. Pitarakis (Istanbul, 2010)1: 91–148.

Bardill, J., "Monuments and Decoration of the Hippodrome in Constantinople," in *Hippodrom/Atmeydanı: İstanbul'un Tarih Sahnesi = Hippodrome/Atmeydani: A Stage for Istanbul's History*, 2 vols., ed. B. Pitarakis (Istanbul, 2010), 1:149–84.

Bardill, J., "Église Saint-Polyeucte à Constantinople: Nouvelle solution pour l'énigme de sa reconstruction," in *Architecture paléochrétienne*, ed. J.-M. Spieser (Gollion, 2011), 77–103.

Bardill, J., *Constantine, Divine Emperor of the Christian Golden Age* (Cambridge, 2012).

Barkan, L., *Unearthing the Past: Archaeology and Aesthetics in the Making of Renaissance Culture* (New Haven, 1999).

Barry, F., "Walking on Water: Cosmic Floors in Antiquity and the Middle Ages," *ArtB* 89 (2017): 627–56.

Barsanti, C., "Note archeologiche su Bisanzio romana," in *Costantinopoli e l'arte delle province orientali*, ed. F. De Maffei, C. Barsanti, and A. Guiglia Guidobaldi (Rome, 1990), 11–72.

Barsanti, C., "Costantinopoli: testimonianze archeologiche di età costantiniana," in *Costantino il grande dall' antichità all'umanesimo: colloquio sul Cristianesimo nel mondo antico, Macerata 18–20 Dicembre 1990*, ed. G. Bonamente and F. Fusco (Macerata, 1992), 115–50.

Barsanti, C., "Le chiese del Grande Palazzo di Costantinopoli," in *Medioevo: La chiesa e il palazzo*, ed. A. C. Quintavalle (Milan, 2007), 87–100.

Barsanti, C., "Un inedito disegno delle rovine del complesso costantinopolitano del "Boukoléon," in *Forme e storia: scritti di arte medievale e moderna per Francesco Gandolfo*, ed. W. Angelelli and F. Pomarici (Rome, 2011), 45–58.

Barsanti, C. and A. Guiglia, "The Byzantine Sculpture of the Ayasofya Müzesi, Istanbul: Ten Years of Researches (1999–2009)," *Ayasofya Müzesi Yıllığı* 13 (2010): 134–54.

Barsanti, C. and A. Guiglia, *The Sculptures of the Ayasofya Müsesi in Istanbul, a Short Guide* (Istanbul, 2010).

Barsanti, C. and A. Guiglia, "*Spolia* in Constantinople's Hagia Sophia from the Age of Justinian to the Ottoman Period: The Phenomenon of Multilayered Reuse," in *Spolia Reincarnated: Afterlives of Objects Materials, and Spaces in Anatolia from Antiquity to the Ottoman Era*, ed. I. Jevtić and S. Yalman (Istanbul, 2018), 97–124.

Bartolfus de Nangeio, "Gesta Francorum Expugnantium Iherusalem," *RHC HOcc* 3 (1866): 490–543.

Bartusis, M. C., *The Late Byzantine Army: Arms and Society, 1204–1453* (Philadelphia, 1992).

Basilakes, N. *Nicephori Basilacae orationes et epistolae*, ed. A. Garzya (Leipzig, 1984).

*Basilicorum Libri LX*, ed. H. J. Scheltema, N. van der Wal and D. Holwerda, 17 vols., ed. H. J. Scheltema, N. van der Wal and D. Holwerda (Groningen, 1955–88).

Bassett, S., *The Urban Image of Late Antique Constantinople* (Cambridge and New York, 2004).

Bauer, F. A., *Stadt, Platz und Denkmal in der Spätantike: Untersuchungen zur Ausstattung des öffentlichen Raums in den spätantiken Städten Rom, Konstantinopel und Ephesos* (Mainz, 1996).

Bauer, F. A., "Urban Space and Ritual: Constantinople in Late Antiquity," *ActaIRNorv* 15 (2001): 27–59.

Bauer, F. A., ed., *Visualisierung von Herrschaft: Frühmittelalterliche Residenzen- Gestalt und Zeremoniell* (Istanbul, 2006).

Baynes, N., "The Supernatural Defenders of Constantinople," in *Byzantine Studies and Other Essays* (London, 1960), 248–60 (= "The Supernatural Defenders of Constantinople," *AB* 67 (1949): 165–77).

Beck, H.-G., *Byzantinisches Gefolgschaftswesen* (Munich, 1965).

Beck, H.-G., *Kirche und theologische Literatur im byzantinischen Reich* (Munich, 1977).

Beck, H.-G., ed., *Studien zur Frühgeschichte Konstantinopels* (Munich, 1973).

Bekar, C., "Hezarfen Hüseyin'in Evrensel Tarihinde Yeni Bir Bizans ve Konstantinopolis Algısı," *XVII. Türk Tarih Kongresi, 15–17 Eylül 2014* (Ankara, 2018), 4: 17–38.

Belke, K., "Tore nach Kleinasien: die Konstantinopel gegenüberliegenden Häfen Chalkedon, Chrysopolis, Hiereia und Eutropiu Limani," in *Die byzantinischen Häfen Konstantinopels*, ed. F. Daim (Mainz, 2016), 161–71.

Bell, P. N., *Social Conflict in the Age of Justinian* (Oxford, 2013).

Belting, H., "Skulptur aus der Zeit um 1300 in Konstantinopel," *MünchJb* 23 (1972): 63–100.

Belting, H., C. Mango, and D. Mouriki, *The Mosaics and Frescoes of St. Mary Pammakaristos (Fethiye Camii) at Istanbul* (Washington, DC, 1978).

Belting, H. and R. Naumann, *Die Euphemia-Kirche am Hippodrom zu Istanbul und ihre Fresken* (Berlin, 1966).

Benjamin of Tudela, *The Itinerary of Benjamin of Tudela, Critical Text, Translation and Commentary*, ed. M. N. Adler (London, 1907).

Benjamin of Tudela, *The Itinerary of Benjamin of Tudela* (Malibu, 1983).

Bennett, D., *Medicine and Pharmacy in Byzantine Hospitals* (Leiden, 2017).

Berg, B. van den, "Homer and the Good Ruler in the 'Age of Rhetoric': Eustathios of Thessalonike on Excellent Oratory," in *Homer and the Good Ruler in Antiquity and Beyond*, ed. J. J. H. Klooster and B. van den Berg (Leiden, 2018), 219–38.

Berger, A., "Die Reliquien der heiligen Euphemia und ihre erste Translation nach Konstantinopel," *Hellenika* 39 (1988): 311–22.

Berger, A., *Untersuchungen zu den Patria Konstantinupoleos* (Bonn, 1988).

Berger, A., "Die Senate von Konstantinopel," *Boreas* 18 (1995): 131–42.

Berger, A., "Zur Topographie der Ufergegend am Goldenen Horn in der byzantinischen Zeit," *IstMitt* 45 (1995): 149–65.

Berger, A., "Tauros e Sigma: Due piazze di Costantinopoli," in *Bisanzio e l'Occidente: Arte, archeologia, storia: Studi in onore di Fernanda de' Maffei* ed. C. Barsanti (Rome, 1996), 17–31.

Berger, A., "Das Chalkun Tetrapylon und Parastaseis, Kapitel 57," *BZ* 90 (1997): 7–12.

Berger, A., "Regionen und Straßen im frühen Konstantinopel," *IstMitt* 47 (1997): 349–414.

Berger, A., "Streets and Public Spaces in Constantinople," *DOP* 54 (2000): 161–72.

Berger, A., "Imperial and Ecclesiastical Processions in Constantinople," in *Byzantine Constantinople: Monuments, Topography and Everyday Life*, ed. N. Necipoğlu (Leiden, 2001), 73–87.

Berger, A., "Sightseeing in Constantinople: Arab Travelers, c. 900–1300," in *Travel in the Byzantine World*, ed. R. Macrides (Aldershot and Burlington, 2002), 179–91.

Berger, A., *Konstantinopel: Geschichte, Topographie, Religion* (Stuttgart 2011).

Berger, A., "The Byzantine Court as a Physical Space", in *The Byzantine Court: Source of Power and Culture*, ed. A. Ödekan E. Akyürek, and N. Necipoğlu (Istanbul, 2013), 3–12.

Berger, A., "Mokios und Konstantin der Große: Zu den Anfängen des Märtyrerkults in Konstantinopel," in *Antecessor: Festschrift für Spyros N. Troianos zum 80. Geburtstag*, ed. V. A. Leontaritou, K. A. Bourdara, and E. S. Papagianni (Athens, 2013), 165–85.

Berger, A., "Städtische Eliten im byzantinischen Raum," in *Städte im lateinischen Westen und im griechischen Osten zwischen Spätantike und Früher Neuzeit*, ed. E. Gruber, M. Popović, M. Scheutz, and H. Weigl (Vienna, 2016), 165–75.

Berger, A., "Magical Constantinople: Statues, Legends, and the End of Time," *Scandinavian Journal of Byzantine and Modern Greek Studies*, 2 (2016): 9–29.

Berger, A., *The Byzantine Neighborhood: Urban Space and Political Action*, ed. B. Anderson and F. Kondyli, 2022.

Berger, A., ed. and trans. *Accounts of Medieval Constantinople, the Patria* (Washington, DC, 2013).

Bergmann, B., "Introduction," in *The Art of Ancient Spectacle*, ed. B. Bergmann and C. Kondoleon (Washington, DC, 1999), 9–35.

Bernard, F., *Writing and Reading Secular Poetry in Byzantium, 1025–1081* (Oxford, 2014).

Bernard, F., "Educational Networks in the Letters of Michael Psellos," in *The Letters of Psellos*, ed. M. Lauxtermann and M. Jeffreys (Oxford, 2017), 13–41.

Bertolini, O., "Per la storia delle diaconie romane nell'alto medioevo sino alla fine del secolo VIII," *Archvio della Società Romana di Storia Patria* 70 (1947): 1–146.

Bertolotto, G., ed. "Nuova Serie di documenti sulle relazioni di Genova con l'Impero bizantino," *Atti della Societa Ligure di Storia Patria* 28 (1898): 343–570.

Bessi, B., "Cristoforo Buondelmonti: Greek Antiquities in Florentine Humanism," *The Historical Review* 9 (2012): 63–76.

Bican Yazıcıoğlu, A., *Dürr-i Meknun = Saklı Inciler*, ed. N. Sakaoğlu (Istanbul, 1999).

Bintliff, J. L., "The Paradoxes of Late Antiquity: A Thermodynamic Solution," *AntTard* 20 (2012): 69–73.

Bisaha, N., *Creating East and West: Renaissance Humanists and the Ottoman Turks* (Philadelphia, 2006).

Bitlisi, I., *Heşt Behişt, VII. Ketibe: Fatih Sultan Mehmed Devri 1451–1481*, ed. and trans. M. I. Yıldırım (Ankara, 2013).

Blöndal, S., translated, revised, and rewritten by B. S. Benedikz, *The Varangians of Byzantium*, trans., revised, and rewritten by B. S. Benedikz (Cambridge, 1978).

Boeck, E., "The Power of Amusement and the Amusement of Power: The Princely Frescoes of St Sophia, Kiev, and Their Connections to the Byzantine World," in *Greek Laughter and Tears: Antiquity and After*, ed. M. Alexiou and D. Cairns (Edinburgh, 2017), 243–62.

Bolognesi Recchi-Franceschini, E. "The Great Palace of Constantinople," in *Neue Forschungen und Restaurierungen im byzantinische Kaiserpalast von Istanbul*, ed. W. Jobst, R. Kastler, and V. Scheibelreiter (Vienna, 1999), 9–16.

Bolognesi Recchi-Franceschini, E., *Il Gran Palazzo degli Imperatori di Bisanzio* (Istanbul, 2000).

Bolognesi Recchi-Franceschini, E., M. König, and E. Riemer, eds., *Palatia: Kaiserpaläste in Konstantinopel, Ravenna und Trier* (Trier, 2003).

Bond, S. E., "Mortuary Workers, the Church, and the Funeral Trade in Late Antiquity," *JLA* 6 (2013): 135–51.

Bonfil, R., et al., eds., *Jews in Byzantium: Dialectics of Minority and Majority Cultures* (Leiden and Boston, 2012).

Bornert, R., *Les commentaires byzantins de la divine liturgie du VIIe au XVe siècle* (Paris, 1966).

Borsari, S., "Pisani a Bisanzio nel XII secolo," *Bollettino Storico Pisano* 60 (1991): 59–75.

Boulgaris, E., Ἰωσὴφ μοναχοῦ τοῦ Βρυεννίου τὰ εὑρεθέντα, vol. 2 (Leipzig, 1768).

Bouras, C., "The Impact of Frankish Architecture on Thirteenth-Century Byzantine Architecture," in *The Crusades from the Perspective of Byzantium and the Muslim World*, ed. A. E. Laiou and R. P. Mottahedeh (Washington, DC, 2001), 247–62.

Bourdieu, P., *Distinction* (London, 1984).

Bourne, M., "Francesco II Gonzaga and Maps as Palace Decoration in Renaissance Mantua," *Imago Mundi* 51 (1999): 51–82.

Bréhier, L. *L'Église et l'Orient au Moyen Age: Les Croisades* (Paris, 1928).

Brett, G., W. J. Macaulay, and R. B. K. Stevenson, *The Great Palace of the Byzantine Emperors: First Report* (Oxford, 1947).

Brock, S., "A Medieval Armenian Pilgrim's Description of Constantinople," *REArm* 4 (1967): 81–102.

Brock, S., "Rabban Ṣauma à Constantinople," in *Mémorial Mgr Gabriel Khouri-Sarkis (1898–1968)* (Louvain, 1969), 245–53.

Brown, P., "The Rise and Function of the Holy Man in Late Antiquity," *JRS* 61 (1971): 80–101.

Brown, P., *Poverty and Leadership in the Late Roman Empire* (Hanover and London, 2002).

Browning, R., "The Correspondence of a Tenth-Century Byzantine Scholar," *Byzantion* 24 (1954): 397–452.

Browning, R., "The Patriarchal School at Constantinople in the Twelfth Century," *Byzantion* 32 (1962): 167–201.

Browning, R., "The Patriarchal School at Constantinople in the Twelfth Century," *Byzantion* 33 (1963): 11–40.

Browning, R. "Byzantine Scholarship," *Past and Present* 28 (1968): 3–22.

Browning, R., "Enlightenment and Repression in Byzantine Scholarship in the Eleventh and Twelfth Centuries," *Past and Present* 69 (1975): 3–23.

Browning, R., "Homer in Byzantium," *Viator* 8 (1975): 1–5.

Browning, R., "Teachers," in *The Byzantines*, ed. G. Cavallo (Chicago, 1997), 105–6.

Brubaker, L. and K. Linardou, eds., *Eat, Drink, and Be Merry (Luke 12:19): Food and Wine in Byzantium* (Aldershot and Burlington, 2007).

Brummett, P., *Mapping the Ottomans: Sovereignty, Territory, and Identity in the Early Modern Mediterranean* (Cambridge, 2015).

Buchwald, H., "Lascarid Architecture," *JÖB* 28 (1979): 261–96.

Buondelmonti, C., *Description des îles de l'Archipel par Christophe Buondelmonti*, trans. E. Legrand (Paris, 1897).

Buondelmonti, C., *Descriptio insulae Cretae*, ed. M.-A. van Spitael (Herakleion, 1981).

Buondelmonti, C., *Liber Insularum archipelagi*, ed. I. Siebert and M. Plassmann (Wiesbaden, 2005).

Buondelmonti, C., *Description of the Aegean and Other Islands*, ed. and trans. E. Edson (New York, 2018).

Bühl, G., *Constantinopolis und Roma: Stadtpersonifikationen der Spätantike* (Kilchberg and Zurich, 1995).

Burke, P., *The European Renaissance: Centers and Peripheries* (London, 1998).

Bury, J. B., *The Imperial Administrative System in the Ninth Century: With a Revised Text of the Kletorologion of Philotheos* (London, 1911; reprint, New York, 1958).

Çağaptay, S., "How Western Is It? The Palace at Nymphaion and Its Architecture," in *Change in the Byzantine World in the Twelfth and Thirteenth Centuries*, ed. E. Akyürek, N. Necipoğlu, and A. Ödekan (Istanbul, 2010), 357–62.

Cameron, A., *Porphyrius the Charioteer* (Oxford, 1973).

Cameron, A., *Circus Factions: Blues and Greens at Rome and Byzantium* (Oxford, 1976).

Cameron, A., *Procopius and the Sixth Century* (London, 1985).

Cameron, A., 'Old and New Rome, Roman Studies in Sixth-Century Constantinople', in *Transformations of Late Antiquity*, ed. P. Rousseau and M. Papoutsakis (Aldershot, 2009), 15–36.

Cameron, A. and J. Herrin, eds., *Constantinople in the Early Eighth Century: The Parastaseis Syntomai Chronikai* (Leiden, 1984).

Cameron, Av., *Arguing It Out* (Budapest, 2016).

Caner, D., *Wandering, Begging Monks: Spiritual Authority and the Promotion of Monasticism in Late Antiquity* (Berkeley, 2002).

Caner, D., "Charitable Ministrations (Diakoniai), Monasticism, and the Social Aesthetic of Sixth-Century Byzantium," in *Charity and Giving in Monotheistic Religions*, ed. M. Frenkel and Y. Lev (Berlin and New York, 2009), 45–73.

Cantino-Wataghin, G. and J.-P. Caillet, eds., *Le voyage dans l'Antiquité Tardive: réalités et images, AntTard* 24 (2016).

Carile, A., "Funerali e sepolture imperiali a Costantinopoli fra realtà e leggenda," *Nea Rhome, rivista di ricerche bizantinistiche* 9 (2012): 43–57.

Carnoy, H. and J. Nicolaïdès, eds., *Folklore de Constantinople* (Paris, 1894).

Carr, A.-M., "Icons and the Object of Pilgrimage in Middle Byzantine Constantinople," *DOP* 56 (2002): 75–92.

Carrié, J.-M., "Were Late Roman and Byzantine Economies Market Economies? A Comparative Look at Historiography," in *Trade and Markets in Byzantium*, ed. C. Morrisson (Washington, DC, 2012), 13–26.

Carte di Verona, *Le carte dei lebbrosi di Verona tra XII e XIII secolo*, ed. A. Rossi Saccomani with introduction by G. De Sandra Gasparini (Padua, 1989), 146–50.

Casale, G., "Did Alexander the Great Discover America? Debating Space and Time in Renaissance Istanbul," *Renaissance Quarterly* 72 (2019): 863–909.

Caseau, B., "L'exercise de la charité à Byzance d'après les sceaux et les tessères (Ve–XIIe siècles)," *TM* 21.1 (2017): 31–52.

Cecaumenus, *Strategikon*, ed. M. D. Spadaro in "Raccomandazioni e consigli di un galantuomo," *Ελληνικά* 2 (1998): 44–242.

Çeçen, K., *The Longest Roman Water Supply Line* (Istanbul, 1996).

Çeçen, K., *Sinan's Water Supply System in Istanbul* (Istanbul, 1996).

Cerasi, M., "The Urban and Architectural Evolution of the Istanbul Divanyolu: Urban Aesthetics and Ideology in Ottoman Town Planning," *Muqarnas* 22 (2005): 204–6.

Cevizli, A. G., "Mehmed II, Malatesta, and Matteo De' Pasti," *Renaissance Studies* 31 (2017): 43–65.

Charanis, P., "The Monk as an Element in Byzantine Society," *DOP* 25 (1971): 61–84.

Chastagnol, A., *La Préfecture Urbaine à Rome Sous le Bas-Empire* (Paris, 1960).

Chatzilazarou, D., "Le centre monumental de Constantinople, espace de synthèse des traditions urbaines gréco-romaines," in *Constantinople réelle et imaginaire: autour de l'œuvre de Gilbert Dagron* (*TM* 21.1), ed. C. Morrisson and J.-P. Sodini (Paris, 2018), 35–54.

Cheynet, J.-C., "L'Éparque: Correctifs et Additifs," *BSl* 45 (1984), 50–4.

Chitwood, Z., *Byzantine Legal Culture and the Roman Legal Tradition, 867–1056* (Cambridge, 2017).

Choniates, M., *Michael Akominatou tou Choniatou ta sozomena*, 2 vols., ed. S. Lampros (Athens, 1879–80, reprint Groningen, 1968).

Choniates, N., *Nicetae Choniatae, Historia*, ed. I. A. van Dieten (Berlin, 1975).

Christopher of Mytilene and John Mauropus, *Poems of Christopher of Mytilene and John Mauropus*, ed. F. Bernard and C. Livanos (Cambridge, MA, 2018).

Christophilopoulou, A., *Βυζαντινὴ Ἱστορία*, 2nd ed., 3 vols. (Thessalonike, 1992).

*Chronicon Paschale*, ed. L. Dindorf (Bonn, 1832).

Chrysoloras, M., Epistolae, *PG* 156 (1866): 24–60.

Chrysostomides, J., "Venetian Commercial Privileges under the Palaeologi," *Studi veneziani* 12 (1970): 267–356.

Ciggaar, K. N., "Une description anonyme de Constantinople du XIIe siècle," *REB* 31 (1973): 335–54.

Ciggaar, K. N., "Description de Constantinople par un pèlerin anglaise," *REB* 34 (1976): 211–68.

Ciggaar, K. N., "Une description de Constantinople dans le *Tarragonensis 55*," *REB* 53 (1995): 117–40.

Ciggaar, K. N., *Western Travellers to Constantinople: The West and Byzantium, 962–1204 – Cultural and Political Relations* (Leiden, New York, and Cologne, 1996).

Ciggaar, K., "Bilingual Word Lists and Phrase Lists: For Teaching or for Travelling?" in *Travel in the Byzantine World*, ed. R. Macrides (Aldershot and Burlington, 2002), 165–78.

Ciggaar, K. N., "Visitors from North-Western Europe to Byzantium – Vernacular Sources: Problems and Perspectives," *ProcBrAc* 132 (2007): 123–55.

Clark, L. R. and N. Um, "The Art of Embassy: Situating Objects and Images in the Early Modern Diplomatic Encounter," *Journal of Early Modern History* 20 (2016): 2–18.

Clavijo, R. G., *Clavijo Embassy to Tamerlane 1403–1406*, trans. G. le Strange (New York and London, 1928) (= Clavijo, *Embassy to Tamerlane* (Oxon, 2005)).

Clavijo, R. G., *Embajada a Tamorlan: estudio y edición de un manuscrito del siglo XV*, ed. F. Lopez Estrada (Madrid, 1943).

Clines, R. J., *Ancient Others: Barbarians in the Italian Renaissance* (forthcoming).

Congdon, E. A., "Imperial Commemoration and Ritual in the Monastery of Christ Pantokrator," *RÉB* 54 (1996): 161–99.

Constantelos, D. J., *Byzantine Philanthropy and Social Welfare*, 2nd ed. (New Rochelle, 1991).

Constantelos, D. J., *Poverty, Society and Philanthropy in the Late Medieval Greek World* (New Rochelle, 1992).

Constantine Porphyrogennetos, *De ceremoniis aulae byzantinae*, ed. J. J. Reiske, 2 vols. (Bonn, 1829–30).

Constantine Porphyrogennetos, *Le livre des cérémonies*, ed. A. Vogt, 2 vols. (Paris, 1935–9).

Constantine Porphyrogennetos, *Three Treatises of Imperial Military Expeditions*, ed. J. F. Haldon (Vienna, 1990).

Constantine Porphyrogennetos, *Book of Ceremonies*, ed. J. J. Reiske (Bonn, 1829), reproduced with English translation and same pagination by A. Moffatt and M. Tall, 2 vols. (Canberra, 2012).

Constantinides, C. N., *Higher Education in Byzantium in the Thirteenth and Early Fourteenth Centuries (1204–ca. 1310)* (Nicosia, 1982).

Cracco Ruggini, L., "Collegium e corpus: la politica economica nella legislazione e nella prassi," in *Istituzioni giuridiche e realtà politiche nel tardo impero (III–IV sec. d. c)*, ed. G. G. Archi (Milan, 1976), 63–94.

Cribiore, R., *The School of Libanius* (Princeton, 2007).

Croke, B., *Count Marcellinus and his Chronicle* (Oxford, 2001).

Croke, B., "Justinian's Constantinople," in *The Cambridge Companion to the Age of Justinian*, ed. M. Maas (Cambridge, 2005), 60–86.

Croke, B., "Leo I and the Palace Guard," *Byzantion* 75 (2005): 117–51.

Croke, B., "Justinian, Theodora, and the Church of Saints Sergius and Bacchus," *DOP* 60 (2006): 25–63.

Croke, B., "Uncovering Byzantium's Historiographical Audience," in *History as Literature in Byzantium*, ed. R. Macrides (Farnham and Burlington, 2010), 25–53.

Croke, B., "Reinventing Constantinople: Theodosius I's Imprint on the Imperial City," in *From the Tetrarchs to the Theodosians: Later Roman History and Culture, 284–350*, ed. S. McGill, C. Sogno, and E. Watts (Cambridge, 2010), 241–64.

Crow, J. "The Long Walls of Thrace," in *Constantinople and Its Hinterland*, ed. C. Mango and G. Dagron (Aldershot, 1995), 109–24.

Crow, J., "The Infrastructure of a Great City: Earth, Walls and Water in Late Antique Constantinople," in *Technology in Transition A.D. 300–650*, ed. L. Lavan, E. Zanini, and A. Sarantis (Leiden and Boston, 2007), 251–85.

Crow, J., "Water and Late Antique Constantinople," in *Two Romes: Rome and Constantinople in Late Antiquity*, ed. L. Grig and G. Kelly (Oxford, 2012), 116–35.

Crow, J., "Blessing or Security? Understanding the Christian Symbols of a Monumental Aqueduct Bridge in the Hinterland of Late Antique Constantinople," in *Graphic Signs of Power and Faith in Late Antiquity and the Early Middle Ages: Essays on Early Graphicacy*, ed. I. Garipzanov, C. Goodson, and H. Maguire (Turnhout, 2017), 147–74.

Crow, J., "Recent Research on the Anastasian Wall in Thrace and Late Antique Linear Barriers around the Black Sea," in *Roman Frontier Studies 2009*, ed. N. Hodgson, P. Bidwell, and J. Schachtmann (Oxford, 2017), 131–8.

Crow, J., "The Imagined Water Supply of Constantinople, New Approaches," *TM* 22.1 (2018): 211–36.

Crow, J., "The Wonderful Works, a History of Bridges on the Thracian Aqueducts," in *Crossing Bridges in Byzantium and Beyond*, ed. G. Fingarova and A. Külzer (forthcoming).

Crow, J., J. Bardill, and R. Bayliss, *The Water Supply of Byzantine Constantinople* (London, 2008).

Cullhed, E., "The Blind Bard and 'I': Homeric Biography and Authorial Personas in the Twelfth Century," *BMGS* 38 (2014): 49–67.

Ćurčić, S., "Design and Structural Innovation in Byzantine Architecture before Hagia Sophia," in *Hagia Sophia from the Age of Justinian to the Present*, ed. R. Mark and A. Ş. Çakmak (Cambridge, 1992), 16–38.

Ćurčić, S., *Architecture in the Balkans from Diocletian to Süleyman the Magnificent* (New Haven, 2010).

Ćurčić, S., "Georgios Palaiologos Kantakouzenos (1390–c. 1459): An Unknown Late Byzantine Architect," in Ἥρως Κτίστης: Μνήμη Χαράλαμπου Μπούρα, ed. M. Korres et al. (Athens, 2018), 139–52.

Cutler, A., "From Loot to Scholarship: Changing Modes in the Italian Response to Byzantine Artifacts, 1200–1750," *DOP* 49 (1995): 237–67.

Cutler, A. and P. Niewöhner, "Towards a History of Byzantine Ivory Carving from the Late Sixth to the Late Ninth Century," in *Mélanges Catherine Jolivet-Lévy*, ed. B. Pitarakis et al. (Paris, 2016), 89–108.

Daffara, D., "L'edificio di Gülhane a Costantinopoli," *Thiasos* 5 (2016): 69–88.

Dagron, G., "Les moines et la ville: Le monachisme à Constantinople jusqu'au concile de Chalcédoine (451)," *TM* 4 (1970): 227–76.

Dagron, G., "Le christianisme dans la ville," *DOP* 31 (1977): 1–25.

Dagron, G., *Naissance d'une capitale: Constantinople et ses institutions, 330–451* (Paris, 1974; 2nd ed. Paris, 1984).

Dagron, G., *Constantinople imaginaire: Études sur le recueil des Patria* (Paris, 1984).

Dagron, G., "Constantinople: Les sanctuaires et l'organisation de la vie religieuse," in *Actes du XIe congrès international d'archéologie chrétienne* (Paris, 1989), 1069–1085.

Dagron, G., "Poissons, pêcheurs et poissonniers de Constantinople," in *Constantinople and Its Hinterland*, ed. C. Mango and G. Dagron (Aldershot, 1995), 57–73.

Dagron, G., "L'organisation et le déroulement des courses d'après le *Livre de Cérémonies*," *TM* 13 (2000): 3–200.

Dagron, G., "The Urban Economy, Seventh–Twelfth Centuries," in *EHB* 2: 393–461.

Dagron, G. *Emperor and Priest: The Imperial Office in Byzantium* (Cambridge, 2003).

Dagron, G. "From One Rome to the Other," in *Hippodrome/Atmeydanı*, 2 vols., ed. B. Pitarakis (Istanbul, 2010), 1: 29–35.

Dagron, G., *L'hippodrome de Constantinople: Jeux, peuple et politique* (Paris, 2011)

Dagron, G., "L'organisation et le déroulement des courses d'aprés le *Livre de Cérémonies*", *TM* 13 (2000): 3–200

Dagron, G. *Emperor and Priest: The Imperial Office in Byzantium* (Cambridge, 2003).

Dagron, G. "From One Rome to the Other," in *Hippodrome/Atmeydani*, 2 vols., ed. B. Pitarakis (Istanbul, 2010), vol. 1, 29–35.

Dalby, A., "Some Byzantine Aromatics," in *Eat Drink and Be Merry (Luke 12:19): Food and Wine in Byzantium*, ed. L. Brubaker and K. Linardou (Aldershot and Burlington, 2007), 51–7.

Dalché, G., "The Reception of Ptolemy's Geography," in *The History of Cartography*, 3 vols., ed. D. Woodward (Chicago, 2007), 3: 285–364.

Dalgiç, Ö., "Early Floor Mosaics in Istanbul," in *Mosaics of Anatolia*, ed. G. Sözen (Istanbul, 2011), 101–12.

Dalgiç, Ö., "The Triumph of Dionysus in Constantinople: A Late Fifth-Century Century Mosaic in Context," *DOP* 69 (2015): 15–47.

Dally, O. and C. J. Ratté, eds., *Archaeology and the Cities of Asia Minor in Late Antiquity* (Ann Arbor, 2011).

Dalman, K. O., *Der Valensaquäduct in Konstantinopel* (Bamberg, 1933).

Dana, M., "'Le banquet des sophistes': représentation funéraire, représentation sociale sur les stèles de Byzance aux époques hellénistique et impériale," in Studia Universitatis "Babeş-Bolyai," *Historia* 59.1 (2014): 345–71.

Dankoff, R., S. A. Kahraman, and Y. Dağlı, eds., *Evliya Çelebi Seyahatnâmesi* (Istanbul, 2006).

Dark, K. R., *Byzantine Pottery* (Charleston, 2001).

Dark, K. R. "Houses, Streets, and Shops in Byzantine Constantinople from the Fifth to the Twelfth Centuries," *JMedHist* 30.2 (2004): 83–107.

Dark, K. R., ed., *Secular Buildings and the Archaeology of Everyday Life in the Byzantine Empire* (Oxford, 2004).

Dark, K. R., "Roman Architecture in the Great Palace of the Byzantine Emperors at Constantinople during the Sixth to Ninth Centuries," *Byzantion* 77 (2008): 87–105.

Dark, K. R. and J. Kostec, "The Hagia Sophia Project in Istanbul," *Bulletin of British Byzantine Studies*, 35 (2009): 56–68.

Dark K. R. and J. Kostec, "The Hagia Sophia Project in Istanbul," *Bulletin of British Byzantine Studies*, 36 (2010): 40–9.

Dark, K. R. and J. Kostec, "The Hagia Sophia Project in Istanbul," *Bulletin of British Byzantine Studies*, 37 (2011): 48–68.

Dark, K. R. and F. Özgümüş, *Constantinople: Archaeology of a Byzantine Megapolis – Final Report on the Istanbul rescue Archaeology Project 1998–2004* (Oxford, 2013).

Debby, N. B.-A., "Crusade Propaganda in Word and Image in Early Modern Italy," *Renaissance Quarterly* 67 (2014): 503–43.

Decker, M. J., *The Byzantine Dark Ages* (London, 2016).

Deckers, J. and Ü. Serdaroğlu, "Das Hypogäum beim Silivri-Kapi in Istanbul," *JbAC* 36 (1993): 140–63.

DeLaine, J., *The Baths of Caracalla: A Study in the Design, Construction, and Economics of Large-Scale Building Projects in Imperial Rome* (Portsmouth, RI, 1997).

Delbrueck, R., *Die Consulardiptychen und verwandte Denkmäler* (Berlin, 1929).

Delehaye, H., *Deux typica byzantins de l'époque des Paléologues* (Brussels, 1921).

Delehaye, H., *Les Saints Stylites* (Brussels, 1923).

Delouis, O., "Écriture et réécriture au monastère de Stoudios à Constantinople (IXᵉ–Xᵉ s.): quelques remarques," in *Remanier, métaphraser: Fonctions et techniques de la réécriture dans le monde byzantin*, ed. S. Marjanovich-Dushanich (Belgrade, 2011), 101–10.

Demangel, R. and E. Mamboury, *Le quartier des Manganes et la première région de Constantinople* (Paris, 1939).

Denker, A., "The Great Palace," in *Byzantine Palaces in Istanbul*, ed. G. Baran Çelik et al. (Istanbul, 2011), 11–69.

Denker, A., "Excavations at the Byzantine Great Palace in the Area of the Old Sultanahmet Jail," in *The Byzantine Court: Source of Power and Culture*, ed. A. Ödekan et al. (Istanbul, 2013), 13–18.

Déroche, V., "Quand l'ascèse devient péché: Les excès dans le monachisme byzantin d'après les témoignages contemporains," *Kentron* 23 (2007): 167–78.

Dey, H. W., *The Afterlife of the Roman City: Architecture and Ceremony in Late Antiquity and the Early Middle Ages* (Cambridge, 2015).

Di Giacomo, S., *Il Conservatorio dei poveri di Gesù Cristo e quello di S. M. di Loreto* (Naples, 1928).

Dijkstra, J. and G. Greatrex, "Patriarchs and Politics in Constantinople in the Reign of Anastasius (with a Reedition of *O. Mon. Epiph.* 59)," *Millennium* 6 (2009): 223–64.

Diller, A., "The Greek Codices of Palla Strozzi and Guarino Veronese," *JWarb* 24 (1961): 313–21.

Dimopoulos, J., "Trade of Byzantine Red Wares, End of the 11th–13th Centuries," in *Byzantine Trade, 4th–12th Centuries*, ed. M. M. Mango (Farnham, 2009), 179–90.

Dionysios of Byzantion, *Dionysii Byzantii Anaplus Bospori*, ed. R. Güngerich (Berlin, 1958).

Dirimtekin, F., "Adduction de l'eau à Byzance dans la région dite 'Bulgarie'," *CahArch* 10 (1959): 217–43.

Dobschütz, E. von, "Methodios und die Studiten: Strömungen und Gegenströmungen in der Hagiographie des 9. Jahrhunderts," *BZ* 18 (1909): 41–105.

Doukas, *Istoria Turco-Bizantina*, ed. V. Grecu (Bucharest 1958).

Doukas, *Decline and Fall of Byzantium to the Ottoman Turks*, trans. H. Magoulias (Detroit, 1975).

Downey, G., *Constantinople in the Age of Justinian* (Norman, 1960).

Drocourt, N., *Diplomatie sur le Bosphore: Les ambassadeurs étrangers à Constantinople*, 2 vols. (Paris, 2015).

Drpić, I., "Manual I Komnenos and the Stone of Unction," *BMGS* 43 (2019): 60–82.

Du Cange, C. du Fresne, *Historia byzantina duplici commentario illustrata* (Paris, 1680; reprint Brussels, 1964).

Du Cange, C. du Fresne, *Glossarium ad scriptores mediae et infimae Latinitatis* (Frankfurt, 1681).

Du Cange, C. du Fresne, *Glossarium ad scriptores mediae et infimae graecitatis* (Lyon, 1688).

Ducellier, A. and M. Balard, eds., *Constantinople 1054–1261: tête de la chrétienté, proie des latins, capitale grecque* (Paris, 1996).

Durak, K., "Commerce and Networks of Exchange between the Byzantine Empire and the Islamic Near East from the Early Ninth Century to the Arrival of the Crusaders" (PhD dissertation, Harvard University, 2008).

Duran, J. and B. Flusin, *Byzance et les reliques du Christ* (Paris, 2004).

Durliat, J., *De la ville antique à la ville byzantine: Le problème des subsistances* (Paris, 1990).

Durliat, J., "L'approvisionnement de Constantinople," in *Constantinople and Its Hinterland*, ed. C. Mango and G. Dagron (Aldershot, 1995), 19–33.

Durliat, J. and A. Guillou, "Le tarif d'Abydos (vers 492)," *BCH* 108 (1984): 581–98.

Duyuran, R., "Mosaiques découvertes près de la prefecture d'Istanbul," *Istanbul Arkeoloji Müzesi Yıllığı* 9 (1960): 70–2.

Dyggve, E., "The Origin of the Urban Churchyard," *ClMed* 13(1952): 147–58.

Eastmond, A., "Consular Diptychs, Rhetoric and the Languages of Art in Sixth-Century Constantinople," *AH* 33 (2010): 742–65.

Ebersolt, J., *Le Grand Palais de Constantinople et le Livre des Cérémonies* (Paris, 1910).

Ebersolt, J., *Constantinople Byzantine et les Voyageurs du Levant* (Paris, 1918; reprint, London, 1986).

Ebersolt, J., *L'Église et l'Orient au Moyen Age: Les Croisades* (Paris, 1928).

Eck, W., *Roma Caput Mundi – the Eternal City as Monument and Idea: The Elite of Empire in the Public Space of the Capital Rome* (Wellington, 2001).

Efendi, H. H., *Telhîsü'l-beyân Fî Kavânîn-i Âl-i Osmân*, ed. S. İlgürel (Ankara, 1998).

Effenberger, A., "Die Klöster der beiden Kyrai Martha und die Kirche des Bebaia Elpis-Klosters in Konstantinopel," *Millennium* 3 (2006): 255–94.

Effenberger, A., "Das Berliner 'Kugelspiel'," *JbBM* 49 (2007): 27–56.

Effenberger, A., "Zu den Gräbern in der Pammakaristoskirche," *Byzantion* 77 (2007): 170–96.

Effenberger, A., "Brücken über das Goldene Horn," *Millennium* 15 (2018): 157–75.

Effenberger, A. and N. Asutay-Effenberger, "Zum Verlauf der Konstantinsmauer zwischen Marmarameer und Bonoszisterne und zu den Toren und Straßen," *JÖB* 59 (2009): 1–29.

Efthymiadis, S., "Le panégyrique de Théophane le Chronographe par S. Théodore Studite (BHG 1792b)," *AB* 31 (1993): 259–90.

Ehrhard, M., "Le Livre du pèlerin d'Antoine de Novgorod," *Romania* 58 (1932): 44–65.

El-Cheikh, N. M., *Byzantium Viewed by the Arabs* (Cambridge, MA, 2004).

Elm, S., *Virgins of God: The Making of Asceticism in Late Antiquity* (Oxford, 1994).

Emecen, F. M., *Fetih Ve Kıyamet, 1453: İstanbul'un Fethi Ve Kıyamet Senaryolan* (Istanbul, 2012).

Emecen, F. M., "1455 Tarihli Istanbul ve Galata Tahririnin Kayıp Sayfaları," *The Journal of Ottoman Studies* 56 (2020): 287–317.

Ephraim of Ainos, *Ephraem Aenii Historia Chronaca*, ed. O. Lampsides (Athens, 1990).

Erdeljan, J., *Chosen Places: Constructing New Jerusalems in Slavia Orthodoxa* (Leiden and Boston, 2017).

Ergin, N. and Magdalino, P., *Istanbul and Water* (Leuven, 2015).

Ergin, O., ed., *Fatih Sultan Mehmed'in vakfiyeleri* (Istanbul, 1945).

Ergin, N. and Magdalino, P. *Istanbul and Water* (Leuven, 2015).

Ermilov, P., "'Satanic Heresy': On One Topic in Anti-Armenian Polemic," in *Orthodoxy and Heresy in Byzantium: The Definition and the Notion of Orthodoxy and Some Other Studies on the Heresies and the Non-Christian Religions*, ed. A. Rigo and P. Ermilov (Rome, 2010), 79–90.

Eusebius of Caesarea, *Life of Constantine*, ed. and trans. Av. Cameron and S. Hall (Oxford, 1999).

Eustathios of Thessalonike, *Eustathios of Thessalonike: Commentary on Homer's Odyssey*, 2 vols., ed. E. Cullhed (Uppsala, 2016).

Evliya Çelebi. *Evliya Çelebi Seyahatnâmesi*, ed. R. Dankoff, S. A. Kahraman, and Y. Dağlı (Istanbul, 2006).

Eyice, S., "Un palais byzantin construit d'après les plans des palais abbasides: Le palais de Bryas," *Belleten* 23 (1959): 79–104.

Fagan, B. *Elixir, a Human History of Water* (London, 2011).

Featherstone, M., "The Chrysotriklinos as Seen through De Cerimoniis," in *Zwischen Polis, Provinz und Peripherie: Beiträge zur byzantinischen Geschichte und Kultur*, ed. A. Monchizadeh and L. M. Hoffmann (Wiesbaden, 2005), 845–52.

Featherstone, M., "The Great Palace as Reflected in De Ceremoniis," in *Visualisierung von Herrschaft: Frühmittelalterliche Residenzen. Gestalt und Zeremoniell*, ed. F. A. Bauer (Istanbul, 2006), 47–61.

Featherstone, M., "Der Große Palast von Konstantinopel: Tradition oder Erfindung?" *BZ* 106 (2013): 119–38.

Featherstone, M., "Space and Ceremony in the Great Palace of Constantinople under the Macedonian Emperors," in *Le corti nell'alto Medioevo, Spoleto 24–9 aprile 2014*, 2 vols. (Spoleto, 2015), 2: 587–610.

Featherstone, M., "The Everyday Palace in the Tenth Century," in *The Emperor's House: Palaces from Augustus to the Age of Absolutism*, ed. J. M. Featherstone, J.-M. Spieser, G. Tanman, and U. Wulf-Rheidt (Berlin, 2015), 149–58.

Featherstone, M., "Theophilus's Margarites: The 'Apsed Hall' of the Walker Trust?," in *"Di Bisanzio dirai ciò che è passato, ciò che passa e che sarà." Scritti in onore die Alessandra Guiglia*, ed. S. Pedone and A. Paribeni (Rome, 2018), 173–86.

Featherstone, M., J.-M. Spieser, G. Tanman, and U. Wulf-Rheidt, eds., *The Emperor's House: Palaces from Augustus to the Age of Absolutism* (Berlin and Boston, 2015).

Feissel, D., "Aspects de l'immigration à Constantinople d'áprès les épitaphes protobyzantines," in *Constantinople and its Hinterland*, ed. C. Mango and G. Dagron (Aldershot and Burlington, 1995), 367–78.

Feist, S., *Die byzantinische Sakralarchitektur der Dunklen Jahrhunderte* (Wiesbaden, 2019).

Fenster, E., *Laudes Constantinopolitanae* (Munich, 1968).

Fıratlı, N., *Les stèles funeraires de Byzance Gréco-Romaine, avec l'édition et l'index commenté des épitaphes par Louis Robert* (Paris, 1964).

Firdevsi, *Süleymānnāme*, v.1, T. 406, Chester Beatty Library, Dublin.

Fischer, E. H., *Melchior Lorck*, 4 vols. (Copenhagen, 2009–15).

Fleischer, C. H., "A Mediterranean Apocalypse: Prophecies of Empire in the Fifteenth and Sixteenth Centuries," *JESHO* 61 (2018): 18–90.

Fleming, J. D., ed., *The Invention of Discovery 1500–1700* (Florence, 2011).

Flusin, B., "Construire une nouvelle Jérusalem: Constantinople et ses reliques," in *Orient dans l'histoire religieuse de l'Europe*, ed. M. A. Amir-Moezzi and J. Scheid (Turnhout, 2000), 51–70.

Flusin, B., "Les reliques de la Sainte-Chapelle et leur passé impérial à Constantinople," in *Le trésor de la Sainte-Chapelle*, ed. J. Durand, M.-P. Laffitte, and D. Giovannoni (Paris, 2001), 20–36.

Flusin, B., "Les cérémonies de l'exaltation de la Croix à Constantinople au Xie siècle d'après la *Dresdensis* A 104," in *Byzance et les reliques du Christ*, ed. J. Durand and B. Flusin (Paris, 2004) 61–89.

Flusin, B. and M. Detoraki, " Les histories édifiantes de Constantinople," in *Constantinople réelle et imaginaire, autour de l'œuvre de Gilbert Dagron*, ed. C. Morrisson and J.-P. Sodini (Paris, 2018), 509–65.

Foka, A., "Gender Subversion and the Early Christian East: Reconstructing the Byzantine Comic Mime," in *Laughter, Humor, and the (Un)Making of Gender: Historical and Cultural Perspectives*, ed. A. Foka and J. Liliequist (New York, 2015), 65–83.

Forchheimer, P. and J. Strzygowski, *Die Byzantinischen Wasserbehälter von Konstantinopel* (Vienna, 1893).

Foss, C., "The Cities of Pamphylia in the Byzantine Age," in *Cities, Fortresses, and Villages of Byzantine Asia Minor*, ed. C. Foss (London, 1996) no. II.

Foss, C. and J. A. Scott, "Sardis," *EHB* 2: 615–22.

Foss, C. and D. Winfield, *Byzantine Fortifications: An Introduction* (Pretoria, 1986).

Franchetti Pardo, V., "Da Bisanzio a Costantinopoli: profilo storico-urbanistico della capitale imperiale; dalle origini a Giustiniano," in *Bisanzio, Costantinopoli, Istanbul*, ed. T. Velmans (Milan, 2008), 13–38.

Franchi di Cavalieri, P., "Una pagina di storia bizantina del secolo IV: il martirio dei santi notari," *AB* 64 (1946): 132–75.

Franciosi, E., *Riforme istituzionali e funzioni giurisdizionali nelle novelle di Giustiniano: Studi su Nov. 13 e Nov. 80* (Milan, 1998).

François, V., "A Distribution Atlas of Byzantine Ceramics: A New Approach to the Pottery Trade in Byzantium," in *Trade in Byzantium*, ed. P. Magdalino and N Necipoğlu (Istanbul, 2016), 143–56.

Frankopan, P., "Byzantine Trade Privileges to Venice in the Eleventh Century: The Chrysobull of 1092," *JMedHist* 30.2 (2004): 135–60.

Freely, J., *Monuments of Byzantine Constantinople* (Cambridge, 2004).

Freely, J., and A. S. Çakmak, *Byzantine Monuments of Istanbul* (Cambridge, 2004).

Fulcher of Chartres. *A History of the Expedition to Jerusalem, 1095–1127*, trans. Frances Rita Ryan (Sisters of St. Joseph), ed. with an introduction by H. S. Fink (Knoxville, TN, 1969).

Gabrielsen, V., "Trade and Tribute: Byzantion and the Black Sea Straits," in *The Black Sea in Antiquity: Regional and Interregional Economic Exchanges*, ed. V. Gabrielsen and J. Lund (Aarhus, 2007): 287–324.

Ganchou, T., "'La tour d'Irène' (Eirene Kulesi) à Istanbul: le palais de Loukas Notaras?" in *Οὗ δῶρόν εἰμι τὰς γραφὰς βλέπων νόει: Mélanges Jean-Claude Cheynet*, ed. B. Caseau, V. Prigent, and A. Sopracasa (Paris, 2017), 169–256.

Garland, L., "Street-Life in Constantinople: Women and the Carnivalesque," in *Byzantine Women: Varieties of Experience 800–1200*, ed. L. Garland (Aldershot, 2006), 163–76.

Garnsey, P. and C. Whittaker, "Trade, Industry, and the Urban Economy," in *CAH* 13, ed. A. Cameron and P. Garnsey (Cambridge, 2007), 312–37.

Gaul, N., *Thomas Magistros und die spätbyzantinische Sophistik* (Mainz, 2011), 272–4.

Gaul, N., "Rising Elites and Institutionalization – *Ēthos/Mores* – 'Debts' and Drafts," in *Networks of Learning*, ed. S. Steckel, N. Gaul, and M. Grünbart (Berlin, 2015), 235–80.

Gaul, N., "All the Emperor's Men (and His Nephews)," *DOP* 70 (2017): 245–70.

Gaul, N., "Performative Reading in the Late Byzantine *Theatron*," in *Reading in the Byzantine Empire and Beyond*, ed. T. Shawcross and I. Toth (Cambridge, 2018), 215–34.

Gautier, P., "L'édit d'Alexis I^er Comnène sur la réforme du clergé," *REB* 31 (1973): 165–201.

Gautier, P., "Le Typikon du Christ Sauveur Pantocrator," *REB* 32 (1974): 1–145.

Gautier, P., "La Diataxis de Michel Attaliate," *REB* 39 (1981): 5–143.

Genesios, *Regnum Libri quattuor*, ed. A. Lesmüller-Wiener and H. Thurn (Berlin and New York, 1978).

George the Monk, *Chronicle, Georgi Monachi Chronicon*, ed. C. de Boor (Leipzig, 1904).

Gerola, G., "Le vedute di Costantinopoli di Cristoforo Buondelmonti," *SBN* 3 (1931): 247–79.

Gerstel, S. E. J., "An Alternate View of the Late Byzantine Sanctuary Screen," in *Thresholds of the Sacred: Architectural, Art Historical, Liturgical, and Theological Perspectives on Religious Screens, East and West*, ed. S. E. J. Gerstel (Washington, DC, 2006), 135–61.

Giatsis, S., "The Organization of Chariot-Racing in the Great Hippodrome of Byzantine Constantinople," *International Journal of the History of Sport* 17 (2000): 36–68.

Gibb, H. A. R., trans. and ed., *Ibn Battuta, Travels in Asia and Africa 1325–1354* (London, 1929).

Gilles, P., *De topographia Constantinopoleos et de illius antiquitatibus libri quattuor* (Lyon, 1561).

Gilles, P., *The Antiquities of Constantinople, Based on the Translation by John Ball*, ed. R. G. Musto (New York, 1988).

Gilles, P. *Pierre Gilles' Constantinople: A Modern English Translation*, ed. and trans. K. Byrd (New York, 2008).

Giorgi, E., *Archeologia dell'acqua a Gortina di Creta in età protobizantina* (Oxford, 2016).

Girgin, Ç., "La porte monumentale trouvée dans les fouilles près de l'ancienne prison de Sultanahmet," *Anatolia antiqua* 16 (2008): 259–90.

Gkoutzioukostas, A., *Ο θεσμός του κοιαίστωρα του ιερού παλατίου: Η γένεση, οι αρμοδιότητες και η εξέλιξή του* (Thessalonike, 2001).

Gkoutzioukostas, A., *Η απονομή δικαιοσύνης στο Βυζάντιο. Τα κοσμικά δικαιοδοτικά όργανα και δικαστήρια της πρωτεύουσας (9ος–12ος αι.)* (Thessalonike, 2004).

Gkoutzioukostas, A., *"Ο πραίτωρ του δήμου/των δήμων,"* Βυζαντινά 24 (2004): 133–66.

Gkoutzioukostas, A., "The Praitor Mentioned in the History of Leo the Deacon and the Praitor of Constantinople: Previous and Recent Considerations," Βυζαντιακά 25 (2005–6): 103–15.

Gkoutzioukostas, A., *"Πολιτάρχης και πολιταρχία στα Θαύματα του Αγίου Δημητρίου και σε άλλες βυζαντινές πηγές,"* Βυζαντινά 27 (2007): 165–85.

Gofas, D., "The Byzantine Law of Interest," in *EHB* 3: 1095–104.

Goitein, S. D., *Mediterranean Society: The Jewish Communities of the Arab World as Portrayed in the Documents of the Cairo Geniza*, 6 vols. (Berkeley, 1967).

Golvin, J.-C. and F. Fauquet, "L'hippodrome de Constantinople: Essai de restitution architecturale du dernier état du monument," *AntTard* 15 (2007): 181–214.

Gouillard, J., "Quatre procès de mystiques à Byzance (vers 960–1143): Inspiration et autorité," *REB* 36 (1978): 5–81.

Graf, F., *Roman Festivals in the Greek East from the Early Empire to the Middle Byzantine Era* (Cambridge, 2015).

Graham, B., and R. Van Dam, "Modelling the Supply of Wood Fuel in Ancient Rome," in *Environment and Society in the Long Late Antiquity*, ed. A. Izdebski and M. Mulryan (Leiden, 2019), 148–59.

Greatrex, G., "Procopius and Agathias on the Defences of the Thracian Chersonese," in *Constantinople and Its Hinterland*, ed. C. Mango and G. Dagron (Aldershot, 1995), 125–9.

Greatrex, G., "The *Nika Riot*: A Reappraisal," *JHS* 117 (1997): 60–86.

Gregoras, N., *Nicephori Gregorae Byzantina Historia*, 3 vols., ed. L. Schopen (Bonn, 1829–55).

Gregorius II patriarcha, *Epistulae*, ed. S. Eustratiades (Alexandria, 1910).

Gregory of Cyprus, *Laudatio Michaelis Palaeologi*, PG 142 (1865): 345–86.

Gregory of Nazianzos, *De pauperum amore (Oratio XIV)*, PG 35: 857–909. English translation in *The Sunday Sermons of the Great Fathers*, 4 vols., trans. M. F. Toul (Chicago, 1963) PG 4 (1857): 43–64.

Gregory of Nazianzos, *In Pentecosten*, PG 36 (1858): 428–52.

Grierson, P., "The Tombs and Obits of the Byzantine Emperors (337–1042)," *DOP* 16 (1962): 3–63.

Grotesend, C. L., "Die Edelherren von Boldensele oder Boldensen," *Zeitschrift des historischen Vereins für Niedersachsen 1852* (1855): 209–92.

Grünbart, M., "Store in a Cool and Dry Place: Perishable Goods and Their Preservation in Byzantium," in *Eat, Drink, and Be Merry (Luke 12:19): Food and Wine in Byzantium*, ed. L. Brubaker and K. Linardou (Aldershot, 2007), 39–49.

Guidi, M., "Un ΒΙΟΣ di Costantino," *RendLinc* 5.16 (1907): 304–40, 637–62.

Guilhembet, J.-P., "La densité des domus et des insulae dans les XIV régions de Rome selon les Régionnaires: représentations cartographiques," *MEFRA* 108 (1996): 7–26.

Guilland, R., "Le Prétoire. Τὸ πραιτώριον," *Ελληνικά* 17 (1962): 100–4 (= R. Guilland, *Études de topographie de Constantinople Byzantine*, 2 vols. (Berlin and Amsterdam, 1969), 2: 36–9.

Guilland, R., *Études de topographie de Constantinople byzantine*, 2 vols. (Berlin/ Amsterdam, 1969).

Guilland, R., "Études sur l'histoire administrative de l'empire byzantin: L'Éparque. I. Léparque de la ville – Ὁ ἔπαρχος τῆς πόλεως," *BSl* 41 (1980): 17–32, 145–80.

Guilland, R., "Études sur l'histoire administrative de l'empire byzantin: L'Éparque. III. L'Apoeparque – ἀπὸ ἐπάρχων," *BSl* 43 (1982): 30–44.

Güngerich, R., ed., *Dionysii Byzantii Anaplus Bospori* (Berlin, 1927).

Günsesin, N., "Medieval Trade in the Sea of Marmora: The Evidence of Shipwrecks," in *Travel in the Byzantine World*, ed. R. Macrides (Aldershot and Burlington, 2002), 125–35.

Günsenin, N., "Ganos Wine and Its Circulation in the 11th Century," in *Byzantine Trade, 4th–12th Centuries*, ed. M. M. Mango (Farnham, 2009), 145–53.

Günsenin, N., "La typologie des amphores Günsenin: Une mise au point nouvelle," *Anatolia Antiqua* 26 (2018): 89–124.

Günther, H., "L'idea di Roma antica nella 'Roma instaurata' di Flavio Biondo," in *Le due Rome del Quattrocento*, ed. S. Rossi (Rome, 1997), 380–93.

Gunther of Pairis, *Hystoria Constantinopolitana: Untersuchung und kritische Ausgabe*, ed. P. Orth (Hildesheim, 1994).

Guran, P., "The Byzantine 'New Jerusalem'," in *New Jerusalems: The Translation of Sacred Spaces*, ed. A. Lidov (Moscow, 2006), 17–23.

Guran, P., "The Constantinople: New Jerusalem at the Crossing of Sacred Space and Political Theology," in Новы Иерусалимы: Иеротолу и Иконография *[New Jerusalems: Hierotopy and Iconography]*, ed. A. Lidov (Moscow, 2009), 35–55.

Haldon, J. *Byzantine Praetorians: An Administrative, Institutional and Social Survey of the Opsikion and Tagmata, c. 580–900* (Bonn, 1984).

Haldon, J., *Byzantium in the Seventh Century* (Cambridge, 1990).

Haldon, J., "Strategies of Defence, Problems of Security: The Garrisons of Constantinople in the Middle Byzantine Period," in *Constantinople and Its Hinterland*, ed. C. Mango and G. Dagron (Aldershot and Burlington, 1994), 143–55.

Haldon, J., *Warfare, State and Society in the Byzantine World, 565–1204* (London, 1999).

Haldon, J., "Production, Distribution and Demand in the Byzantine World, c. 660–840," in *The Long Eighth Century: Production, Distribution and Demand*, ed. I. L. Hansen and C. Wickham (Leiden, 2000), 225–64.

Haldon, J., ed., *A Social History of Byzantium* (Chichester and Malden, 2009).

Haldon, J. "Commodities and Traffic Routes: Results and Prospects, Current Problems and Current Research," in *Handelsgüter und Verkehrswege: Aspekte der Warenversorgung im östlichen Mittelmeer (4. Bis 15. Jahrhundert)*, ed. E. Kislinger, J. Koder, and A. Külzer (Vienna, 2010), 289–94.

Haldon, J., *The Empire That Would Not Die* (Cambridge, MA, 2016).

Halkin, F., "Saint Sampson le xénodoque de Constantinople," *Rivista di studi bizantini e neoellenici*, n.s. 14–16 (1977–9): 6–17.

Halkin, F., ed. *Hagiologie Byzantine* (Brussels, 1986).

Hall, E., "Introduction: Pantomime, a Lost Chord of Ancient Culture," in *New Directions in Ancient Pantomime*, ed. E. Hall and R. Wyles (Oxford, 2008), 1–40.

Hallensleben, H., "Untersuchungen zur Baugeschichte der ehemaligen Pammakaristoskirche der heutigen Fethiye Camii in Istanbul," *IstMitt* 13.14 (1963–4): 128–93.

Hamadeh, S. and Ç. Kafescioğlu, eds., *A Companion to Early Modern Istanbul* (Leiden, 2021).

Hanell, K., *Megarische Studien* (Lund, 1934).

Harper, K., *The Fate of Rome: Climate, Disease, and the End of Empire* (Princeton, 2017).

Harris, J., *Constantinople: Capital of Byzantium* (London and New York, 2007).

Harrison, M., *A Temple for Byzantium: The Discovery and Excavation of Anicia Juliana's Palace-Church in Istanbul* (Austin, 1989).

Harrison, M. and G. R. J. Lawson, "The Mosaics in Front of the Vilayet Building in Istanbul," *Istanbul Arkeoloji Müzesi Yıllığı* 13.14 (1966): 216–18.

Harrison, R. M., *A Temple for Byzantium: The Discovery and Excavation of Anicia Juliana's Palace-Church in Istanbul* (Austin, 1989).

Haskins, C. H., "A Canterbury Monk at Constantinople, c. 1090," *English Historical Review* 25 (1910): 293–5.

Hasse-Ungeheuer, A., *Das Mönchtum in der Religionspolitik Kaiser Justinians I: Die Engel des Himmels und der Stellvertreter Gottes auf Erden* (Berlin, 2016).

Hatlie, P., *Monks and Monasteries of Constantinople, 350–850* (Cambridge, 2007).

Havaux, M., "Théodose II, Constantinople et l'Empire: une nouvelle lecture de la Notitia urbis Constantinopolitanae," *RH* 681 (2017): 3–54.

Hawkes-Teeples, S., ed. and trans., *St. Symeon of Thessalonika: The Liturgical Commentaries* (Toronto, 2010).

Hayes, J. W., *Excavations at Saraçhane in Istanbul*, 2 vols. (Princeton, 1992).

Heather, P., "New Men for New Constantines? Creating an Imperial Elite in the Eastern Mediterranean," in *New Constantines: The Rhythm of Imperial Renewal in Byzantium 4th–13th Centuries*, ed. P. Magdalino (Aldershot and Burlington, 1994), 11–33.

Heather, P., "Themistius: A Political Philosopher," in *The Propaganda of Power*, ed. M. Whitby (Leiden, 1998), 125–50.

Heather, P. and D. Moncur, *Politics, Philosophy, and Empire in the Fourth Century: Select Orations of Themistius* (Liverpool, 2001).

Heher, D., "Der Boukoleonhafen und die angrenzenden Palaststrukturen," *JÖB* 64 (2014): 119–37.

Heher, D., "Der Palasthaften des Bukoleon," in *Die byzantinischen Häfen Konstantinopels*, ed. F. Daim (Mainz, 2016), 67–88.

Heisenberg, A., *Nikolaos Mesarites Die Palastrevolution des Johannes Komnenos* (Würzburg, 1907).

Heisenberg, A., *Grabeskirche und Apostelkirche* (Leipzig, 1908).

Hellenkemper, H., "Politische Orte? Kaiserliche Sommerpaläste in Konstantinopel," in *The Emperor's House: Palaces from Augustus to the Age of Absolutism*, ed. M.

Featherstone, J.-M. Spieser, G. Tanman, and U. Wulf-Rheidt (Berlin, 2015), 243–56.

Hendy, M. F., *Studies in the Byzantine Monetary Economy c. 300–1450* (Cambridge, 1985).

Hendy, M. F., "'Byzantium, 1081–1204': The Economy Revisited Twenty Years on," in M. Hendy, *The Economy, Fiscal Administration and Coinage of Byzantium* (Aldershot, 1989), no. III.

Hennessy, C., "Young People in Byzantium," in *A Companion to Byzantium*, ed. L. James (Malden, 2010), 81–92.

Herklotz, I., *"Sepulcra" e "Monumneta" del medioevo*, 2nd ed. (Rome, 1990).

Herman, E., "The Secular Church," in *CMH* 4, *The Byzantine Empire, Part II: Government, Church and Civilization*, ed. J. M. Hussey (Cambridge, 1967), 105–34.

Herrin, J., "Constantinople and the Treatment of Hostages, Refugees and Exiles During Late Antiquity," in *Constantinople réelle et imaginaire: autour de l'œuvre de Gilbert Dagron*, ed. C. Morrisson and J.-P. Sodini (Paris, 2018).

Hesseling, D.-C. and H. Pernot, eds., *Poèmes prodromiques en grec vulgaire* (Amsterdam, 1910).

Hetherington, P., "Vecchi e non antichi: Differing Responses to Byzantine Culture in Fifteenth-Century Tuscany," *Rinascimento* 32 (1992): 203–11.

Heyd, W., *Histoire du commerce du Levant au moyen-âge*, 2 vols. (Leipzig, 1885).

Hezarfen Hüseyin Efendi, *Tenḳīḥü't-Tevārīḥ*, Paris, Bibliothèque nationale œuvrence, Supplément turc 136 (1674–5).

Hezarfen Hüseyin Efendi, *Telhîsü'l-beyân Fî Kavânîn-i Âl-i Osmân*, ed. S. İlgürel (Ankara, 1998).

Hilsdale, C., *Byzantine Art in an Age of Diplomacy in an Age of Decline* (Cambridge, 2014).

Holman, S., ed., *Wealth and Poverty in Early Church and Society* (Grand Rapids, 2008).

Homo, L. P., *Rome impériale et l'urbanisme dans l'antiquité* (Paris, 1951).

Hopkins, K., "The Political Economy of the Roman Empire," in *The Dynamics of Ancient Empires: State Power from Assyria to Byzantium*, ed. I. Morris and W. Scheidel (Oxford, 2009), 178–203.

Hörandner, W., A. Rhoby, and N. Zagklas, eds., *A Companion to Byzantine Poetry* (Leiden, 2019).

Horden, P., "How Medicalized Were Byzantine Hospitals?" in *Sozialgeschichte Mittelalterischer Hospitäler*, ed. N. Bulst and K.-H. Spieß (Ostefildern, 2007), 213–35.

Horna, K., "Eine unedierte Rede des Konstantin Manasses," *Wiener Studien* 28 (1906): 171–204.

Howard-Johnston, J. D., "The Siege of Constantinople in 626," in *Constantinople and Its Hinterland*, ed. C. Mango and G. Dagron (Aldershot, 1995), 131–42.

Howard-Johnston, J. D., *Witnesses to a World Crisis: Historians and Histories of the Middle East in the Seventh Century* (Oxford, 2010).

Hughes, B., *Istanbul: A Tale of Three Cities* (London, 2017).

Hyrtakenos, T. *The Letters of Theodoros Hyrtakenos*, ed. A. Karpozilos and G. Fatouros (Athens, 2017).

Ibn Kemal, *Tevâlih-i Âl-i Osman, VII. Defter*, ed. Ş. Turan (Ankara, 1957).

İnalcık, H., *The Survey of Istanbul 1455: The Text, English Translation, Analysis of the Text, Documents* (Istanbul, 2012).

Ioannes Lydus, *Des magistratures de l'État romain/De magistratibus populi Romani*, ed. M. Dubuisson and J. Schamp, 2 vols. (Paris, 2006).

Isaac, B., *The Greek Settlements in Thrace until the Macedonian Conquest* (Leiden, 1986).

Isendahl, C. and S. Barthel, "Archaeology, History, and Urban Food Security: Integrating Cross-Cultural and Long-Term Perspectives," in *Routledge Handbook of Landscape and Food*, ed. J. Zeunert and T. Waterman (London, 2018), 61–72.

*Itinerarium Peregrinorum et Gesta regis Richardi*, ed. W. Stubbs (London 1864).

Iuliano, M., "Melchior Lorck's Constantinople in the European Context," in *Melchior Lorck*, 4 vols., ed. E. H. Fischer (Copenhagen, 2009), 4: 25–65.

Jacoby, D., "La population de Constantinople à l'époque byzantine: un problème de démographie urbaine," *Byzantion* 31 (1961): 81–109.

Jacoby, D., "Les quartiers juifs de Constantinople à l'époque byzantine," *Byzantion* 37 (1967): 167–227.

Jacoby, D., "Silk in Western Byzantium before the Fourth Crusade," *BZ* 84.2 (1992): 452–500.

Jacoby, D., "Italian Privileges and Trade in Byzantium before the Fourth Crusade: A Reconsideration," *Annuario de estudios medievales* 24 (1994): 349–68.

Jacoby, D. "The Jews of Constantinople and Their Demographic Hinterland," in *Constantinople and Its Hinterland*, ed. C. Mango and G. Dagron (Aldershot, 1995), 221–32.

Jacoby, D., "Silk Crosses the Mediterranean," in *Le vie del Mediterraneo; Idee, uomini, oggetti (secoli XI–XVI)*, ed. G. Airaldi (Genoa, 1997), 35–79.

Jacoby, D., "Byzantine Outsider in Trade," in *Strangers to Themselves: The Byzantine Outsider*, ed. D. Smythe (Aldershot, 2000), 129–47.

Jacoby, D., "Byzantine Trade with Egypt from the Mid-Tenth Century to the Fourth Crusade," *Thesaurismata* 30 (2000): 25–77.

Jacoby, D., "The Venetian Quarter of Constantinople from 1082 to 1261: Topographical Considerations," in *Novum Millennium: Studies on Byzantine History and Culture Dedicated to Paul Speck*, ed. C. Sode and S. Takács (Aldershot, 2001), 153–70.

Jacoby, D., "Venetian Settlers in Latin Constantinople (1204–1261): Rich or Poor?" in *Byzantium, Latin Romania and the Mediterranean*, ed. D. Jacoby (Aldershot, 2001), no VII.

Jacoby, D., "The Urban Evolution of Latin Constantinople, 1204–1261," in *Byzantine Constantinople: Monuments, Topography and Everyday Life*, ed. N. Necipoğlu (Leiden, 2001), 277–97.

Jacoby, D., "The Venetian Government and Administration in Latin Constantinople, 1204–1261: A State within a State," in *Quarta crociata: Venezia – Bisanzio – Impero Latino*, 2 vols., ed. G. Ortalli, G. Ravegnani, and P. Schreiner (Venice, 2006), 1: 19–79.

Jacoby, D., "The Greeks of Constantinople under Latin Rule," in *The Fourth Crusade: Event, Aftermath, and Perceptions*, ed. T. Madden (Aldershot, 2008), 53–73.

Jacoby, D., "Venetian Commercial Expansion in the Eastern Mediterranean, 8th–11th Centuries," in *Byzantine Trade, 4th–12th Centuries: The Archaeology of Local, Regional, and International Exchange*, ed. M. M. Mango (Aldershot, 2009), 371–91.

Jacoby, D., "Mediterranean Food and Wine for Constantinople: The Long-Distance Trade, Eleventh to Mid-fifteenth Century," in *Handelsgüter und Verkehrswege, Aspekte der Warenversorgung im östliche Mittelmeeraum (4. Bis 15. Jahrhundert)*, ed. E. Kislinger, J. Koder, and A. Küzler (Vienna, 2010), 127–47.

Jacoby, D., *Travelers, Merchants and Settlers in the Eastern Mediterranean, 11th–14th centuries* (Farnham, 2014).

Jacoby, D., "Constantinople as Commercial Transit Center, Tenth to Mid-fifteenth Century," in *Trade in Byzantium*, ed. P. Magdalino, N Necipoğlu, and I. Jevtić (Istanbul, 2016), 193–210.

Jacoby, D., "Pisan Presence and Trade in Late Byzantium," in *Koinotaton Doron: Das späte Byzanz zwischen Machtlosigkeit und kultureller Blüte*, ed. A. Berger, S. Mariev, G. Prinzing, and A. Riehle (Berlin, 2016), 47–59.

James, L. and R. Webb, ""To Understand Ultimate Things and Enter Secret Places': Ekphraseis and Art in Byzantium'," *AH* 14.2 (1991): 1–17.

Janin, R., *Constantinople byzantine* (Paris, 1950).

Janin, R., *Constantinople byzantine: Développement urbain et répertoire topographique*, 2nd ed. (Paris, 1964).

Janin, R., *La géographie ecclésiastique de l'empire byzantin, I: Le siège Constantinople et le p œuvreecuménique, 3: Les églises <sup>e</sup>t les monastères*, 2nd ed. (Paris, 1969).

Jankowiak, M., "The First Arab Siege of Constantinople," *TM* 17 (2013): 237–320.

Jeffreys, E., *Digenis Akritis: The Grottaferrata and Escorial Versions* (Cambridge, 1998).

Jeffreys, E., trans., *Four Byzantine Novels* (Liverpool, 2012).

Jobst, W., R. Kastler, and V. Scheibelreiter, *Neue Forschungen und Restaurierungen im byzantinischen Kaiserpalast von Istanbul* (Vienna, 1999).

Johnson, M. J., *The Roman Imperial Mausoleum in Late Antiquity* (Cambridge, 2009).

Johnson, M. J., "Constantine's Apostoleion: A Reappraisal," in *The Holy Apostles: A Lost Monument, a Forgotten Project, and the Presentness of the Past*, ed. M. Mullett and R. G. Ousterhout (Washington, DC, 2020), 79–98.

Jones, A. H. M., *The Later Roman Empire, 284–602: A Social, Economic and Administrative Survey*, 3 vols. (Oxford, 1964).

Jones, A. R. and M. Rosenthal, *The Clothing of the Renaissance World: Europe, Asia, Africa, the Americas; Cesare Vecellio's Habiti Antichi et Moderni* (London, 2008).

Joranson, E., "The Great German Pilgrimage of 1064–1065," in *The Crusades and Other Essays Presented to Dana C. Munro by His Former Students*, ed. L. J. Paetow (New York, 1928), 3–43.

Joranson, E., "The Problem of the Spurious Letter of Emperor Alexius to the Count of Flanders," *AHR* 55 (1950): 811–32.

Jordan, R. and R. Morris, *The Hypotyposis of the Monastery of the Theotokos Evergetis, Constantinople (11th–12th Centuries)* (Farnham and Burlington, 2012).

Jordanes, *Iordanes Romana et Getica*, ed. T. Mommsen (Berlin, 1882).

Jordanov, I., "Preslav," in *EHB*, 2: 667–71.

Kafadar, Ç., *Between Two Worlds: The Construction of the Ottoman State* (Berkeley, 1995).

Kafescioğlu, Ç., *Constantinopolis/Istanbul: Cultural Encounter, Imperial Vision, and the Construction of the Ottoman Capital* (University Park, 2009).

Kafescioğlu, Ç., "Picturing the Square, the Streets, and Denizens of Early Modern Istanbul: Practices of Urban Space and Shifts in Visuality," *Muqarnas*, 37 (2020).

Kalavrezou, I., "Helping Hands for the Empire: Imperial Ceremonies and the Cult of Relics at the Byzantine Court," in *Byzantine Court Culture from 829 to 1204*, ed. H. Maguire (Washington, DC, 1997), 53–79.

Kaldellis, A., *The Argument of Psellos' Chronographia* (Leiden, 1999).

Kaldellis, A., *Procopius of Caesarea: Tyranny, History, and Philosophy at the End of Antiquity* (Philadelphia, 2004).

Kaldellis, A., *The Byzantine Republic, People and Power in New Rome* (Cambridge, 2015).

Kaldellis, A., *Streams of Gold, Rivers of Blood: The Rise and Fall of Byzantium, 955 A.D. to the First Crusade* (Oxford, 2017).

Kaldellis, A., *Romanland: Ethnicity and Empire in Byzantium* (Cambridge, MA, 2019).

Kaldellis, A., "Civic Identity and Civic Participation in Constantinople," in *Civic Identity and Civic Participation in Late Antiquity and the Early Middle Ages*, ed. H. G. E. Rose and C. Brelaz, 2021.

Kalevrezou, I., "Helping Hands for Empire: Imperial Ceremonies and the Cult of Relics at the Byzantine Court," in *Byzantine Court Culture from 829 to 1204*, ed. H. Maguire (Washington, DC, 1997), 53–80.

Kallistos, A., *Monodia de Constantinopoli capta*, PG 161: 1132–42.

Kalogeras, N. M., "Byzantine Childhood Education and Its Social Role from the Sixth Century until the End of Iconoclasm" (PhD thesis, University of Chicago, 2000).

Kaplan, M., "Le ventre de l'Empire," in *Constantinople 1054–1261: tête de la chrétienté, proie des latins, capitale grecque*, ed. A. Ducellier and M. Balard (Paris, 1996), 86–103.

Kaplan, M., "Les artisans dans la société de Constantinople aux VIIe–XIe siècles," in *Byzantine Constantinople: Monuments, Topography and Everyday Life*, ed. N. Necipoğlu (Leiden, 2001), 245–60.

Kaplony, A., *Konstantinopel und Damascus: Gesandschaften und Vertägen zwischen Kaisern und Khalifen 639–750* (Berlin, 1996).

Karamani-Pekin, A., ed., *8000 Years Brought to Day Light: Marmaray, Metro, Sultanahmet Excavations* (Istanbul, 2007).

Karamani-Pekin, A., *Stories from the Hidden Harbor: The Shipwrecks of Yenikapı* (Istanbul, 2013).

Karpozilos, A., "The Correspondence of Theodore Hyrtakenos," *JÖB* 40 (1990): 275–84.

Karydis, N., "Justinian's Church of the Holy Apostles: A New Reconstruction Proposal," in *The Holy Apostles: A Lost Monument, a Forgotten Project, and the Presentness of the Past*, ed. M. Mullett and R. G. Ousterhout (Washington, DC, 2020), 99–130.

Katib Çelebi, *Târih-i Kostantiniyye ve Kayâsire*, ed. İ. Solak (Konya, 2009).

Katib Çelebi, *Katip Çelebi'nin Yunan Roma ve Hristiyan tarihi hakkındaki risalesi: (İrşâdü'l-Hayârâ ilâ Târîhi'l-Yûnân ve'r-Rûm ve'n-Nasârâ)*, ed. B. Yurtoğlu (Ankara, 2012).

Kazan, G., "What's in a Name? Constantinople's Lost 'Golden Gate' Reconsidered," in *Discipuli Dona Ferrentes: Glimpses of Byzantium in Honour of Marlia Mundell Mango*, ed. T. Papacostas and M. Parani (Turnhout, 2017), 291–320.

Kazhdan, A. P. and G. Constable, *People and Power in Byzantium* (Washington, DC, 1982).

Kazhdan, A. P. and A. Epstein, *Change in Byzantine Culture in the Eleventh and Twelfth Centuries* (Berkeley, 1985).

Kazhdan, A. P. and M. McCormick, "The Social World of the Byzantine Court," in *Byzantine Court Culture from 829 to 1204*, ed. H. Maguire (Washington, DC, 1997), 167–97.

Kedrenos, G., *Georgius Cedrenus*, 2 vols., ed. I Bekker (Bonn, 1838–9).

Kepetzi, V., "Scenes of Performers in Byzantine Art, Iconography, Social and Cultural Milieu: The Case of Acrobats," in *Medieval and Early Modern Performance in the Eastern Mediterranean*, ed. A. Öztürkmen and E. Birge Vitz (Turnhout, 2014), 345–8.

Khitrowo, Mme. B. de [Sofiia Petrovna], *Itinéraires russe in Orient* (Geneva, 1889; reprint Osnabrück, 1966).

Kidonopoulos, V., *Bauten in Konstantinopel 1204–1328: Verfall und Zerstörung, Restaurierung, Umbau und Neubau von Profan- und Sakralbauten* (Wiesbaden, 1994).

Kidonopoulos, V., "The Urban Physiognomy of Constantinople from the Latin Conquest through the Palaiologan Era," in *Byzantium, Faith and Power (1261–1557)*:

*Perspectives on Late Byzantine Art and Culture*, ed. S. T. Brooks (New York, 2006), 98–117.

Kim, D. Y., "Gentile in Red," *I Tatti Studies* 18 (2015): 157–92.

Kingsley, S. and Decker, M., "New Rome, New Theories on Inter-regional Exchange: An Introduction to the East Mediterranean Economy in Late Antiquity," in *Economy and Exchange in the East Mediterranean during the Late Antiquity*, ed. S. Kingsley and M. Decker (Oxford, 2001), 1–27.

Kinnamos, J., *Ioannis Cinnami epitome rerum ab Ioanne et Alexio Comnenis gestarum*, ed. A. Meineke, *CSHB* 26 (Bonn, 1836).

Kislinger, E., "Taverne, alberghi, e filantropia ecclesiastica a Bizanzio," *Atti della Accademia delle Scienze di Torino* 120 (1986): 83–96.

Kislinger, E., "Gewerbe im späten Byzanz," in *Handwerk und Sachkultur im Spätmittelalter*, ed. R. Sprandel (Vienna, 1988), 103–26.

Kislinger, E., "Zur Lage der Leproserie des Pantokrator-Typikon," *JÖB* 42 (1992): 171–4.

Kislinger, E., J. Koder, and A. Küzler, eds., *Handelsgüter und Verkehrswege, Aspekte der Warenversorgung im östliche Mittelmeeraum (4. Bis 15. Jahrhundert)* (Vienna, 2010).

Kızıltan, Z., ed., *Istanbul: 8,000 Years Brought to Daylight: Marmaray, Metro Sultanahmet Excavations* (Istanbul, 2007).

Klein, H., "Constantine, Helena and the Cult of the True Cross in Constantinople," in *Byzance et les réliques du Christ*, ed. B. Flusin and J. Durand (Paris, 2004), 31–59.

Klein, H., "Sacred Relics and Imperial Ceremonies at the Great Palace of Constantinople," in *Visualisierung von Herrschaft: Frühmittelalterliche Residenzen – Gestalt und Zeremoniell*, ed. F. A. Bauer (Istanbul, 2006), 79–99.

*Kletorologion of Philotheos*, in *Les listes de préséance byzantines des IXe et Xc siècles: Introduction, téxte, traduction et commentaire*, ed. N. Oikonomides (Paris, 1972), 67–235.

Kline, G. R., *The Voyage d'Outremer by Bertrandon de la Broquière. Edited, Translated, and Annotated with an Introduction and Maps* (New York, Bern, and Frankfurt am Main, 1988).

Köç, A., ed., *Osmanlı Arşiv Belgelerinde Sultangazi* (İstanbul, 2012).

Kocabaş, U., *Yenikapı Shipwrecks* (İstanbul, 2008).

Koder, J., ed., *Das Eparchenbuch Leons des Weisen*, CFHB, 33 (Vienna, 1991).

Koder, J., "Fresh Vegetables for the Capital," in *Constantinople and Its Hinterland*, ed. C. Mango and G. Dagron (Aldershot, 1995), 49–56.

Koder, J., "Maritime Trade and the Food Supply of Constantinople in the Middle Ages," in *Travel in the Byzantine World*, ed. R. Macrides (Aldershot, 2002), 109–24.

Koder, J., "Stew and Salted Meat: Opulent Normality in the Diet of Every Day?" in *Eat, Drink, and Be Merry (Luke 12:19): Food and Wine in Byzantium*, ed. L. Brubaker and K. Linardou (Aldershot, 2007), 59–72.

Koder, J., "The Authority of the Eparchos in the Markets of Constantinople (According to the Book of the Eparch)," in *Authority in Byzantium*, ed. P. Armstrong (Abingdon and New York, 2013), 83–108.

Komnene, A., *Anna Comnène: Alexiade*, 3 vols., ed. B. Leib (Paris, 1934–45), trans. E. W. Sewter (Baltimore, 1969).

Komnene, A., *Annae Comnenae Alexias* ed. D. R. Reinsch and A. Kambylis (Berlin, 2001).

Komnene, A., *The Alexiad*, trans. E. R. A. Sewter (London, 1969; rev. ed., P. Frankopan, London, 2009).

Konrad, C., "Beobachtungen zur Architektur und Stellung des Säulenmonuments in Istanbul- Cerrahpasa – 'Arkadiussäule'," *IstMitt* 51 (2001): 319–401.

Kontogiannopoulou, A., *Η εσωτερική πολιτική του Ανδρονίκου Β΄ Παλαιολόγου (1282–1328): Διοίκηση – Οικονομία* (Thessalonike, 2004).

Kosiński, R., *The Emperor Zeno: Religion and Politics* (Cracow, 2010).

*Kosmas und Damianos*, ed. L. Deubner (Leipzig and Berlin, 1907).

Kostenec, J., "The Heart of the Empire: The Great Palace of the Byzantine Emperors Reconsidered," in *Secular Buildings and the Archaeology of Everyday Life in the Byzantine Empire*, ed. K. Dark (Oxford, 2004), 4–36.

Kotzabassi, S., ed., *The Pantokrator Monastery in Constantinople* (Boston, 2013).

Kountoura-Galake, E., "Legend and Reality: The Case of Oikoumenikos Didaskalos in the Early Palaiologan Period," in *Hypermachos*, ed. C. Stavrakos, A.-K. Wassiliou, and M. K. Krikorian (Wiesbaden, 2008), 173–86.

Krallis, D., *Michael Attaleiates and the Politics of Imperial Decline in Eleventh-Century Byzantium* (Tempe, 2012).

Krausmüller, D., "The Athonite Monastic Tradition during the Eleventh and Early Twelfth Centuries," in *Mount Athos and Byzantine Monasticism*, ed. A. Bryer and M. Cunningham (Aldershot, 1996), 57–65.

Krausmüller, D., "The Triumph of Hesychasm," in *The Cambridge History of Christianity*, Vol. 5, *Eastern Christianity*, ed. M. Angold (Cambridge, 2006), 101–26.

Krausmüller, D., "Decoding Monastic Ritual: Auto-installation and the Struggle for the Spiritual Autonomy of Byzantine Monasteries in the Eleventh and Twelfth Centuries," *JÖB* 58 (2008): 75–86.

Krausmüller, D., "Chastity or Procreation? Models of Sanctity for Byzantine Laymen During the Iconoclastic and Post-iconoclastic Period," *Journal for Late Antique Religion and Culture* 7 (2013), 49–68.

Krausmüller, D., "Liturgical Innovation in Eleventh- and Twelfth-Century Constantinople: Hours and Inter-hours in the Evergetis *Typikon*, Its 'Daughters' and its 'Grand-Daughters'," *REB* 71 (2013): 149–72.

Krausmüller, D., "Diorasis Denied: Opposition to Clairvoyance in Byzantium from Late Antiquity to the Eleventh Century," *JÖB* 65 (2015): 111–28.

Krausmüller, D., "Can Human Beings Know the Hour of Their Own Death or of the Death of Others? A Ninth-Century Controversy and Its Historical Context," *ZRVI* 53 (2016): 63–82.

Krausmüller, D., "From Individual Almsgiving to Communal Charity: The Impact of the Middle Byzantine Monastic Reform Movement on the Life of Monks," *JÖB* 66 (2016): 111–26.

Krausmüller, D., "'Monks Who Are Not Priests Do Not Have the Power to Bind and to Loose': The Debate about Confession in Eleventh- and Twelfth-Century Byzantium'," *BZ* 109 (2016): 703–32.

Krausmüller, D., "Multiple Hierarchies: Servants and Masters, Monastic Officers, Ordained Monks, and Wearers of the Great and the Small Habit at the Stoudios Monastery (10th–11th Centuries)," *BSl* 74 (2016): 92–114.

Krausmüller, D., "From Competition to Conformity: Saints' Lives, *Typika*, and the Byzantine Monastic Discourse of the Eleventh Century," in *Byzantium in the Eleventh Century: Being In-Between*, ed. M. D. Lauxtermann and M. Whittow (Abingdon and New York, 2017), 199–215.

Krausmüller, D., "Nobody Has Ever Seen God: The Denial of the Possibility of Mystical Experiences in Eighth- and Eleventh-Century Byzantium," *Journal of Late Antique Religion and Culture* 11 (2017): 65–73.

Krausmüller, D., "Take No Care for the Morrow! The Rejection of Landed Property in Eleventh- and Twelfth-Century Byzantine Monasticism," *BMGS* 42 (2018): 45–57.

Krausmüller, D., "An Embattled Charismatic: Assertiveness and Invective in Nicetas Stethatos' *Spiritual Centuries*," *BMGS* 44 (2020): 106–23.

Krausmüller, D. and O. Grinchenko, "The Tenth-Century Stoudios *Typikon* and Its Impact on Eleventh- and Twelfth-Century Byzantine Monasticism," *JÖB* 63 (2013): 153–75.

Krischen, F. and T. von Lüpke, *Die Landmauer von Konstantinopel* (Berlin, 1938).

Kuban, D., *Istanbul, an Urban History: Byzantion, Constantinopolis, Istanbul* (Istanbul, 1996).

Kuran, A., *Sinan: The Grand Old Master of Ottoman Architecture* (Istanbul, 1987).

Kyle, D. G., *Sport and Spectacle in the Ancient World*, 2nd ed. (Chichester, 2015).

Kyritses, D. "The Byzantine Aristocracy in the Thirteenth and Early Fourteenth Centuries" (PhD thesis, Harvard University, 1997).

Laiou, A. E., "The Provisioning of Constantinople during the Winter of 1306–1307," *Byzantion* 37 (1967): 91–113.

Laiou, A. E., *Constantinople and the Latins: The Foreign Policy of Andronicus II, 1281–1328* (Cambridge, MA, 1972).

Laiou, A. E., "The Byzantine Economy in the Mediterranean Trade System: 13th–15th Centuries," *DOP* 34 (1980): 177–222.

Laiou, A. E., "The Festival of 'Agathe': Comments on the Life of Constantinopolitan Women," in *Byzantium: Tribute to Andreas N. Stratos*, ed. N. A. Stratos (Athens, 1986), 111–22.

Laiou, A. E., "Women in the Marketplace of Constantinople (10th–14th Centuries)," in *Byzantine Constantinople: Monuments, Topography and Everyday Life*, ed. N. Necipoğlu (Leiden, 2001), 261–73.

Laiou, A. E., et al., *The Economic History of Byzantium from the Seventh through the Fifteenth Century*, 3 vols. (Washington, DC, 2002).

Laiou, A. E., "Exchange and Trade, Seventh–Twelfth Centuries," in *EHB* 2: 697–770.

Laiou, A. E. "Constantinople sous les Paléologues," in *Le monde byzantin*, Vol. 3, *Byzance et ses voisins 1204–1453*, ed. A. Laiou and C. Morrisson (Paris, 2011).

Laiou, A. E. and Morrisson, C., *The Byzantine Economy* (Cambridge, 2007).

Laiou, A. E., ed., *The Economic History of Byzantium: From the Seventh through the Fifteenth Century* (Washington, DC, 2002).

Laiou-Thomadakis, A. E., "The Greek Merchant of the Palaeologan Period: A Collective Portrait," *Praktika tes Akademias Athenon* 57 (1982): 96–132.

Łajtar, A., *Die Inschriften von Byzantion* (Bonn, 2000).

Laniado, A., *Ethnos et droit dans le monde protobyzantin, Ve–VIe siècle: Fédérés, paysans et provinciaux à lumière d'une scholie juridique de l'époque de Justinien* (Geneva, 2015).

Lannoy, G., *Oeuvres de Ghillebert de Lannoy, voyageur, diplomate et moraliste*, ed. C. Potvin (Louvain, 1878).

Lassner, J., *The Topography of Baghdad in the Early Middle Ages: Text and Studies* (Detroit, 1970).

Lauxtermann, M., "The Intertwined Lives of Michael Psellos and John Mauropous," in *The Letters of Psellos*, ed. M. Lauxtermann and M. Jeffreys (Oxford, 2017), 89–127.

Lavan, L., E. Zanini, and A. Sarantis, *Technology in Transition AD 300–650* (Leiden and Boston, 2007).

Le Grand, L. ed. *Statuts d'Hôtels-Dieu et de léproseries; recueil de textes du XIIe au XIVe siècle* (Paris, 1901).

Leal, K. A., "The Ottoman State and the Greek Orthodox of Istanbul: Sovereignty and Identity at the Turn of the Eighteenth Century" (PhD dissertation, Harvard University, 2003).

Lee, A. D., *From Rome to Byzantium AD 363 to 565* (Edinburgh, 2013).

Lefort, J., "The Rural Economy, Seventh–Twelfth Centuries," in *EHB*, 1: 231–311.

Lehmann-Haupt, C. F., "Pausanias, Heros Ktistes von Byzanz," *Klio* 17 (1921): 59–73.

Lemerle, P., "Elèves et Professeurs à Constantinople au Xe Siècle," *CRAI* 113.4 (1969): 576–87.

Lemerle, P., *Le premier humanisme byzantine* (Paris, 1971) (= *Byzantine Humanism: The First Phase*, trans. H. Lindsay and A. Moffat (Canberra, 1986)).

Lemerle, P., *Cinq études sur le XIe siècle byzantin* (Paris, 1977).

Lemerle, P., "Le gouvernement de philosophes," in *Cinq études sur le XIᵉ siècle byzantine*, P. Lemerle (Paris, 1977), 193–248.

Lenski, N., "Assimilation and Revolt in the Territory of Isauria, from the 1st Century BC to the 6th Century AD," *JESHO Orient* 42.4 (1999): 413–65.

Leo Diaconus, *Leonis diaconi Caloënnis historia libri decem et liber de Velitatione Bellica*, CSHB, vol. 5 (Bonn, 1828). English translation: *The History of Leo the Deacon: Byzantine Military Expansion in the Tenth Century*, trans. A.-M. Talbot and D. Sullivan (Washington, DC, 2005).

Leo, Metropolitan of Synada, *The Correspondance of Leo, Metropolitan of Synada and Syncellus*, ed. M. Vinson (Washington, DC, 1985).

Leontsini, M., "Views Regarding the Use of the Syrian Language in Byzantium during the 7th Century," *Graeco-Arabica* 9–10 (2004): 235–48.

Leroy, J., "La vie quotidienne du moine studite," *Irénikon* 27 (1954): 21–50.

Leroy, J., *Studitisches Mönchtum: Spiritualität und Lebensform* (Graz, 1969).

Leszka, M. B., "The Role of the Constantinopolitan Patriarch at the Early Byzantine Emperors' Court," *Acta Universitatis Lodziensis, Folia Historica* 56 (1996): 137–58.

Lewis, G. H., "The Sociology of Popular Culture," *Current Sociology* 26 (1978): 3–64.

Libanius, *Orationes*, 4 vols., ed. R. Foerster, *Libanii opera* (Leipzig, 1903).

*Liber Diurnus Romanorum Pontificum*, ed. H. Foerster (Bern, 1958).

*Liber Pontificalis: texte, introduction, et commentaire*, 3 vols., ed. L. Duchesne (Paris, 1886–1957).

Lidov, A., ed., *New Jerusalems: The Translation of Sacred Spaces* (Moscow, 2006).

Lidov, A., "Spatial Icons: The Miraculous Performance with the Hodegetria of Constantinople," in Иеротопиа: Создание Сакралыьх Простанств в Византии и Древней Руси *[Hierotopy: The Creation of Sacred Spaces in Byzantium and Medieval Russia]*, ed. A. Lidov (Moscow, 2006), 349–72.

Lilie, R.-J., *Handel und Politik zwischen dem byzantinischen Reich und den italienischen Kommunen Venedig, Pisa und Genua in der Epoche der Komnenen und der Angeloi (1081–1204)* (Amsterdam, 1984).

Lim, R., "Consensus and Dissensus on Public Spectacles in Early Byzantium," *ByzF* 24 (1997): 159–79.

Liutprand of Cremona, *Liutprandi Cremonensis Opera omnia: Relatio de legatione Constantinopolitana*, ed. P. Chiesa (Turnhout, 1998).

Liutprand of Cremona, *Complete Works of Liutprand of Cremona*, ed. and trans. P. Squatriti (Washington, DC, 2007).

Livingston, R. A., "Material Analysis of the Masonry of the Hagia Sophia Basilica, Istanbul," in *Soil Dynamics and Earthquake Engineering VI, WIT Transactions on the Built Environment 3*, ed. A. Ş. Çakmak and C. A. Brebbia (Southampton and Boston, 1993), 849–65, www.witpress.com/elibrary/wit-transactions-on-the-builtenvironment/3/13470.

Lopez, R. S., "The Role of Trade in the Economic Readjustment of Byzantium in the Seventh Century," *DOP* 13 (1959): 67–85.

Loseby, S. T., "The Mediterranean Economy," in *NCMH: 1, c.500–c.700*, ed. P. Fouracre (Cambridge, 2005), 605–38.

Loukopoulou, L. D., "Colons et indigénes dans la Thrace Propontique," *Klio* 71 (1989): 78–83.

Loukopoulou, L. D., *Contribution à l'histoire de la Thrace Propontique durant la periode archaique* (Athens, 1989).

Lugovyi, O., "The Chrysobullos of 1189 and the History of German and French Quarters of Constantinople," in *Proceedings of the Symposium on City Ports from the Aegean to the Black Sea: Medieval-Modern Networks*, ed. F. Karagianni and U. Kocabas (Istanbul, 2015), 71–80.

Maas, M., *John Lydus and the Roman Past* (London, 1992).

Macaraig, N., *Çemberlitaş Hamami in Istanbul: The Biographical Memoir of a Turkish Bath* (Edinburgh, 2018).

Machado, C., "Aristocratic Houses and the Making of Late Antique Rome and Constantinople," in *Two Romes: Rome and Constantinople in Late Antiquity*, ed. L. Grig and G. Kelly (Oxford, 2012), 136–60.

Macrides, R. "Killing, Asylum and the Law in Byzantium," *Speculum* 63 (1988): 509–38.

Macrides, R., "Constantinople: The Crusaders' Gaze," in *Travel in The Byzantine World*, ed. R. Macrides (Aldershot, 2002), 193–212.

Macrides, R., "The Citadel of Constantinople," in *Cities and Citadels in Turkey from the Iron Age to the Seljuks*, ed. S. Redford and N. Ergin (Leuven, 2013), 277–304.

Macrides, R., "The 'Other' Palace in Constantinople: The Blachernai," in *The Emperor's House, Palaces from Augustus to the Age of Absolutism*, ed. M. Featherstone, J.-M. Spieser, G. Tanman, and U. Wulf-Rheidt (Berlin, 2015), 159–68.

Macrides, R. and P. Magdalino, "The Architecture of Ekphrasis: Construction and Content of Paul the Silentiary's Poem on Hagia Sophia," *BMGS* 12 (1988): 47–82.

Macrides, R., ed., *Travel in the Byzantine World* (Aldershot, 2002).

Madden, T. F., "The Fires of the Fourth Crusade in Constantinople, 1203–1204: A Damage Assessment," *BZ* 84–5 (1992): 72–93.

Madden, T. F., "The Chrysobull of Alexius I Comnenus to the Venetians: the Date and the Debate," *JMedHist* 28.2 (2002): 199–204.

Madden, T. F., *Istanbul* (New York, 2016).

Madden, T. F., ed., *The Fourth Crusade: Event, Aftermath, Perceptions* (Aldershot, 2008).

Magdalino, P. "Manuel Komnenos and the Great Palace," *BMGS* 4.1 (1978): 101–14.

Magdalino, P., "The Byzantine Aristocratic *Oikos*," in *The Byzantine Aristocracy IX to XII Centuries*, ed. M. Angold (Oxford, 1984), 92–111.

Magdalino, P., "Observations on the Nea Ekklesia of Basil I," *JÖB* 37 (1987): 51–64.

Magdalino, P., "The Bath of Leo the Wise and the 'Macedonian Renaissance' Revisited," *DOP* 42 (1988): 97–118.

Magdalino, P., "Church, Bath, and Diakonia in Medieval Byzantium," in *Church and People in Byzantium*, ed. R. Morris (Birmingham, 1990), 165–88.

Magdalino, P., *The Empire of Manuel I Komnenos, 1143–1180* (Cambridge, 1993).

Magdalino, P., "The Grain Supply of Constantinople, Ninth–Twelfth Centuries," in *Constantinople and Its Hinterland*, ed. C. Mango and G. Dagron (Aldershot, 1995), 35–47 (= "The Grain Supply of Constantinople, NinthTwelfth Centuries," in *Studies on the History and Topography of Byzantine Constantinople*, ed. P. Magdalino (Aldershot and Burlington, 2007), no. IX). IX.

Magdalino, P., *Constantinople Médiévale: Études sur l'évolution des structures urbaines* (Paris, 1996) (= "Medieval Constantinople," in *Studies on the History and Topography of Byzantine Constantinople*, ed. P. Magdalino (Aldershot, 2007), no. I).

Magdalino, P., "The Reform Edict of 1107," in *Alexios I Komnenos*, ed. M. Mullett and D. C. Smythe (Belfast, 1996), 199–218.

Magdalino, P., "The Maritime Neighborhoods of Constantinople: Commercial and Residential Functions, Sixth to Twelfth Centuries," *DOP* 54 (2000): 209–26.

Magdalino, P., "Aristocratic Oikoi in the Tenth and Eleventh Regions of Constantinople," in *Byzantine Constantinople: Monuments, Topography and Everyday Life*, ed. N. Necipoğlu (Leiden, 2001), 53–69.

Magdalino, P., "Medieval Constantinople: Built Environment and Urban Development," *EHB*, 2: 529–37.

Magdalino, P., "L'Église du Phare et les reliques de la Passion à Constantinople (VIIe/VIIe–XIIIe siècles)," in *Byzance et les reliques du Christ*, ed. J. Durand and B. Flusin (Paris, 2004), 15–30.

Magdalino, P., "Constantine V and the Middle Age of Constantinople," in *Studies on the History and Topography of Byzantine Constantinople*, ed. P. Magdalino (Aldershot and Burlington, 2007), no. IV.

Magdalino, P., "Isaac II, Saladin, and Venice," in *The Expansion of Orthodox Europe: Byzantium, the Balkans and Russia*, ed. J. Shepard (Aldershot and Burlington, 2007), 93–106.

Magdalino, P., "Medieval Constantinople," in *Studies on the History and Topography of Byzantine Constantinople*, ed. P. Magdalino (London, 2007).

Magdalino, P., *L'Orthodoxie des astrologues* (Paris, 2007).

Magdalino, P., "Psueo-Kodinos' Constantinople," in *Studies on the History and Topography of Byzantine Constantinople*, ed. P. Magdalino (Aldrshot and Burlington, 2007), no. XII.

Magdalino, P., *Studies in the History and Topography of Byzantine Constantinople* (Aldershot and Burlington, 2007).

Magdalino, P., "Court Society and Aristocracy," in *Social History of Byzantium*, ed. J. Haldon (Chichester, 2009), 212–33.

Magdalino, P., "The Harbors of Byzantine Constantinople," in *Stories from the Hidden Harbor, Shipwrecks of Yenikapı*, ed. Z. Kızıltan (Istanbul, 2013), 11–15.

Magdalino, P., "Power Building and Power Space in Byzantine Constantinople: The Ethics and Dynamics of Construction and Conservation in the Byzantine Court," in *The Byzantine Court: Source of Power and Culture*, ed. A. Ödekan et al. (Istanbul, 2013): 55–62.

Magdalino, P., "The People and the Palace," in *The Emperor's House: Palaces from Augustus to the Age of Absolutism*, ed. M. Featherstone, J-M. Spieser, G. Tanman, U. Wulf-Rhiedt (Berlin and Boston, 2015): 169–80.

Magdalino, P., "The Culture of Water in the 'Macedonian Renaissance'," in *Fountains and Water Culture in Byzantium*, ed. B. Shilling and P. Stephenson (Cambridge, 2016), 130–44.

Magdalino, P., "The House of Basil the Parakoimomenos," in *Le saint, le moine et le paysan, Mélanges d'histoire byzantine offerts à Michel Kaplan*, ed. O. Delouis, S. Métivier, and P. Pagès (Paris, 2016), 323–8.

Magdalino, P., "The Merchant of Constantinople," in *Trade in Byzantium*, ed. P. Magdalino and N. Necipoğlu (Istanbul, 2016), 181–91.

Magdalino, P., "Neighbourhoods in Byzantine Constantinople," in *Hinter den Mauern und auf dem offenen Land: Neue Forschungen zum Leben im byzantinischen Reich*, ed. F. Daim and J. Drauschke (Mainz, 2016), 23–30.

Magdalino, P., "The House of Basil the Parakoimomenos," in *Le saint, le moine et le paysan, Mélanges d'histoire byzantine offerts à Michel Kaplan*, ed. O. Delouis, S. Métivier, and P. Pagès (Paris, 2016), 323–8.

Magdalino, P., "Constantinople in the Age of Constantine VII Porphyrogennetos," in *Center, Province and Periphery in the Age of Constantine VII Porphyrogennetos*, ed. N. Gaul, V. Menze and C. Bálint (Wiesbaden, 2018), 39–54.

Magdalino, P., "Renaissances d'une capitale: l'urbanisme constantinopolitain des dynasties impériales," *TM* 22.1 (2018): 55–77.

Magdalino, P., "Modes of Reconstruction in Byzantine Constantinople," in *Reconstruire les villes, temps et espaces réappropriés*, ed. E. Capet et al. (Turnhout, 2019), 255–68.

Magdalino, P. "Around and About the Holy Apostles," in *The Holy Apostles: A Lost Monument, a Forgotten Project, and the Presentness of the Past*, ed. M. Mullett and R. G. Ousterhout (Washington, DC, 2020), 131–42.

Magdalino, P. and N. Ergin, eds., *Istanbul and Water* (Leuven, 2015).

Magdalino, P. and N. Necipoğlu, eds., *Trade in Byzantium* (Istanbul, 2016).

Magoulias, H., "The Lives of the Saints as Sources of Data for the History of Commerce in the Byzantine Empire in the VIth and VIIth Cent.," *Kleronomia* 4 (1971): 303–30.

Maguire, E. D. and H. Maguire, *Other Icons: Art and Power in Byzantine Secular Culture* (Princeton, 2007).

Maguire, H., "Gardens and Parks in Constantinople," *DOP* 54 (2000): 251–64.

Maguire, H. and R. Ousterhout, "Introduction: Constantinople: The Fabric of the City," *DOP* 54 (2000): 157–9.

Maguire, H., ed., *Byzantine Court Culture from 829 to 1204* (Washington, DC, 1997).

Maier, J., "Francesco Rosselli's Lost View of Rome," *ArtB* 94 (2012): 395–411.

Maier, J., *Rome Measured and Imagined, Early Modern Maps of the Eternal City* (Chicago, 2015).

Mainstone, R. J., *Hagia Sophia: Architecture, Structure, and Liturgy of Justinian's Great Church* (New York, 1988).

Majeska, G. P., "A Medallion of the Prophet Daniel in the Dumbarton Oaks Collection," *DOP* 28 (1974): 361–6.

Majeska, G. P., *Russian Travelers to Constantinople in the Fourteenth and Fifteenth Centuries* (Washington, DC, 1984).

Majeska, G. P., "Russian Pilgrims in Constantinople," *DOP* 56 (2002): 93–108.

Maksimović, L. *The Byzantine Provincial Administration under the Palaiologoi* (Amsterdam, 1988).

Malmberg, S. "Dazzling Dining: Banquets as an Expression of Imperial Legitimacy" (PhD dissertation, Uppsala University, 2003).

Malmberg, S., "Dazzling Dining: Banquets as an Expression of Imperial Legitimacy," in *Eat, Drink, and Be Merry (Luke 12:19): Food and Wine in Byzantium*, ed. L. Brubaker and K. Linardou (Aldershot, 2007), 75–91.

Mamboury, E. and T. Wiegand, *Die Kaiserpaläste von Konstantinopel zwischen Hippodrom und Marmara-Meer* (Berlin, 1934).

Manasses, C., *Constantini Manassis Breviarium*, ed. I. Bekker (Bonn, 1837).

Manasses, C., "Encomium on Nikephoros Komnenos," ed. E. Kurtz, in *VizVrem* 17, ed. E. Kurtz (1910): 302–22.

Mango, C., *The Brazen House: A Study of the Vestibule of the Imperial Palace of Constantinople* (Copenhagen, 1959).

Mango, C., "Antique Statuary and the Byzantine Beholder," *DOP* 17 (1963): 55–75.

Mango, C., "Constantinopolitana," *JDAI* 80 (1965): 305–36.

Mango, C., *Byzantine Architecture* (New York, 1976).

Mango, C., "The Date of the Studius Basilica at Istanbul," *BMGS* 4 (1978): 115–22.

Mango, C., "Daily Life in Byzantium," *JÖB* 31/1 (1982): 337–53.

Mango, C., "A Daniel Apocalypse of 716/717," *Rivista di studi bizantini e slavi* 2 (1982): 297–313.

Mango, C., *Le développement urbain de Constantinople (IVe–VIIe siècles)* (Paris, 1985; reprint with addenda, 1990).

Mango, C., "Constantine's Mausoleum and the Translation of Relics," *BZ* 83 (1990): 51–61.

Mango, C., "The Palace of Marina, the Poet Palladas and the Bath of Leo VI," in *Euphrosynon: aphieroma ston Manoli Chatzidaki*, ed. E. Kypraiou (Athens, 1991), 1: 321–30.

Mango, C., "Byzantine Writers on the Fabric of Hagia Sophia," in *Hagia Sophia from the Age of Justinian to the Present*, ed. R. Mark and A. Ş. Çakmak (Cambridge, 1992), 41–56.

Mango, C., "Columns of Justinian and his Successors," in *Studies on Constantinople*, C. Mango (Aldershot 1993) no. X.

Mango, C. "The Development of Constantinople as an Urban Centre," in *Studies on Constantinople*, C. Mango (Aldershot, 1993), no. I (= *The 17th International Byzantine Congress: Main Papers* (New Rochelle, NY, 1986), 117–36).

Mango, C., "Justinian's Equestrian Statue," in *Studies on Constantinople*, C. Mango (Aldershot, 1993) no. XI (= Letter to the Editor, *Art Bulletin* 41.4 (1959): 351–6).

Mango, C., *Studies on Constantinople* (Aldershot, 1993).

Mango, C., "Ancient Spolia in the Great Palace of Constantinople," in *Byzantine East, Latin West: Art-Historical Studies in Honor of Kurt Weitzmann*, ed. C. Moss and K. Kiefer (Princeton, 1995), 645–9.

Mango, C., "The Water Supply of Constantinople," in *Constantinople and Its Hinterland*, ed. C. Mango and G. Dagron (Aldershot, 1995), 9–18.

Mango, C., "The Palace of the Boukoleon," *CahArch* 45 (1997): 41–50.

Mango, C., "The Relics of St. Euphemia and the Synaxarion of Constantinople," *BollGrott* 53 (1999): 79–87.

Mango, C., "The Triumphal Way of Constantinople and the Golden Gate," *DOP* 54 (2000): 173–88.

Mango, C., "The Shoreline of Constantinople in the Fourth Century," in *Byzantine Constantinople: Monuments, Topography and Everyday Life*, ed. N. Necipoğlu (Leiden, 2001), 17–28.

Mango, C., "Le mystère de la XIVe région de Constantinople," in *Mélanges Gilbert Dagron*, ed. V. Déroche (Paris, 2002) 449–55.

Mango, C., "Septime Sévère et Byzanc," *CRAI* 147.2 (2003): 593–608.

Mango, C., "Introduction," in *Byzance et les reliques du Christ*, ed. J. Durand and B. Flusin (Paris, 2004), 11–14.

Mango, C., "A History of the Hippodrome of Constantinople," in *Hippodrome/Atmeydanı*, 2 vols., ed. B. Pitarakis (Istanbul, 2010), 1: 36–44.

Mango, C. and G. Dagron, eds., *Constantinople and Its Hinterland* (Aldershot, 1995).

Mango, M. M., "The Commercial Map of Constantinople," *DOP* 54 (2000): 189–207.

Mango, M. M., "Beyond the Amphora: Non-ceramic Evidence for Late Antique Industry and Trade," in *Economy and Exchange in the East Mediterranean during the Late Antiquity*, ed. S. Kingsley and M. Decker (Oxford, 2001), 87–106.

Maniatis, G. "The Byzantine Cheesemaking Industry," *Byzantion* 84 (2014): 257–84.

Manners, I. R., "Constructing the Image of a City: The Representation of Constantinople in C. Buondelmonti *Liber Insularum Archipelagi*," *Annals of the Association of American Geographers* 87 (1997): 72–102.

Manolopoulou, V., "Processing Emotion: Litanies in Byzantine Constantinople," in *Experiencing Byzantium*, ed. C. Nesbitt and M. Jackson (Farnham, 2013), 153–71.

Mansel, A. M., "Les fouilles de Rhegion près d'Istanbul," in *Actes du VIe Congrès International d'Etudes Byzantines*, 2 vols., ed. Comité français des études byzantines (Paris, 1951), 2: 256–60.

Manuzio, A., *The Greek Classics*, ed. and trans. N. Wilson (Cambridge, MA, 2016).

Maraval, P., *Lieux saints et pèlerinages d'Orient: Histoire et géographie des origines à la conquête arabe* (Paris, 1985).

Marciniak, P., "The Byzantine Performative Turn," in *Within the Circle of Ancient Ideas and Virtues: Studies in Honour of Professor Maria Dzielska*, ed. K. Twardowska, et al. (Krakow, 2014), 423–30.

Marciniak, P., "How to Entertain the Byzantines: Some Remarks on Mimes and Jesters in Byzantium," in *Medieval and Early Modern Performance in the Eastern Mediterranean*, ed. A. Öztürkmen and E. Birge Vitz (Turnhout, 2014), 125–48.

Margolis, O., *Aldus Manutius: A Cultural History* (forthcoming).

Maridaki-Karatza, O., "Legal Aspects of the Financing of Trade," in *EHB*, 3: 1105–20.

Marinescu, C. A., "Making and Spending Money along the Bosporus: The Lysimachi Coinages Minted by Byzantium and Chalcedon and Their Socio-cultural Context" (PhD dissertation, Columbia University, 1996).

Marinis, V., "Tombs and Burials in the Monastery *tou Libos* in Constantinople," *DOP* 63 (2009): 147–66.

Marinis, V., *Architecture and Ritual in the Churches of Constantinople, Ninth–Fifteenth Centuries* (Cambridge, 2014).

Marinis, V., "The *Historia Ekklesiastike kai Mystike Theoria*: A Symbolic Understanding of the Byzantine Church Building," *BZ* 108 (2015): 753–70.

Markopoulos, A., *Anonymi professoris epistulae* (Berlin, 2000).

Markopoulos, A., "Education," in *The Oxford Handbook of Byzantine Studies*, ed. E. Jeffrey, J. Haldon, and R. Cormack (Oxford, 2008), 785–95.

Markopoulos, A., "In Search for 'Higher Education' in Byzantium," *ZRVI* 50 (2013): 29–44.

Martin, M. E., "The Venetians in the Byzantine Empire before 1204," *ByzF* 13 (1988): 201–14.

Mateos, J., *The Liturgy of the Word* (Fairfax, VA, 2016).

Mateos, J., ed., *Le typicon de la Grande Église. MS Sainte-Croix no. 40, Xe siècle*, Vol. 1, *Le cycle des douze mois* (Rome, 1962).

Mathews, T. F., *The Early Churches of Constantinople: Architecture and Liturgy* (University Park, 1971).

Mathews, T. F., "The Palace Church of Sts. Sergius and Bacchus in Constantinople," in *Archaeology in Architecture: Studies in Honor of Cecil L. Striker*, ed. J. J. Emerick and D. M. Deliyannis (Mainz, 2005), 137–41.

Mathews, T. F. and A.-C. Daskalakis-Mathews, "Islamic-Style Mansions in Byzantine Cappadocia and the Development of the Inverted T-Plan," *JSAH* 56.3 (1997): 294–315.

Matschke, K.-P., "Rolle und Aufgabe des Gouverneurs von Konstantinopel in der Palaiologenzeit," *Byzantinobulgarica* 3 (1969): 81–110.

Matschke, K.-P., "Rolle und Aufgaben der Demarchen in der spätbyzantinischen Hauptstadt," *Jahrbuch für Geschichte des Feudalismus* 1 (1977): 211–31 (= *Das spätbyzanische Konstantinopel*, 153–87).

Matschke, K.-P., "Builders and Building in Late Byzantine Constantinople," in *Byzantine Constantinople: Monuments, Topography and Everyday Life*, ed. N. Necipoğlu (Leiden, 2001): 315–28.

Matschke, K.-P., "Commerce, Trade, Markets, and Money, Thirteenth–Fifteenth Centuries," in *EHB* 2: 771–806.

Matschke, K.-P., "Late Byzantine Urban Economy, Thirteenth–Fifteenth Centuries," in *EHB* 2: 463–95.

Matschke, K.-P., *Das spätbyzantinische Konstantinopel: Alte und neue Beiträge zur Stadtgeschichte zwischen 1261 und 1453* (Hamburg, 2008).

Matthews, J., "*Notitia Urbis Constantinopolitanae*," in *Two Romes: Rome and Constantinople in Late Antiquity*, ed. L. Grig and G. Kelly (Oxford, 2012), 81–115.

McCall, T. and S. Roberts, "Art and the Material Culture of Diplomacy," in *Italian Renaissance Diplomacy*, ed. M. Azzolini and I. Lazarini (Toronto, 2017), 214–33.

McGeer, E., *Sowing the Dragon's Teeth: Byzantine Warfare in the Tenth Century* (Washington, DC, 1995).

McVey, K. E., "Spirit Embodied: The Emergence of Symbolic Interpretations of Early Christian and Byzantine Architecture," in *Architecture as Icon: Perception and Representation of Architecture in Byzantine Art*, ed. S. Ćurčić and E. Hadjitryphonos (Princeton, 2010), 38–71.

Meijer, F., *Chariot Racing in the Roman Empire: Spectacles in Rome and Constantinople* (Baltimore, 2010).

Mercati, S. G., "Santuari de reliquie costantinopolitane secondo il codice Ottoboniano Latino 169 prima della conquista Latina (1204)," *RendPontAcc* 3.12 (1936): 133–56.

Mergiali, S., *L'enseignement et les lettrés pendant l'époque des Paléologues (1261–1453)* (Athens, 1996).

Merkelbach, R., ed., *Die Inschriften von Kalchedon* (Bonn, 1980).

Merle, H., *Die Geschichte des Städte Byzantion und Kalchedon, von ihrer Gründung biz zum Eingriefen der Römer in die Verhältnisse des Ostens* (Kiel, 1916).

Merlet, R. and M. Jusselin, eds., *Cartulaire de la léproserie du Grand-Beaulieu et du prieuré de Notre-Dame de la Bourdenière* (Chartres, 1990).

Mesarites, N. *Die Palastrevolution von Johannes Komnenos*, ed. A. Heisenberg (Würzburg, 1907).

Mesarites, N., "Description of the Church of the Holy Apostles," §42, *Grabskirche und Apostelkirche*, ed. A. Heisenberg (Leipzig, 1908), 2: 90–4.

Mesarites, N., *Nicholas Mesarites: His Life and Works*, trans. M. Angold (Liverpool, 2017), 129–31.

Meserve, M., *Empires of Islam in Renaissance Historical Thought* (Cambridge, MA, 2008).

Metivier, S., "Note sur l'hippodrome de Constantinople vu par les Arabes," *TM* 13 (2000), 175–80.

Metzger, C., "Tissus et culte des relique," *AntTard* 12 (2004): 183–6.

Meyendorff, P., *St. Germanus of Constantinople: On the Divine Liturgy* (Crestwood, 1984).

Meyer-Plath, B. and A. M. Schneider, *Die Landmauer von Konstantinopel*, 2 vols. (Berlin, 1943; reprint 1974).

Miklosich, F. and I. Müller, eds., *Acta et diplomata graeca medii aevi sacra et profana*, 6 vols. (Vienna, 1860–90; reprint Athens, 1961).

Millar, F., *A Greek Roman Empire: Power and Belief under Theodosius II, 408–50* (Berkeley, 2006).

Miller, N., *Mapping the City: The Language and Culture of Cartography in the Renaissance* (London, 2003).

Miller, T. S., *The Birth of the Hospital in the Byzantine Empire* (Baltimore, 1985; revised edition, 1997).

Miller, T. S., "The Sampson Xenon," *ByzF* 15 (1990): 101–35.

Miller, T. S., "The Legend of Saint Zotikos according to Constantine Akropolites," *AB* 112 (1994): 339–76.

Miller, T. S., *The Orphans of Byzantium: Child Welfare in the Christian Empire* (Washington, DC, 2003).

Miller, T. S., "Two Teaching Texts from the Twelfth-Century Orphanotropheion," in *Byzantine Authors, Literary Activities and Preoccupations: Texts and Translations Dedicated to the Memory of Nicolas Oikonomides*, ed. J. Nesbitt (Leiden and Boston, 2003), 9–20.

Miller, T. S., "Medical Thought and Practice," in *The Cambridge Intellectual History of Byzantium*, ed. A. Kaldellis and N. Siniossoglou (Cambridge, 2017), 252–65.

Miller, T. S. and J. Nesbitt, *Walking Corpses: Leprosy in Byzantium and the Medieval West* (Ithaca, NY, 2014).

*Miracles of St. Artemius*, ed. and trans. V. Crisafulli and J. Nesbitt (Leiden, 1997).

Moeglin, J.-M. and A. Péquinot, *Diplomatie et 'Relations Internationales' au Moyen Age (IXe–XVe siècle)* (Paris, 2017).

Mordechai, L., and M. Eisenberg, "Rejecting Catastrophe: The Case of the Justinianic Plague," *Past and Present* 244 (2019): 3–50.

Moreno, A., "Hieron: The Ancient Sanctuary at the Mouth of the Black Sea," *Hesperia* 77 (2008): 655–709.

Moreno Gallo, I., "Roman Water Supply Systems, a New Approach," in *De aquaeductu atque aqua urbium Lyciae, Pamphyliae, Pisidiae, the Legacy of Sextus Julius Frontinus*, ed. G. Wiplinger (Leuven, 2016), 117–27.

Morrisson, C., "Trading in Wood in Byzantium: Exchange and Regulations," in *Trade in Byzantium*, ed. P. Magdalino and N. Necipoğlu (Istanbul, 2016), 105–27.

Morrisson C. and J.-P. Sodini, "The Sixth-Century Economy," in *EHB* 1: 165–220.

Morrisson, C., ed., *Le monde byzantine I: L'Empire romain d'orient (330–641)* (Paris, 2004).

Morrisson, C., ed., *Trade and Markets in Byzantium* (Washington, DC, 2012).

Morrisson, C. and J.-P. Sodini, eds., *Constantinople réelle et imaginaire: autour de l'œuvre de Gilbert Dagron*, TM 22.1 (2018).

Moustakas, K., "Μεθοδολογικά ζητήματα στην προσέγγιση των πληθυσμιακών μεγεθών της υστεροβυζαντινής πόλης," in *Οι βυζαντινές πόλεις (8ος-15ος αιώνας): Προοπτικές της έρευνας και ερευνητικές προσεγγίσεις*, ed. T. Kiousopoulou (Rethymno, 2012), 225–51.

Mueller-Jourdan, P., *Typologie spatio-temporelle de l'ecclesia byzantine: la mystagogie de Maxime le Confesseur dans la culture philosophique de l'antiquité tardive* (Leiden and Boston, 2005).

Müller, A. E., "Getreide für Konstantinopel: Überlegungen zu Justinians Edikt XIII als Grundlage für Aussagen zur Einwohnerzahl Konstantinopels im 6. Jahrhundert," *JÖB* 43 (1993): 1–20.

Müller, G., ed., *Documenti sulle relazioni delle città toscane coll'Oriente cristiano e coi Turchi fino all'anno 1531* (Florence, 1879).

Müller-Wiener, W., *Bildlexikon zur Topographie Istanbuls: Byzantion, Konstantinupolis, Istanbul bis zum Beginn d. 17. Jh.* (Tübingen, 1977).

Mullett, M., "Aristocracy and Patronage," in *The Byzantine Aristocracy, IX–XIII Centuries*, ed. M. Angold (Oxford, 1984), 173–201.

Mullett, M., "No Drama, No Poetry, No Fiction, No Readership, No Literature," in *A Companion to Byzantium*, ed. L. James (Marden, 2010), 227–38.

Mullett, M. and R. G. Ousterhout, eds., *The Holy Apostles: A Lost Monument, a Forgotten Project, and the Presentness of the Past* (Washington, DC, 2020).

Murphey, R., "Provisioning Istanbul: The State and Subsistence in the Early Modern Middle East," *Food and Foodways* 2 (1988): 217–63.

Nagel, A. and C. Wood, *Anachronic Renaissance* (Cambridge, MA, 2010).

Naumann, R., "Vorbericht über die Ausgrabungen zwischen Mese und Antiochus-Palast 1964 in Istanbul," *IstMitt* 15 (1965): 135–48.

Naumann, R., "Der antike Rundbau beim Myrelaion und der Palast Romanos I. Lekapenos," *IstMitt* 16 (1966): 199–216.

Necipoğlu, G., "The Life of an Imperial Monument: Hagia Sophia after Byzantium," in *Hagia Sophia from the Age of Justinian to the Present*, ed. R. Mark and A. S. Çakmak (Cambridge, 1992), 195–225.

Necipoğlu, G., *The Age of Sinan: Architectural Culture in the Ottoman Empire* (London, 2005).

Necipoğlu, G., "Visual Cosmopolitanism and Creative Translation: Artistic Conversations with Renaissance Italy in Mehmed II's Constantinople," *Muqarnas* 29 (2012): 1–81.

Necipoğlu, G., "Connectivity, Mobility, and Mediterranean 'Portable Archaeology': Pashas from the Dalmatian Hinterland as Cultural Mediators," in *Dalmatia and the Mediterranean: Portable Archeology and the Poetics of Influence*, ed. A. Payne (Leiden, 2013), 313–81.

Necipoğlu, N., "Ottoman Merchants in Constantinople during the First Half of the Fifteenth Century," *BMGS* 16 (1992): 158–69.

Necipoğlu, N., "Economic Conditions in Constantinople during the Siege of Bayezid I (1394–1402)," in *Constantinople and Its Hinterland*, ed. C. Mango and G. Dagron (Aldershot, 1995), 157–67.

Necipoğlu, N., *Byzantium between the Ottomans and the Latins: Politics and Society in the Late Empire* (Cambridge, 2009).

Necipoğlu, N., "Gennadios Scholarios and the Patriarchate: A Reluctant Patriarch on the 'Unhappy Throne'," in *The Holy Apostles: A Lost Monument, a Forgotten Project, and the Presentness of the Past*, ed. M. Mullet and R. G. Ousterhout (Washington, DC, 2020), 237–46.

Necipoğlu, N., ed., *Byzantine Constantinople: Monuments, Topography and Everyday Life* (Leiden, 2001).

Nedungatt, G. and M. Featherstone, eds., *The Council in Trullo Revisited* (Rome, 1995).

Neil, B., *Seventh-Century Popes and Martyrs: The Political Hagiography of Anastasius Bibliothecarius* (Turnhout, 2006).

Nelson, R., "Byzantium and the Rebirth of Art and Learning in Italy and France," in *Byzantium: Faith and Power (1261–1557)*, ed. H. C. Evans (New York, 2004), 515–23.

Nelson, R., "Byzantine Art in the Italian Renaissance," in *Heaven and Earth: Art of Byzantium in Greek Collections*, ed. A. Drandaki, D. Papanikola-Bakirtzi, and A. Tourta (Los Angeles, 2014), 327–35.

Nesbitt, J., "Byzantine Copper Tokens," in *SBS* 1, ed. N. Oikonomides (Washington, DC, 1987): 67–75.

Nesbitt, J., "The Orphanotrophos: Some Observations on the History of the Office in Light of Seals," *SBS* 8, ed. J.-C. Cheynet and C. Soda (Munich and Leipzig, 2003): 51–62.

Nesbitt, J., "St. Zotikos and the Early History of the Office of Orphnaotrophos," in *Byzantine State and Society: In Memory of Nikos Oikonomides*, ed. A. Avramea, A. Laiou, and E. Chrysos (Athens, 2003), 417–22.

Nesbitt, J. and T. S. Miller, *Walking Corpses: Leprosy in Byzantium and the Medieval West* (Ithaca, NY, 2014).

Nesbitt, J., ed., *Byzantine Authors, Literary Activities and Preoccupations: Texts and Translations Dedicated to the Memory of Nicolas Oikonomides* (Leiden and Boston, 2003).

Neuman, G. A., "Ludolphus de Sudheim, *De Itinere Terre Sancte*," *AOL* 2 (1882): *Voyages*, 3: 305–77.

Newton, C. T., *Travels and Discoveries in the Levant*, 2 vols. (London, 1865).

Nicol, D., *Byzantium and Venice: A Study in Diplomatic and Cultural Relations* (Cambridge, 1988).

Nicol, D., *The Last Centuries of Byzantium, 1261–1453* (Cambridge, 2004).

Niewöhner, P., "Der frühbyzantinische Rundbau beim Myrelaion in Konstantinopel. Kapitelle, Mosaiken und Ziegelstempel," *IstMitt* 60 (2010): 411–59.

Niewöhner, P., "The Rotunda at the Myrelaion in Constantinople: Pilaster Capitals, Mosaics, and Brick Stamps," in *The Byzantine Court: Source of Power and Culture*, ed. A. Ödekan, E. Akyürek, and N. Necipoğlu (Istanbul, 2013), 25–36.

Niewöhner, P., "Historisch-topographische Überlegungen zum Trierer Prozessionselfenbein, dem Christusbild an der Chalke, Kaiserin Irenes Triumph im Bilderstreit und der Euphemiakirche am Hippodrom," *Millennium* 11 (2014): 261–88.

Niewöhner, P., "The Late Late Antique Origins of Byzantine Palace Architecture," in *The Emperor's House: Palaces from Augustus to the Age of Absolutism*, ed. M. Featherstone, J-M. Spieser, G. Tanman, and U. Wulf-Rhiedt (Berlin, 2015), 31–52.

Niewöhner, P., "The Decline and Afterlife of the Roman Entablature: The Collection of the Archaeological Museum Istanbul and other Byzantine Epistyles and Cornices from Constantinople," *IstMitt* 67 (2017): 237–328.

Niewöhner, P., "Houses," in *The Archaeology of Byzantine Anatolia*, ed. P. Niewöhner (New York, 2017), 39–59.

Nikephoras, *Nikephoros, Patriarch of Constantinople, Short History*, trans. C. Mango (Washington, DC, 1990).

Nikephoras, *The Life of St. Andrew the Fool*, 2 vols., ed. L. Rydén (Uppsala, 1995).

Nikephoros, Patriarch of Constantinople, *Opuscula historica* ed. C. de Boor (Leipzig, 1880).

Nixon, L. and S. Price, "The Size and Resources of Greek Cities," in *The Greek City, from Homer to Alexander*, ed. O. Murray and S. Price (Oxford, 1990), 137–70.

Noailles, P. and A. Dain, ed. and trans., *Les novelles de Léon VI le Sage* (Paris, 1944).

Norman, A. F., *Themistii orationes qui supersunt* (Leipzig, 1965).

*Notitia Dignitatum*, ed. C. Neira Faleiro (Madrid, 2004).

Nutton, V., "Essay Review," *Medical History* 30 (1986): 218–21.

Ödekan, A., E. Akyürek, and N. Necipoğlu, eds., *The Byzantine Court: Source of Power and Culture* (Istanbul, 2013).

Odo of Deuil, *De profectione Ludovici VII in orientem: The Journey of Louis VII to the East*, ed. and trans. V. G. Berry (New York, 1948).

Oikonomides, N., *Les listes de préséance byzantines des IXe et Xe siècles* (Paris, 1972).

Oikonomides, N., "Quelques boutiques de Constantinople au Xe s.: prix, loyers, imposition (Cod. Patmiacus 171)," *DOP* 26 (1972): 345–56.

Oikonomides, N., *Hommes d'affaires grecs et latins à Constantinople: XIIIe–XVe siècles* (Montreal, 1979).

Oikonomides, N., "Un vast atelier: artisans et marchands," in *Constantinople 1054–1261: tête de la chrétienté, proie des latins, capitale grecque*, ed. A, Ducellier and M. Balard (Paris, 1996), 104–35.

Oikonomides, N., "The Economic Region of Constantinople: From Directed Economy to Free Economy, and the Role of the Italians," in *Europa medievale e mondo bizantino*, ed. G. Arnaldi and G. Cavallo (Rome, 1997), 221–38.

Oikonomides, N., "Entrepreneurs," in *The Byzantines*, ed. G. Cavallo (Chicago, 1997), 144–71.

Oikonomides, N., "Title and Income at the Byzantine Court," in *Byzantine Court Culture from 829 to 1204*, ed. H. Maguire (Washington, DC, 1997), 199–215.

Oikonomides, N. and E. Zachariadou, *Social and Economic Life in Byzantium* (Aldershot, 2004).

Öncü, E. and S. Çömlekçi, "Yenikapı Kazıları ve Bizans Dönemi Amphora Buluntuları," *XIth Congress Aiecm3 on Medieval and Modern Period Mediterranean Ceramics Proceedings*, 2 vols., ed. F. Yenişehirlioğlu (Ankara, 2018) 1: 15–28.

Oreskov, P. N., "Vizantijski starini okolo Carigrad," *SpBAN* 10 (1915): 71–118.

Östenberg, I., S. Malmberg, and J. Bjørnebye, eds., *The Moving City: Processions, Passages and Promenades in Ancient Rome* (London, 2015).

Ousterhout, R., "Observations on the 'Recessed Brick' Technique during the Palaeologan Period," *Archaiologikon Deltion* 39 (1984): 163–70.

Ousterhout, R., *The Architecture of the Kariye Camii in Istanbul* (Washington, DC, 1987).

Ousterhout, R., "Building Medieval Constantinople," in *Proceedings of the PMR Conference* 19–20 (1994–6): 35–67.

Ousterhout, R., "Temporal Structuring in the Chora Parekklesion," *Gesta* 34 (1995): 63–76.

Ousterhout, R., *Master Builders of Byzantium* (Princeton, 1999).

Ousterhout, R., "Contextualizing the Later Churches of Constantinople: Suggested Methodologies and a few Examples," *DOP* 54 (2000): 241–50.

Ousterhout, R., "Study and Restoration of the Zeyrek Camii in Istanbul: First Report, 1997–1998," *DOP* 54 (2000): 265–70.

Ousterhout, R., "Architecture, Art, and Komnenian Ideology at the Pantokrator Monastery," in *Byzantine Constantinople: Monuments, Topography and Everyday Life*, ed. N. Necipoğlu (Leiden, 2001), 133–50.

Ousterhout, R., *The Art of the Kariye Camii* (London, 2002).

Ousterhout, R., "Byzantine Funerary Architecture of the Twelfth Century," in *Drevnerulskoe iskustvo: Rusi i stranii byzantinskogo mira XII vek* (St. Petersburg, 2002), 9–17.

Ousterhout, R., "The East, the West, and the Appropriation of the Past in Early Ottoman Architecture," *Gesta* 43(2004): 165–76.

Ousterhout, R., "Constantinople and the Construction of Medieval Urban Identity," in *The Byzantine World*, ed. P. Stephenson (London and New York, 2010), 334–51.

Ousterhout, R. "Aesthetics and Politics in the Architecture of Justinian," *TM* 22.1 (2018): 103–20.

Ousterhout, R., *Eastern Medieval Architecture: The Building Traditions of Byzantium and Neighboring Lands* (Oxford, 2019).

Pachymeres, G., *Relation Historiques*, 5 vols., ed. A. Failler (Paris 1984–2000).

Palágyi, T., "Between Admiration, Anxiety, and Anger: Views on Mimes and Performers in the Byzantine World," in *Medieval and Early Modern Performance in the Eastern Mediterranean*, ed. A. Öztürkmen and E. Birge Vitz (Turnhout, 2014), 149–65.

*Palestine Pilgrims Text Society*, 15 vols. (London, 1887–97).

Palladios, *Dialogue sur la vie de Jean Chrysostome: Introduction, texte critique, traduction française, et notes*, 2 vols., ed. and trans. A.-M. Malingrey with P. Leclercq (Paris, 1988).

Papadopoulos-Kerameus, A., "Vita Antonii junioris," *Provoslavnij Palestinskij Sbornik* 19 (1907): 186–216.

Papakonstantinou, Z., "Work and Leisure," in *A Cultural History of Work in Antiquity*, ed. E. Lytle (London, 2018), 159–71.

Papanikola-Bakirtzis, D., ed., *Daily Life in Byzantium* (Athens, 2002).

Pargoire, J., "Saint-Mamas, le quartier des Russes à Constantinople," *Échos d'Orient* 11.71 (1908): 203–310.

Paribeni, A., "Le sigle dei marmorari e l'organizzazione del cantiere," in *S. Sofia di Costantinopoli: L'arredo marmoreo della Grande Chiesa giustinianea*, ed. A. Guiglia Guidobaldi and C. Barsanti (Vatican City, 2004), 651–734.

Parnell, D. A., "Spectacle and Sport in Constantinople in the Sixth Century CE," in *A Companion to Sport and Spectacle in Greek and Roman Antiquity*, ed. P. Christesen and D. G. Kyle (London, 2013), 633–45.

"Passion des saints Adrien et Natalie," in *Hagiologie Byzantine*, ed. F. Halkin (Brussels, 1986), 47–55.

Patala, Z., "Les chants grecs du *Liber Politicus* du chanoine Benoît," *Byzantion* 66 (1996): 512–30.

Paton, W. R., trans., *Anthologia Graeca* I.10 (Cambridge, MA, 1916).

Pentcheva, B., *Icons and Power: The Mother of God in Byzantium* (University Park, 2006).

Pentcheva, B. V., *Hagia Sophia: Sound, Space, and Spirit in Byzantium* (University Park, 2017).

Pérez Martín, I., "Le conflit de l'union des églises (1274) et son reflet dans l'enseignement supérieur de Constantinople," *BSl* 56 (1995): 411–22.

Perisanidi, M., "Entertainment in the Twelfth-Century Canonical Commentaries:
Were Standards the Same for Byzantine Clerics and Laymen?" *BMGS* 38 (2014):
185–200.

Pertusi, A., *La Caduta Di Costantinopoli* (Rome, 1976).

Peschlow, U., *Die Irenenkirche in Istanbul* (Tübingen, 1977).

Peschlow, U., "Eine wiedergewonnen byzantinische Ehrensäule in Istanbul," in *Studien
zur spätantiken und byzantinischen Kunst*, ed. O. Feld (Bonn 1986), 1: 21–33.

Peschlow, U., "Die befestigte Residenz von Mermerkule," *JÖB* 51 (2001): 385–401.

Peschlow, U., "Dividing Interior Space in Early Byzantine Churches: The Barriers
between the Nave and Aisles," in *Thresholds of the Sacred: Architectural, Art Historical,
Liturgical, and Theological Perspectives on Religious Screens, East and West*, ed. S. E. J.
Gerstel (Washington, DC, 2006), 53–71.

Petit, L., "Monodie de Nicétas Eugénianos sur Théodore Prodrome," *Vizantinijskij
Vremennik* 9 (1902): 446–63.

Petit, L., "Monodie de Theodore Prodrome sur Étienne Skylitzès métropolitain de
Trébizonde," *Bulletin d'Institut archéologique russe à Constantinople/Izvestija Russkogo
Arheologiçeskogo Instituta v Konstantinopole* 6 (1903): 1–13.

Petit, L., "Typikon du monastère de la Kosmosotira près d'Ainos (1152)," *Bulletin
d'Institut archéologique russe à Constantinople/Izvestija Russkogo Arheologiçeskogo
Instituta v Konstantinopole*, 11 (1908): 17–75. English trans. N. Ševčenko *BMFD* 2,
782–858.

Philippides, M. and W. Hanak, *The Siege and the Fall of Constantinople in 1453:
Historiography, Topography and Military Studies* (Abingdon and New York, 2011).

Philostorgios, *Philostorgious: Kirchengeschichte*, ed. J. Bidez (Berlin, 1981).

Philotheos Kokkinos, Φιλοθέου τοῦ Κοκκίνου Ἁγιολογικὰ ἔργα, ed. D. G. Tzames
(Thessalonike, 1985).

Philotheos of Selymbria, *Speech on St Agathonikos*, in PG 154: 1230–40.

Photios [Photius], Patriarch of Constantinople, *The Homilies of the Patriarch Photius*, trans.
C. Mango (Cambridge, MA, 1958).

Pincherle, M., *Vivaldi: Genius of the Baroque*, trans. C. Hatch (New York, 1957).

Pitarakis, B., "The Material Culture of Childhood in Byzantium," in *Becoming
Byzantine: Children and Childhood in Byzantium*, ed. A. Papaconstantinou and A.-
M. Talbot (Washington, DC, 2009), 167–251.

Pitarakis, B., ed., Hippodrom/Atmeydanı: İstanbul'un Tarih Sahnesi *[Hippodrome/
Atmeydani: A Stage for Istanbul's History]*, 2 vols. (Istanbul, 2010).

Pott, T., *Byzantine Liturgical Reform* (Crestwood, NY, 2010).

Poulter, A., "The Use and Abuse of Urbanism in the Danubian Provinces during the
Later Roman Empire," in *The City in Late Antiquity*, ed. J. Rich (London, 2001), 99–
135.

Preger, T., "Studien zur Topographie Konstantinopels. III. Die Konstantinsmauer," *BZ*
19 (1910): 450–61.

Prinzing, G. and P. Speck, "Fünf Localitäten in Konstantinopel," in *Studien zur
Frühgeschichte Konstantinopels*, ed. H.-G. Beck (Munich, 1973), 179–227.

Prodromos, *Eisiterios orphanotropho Alexio Aristeno*, PG 133 (1864): 1268–74.

Prokopios, *De Aedificia*, ed. J. Haury (Leipzig, 1913).

Prokopios, *The Anecdota or Secret History*, ed. and trans. H. B. Dewing (London, 1954).

Prokopios, *Historia Arcana*, ed. J. Haury and G. Wirth, *Procopii Caesariensis opera omnia*, 3 vols. (Leipzig, 1963).

Psellos, M., *Michele Psello, Epistola a Michele Cerulario*, ed. U. Criscuolo (Naples, 1973).

Psellos, M., *Michaelis Pselli oratoria minora*, ed. A. R. Littlewood (Leipzig, 1985).

Psellos, M., *Chronographia*, ed. V. Karales (Athens, 1992).

Psellos, M., *Michael Psellus: Orationes Panegyricae*, ed. G. Dennis (Stuttgart and Leipzig, 1994).

Psellos, M., *Chronographia*, ed. D.-R. Reinsch, *Millenium Studies* 51 (Berlin and Boston, 2014).

Psellos, M., *Michael Psellus: Orationes funebres*, ed. I. Polemis (Berlin, 2014).

Psellos, M., *Psellos and the Patriarchs*, trans. I. Polemis (Notre Dame, 2015).

Psellos, M. *Michael Psellus: Epistulae*, ed. S. Papaioannou (Leipzig, 2019).

Pseudo-Kodinos, *Traité des offices*, ed. J. Verpeaux (Paris, 1966).

Pseudo-Kodinos, *Pseudo-Kodinos and the Constantinopolitan Court: Offices and Ceremonies*, ed. and trans. R. Macrides, J. A. Munitiz, and D. Angelov (Farnham, 2013).

Pseudo-Martyrios, *Oratio funebris in laudem Sancti Ioannis Chrysostomi: Epitaffio attribuito a Martirio di Antiochia*, ed. M. Wallraff, Italian trans. C. Ricci (Spoleto, 2007).

Puchner, W., "Acting in the Byzantine Theater: Evidence and Problems," in *Greek and Roman Actors: Aspects of an Ancient Profession*, ed. P. Easterling and E. Hall (Cambridge, 2002), 304–24.

Puchner, W., *Greek Theatre between Antiquity and Independence* (Cambridge, 2017).

Puk, A., *Das römische Spielewesen in der Spätantike* (Berlin, 2014).

Queller, D. E. and T. F. Madden, *The Fourth Crusade: The Conquest of Constantinople* (Philadelphia, 1997).

Raby, J., "Mehmed the Conqueror's Greek Scriptorium," *DOP* 37 (1983): 15–34.

Raby, J., "From the Founder of Constantinople to the Founder of Istanbul: Mehmed the Conqueror, Fatih Camii, and the Church of the Holy Apostles," in *The Holy Apostles: A Lost Monument, a Forgotten Project, and the Presentness of the Past*, ed. M. Mullet and R. Ousterhout (Washington, DC, 2020), 247–85.

Rapp, C., "Literary Culture in the Age of Justinian," in *The Cambridge Companion to the Age of Justinian*, ed. M. Maas (Cambridge, 2005), 379–82.

Raub Vivian, M., "The World of Daniel the Stylite: Rhetoric, Religion, and Relationships in the Life of the Pillar Saint," in *The Rhetoric of Power in Late Antiquity: Religion and Politics in Byzantium, Europe and the Early Islamic World*, ed. E. De Palma Digeser, R. M. Frakes, and J. Stephens (London, 2010), 147–66.

Redford, S., "Constantinople, Konya, Conical Kiosks, Cultural Confluence," in *The Byzantine Court, Source of Power and Culture*, ed. A. Ödekan, E. Akyürek, and N. Necipoğlu (Istanbul, 2013), 41–7.

Redford, S. and N. Ergin, eds. *Cities and Citadels in Turkey from the Iron Age to the Seljuks* (Leuven, 2013).

Reinert, S. W., "The Muslim Presence in Constantinople, 9th–15th Centuries: Some Preliminary Observations," in *Studies on the Internal Diaspora of the Byzantine Empire*, ed. H. Ahrweiler and A. E. Laiou (Washington, DC, 1998), 125–50.

Reinsch, D. R., "The History of Editing Byzantine Historiographical Texts," in *The Byzantine World*, ed. P. Stephenson (London and New York, 2010), 435–44.

Riant, P. E. D. *Exuviae sacrae constantinopolitanae: Fasciculus documentorum ecclesiasticorum, ad byzantine lipsana in Occidentem saeculo XIIIe translate, spectantium*, 3 vols. (Paris and Leipzig, 1877–1904).

Ricci, A., "Rediscovery of the Patriarchal Monastery of Satyros (Küçükyalı, Istanbul): Architecture, Archaeology and Hagiography," *Bizantinistica: Rivista di Studi Bizantini e Slavi*, 2nd ser. 19 (2018): 247–76.

Rice, D. T., "Excavations at Bodrum Camii, 1930," *Byzantion* 8 (1933): 151–74.

Rice, D. T., ed., *The Great Palace of the Byzantine Emperors: Second Report* (Edinburgh, 1958).

Richard, J., "Le transport outre-mer des croisés et des pèlerins," in *Maritime Aspects of Migration*, ed. K. Friedland (Cologne and Vienna, 1989), 27–44.

Risse, G. B., *Mending Bodies, Saving Souls: A History of Hospitals* (New York, 1999).

Ristovska, N., "Distribution Patterns of Middle Byzantine Painted Glass," in *Byzantine Trade, 4th–12th Centuries*, ed. M. M. Mango (Farnham, 2009), 199–220.

Rizos, E., ed., *New Cities in Late Antiquity: Documents and Archaeology* (Turnhout, 2017).

Robbert, L. B., "Rialto Businessmen and Constantinople, 1204–1261," *DOP* 49 (1995): 43–58.

Robert of Clari. *The Conquest of Constantinople*, trans. with introduction and notes by E. H. McNeal (New York, 1964) (= Medieval Academy Reprints for Teaching 36 (Toronto, Buffalo and London, 1996)).

Roberts, S., *Printing a Mediterranean World: Florence, Constantinople, and the Renaissance of Geography* (Cambridge, MA, 2013).

Roberts, S., "The Lost Map of Matteo de' Pasti," *Journal of Early Modern History* 20 (2016): 19–38.

Robertus Monachus. "Historia Iherosolimitana," *RHC HOcc* 3 (1866): 721–882.

Robu, A., *Mégare et les établissements mégariens de Sicile, de Propontide, et du Pont-Euxin: Histoire et institutions* (Berne, 2014).

Rodini, E., "The Sultan's True Face," in *The Image of the Turk and Islam in the Western Eye*, ed. J. Harper (Burlington, 2011), 21–40.

Rojek, C., *Leisure and Culture* (New York, 2000).

Rossi Saccomani, A., *Le Carte dei lebbrosi di Verona tra XII e XIII secolo* (Padua, 1989).

Roueché, C., "Entertainments, Theatre, and Hippodrome," in *OHBS*, 677–84.

Roueché, C., "Spectacles in Late Antiquity: Some Observations," *AntTard* 15 (2007): 59–64.

Roueché, C., "The Factions and Entertainment," in *Hippodrom/Atmeydanı: İstanbul'un Tarih Sahnesi = Hippodrome/Atmeydani: A Stage for Istanbul's History*, 2 vols. ed. B. Pitarakis (Istanbul, 2010), 1: 50–64.

Rousseau, P., "Eccentrics and Coenobites in the Late Roman East," in *Conformity and Non-conformity in Byzantium*," *ByzF* 34 (1997):35–50.

Ruggeri, F., M. Crapper, J. R. Snyder, and J. Crow, "GIS Based Assessment of the Byzantine Water Supply System of Constantinople," *Water Science and Technology: Water Supply* 17.6 (2017): 1534–43.

Runciman, S., "The Country and Suburban Palaces of the Emperors", in *Charanis Studies: Essays in Honor of Peter Charanis*, ed. A. E. Laiou-Thomadakis (New Brunswick, 1980), 219–28.

Russell, T., *Byzantium and the Bosporus: A Historical Study from the Seventh Century BC until the Foundation of Constantinople* (Oxford, 2017).

Rüstem, Ü., "*Spolia* and the Invocation of History in Eighteenth-Century Istanbul," in *Spolia Reincarnated: Afterlives of Objects Materials, and Spaces in Anatolia from Antiquity to the Ottoman Era*, ed. I. Jevtić and S. Yalman (Istanbul, 2018), 289–308.

Ruvoldt, M., "Sacred to Secular, East to West: The Renaissance Study and Strategies of Display," *Renaissance Studies* 20 (2006): 640–57.

Şahin, K. "Constantinople and the End Time: The Ottoman Conquest as a Portent of the Last Hour," *Journal of Early Modern History* 14 (2010): 317–54.

Saliou, C., *Le traité d'urbanisme de Julien d'Ascalon: Droit et architecture en Palestine au VIe siècle* (Paris, 1996).

Saliou, C., "Construire en capitale: la loi de Zénon sur la construction privée à Constantinople (CJ VIII, 10, 12), une relecture," in *Constantinople réelle et imaginaire: autour de l'oeuvre de Gilbert Dagron (TM 22.1)*, ed. C. Morrisson and J.-P. Sodini (Paris, 2018), 79–102.

Saradi, H., "Constantinople and Its Saints, IVth–VIIth Centuries," *Studi Medievali* 36.1 (1995): 87–110.

Saradi, H., "The Use of Ancient Spolia in Byzantine Monuments: The Archaeological and Literary Evidence," *International Journal of the Classical Tradition* 3.4 (1997): 395–423.

Saradi, H., "Space in Byzantine Thought," in *Architecture as Icon: Perception and Representation of Architecture in Byzantine Art*, ed. S. Ćurčić and E. Chatzetryphonos (Princeton, 2010), 73–105.

Sathas, K., *Mesaionike Bibliotheke/Μεσαιωνικὴ Βιβλιοθήκη*, 7 vols. (Venice, Athens, and Paris, 1872–94; reprinted Athens, 1972).

Schibille, N., *Hagia Sophia and the Byzantine Aesthetic Experience* (Farnham and Burlington, 2014).

Schiltberger, J., *The Bondage and Travels of Johann Schiltberger in Europe, Asia, and Africa 1396–1427*, ed. and trans. J. Buchan Telfer (New York, 1970).

Schlange-Schöningen, H., *Kaisertum und Bildungswesen im spätantiken Konstantinopel* (Stuttgart, 1995).

Schmidt, B., *Inventing Exoticism: Geography, Globalism, and Europe's Early Modern World* (Philadelphia, 2015).

Schnath, G., "Drei niedersächsische Sinaipilger um 1330," in *Festschrift Percy Ernst Schramm*, 2 vols., ed. P. Classen (Wiesbaden, 1964), 1: 464–71.

Schneider, A. M., "Mauern und Tore am Goldenen Horn zu Konstantinopel," *NachrGött* (1950): 65–107.

Schneider, A. M., "Die Blachernen," *Oriens* 4 (1951): 82–120.

Schneider, A. M. and M. I. Nomidis, *Galata, topographisch-archäologischer Plan* (Istanbul, 1944).

Schreiner, A. P., "Die Organisation byzantinischer Kaufleute und Handwerker," in *Untersuchungen zu Handel und Verkehr der vor- und frühgeschichtlichen Zeit in Mittel- und Nordeuropa*, ed. H. Jankuhn and E. Ebel (Göttingen, 1989), 44–61.

Schreiner, A. P., "The Architecture of Aristocratic Palaces in Constantinople in Written Sources," in *The Byzantine Court, Source of Power and Culture*, ed. A. Ödekan, E. Akyürek, and N. Necipoğlu (Istanbul, 2013), 53–6.

Schwartz, E., ed., *Kyrillos von Skythopolis* (Leipzig, 1939).

*Scriptores originum Constantinopolitanarum*, 2 vols., ed. T. Preger (Leipzig, 1907).

Ševčenko, I., ed. and trans., *Theophanis Continuati liber V, Vita Basilii imperatoris*, CFHB 42 (Boston and Berlin, 2011).

Ševčenko, N., "The Tomb of Manuel I Komnenos, Again," in *First International Byzantine Studies Symposium*, ed. A. Ödekan, E. Akyürek, and N. Necipoğlu (Istanbul, 2010), 609–16.

Seyyid Lokman bin Hüseyin, *Lokman Tārīḫ-i Sulṭān Süleymān*, T413, Chester Beatty Library, Dublin.

Seyrig, H., "Monnaies hellénistiques de Byzance et de Calcédoine," in *Essays in Greek Coinage Presented to Stanley Robinson*, ed. C. M. Kraay and G. K. Jenkins (Oxford, 1968), 183–200.

Sezer, Y., "The Architecture of Bibliophilia: Eighteenth-Century Ottoman Libraries" (PhD dissertation, Massachusetts Institute of Technology, 2016).

Shepard, J., "Constantinople, Gateway to the North," in *Constantinople and Its Hinterland*, ed. C. Mango and G. Dagron (Aldershot, 1995), 243–60.

Shepard, J., "'Mists and Portals': The Black Sea's North Coast," in *Byzantine Trade, 4th–12th Centuries*, ed. M. M. Mango (Farnham, 2009), 421–41.

Shopov, A., "Urban Agriculture," *A Companion to Early Modern Istanbul*, ed. S. Hamadeh and Ç. Kafescioğlu (Leiden, 2021).

Sidéris, G., "Lèpre et lépreux à Constantinople: Maladie, épidémie et idéologie impériale à Byzance," in *La Paléodémographie: Mémoire d'os, mémoire d'hommes*, ed. L. Buchet, C. Dauphin, and I. Séguy (Antibes, 2006), 187–207.

Siebert, I. and M. Plassmann, eds., *Cristoforo Buondelmonti, Liber insularum archipelagi* (Wiesbaden, 2005).

Sinnigen, W. G., *The Officium of Urban Prefecture during the Later Roman Empire* (Rome, 1957).

Skhirtladze, Z., "The Image of the Virgin on the Sinai Hexaptych and the Apse Mosaic of Hagia Sophia, Constantinople," *DOP* 68 (2014): 369–86.

Skinner, A., "The Early Development of the Senate of Constantinople," *BMGS* 32 (2008): 128–48.

Skylitzes, J., *Ioannis Scylitzae Synopsis Historiarum*, CFHB 5, ed. H. Thurn (Berlin and New York, 1973).

Skylitzes, J., *John Skylitzes: A Synopsis of Byzantine History 811–1057*, trans. John Wortley (Cambridge, 2010).

Skylitzes Continuatus, *He synecheia tes Chronographias tou Ioannou Skylitse*, ed. E. T. Tsolakes (Thessalonike, 1968).

Smits van Waesberghe, J., "Neues über die Schola Cantorum zum Rom," in *Zweiter internationaler Kongress für katholische Kirchenmusik (Wien 4–10 Oktober 1954)* (Vienna, 1955), 111–19.

Smrylis, K., "Trade Regulation and Taxation in Byzantium, Eleventh-Twelfth Centuries," in *Trade in Byzantium*, ed. N. Necipoğlu and P. Magdalino, with the assistance of I. Jevtić (Istanbul, 2016), 65–87.

Snyder, J. R., "Manipulating the Environment: The Impact of the Construction of the Water Supply of Constantinople," in *A Most Pleasant Scene and an Inexhaustible Resource? Steps Towards Environmental History of the Byzantine Empire*, ed. H. Baron and F. Daim (Mainz, 2017), 169–85.

Sodini, J.-P., "Le commerce des marbres à l'époque protobyzantine, I: IVᵉ–VIIᵉ siècle," in *Hommes et richesses dans l'Empire byzantine, IVᵉ–VIIᵉ siècle*, 2 vols. (Paris, 1989), 1: 163–86.

Sodini, J.-P., "Productions et échanges dans le monde protobyzantin (IVᵉ–VIIᵉ siècle): le cas de la céramique," in *Byzanz als Raum*, ed. K. Belke, F. Hild, J. Koder, and P. Soustal (Vienna, 2000), 181–208.

Sodini, J.-P., "Marble and Stoneworking in Byzantium, Seventh-Fifteenth Centuries," in *EHB* 1: 129–46.

Sokrates, *Sokrates: Kirchengeschichte*, ed. G. C. Hansen (Berlin, 1995).

Sorlin, I., "Les traités de Byzance avec la Russie au Xe siècle (I)," *Cahiers du monde russe et sovietique* 2 (1961): 313–60.

Sozomenos, *Sozomenos: Kirchengeschichte*, ed. J. Bidez, introduction and index by G. C. Hansen (Berlin, 1960).

Speck, P., *Die Kaiserliche Universität von Konstantinopel* (Berlin, 1974).

Speck, P., "Urbs, quam Deo donavimus," *Boreas* 18 (1995): 143–73.

Speck, P., "Konstantins Mausoleum," *Varia* 7, ed. P. Speck (Bonn, 2000), 113–56.

Spingou, F., "Snapshot from the Eleventh Century: The Lombards from Bari, a Chartularios from Petra, and the Complex of the Mangana," *BMGS* 39 (2015): 50–65.

Stathakopoulos, D., *Famine and Pestilence in the Late Roman and Early Byzantine Empire* (Aldershot, 2004), 10–54.

Stathakopoulos, D., "Between the Field and the Plate: How Agricultural Products Were Processed into Food," in *Eat Drink and Be Merry (Luke 12:19): Food and Wine in Byzantium*, ed. L. Brubaker and K. Linardou (Farnham, 2007), 27–38.

Stathakopoulos, D., "Population, Demography, and Disease," in *OHBS*, 309–16.

Stavrakios Chartophylax, *Speech on the Miracles of St Demetrios*, ed. I. Iberitis, *Makedonika* 1 (1940): 334–76.

Stebbins, R., "The Sociology of Entertainment," in *21st Century Sociology: A Reference Handbook*, ed. C. D. Bryant and D. L. Peck (Thousand Oaks, 2007), 178–85.

Steckel, S., N. Gaul, and M. Grünbart, eds., *Networks of Learning: Perspectives on Scholars in Byzantine East and Latin West, c. 1000–1200* (Berlin, 2015).

Steiner, A., *Untersuchungen zu einem anonymen byzantinischen Briefcorpus des 10. Jahrhunderts* (Frankfurt, 1987).

Stephenson, P., ed., *The Byzantine World* (London and New York, 2010).

Stephenson, P., "The Rise of the Middle Byzantine Aristocracy and the Decline of the Imperial State," in *The Byzantine World*, ed. P. Stephenson (London, 2010), 22–33.

Stephenson, P., *The Serpent Column* (Oxford, 2016).

Stephenson, P. and R. Hedlund, "Monumental Waterworks in Late Antique Constantinople," in *Fountains and Water Culture in Byzantium*, ed. B. Shilling and P. Stephenson (Cambridge, 2016), 36–54.

Stiernon, D., " Le quartier de Xérolophos à Constantinople et les reliques vénitiennes du Saint Athanase," *REB* 19 (1961): 165–88.

Stilbes, C., *Poemata*, eds. J. Diethart and W. Hörandner (Munich and Leipzig, 2005). English trans. and commentary by T. S. Miller, "Death in a Xenon?" in *S. Realia Byzantina*, ed. S. Kotzabassi and G. Mavromatis (Berlin and New York, 2009).

Stone, A. F., "Eustathios and the Wedding Banquet for Alexios Porphyrogennetos," in *Feast, Fast or Famine: Food and Drink in Byzantium*, ed. W. Mayer and S. Trzcionka (Brisbane, 2005), 33–42.

Striker, C. L., *The Myrelaion (Bodrum Camii) in Istanbul* (Princeton, 1981).

Striker, C. L. and D. Kuban, *Kalenderhane in Istanbul*, 2 vols. (Mainz, 1997–2007).

Striker, C. L., J. M. Russell, and J. C. Russell, "Quantitative Indications about Church Building in Constantinople, 325–1453 A.D.," *Architectura* 38 (2008): 1–12.

Strube, C., "Der Begriff Domus in der Notitia Urbis Constantinopolitana," in *Studien zur Frühgeschichte Konstantinopels*, ed. H.-G. Beck (Munich, 1973), 121–34.

Sturluson, S., *Heimskringla, Part Two: Sagas of the Norse Kings*, trans. S. Laing, revised with introduction and notes by P. Foote (London, 1961).

*Suidae Lexicon*, 5 vols., ed. A. Adler (Leipzig, 1928–38).

Sullivan, D., "A Byzantine Instructional Manual on Siege Defense: The De obsidione toleranda – Introduction, English Translation and Annotations," in *Byzantine Authors: Literary Activities and Preoccupations*, ed. J. W. Nesbitt (Leiden, 2003), 139–266.

Sweetenham, C., trans., *Robert the Monk's History of the First Crusade, Historia Iherosolimitana* (Aldershot and Burlington, 2005).

Symeon, Archbishop of Thessalonike, *The Liturgical Commentaries*, ed. and trans. S. Hawkes-Teeples (Toronto, 2010).

Symeon Logothete, *Symeonis Magistri et Logothetae chronicon*, CFHB 44/1, ed. S. Wahlgren (Berlin and New York, 2006), 301.

Synesios of Cyrene, *Letters*, ed. A. Garzya (Rome, 1979).

Taft, R. F., "The Liturgy of the Great Church: An Initial Synthesis of Structure and Interpretation on the Eve of Iconoclasm," *DOP* 34–5 (1980–1): 45–75.

Taft, R. F., *The Byzantine Rite: A Short History* (Collegeville, 1992).

Taft, R. F., "Women at Church in Byzantium: Where, When – and Why?" *DOP* 52 (1998): 27–87.

Taft, R. F., *The Communion, Thanksgiving, and Concluding Rites* (Rome, 2008).

Taft, R. F. and S. Parenti, *Il Grande Ingresso* (Grottaferrata, 2014).

Tafur, P., *Pero Tafur, Travels and Adventures 1435–1439*, ed. and trans. M. Letts (New York and London, 1926).

Talbot, A.-M., *The Correspondence of Athanasius I Patriarch of Constantinople* (Washington, DC, 1975).

Talbot, A.-M., "The Restoration of Constantinople under Michael VIII," *DOP* 47 (1993): 243–61.

Talbot, A.-M., "The Posthumous Miracles of St. Photeine," *AB* 112 (1994): 85–104.

Talbot, A.-M., "Introduction," *DOP* 56 (2002): 59–61.

Talbot, A.-M., "Mealtime in Monasteries: The Culture of the Byzantine Refectory," in *Eat Drink and Be Merry (Luke 12:19): Food and Wine in Byzantium*, ed. L. Brubaker and K. Linardou (Farnham, 2007): 109–25.

Talbot, A-M., *Varieties of Monastic Experience in Byzantium, 800–1453* (Notre Dame, 2019).

Tansuğ, S., *Şenlikname Düzeni* (Istanbul, 2018; first edition 1961).

Tanyeli, U., "Sinan ve Antik Dünyanın Mirası," *Uluslararası Mimar Sinan Sempozyumu Bildirileri*, ed. A. Aktaş-Yasa (Ankara, 1996), 87–98.

Tate, G., "Les métiers dans les villages de la Syrie du Nord," *Ktema* 16 (1991): 73–8.

Teall, J. L., "The Grain Supply of the Byzantine Empire, 330–1025," *DOP* 13 (1959): 87–139.

Themistios, *Themistii orationes quae supersunt*, 3 vols., ed. H. Schenkel and G. Downey (Leipzig, 1965).

Theodore Studites, *Theodori Studitae epistulae*, ed. G. Fatouros (Berlin and New York, 1992).

Theodoros Anagnostes, *Theodoros Anagnostes: Kirchengeschichte*, ed. G. C. Hansen (Berlin, 1971).

Theophanes, *Theophanes Continuatus*, ed. I. Bekker (Bonn, 1838).

Theophanes, *Chronicle*, trans. H. Turtledove (Philadelphia, 1982).

Theophanes, *The Chronicle of Theophanes Confessor*, trans. C. Mango and R. Scott (Oxford, 1997).

Theophanes Continuatus, *Theophanis Continuati Liber V Vita Basilii Imperatoris*, CFHB 42, ed. and trans. I. Ševčenko (Boston and Berlin, 2011).

Theophanes Continuatus, *Theophanis Continuati Libri I–IV*, CFHB 53 ed. M. Featherstone and J. Signes Codoñer (Boston and Berlin, 2015).

Theophylaktos, Archbishop of Ohrid, *Théophylacte d'Achrida: Discours, Traités, Poé-sies*, ed. P. Gautier (Thessalonike, 1980).

Theophylaktos Simokattes, *Historiae*, ed. C. de Boor, revised P. Wirth (Stuttgart, 1974).

Thomas, J. P., *Private Religious Foundations in the Byzantine Empire* (Washington, DC, 1987).

Thomas, J. P. and A. C. Hero, *Byzantine Monastic Foundation Documents: A Complete Translation of the Surviving Founders' "Typika" and Testaments*, ed. J. Thomas and A. C. Hero (Washington, DC, 2000)

Thomov, T. and A. Ilieva, "The Shape of the Market: Mapping the Book of the Eparch," *BMGS* 22.1 (1998): 105–16.

Tinnefeld, F., "Zum profanen Mimos in Byzanz nach dem Verdikt des Trullanums," *Byzantina* 6 (1974): 321–43.

Tinnefeld, F., "Der Blachernenpalast in Schriftquellen der Palaiologenzeit," in *Lithostroton: Studien zur byzantinischen Kunst und Geschichte. Festschrift für Marcell Restle*, ed. B. Borkopp and T. Steppan (Stuttgart, 2000), 277–85.

Tolias, G., "*Isolarii*, Fifteenth to Seventeenth Century," in *The History of Cartography*, 3 vols., ed. D. Woodward (Chicago, 2007), 3: 263–84.

Tougher, S., *The Eunuch in Byzantine History and Society* (London and New York, 2008).

Tougher, S., "Having Fun in Byzantium," in *A Companion to Byzantium*, ed. L. James (Chichester, 2010), 135–45.

Toynbee, J. M. C., *Death and Burial in the Roman World* (Ithaca, NY, 1971).

Trigger, B., "Monumental Architecture: A Thermodynamic Explanation of Symbolic Behaviour," *World Archaeology* 22.2 (1990): 119–32.

Tülek, F., "A Fifth Century Floor Mosaic and a Mural of the Virgin of Pege in Constantinople," *CahArch* 52 (2005–8): 23–30.

Tunay, M. I., "Byzantine Archaeological Findings in Istanbul during the Last Decade," in *Byzantine Constantinople: Monuments, Topography and Everyday Life*, ed. N. Necipoğlu (Leiden, 2001), 217–31.

Turnbull, S., *The Walls of Constantinople AD 324–1453* (Oxford, 2004).

Turner, H. J. M., *St. Symeon the New Theologian and Spiritual Fatherhood* (Leiden, New York, and Cologne, 1990).

Tzetzes, I. *Ioannis Tzetzae epistolae*, ed. P. A. M. Leone (Leipzig, 1972).

Underwood, P., *The Kariye Djami*, Vol. 1, *Historical Introduction and Description of the Mosaics and Frescoes* (New York, 1966).

Van Dam, R., *Rome and Constantinople: Rewriting Roman History during Late Antiquity* (Waco, 2010).

Van Millingen, A., *Byzantine Constantinople: The Walls of the City and Adjoining Historical Sites* (London, 1899).

Van Millingen, A., *Byzantine Churches in Constantinople: Their History and Architecture* (London, 1912).

Van Minnen, P., "Medical Care in Late Antiquity," *Cleo Medica* 27 (1995): 153–69.

Van Rooy, R., "Teaching Grammar in 11th-Century Constantinople: Michael Psellus on the Greek 'Dialects'," *BZ* 109.1 (2016): 207–22.

Vanderspoel, J., *Themistius and the Imperial Court* (Ann Arbor, 1995).

Vasari, G., *Le vite de più eccellenti pittori scultori e architettori, nelle redazioni del 1550 e 1568*, 2 vols., ed. R. Bettarini (Florence, 1966).

Vasiliev, A., "Harun ibn Yahya and His Description of Constantinople," *Seminarium Kondakovium* 5 (1932): 149–64.

Vasiljevskij, V., "Dva nadgrobuykh stikhothorenija Simeona Logofeta," *Vizantijskij Vremmenik* 3 (1896): 574–8.

Verzone, P., *Palazzi e domus: dalla tetrarchia al VII secolo*, ed. D. de Bernardi Ferrero (Rome, 2011).

Vetters, H., "Das Baugesetz Zenons für Konstantinopel," *IstMitt* 39 (1989): 575–84.

*Vie de Saint Cyrille le Philéote, Moine Byzantin: Introduction, téxte critique, traduction et notes*, ed. É. Sargolos (Brussels, 1964).

Vin, J. P. A. van der, *Travellers to Greece and Constantinople: Ancient Monuments and Old Traditions in Medieval Travellers' Tales*, 2 vols. (Istanbul, 1980).

*Vita Auxentii*, PG 114 (1903): 1377–436.

*Vita Danielis Stylitae*, ed. H. Delehaye, *Les Saints Stylites* (Brussels, 1923).

*Vita Dionysii Athonitae*, ed. B. Laourdas (Athens, 1956).

"Vita S. Ioannicii, auctore Petro monacho", in *AASS*, Novembris II/1 (Brussels, 1894), 384–405.

*Vita Sancti Lucae Stylitae*, in *Les Saints Stylites*, ed. H. Delehaye (Brussels, 1923).

*Vita Petri Argivorum*, ed. A. Mai, in *Patrum nova bibliotheca*, 10 vols. (Rome, 1844–1905), 1–17.

*Vita Sampsonis II*, PG 115 (1899): 277–308.

*Vita Zotici II*, ed. T. S. Miller, "The Legend of Saint Zotikos According to Constantine Akropolites," *AB* 112 (1994): 339–76.

Vocotopoulos, P. L., "The Concealed Course Technique: Further Examples and Few Remarks," *JÖB* 28 (1979): 247–60.

Von Suchem, L. *Description of the Holy Land, and of the Way Thither, Written in 1350*, trans. Aubrey Stewart (London, 1895).

Vroom, J., "Byzantine Sea Trade in Ceramics: Some Case Studies in the Eastern Mediterranean (ca. Seventh–Fourteenth Centuries)," *Trade in Byzantium*, ed. P. Magdalino and N Necipoğlu (Istanbul, 2016), 157–79.

Vryonis, S., "Byzantine Dēmokratia and the Guilds in the Eleventh Century," *DOP* 17 (1963): 287–314.

Vryonis, S., "Byzantine Constantinople and Ottoman Istanbul: Evolution in a Millennial Imperial Iconography," in *The Ottoman City and Its Parts: Urban Structure and Social Order*, ed. I. Bierman, R. A. Abou-El-Haj, and D. Preziosi (New Rochelle, 1991), 13–52.

Walker, A., *The Emperor and the World: Exotic Elements and the Imaging of Byzantine Imperial Power, Ninth to Thirteenth Centuries C.E.* (Cambridge, 2012).

Wallraff, M., "Markianos: Ein prominenter Konvertit vom Novatianismos zur Orthodoxie," *Vigilae Christianae* 52 (1998): 1–29.

Ward, K., M. Crapper, K. Altuğ, and J. Crow, "The Byzantine Cisterns of Constantinople," *Water Science and Technology: Water Supply* 17.6 (2017): 1499–506.

Ward, K., J. Crow, and M. Crapper, "Water-Supply Infrastructure of Byzantine Constantinople," *JRA* 30 (2017): 175–95.

Ward-Perkins, J. B., "Notes on the Structure and Building Methods of Early Byzantine Architecture," in *The Great Palace of the Byzantine Emperors: Second Report*, ed. D. Talbot Rice (Edinburgh, 1958), 52–104.

Watts, E., "Justinian, Malalas, and the End of Athenian Philosophical Teaching in A.D. 529," *JRS* 94 (2004): 168–82.

Webb, R., "The Aesthetics of Sacred Space: Narrative, Metaphor and Motion in Ekphraseis of Church Buildings," *DOP* 53 (1999): 59–74.

Webb, R., "Ekphrasis, Amplification and Persuasion in Procopius' *Buildings*," *AntTard* 8 (2000): 67–71.

Webb, R., "Female Entertainers in Late Antiquity," in *Greek and Roman Actors: Aspects of an Ancient Profession* (Cambridge, 2002), 282–303.

Webb, R., "Mime and the Dangers of Laughter in Late Antiquity," in *Greek Laughter and Tears: Antiquity and After*, ed. M. Alexiou and D. Cairns (Edinburgh, 2017), 219–31.

Westbrook, N. "The Account of the Nika Riot as Evidence for Sixth-Century Constantinopolitan Topography," *Journal of the Australian Early Medieval Association* 7 (2011): 33–54.

Whitby, M., "The St. Polyeuktos Epigram (AP I.10): A Literary Perspective," in *Greek Literature in Late Antiquity: Dynamism, Didacticism, Classicism*, ed. S. F. Johnson (Aldershot and Burlington, 2006), 159–87.

Wickham, C., *Framing the Early Middle Ages: Europe and the Mediterranean, 400–800* (Oxford, 2005).

Wilkinson, J., *Jerusalem Pilgrimage 1099–1185* (London, 1988).

Wilkinson, J., *Egeria's Travels*, 3rd ed. (Warminster, 1999).

Wilkinson, J., *Jerusalem Pilgrims before the Crusades* (Warminster, 2002).

William of Tyre, *A History of Deeds Done beyond the Sea by William, Archbishop of Tyre*, 2 vols., trans. and annotated E. A. Babcock and A. C. Krey (New York, 1943).

Wilson, B., "Assembling the Archipelago: *Isolarii* and the Horizons of Early Modern Public Making," in *Making Space Public in Early Modern Europe*, ed. A. Vanhaelen and J. P. Ward (New York, 2013), 101–26.

Wilson, N. G., *Scholars of Byzantium* (London, 1983; revised ed., 1996).

Witakowski, W., *Pseudo-Dionysios of Tel-Mahre: Chronicle (Known Also as the Chronicle of Zuqnin), Part III* (Liverpool, 1996).

Wolska-Conus, W., "Les écoles de Psellos et Xiphilin sous Constantin IX Monomaque," *TM* 6 (1976): 223–43.

Woodfin, W. T., "A Majestas Domini in Middle-Byzantine Constantinople," *CahArch* 51 (2003–4): 45–53.

Wortley, J., "Relics and the Great Church," *BZ* 99 (2006): 631–47.

Wulf-Rheidt, U., "The Palace of the Roman Emperors on the Palatine," in *The Emperor's House, Palaces from Augustus to the Age of Absolutism*, ed. M. Featherstone, J.-M. Spieser, G. Tanman, and U. Wulf-Rheidt (Berlin and Boston, 2015), 3–18.

Wulzinger, C., "Byzantinische Substruktionsbauten Konstantinopels," *JDAI* 28 (1913): 370–95.

Wulzinger, K., *Byzantinische Baudenkmäler zu Konstantinopel auf der Seraispitze, die Nea, das Tekfur- Serai und das Zisternenproblem* (Hannover, 1925).

Yazıcıoğlu Ahmed Bican, *Dürr-i Meknun = Saklı İnciler*, ed. N. Sakaoğlu (Istanbul, 1999).

Yenişehirlioğlu, F., "Les fours et la production des céramiques du palais de Tekfur a Istanbul," in *Actas del VIII Congreso Internacional de Cerámica Medieval*, 2 vols., ed. J. Zozaya (Ciudad Real, 2009), 2: 617–32.

Yenişehirlioğlu, F. "İbrahim Pasha and Sculpture as Subversion in Art," in *Hippodrom/ Atmeydanı: A Stage for Istanbul's History*, 2 vols., ed. B. Pittarakis (Istanbul, 2010), 2: 111–27.

Yerasimos, S., *La fondation de Constantinople et de Sainte-Sophie dans les traditions turques: Légendes d'empire* (Istanbul and Paris, 1990).

Yerasimos, S., "La fondation d'Istanbul ottomane," in *7 Centuries of Ottoman Architecture: A Supra National Heritage*, ed. N. Akın, A. Batur, and S. Batur (Istanbul, 1999), 205–24.

Yılmaz, H. F., U. M. Ermiş, and F. Özgümüş, "Report of the New Findings from Byzantine Istanbul," *IstMitt* 67 (2017): 329–56.

Zachariah of Mitylene, *The Syriac Chronicle*, trans. J. F. Hamilton and E. W. Brooks (London, 1899).

Zanini, E., "Materiali e tecniche costruttive degli edifici costantinopolitani in età paleologa: un approccio archeologico," in *L'arte bizantina nel tempo dei Paleologi 1261–1453*, ed. A. Iacobini and M. della Valle (Rome, 1999), 301–20.

Zanini, E., "Technology and Ideas: Architects and Master-Builders in Early Byzantine World," in *Technology in Transition A.D. 300–65*, ed. L. Lavan, E. Zanini, and A. Sarantis (Leiden and Boston, 2007), 381–405.

Zanini, E., "The 'Byzantine District' of Gortyn (Crete) and the End of a/the Mediterranean city," in *Byzantine Greece: Microcosm of Empire?*, ed. A. Dunn (Abingdon, 2021).

Zepos, J. and P. Zepos, eds., *Jus graecoromanum*, 8 vols. (Athens, 1931; reprint Aalen, 1962).

Zonaras, J., *Epitomae historiarum*, 3 vols., ed. M. Pinder and T. Büttner (Bonn, 1841–97).

Zosimos, *Histoire nouvelle*, 3 vols., ed. and trans. F. Paschoud (Paris, 1971).

Zuckerman, C., *Du village à l'empire: Autour du régistre fiscale d'Aphroditô (525/526)* (Paris 2004).

# INDEX